THE
UNITED STATES
IN THE WORLD
POLITICAL ECONOMY

Stephen J. Wayne
Georgetown University
Consulting Editor

THE
UNITED STATES
IN THE WORLD
POLITICAL ECONOMY

Edited by
THEODORE RUETER
University of Wisconsin—Madison

McGraw-Hill, Inc.
New York   St. Louis   San Francisco   Auckland   Bogotá   Caracas
Lisbon   London   Madrid   Mexico City   Milan   Montreal   New Delhi
San Juan   Singapore   Sydney   Tokyo   Toronto

THE UNITED STATES IN THE WORLD POLITICAL ECONOMY

This book is printed on acid-free paper.

1 2 3 4 5 6 7 8 9 0 DOC DOC 9 0 9 8 7 6 5 4 3

ISBN 0-07-054259-7

This book was set in Melior by Ruttle, Shaw & Wetherill, Inc.
The editors were Peter Labella and Fred H. Burns;
the production supervisor was Kathryn Porzio.
The cover was designed by Carla Bauer.
R. R. Donnelley & Sons Company was printer and binder.

Library of Congress Cataloging-in-Publication Data

The United States in the world political economy /edited by Theodore Rueter.
       p.   cm.
   Includes bibliographical references and index.
   ISBN 0-07-054259-7 (alk. paper)
     1. United States—Foreign economic relations.   2. United States—
Commercial policy.   3. International economic relations.
I. Rueter, Theodore.
HF1455.U524   1994
337.73—dc20   93-1129

About the Editor

Theodore Rueter is adjunct professor of political science at the University of Wisconsin—Madison. He has also taught at Middlebury College, Georgetown University, Smith College, and the University of Minnesota. He is the author of *Carter vs. Ford: The Counterfeit Debates of 1976; Teaching Assistant Strategies: An Introduction to College Teaching;* and *The Minnesota House of Representatives and the Professionalization of Politics.* His articles have appeared in *World Politics, Journal of Politics, Armed Forces and Society, The New York Times,* and *The Boston Globe.* He recently completed a novel, *Balance of Power,* which concerns conflict between the United States and Japan.

Contents

Contributors

David Alan Aschauer is Elmer E. Campbell Professor of Economics at Bates College.

Robert E. Baldwin is professor of economics at the University of Wisconsin—Madison.

Daniel Bell is Professor Emeritus of Sociology at Harvard University.

C. Fred Bergsten is director of the Institute for International Economics.

Barry Bluestone is professor of political economy at the University of Massachusetts—Boston.

Clemens Boonekamp is a senior economist in the Geneva office of the International Monetary Fund.

Richard G. Darman was director of the U.S. Office of Management and Budget.

Rudiger W. Dornbusch is the Ford International Professor of Economics at the Massachusetts Institute of Technology.

Gerald Epstein is assistant professor of economics at the University of Massachusetts at Amherst, and staff economist for the Center for Popular Economics.

Aaron L. Friedberg is assistant professor of politics and international affairs at Princeton University.

Roger H. Gordon is professor of economics at the University of Michigan.

Stephan Haggard is associate professor of government at Harvard University.

Bennett Harrison is visiting professor of political economy at Carnegie–Mellon University.

Esmail Hosseinzadeh is assistant professor of economics at Drake University.

G. John Ikenberry is assistant professor of politics and international affairs at Princeton University.

Shintaro Ishihara is a member of the Standing Committee on Foreign Affairs of the Japanese Diet.

H. B. Junz is the director of the Geneva office of the International Monetary Fund.

Robert Kudrle is professor and director of the Freeman Center for International Economic Policy at the Hubert Humphrey Institute of Public Affairs at the University of Minnesota.

Wei Li is a graduate student in economics at the University of Michigan.

Robert J. Lieber is professor and chairman of the Department of Government at Georgetown University.

Helen Milner is assistant professor of political science at Columbia University.

Phedon Nicolaides is a research fellow at the Royal Institute of International Affairs in London.

Joseph S. Nye, Jr., is director of the Center for Science and International Affairs at the Kennedy School of Government at Harvard University.

James Poterba is associate professor of economics at the Massachusetts Institute of Technology.

Clyde Prestowitz is president of the Economic Policy Institute; he was formerly Counselor for Japan Affairs to the U.S. Secretary of Commerce.

Jeffrey J. Schott is a research fellow at the Institute for International Economics.

Susan Strange is a professor at the London School of Economics.

Lawrence H. Summers is Nathaniel Ropes Professor of Political Economy at Harvard University, as well as chief economist for the World Bank.

Howard M. Wachtel is professor of economics at the American University, as well as a fellow at the Transnational Institute.

Willi Wapenhans is vice president of the World Bank's Europe, Middle East, and North Africa Region.

Preface

The readings in *The United States in the World Political Economy* explore the major issues facing America as an international economic power. This book can be used in courses on international political economy, international relations, American foreign policy, international economics, macroeconomics, international relations theory, and American studies.

This volume features articles from some of the most prominent analysts of international political economy, including Daniel Bell, C. Fred Bergsten, Barry Bluestone, Richard Darman, Bennett Harrison, Shintaro Ishihara, Robert Lieber, Joseph Nye, Clyde Prestowitz, and Susan Strange. I have chosen selections from political scientists, economists, and policymakers. I have attempted to select readable, policy-oriented articles from a wide range of ideological perspectives.

The readings examine a variety of topics: American hegemonic decline, the American budget deficit, the structural basis of the American economy, U.S./Japanese economic relations, the distribution of international economic power, the American economy and international trade, the American economy and international investment, the political economy of international debt, and the future of the world political economy. They provide an overview of such issues as American infrastructure, industrial policy, Japanese economic policy, the Persian Gulf war, economic reform in Eastern Europe and Russia, Chinese economic behavior, the "Four Tigers" of Asia, the rise of regionalism in world trade, and the GATT talks.

Organization

The readings are organized into nine chapters. Following the introductory essay, the first chapter examines the role of the United States as the leader of the world economy, including recent changes. The next two chapters examine factors internal to the American economy, such as public infrastructure and the federal budget deficit. Chapters 4 and 5 consider American relations with Japan, OPEC, the Group of Seven, the former Soviet Union, Eastern Europe, the Newly Industrializing Countries of East Asia, and China. The next three chapters investigate the relationship between the American economy and three sectors of the world economy: trade, investment, and debt. Finally, the last chapter concerns the future of the world political economy.

Themes

This volume has two themes. One is that the United States is the most important actor in the world political economy. The United States has the world's largest economy, it is the key player in global economic institutions, it holds the world's dominant reserve currency, and it is the world's largest debtor nation (after having been the world's largest creditor nation). Therefore, it is appropriate to view international political economy from an American-centered perspective.

The second theme is the close relationship between domestic politics and international economics. There are domestic sources of international economic policy as well as international sources of domestic economic policy. Political factors affect economic policy, and vice versa.

These interactions were evident in the 1992 American election. Bill Clinton made the economy his central campaign issue. Indeed, a sign in the "War Room" at his campaign headquarters reminded his staffers, "It's the economy, stupid."

Clinton's election may portend changes in American international economic policy. He promised to press for a "stronger, sharper" trade bill, to "work more aggressively to open foreign markets to American goods and services," to renegotiate the North American Free Trade Accord, and to abolish tax breaks for American corporations "that shut down their plants in America and ship American jobs overseas."

Clinton's campaign rhetoric was consistent with economic nationalism, an ideology supported by Rust Belt congressmen, smokestack industries dependent upon government help, and industrial unions. Economic nationalism calls for regulation of foreign investment, direct assistance to American firms, and a militant trade strategy to open up Asian markets.

Several prominent members of the Clinton administration are advocates of industrial policy and economic nationalism. Laura D'Andrea Tyson, an economist at the University of California, Berkeley, is the head of Clinton's Council of Economic Advisers. She has edited books on trade and employment, American international competitiveness, and Japan's economic performance. Her latest book is *Who's Bashing Whom? Trade Conflicts in High-Technology Industries* (1993).

Ira Magaziner, another advocate of industrial policy, is on Clinton's White House staff. Magaziner is author or co-author of *Japanese Industrial Policy* (1981), *Minding America's Business: The Decline and Rise of the American Economy* (1983, with Robert Reich), and *The Silent War: Inside the Global Business Battles Shaping America's Future* (1989).

Robert Reich, Clinton's Secretary of Labor, is an advocate of improved worker training, greater American investment, and closer relations between labor and management. He has written *The Next American Frontier* (1983), *Tales of a New America* (1987), *The Resurgent Liberal* (1989), and *The Work of Nations: Preparing Ourselves for the 21st Century* (1991).

In February 1992, President Clinton presented his program to rejuvenate the nation's economy. He proposed extending federal unemployment benefits, creating an investment tax credit, and spending $16 billion on new public works projects.

Clinton also called for austerity measures. He proposed establishing a broad-based energy tax, increasing the tax rate on Social Security benefits, increasing the top rate for individual and corporate income taxes, reducing domestic and military spending, and decreasing federal employment and administrative costs.

Economic policy will continue to be a major issue in American politics. One objective of this volume is to improve the quality of the public debate.

Acknowledgments

I wish to thank several individuals for their assistance in the preparation of this book. In graduate school, I learned the subject of international political economy from Barbara Stallings of the University of Wisconsin–Madison and Charles Lipson of the University of Chicago. I also learned from several colleagues, including David Rosenberg of Middlebury College, Robert Lieber of Georgetown University, and Charles Robertson of Smith College.

I also wish to thank my students, particularly those enrolled in Political Science 304 at Middlebury College and Government 488 at Georgetown University. Stephen Holmes, formerly of Middlebury College (now of The Brock Group in Washington) provided much information, as did Tom Kalil, formerly of the University of Wisconsin–Madison (now of the National Economic Council in the White House).

Thanks are also due to those who reviewed this manuscript and offered helpful suggestions: Vincent Ferraro, Mount Holyoke College; Richard Jankowski, University of Arizona; Michael A. Lanius, Central Washington University; Frederic S. Pearson, Wayne State University; Brian Pollins, Ohio State University; Herman Schwartz, University of Virginia; and Daniel Unger, Georgetown University.

Finally, I am grateful to Peter Labella, Tamara Metz, Bert Lummus, Bill Barter, and Fred Burns of McGraw-Hill for providing much encouragement and support.

Theodore Rueter

Introduction: The Nature of International Political Economy

My purpose in this essay is to provide an introduction to the field of international political economy (IPE). I will review the significance of international economic issues in American politics, historical change in the IPE, leading theories of IPE, and competing levels of analysis in IPE.

International political economy may be defined as the relationship between international politics and international economics. The academic discipline of IPE is becoming increasingly prominent, creating greater unity between the fields of political science and economics.

INTERNATIONAL ECONOMIC ISSUES AND AMERICAN POLITICS

The growing popularity of IPE parallels the increasing significance of international economic issues in American politics. The agenda of international relations is no longer limited to the "high politics" issues of national security, alliances, and armaments. Increasingly, the agenda of international relations consists of "low politics" issues, such as foreign direct investment, oil imports, and the balance of payments.

American public concern about the economy grew substantially in the 1970s—a decade which witnessed the Arab oil embargo, a global recession, the final years of the Vietnam war, the end of the Bretton Woods system of international finance, and the Islamic revolution in Iran.

Public concern about the economy may be grouped into three areas. The first is deficits. For the last twenty years, the United States has regularly run a federal budget deficit, a trade deficit, and a balance-of-payments deficit. Many analysts argue that each deficit is the result of the nature of the American political economy. The federal budget deficit may be seen as the result of the structural inability of the American political system to impose costs and resist interest group pressures. The trade deficit may be seen as the consequence of the failure of the American economic system to modernize plants and equipment and to improve the quality of the labor force. Finally, the balance-of-payments deficit may be seen as the result of the foreign direct investments of American-based multinational corporations, as well as the international role of the dollar.

The second general area of concern is American competitiveness. In the 1990s and beyond, the United States faces stiff competition from Japan, Germany, the European Economic Community (EEC), and the Newly Industrializing Countries (NICs), such as the "Asian tigers" of Hong Kong, Taiwan, and Singapore. The American economy has lost world market shares as well as manufacturing facilities. American growth rates and productivity rates have declined. Barry Bluestone and Bennett Harrison call the loss of American industrial capacity and high-wage jobs "the deindustrialization of America." In an interdependent world economy, the availability of low-wage labor depresses the market power of high-wage labor. While the American economy has created millions of jobs in the last twenty years, many of these jobs are part-time, seasonal, or low-paying (and they are often without health insurance or other benefits).

Concern about American competitiveness may also be viewed from a sectoral perspective. Much of the debate over seeming American economic decline concerns the ability of specific American industries—such as steel, automobiles, semiconductors, and agriculture—to compete in the global marketplace.

A third area of public concern about the American economy involves national autonomy. Critics of excessive foreign direct investment in America fear loss of control of strategic industries. Economic nationalists also fear American dependency on foreign sources of natural resources, especially petroleum. Finally, it may be argued that the United States has lost control of its national borders, as evidenced by the wave of drugs and illegal immigrants entering the nation.

American economic problems have inspired numerous proposals for change. Several ideas have been offered to deal with the federal budget deficit, including a balanced budget Constitutional amendment, a line-item presidential veto, and congressional term limitations. The theory behind each proposal is that Congress is institutionally incapable of passing a balanced budget, due to the constant pressure to spend federal dollars in order to satisfy constituents, interest groups, and political action committees. However, defenders of Congress note that neither President Ronald Reagan (1981–1989) nor President George Bush (1989–1993) ever submitted a balanced budget to Congress. Other proposals for resolving the federal budget deficit are more dramatic, such as cutting deeply into military spending or middle-class entitlement programs (including Social Security).

Of course, these deficit-reduction measures would do nothing about the federal *debt*—the aggregate of past deficits. The United States national debt is now about $4 trillion. Interest on the national debt takes about 15 percent of the federal budget.

Several proposals have also been made to deal with the American trade deficit. One approach looks to address external sources of the American trade deficit. These include agricultural subsidies within the EEC and nontariff barriers to trade by Japan (such as health specifications, inspection requirements, and safety regulations). Many "Japan bashers" support the imposition of retaliatory tariffs (or even quotas) against Japanese exports to the United States.

Another externally directed approach to the trade deficit is "managed trade." Under "voluntary export restraints" or "orderly marketing agreements," a nation "voluntarily" limits its exports of a particular product to another country. These devices are becoming increasingly prevalent.

The internal approach to the American trade deficit (and other economic problems) looks to methods of improving American education and job training, as well as America's infrastructure (such as roads and bridges). The biggest problem with the internal approach is that it would not yield significant results in the short run.

The fear that America is experiencing economic decline has affected the rhetoric of American politics. One response of the Democratic party is to employ the politics of class. In a period of economic expansion, the middle class may be expected to identify more with the upper class than with the lower class. During a time of retrenchment, however, many members of the middle class begin to worry that their economic status will plunge. Many Democratic office seekers stress the need to institute national health insurance and expand job-creation efforts.

American economic decline has also spurred a neo-isolationist impulse within the Democratic party. Many Democrats have criticized President Bush for his seeming preoccupation with foreign affairs. Also, some congressional Democrats have proposed the financing of expanded national health care through cutbacks in foreign aid.

While Democrats have been focusing on class divisions within the American polity, Republicans have been focusing on the politics of race. Many Republican officeholders have argued strongly against affirmative action, crime, and welfare dependency; each of these terms may be viewed as a racial code.

HISTORICAL CHANGE IN IPE

Many analysts regard the year 1648 as the beginning of the modern world political system. After the Thirty Years War, the Treaty of Westphalia established the contemporary system of nation-states and sovereignty. Immanuel Wallerstein argues that the seventeenth century was the beginning of the modern world capitalist system as well.

The international capitalist system involves production for sale in a market, in order to maximize profits for the producer. It also entails an internal division of labor and an international division of labor. According to standard analyses, capitalists seek to accumulate surplus value on a world scale, and the international capitalist economy forces all states to act similarly. Capital accumulation is the goal of nation-states as well as capitalists.

Of course, not all states are equally adept at this task. Since the outset of the world capitalist system, dominant states, or hegemons, have appeared, such as Spain, the Netherlands, Great Britain, and the United States.

In the nineteenth century, Great Britain was the world's dominant economic power. Many historians have contended that "the sun never set on the British empire." The British used a system of military power, formal colonialization, and international trade and investment to sustain their dominance. The British pressed their "comparative advantage" in numerous sectors—what critics called "the imperialism of free trade."

The period of American economic hegemony had its genesis during the interwar period. After World War I, the United States gradually began to equal and then surpass European states as the world's largest economy. However, the United States did not *act* like a hegemon during this period. A protectionist Congress rejected the 1934 Reciprocal Trade Act, reflecting the same biases that led it to pass the protectionist Smoot-Hawley Act (which helped cause the Great Depression).

By the end of World War II, however, the United States was clearly the world's strongest economic (and military) power. The United States created a series of institutions to support the American postwar vision. The Bretton Woods conference of 1944 created the International Monetary Fund (IMF) and the World Bank, in order to provide liquidity and foster development within the world economy. Bretton Woods also established the dollar as the world's reserve currency, and linked the dollar to gold. In 1947, the United States helped establish the General Agreement on Tariffs and Trade (GATT), in order to create rules to govern international trade and foster economic liberalism. Also, the Marshall Plan provided significant aid to Western European countries, in order to reconstruct their devastated economies (and thus lessen their possible leftist temptations).

The United States also played a strong role in creating two political institutions—the North Atlantic Treaty Organization (NATO) and the United Nations (UN). NATO, established in 1949, institutionalized a system of collective defense for the nations of Western Europe. Under the treaty, America pledged to come to the defense of Western Europe, even to the point of employing nuclear weapons (called the doctrine of "first use"). Also, the establishment of the UN reinforced the power of the victors in World War II (the United States, Great Britain, France, the Soviet Union, and China) by granting them a permanent right of veto within the Security Council.

While the genesis of American hegemony is clear, pinpointing the date of its decline (or termination) is much more difficult. One candidate is the Vietnam war. By the time of the Tet offensive in January 1968, the American public had turned against the war. By the Paris Peace Agreement of January 1973, America had lost 58,000 soldiers in combat and had spent hundreds of billions of dollars. Vietnam was the first military defeat experienced by the United States; the fall of Saigon in 1975 was particularly humiliating.

Also, Vietnam played a strong role in creating massive federal budget deficits. President Johnson financed the Vietnam war by taking advantage of America's role as world monetary hegemon—by printing dollars. The Federal Reserve Board's expansionary monetary policy led to the massive spread of dollars throughout the world, known as "Eurodollars."

The excessive international spread of the dollar led to the "Nixon shocks," another possible demarcation of the end of American hegemony. On August 15, 1971, President Richard Nixon (1969–1974) removed the link between the dollar and gold, instituted a 90-day wage and price freeze, and imposed a 10 percent import surcharge. Nixon took these actions because of inflation, the depreciating value of the dollar, and the threat that foreign central banks might turn in their dollars for gold in massive amounts. By 1971, there were more Eurodollars around the globe than there was gold in Fort Knox to support them. By closing the gold window, Nixon unilaterally abrogated the most important element of the Bretton Woods agreement. After several rounds of international negotiations, the international capitalist community established a system of flexible exchange rates to replace the previous system of fixed exchange rates.

The Arab oil embargo is another possible demarcation of the end of American economic hegemony. In 1973, OPEC suspended oil exports to the United States, in retaliation for American support of Israel. As a consequence of this action, world oil prices quadrupled and American unemployment skyrocketed. Millions of American motorists spent time in long lines at gas stations. Many states imposed limited forms of gasoline rationing.

Several events during the administration of President Jimmy Carter (1977–1981) were consistent with the pattern of American decline. First and foremost was the national indignity experienced as a result of the Iranian hostage crisis. Fifty-two American citizens were held hostage for 444 days in the American Embassy, in blatant violation of international law. In April 1980, President Carter ordered a rescue mission, "Desert One," which failed dramatically. After the fall of the Shah, Iran greatly reduced its oil production, resulting in "oil price shock II." Increased global oil prices contributed to 20 percent interest rates in 1980.

A number of events during the Reagan administration may also be regarded as indicators of American economic decline. Most prominently, the Reagan administration oversaw the transformation of the American economy from the world's largest creditor to the world's largest debtor. This was largely due to "Reaganomics," which cut federal income tax rates sharply, especially for the wealthy. Meanwhile, President Reagan instituted large increases in military spending.

The theoretical foundation of Reaganomics was "supply-side economics." According to this view, a reduction in marginal tax rates would actually *increase* tax revenues, by increasing incentives to work and produce. Similarly, the Reagan ideological revolution entailed extensive deregulation of the economy. Also, the Reagan administration attempted to spread its economic and social gospel to the third world.

Another significant event during the Reagan administration was the beginning of the international debt crisis. On August 30, 1982, Mexico stunned the world by announcing that it could not meet the interest payments on its foreign loans, owed to 1,400 banks. Mexico's declaration prompted similar proclamations by other nations. The United States and the IMF undertook a series of debt payment rescheduling plans; this process is very much in effect today.

Finally, the Reagan administration was witness to the stock market crash of October 1987, known as "Black Monday," set off by American criticism of Western European interest rate policy. The events of Black Monday gave at least temporary credence to the predictions of two best-sellers: Ravi Batra's *The Great Depression of 1990,* and Paul Erdman's novel, *The Panic of '89.*

The United States faces severe economic challenges in the 1990s. America continues to run a massive trade deficit with Japan, and Japanese direct investment in the United States is increasing rapidly. Germany is now reunified and has become Europe's preeminent economic powerhouse. The agreement unifying the twelve economies of the EEC took effect on December 31, 1992. While this agreement greatly simplifies trade regulations (and could thus assist American exporters), it also threatens to exclude outsiders from European trade.

Other developments are equally foreboding. The collapse of the Soviet Union and the demise of the Warsaw Pact create great opportunities for deep reductions in American defense spending. However, these developments could also threaten American security and economic interests. The potential spread of nuclear weapons to former Soviet republics could create prospects for their use. Indeed, there were reports that the eight leaders of the August 1991 coup against Mikhail Gorbachev had control of the Soviet nuclear code. Further, the apparent end of the international system of nuclear bipolarity has lessened inhibitions against hypernationalism in Europe. Finally, the collapse of the Russian economy is necessitating a large-scale bailout by the West.

THEORIES OF INTERNATIONAL POLITICAL ECONOMY

There are three dominant theoretical traditions in IPE: liberalism, Marxism, and mercantilism. Each theory makes differing assumptions about the role of the state and the nature of capitalism.

Economic liberalism holds that free markets and free trade will maximize global prosperity, thereby reducing economic and political conflict. Liberals contend that the state should play a very limited role in the operation of the economy.

The intellectual forefathers of liberalism are Adam Smith and David Ricardo. Smith, an eighteenth-century Scottish economist, is often regarded as the founder of modern economic theory. He wrote *The Wealth of Nations*

(1776), which discusses the relationship between order and freedom, analyzes economic processes, and attacks governmental restrictions on free trade.

Smith believed that free trade and a self-regulating economy would result in social progress. He contended that the proper role of government was limited to preserving law and order, enforcing justice, defending the nation, and providing for a few social needs that could not be met through the market.

David Ricardo, in *Principles of Political Economy and Taxation* (1817), contributed the concept of "comparative advantage" to liberal capitalism. Ricardo argued that international society should be organized according to relative efficiencies. According to this theory, countries should specialize in their most efficient industries and trade with other states for their other needs. In his famous example, Ricardo demonstrated that if Britain traded its cloth for Portuguese wine, both would be better off—even if Britain was more efficient at producing both cloth and wine.

Liberalism sees a world of natural harmony and mutuality of interests. The fundamental principle of neoclassical economics is the natural equilibrium between supply and demand. Jean-Baptiste Say, in *A Treatise on Political Economy* (1834), put forth Say's Law—supply creates its own demand, fostering a natural equilibrium. Cordell Hull, Secretary of State under President Franklin D. Roosevelt (1933–1945), claimed that "when trade crosses borders, armies won't."

The concept of *economic liberalism* has a strong role in contemporary international relations theory. Such scholars as Robert Keohane and Joseph Nye have advanced the theory of "interdependence," which is a challenge to Marxist notions of hegemony, dominance, and exploitation. *Interdependence,* according to Keohane and Nye, may be defined as sensitivity (being affected by the actions of other nations) or vulnerability (being susceptible to the aggressive economic actions of other nations).

More recently, many scholars have explored the conditions under which nations can "cooperate under anarchy." In contrast to the realist concept of Hobbesian pessimism, the theory of neoliberal institutionalism holds that states can cooperate, especially if they form "regimes." *Regimes* may be defined as the rules, principles, procedures, and customs governing an issue area. Regimes have been established, either formally or informally, in such areas as trade, money, oceans, and space.

The second grand theory of IPE is *Marxism.* Marxist theory has been generated by Karl Marx, Friedrich Engels, Rosa Luxemburg, Nikolay Ivanovich Bukharin, Rudolf Hilferding, V. I. Lenin, Paul Baran, and Paul Sweezy. Contemporary "dependency" theory has been devised by Raul Prebisch, Osvaldo Sunkel, Andre Gunder Frank, Emmanuel Arghiri, and Theotonio dos Santos.

Marxist economic theory may be summarized with reference to several "laws." Perhaps the most important Marxist law is that of *disproportionality.* Whereas liberal economics sees a tendency toward natural equilibrium in the economy, Marxist analysis sees disequilibrium, which is caused by the crisis of overproduction and underconsumption. This crisis occurs because capitalists, acting rationally, attempt to pay workers as little as possible. While this behavior is rational for individual capitalists, the systemic result is irrational, since, collectively, workers cannot afford to purchase the products they produce.

Another Marxist concept is the law of the *accumulation and concentration of capital.* According to Marxist analysis, the motivating force of capitalism is the drive for profits. Therefore, it is necessary for individual capitalists to accumulate and invest. Also, capitalists must increase their efficiency in order to avoid economic extinction. The natural evolution of capitalism is thus the increasing concentration of wealth in the hands of the efficient few, and the growing impoverishment of the many.

Marxists also point to the *falling rate of profit* as an inexorable law of capitalism. According to this law, the rate of return declines as capital accumulates and becomes more abundant, thereby decreasing the incentive to invest. The pressure of competition forces capitalists to increase efficiency and productivity through investment in new labor-saving technology (what Rosa Luxemburg calls the "rising organic composition of capital"). However, this will increase unemployment, in turn leading to decreased incentives to invest, thereby decreasing rates of return on capital.

Still another Marxist economic concept is *imperialism*. Imperialist theory holds that, as capitalist economies mature (and become more monopolistic) and as profit rates fall, capitalist economies are compelled to seize colonies and create dependencies to serve as markets, investment outlets, and sources of food and raw materials. Lenin, in *Imperialism: The Highest Stage of Capitalism* (1917), argued that World War I was the result of capitalist competition for markets. Lenin also wrote about the special role of banks in integrating production and finance and in integrating the capitalist world economy through the export of capital.

Marxists also employ the law of *uneven development.* This law holds that because capitalist economies grow and accumulate at differential rates, a capitalist system can never be stable for more than short periods of time. Lenin believed that all capitalist alliances were temporary, reflecting momentary balances of power that would inevitably be undermined by the process of uneven development. Interimperialist rivalry would take place over colonial territories.

A further Marxist concept is the law of *unequal exchange,* or declining terms of trade. Economic structuralists maintain that a liberal capitalist world economy tends to preserve or increase inequities between developed and less developed countries. In their view, the terms of trade inherently favor manufactured goods over agriculture goods. Therefore, early industrializers have a strong and growing advantage over late industrializers. The world capitalist system is thus in a self-perpetuating state of underdevelopment.

A further Marxist economic concept is the law of *one price.* According to this law, identical goods will tend to have the same price in any world market. The implication of the law of one price is that capitalism destroys all other modes of production, creating one integrated world market.

The final Marxist law is *historical materialism*—the methodology of Marxism. Historical materialism holds that social systems experience transition and development, according to dialectical logic. Marx contended that the capitalist system was the result of a natural historical process, beginning with slavery. Slavery was replaced by communalism, which was replaced by feudalism, which was replaced by capitalism. In the future, capitalism would crumble, since it contained the seeds of its own destruction. Capitalism would thus eventually be replaced by socialism, which would give way to the ultimate historical form, communism. Communist society would be classless and would witness the withering away of the state. It would be governed by the creed, "From each according to his ability, to each according to his need."

The concept of materialism, in Marxist terms, focuses on earth, productivity, and production. Materialism is opposed to the idealist concept that ideas are an independent social force. Indeed, Marx referred to the "phantoms of the human brain." For Marx, capitalism was fated to self-destruct, regardless of the ruminations of philosophers.

The third theoretical tradition in international political economy is *mercantilism*. Mercantilism may be regarded as the "realist" theory of international relations, applied to international economics. Mercantilists believe that the state is the central unit of analysis, that the role of the state is to strengthen national power, and that international economic conflict is inevitable.

One of the original mercantilist theorists was Alexander Hamilton, the first American Secretary of the Treasury. In 1791, Hamilton submitted *Report on the Subject of Manufactures* to the U.S. House of Representatives. The report stressed the importance of industrial manufacturing and national self-sufficiency. Hamilton wrote that "not only the wealth, but the independence and security of a country, appear to be materially connected with the prosperity of manufactures. Every nation ought to possess within itself all the essentials of national supply. These comprise the means of subsistence, habitation, clothing, and defense."

In 1841, Friedrich List, a German nationalist, wrote *The National Political System of Political Economy.* List expressed his opposition to British hegemony, which was based on low-cost British exports. List charged that the British ideological commitment to "free trade" was simply a means of advancing Great Britain's own economic interests. He contended that the law of *comparative advantage* was merely a rationalization of the existing international division of labor. List advocated several measures to improve Germany's ability to compete with Great Britain, including political unification, the construction of railroads, and high tariff barriers. He favored greater emphasis on German industry and manufacturing, and less on agriculture.

Perhaps the most significant contemporary mercantilist theorist is Robert Gilpin, a professor of politics and international affairs at Princeton. In 1975, Gilpin wrote *U.S. Power and the Multinational Corporation,* which argued that American corporations were spreading wealth, resources, and technology to the rest of the world, to the detriment of the United States.

Gilpin further developed his mercantilist analysis in *War and Change in World Politics* (1981). In this book, Gilpin set forth a general theory of change in international systems. He contended that hegemonic countries, historically, have lost their relative power, due to both external and internal factors.

Internally, argued Gilpin, hegemonic powers are subject to the law of *industrial growth,* which posits that there is a tendency for the growth impulses of any innovation to come to an end. Thus, industrial innovators gradually lose their competitive advantage.

Another internal cause of hegemonic decline is the law of the *increasing cost of war.* Adam Smith noted that expenditures on preparation for war tend to increase as a civilization ages. This is due to the fact that an established political and economic power has a large investment in the maintenance of the status quo.

Finally, Gilpin points to the corrupting influence of affluence as an internal cause of economic decline. In modern societies, economic prosperity has often resulted in the loss of moral values, thereby lessening economic productivity.

Gilpin also identifies several external causes of hegemonic decline. One is the international diffusion of technology. As patents expire, as less developed countries insist on co-production agreements as a condition of direct foreign investment, and as foreign countries improve their educational systems, the technological leadership of the hegemon begins to wane.

Gilpin also points to the costs of empire as an external source of decline. Military dominance—which can be very expensive—has often been a prerequisite to economic dominance. Also, hegemons have typically been required to provide economic aid to their allies, and to allow trade discrimination by their trading partners, all for the purpose of maintaining the stability of the system. Eventually, however, the hegemon cannot afford these burdens, and begins to reduce military spending, cut foreign aid, and retaliate against discriminatory trade practices. Hegemons often take these measures in order to hold off the challenge from a rising power.

LEVELS OF ANALYSIS IN INTERNATIONAL POLITICAL ECONOMY

IPE may be understood from various perspectives, or levels of analysis. Kenneth Waltz, in *Man, the State, and War,* analyzed the causes of war according to three levels of analysis: the individual, the nation-state, and the international system. His typology has been widely employed in international relations scholarship.

The *individual* level of analysis, applied to IPE, looks to microeconomic factors, such as the behavior of individual capitalists, farmers, laborers, shopkeepers, and entrepreneurs. It also encompasses the behavior of individual heads of state, as well as their relationships with other world leaders.

Clearly, the individual level of analysis has limited utility in analyzing IPE. There is little doubt that national and international factors are far more consequential than the actions of individuals.

The second level of analysis is the *nation-state*. This perspective may be disaggregated in various ways. The first subdivision concerns the state itself as an independent variable. The state is a central concept in political science and in IPE. Analysts of IPE seek to understand the role of the state, the relative autonomy of the state, and the nature of state interests. Stephen Krasner, for example, argues that the American state has followed its own interests in postwar trade and oil policy.

Another approach at the nation-state level of analysis is to examine the condition and relationship of particular states. For example, an analyst could examine the state of the British national economy, or the economic relationship between South Korea and Germany.

Further, the nation-state level of analysis may be applied to intergovernmental organizations, such as the UN, the IMF, and the World Bank. Each of these organizations, of course, is composed of individual nation-states.

In addition, nation-states may be analyzed according to their capabilities in particular sectors. These include such key industries as energy, automobiles, steel, computers, semiconductors, banking, and agriculture.

Finally, it is useful to transpose the second level of analysis. The "second image reversed" examines the international sources of domestic policy, such as capital mobility, labor mobility, and immigration, as well as international inflation rates, international unemployment rates, and international interest rates.

Waltz's third perspective on international relations is the *systemic* level of analysis. This perspective stresses the international distribution of power and the imperatives of the international system as the most critical explanatory variables.

These are several possible international distributions of power. One is hegemony, or unipolarity, under which one state is dominant. Another possibility is bipolarity, under which two states exert joint control over the international system. Finally, the distribution of power could be multipolar.

One of the central theories of IPE (which employs the systemic level of analysis) is the hegemonic stability thesis. This concept holds that there is a strong relationship between the existence of an international hegemon and the pursuit of "liberal" policies (defined as free markets and free trade) in the world economy. Conversely, an international economic system with a declining hegemon or no hegemon will become increasingly illiberal. Many analysts argue that the United States can no longer afford such hegemonic burdens as foreign aid and the defense of Western Europe and Japan.

While Waltz popularized the three preceding levels of analysis, there are other perspectives. One is to focus on *international classes.* Under a Marxist approach, the most important issue in IPE is the relative bargaining power between the bourgeoisie and the proletariat, as well as the international linkages between classes. Marxist methodology also places emphasis on the power of multinational corporations.

Yet another level of analysis is *ideology.* This viewpoint is often consistent with Marxism. Marxists (such as Antonio Gramsci) stress the role of ideological hegemony in maintaining political and economic systems. One such doctrine is trilateralism, which seeks to build transnational alliances between the economies of Western Europe, Japan, and the United States, in the name of bolstering capitalism.

A further analytical perspective is *gender.* Feminist analysts of international relations argue that such realist concepts as power, security, force, and international anarchy reflect male attitudes. Feminist international relations theory stresses cooperation, interdependence, and mutual interests. Feminist scholars also emphasize the effect of the international political and economic system on women.

The readings in this collection employ a wide variety of theoretical and analytical perspectives. They also assess the significance of economic issues in American politics and consider the future of the world economy.

CHAPTER 1
American Hegemonic Decline?

The articles in this section examine whether America has declined as a world economic power. John Ikenberry explores American policies toward European postwar reconstruction in order to understand the origins and nature of American hegemony. He reviews such concepts as hegemonic power, liberal internationalism, the postwar international order, Bretton Woods, the Marshall Plan, Europe as a third force, NATO, and embedded liberalism. Contrary to conventional wisdom, Ikenberry argues that postwar American power "was unprecedented, but it was not unalloyed." In the end, he says, the United States had to settle for "an institutionalized relationship that diverted American resources to Europe in the form of a security commitment, allowing Europeans to employ their more scarce resources elsewhere. . . ." While America had overwhelming economic and military superiority after World War II, it was less successful in carrying out postwar policies than often thought.

In the next selection, Joseph Nye discusses recent theories concerning the decline of the United States. He contends that such theories are based on vague definitions, and that basic distinctions between the terms "power," "balance of power," and "hegemony" must be recognized. His fundamental point is that while the United States has lost "hard" power (the ability to command or coerce, possibly through threats), it still has ample "soft" power (the ability to set the agenda or co-opt opposition, through culture, ideology, or institutions). In his view, the United States is still the predominant actor on the world stage. He states that "the real problems of the post-Cold War world will not be new challenges for hegemony, but the new challenges of transnational interdependence."

Finally, Aaron Friedberg probes the question of whether the United States is strategically "overextended." He reviews two prominent books on the theory and history of hegemonic decline: David Calleo, *Beyond American Hegemony: The Future of the Western Alliance* and Paul Kennedy, *The Rise and Fall of the Great Powers.* Calleo argues that the United States should lessen its military commitment to Europe, in order to improve the American economy and maintain international economic stability. Kennedy's thesis is that great powers, historically, have tended to decline over time. Friedberg's argument is that defense spending bears only a small part of the responsibility for present American economic problems. He contends that the proper level of American defense spending is a *political* question, not an *economic* one.

1.   Rethinking the Origins of American Hegemony*

G. John Ikenberry

In recent years no topic has occupied the attention of scholars of international relations more than that of American hegemonic decline. The erosion of American economic, political, and military power is unmistakable. The historically unprecedented resources and capabilities that stood behind United States early postwar diplomacy, and that led Henry Luce in the 1940s to herald an "American century," have given way to an equally remarkable and rapid redistribution of international power and wealth. In the guise of theories of "hegemonic stability," scholars have been debating the extent of hegemonic decline and its consequences.[1]

Although scholars of international political economy have analyzed the consequences of American hegemonic decline, less effort has been directed at examining the earlier period of hegemonic ascendancy. Theorists of hegemonic power and decline pass rather quickly over the early postwar period. In rather superficial fashion, it is assumed that the United States used its power to organize the operation of the non-Communist international system—to "make and enforce the rules for the world political economy" as one scholar put it.[2] While the rest of the industrialized world lay in economic and political ruin, American resources and capabilities were at their peak. Out of these historical circumstances, the conventional view suggests, the United States got its way and created a postwar order of its choosing.

This conventional view, wielded by those scholars more interested in hegemonic decline, requires closer attention; and so it is useful to reexamine the origins and character of American power in the early postwar era. The questions are several: How was U.S. hegemonic power used after World War II in constructing the postwar world order? How successful

* The author wishes to thank John Lewis Gaddis, Lloyd Gardner, and Klaus Knorr for helpful comments and suggestions. An earlier version of the paper was presented to a seminar on Postwar American Foreign Policy at Rutgers University. Research was supported by funds from the J. Howard Pew Freedom Trust and the Center of International Studies, Princeton University.

[1] Recent discussions of the implications of American decline include Robert Gilpin, "American Policy in the Post-Reagan Era," *Daedalus* 116 (Summer 1987): 33–67; and Paul Kennedy, *The Rise and Fall of the Great Powers* (New York: Random House, 1988); David P. Calleo, *Beyond American Hegemony: The Future of the Western Alliance* (New York: Basic Books, 1987).

SOURCE: Reprinted with permission from *Political Science Quarterly*, vol. 104, no. 3, Fall 1989, pp. 375–400.

[2] Robert O. Keohane, *After Hegemony: Cooperation and Discord in the World Political Economy* (Princeton, N.J.: Princeton University Press, 1984), 37.

was the United States in creating a postwar order of its choosing? What did the United States want and what did it get in the early postwar years? Most importantly, what does a hegemonic state, such as the United States, do when it is being hegemonic?

The answers to these questions require us to rethink the nature of American hegemonic power. I argue that the United States got both less than it wanted and more than it bargained for in the early postwar period. In terms of the ideals and plans it originally articulated, the United States got much less than it wanted; in terms of direct involvement in leading the postwar western system, it got much more involved than it wanted. The United States was clearly hegemonic and used its economic and military position to construct a postwar order. But that order was not really of its own making. There was less exercise of coercion than is commonly assumed in the literature of hegemonic power, and where it was used, it was less successful than often thought.

I want to make three general points. First, the early efforts by the United States to build a postwar liberal multilateral system largely failed. Those efforts, in part attractive to the United States because they did not require a direct political or military presence in Europe, failed because of the rise of the East-West struggle and the underestimated problems of postwar economic and political reconstruction in Europe. Second, at each step along the way, the United States sought to minimize its direct (that is, formal, hierarchical) role in Europe. It was the European governments that sought to elicit and influence the projection of U.S. power into Europe—and they did so primarily for security and resource reasons. In short, U.S. hegemony in Europe was largely an empire by invitation. Third, while European nations sought to promote U.S. involvement in Europe, they also acted to rework the liberal, multilat-

eral ideas that initially propelled the United States during and after World War II. In effect, the European nations successfully modified liberal multilateralism into a welfare state liberalism (or embedded liberalism). The United States tried to use its power to create a system that would allow it to stay out of Europe—a sort of self-regulating and automatic international political economy. This failed, and the United States was drawn into a more direct role in Europe, defending a system that the Europeans themselves effectively redefined.

This article traces the evolution of U.S. policy as it reveals the mechanisms and limits of hegemonic power. U.S. policy traveled through different phases: the one world ideals of liberal multilateralism (1941–1947); the shift to a two worlds concept and the attempt to build a United Europe (1947–1950); and the subsequent emergence of an ongoing and direct American political and security presence in Europe—an empire by invitation. A close historical reading of policy change suggests the need to rethink the nature and limits of U.S. hegemonic power.

THEORIES OF HEGEMONIC POWER

The central claim of hegemonic stability theory is that a single Great Power is necessary to create and sustain order and openness in the international political economy. Accordingly, *Pax Britannica* and *Pax American* both represent historical eras when a hegemonic power held sway and used its dominant position to ensure an orderly and peaceful international system. Reflecting this position, Robert Gilpin argues that "Great Britain and the United States created and enforced the rules of a liberal international economic order."[3] Likewise, as the

[3] Robert Gilpin, *War and Change in World Politics* (New York: Cambridge University Press, 1981), 145.

power of these hegemonic nations declines, so also does the openness and stability of the international economic system. The decline of Britain's nineteenth-century order foreshadowed the decline of America's postwar system. In each era it was the dominant role of the hegemonic nation that ensured order and liberal relations among nations.

This thesis draws powerful conceptual links between the rise and decline of nations and the structure of international relations. Scholarly interest in this type of argument was stimulated by the writings of Charles Kindleberger and Robert Gilpin. In a study of the sources of the Great Depression, Kindleberger argued that the stability of the pre-World War I international political economy rested on the leadership of Britain.[4] This leadership role involved the provision of a variety of collective goods, in particular the willingness of Britain to extend credit abroad and to maintain open markets at home. In the midst of falling commodity prices beginning in 1927 and the emerging shortage of international credit, the United States failed to act in a counter-cyclical manner to reverse the flow of funds and raised protectionist barriers. The collapse of the system in the interwar period was due to the absence of a hegemonic leader able and willing to maintain open markets for surplus goods and capable of maintaining the flow of capital. Kindleberger argues that the return to mercantilist relations in the interwar period was largely due to the inability of a weakened Britain to continue to play this leadership role and the unwillingness of the United States to take up these international responsibilities.

Similarly, Robert Gilpin developed a theory of global leadership emphasizing the active role of the hegemonic nation

in creating and sustaining international economic and political order.[5] The rise of a hegemonic nation, Gilpin argues, "resolves the question of which state will govern the system, as well as what ideas and values will predominate, thereby determining the ethos of succeeding ages."[6] In this formulation, the hegemonic nation dominates the creation of the rules and institutions that govern international relations in a particular age. Gilpin's argument was that Britain undermined its own economic base of hegemonic power by investing heavily in overseas production at the expense of its own economy.[7] In the twentieth century, moreover, the United States was in danger of repeating the cycle of hegemonic decline and instability.[8]

In these studies and in the literature on hegemonic stability that they continue to inspire, attempts are made to find systematic links between the prevailing distribution of power (that is, military capabil-

[4] Charles P. Kindleberger, *The World in Depression, 1929–39* (Berkeley: University of California Press, 1973).

[5] Gilpin, *War and Change.* An earlier formulation of hegemonic power emphasizing similarities in the rise and decline of *Pax Britannica* and *Pax Americana* is in Gilpin, *U.S. Power and the Multinational Corporation* (New York: Basic Books, 1975).

[6] Gilpin, *War and Change,* 203.

[7] Gilpin, *U.S. Power and the Multinational Corporation.*

[8] Gilpin notes: "Much as it happened in the latter part of the nineteenth century and the interwar period, the relative decline of the dominant economy and the emergence of new centers of economic power have led to increasing economic conflicts. During such periods of weak international leadership, international economic relations tend to be characterized by a reversion to mercantilism (economic nationalism), intense competition and bargaining among economic powers, and the fragmentation of the liberal interdependent world economy into exclusive blocs, rival nationalisms, and economic alliances." "Economic Interdependence and National Security in Historical Perspective" in Klaus Knorr and Frank N. Trager, eds., *Economic Issues and National Security* (Lawrence: Regents Press of Kansas, 1977), 61.

ities, control over trade, capital, and raw materials) and the organization of international political and economic processes. In doing so, these theories share several assumptions. First, they tend to conceive of power in traditional resource terms. Reflecting this position, Robert Keohane defines hegemony as "preponderance of material resources."[9] Thus, the constitutive elements of hegemonic power, as it relates to the world political economy, include control over raw materials, markets, and capital as well as competitive advantages in highly valued goods. Second, according to this perspective, these material resources provide the means for the hegemon to "make and enforce the rules for the world political economy."[10] Power is exercised by the hegemon primarily through the use of coercion, inducements, or sanctions. In effect, power is manifest as arm twisting.

While sharing these basic assumptions, scholars working in this tradition disagree over the manner in which hegemonic power is exercised.[11] Some writers, such as Kindleberger, see that power as basically benign, centering around the provision of public goods and leadership.[12] The image of the hegemon in this formulation is that of an enlightened leader, submerging narrow and short-term national interests to the preservation of a well-ordered and mutually beneficial international system. Others stress the importance of self-regarding actions by the hegemon directed at the creation and enforcement of the essential rules of the system.[13] Here the image is of a much more coercive hegemon, structuring the system to strengthen its own international economic position.

The debate within this literature tends to focus on the implications of the loss of American hegemonic power. The questions at this level are two-fold. One concerns the manner and extent to which the loss of hegemonic power has impacts on international regimes. The debate here is about how autonomous and powerful regimes may be as an independent force for order and openness, even with the declining hegemon playing a less constructive role.[14] A second debate asks the prior question of the extent to which the United States has in fact lost its hegemonic capabilities.[15]

This literature provides fertile ground for research on American power in the

---

[9] Keohane, *After Hegemony,* 32.

[10] Ibid, 37.

[11] Duncan Snidal makes a distinction between hegemony that is benign and exercised by persuasion, hegemony that is benign but exercised by coercion, and hegemony that is coercive and exploitive. Snidal, "Hegemonic Stability Theory Revisited," *International Organization* 39 (Autumn 1985). In another effort to distinguish between types of hegemonic power, Hirsch and Doyle note those of cooperative leadership, hegemonic regime, and imperialism. See Fred Hirsch and Michael Doyle, *Alternatives to Monetary Disorder* (New York: McGraw-Hill, 1977), 27.

[12] Kindleberger, *World in Depression*; see also Kindleberger, "Dominance and Leadership in the International Economy," *International Studies Quarterly* 25 (June 1981): 242–54.

[13] Gilpin, *War and Change*; Stephen Krasner, "State Power and the Structure of International Trade," *World Politics* 28 (April 1976): 317–43.

[14] For an overview of this literature see Stephan Haggard and Beth Simmons, "International Regimes," *International Organization* 41 (Summer 1987). Some scholars, employing a sociological perspective, focus on the role of regimes as institutions that inform the process by which nations define and pursue their interests. See Stephen Krasner, ed., *International Regimes* (Ithaca, N.Y.: Cornell University Press, 1983). Others have developed microeconomic models that relate the maintenance of regimes to strategic interactions of states. See Keohane, *After Hegemony.*

[15] Bruce Russett, "The Mysterious Case of Vanishing Hegemony; or Is Mark Twain Really Dead?" *International Organization* 39 (Spring 1985); Susan Strange, "The Persistent Myth of Lost Hegemony," *International Organization* 41 (Autumn 1987).

postwar period by drawing bold lines between the rise and decline of nations and the international political economy. Its power is in its simplicity, and the images it presents are evocative. Nonetheless, it suffers from at least two problems—one theoretical and the other historical. Theoretically, the literature suffers from the absence of a clear theoretical understanding of the manner in which hegemonic power is manifest as it promotes international order and openness. The mechanisms and the texture of hegemonic power has not been captured in the literature. Susan Strange notes that "we have not clearly understood the alternative ways hegemons exercise power and the alternative uses to which their power may be put."[16] What factors determine when and how the rich and militarily strong nations are able to convert their power into hegemonic domination? Through what mechanisms and processes does power manifest itself? Why do some states come to accept, even invite, the rule of the hegemon, while others resist? And how do the goals of the hegemon change in the process of building international order? These questions remain unanswered because the focus of hegemonic stability theory remains fixed on the material resources of power and fails to explore the larger dimensions of power.

The second problem is historical. As noted above, the literature on hegemonic stability passes very briefly over the early phases of the cycle of rise and decline. In particular, it is assumed that the rules and institutions that emerged in the early postwar period are essentially the creations of the United States. The unprecedented position of the United States gave it a unique historical license to create international order on its own terms, or so it is thought. We are left only to trace the

course of that power and analyze the fate of the rules and institutions it fathered. This image is a distortion: it is, to borrow Dean Acheson's memorable phrase, a view that is "clearer than the truth." And it serves to mislead the subsequent inquiry into the processes of hegemonic decline. If the capabilities of the United States in the early postwar period were less overpowering than commonly assumed, and if that power was exercised in less direct ways, this is important for the way we are to judge the current period of decline.

The Limits of American Postwar Power

Viewed in terms of material capabilities, the United States did occupy an overwhelmingly powerful position at the close of the war. The disparity in resources and capabilities was huge, not only in general aggregate economic and military terms, but also in the wide assortment of resources the United States had at its disposal. As early as 1900 the United States was already the world's largest industrial producer; on the eve of World War I the United States had twice the share of world industrial production as Britain and Germany, its nearest industrial rivals. This trend toward economic dominance was rendered more pronounced by the war itself, which destroyed the industrial base of the European economies and further expanded the American counterpart.[17]

The unprecedented nature of the American position is reflected in comparisons with British economic strength in the nineteenth century. While the British in 1870, at the zenith of their power, possessed 32 percent of the global distri-

[16] Strange, "The Persistent Myth of Lost Hegemony," 555.

[17] U.S. national output more than doubled in real terms during the war: American GNP rose from $91 billion in 1939 to $210 billion in 1945.

bution of industrial production, the United States held 48 percent of the global share in 1948. The scope of British and American power, in their respective eras, is often found to be similar; yet in terms of the preponderance of material resources, American power was much greater.

As the hegemonic account of the early postwar period suggests, the United States did employ its resources to help shape the global political and economic order. American oil reserves were used in the 1950s and 1960s to make up for global shortfalls triggered by a series of crises and embargoes in the Middle East. Lend-lease arrangements and loans were used to influence British commercial policy immediately after the war. Foreign aid was used to influence European monetary policy in the 1950s.[18] An entire range of postwar rulemaking and institution-building exercises were influenced and supported by the American resort to inducements and coercion, all backed by U.S. resource capabilities.

Closer historical scrutiny of the period suggests that the absence of success by the United States in implementing its liberal designs for order was more pervasive than the hegemonic account allows. American officials consistently were forced to modify their plans for a liberal, multilateral order; and they often found themselves at a loss in attempting to draw others into such a system.

In the various commercial negotiations after the war, the United States was unable or unwilling to pursue consistent liberal policies. The most ambitious efforts at trade liberalization, embodied in the International Trade Organization proposal, were blocked by the United States

Congress.[19] The General Agreement on Tariffs and Trade (GATT) that did survive was less extensive, contained escape clauses and exemptions, and left agriculture trade outside the multilateral framework. In areas such as maritime rights and shipping, as Susan Strange notes, the United States also pursued less than liberal policies.[20] Moreover, despite the unprecedented power position of the United States, holding the dollars and relief funds desperately needed in Britain and on the continent, American officials were less than successful in persuading Europe to embrace U.S. policies. In a recent study, Michael Mastanduno finds that the United States was surprisingly ineffective in convincing Europe to adopt its hardline East-West trade strategies.[21] Moreover, the U.S. was unable to push the European governments toward full-scale economic integration, despite its continued efforts and the massive aid of the Marshall Plan.

FROM LIBERAL MULTILATERALISM TO A UNITED EUROPE

The unprecedented opportunity for the United States to construct a postwar international order congenial with its interests and ideals was not wasted. The order that took shape in the late 1940s, however, was not what wartime planners had envisaged or sought to implement during and immediately after the war. The one world of American wartime planning gave way to efforts to build Europe into an independent center of global power;

[18] Krasner, "American Policy and Global Economic Stability" in William P. Avery and David P. Rapkin, eds., *America in a Changing World Political Economy* (New York: Longman, 1982), 32.

[19] This does not in itself argue against the presence of hegemonic power, but it does suggest the importance of congenial domestic coalitions to support its exercise.
[20] Strange, "The Persistent Myth of Lost Hegemony," 560–61.
[21] Michael Mastanduno, "Postwar East-West Trade Strategy," *International Organization* 42 (Winter 1987/88).

these revised plans, signaled by the Marshall Plan, in turn gave way to a bipolar system and the active courtship by Europe of American hegemonic leadership.

The chief focus of wartime planners was the construction of a postwar economy based on liberal, multilateral designs. The primacy of economic planning reflected both principle and prudence. It was part of the liberal faith that if the economic foundation were properly laid, the politics would follow. "If goods can't cross borders, soldiers will" was the slogan of the time, capturing the liberal faith.

The absence of postwar political and military planning also followed from more explicit wartime constraints. Franklin D. Roosevelt's vision of Great Power postwar cooperation held sway, an approach difficult to break with as long as the war persisted. Well into 1947 the idea that postwar order would be one world, with collective security and a liberal international economy, continued to drive policy in the Roosevelt and Truman administrations.

Domestic considerations, moreover, made a large-scale peacetime military commitment to Europe and a spheres-of-influence policy difficult to sustain.[22] A liberal, multilateral system would allow the United States to project its own ideals onto a world where depression and war had clearly demonstrated the bankruptcy of European ideas of spheres of influence and economic nationalism. If the United States could no longer isolate itself from the affairs of Europe, it would need to alter the terms of international politics. Only on this basis would congressional and public opinion allow the United States to play an internationalist role. A liberal, multilateral system, once established, would be self-regulating and would not require direct American involvement in Europe. For an American public eager to see its troops return home, ideals and prudence reinforced the initial American designs for postwar order.

The Failure of Liberal Multilateralism

The tenets of liberal multilateralism were several: trade and financial relations are best built around multilateral rather than bilateral or other partial arrangements; commercial relations are to be conducted primarily by private actors in markets; and states are to become involved in setting the domestic and international institutional framework for trade and financial relations, both participating in liberalizing international negotiations and facilitating domestic adjustment to international economic change.[23]

American officials involved in economic planning in the Departments of State and Treasury were strikingly in accord on the need for the creation of international institutions to support liberal,

[22] Franz Schurmann argues that the isolationist heritage made a postwar internationalist strategy difficult to sustain unless it was clothed in liberal ideals. The reluctance of portions of American public opinion to get involved in the atavistic power politics of Europe weighed heavily on foreign policy officials. Such involvement, it was argued, had a corrupting influence on the exceptionalism of American politics. Internationalism, consequently, would need to involve reforming and remaking European power politics in an American image—to export American exceptionalism. Schurmann, *The Logic of World Power* (New York: Pantheon, 1974).

[23] American liberal multilateral ideas have long historical roots. They can be traced to John Hay's "Open Door" and to the third of Woodrow Wilson's Fourteen Points: "the removal, so far as possible, of all economic barriers." Richard N. Gardner's study remains the most comprehensive account of these ideas and their fate in postwar economic diplomacy. Gardner, *Sterling-Dollar Diplomacy: The Origins and the Prospects of Our International Economic Order* (New York: McGraw-Hill, 1969).

multilateral economic relations. All were influenced by the failures after World War I: the lack of preparation, the failure of American participation in the League of Nations, the inadequacy of attention to economic problems.[24] "The postwar planners were united in their determination to break with the legacy of economic nationalism. . . . They recognized that the United States, despite its comparative self-sufficiency, had a very great stake in the economic well-being of the rest of the world, not only because it needed foreign markets for the produce of its factories and farms, but because it needed a healthy environment on which to base its efforts at world peace."[25]

Most of the American wartime efforts to insure a liberal, multilateral system were directed at Britain. British economic planners were generally sympathetic to American liberal, multilateral ideas; but outside of the government, political groups and individuals were profoundly divided. On the Left, free markets were associated with unemployment and social injustice. Segments of British industry feared competition with American industry. On the Right, liberal multilateralism was a threat to the Imperial Preference system (providing privileged trade relations among commonwealth nations) and the remains of the British Empire.[26] In various ways these groups favored national, bilateral, or regional economic relations.

Directed primarily at dismantling British Imperial Preferences, American officials resorted to several bargaining tools and advantages. In 1941 Lend-Lease negotiations, the United States sought to tie aid to the removal of discriminatory British trade practices.[27] Compromises were

achieved, and the British were able to resist a firm commitment to multilateral principles.[28]

The most far-reaching discussions between the United States and Britain over the principles and mechanisms of postwar economic order were agreed upon at the 1944 Bretton Woods conference in New Hampshire.[29] In these monetary negotiations, the British-American differences were considerable in regard to the provision for liquidity and the allocation of responsibility for adjustment between creditor and debtor countries. The British emphasized the primacy of national control over fiscal and monetary policy, the importance of biasing the arrangements toward economic expansion, and the need for a large international reserve and relatively easy terms of access to adjustment funds.

In the compromise agreement that created the charters of the International Monetary Fund and the International Bank for Reconstruction and Development (World Bank), major differences of perception remained between the British and Americans. In the American Senate debate, administration officials gave the impression that the institutional foundations have been laid for a liberal, multilateral system. Further funds would not be necessary for British economic reconstruction, and a British commitment to nondiscrimination had been achieved. The British, for their part, understood

[24] Ibid., 4.
[25] Ibid., 12.
[26] Ibid., 31–35.
[27] Article Seven to the Mutual Aid Agreement was the object of these negotiations.

[28] Gardner, *Sterling-Dollar Diplomacy,* 68. On American wartime efforts to extract British concessions on the postwar trading system, see Lloyd C. Gardner, "Will Clayton, the British Loan, and the Political Economy of the Cold War" in Gardner, *Architects of Illusion: Men and Ideas in American Foreign Policy, 1941–1949* (Chicago: Quadrangle Books, 1970), 113–38.
[29] For systematic accounts of these monetary agreements, see Gardner, *Sterling-Dollar Diplomacy;* and Armand Van Dormael, *Bretton Woods: Birth of a Monetary System* (London: Macmillan, 1978).

that the United States had committed itself to helping Britain in what would be
a lengthy economic transition period,
and that the American government
would make the sacrifices necessary to
insure postwar economic expansion.[30]

At the same time that British-American
negotiations dealt with monetary arrangements, the framework for international trade was also debated. In 1945 a
set of proposals were worked out between the two countries on commercial
policy. British reluctance to endorse the
full array of American proposals for non-
discriminatory trade and multilateral tariff reductions were similar to those in the
monetary area. The British were not prepared to eliminate the Imperial Preference arrangements. Concerns about employment and economic stability made
the British cautious of a full-blown, liberal trading system.[31]

Further efforts by the United States to
use its economic preeminence to alter
British commercial and monetary practices came during consideration of the
British loan in 1945–1946. The core of
this effort was to gain a British pledge to
lift discriminatory controls earlier than
mandated by the Bretton Woods agreement. Negotiations over the British loan
provided the most coercive use of American power for liberal, multilateral purposes during this period. Reflecting the
attitude of Congress on this issue, a congressional report argued that "the advantages afforded by the United States loans
and other settlements are our best bargaining asset in securing political and
economic concessions in the interest of

world stability."[32] The British found little room to reject the conditions of the
loan.[33]

Under the terms of the Anglo-American Financial Agreement, the British
were obliged to make sterling externally
convertible. Yet this action led in only six
weeks to a massive drain on British reserves, forcing the suspension of con-
vertibility. Despite its commanding bargaining position, the United States was
unable to bring Britain into a multilateral
order. Moreover, the chief political
strength of the British (and the Europeans
generally) in resisting American designs
was their economic weakness. The early
move toward multilateralism would not
be possible.

Throughout the 1944–1947 period, the
United States attempted to build a framework for international economic relations with the reconstruction of multilateral trade as its centerpiece. This
objective largely failed. The most basic
obstacle in the way of American policy
was the economic and political dislocation of the war itself. The American proposals required, as Richard Gardner
maintains, a reasonable state of economic
and political equilibrium. "The multilateral system could not be achieved unless
individual nations were in approximate
balance with the world as a whole. Unfortunately the post-war planners did not
foresee the full extent of the measures
necessary to achieve such balances after
the destruction and dislocation of the
Second World War. . . . The institutions
they built for the achievement of multilateralism were not designed to with-
stand the unfavorable pressures of the
post-war transition period."[34] The objectives of the hegemonic power were not in

[30] For a summary of differences in Ameri-
can and British understandings of Bretton
Woods, see Gardner, *Sterling-Dollar Diplo-
macy,* 143–44. See also Alfred E. Eckes, Jr., *A
Search for Solvency: Bretton Woods and the
International Monetary System, 1941–1971*
(Austin: University of Texas Press, 1975); and
Van Dormael, *Bretton Woods.*

[31] Gardner, *Sterling-Dollar Diplomacy,* 158.

[32] Quoted in ibid., 198.

[33] See Robin Edmonds, *Setting the Mould:
The United States and Britain 1945–1950*
(New York: Norton, 1986), chap. 8.

[34] Gardner, *Sterling-Dollar Diplomacy,* 382.

balance with the power and influence at its disposal.

Moreover, in the rush to international economic rulemaking, important differences were masked concerning the proper role of governments in promoting full employment, price stability, and social welfare. These differences would reappear as the transition period of reconstruction and alliance building ended in the late 1940s.

Finally, there was the problem of the emergence of U.S.–Soviet hostilities. Ernst H. Van Der Beugel notes: "The political hopes of the United States were shattered by the nature of Soviet policy. The total ruin of Europe destroyed the hope of economic stability.[35] Taken together, the early efforts to usher in a period of liberal multilateralism were thwarted by the same forces that destroyed the wartime vision of one world. American officials were determined not to repeat the errors of World War I, but the plans themselves would need revision. In the end, as Richard Gardner notes, the assumptions of an early return to political and economic equilibrium were unfounded.[36] In political terms, the postwar world was moving toward two worlds, not one. In economic terms, the Europeans suffered from a severe dollar shortage, importing as much as seven times the value of goods they were exporting to the United States.

The Marshall Plan and a European Third Force

As the difficulties of implementing the liberal, multilateral proposals became evident, American policy began to involve efforts to bolster the political and eco-

nomic foundations of Europe—to create in effect a third force. Burton Berry, a career Foreign Service officer, noted in July 1947 that it was time to "drop the pretense of one world."[37] The need to search for a new approach to Europe was underscored by State Department official Charles Bohlen:

The United States is confronted with a condition in the world which is at direct variance with the assumptions upon which, during and directly after the war, major United States policies were predicated. Instead of unity among the great powers—both political and economic—after the war, there is complete disunity between the Soviet Union and the satellites on one side and the rest of the world on the other. There are, in short, two worlds instead of one. Faced with this disagreeable fact, however much we may deplore it, the United States in the interest of its own well-being and security and those of the free non-Soviet world must reexamine its major policy objectives.[38]

American officials were forced to attend to the balance of power in Europe. Accordingly, the new policy emphasis—embodied in the proposals for a European Recovery Program (what became known as the Marshall Plan)—was to establish a strong and economically integrated Europe.[39] Importantly, the policy shift was

[35] Ernst H. Van Der Beugel, *From Marshall Aid to Atlantic Partnership: European Integration as a Concern of American Foreign Policy* (Amsterdam: Elsevier Publishing Co., 1966), 19.

[36] Gardner, *Sterling-Dollar Diplomacy,* 294.

[37] Quoted in John Gaddis, "Spheres of Influence: The United States and Europe, 1945–1949" in Gaddis, *The Long Peace* (New York: Oxford University Press, 1987), 57.

[38] Bohlen memorandum, 30 August 1947, *Foreign Relations of the United States* [henceforth FRUS] 1947 (Washington, D.C.: U.S. Government Printing Office, 1973), vol. 1, 763–64.

[39] On the role of Europe in American wartime planning and the "relative indifference of the administration to regionalist ideas," see Max Beloff, *The United States and the Unity of Europe* (Washington, D.C.: Brookings Institution, 1963), chap. 1.

not to a sphere-of-influence approach with a direct and ongoing American military and political presence in Europe. Rather, the aim was to build Europe into an *independent* center of military and economic power, a third force.

This new policy was advanced by several groups within the State Department.[40] The new emphasis on building centers of power in Europe was a view George Kennan had already held, and it was articulated with some vigor by Kennan's Policy Planning staff, newly organized in May 1947. "It should be a cardinal point of our policy," Kennan argued in October 1947, "to see to it that other elements of independent power are developed on the Eurasian land mass as rapidly as possible in order to take off our shoulders some of the burden of 'bipolarity.' "[41]

Kennan's Policy Planning staff presented its first recommendations to Secretary of State George Marshall on 23 May 1947. Their emphasis was not on the direct threat of Soviet activities in Western Europe, but on the war-ravaged economic, political, and social institutions of Europe that made communist inroads possible. An American effort to aid Europe "should be directed not to combatting communism as such, but to the restoration of the economic health and vigor of European society."[42] In a later memorandum the Policy Planning staff argued

that the program should take the form of a multilateral clearing system to lead to the reduction of tariffs and trade barriers and eventually to take the form of a European Customs Union.[43] Moreover, the Policy Planning staff argued that the initiative and responsibility for the program should come from the Europeans themselves. This group clearly envisaged a united and economically integrated Europe standing on its own apart from both the Soviet sphere and the United States.[44] "By insisting on a joint approach," Kennan later wrote, "we hoped to force the Europeans to think like Europeans, and not like nationalists, in this approach to the economic problems of the continent."[45]

Another group of State Department officials working on European recovery prepared a memorandum of major importance in May 1947 that outlined objectives of American foreign aid.[46] The chief objective of U.S. policy, they argued, should be to strengthen the political and economic countries of Europe and by so doing create the conditions in Europe to induce the Soviets to negotiate with the West rather than continue a policy of unilateral expansion. The objective was to foster a strong and economically

---

[40] See Beugel, *From Marshall Plan to Atlantic Partnership*, 41–45. For a fascinating account of the emerging policy views of State Department and other top government officials concerning the rebuilding of Europe, see Walter Isaacson and Evan Thomas, *The Wise Men: Six Friends and the World They Made* (New York: Simon and Schuster, 1987), 402–418.

[41] Kennan to Cecil B. Lyon, 13 October 1947, Policy Planning Staff Records. Quoted in Gaddis, "Spheres of Influence," 58.

[42] Kennan quotes the memorandum in his memoirs. George Kennan, *Memoirs: 1925–1950* (Boston: Little, Brown, 1967), 336.

[43] Beugel, *From Marshall Plan to Atlantic Partnership*, 43.

[44] Kennan, *Memoirs: 1925–1950*, 325–353; *FRUS, 1947*, III: 223–230.

[45] Kennan, *Memoirs: 1925–1950*, 337.

[46] The document was dated 12 June 1947, a week after Marshall's Harvard speech; but the main ideas were circulated earlier. This group, composed of H. van D. Cleveland, Ben T. Moore, and Charles Kindleberger, prepared the memorandum for a major State-War-Navy Coordinating Committee report. Parts of the document are reprinted in Charles P. Kindleberger, *Marshall Plan Days* (Boston: Allen & Unwin, 1987), 4–24. See also Michael Hogan, "European Integration and the Marshall Plan" in Stanley Hoffman and Charles Maier, eds., *The Marshall Plan: A Retrospective* (Boulder, Colo.: Westview Press, 1984), 4–5.

integrated Europe. Moreover, the memorandum argued that U.S. policy should be directed at increasing the western orientation of European leaders. In France, Italy, and Germany, in particular, policy should be directed at preventing leaders from drifting to the extreme Left or Right. A European recovery program, these officials argued, would need to stress political and ideological as well as economic objectives. In summarizing the document, Beugel notes that in meeting these objectives a "purely economic program would be insufficient. Non-communist Europe should also be provided with possible goals to help fill the present ideological and moral vacuum. The only possible ideological content of such a program was European unity."[47] The idea of a united Europe was to provide the ideological bulwark for European political and economic reconstruction.

Other State Department voices echoed the call for a shift in policy. Under Secretary of State William Clayton returned from Europe on 19 May alarmed by the economic distress of Europe. In a memorandum to Acheson and Marshall, Clayton argued that the United States had underestimated the destruction of Europe's economy and stressed the need for immediate and large-scale action.[48] On 8 May Under Secretary Acheson took the occasion of a public speech to outline the imperatives of European recovery and foreshadowed the Marshall Plan.[49]

The public turning point in U.S. policy came on 5 June 1947 with Marshall's speech at Harvard University. The American government was now ready to play a much more direct and systematic role in European reconstruction. Yet State Department officials, in a theme echoed throughout this period, were insistent that European leaders themselves take responsibility for organizing the program. At a State Department meeting on 29 May 1947, for example, Kennan "pointed out the necessity of European acknowledgement of responsibility and parentage in the plan to prevent the certain attempts of powerful elements to place the entire burden on the United States and to discredit it and us by blaming the United States for all failures." Similarly, Bohlen noted that the United States had to balance the "danger of appearing to force 'the American way' on Europe and the danger of failure if the major responsibility is left to Europe." The United States would need to make it clear to the Europeans, Bohlen argued, that "the only politically feasible basis on which the United States would be willing to make the aid available is substantial evidence of a developing overall plan for economic cooperation by the Europeans themselves, perhaps an economic federation to be worked out over 3 or 4 years."[50]

A policy of fostering European independence rather than a spheres-of-influence policy had both practical and

---

[47] Beugel, *From Marshall Plan to Atlantic Partnership*, 45.

[48] "The European Situation," Memorandum by the Under Secretary of State for Economic Affairs, *FRUS, 1947,* III: 230–232. Joseph Jones argues that this report had a decisive influence on Marshall's speech and may have prompted the speech itself. *The Fifteen Weeks* (New York: Viking Press, 1955), 203. Clayton's memo reportedly moved Marshall to confirm his tentatively scheduled appointment to speak at Harvard's commencement exercises. The next day Marshall gave a copy of Clayton's memorandum and Kennan's Policy Planning paper to Bohlen and instructed hm to write a speech that would invite Europe to request American aid.

[49] Summarized by Beugel, *From Marshall Plan to Atlantic Partnership*, 47–49; also see Dean Acheson, *Present at the Creation* (New York: New American Library, 1966), 227–230.

[50] "Summary of Discussion on Problems of Relief, Rehabilitation and Reconstruction of Europe," 29 May 1947, *FRUS, 1947,* III: 235.

ideological considerations. Within the Truman administration some officials stressed the policy's importance in strengthening European democracies against communist subversion. Others focused on its usefulness in rebuilding Franco-German relations. Still others found the policy important in promoting expanded production and stability of the European economy.

There were also domestic political reasons for administration support for a united Europe. Congress and American public opinion were in 1947 still wary of permanent political and military commitments to Europe. Such domestic considerations are evident in discussions by Truman administration officials as they prepared to sell the Marshall Plan aid program to Congress. In the foreign assistance legislation that funded the European Recovery Program, Congress made greater European unification a condition for aid.[51]

The idea of a united Europe also fit well with American ideals. "The vague uneasiness and even irritation about the fragmentation of the old world and the genuine desire to transplant the American image to the shattered European countries were translated into a plan and subsequent action." Moreover, State Department officials felt that by encouraging independence and self-determination in Europe, the emergence of democratic institutions would be more likely to succeed. John Gaddis summarizes this notion: "the view in Washington persisted throughout the late 1940s that the viability of political systems depended in large part upon their autonomy, even spontaneity. For this reason, Americans were willing to tolerate a surprising amount of

diversity within the anti-Soviet coalition."[52]

The European Recovery Program put the economic and political reconstruction of Europe into a security framework. It was at this juncture that Kennan's ideas most resonated with official U.S. policy. The crisis of Europe, according to these officials, was not due to the pressure of communist activities. Policy Planning and the others believed that "the present crisis resulted in large part from the disruptive effects of the war on the economic, political and social structure of Europe."[53]

European responses to American efforts to assist in economic and political reconstruction were initially quite enthusiastic. British Foreign Minister Ernest Bevin, listening to Marshall's speech on the BBC, accepted the offer of assistance immediately; and he quickly traveled to Paris to begin consultations with the French. The new attitude toward European unity was later reaffirmed by Bevin on 22 January 1948. Announcing that the time had arrived for a new consolidation of Western Europe, Bevin argued for an association of the "historic members of European civilization." United States officials welcomed Bevin's speech as a signal of European initiative.[54]

The major product of the early negotiations among European officials was the Organization for European Economic Cooperation (OEEC), which came into being on 5 June 1948. At each step along the way, the United States used its economic strength, primarily in the form of dollar aid, to promote European unity, while at

---

[51] Section 102(a) of the Economic Cooperation Act of 1948, as amended, stated that: "It is further declared to be the policy of the people of the US to encourage the unification of Europe. . . ."

[52] Gaddis, "Spheres of Influence," 59. See also Michael J. Hogan, The Marshall Plan: America, Britain, and the Reconstruction of Western Europe, 1947–1952 (New York: Cambridge University Press, 1987).

[53] Beugel, From Marshall Plan to Atlantic Partnership, 42.

[54] Ibid., 121–122.

the same time attempting to remain outside the negotiations. In addition to organizations devoted to the administration of U.S. aid, monetary and trade liberalization agreements were also forged.

Yet the building of a third force, the central objective of American policy between 1947 and 1950, fell short of American hopes. Disagreements between the British and the French over the extensiveness of supranational political authority and economic integration left the early proposals for unity unfulfilled. W.W. Rostow notes: "[B]ecause the British opposed it, because the economic requirements of unity did not converge with requirements for prompt recovery, and because the United States was unclear as to how its influence should be applied—the Marshall Plan did not succeed in moving Western Europe radically towards unity."[55]

In late 1949 a tone of urgency was heard in State Department discussions of European integration. In a memorandum written by Secretary of State Acheson, shifts in administration thinking were evident. With British reluctance to lead a movement toward European integration, Acheson noted that "[t]he key to progress towards integration is in French hands." Moreover, Acheson was willing to settle for integration on the continent itself and introduced the possibility of American participation in the Organization of European Economic Cooperation. Yet on these revised terms the United States continued to push for integration that would involve "some merger of sovereignty."[56]

The United States wanted to encourage an independent Europe—a third force—and not to establish an American sphere of influence. Yet the Europeans could not agree among themselves to organize such a center of global power; the United States, despite its hegemonic power, could not see to its implementation. Just as in the earlier phase, when the goal of U.S. policy was that of global, liberal multilateralism, severe limits of U.S. power were experienced. Beugel makes this point:

In dealing with sovereign states, even if these states are impoverished and politically and economically impotent, as was the case in Europe during the first years of the Marshall Plan, there is a limit beyond which even a country of the unique power of the United States cannot go in imposing far-reaching measures such as those leading to European integration.[57]

The irony is that while the United States was unwilling and probably unable to use more direct coercive power to encourage European unity, European resistance was not to the use of American power but to the ends toward which it was to be put. The United States wanted to avoid a direct, ongoing security commitment to Western Europe and the emergence of a sphere of influence that such a policy would entail. Yet as East-West tensions increased and as British and continental governments frustrated plans for a geopolitical third force, a new phase of American policy unfolded. Europe actively courted the extension of

---

[55] W. W. Rostow, *The United States in the World Arena: An Essay in Recent History* (New York: Harper & Row, 1960) 216. See also Alan S. Milward, *The Reconstruction of Western Europe, 1945–51* (Berkeley: University of California Press, 1984).

[56] "The Secretary of State to the Embassy in France," 19 October 1949, *FRUS, 1949,* IV:

469–472. In the subsequent meeting of American ambassadors in Paris, agreement was reached among them that European integration could not proceed without British participation.

[57] Beugel, *From Marshall Plan to Atlantic Partnership,* 220–21.

American power and, in the guise of NATO, a subordinate position in an American sphere of influence.

THE "PULL" OF EUROPE: EMPIRE BY INVITATION

In 1947 and the following years, the United States appeared to hold the military and economic power needed to shape the terms of European reconstruction. With a monopoly on the atomic bomb, a massive (although demobilizing) standing army, and an industrial economy enlarged by the war, the United States appeared to have all the elements of hegemonic power. Moreover, the United States had what Europeans needed most: American dollars. "More and more as week succeeds week," the *Economist* noted in May 1947, "the whole of European life is being overshadowed by the great dollar shortage. The margin between recovery and collapse throughout Western Europe is dependent at this moment upon massive imports from the U.S."[58]

It is all the more striking, therefore, how successful the European governments were at blunting and redirecting American policy toward Europe. This resistance by Europe to the construction of a third force had several sources and differed from country to country. Each sought to use American hegemonic power for its own national purposes. At the same time, the same considerations that led to the rejection of a full-blown united Europe prompted these same governments to encourage a direct American political and security presence in Europe.

The British were the most resistant to a united Europe. Britain initially reacted positively to the larger political objectives of Marshall Plan aid. A secret Cabinet session in March 1948 concluded that Britain "should use United States aid

to gain time, but our ultimate aim should be to attain a position in which the countries of western Europe could be independent both of the United States and of the Soviet Union."[59] Yet as a practical matter, the British resisted significant steps in that direction. In a meeting of American ambassadors in Europe in October 1949, David Bruce argued: "We have been too tender with Britain since the war: she has been the constant stumbling block in the economic organization of Europe. . . ."[60]

The British were eager to maintain their special relationship with the United States, but feared it would be undermined by the emergence of a confederation with European countries. Moreover, the political and economic burdens of sustaining a European center of power would only further strain the British Commonwealth system. As with several of the other European countries, the British also feared the eventual dominance of Germany or even Russia in a unified Europe. These considerations implied the need for more, not less, American involvement in postwar Europe, particularly in the form of the NATO security relationship. As David Calleo has recently noted: "NATO seemed an ideal solution. With American commanders and forces taking primary responsibility for European ground defense, no question would remain about America's willingness to come to Europe's aid. Britain could reserve for itself those military and naval commands needed to retain control over its own national defense."[61] Indeed, in 1952 the British sought to reduce the

---

[58] *The Economist,* 31 May 1947.

[59] Quoted in Gaddis, "Sphere of Influence," 66.

[60] "Summary Record of a Meeting of United States Ambassadors at Paris," 21–22 October 1949, *FRUS, 1949,* IV: 492.

[61] David P. Calleo, *Beyond American Hegemony: The Future of the Western Alliance* (New York: Basic Books, 1988), 35.

role of the OEEC and transfer its functions to NATO—an attempt to build the Atlantic relationship at the expense of European unity.[62]

British officials were more concerned with preventing a return by the United States to an isolationist position than with an overbearing American hegemonic presence in Europe. "The fear was not of American expansionism," Gaddis notes, "but of American isolationism, and much time was spent considering how such expansionist tendencies could be reinforced."[63] It is no surprise, therefore, that in encouraging the United States to lead a security protectorate of Europe, the British began to stress the seriousness of the Soviet threat in Europe. In January 1948, British Foreign Minister Ernest Bevin warned Washington of "the further encroachment of the Soviet tide" and the need to "reinforce the physical barriers which still guard Western civilization."[64]

The French also sought to put American resources to their own national purposes and encourage an Atlantic security relationship. To be sure, France was more sympathetic to American ideas of European integration. Integration was useful in fostering French-dominated coalitions of governments in Western Europe. A political and economic union would also allow France to have some influence over the reemergence of the German economy as well as tie Germany

to a larger regional framework.[65] At the same time, however, the French also had an interest in encouraging a larger American security relationship with Europe. NATO, even more than a European community, would serve to contain Germany and the Soviets. Moreover, as with Britain, an American presence would free French resources, otherwise tied up in European defense, for purposes of preserving the remains of its colonial empire.[66]

Germany also supported American leadership of NATO. For West Germany's Chancellor Konrad Adenauer, the Atlantic security relationship was a means of rebuilding German sovereignty and equality on the continent. Germany had less room for maneuver than Britain or France. But participation in regional integration and NATO served the goals of political and economic reconstruction.[67]

In late 1947, efforts intensified by Europeans to draw the United States into a security relationship. British Foreign Minister Bevin outlined his ideas on military cooperation to Secretary of State Marshall on 15 December 1947. A regional European organization centered around Britain, France, and the Benelux countries would be linked to the other Western European countries and to the United States. Marshall signaled his interest in the plan but later indicated that the United States could not presently make any commitments.[68] Other Euro-

[62] Beloff, *The United States and the Unity of Europe*, 69.

[63] John Lewis Gaddis, "The Emerging Post-Revisionist Synthesis on the Origins of the Cold War," *Diplomatic History* 7 (Summer 1983). This statement is based, at least in part, on newly opened records of the British Foreign Office.

[64] "Summary of a Memorandum Representing Mr. Bevin's Views on the Formation of a Western Union," enclosed in Inverchapel to Marshall, 13 January 1948, *FRUS, 1948*, III: 4–6.

[65] See Maier, "Supranational Concepts and National Continuity in the Framework of the Marshall Plan," 34.

[66] Calleo, *Beyond American Hegemony*, 35. See also Michael M. Harrison, *The Reluctant Ally: France and Atlantic Security* (Baltimore: Johns Hopkins University Press, 1981).

[67] Calleo, *Beyond American Hegemony*, 35.

[68] Memorandum by the British Foreign Office, undated, *FRUS, 1947*, 111: 818–819. See also Geir Lundestad, *America, Scandinavia, and the Cold War, 1945–1949* (New York: Columbia University Press, 1980), 171–72.

30   G. John Ikenberry

pean officials, such as Belgian Prime
Minister (and Foreign Minister) Paul-
Henri Spaak, were also calling for Amer-
ican military cooperation.[69]

Bevin's urgings were given prominence in his 22 January 1948 speech in
the House of Commons. Later Bevin
argued that European defense efforts
would not be possible without American assistance. "The treaties that are
being proposed cannot be fully effective
nor be relied upon when a crisis arises
unless there is assurance of American
support for the defense of Western
Europe."[70]

The French also sought to draw the
United States into playing a military role
in Western Europe. Foreign Minister
Georges Bidault called upon the United
States "to strengthen in the political field,
and as soon as possible in the military
one, the collaboration between the old
and the new worlds, both so jointly responsible for the preservation of the only
valuable civilization."[71]

Some officials in the Truman administration, such as Director of the Office of
European Affairs John D. Hickerson,
were urging military cooperation with
Western Europe.[72] Others, most notably
George Kennan, resisted the idea of a military union, arguing that it would be de-

structive of the administration's goal of
European unity.[73] The official position of
the Truman administration during this
period was ambiguous: it was sympathetic to European concerns but reluctant
to make a commitment. After repeated
British attempts to obtain an American
pledge of support, Under Secretary Robert Lovett informed the British ambassador that the Europeans themselves must
proceed with discussions on European
military cooperation. Only afterward
would the United States consider its relationship to these initiatives.[74] The British, undeterred, continued to insist on
American participation in plans for
Western European defense.

It was not until 12 March, after the
coup in Czechoslovakia, which demonstrated the Soviet hold on East Europe,
and the further deterioration of East-West
relations, that the United States agreed to
engage in joint talks with the West Europeans on an "Atlantic security system."[75]
In the months that followed, American
and European differences narrowed,
largely with the United States coming to
agree on an integrated security system
with itself at the center.

Taken together, the United States and
State Department officials such as George
Kennan were much more eager to see an
independent Europe than the Europeans
themselves. In the end, the European governments were not willing to take the
risks, expend the resources, or resolve
the national differences that would necessarily be a part of an independent,
third force. Political life within an American hegemonic system and a bipolar

[69] Lundestad, *America, Scandinavia, and the Cold War, 1945–1949*, 172.

[70] *FRUS, 1948*, III: 14. In his memoirs, British Prime Minister C. R. Attlee referred to the "making of the Brussels treaty and the Atlantic Pact" as "the work of Bevin." Attlee, *As It Happened* (London: Heinemann, 1954), 171. See also Escott Reid, *Time of Fear and Hope: The Making of the North Atlantic Treaty, 1947–1949* (Toronto: McClelland and Stewart, 1977).

[71] Quoted in Lundestad, "Empire by Invitation? The United States and Western Europe, 1945–1952," *Journal of Peace Research* 23 (1986): 270.

[72] Hickerson memorandum, *FRUS, 1948*, III: 6–7.

[73] Kennan memorandum to Secretary of State, 20 January 1948, *FRUS, 1948*, III: 7–8. See also Kennan, *Memoirs: 1925–1950*, 397–406.

[74] Lovett to Inverchapel, 2 February 1948, *FRUS, 1948*, III: 17–18.

[75] Ibid., III: 48.

world was the more acceptable alternative.

Part of the reason for this "craving for dependence,"[76] as David Calleo has recently put it, is that the European nations, except perhaps for Germany, were able to develop the means for maneuver within that American hegemonic system. Such was the case for Britain, as it is noted by Charles Maier:

> Within the American "hegemony" Britain preserved as much of her Commonwealth position, her shielding of her balance of payments, as possible. She also played what might be termed the "Polybian" strategy, attempting to become the Greeks in America's Roman empire, wagering on the "special relationship" to prolong their influence and status.[77]

The more general point is that the European encouragement of an American presence in Europe served a variety of national needs. The room for maneuver within that hegemonic system ensured that those needs would at least in part be met. Moreover, to tie the United States to a formal security relationship with Europe would provide a much more effective basis for the Europeans to influence and shape the American exercise of hegemonic power than would be the case with a less encumbered America. Even as Britain and the continental governments invited America's political and military presence in Europe, it ensured that the international economic system that would attend that new relationship was sufficiently based on European terms.

FROM LIBERAL MULTILATERALISM TO "EMBEDDED LIBERALISM"

The United States failed in its initial attempt to bring liberal multilateralism to Europe. The coercive use of American hegemonic power, most explicitly evident in the British loan, was largely self-defeating. The Marshall Plan represented a shift in policy toward regional reconstruction and a politically independent and integrated Europe. The Europeans took the aid but declined the invitation to move toward a third force in a multipolar world. At the same time, as we have seen, the Europeans (with leadership from British Foreign Minister Bevin) actively sought to extend the American security presence to Western Europe.

The United States was prevailed upon to defend a grouping of western industrial democracies. But what kind of grouping? In late 1949 officials within the Truman administration were uncertain. "It is not yet clear," Acheson argued, "what is the most desirable ultimate pattern of deeper international association of the United States, British Commonwealth, and Europe, and I do not believe that anyone should blueprint a course far ahead with any great rigidity."[78] Nonetheless, even as American policy shifted, the Truman administration clung to a now more distant objective of liberal multilateralism. Liberal economic internationalism, although initially blocked by the imperatives of European reconstruction and the unfolding cold war, were not abandoned, at least in rhetoric. William Clayton noted this in a broadcast on 22 November 1947: "The Marshall Plan, or the European Recovery Program, has to do with the short-term emergency

[76] Calleo, *Beyond American Hegemony,* 35.
[77] Maier, "Supranational Concepts and National Continuity in the Framework of the Marshall Plan," 34.

[78] "The Secretary of State to the Embassy in France," 19 October, 1949, *FRUS, 1949,* IV: 469.

needs of one part of the world. The International Trade Organization has to do with long-range trade policies and trade of all the world. They are highly complementary and interrelated."[79]

This observation was more a hope than anything else. The Marshall Plan was not simply an interim step to place the European economies in a position to participate in a system based on earlier elaborated American plans for liberal multilateralism. Rather, the working out of these policy shifts served to alter the substantive character of those liberal, multilateral designs. This policy retreat and what it reveals about American hegemonic power is noted by Fred Hirsch and Michael Doyle:

The limited capacity of the United States to determine the international economic order actually in force, even at the peak of American military-economic predominance in the immediate aftermath of World War II, is a striking indication of the extent to which relationships between the United States and other major Western powers at this time fell short of unqualified American hegemony. For the striking fact is that the United States was not able to impose its preferred multilateral trading order on the major trading countries. It was able to set the frame for such an order, as embodied in the major provisions of the IMF [International Monetary Fund] and the proposed International Trade Organization (ITO). But these provisions themselves had to be considerably modified, as compared with the original United States proposals, to make them acceptable to other governments. The original United States conception was thus weakened substantially by the resulting allow-

ance made for transitional provisions, for exceptions to nondiscrimination and absence of restrictions, and for the ultimate escape by countries from the discipline of the international system through exchange adjustment.[80]

Throughout the period, these concessions and compromises were indirect and were manifest as the United States sought to promote political stability and noncommunist regimes in Western Europe. The effort to encourage noncommunist alternatives in continental Europe was pursued from many quarters of the American government. At the State Department Charles Bohlen argued in 1946 that the United States should direct the Left in democratic directions. "It is definitely in the interest of the United States to see that the present left movement throughout the world, which we should recognize and even support, develops in the direction of democratic as against totalitarian systems."[81] Later, George Kennan argued that the Marshall Plan itself was the key to building the strength of anticommunist forces.[82] Where serious communist parties contended for power, such as in Italy and France, the United States was willing to come to the aid of all parties to their right, including socialists.

United States involvement in support of noncommunist forces in Italy during the crucial 1948 national elections reveals this strategy. An immediate aim during this period was the bolstering of the noncommunist Italian Socialists. The American ambassador, James Dunn, searched for ways to channel funds to strengthen the fragile political base of the

[79] Quoted in Beloff, *The United States and the Unity of Europe,* 28.

[80] Hirsch and Doyle, *Alternatives to Monetary Disorder,* 29.
[81] Quoted in Gaddis, "Dividing Adversaries" in Gaddis, *The Long Peace,* 150.
[82] Ibid., 154.

Socialists as well as those to the right.[83]
The attempt was made to prevent the Italian Socialist Party from joining the ranks
of the communist-led electoral alliance.
In the end, with massive American covert
aid and threats of the cut-off of Marshall
Plan assistance, the Christian Democrats
won a commanding electoral victory and
a majority in parliament.

The primacy of stability in Western Europe, built around noncommunist political parties, had larger ramifications for
American foreign economic policy. Indirectly, at least, this commitment meant
that the United States would need to accommodate social democratic goals in
the construction of international economic order. The successful political reconstruction of Europe meant not just a
delay in the realization of liberal, multilateral goals, but their permanent
alteration.

Although not framed as an explicit
shift in international economic objectives, the United States did gradually
move to accept a modified liberal, multilateral order. For the most part this took
the form of exemptions and abridgements
in trade and financial arrangements. Together, these compromises allowed a
larger measure of national economic autonomy and a stronger role of the state in
pursuing full employment and social
welfare. The discipline of the international market would be softened by the
welfare state. The differences between
Britain and the United States over postwar economic arrangements were representative of the larger American-European split. At each turn during
negotiations over monetary and trade
rules and institutions, Britain sought arrangements that would be congenial with

an expanded domestic state role in employment and social welfare.

Compromises between multilateralism
in international economic relations and
state intervention in the domestic economy and society are what John Ruggie
has termed "embedded liberalism."[84]
The task of postwar institutional reconstruction," Ruggie argues, was to "devise
a framework which would safeguard and
even aid the quest for domestic stability
without, at the same time, triggering the
mutually destructive external consequences that had plagued the interwar
period."[85] In other words, rules would be
devised to allow for nondiscrimination in
commercial and monetary relations, but
also to facilitate the welfare state.

Ruggie argues that a loose consensus
existed among the industrial democracies, even during the war, on the need to
make compromises between postwar liberal multilateralism and domestic interventionism. This was the case, however,
only at the most general level. The types
of compromises were achieved in piecemeal fashion over the course of the entire
1940s. European countries gave ground
on the American insistence that multilateralism be at the core of international
economic arrangements. The United
States came to accept the need to protect
newly emerging Keynesian economic
policies and the provisions of the welfare
state. But these compromises were less
explicit and negotiated than a product of

[83] James Edward Miller, *The United States and Italy, 1940–1950: The Politics and Diplomacy of Stabilization* (Chapel Hill: University of North Carolina Press, 1986), 243–49.

[84] John Gerard Ruggie, "International Regimes, Transactions, and Change: Embedded Liberalism in the Postwar Economic Order," *International Organization* 36 (Spring 1982): 379–415. See also Robert Keohane, "The World Political Economy and the Crisis of Embedded Liberalism" in John H. Goldthorpe, ed., *Order and Conflict in Contemporary Capitalism: Studies in the Political Economy of Western European Nations* (Oxford, Eng.: Clarendon Press, 1984), 15–38.

[85] Ruggie, "International Regimes, Transactions, and Change," 393.

the failure of such instruments of liberal multilateralism as the Anglo-American Financial Agreement and the International Trade Organization.

At each stage of negotiation the British sought to make American monetary and commercial proposals contingent on expanded production and employment. Behind Britain's conditional response to American initiatives were various factions on the Left and Right that opposed liberal multilateralism.[86] Uniting these groups was a skepticism of economic liberalism at home or abroad. A British newspaper of the day noted: "We must . . . reconcile ourselves once and for all to the view that the days of *laissez-faire* and the unlimited division of labor are over; that every country—including Great Britain—plans and organizes its production in the light of social and military needs, and that the regulation of this production by such 'trade barriers' as tariffs, quotas, and subsidies is a necessary and integral part of this policy."[87]

In British debates on the various trade and financial agreements, as Gardner notes, officials "devoted considerable efforts to showing that full employment and domestic planning would not be impeded by the multilateral arrangements."[88] In negotiations over the ITO these concerns were manifest in safeguards and escape clauses, in the removal of agriculture from the framework, and in transition periods to multilateralism. As one British official noted in discussions over trade arrangements, "there must be in the international settlement which we are now devising sufficient escape clauses, let-outs, special arrangements, call them what you will, which will en-

able those countries which are adopting internal measures for full employment to protect themselves. . . ."[89]

These efforts to protect domestic economic and social obligations of the state came primarily from Britain and the other European countries. The Europeans themselves were crucial in recasting the terms of liberal multilateralism—if only in resisting, modifying, and circumventing American proposals. In insisting on the primacy of domestic stability in the development of international economic rules and institutions, the Europeans (and most importantly the British) successfully recast the character of postwar economic order. The story of postwar international political economy is as much that of the triumph of the welfare state as of the halting and partial emergence of liberal multilateralism.

CONCLUSION

The structure of the early postwar system bears the profound marks of American ideas and the projection of its power; about this there is no dispute. The task here has been to reconsider the conventional understanding of that power and the fate of those ideas. American power was unprecedented, but it was not unalloyed. The United States was not able to implement the full range of its proposals for postwar order; but it did get drawn into a larger hegemonic role in Europe than it anticipated or wanted. In understanding this duality of the American postwar experience, we are better able to appreciate the substance, scope, and limits of American hegemonic power.

The failure of the first efforts at multilateralism and the failure of policies to promote European unity say a great deal about the character of American hegemonic power after the war. The direct use

---

[86] See Gardner, *Sterling-Dollar Diplomacy*, 30–35.

[87] *The Times* (London), 11 January 1941. Quoted in Gardner, *Sterling-Dollar Diplomacy*, 31.

[88] Gardner, *Sterling-Dollar Diplomacy*, 234.

[89] Ibid., 277.

of American power to coerce European acceptance of liberal, multilateral designs (seen most clearly in the British loan episode) were singularly unsuccessful. Less direct methods of pursuing even a revised plan for European regional cooperation also fell short. The purpose of the Marshall Plan was to restore the political confidence of the Europeans. Yet as Gaddis notes, once this was the objective, it was the Europeans who could dictate what it would take to produce confidence.[90] In the end, this required a direct American military commitment.

The Europeans wanted a stronger and more formal hegemonic system than the United States was initially willing to provide. The initial one world plans of collective security and economic universalism would have been a very cost-effective form of *Pax Americana.* The obligations to Europe would have been minimal and they would have accorded with prevailing U.S. congressional and popular public opinion. The system, once constituted, was envisaged to be self-regulating. Given American economic size and competitiveness, this global open door would both serve its own interests and resonate with time-honored American liberal ideas of politics and economics. However, not only were the assumptions behind this vision of postwar order wrong, but the United States, despite its preponderance of economic and military resources, was unable to implement its essential parts.

The revised strategy of a European third force and the construction of a multipolar order was equally elusive. It again revealed the limits of American postwar power. These limits were recognized by many of the American officials themselves. In promoting the idea of a united Europe in the context of Marshall Plan aid, the Truman administration insisted that Europe itself take the initiative. More direct American pressure would have been self-defeating, but its absence also ensured that the Europeans could set the limits on cooperation and integration. It was the very weakness of the European economies and societies that prevented the United States from translating its array of power resources into bargaining assets. The United States could not push too hard. The Europeans, in turn, could set the terms upon which to pull the United States into economic and security relationships.

In the end the United States had to settle for a more traditional form of empire—a *Pax Americana* with formal commitments to Europe. The result was an institutional relationship that diverted American resources to Europe in the form of a security commitment, allowing the Europeans to employ their more scarce resources elsewhere and providing the ongoing institutional means for the Europeans to influence and render predictable American hegemonic power. In blunting and altering the substantive character of international economic relations to ensure the survival of budding welfare states, the Europeans succeeded in drawing the United States into protecting a system that they were able to effectively redefine. As students of empire have often noted, the flow of ideas and influence between empirical center and periphery works in both directions.[91] Unable to secure a less formal and more ambitious *Pax Americana,* the United States found itself experiencing the similar two-way flow of ideas and influence.

The sequence of shifts in American policy toward postwar order is often understood as a set of adjustments to the emergence of East-West hostilities. It was the rise of perceptions of threat from the

---

[90] Gaddis, "Spheres of Influence," 62.

[91] See Michael W. Doyle, *Empires* (Ithaca, N.Y.: Cornell University Press, 1986).

Soviet Union that forced the compromises and that shifted the center of gravity from economic-centered postwar designs to security-centered designs. There are at least two problems with this understanding. First, this interpretation obscures the failures of American policy and the limited ability of the United States to exercise hegemonic power on its own terms. The focus on failure to implement policy in the first two phases of U.S. policy reveals these limits and the striking ability with which the Europeans could resist American initiatives from a position of weakness.

Second, perhaps more fateful for the way in which American policy unfolded after World War II was the utter collapse of Great Britain, not the rise of the Soviet Union. In a meeting of American ambassadors in Paris in the autumn of 1949, John J. McCloy, the high commissioner for Germany, argued that perhaps too much emphasis had been given to "the increase of Russian power in the world

and too little thought to the enormously important factor that is the collapse of the British Empire."[92] Scholars may have suffered a similar problem. This decline of British power, recognized for decades, accelerated by the destruction of the war, and taking a dramatic turn in 1947, was crucial in weakening the overall political and economic position of Europe in the late 1940s. If the argument made above has merit, it was precisely the weakness of Britain and continental Europe that undermined the ability of the United States to successfully employ its hegemonic position after the war. Ironically, it might well be the case that less disparity in the relationship between Europe and the United States after the war could possibly have provided the basis for the realization of more of the American postwar agenda.

[92] "Summary Record of a Meeting of United States Ambssadors at Paris," 21–22 October 1949, *FRUS, 1949,* IV: 485.

2.   The Changing Nature of World Power

Joseph S. Nye, Jr.

Power in international politics is like the weather. Everyone talks about it, but few understand it. Just as farmers and meteorologists try to forecast storms, so do leaders and analysts try to understand the dynamics of major changes in the distribution of power among nations. Power transitions affect the fortunes of individual nations and are often associated with the cataclysmic storms of world war. But before we can examine theories of hegemonic transition—that is, some of the

SOURCE: Reprinted with permission from *Political Science Quarterly,* vol. 105, no. 2, Summer 1990, pp. 177–192.

leading efforts to predict big changes in the international political weather—we first need to recognize some basic distinctions among the terms *power, balance of power,* and *hegemony.*

POWER

Power, like love, is easier to experience than to define or measure. Power is the ability to achieve one's purposes or goals. The dictionary tells us that it is the ability to do things and to control others. Robert Dahl, a leading political scientist, defines power as the ability to get others to do what they otherwise would not do.[1] But when we measure power in terms of the changed behavior of others, we have to know their preferences. Otherwise, we may be as mistaken about our power as was the fox who thought he was hurting Brer Rabbit when he threw him into the briar patch. Knowing in advance how other people or nations would behave in the absence of our efforts is often difficult. The behavioral definition of power may be useful to analysts and historians who devote considerable time to reconstructing the past, but to practical politicians and leaders it often seems too ephemeral. Because the ability to control others is often associated with the possession of certain resources, political leaders commonly define power as the possession of resources. These resources include population, territory, natural resources, economic size, military forces, and political stability, among others.[2] The virtue of this definition is that it makes power appear more concrete, measurable, and predictable than does the behavioral definition. Power in this sense means holding the high cards in the international poker game. A basic rule of poker is that if your opponent is showing cards that can beat anything you hold, fold your hand. If you know you will lose a war, don't start it.

Some wars, however, have been started by the eventual losers, which suggests that political leaders sometimes take risks or make mistakes. Often the opponent's cards are not all showing in the game of international politics. As in poker, playing skills, such as bluff and deception, can make a big difference. Even when there is no deception, mistakes can be made about which power resources are most relevant in particular situations (for example, France and Britain had more tanks than Hitler in 1940, but Hitler had greater maneuverability and a better military strategy). On the other hand, in long wars when there is time to mobilize, depth of territory and the size of an economy become more important, as the Soviet Union and the United States demonstrated in World War II.

Power conversion is a basic problem that arises when we think of power in terms of resources. Some countries are better than others at converting their resources into effective influence, just as some skilled card players win despite being dealt weak hands. Power conversion is the capacity to convert potential power, as measured by resources, to realized power, as measured by the changed behavior of others. Thus, one has to know about a country's skill at power conversion as well as its possession of power resources to predict outcomes correctly.

Another problem is determining which resources provide the best basis for power in any particular context. In earlier periods, power resources were easier to judge. According to historian A. J. P. Taylor, traditionally "the test of a Great Power is . . . the test of strength for war."[3]

---

[1] Robert A. Dahl, *Who Governs? Democracy and Power in an American City* (New Haven, Conn.: Yale University Press, 1961). See also James March, "The Power of Power" in David Easton, ed., *Varieties of Political Theory* (New York: Prentice Hall, 1966), 39–70; Herbert Simon, *Models of Man* (New York: John Wiley, 1957); and David Baldwin, "Power Analysis and World Politics," *World Politics* 31 (January 1979): 161–94.

[2] See Ray S. Cline, *World Power Assessment* (Boulder, Colo.: Westview Press, 1977); Hans J. Morgenthau, *Politics among Nations* (New York: Alfred Knopf, 1955), chap. 9; and Klaus Knorr, *The Power of Nations* (New York: Basic Books, 1975), chaps. 3, 4.

[3] A. J. P. Taylor, *The Struggle for Mastery in Europe, 1848–1918* (Oxford, Eng.: Oxford University Press, 1954), xxix.

For example, in the agrarian economies of eighteenth-century Europe, population was a critical power resource because it provided a base for taxes and recruitment of infantry. In population, France dominated Western Europe. Thus, at the end of the Napoleonic Wars, Prussia presented its fellow victors at the Congress of Vienna with a precise plan for its own reconstruction in order to maintain the balance of power. Its plan listed the territories and populations it had lost since 1805, and the territories and populations it would need to regain equivalent numbers.[4] In the prenationalist period, it did not much matter that many of the people in those provinces did not speak German or felt themselves to be German. However, within half a century, nationalist sentiments mattered very much. Germany's seizure of Alsace-Lorraine from France in 1870, for example, made hope of any future alliance with France impossible.

Another change that occurred during the nineteenth century was the growing importance of industry and rail systems that made rapid mobilization possible. In the 1860s, Bismarck's Germany pioneered the use of railways to transport armies for quick victories. Although Russia had always had greater population resources than the rest of Europe, they were difficult to mobilize. The growth of the rail system in Western Russia at the beginning of the twentieth century was one of the reasons the Germans feared rising Russian power in 1914. Further, the spread of rail systems on the Continent helped deprive Britain of the luxury of concentrating on naval power. There was no longer time, should it prove necessary, to insert an army to prevent another great power from dominating the Continent.

The application of industrial technol-ogy to warfare has long had a powerful impact. Advanced science and technology have been particularly critical power resources since the beginning of the nuclear age in 1945. But the power derived from nuclear weapons has proven to be so awesome and destructive that its actual application is muscle-bound. Nuclear war is simply too costly. More generally, there are many situations where any use of force may be inappropriate or too costly. In 1853, for example, Admiral Matthew C. Perry could threaten to bombard Japan if it did not open its ports for supplies and trade, but it is hard to imagine that the United States could effectively threaten force to open Japanese markets today.

The Changing Sources of Power

Some observers have argued that the sources of power are, in general, moving away from the emphasis on military force and conquest that marked earlier eras. In assessing international power today, factors such as technology, education, and economic growth are becoming more important, whereas geography, population, and raw materials are becoming less important. Kenneth Waltz argues that a 5-percent rate of economic growth in the United States for three years would add more to American strength than does our alliance with Britain.[5] Richard Rosecrance argues that since 1945, the world has been poised between a territorial system composed of states that view power in terms of land mass, and a trading system "based in states which recognize that self-sufficiency is an illusion." In the past, says Rosecrance, "it was cheaper to seize another state's territory by force than to develop the sophisticated economic and trading apparatus needed to

[4] Edward V. Gulick, *Europe's Classical Balance of Power* (New York: W. W. Norton, 1955), 248–51.

[5] Kenneth N. Waltz, *Theory of International Politics* (Reading, Mass.: Addison-Wesley, 1979), 172.

derive benefit from commercial exchange with it."[6]

If so, perhaps we are in a "Japanese period" in world politics. Japan has certainly done far better with its strategy as a trading state after 1945 than it did with its military strategy to create a Greater East Asian Co-Prosperity sphere in the 1930s. But Japan's security via-à-vis its large military neighbors—China and the Soviet Union—depends heavily on U.S. protection. In short, even if we can define power clearly, it still has become more difficult to be clear about the relationship of particular resources to it. Thus, we cannot leap too quickly to the conclusion that all trends favor economic power or countries like Japan.

Like other forms of power, economic power cannot be measured simply in terms of tangible resources. Intangible aspects also matter. For example, outcomes generally depend on bargaining, and bargaining depends on relative costs in particular situations and skill in converting potential power into effects. Relative costs are determined not only by the total amount of measurable economic resources of a country but also by the degree of its interdependence in a relationship. If, for example, the United States and Japan depend on each other but one is less dependent than the other, that asymmetry is a source of power. The United States may be less vulnerable than Japan if the relationship breaks down, and it may use that threat as a source of power.[7] Thus, an assessment of Japanese and American power must look not only

at shares of resources but also at the relative vulnerabilities of both countries.

Another consideration is that most large countries today find military force more costly to apply than in previous centuries. This has resulted from the dangers of nuclear escalation, the difficulty of ruling nationalistically awakened populations in otherwise weak states, the danger of rupturing profitable relations on other issues, and the public opposition in Western democracies to prolonged and expensive military conflicts. Even so, the increased cost of military force does not mean that it will be ruled out. To the contrary, in an anarchic system of states where there is no higher government to settle conflicts and where the ultimate recourse is self-help, this could never happen. In some cases, the stakes may justify a costly use of force. And, as recent episodes in Grenada and Libya have shown, not all uses of force by great powers involve high costs.[8]

Even if the direct use of force were banned among a group of countries, military force would still play an important political role. For example, the American military role in deterring threats to allies, or of assuring access to a crucial resource such as oil in the Persian Gulf, means that the provision of protective force can be used in bargaining situations. Sometimes the linkage may be direct; more often it is a factor not mentioned openly but present in the back of statesmen's minds.

In addition, there is the consideration that is sometimes called "the second face of power."[9] Getting other states to change

[6] Richard N. Rosecrance, *The Rise of the Trading State* (New York: Basic Books, 1986), 16, 160.

[7] Robert O. Keohane and Joseph S. Nye, Jr., *Power and Interdependence* (Boston: Little, Brown, 1977), chap. 1. See also R. Harrison Wagner, "Economic Interdependence, Bargaining Power and Political Influence," *International Organization* 41 (Summer 1988): 461–84.

[8] Keohane and Nye, *Power and Interdependence,* 27–29; Robert O. Keohane and Joseph S. Nye, Jr., "Power and Interdependence Revisited," *International Organization* 41 (Autumn 1987): 725–53.

[9] Peter Bachrach and Morton S. Baratz, "Decisions and Nondecisions: An Analytical Framework," *American Political Science Review* 57 (September 1963):632–42. See also Richard Mansbach and John Vasquez, *In*

might be called the directive or commanding method of exercising power. Command power can rest on inducements ("carrots") or threats ("sticks"). But there is also an indirect way to exercise power. A country may achieve the outcomes it prefers in world politics because other countries want to follow it or have agreed to a system that produces such effects. In this sense, it is just as important to set the agenda and structure the situations in world politics as it is to get others to change in particular situations. This aspect of power—that is, getting others to want what you want—might be called indirect or co-optive power behavior. It is in contrast to the acive command power behavior of getting others to do what you want.[10] Co-optive power can rest on the attraction of one's ideas or on the ability to set the political agenda in a way that shapes the preferences that others express. Parents of teenagers know that if they have structured their children's beliefs and preferences, their power will be greater and will last longer than if they had relied only on active control. Similarly, political leaders and philosophers have long understood the power that comes from setting the agenda and determining the framework of a debate. The ability to establish preferences tends to be associated with intangible power resources such as culture, ideology, and institutions. This dimension can be thought of as soft power, in

contrast to the hard command power usually associated with tangible resources like military and economic strength.[11]

Robert Cox argues that the nineteenth-century *Pax Britannica* and the twentieth-century *Pax Americana* were effective because they created liberal international economic orders, in which certain types of economic relations were privileged over others and liberal international rules and institutions were broadly accepted. Following the insights of the Italian thinker Antonio Gramsci, Cox argues that the most critical feature for a dominant country is the ability to obtain a broad measure of consent on general principles—principles that ensure the supremacy of the leading state and dominant social classes—and at the same time to offer some prospect of satisfaction to

---

Search of Theory: A New Paradigm for Global Politics (Englewood Cliffs, N.J.: Prentice Hall, 1981).

[10] Susan Strange uses the term *structural power,* which she defines as "power to shape and determine the structures of the global political economy" in *States and Markets* (New York: Basil Blackwell, 1988), 24. My term, *co-optive power,* is similar in its focus on preferences but is somewhat broader, encompassing all elements of international politics. The term *structural power,* in contrast, tends to be associated with the neo-realist theories of Kenneth Waltz.

[11] The distinction between hard and soft power resources is one of degree, both in the nature of the behavior and in the tangibility of the resources. Both types are aspects of the ability to achieve one's purposes by controlling the behavior of others. Command power—the ability to change what others *do*—can rest on coercion or inducement. Co-optive power—the ability to shape what others *want*—can rest on the attractiveness of one's culture and ideology or the ability to manipulate the agenda of political choices in a manner that makes actors fail to express some preferences because they seem to be too unrealistic. The forms of behavior between command and co-optive power range along this continuum:

Command   coercion   inducement
  power
      agenda-setting   attraction   Co-optive
                                    power

Further, soft power resources tend to be associated with co-optive power behavior, whereas hard power resources are usually associated with command behavior. But the relationship is imperfect. For example, countries may be attracted to others with command power by myths of invincibility, and command power may sometimes be used to establish institutions that later become regarded as legitimate. But the general association is strong enough to allow the useful shorthand reference to hard and soft power resources.

the less powerful. Cox identifies Britain from 1845 to 1875 and the United States from 1945 to 1967 as such countries.[12] Although we may not agree with his terminology or dates, Cox has touched a major point: soft co-optive power is just as important as hard command power. If a state can make its power legitimate in the eyes of others, it will encounter less resistance to its wishes. If its culture and ideology are attractive, others will more willingly follow. If it can establish international norms that are consistent with its society, it will be less likely to have to change. If it can help support institutions that encourage other states to channel or limit their activities in ways the dominant state prefers, it may not need as many costly exercises of coercive or hard power in bargaining situations. In short, the universalism of a country's culture and its ability to establish a set of favorable rules and institutions that govern areas of international activity are critical sources of power.[13] These soft sources of power are becoming more important in world politics today.

Such considerations question the conclusion that the world is about to enter a Japanese era in world politics. The nature of power is changing and some of the changes will favor Japan, but some of them may favor the United States even more. In command power, Japan's economic strength is increasing, but it remains vulnerable in terms of raw materials and relatively weak in terms of military force. And in co-optive power, Japan's culture is highly insular and it has yet to develop a major voice in international institutions. The United States, on the other hand, has a universalistic popular culture and a major role in inter-

national institutions. Although such factors may change in the future, they raise an important question about the present situation: What resources are the most important sources of power today? A look at the five-century-old modern state system shows that different power resources played critical roles in different periods. (See Table 2.1.) The sources of power are never static and they continue to change in today's world.

In an age of information-based economies and transnational interdependence, power is becoming less transferable, less tangible, and less coercive. However, the transformation of power is incomplete. The twenty-first century will certainly see a greater role for informational and institutional power, but military force will remain an important factor. Economic scale, both in markets and in natural resources, will also remain important. As the service sector grows within modern economies, the distinction between services and manufacturing will continue to blur. Information will become more plentiful, and the critical resource will be the organizational capacity for rapid and flexible response. Political cohesion will remain important, as will a universalistic popular culture. On some of these dimensions of power, the United States is well endowed; on others, questions arise. But even larger questions arise for the other major contenders—Europe, Japan, the Soviet Union, and China. But first we need to look at the patterns in the distribution of power—balances and hegemonies, how they have changed over history, and what that implies for the position of the United States.

BALANCE OF POWER

International relations is far from a precise science. Conditions in various periods always differ in significant details, and human behavior reflects personal choices. Moreover, theorists often

---

[12] Robert W. Cox, *Production, Power, and World Order* (New York: Columbia University Press, 1987), chaps. 6, 7.
[13] See Stephen D. Krasner, *International Regimes* (Ithaca, N.Y.: Cornell University Press, 1983).

Table 2.1   Leading States and Major Power Resources, 1500s–1900s

Period	Leading State	Major Resources
Sixteenth century	Spain	Gold bullion, colonial trade, mercenary armies, dynastic ties
Seventeenth century	Netherlands	Trade, capital markets, navy
Eighteenth century	France	Population, rural industry, public administration, army
Nineteenth century	Britain	Industry, political cohesion, finance and credit, navy, liberal norms, island location (easy to defend)
Twentieth century	United States	Economic scale, scientific and technical leadership, universalistic culture, military forces and alliances, liberal international regimes, hub of transnational communication

suffer from writing in the midst of events, rather than viewing them from a distance. Thus, powerful theories—those that are both simple and accurate—are rare. Yet political leaders (and those who seek to explain behavior) must generalize in order to chart a path through the apparent chaos of changing events. One of the longest-standing and most frequently used concepts is balance of power, which eighteenth-century philosopher David Hume called "a constant rule of prudent politics."[14] For centuries, balance of power has been the starting point for realistic discussions of international politics.

To an extent, balance of power is a useful predictor of how states will behave; that is, states will align in a manner that will prevent any one state from developing a preponderance of power. This is based on two assumptions: that states exist in an anarchic system with no higher government and that political leaders will act first to reduce risks to the independence of their states. The policy of balancing power helps to explain why in modern times a large state cannot grow forever into a world empire. States seek to increase their powers through internal growth and external alliances. Balance of power predicts that if one state appears to grow too strong, others will ally against it so as to avoid threats to their own independence. This behavior, then, will preserve the structure of the system of states.

However, not all balance-of-power predictions are so obvious. For example, this theory implies that professions of ideological faith will be poor predictors of behavior. But despite Britain's criticism of the notorious Stalin-Hitler pact of 1939, it was quick to make an alliance with Stalin's Soviet Union in 1941. As Winston Churchill explained at the time, "If I learned that Hitler had invaded Hell, I would manage to say something good about the Devil in the House of Commons."[15] Further, balance of power does not mean that political leaders must maximize the power of their own states in the

[14] David Hume, "Of the Balance of Power" in Charles W. Hendel, ed., *David Hume's Political Essays* (1742; reprint, Indianapolis, Ind.: Bobbs-Merrill, 1953), 142–44.

[15] Quoted in Waltz, *International Politics,* 166.

short run. Bandwagoning—that is, joining the stronger rather than the weaker side—might produce more immediate spoils. As Mussolini discovered in his ill-fated pact with Hitler, the danger in bandwagoning is that independence may be threatened by the stronger ally in the long term. Thus, to say that states will act to balance power is a strong generalization in international relations, but it is far from being a perfect predictor.

Proximity and perceptions of threat also affect the way in which balancing of power is played out.[16] A small state like Finland, for instance, cannot afford to try to balance Soviet power. Instead, it seeks to preserve its independence through neutrality. Balance of power and the proposition that "the enemy of my enemy is my friend" help to explain the larger contours of current world politics, but only when proximity and perceptions are considered. The United States was by far the strongest power after 1945. A mechanical application of power balance might seem to predict an alliance against the United States. In fact, Europe and Japan allied with the United States because the Soviet Union, while weaker in overall power, posed a proximate threat to its neighbors. Geography and psychology are both important factors in geopolitics.

The term *balance of power* is sometimes used not as a prediction of policy but as a description of how power is distributed. In the latter case, it is more accurate to refer to the distribution of power. In other instances, though, the term is used to refer to an evenly balanced distribution of power, like a pair of hanging scales. The problem with this usage is that the ambiguities of measuring power make it difficult to determine when an equal balance exists. In fact, the major concerns in world politics tend to arise from inequalities of power, and particularly from major changes in the unequal distribution of power.

HEGEMONY IN MODERN HISTORY

No matter how power is measured, an equal distribution of power among major states is relatively rare. More often the processes of uneven growth, which realists consider a basic law of international politics, mean that some states will be rising and others declining. These transitions in the distribution of power stimulate statesmen to form alliances, to build armies, and to take risks that balance or check rising powers. But the balancing of power does not always prevent the emergence of a dominant state. Theories of hegemony and power transition try to explain why some states that become preponderant later lose that preponderance.

As far back as ancient Greece, observers attempting to explain the causes of major world wars have cited the uncertainties associated with the transition of power. Shifts in the international distribution of power create the conditions likely to lead to the most important wars.[17] However, while power transitions provide useful warning about periods of heightened risk, there is no iron law of hegemonic war. If there were, Britain and the United States would have gone to war at the beginning of this century, when the Americans surpassed the British in economic and naval power in the Western Hemisphere. Instead, when the United States backed Venezuela in its

---

[16] Stephen M. Walt, "Alliance Formation and the Balance of Power," *International Security* 9 (Spring 1985): 3–43. See also by Walt, *The Origins of Alliances* (Ithaca, N.Y.: Cornell University Press, 1987), 23–26, 263–66.

[17] A. F. K. Organski and Jack Kugler, *The War Ledger* (Chicago: University of Chicago Press, 1980), chap. 1.

boundary dispute with British Guyana in 1895, British leaders appeased the rising American power instead of going to war with it.[18]

When power is distributed unevenly, political leaders and theorists use terms such as *empire* and *hegemony*. Although there have been many empires in history, those in the modern world have not encompassed all major countries. Even the British Empire at the beginning of this century encompassed only a quarter of the world's population and Britain was just one of a half-dozen major powers in the global balance of power. The term *hegemony* is applied to a variety of situations in which one state appears to have considerably more power than others. For example, for years China accused the Soviet Union of seeking hegemony in Asia. When Soviet leader Mikhail Gorbachev and Chinese leader Deng Xiaoping met in 1989, they pledged that "neither side will seek hegemony in any form anywhere in the world."[19]

Although the word comes from the ancient Greek and refers to the dominance of one state over others in the system, it is used in diverse and confused ways. Part of the problem is that unequal distribution of power is a matter of degree, and there is no general agreement on how much inequality and what types of power constitute hegemony. All too often, hegemony is used to refer to different behaviors and degrees of control, which obscures rather than clarifies that analysis. For example, Charles Doran cites aggressive military power, while Robert Keohane looks at preponderance in economic resources. Robert Gilpin

sometimes uses the terms *imperial* and *hegemonic* interchangeably to refer to a situation in which "a single powerful state controls or dominates the lesser states in the system"[20] British hegemony in the nineteenth century is commonly cited even though Britain ranked third behind the United States and Russia in GNP and third behind Russia and France in military expenditures at the peak of its relative power around 1870. Britain was first in the more limited domains of manufacturing, trade, finance, and naval power.[21] Yet theorists often contend that "full hegemony requires productive, commercial, and financial as well as political and military power."[22]

Joshua Goldstein usefully defines hegemony as "being able to dictate, or at least dominate, the rules and arrangements by which international relations, political and economic, are conducted. . . . Economic hegemony implies the ability to center the world economy around itself. Political hegemony means being able to dominate the world militarily."[23] However, there are still two important questions to be answered with regard to how the term *hegemony* is used. First,

[20] Charles F. Doran, *The Politics of Assimilation: Hegemony and Its Aftermath* (Baltimore: Johns Hopkins University Press, 1971), 70; Robert O. Keohane, *After Hegemony* (Princeton, N.J.: Princeton University Press, 1984), 32; Robert Gilpin, *War and Change in World Politics* (New York: Cambridge University Press, 1981), 29.
[21] Bruce M. Russett, "The Mysterious Case of Vanishing Hegemony; or, Is Mark Twain Really Dead?" *International Organization* 39 (Spring 1985): 212.
[22] Robert C. North and Julie Strickland, "Power Transition and Hegemonic Succession" (Paper delivered at the meeting of the International Studies Association, Anaheim, Calif., March-April 1986), 5.
[23] Joshua S. Goldstein, *Long Cycles: Prosperity and War in the Modern Age* (New Haven, Conn.: Yale University Press, 1988), 281.

[18] Stephen R. Rock, *Why Peace Breaks Out: Great Power Rapprochement in Historical Perspective* (Chapel Hill; University of North Carolina Press, 1989).
[19] "New Era Declared as China Visit Ends," *International Herald Tribune,* 19 May 1989.

what is the scope of the hegemon's control? In the modern world, a situation in which one country can dictate political and economic arrangements has been extremely rare. Most examples have been regional, such as Soviet power in Eastern Europe, American influence in the Caribbean, and India's control over its small neighbors—Sikkim, Bhutan, and Nepal.[24] In addition, one can find instances in which one country was able to set the rules and arrangements governing specific issues in world politics, such as the American role in money or trade in the early postwar years. But there has been no global, system-wide hegemon during the past two centuries. Contrary to the myths about *Pax Britannica* and *Pax Americana,* British and American hegemonies have been regional and issue-specific rather than general.

Second, we must ask what types of power resources are necessary to produce a hegemonic degree of control. Is military power necessary? Or is it enough to have preponderance in economic resources? How do the two types of power relate to each other? Obviously, the answers to such questions can tell us a great deal about the future world, in which Japan may be an economic giant and a military dwarf while the Soviet Union may fall into the opposite situation. A careful look at the interplay of military and economic power raises doubt about the degree of American hegemony in the postwar period.[25]

[24] James R. Kurth, "Economic Change and State Development" in Jan Triska, ed., *Dominant Powers and Subordinate States: The United States in Latin America and the Soviet Union in Eastern Europe* (Durham, N.C.: Duke University Press, 1986), 88.

[25] The distinction between definitions in terms of resources or behavior and the importance of indicating scope are indicated in the following table. My usage stresses behavior and broad scope.

Theories of Hegemonic Transition and Stability

General hegemony is the concern of theories and analogies about the instability and dangers supposedly caused by hegemonic transitions. Classical concerns about hegemony among leaders and philosophers focus on military power and "conflicts precipitated by the military effort of one dominant actor to expand well beyond the arbitrary security confines set by tradition, historical accident, or coercive pressures."[26] In this approach, hegemonic preponderance arises out of military expansion, such as the efforts of Louis XIV, Napoleon, or Hitler to dominate world politics. The important point is that, except for brief periods, none of the attempted military hegemonies in modern times has succeeded. (See Table 2.2) No modern state has been able to develop sufficient military power to transform the balance of power into a long-lived hegemony in which one state could dominate the world militarily.

More recently, many political scientists have focused on economic power as a source of hegemonic control. Some define hegemonic economic power in terms of resources—that is, preponderance in

Approaches to Hegemony

	Power Resources
Political/military hegemony	Army/navy (Modelski)
Economic hegemony	Raw materials, capital, markets, production (Keohane)

Power Behavior	Scope
Define the military hierarchy (Doran)	Global or regional
Set rules for economic bargains (Goldstein)	General or issue-specific

[26] Doran, *Politics of Assimilation,* 15.

Table 2.2   Modern Efforts at Military Hegemony

State Attempting Hegemony	Ensuring Hegemonic War	New Order after War
Hapsburg Spain	Thirty Years' War, 1618–1648	Peace of Westphalia, 1648
Louis XIV's France	Wars of Louis XIV	Treaty of Utrecht, 1713
Napoleon's France	1792–1815	Congress of Vienna, 1815
Germany (and Japan)	1914–1945	United Nations, 1945

Source: Charles F. Doran, *The Politics of Assimilation: Hegemony and Its Aftermath* (Baltimore: Johns Hopkins University Press, 1971), 19–20.

control over raw materials, sources of capital, markets, and production of goods. Others use the behavioral definition in which a hegemon is a state able to set the rules and arrangements for the global economy. Robert Gilpin, a leading theorist of hegemonic transition, sees Britain and America, having created and enforced the rules of a liberal economic order, as the successive hegemons since the Industrial Revolution.[27] Some political economists argue that world economic stability requires a single stabilizer and that periods of such stability have coincided with periods of hegemony. In this view, *Pax Britannica* and *Pax Americana* were the periods when Britain and the United States were strong enough to create and enforce the rules for a liberal international economic order in the nineteenth and twentieth centuries. For example, it is often argued that economic stability "historically has occurred when there has been a sole hegemonic power; Britain from 1815 to World War I and the United States from 1945 to around 1970. ... With a sole hegemonic power, the rules of the game can be established and enforced. Lesser countries have little choice but to go along. Without a hegemonic power, conflict is the order of the day."[28] Such theories of hegemonic stability and decline are often used to predict that the United States will follow the experience of Great Britain, and that instability will ensue. Goldstein, for example, argues that "we are moving toward the 'weak hegemony' end of the spectrum and . . . this seems to increase the danger of hegemonic war."[29]

I argue, however, that the theory of hegemonic stability and transition will not tell us as much about the future of the United States. Theorists of hegemonic stability generally fail to spell out the causal connections between military and economic power and hegemony. As already noted, nineteenth-century Britain was not militarily dominant nor was it the world's largest economy, and yet Britain is portrayed by Gilpin and others as hegemonic. Did Britain's military weakness at that time allow the United States and Russia, the two larger economies, to remain mostly outside the liberal system of free trade? Or, to take a twentieth-century puzzle, did a liberal international economy depend on postwar American military strength or only its economic power? Are both conditions necessary to-

[27] Keohane, *After Hegemony,* 32; Gilpin, *War and Change,* 144.

[28] Michael Moffitt, "Shocks, Deadlocks and Scorched Earth: Reaganomics and the Decline of U.S. Hegemony," *World Policy Journal* 4 (Fall 1987): 576.
[29] Goldstein, *Long Cycles,* 357.

day, or have modern nations learned to cooperate through international institutions?

One radical school of political economists, the neo-Marxists, has attempted to answer similar questions about the relationship between economic and military hegemony, but their theories are unconvincing. For example, Immanuel Wallerstein defines hegemony as a situation in which power is so unbalanced that

> one power can largely impose its rules and its wishes (at the very least by effective veto power) in the economic, political, military, diplomatic, and even cultural arenas. The material base of such power lies in the ability of enterprises domiciled in that power to operate more efficiently in all three major economic arenas—agro-industrial production, commerce, and finance.[30]

According to Wallerstein, hegemony is rare and "refers to that short interval in which there is simultaneously advantage in all three economic domains." At such times, the other major powers become "*de facto* client states." Wallerstein claims there have been only three modern instances of hegemony—in the Neth-

erlands, 1620–1650; in Britain, 1815–1873; and in the United States, 1945–1967. (See Table 2.3.) He argues that "in each case, the hegemony was secured by a thirty-year-long world war," after which a new order followed—the Peace of Westphalia after 1648; the Concert of Europe after 1815; and the United Nations–Bretton Woods system after 1945.[31] According to this theory, the United States will follow the Dutch and the British path to decline.

The neo-Marxist view of hegemony is unconvincing and a poor predictor of future events because it superficially links military and economic hegemony and has many loose ends. For example, contrary to Wallerstein's theory, the Thirty Years' War *coincided* with Dutch hegemony, and Dutch decline began with the Peace of Westphalia. The Dutch were not militarily strong enough to stand up to the British on the sea and could barely defend themselves against the French on land, "despite their trade-derived wealth."[32] Further, although Wallerstein argues that British hegemony began after the Napoleonic Wars, he is not clear about how the new order in the balance of power—that is, the nineteenth-century Concert of Europe—related to Britain's supposed ability to impose a global free-trade system. For example, Louis XIV's France, which many historians view as

[30] Immanuel M. Wallerstein, *The Politics of the World-Economy: The States, the Movements, and the Civilizations: Essays* (New York: Cambridge University Press, 1984), 38, 41.

[31] Ibid.
[32] Goldstein, *Long Cycles,* 317.

Table 2.3   A Neo-Marxist View of Hegemony

Hegemony	World War Securing Hegemony	Period of Dominance	Decline
Dutch	Thirty Years' War, 1618–1648	1620–1650	1650–1672
British	Napoleonic War, 1792–1815	1815–1873	1873–1896
American	World Wars I and II, 1914–1945	1945–1967	1967–

Source: Immanuel Wallerstein, *The Politics of the World Economy* (New York: Cambridge University Press, 1984). 41–42.

the dominant military power in the second half of the seventeenth century, is excluded from Wallerstein's schema altogether. Thus, the neo-Marxist historical analogies seem forced into a Procrustean ideological bed, while other cases are left out of bed altogether.

Others have attempted to organize past periods of hegemony into century-long cycles. In 1919, British geopolitician Sir Halford Mackinder argued that unequal growth among nations tends to produce a hegemonic world war about every hundred years.[33] More recently, political scientist George Modelski proposed a hundred-year cyclical view of changes in world leadership. (See Table 2.4.) In this view, a long cycle begins with a major global war. A single state then emerges as the new world power and legitimizes its preponderance with postwar peace treaties. (Preponderance is defined as having at least half the resources available for global orderkeeping.) The new leader supplies security and order for the international system. In time, though, the leader loses legitimacy, and deconcentration of power leads to another global war. The new leader that emerges from that

war may not be the state that challenged the old leader but one of the more innovative allies in the winning coalition (as, not Germany, but the United States replaced Britain). According to Modelski's theory, the United States began its decline in 1973.[34] If his assumptions are correct, it may be Japan and not the Soviet Union that will most effectively challenge the United States in the future.

Modelski and his followers suggest that the processes of decline are associated with long waves in the global economy. They associate a period of rising prices and resource scarcities with loss of power, and concentration of power with falling prices, resource abundance, and economic innovation.[35] However, in linking economic and political cycles, these theorists become enmeshed in the controversy surrounding long cycle theory. Many economists are skeptical about the empirical evidence for alleged long economic waves and about dating histor-

[33] Halford J. Mackinder, *Democratic Ideals and Reality: A Study in the Politics of Reconstruction* (New York: Henry Holt and Co., 1919), 1–2.

[34] George Modelski, "The Long Cycle of Global Politics and the Nation-State," *Comparative Studies in Society and History* 20 (April 1978): 214–35; George Modelski, *Long Cycles in World Politics* (Seattle: University of Washington Press, 1987).

[35] William R. Thompson, *On Global War: Historical Structural Approaches to World Politics* (Columbia: University of South Carolina Press, 1988), chaps. 3, 8.

Table 2.4   Long Cycles of World Leadership

Cycle	Global War	Preponderance	Decline
1495–1580	1494–1516	Portugal, 1516–1540	1540–1580
1580–1688	1580–1609	Netherlands, 1609–1640	1640–1688
1688–1792	1688–1713	Britain, 1714–1740	1740–1792
1792–1914	1792–1815	Britain, 1815–1850	1850–1914
1914–	1914–1945	United States, 1945–1973	1973–

Source: George Modelski, *Long Cycles in World Politics* (Seattle: University of Washington Press, 1987), 40, 42, 44, 102, 131, 147.

ical waves by those who use the concept.[36]

Further, we cannot rely on the long-cycle theory to predict accurately the American future. Modelski's treatment of political history is at best puzzling. For example, he ranks sixteenth-century Portugal as a hegemon rather than Spain, even though Spain controlled a richer overseas empire and swallowed up Portugal a century later. Likewise, Britain is ranked as a hegemon from 1714 to 1740, even though eighteenth-century France was the larger power. Modelski's categories are odd in part because he uses naval power as the sine qua non of global power, which results in a truncated view of military and diplomatic history. Although naval power was more important for countries that relied on overseas possessions, the balance in Europe depended on the armies on the continent. Britain could not afford to ignore its armies on land and rely solely on its naval power. To preserve the balance of power, Britain had to be heavily involved in land wars on the European continent at the beginning of the eighteenth, nineteenth, and twentieth centuries. More specifically, Modelski underrates the Spanish navy in the sixteenth century as well as the French navy, which outnumbered Britain's, in the late seventeenth century.[37] Some major wars, such as the Thirty Years' War and the Anglo-French wars of the eighteenth century, are excluded altogether from Modelski's organization of history.

Vague definitions and arbitrary schematizations alert us to the inadequacies of such grand theories of hegemony and decline. Most theorists of hegemonic transition tend to shape history to their own theories by focusing on particular power resources and ignoring others. Examples include the poorly explained relationship between military and political power and the unclear link between decline and major war. Since there have been wars among the great powers during 60 percent of the years from 1500 to the present, there are plenty of candidates to associate with any given scheme.[38] Even if we consider only the nine general wars that have involved nearly all the great powers and produced high levels of casualties, some of them, such as the Seven Years' War (1755–1763), are not considered hegemonic in any of the schemes. As sociologist Pitirim Sorokin concludes, "no regular periodicity is noticeable."[39] At best, the various schematizations of hegemony and war are only suggestive. They do not provide a reliable basis for predicting the future of American power or for evaluating the risk of world war as we enter the twenty-first century. Loose historical analogies about decline and falsely deterministic political theories are not merely academic: they may lead to inappropriate policies. The real problems of a post-cold-war world will not be new challenges for hegemony, but the new challenges of transnational interdependence.

[36] Richard N. Rosecrance, "Long Cycle Theory and International Relations," *International Organization* 41 (Spring 1987): 291–95. An interesting but ultimately unconvincing discussion can be found in Goldstein, *Long Cycles.*
[37] Paul Kennedy, *The Rise and Fall of the Great Powers: Economic Change and Military Conflict from 1500 to 2000* (New York: Random House, 1987), 99.

[38] Jack S. Levy, "Declining Power and the Preventive Motivation for War," *World Politics* 40 (October 1987): 82–107. See also Jack S. Levy, *War in the Modern Great Power System, 1495–1975* (Lexington: University of Kentucky Press, 1983), 97.
[39] Pitirim Aleksandrovich Sorokin, *Social and Cultural Dynamics: A Study of Change in Major Systems of Art, Truth, Ethics, Law and Social Relationships* (1957; reprint, Boston: Porter Sargent, 1970), 561.

3. The Political Economy of American Strategy*

Aaron L. Friedberg

The study of the relationship between economics and strategy points in two different directions. On one hand, there is the problem of *extraction*—the ways in which the resources of a city, state, or empire can be mobilized and converted into the implements of military power. On the other, there is the question of *burdens*—how war and the preparations for it may affect the economy of a given political unit. The first issue has been a central preoccupation of statesmen, soldiers, and scholars since ancient times. The second, as Adam Smith anticipated, has become increasingly important as technology has developed, the destructiveness of war has increased, and the extent and cost to the state of peacetime military preparedness have grown.[1]

In the United States, substantial and sustained military expenditures are a relatively recent phenomenon, dating back only 45 years to the close of World War II. The possibility that such spending could disrupt or distort the domestic productive mechanism received a great deal of attention in the late forties and early fifties as Americans began for the first time to contemplate the full implications of a protracted cold war. By the early sixties, however, much of the anxiety about the United States' ability to preserve both economic and military strength, over what was referred to during the Eisenhower years as the "long pull," had begun to fade. It is only in the last ten years or so that these worries have started to reemerge, sparked first by a decade of inflation and recession and, more recently, by fears about the precarious financial foundations and deteriorating industrial competitiveness of the American economy.

Whether the problems of recent decades are in fact the direct result of prolonged high levels of defense expenditure has now become a subject of heated academic and political debate. Many observers are convinced that the United States, if it is to improve its economic performance, will have to make major cutbacks in defense spending. Such cuts, in turn, will be possible only if Washington reduces substantially the array of external commitments it took on in the wake of World War II. The burdens of maintaining its postwar "empire" now seem to be sapping America's economic strength; the key to renewal, in this view, is withdrawal.

The economic case for retrenchment has two separate but related strands. Some analysts argue that, in attempting to uphold its many overseas alliances and

* An earlier version of this paper was presented to the West Point Senior Conference, June 4, 1988. I am grateful to Rebecca Blank, Benjamin Berman, Michael Doyle, David Epstein, Robert Gilpin, Fred Greenstein, James Hines, Jane Katz, Klaus Knorr, Andrew Marshall, Irving Sirken, and Nicholas Zeigler for their comments on earlier drafts of this paper, and to Michael Gilligan for research assistance.

[1] "The military force of the society, which originally cost the sovereign no expence either in time of peace or in time of war, must, in the progress of improvement, first be maintained by him in time of war, and afterwards even in time of peace." Adam Smith, *The Wealth of Nations: Volume II* (Chicago: University of Chicago Press, 1976), 230.

SOURCE: Reprinted with permission of the publisher, The Johns Hopkins University Press, from *World Politics,* vol. 41, no. 3, April 1989, pp. 381–406.

diplomatic commitments, the United States has been led into persistent and harmful fiscal imbalances. Others blame the extended strategic posture and unprecedentedly large defense budgets of the postwar period for disrupting the processes of investment and economic growth, thereby hindering the United States in its competition with the other, less heavily burdened, industrialized countries.

An examination of the logic and the evidence underpinning each of these assertions reveals that both are, in important ways, misleading. At most, defense spending would appear to bear only a small fraction of the responsibility for the fiscal and industrial difficulties that the United States has experienced in the past several years. The argument that, in future, the U.S. must either retrench or face ruin is also incorrect. There is little doubt that the United States can, if it chooses to do so, continue to maintain a substantial and extended defense posture without doing itself grievous economic harm. The question is not so much whether the burden *can* be borne as whether it *should* be borne, and *who,* precisely, should bear it. The range of choice is actually much wider than many recent discussions of the relationship between economics and strategy would seem to suggest.

FISCAL IMBALANCES

Beyond American Hegemony

Since he wrote *The Atlantic Fantasy* in 1970, David Calleo has argued that the existing structure of NATO is unnatural and, over the long-run, unhealthy—both for the United States and for its European allies.[2] Instead of an arrangement in

[2] David P. Calleo, *The Atlantic Fantasy: The U.S., NATO, and Europe* (Baltimore: The Johns Hopkins University Press, 1970).

which the U.S. bears the greatest share of the responsibility for Alliance defense, Calleo has consistently favored arrangements that would shift a larger portion of the burden onto the Europeans themselves. He now maintains that what he calls a policy of "devolution" is not only desirable but essential if the United States wishes to preserve its own domestic health and to maintain the stability of the international economic system.

Although he bases his analysis primarily on a consideration of economic factors, Calleo actually begins with an important observation about the erosion in America's relative military power. After first toying with the idea of trying to match Soviet conventional forces, U.S. strategists in the early 1950s chose to rely instead on America's clear advantage in nuclear weapons. If the Soviets dared to attack a U.S. ally, they were to be met with crushing atomic and thermonuclear retaliation. So long as the Russians lacked any real capability for launching similar strikes against the United States, there was little reason to fear that they would ever initiate hostilities in the first place. If the U.S. retained its overwhelming nuclear superiority, it could defend its allies (or, at least, deter attacks on them) without building up large and expensive conventional forces. This policy of "massive retaliation" was, as Calleo puts it, a way of maintaining American "hegemony on the cheap" (p. 41).

By the late 1950s, the Soviet Union was beginning to deploy forces capable of striking directly at the continental United States. As American invulnerability dwindled, so did the European countries' confidence in the willingness of the U.S. to initiate nuclear war on their behalf. The shifting strategic balance seemed to push the burden of deterrence downward onto the conventional forces of the United States and its allies. This reasoning was first adopted by President Kennedy in the early 1960s and has been adhered to by all successive administrations.

Under Kennedy, the U.S. began once again to expand its conventional forces while urging the Europeans to follow suit. This, in Calleo's account, is where the problems of the present really have their origin. With the exception of a brief period in the late sixties and early seventies, the last 25 years have been marked by a series of efforts by the United States to increase its conventional military power in order to compensate for a loss of strategic nuclear superiority. The problem is that, compared to their nuclear counterparts, conventional forces are quite expensive. As a result (with the exception of the immediate post-Vietnam period), there has tended to be a strong upward pressure on American defense budgets. That pressure, combined with the increasing cost of government-funded social programs, has helped to create the deficits of the last three decades. Since 1961, federal outlays have been permitted to exceed revenues in every year except one (1969). According to Calleo, this abandonment of the traditional principles of fiscal restraint was sanctioned first by a renewed faith in Keynesianism, and then, in the 1980s, by the alluring assumptions of "supply side economics."[3]

Most countries would be prevented from running indefinite budget deficits by the requirements of participating in the international economic system. Unless accompanied by tight monetary policy, deficit spending tends to be inflationary; Calleo explains that, in an open world economy, money will flow away from the national currency of a state with a relatively high inflation rate. Thus, in most cases, "the inflationary country suffers a balance-of-payments deficit and its

currency begins to weaken against other currencies."[4]

In response to these pressures, an "ordinary" country would have to check inflation by balancing its budget or constricting its money supply. But the United States is not an ordinary country. Thanks to the central role of its currency in the world financial system, it has been able to run a "chronic basic balance-of-payments deficit" (p. 83). According to Calleo, this has meant that since the 1960s, the U.S. has been able to escape any external discipline on its increasingly unbalanced domestic fiscal policies. In doing so, however, it has caused serious economic problems for some of its most important allies and trading partners. In the 1960s and 1970s, a combination of budget deficits and loose monetary policy meant that America was essentially exporting inflation (pp. 83–93). During the Reagan administration, continued deficits combined with tight money to produce relatively high real interest rates and a vast influx of foreign funds.[5] Once again, the dollar was propagating the effects of American domestic fiscal irresponsibility internationally.

The chain of causality that Calleo has identified may be summarized as follows: Washington's commitment to the defense of Europe leads to excessive defense spending, which contributes to persistent deficits, which, in turn, encourage international economic instability. The way to set things straight is to go to the source of the problem. The United States must cut into its defense budget by reducing its contribution to NATO. For starters, the U.S. Army should disband five of the ten divisions it currently main-

[3] For a more detailed discussion of these developments, see David P. Calleo, *The Imperious Economy* (Cambridge: Harvard University Press, 1982).

[4] David P. Calleo, "Inflation and American Power," *Foreign Affairs* 59 (Spring 1981), 784.

[5] As Calleo describes it, "American monetary and fiscal policies were sucking capital from Europe, and the consequences were blighting Europe's domestic prosperity" (p. 101).

tains for use in the European theater. Instead of five divisions on the Continent
and five NATO-designated divisions in
reserve at home, the Army should keep
no more than three divisions on the
ground in Europe, with the other two
based in the United States. Whatever gap
this leaves in NATO's ground defenses
should be made up by greater (and more
closely coordinated) British, French, and
German efforts. In addition to their expanded conventional role, the European
powers should also field a more credible
"indigenous deterrent." This could take
a variety of forms, and might even include an independent German nuclear
force (pp. 165, 169, 170).

Putting aside the questions of whether
the changes Calleo proposes are either
strategically desirable or equitable (in
terms of intra-alliance "burden sharing"),
are they, as he concludes, economically
necessary? The crucial link in Calleo's
causal chain is the first one, which con-
nects high defense spending with big
budget deficits. If this link is strong, the
argument stands and the conclusions follow. If it is weak, the situation may be
more complex than it appears at first
glance.

Budgetary outcomes are, of course,
never the *result* of any one thing. They
are, instead, a *resultant* of several sets of
decisions taken simultaneously—about
expenditures, on the one hand, and about
appropriate levels of taxation, on the
other. It therefore makes little sense to
blame defense outlays alone for a particular deficit without reference to what was
going on in other spending categories as
well as on the revenue side of the budget
ledger.

This said, it is clear that, from the early
1960s to the late 1970s, the connection
between defense and deficits was extremely weak. Although military outlays
increased in terms of absolute, current
dollars, they did not grow nearly as
quickly as total government spending or

the economy as a whole. During this period, defense spending actually fell as a
percentage of total government outlays
(from 50 percent in 1960 to 23 percent in
1980) and of gross national product (from
slightly over 9 percent of GNP to 5 percent in the same 20-year interval). (See
Figures 3.1 and 3.2.)

As defense spending went down in relative terms, nondefense spending rose
dramatically from the mid-sixties on. Between 1965 and 1980, nondefense expenditures (not including interest payments
on the national debt) increased from 50
to 68 percent of government outlays and
from 9.5 to 17 percent of GNP. In the nondefense category, so-called "entitlement
programs" (mostly Social Security, Medicare, and pensions) expanded most rapidly. Between 1965 and 1980, payments
to individuals grew from 27 to 47 percent
of total outlays and from 4.6 to 10 percent
of GNP. (See Figures 3.1 and 3.2.)

While government expenditures on defense and nondefense programs together
absorbed an increasing share of gross national product, federal tax revenues
stayed more or less constant as a percentage of GNP. Until the late seventies,
budget receipts grew at the same rate as
the economy, and hovered at around 18
percent of GNP.[6] The confluence of these
trends produced a series of increasing,
but still fairly minor, annual budget deficits. Although they were generally bigger in absolute terms than those of the
preceding decade, the deficits of the seventies were still comparatively small in
relation to the size of the national economy, averaging only 1.7 percent of GNP
each year.[7]

[6] Keith M. Carlson, "Trends in Federal Revenues: 1955–86," *Federal Reserve Bank of St.
Louis Review* 63 (May 1981), 34.
[7] Peter G. Peterson, 'The Morning After,"
The Atlantic Monthly (October 1987), 44. The
real significance of even these larger deficits
was (and is) a subject of debate among econo-

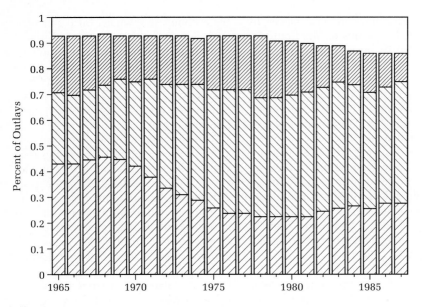

Figure 3.1
Selected Government Outlays as a Percentage of Total Outlay
SOURCES: Outlay figures for 1965–1985 are from *Facts and Figures on Government Finance.*

Except for the Vietnam War years, the 1960s and 1970s marked the continuation of a larger historical tendency toward what one analyst has called the "waning of the warfare state" and the rise of an American "welfare state.''[8] The general upward trend in budget deficits during this period was not, as Calleo candidly acknowledges at various points, the

product of any one thing.[9] Spending of all sorts increased and revenues did not keep pace. On the spending side, however, the expansion in social services played a far more significant part in unbalancing the federal budget than did the much slower growth in defense outlays.

During the 1980s, the connection between defense and deficits has been far stronger; still, defense spending alone cannot be said to have caused the excess of expenditures over revenues. Under the Reagan administration, federal resources were shifted away from those nondefense programs that did not involve payments to individuals and toward defense and

---

mists. One authority has recently argued that conventional methods of calculating the magnitude of the deficit without correcting for inflation are seriously misleading. Properly adjusted, the deficits of the inflationary late 1970s actually appear as real *surpluses.* See Robert Eisner, *How Real Is the Deficit?* (New York: Free Press, 1986). For a review of changing expert opinion on the significance of budget deficits, see Paul G. Peterson, "The New Politics of Deficits," *Political Science Quarterly* 100 (Winter 1985–86), 575–601.

[8] James L. Clayton, "The Fiscal Limits of the Warfare-Welfare State: Defense and Welfare Spending in the United States Since 1900," *Western Political Quarterly* 29 (September 1976), 364–83.

[9] He notes, for example, that "the unbalanced fiscal policy of the 1960s could not, of course, be blamed on military and space spending alone." Concerning the 1970s, he points out that "while U.S. military expenditures did fall in the wake of Vietnam, the rapid growth of domestic social services more than offset that decline" (pp. 87 and 91).

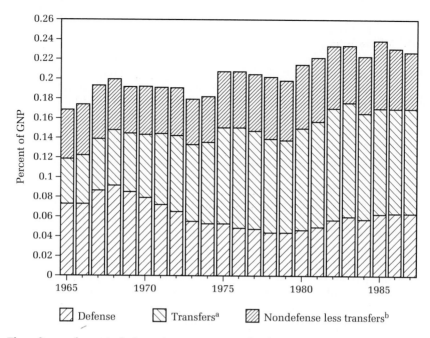

These figures do not include net interest payments by the government.
[a] Includes Veterans Benefits, Social Security benefits, Medicare, Medicaid, and Aid for Families with Dependent Children (AFDC).
[b] Includes government purchases of goods and services that are not directly used for national defense, such as roads, office buildings, and salaries for nondefense personnel.

Figure 3.2
Government Outlays as a Percentage of GNP
SOURCES: Outlay figures for 1965–1985 are from *Facts and Figures on Government Finance.*

interest on the national debt. Between 1980 and 1987, defense increased its share of outlays (from 23 to 28%) and of GNP (from 5 to 6.3%), while nondefense spending (excluding interest) fell from 68 to 58% of outlays and from 15.1 to 13.2% of GNP. Out of this total, transfer payments held steady (at around 47% of outlays and 10.5% of GNP), and cuts were made in funding for such items as energy, education, community development, and public service employment.[10]

[10] Figures were calculated from tables in *The United States Budget in Brief, FY 1989* (Washington, DC: G.P.O., 1988), 102 and 116. For a review of spending on the various com-

Without a change in tax policy, these shifts in expenditures might have produced substantial yearly budget surpluses.[11] In 1981, however, the Reagan administration chose to lower taxes, hoping in the process to stimulate economic growth and to generate the revenues

ponents of the budget during the Reagan years, see *ibid.,* pp. 49–90.
[11] According to Carlson (fn. 6, p. 37), if there had been no change in tax policy, federal budget receipts would by 1986 have equaled 24% of GNP. As things turned out, at that point revenues had fallen to around 18% of GNP while expenditures had risen to around 23%. *Economic Report of the President, 1988* (Washington, DC: G.P.O., 1988), 31.

needed to make up any temporary gap between defense increases and nondefense cuts.[12] In the event, a supply-side dividend of the magnitude that had been predicted (and presumably expected) did not materialize. Tax receipts grew much less quickly than outlays, deficits skyrocketed,[13] debt increased, and interest payments came to claim an increasing share of the national budget and of GNP.[14]

There is nothing about defense expenditures or even defense buildups that causes them inevitably to produce budget deficits. Imbalances result when governments are unable or unwilling to raise taxes or reduce other forms of spending sufficiently to pay for increased military outlays. Even a buildup as big and as rapid as that recently undertaken could conceivably have been carried out without producing massive fiscal imbalances.[15] If the Reagan administration had

reduced taxes less or kept them constant, if it had accelerated defense spending more gradually, or if it had been more successful in slowing the growth of nondefense programs, it could have expanded U.S. military capabilities without increasing the size of the deficit.

The array of possible combinations of taxes and expenditures that might have permitted a fully financed buildup is virtually infinite. Similarly, the imbalances that now exist could, in theory, be brought down through a variety of differently mixed fiscal policies.[16] Deep defense cuts of the sort Calleo proposes would certainly be one way of approaching the problem. In view of the magnitude of the present gap between revenues and expenditures, however, it is unlikely that such reductions would be sufficient, in and of themselves, to bring the federal budget fully into balance. According to projections by the Congressional Budget Office, the deficit could remain at around $150 billion per year into the early 1990s.[17] Calleo estimates that a 50-percent cut in U.S. ground forces in NATO would save "only" $67 billion in annual expenditures (p. 269). As radical as it may seem at first glance, Calleo's proposal is therefore, quite literally, something less than a halfway measure.

Mere devolution will not be sufficient to get rid of the deficit; on the other hand, major changes in military strategy may also not be necessary in order to achieve substantial savings on the defense budget. By slowing the rate of growth in

[12] M. Ishaq Nadiri, "Increase in Defense Expenditure and Its Impact on the U.S. Economy," in David Denoon, ed., *Constraints on Strategy: The Economics of Western Security* (New York: Pergamon-Brassey's, 1986), 33–34.

[13] Deficits averaged $157 billion for the years 1980–1987 and reached a peak of $221 billion in 1986. *Economic Report of the President* (fn. 11), 337. In 1986, the deficit equaled 4.9% of GNP. Peter Peterson (fn. 7), 44.

[14] Interest payments went from 8.8% of outlays and 1.9% of GNP in 1980 to 13.8% and 3.1%, respectively, in 1987. *U.S. Budget in Brief* (fn. 10), 102 and 116.

[15] During the Korean War, for example, defense budgets grew from under 5% of GNP to over 13% between 1950 and 1954 (as compared to a smaller than 2% increase between 1980 and 1987). While the war was going on, however, taxes were increased, civilian spending was permitted to fall as a percentage of GNP and, as a result, deficits increased only slightly. Robert W. DeGrasse, Jr., *Military Expansion, Economic Decline* (New York: Council of Economic Priorities, 1983), 135–37. For a comparison of the Korea, Vietnam, and Reagan buildups, see Lester Thurow, "How to Wreck the Economy," *The New York Review of Books,* May 14, 1981, pp. 3–8.

[16] Whether the aim of the government's policy ought to be the total, automatic elimination of yearly deficits is, of course, another question. For the case against reflexive budget balancing, see Eisner (fn. 7), 145–64. For a history of the balanced budget as a potent political symbol, see James D. Savage, *Balanced Budgets and American Politics* (Ithaca, NY: Cornell University Press, 1988).

[17] For a range of estimates, see *The Economist,* February 20, 1988, pp. 25–26.

annual expenditures from 3 to 2 percent, the Defense Department planned in 1988 to trim an average of $40 billion annually from previously programmed spending.[18] Some civilian analysts have proposed even larger cuts that would still leave about the same number of U.S. ground forces in Europe and Asia.[19] Whatever the risks involved in trying to maintain existing commitments at a lower level of defense effort, a rational strategic planning process would have to weigh them against the possible dangers of a substantial U.S. pullback from its present world position.

Unless the United States gets out of NATO altogether and cuts its military budget in half, dissolving the deficit will probably require some mix of tax increases and reductions in nondefense as well as defense expenditures. There is certainly no shortage of ways in which the federal government could "enhance revenues," whether by "soaking the rich" and taxing "sinners,"[20] by creating a new nationwide consumption tax,[21] or by imposing charges for energy use and environmental pollution.[22] Some of these measures might even have economic and broader societal benefits, whatever their impact on the government's fiscal well-being.

Along with cuts in defense and increases in taxes, civilian spending could also be reduced in a variety of ways. Following the precedent set during the Reagan years, the new administration may choose to slice even more deeply into nondefense, nonentitlement programs.[23] Further savings could also be obtained by restricting the costs of government operations.[24] Alternatively, the Bush administration could try to change the structure

---

[18] "The Pentagon Is Learning to Live With Less," New York Times, April 3, 1988, p. E5.

[19] William Kaufmann has suggested a variety of other reductions (especially in strategic nuclear and naval forces) that could save close to $370 billion over the next five years without requiring a withdrawal of U.S. ground forces from Europe. See David P. Calleo, Harold van B. Cleveland, and Leonard Silk, "The Dollar and the Defense of the West," Foreign Affairs 66 (Spring 1988), 854–55.

[20] By one estimate, increasing the top marginal income tax rate from 28 to 30% could generate $76 billion in additional revenues over the next five years. Adding a 33% bracket would affect only a relatively small number of taxpayers, but could yield almost $30 billion over the same period. Higher taxes on beer, wine, distilled spirits, and cigarettes could bring in over $43 billion between 1989 and 1993. See Reducing the Deficit: Spending and Revenue Options (Washington, DC: Congressional Budget Office, 1988), 285–88 and 351–53.

[21] A flat 5% value-added tax (VAT) would yield almost $460 billion over the next five

years. Even if items like food, housing, and medical care were excluded (to reduce what might otherwise be a disproportionate burden on people with lower incomes), a national VAT would still bring in over $260 billion during the same period (ibid., 342–45). For an analysis of possible taxes on consumption, see Charls E. Walker and Mark A. Bloomfield, eds., The Consumption Tax: A Better Alternative? (Cambridge, MA: Ballinger, 1987). For a variety of other tax proposals, see "Doing the Unthinkable: Six Recipes for Raising Federal Taxes," The New York Times, October 16, 1988, p. F2. Also see Herbert Stein, "Tax the Rich, They Consume Too Much," The New York Times, October 23, 1988, p. F2.

[22] A $5 per barrel fee on domestic and imported oil would bring in $106 billion over five years. An oil import fee alone would yield $41 billion. A 12 cent per gallon increase in the tax on motor fuel would raise $57 billion. Imposing a charge on sulfur dioxide and nitrogen oxide emissions and on the production of hazardous wastes could bring in almost $12 billion in five years. See Reducing the Deficit (fn. 20), 351–56.

[23] For example, cancellation of a planned new NASA space station would eliminate $13 billion in expenditures between 1989 and 1993; elimination of the controversial Superconducting Super Collider particle accelerator would save over $2 billion during the same period. Ibid., 184–85 and 188–89.

[24] A 2% annual cap on pay increases for government employees might save as much as $21 billion over the next five years. Ibid., 259–61.

of entitlement programs that has been built up over the past thirty years. According to one recent estimate, 85 percent of the benefits from those programs are now provided on a "non-means-tested basis"; in other words, they are paid out to individuals regardless of their incomes.[25] The federal government could undoubtedly save a great deal of money if it provided less to those who are already well off.[26] Controlling the rate at which benefits increase (rather than, as under present law, requiring that they rise automatically with the consumer price index) would also serve to slow the growth in social spending; it could be argued that such changes would impose relatively little hardship on any individual recipient.[27]

[25] In 1986, the federal government made payments of $455 billion to individuals, with the majority going to non-means-tested programs like Social Security and Medicare ($271 billion), civil service and military retirement benefits ($47 billion), and agricultural subsidies ($26 billion). By contrast, unemployment compensation amounted to only $18 billion. Peter Peterson (fn. 7), 61.

[26] Former Secretary of Commerce Peter Peterson estimates that, if retirement ages were gradually increased, initial benefits to those in upper income brackets were lowered, and taxes were imposed on benefits that exceed contributions, the federal government could save over $50 billion annually by the year 2000. *Ibid.*, 69.

[27] One proposal calls for limiting cost-of-living adjustments on Social Security, railroad retirement, and other non-means-tested programs to 66% (instead of 100%) of any increase in the consumer price index over the next five years. Offsetting increases could be provided to the recipients of means-tested programs and Medicare benefits. This approach could save over $62 billion; assuming continued moderate inflation, however, it would leave beneficiaries 7% worse off in 1993 than they would have been under full price indexing. *Reducing the Deficit* (fn. 20), 145–49. For an additional discussion of the entitlements issue, see Murray Weidenbaum, *Rendezvous with Reality: The American Economy after Reagan* (New York: Basic Books, 1988), 33–37.

In terms of simple bookkeeping arithmetic, there is obviously no single solution to the deficit problem. Whether the best way to proceed would be to cut spending (either on defense or nondefense items, or on both) or to increase taxes, or some combination of the two is therefore a matter of societal choice; it is a *political* issue rather than, in any sense, a "purely" economic one. Calleo acknowledges this when he admits that there may be alternatives to his plan, but he quickly dismisses these as unacceptable to the American electorate.[28] Although he sometimes seems to suggest that devolution is economically inescapable, in the end he argues that it is the only politically acceptable way of eliminating the deficit.

Even this lesser assertion is not self-evident. Whatever their merits or drawbacks, none of the above measures are so far-fetched as to be inconceivable. In any case, if the fiscal gap is to be narrowed in the years ahead, some changes in taxes and civilian spending are likely, with or without substantial shifts in foreign and defense policy. A major struggle over priorities is therefore quite probable. How that struggle is resolved will depend, among other things, on the coalition-building skill of the president, the balance of power in Congress, the influence of various groups whose interests are inevitably affected by any major change in government fiscal policy, and the impact of unforeseen and unpredictable international events.

To sum up, an American pullback from Europe may be strategically feasible. It

Also see Peter G. Peterson and Neil Howe, *On Borrowed Time: How the Growth in Entitlement Spending Threatens America's Future* (San Francisco: Institute for Contemporary Studies Press, 1988).

[28] See his discussion of "America's Budgetary Dilemma" (pp. 109–26). See also Calleo, Cleveland, and Silk (fn. 19), 851–53.

may be desirable as a way of promoting more equitable burden sharing between the U.S. and its NATO allies. But it is not essential for financial reasons. The United States can put its budgetary house in order without drastic reductions in defense spending, and it may even be able to do so without radical tax increases or extensive cuts in existing social programs. Solvency and world power are not necessarily incompatible.

LONG-TERM EROSION

The Rise and Fall of the Great Powers

Even if the present geopolitical posture of the United States can be maintained without harmful fiscal imbalance, it may be that doing so will still cause long-term damage. Over a sufficiently protracted period, pouring money into defense may weaken the U.S. economy and further erode its international competitive position—even if, year by year, it does not derange the nation's finances. That, at least, is the contention of Paul Kennedy's important and much-discussed book.

Stripped of its rich historical flesh, the skeleton of Kennedy's argument is actually quite simple. Looking back over almost five hundred years of history, Kennedy perceives a recurrent two-step process, driven forward ceaselessly by the engine of uneven economic growth.[29] During any given period, the dominant units of social organization (nation-states in the modern era) have increased their wealth at unequal rates. This pattern of

differential growth is a result of the fact that periodic "technological and organizational breakthroughs" tend to "bring a greater advantage to one society than to another" (pp. xv–xvi).[30]

Although the correlation has not always been exact or immediate, states that have grown wealthier than their competitors have also tended, over time, to become more powerful in military terms. The reasons for this are easy to see. As Kennedy explains it: "Once their productive capacity was enhanced, countries would normally find it easier to sustain the burden of paying for large-scale armaments in peacetime and maintaining and supplying large armies and fleets in wartime." Because "wealth is usually needed to underpin military power," it seems obvious that the more wealth a country has in relation to its neighbors, the greater its potential for obtaining military advantage over them (p. xvi).

Historically, the wealthiest and strongest states have tended to expand their political influence. The superior military might that these countries can generate gives them the capacity to conquer and colonize "peripheral" areas (as Spain, the Netherlands, France, and Great Britain all did in their time) and to defeat other major powers (as the United States

---

[29] The idea that uneven economic development is an important underlying cause of international conflict dates back to Thucydides; it was reintroduced in this century by Lenin. See the discussion in Robert Gilpin, *The Political Economy of International Relations* (Princeton: Princeton University Press, 1987), 54–56.

[30] Kennedy later suggests that "the speed of . . . global economic change has not been a uniform one, simply because growth is itself irregular, conditioned by the circumstance of the individual inventor and entrepreneur as well as by climate, disease, wars, geography, the social framework, and so on" (p. 439). Scholars from a variety of disciplines have tried to explain why it is that growth rates are uneven across countries and why, in any one state, they tend to diminish over time. See Carlo Cipolla, ed., *The Economic Decline of Empires* (London: Methuen, 1970); Mancur Olson, *The Rise and Decline of Nations* (New Haven: Yale University Press, 1982); and Robert Gilpin, *War and Change in World Politics* (New York: Cambridge University Press, 1981).

has done in the twentieth century). Riding the wave of economic development, one state after another has risen to "Great Power" status. But this rise is only half of the story. The ascent of any given country, no matter how powerful it may be at its peak, does not bring the process of economic progress to a close. The forces that, for a time, worked to the advantage of one state will rarely continue to do so for very long. Countries that are left behind during one cycle of development and growth may be able to reassert themselves and perhaps even to pull ahead in subsequent phases. In time, the biggest, fastest-growing states will have their chance to become the world's leading military powers.

Historians, economists, and political scientists have long noted the crucial role of wealth in promoting the accumulation of military power.[31] In explaining the decline of the mighty, however, Kennedy postulates the existence of a less commonly recognized mechanism. As they grow richer and stronger, states typically acquire commitments beyond their own borders. These may take a variety of forms: "dependence on foreign markets and raw materials, military alliances, perhaps bases and colonies." At first, these interests may be relatively easy for a rapidly growing country to defend. With shifts in the locus of economic leadership, however, this happy coincidence of capabilities and commitments is unlikely to last. As Kennedy describes the beginning of this next historical stage: "Other, rival Powers are now economically expanding at a faster rate, and wish in their turn to extend their influence abroad" (p. xxiii). As this happens, the

dominant state will feel increasingly vulnerable. In order to defend its home territory and, even more urgently, its external interests, it will have to undertake larger and more costly defensive efforts. Ironically, these exertions may actually *weaken* a country rather than make it stronger and more secure. As more is spent on defense, the once-dominant power's rate of overall economic growth will slow even further, thereby accelerating the process of relative decline and worsening the country's strategic problems. According to Kennedy: "If too large a proportion of the state's resources is diverted from wealth creation and allocated instead to military purposes, then that is likely to lead to a weakening of national power over the longer term" (p. xvi).

In Kennedy's view, the United States has recently entered the second, downward portion of its trajectory as a Great Power. By the beginning of the twentieth century, the U.S. had surpassed all other states in such measures of economic capability as steel production and energy consumption (pp. 200–202). On the eve of World War I, Americans were enjoying a per capita income greater than that of any other industrialized state (p. 243). Still, despite its crucial role in determining the outcome of that conflict (p. 271), for domestic political reasons the United States remained a latent or "offstage" superpower (p. 320), reluctant to play the military and political role to which it was entitled by its economic prowess.

Only the colossal upheaval of World War II proved sufficient to draw the United States permanently onto the global stage. Emerging in 1945 with enormous economic and military advantages over all possible rivals, America finally began to follow a course that, as Kennedy puts it,

could come as no surprise to those familiar with the history of international politics. With the traditional Great

[31] For a review of early modern thinking on this subject, see Gordon H. McCormick, "Strategic Considerations in the Development of Economic Thought," in Gordon H. McCormick and Richard E. Bissell, ed., *Strategic Dimensions of Economic Behavior* (New York: Praeger, 1984), 3–25.

Powers fading away, it steadily moved into the vacuum which their going created; having become number one, it could no longer contain itself within its own shores, or even its own hemisphere (p. 359).

It matters little whether the United States jumped or was pulled into its new role. Within a very brief period, the country had abandoned its isolationist traditions and acquired a vast assortment of overseas interests and outposts (pp. 389–90). These were easy enough to defend at first, but soon the U.S. began to encounter problems similar to those of all previous "number one" nations. As the Soviet Union and the countries of Europe and Asia recovered from World War II, America's economic edge began to dwindle. Yet, from the early 1950s on, the nation's overseas commitments have remained largely unchanged.

By the 1970s, the United States found itself increasingly in a situation of "imperial overstretch" or "strategical overextension" (p. 515). Because of the scope of its responsibilities, the persistence of the Soviet Union as a major military power (although one that is itself faced with severe economic problems), and the rising costs of weapons systems, the United States has been forced to spend considerable sums on defense (pp. 515–23). At the same time, the massive American economic lead of the 1940s and 1950s has been eaten away at a rapid rate. As a result, the U.S. capacity to carry its assorted burdens is "obviously less than it was several decades ago" (p. 529).

According to Kennedy, the United States is now caught on the horns of a familiar dilemma. If it reduces military spending, it will wind up "feeling vulnerable everywhere." If it attempts to sustain "a very heavy investment in armaments," it can buy greater security in the short run; but, in the process, it may "so erode the commercial competitiveness of the American economy that the nation

will be *less* secure in the long term" (pp. 532–33). Although Kennedy does not spell out the implications for American foreign policy in detail, they seem clear enough. The United States cannot preserve its existing strategic position, nor can it completely reverse the relative erosion in its power. The best that can be hoped for is that American statesmen will "manage" that erosion so that it "takes place slowly and smoothly, and is not accelerated by policies which bring merely short-term advantage but longer-term disadvantage" (p. 534). Kennedy does not say so, but the successful "management" of relative decline would appear to require a withdrawal by the U.S. from all or some of its present commitments and a redirection of the resulting savings from military expenditure to civilian investment. Only in this way can the country hope to hold onto even its "natural" share of the world's wealth and power, which should probably be "16 or 18 percent" as compared to the 40 percent it had acquired by 1945 (p. 533).

At the heart of the second half of Kennedy's general argument—one that he seeks to make not only about the United States, but about the other Great Powers of the past—is the question of whether and under what conditions defense spending may inhibit economic growth. This question is, as Kennedy notes, "a highly controversial one . . . and the evidence does not point simply in one direction" (pp. 531–32). Indeed, according to a recent survey, "the literature offers no clear and simple answer to the question: Does defense spending have an impact on economic performance?"[32]

[32] Steve Chan, "The Impact of Defense Spending on Economic Performance: A Survey of Evidence and Problems," *Orbis* 29 (Summer 1985), 403–34, at 409. For a small sampling of the available literature, see James L. Clayton, ed., *The Economic Impact of the Cold War* (New York: Harcourt Brace, 1970); Lloyd Dumas, *The Overburdened Economy* (Berkeley: University of California Press,

The connection between defense and growth may depend in part on a state's level of economic development. Although their views are controversial, some analysts believe that less developed countries need not suffer and can actually benefit from high levels of military spending.[33] In the short term, at least, the impact of defense expenditures is also a function of domestic economic conditions;[34] an identical expansion in military budgets could stimulate a flagging economy or produce inflation in one already operating at close to full capacity.[35] Using various statistical techniques, a

number of researchers claim to have found a correlation over the long run between large military budgets and low levels of investment or economic growth,[36] but the validity and significance of these results have been questioned by other analysts.[37]

Kennedy is not, of course, interested in all countries under all conditions, but in Great Powers and especially those that have entered into a period of economic decline. On the crucial question as to what part military expenditures may play in bringing on that decline, Kennedy is somewhat vague. At some points he seems to suggest that the difficulties produced by defense spending are simply a function of time and level of effort. Thus he maintains that "the historical record

1986); Mary Kaldor, *The Baroque Arsenal* (New York: Hill & Wang, 1981); Gavin Kennedy, *The Economics of Defence* (London: Faber & Faber, 1975); Kurt W. Rothschild, "Military Expenditure, Exports and Growth," *Kyklos* 26 (No. 4, 1973); 804–14; Bruce Russett, "Defense Expenditures and National Well-Being," *American Political Science Review* 76 (December 1982), 767–77; Dan Smith and Ron Smith, *The Economics of Militarism* (London: Pluto Press, 1983); Harvey Starr, Francis W. Hoole, Jeffrey A. Hart, and John R. Freeman, "The Relationship between Defense Spending and Inflation," *Journal of Conflict Resolution* 28 (March 1984), 103–22; *Report of the U.S. President's Committee on the Economic Impact of Defense and Disarmament* (Washington, DC: G.P.O., 1965).

[33] For an overview of this debate, see *ibid.*, 405–10. See also David K. Whynes, *The Economics of Third World Military Expenditure* (Austin: University of Texas Press, 1979).

[34] One recent study finds, for example, that, "if there can be any single conclusion about the effects of military expenditure on the economy, it must be that it depends on the nature of the expenditure, the prevailing circumstances, and the concurrent government policies." Ron Smith and George Georgiou, "Assessing the Effect of Military Expenditure on OECD Economies: A Survey," *Arms Control* 4 (May 1983), 3–15, at 15.

[35] See, for example, an analysis of the probable macroeconomic impact of the Reagan buildup in *Defense Spending and the Economy* (Washington, DC: Congressional Budget Office, 1983), 9–36.

[36] The claim that defense hurts investment is supported, for example, by a comparison of the 14 OECD countries in Ronald P. Smith, "Military Expenditure and Investment in OECD Countries, 1954–1973," *Journal of Comparative Economics* 4 (March 1980), 19–32. A similar study of 17 industrialized countries between 1960 and 1980 found that "nations with a larger military burden tended to invest less," but it concluded also that there was only "weak evidence that higher military spending correlates with lower real economic growth." DeGrasse (fn. 15), 67–68.

[37] See the critique of Smith and DeGrasse in Gordon Adams and David Gold, *Defense Spending and the Economy: Does the Defense Dollar Make a Difference?* (Washington, DC: Defense Budget Project, July 1987), 14–19. For a brief critical overview of the literature on this question, see David Greenwood, "Note on the Impact of Military Expenditure on Economic Growth and Performance," in Christian Schmidt, ed., *The Economics of Military Expenditures* (New York: St. Martin's, 1987), 98–103. After reviewing the performance of Britain, France, Germany, Japan, and the United States during the nineteenth and twentieth centuries, two researchers have recently concluded that "the defense-investment substitution effect is not quite as prevalent as many think." Karen Rasler and William R. Thompson, "Defense Burdens, Capital Formation, and Economic Growth," *Journal of Conflict Resolution* 32 (March 1988), 81.

suggests that if a particular nation is allocating *over the long term* more than 10 percent (and in some cases—when it is structurally weak—more than 5 percent) of GNP to armaments, that is likely to limit its growth rate" (p. 609; emphasis in original). More typically, he argues that defense becomes a problem only during certain phases of a Great Power's development and, in particular, when it has already begun to experience some erosion in its relative economic and military power. At that point, what he calls "*excessive* arms spending" or "a top-heavy military establishment" (made necessary by strategic overextension which, in turn, was made possible by an earlier, relatively rapid accumulation of national wealth) "will hurt economic growth" or "may slow down the rate of economic growth" (pp. 444 and 445; emphasis in original).

In the end, Kennedy's reflections on the relationship between defense spending and decline come down to a simple and seemingly incontestable observation: once a leading power has begun to slip economically, *for whatever reason,* it will find it increasingly difficult to sustain large (still less, rising) defense burdens. As Kennedy explains it, declining powers are like aging people: "If they spend too much on armaments—or, more usually, upon maintaining at growing cost the military obligations they had assumed in a previous period—they are likely to overstrain themselves, like an old man attempting to work beyond his natural strength" (p. 540).

It may not be possible at this point to make any more powerful, universal generalizations about the economic impact of defense spending. Nevertheless, it may be that the effects of such spending can be determined with precision in particular cases. For the United States, the questions are both empirical and theoretical: First, have the substantial peacetime military expenditures that the U.S. has un-

dertaken since 1945 caused (or at least substantially contributed to) its relative economic decline? Second, if continued, will those expenditures inevitably cause further erosion in the U.S. position?[38]

Although their significance has been contested, the raw facts of the decline of the United States are by now widely accepted.[39] The country's shares of such things as gross world product,[40] world trade,[41] and production of industrial manufactured goods[42] have diminished substantially since the end of World War II. This alone, of course, is not evidence that there is anything wrong with the American economy. In 1945, with the rest of the world in ruins, the United States enjoyed an unnaturally large advantage over all other countries. As the world recovered, the American margin was bound to shrink; indeed, it was that

[38] While Kennedy's work raises both of these issues, it does not provide definitive answers to either one. Although he has sometimes been criticized for doing so, Kennedy does not in fact maintain that postwar military expenditures caused America's economic decline. Indeed, his book contains no direct assessment of what the cumulative impact of that spending has been. As to whether defense spending at existing levels will be sustainable in the future, Kennedy strongly implies that it may not be, but he cannot be said to rule out the possibility altogether.

[39] Some authors have suggested, however, that the U.S. decline is not as severe as the usual indicators would seem to suggest. See Susan Strange, "The Persistent Myth of Lost Hegemony," *International Organization* 41 (Autumn 1987), 551–74, and Bruce Russett, "The Mysterious Case of Vanishing Hegemony; or, Is Mark Twain Really Dead?" *International Organization* 39 (Spring 1985) 207–31.

[40] Down from 25.9% in 1960 to 21.5% in 1980 (Kennedy, p. 436).

[41] Down from 18.4% in 1950 to 13.4% in 1977. See Robert Keohane, *After Hegemony* (Princeton: Princeton University Press, 1984), 36.

[42] Down from around 50% in 1945 to 44.7% in 1953 to 31.5% in 1980 (Kennedy, p. 432).

very recovery which was a principal aim of postwar U.S. policy.[43]

"The real question," Kennedy explains, is not " 'Did the United States have to decline relatively?' but 'Did it have to decline so fast?' " (p. 432). He might have added, Will it continue to decline so rapidly in the future? There were surely good reasons to expect that in the initial postwar era the American economy would grow more slowly than those of its recovering rivals, and that the U.S. would therefore lose part of its initial, overall advantage. What is disturbing from the American point of view is that, in some cases, the difference in economic performance persisted long after the war was over. Throughout the sixties, seventies, and into the eighties, the United States' GNP, GNP per capita, and manufacturing productivity all grew far more slowly than those of Japan. Compared to the European countries, American achievements were more mixed, with the U.S. regaining some advantages by the seventies and eighties.[44]

Analysts have made three different arguments in support of the contention that what they regard as America's *compara-*

tively unimpressive postwar economic performance was due to its *relatively* high level of defense expenditures. Each of these assertions centers on the alleged impact of defense spending on investment. The first (or, in economist Lester Thurow's term, the "quantitative" version of the argument) is simply that military expenditures "crowd out" private investment.[45] This assertion follows from an examination of the national income identity in which a state's GNP is defined as equal to the combined value of its private consumption, private investment, total government spending (including both defense and nondefense expenditures), and net exports.[46] For a given level of national income, if one of these categories goes up, then some or all of the others will have to come down. If consumption, nondefense government spending, and net exports are fixed, if defense spending increases, then investment must decline. But, because investment is the engine of future economic growth, as it diminishes, so too will the rate at which national income expands. Under certain conditions, therefore, high levels of defense spending may lead to slower growth.

Even in the abstract, this connection is

---

[43] In this sense, as one observer has pointed out, "the relative decline in American global economic preeminence occurred not in spite of America but because of America." Zbigniew Brzezinski, "America's New Geostrategy," *Foreign Affairs* 66 (Spring 1988), 693. For a similar argument, see Joseph S. Nye, Jr., "America's Decline: A Myth," *The New York Times,* April 10, 1988, p. 31.

[44] By the seventies, U.S. and average European Community GNP growth rates were about the same, with the U.S. growing somewhat faster in the eighties. U.S. and E.E.C. per capita GNP growth rates converged in the seventies and remained roughly equal in the eighties. After lagging throughout the sixties and seventies, American manufacturing productivity seems finally to be increasing slightly faster than that of France and Germany. For figures, see the Central Intelligence Agency's *Handbook of Economic Statistics, 1987* (Washington, DC: G.P.O., 1987), 39, 40, and 43.

[45] Thurow, "Budget Deficits," in Daniel Bell and Lester Thurow, *The Deficits: How Big? How Long? How Dangerous?* (New York: New York University Press, 1985), 122–24. Kennedy (p. 533) advances a variant of this argument when he suggests that declining world powers tend to "allocate more and more of their resources into the military sector, which in turn squeezes out productive investment and, over time, leads to the downward spiral of slower growth. . . ."

[46] This relationship is usually presented as an equation: $Y = C + I + G + (X - M)$, where

Y = national income
C = consumption
I = investment
G = government expenditures
X = exports
M = imports

not simple or direct. Increasing military expenditures will not lead automatically to diminished investment if, for example, private consumption falls or government spending on nondefense items is reduced by an equivalent amount. On the other hand, cutbacks in military spending will not necessarily promote more rapid economic growth. Reductions in one form of government spending might be made up by increases in the other variety, or, perhaps, by an upsurge in private consumption. In either case, there would be little or no increase in private investment and (assuming for the moment that government spending cannot act as a form of investment), little acceleration in the rate of overall economic expansion.

Since the end of World War II, the United States has spent relatively more on defense than its major allies. During the same period, the portion of U.S. national income devoted to investment has also been comparatively low. To conclude, however, that the first fact is completely responsible for the second would overlook another crucial piece of the equation. In postwar America, both military spending and private consumption have been relatively high.[47] Instead of asserting, as Thurow does, that the U.S. has "essentially taken defense out of investment ever since World War II,"[48] it would be more reasonable to say that, if investment has suffered, it has been at the expense of defense and private consumption combined.[49]

If levels of consumption had been lower in the past, the United States could have sustained higher levels of investment along with actual rates of defense expenditure. In the future, increases in private investment could be achieved through cuts in the shares of national income devoted to defense or nondefense government programs, or by reductions in the level of private consumption.[50] Such shifts could be encouraged by cutbacks in government spending, by changes in the tax laws intended to discourage consumption and promote savings and investment, or by some combination of the two.[51] In any case, claims to

[49] In fact, several comparisons of the composition of U.S. GNP before and after World War II suggest that the level of gross private domestic investment did not change very much (standing, according to one calculation, at around 14 or 15% of GNP in both 1929 and 1969 or, according to another, at 15% in 1930, 1940, 1953, and 1957). The increase in peacetime military expenditures after 1945 seems to have been made up for by a drop in the share of GNP devoted to personal consumption. For the first calculation, see Kenneth E. Boulding, "The Impact of the Defense Industry on the Structure of the American Economy," in Bernard Udis, ed., *The Economic Consequences of Reduced Military Spending* (Lexington: D. C. Heath, 1973), 225–52. For the second, see Charles J. Hitch and Roland M. McKean, *The Economics of Defense in the Nuclear Age* (Cambridge: Harvard University Press, 1963), 39.

[50] The case for cuts in consumption is made in Peter Peterson (fn. 7). For an opposing view that favors reducing defense and increasing "public investment," see Jeff Faux, "America's Economic Future," *World Policy Journal* 5 (Summer 1988), 367–414. See also Robert Eisner, "To Raise the Savings Rate, Try Spending," *New York Times,* August 29, 1988, p. A19.

[51] For an analysis of the various ways in which private and overall national savings might be increased, see Lawrence Summers

[47] According to one calculation for the period 1960–1979, 7.4% of U.S. gross domestic product went to military spending. The figures for Britain, West Germany, and Japan were 5.4%, 3.9%, and .9%, respectively. Fixed capital formation made up 17.6% of GDP in the United States, as compared to 18.4% in Britain, 24.1% in West Germany, and 32.7% in Japan. Private consumption made up 63% of GDP in the United States, versus 62.8% in Britain, 55.6% in West Germany, and 55.4% in Japan. See Kenneth A. Oye, "International Systems Structure and American Foreign Policy," in Kenneth A. Oye, Robert J. Lieber, and Donald Rothchild, eds., *Eagle Defiant* (Boston: Little, Brown, 1983), 10.

[48] Thurow (fn. 45), 123.

the contrary notwithstanding, there is no ironclad trade-off between defense and investment. As economist Charles Schultze has pointed out: "There is no reason in principle why we cannot design the taxes needed to support defense spending so as to depress consumption rather than investment. If we do otherwise, the resulting fall in investment is our own choice and not something inherent in defense spending."[52]

Even if a "quantitative" investment problem can be avoided, there may still be a second, "qualitative" one. Despite descriptions of defense spending as just another form of consumption,[53] the military actually invests billions of dollars each year in research and development.[54] This work, like its counterpart in civilian industry, requires the efforts of highly skilled scientists and engineers. If there were only a fixed number of such people in the United States, and if, for some reason, they preferred involvement in military over civil programs, it is possible that commercial research could suffer and, along with it, the entire economy. According to Lester Thurow, this is precisely what happened throughout much of the postwar period. "The best and the

brightest among America's engineering and science prospects tend to enter military R & D," he maintains, because "it is simply more fun." In this way, "the large U.S. military establishment handicaps future civilian economic success."[55]

Despite such assertions, there is little evidence of a past military "brain drain."[56] Far from being fixed, the number of scientists and engineers has actually grown considerably since the 1960s.[57] The fraction of the total involved either directly or indirectly in defense work is a matter of definition and a subject of debate.[58] A recent survey suggests,

[55] Lester Thurow, "America among Equals," in Sanford Ungar, ed., *Estrangement* (New York: Oxford University Press, 1985), 175. Again, Kennedy (p. 532) makes a similar argument: "If the Pentagon's spending drains off the majority of the country's scientists and engineers from the design and production of goods for the world market while similar personnel in other countries are primarily engaged in bringing out better products for the civilian consumer, then it seems inevitable that the American share of world manufacturing will steadily decline, and also likely that its economic growth rates will be slower than in those countries dedicated to the marketplace. . . ."

[56] It is possible, however, that the effects of such a drain might be subtle, lagged, and hard to measure. Some experts have suggested that the competition for scarce research talent may, in the past, have bid up the cost of R & D and reduced the feasibility of some civilian projects. See Harvey Brooks, "The Strategic Defense Initiative as Science Policy," *International Security* II (Fall 1986), 184. This possibility deserves further study.

[57] After decreasing in the seventies, the number of students receiving degrees of all sorts in science and engineering has increased steadily since the early eighties. The growth in doctoral degrees has, however, been due largely to an influx of foreign graduate students to American universities. The long-term implications of this trend for the U.S. economy are unclear, and depend in part on how many foreign students eventually settle and work in the United States. *National Patterns* (fn. 54), 28–30.

[58] A 1978 National Science Foundation survey found that 16.2% of scientists and engi-

and Chris Carroll, "Why Is U.S. National Savings so Low?" *Brookings Papers on Economic Activity* 2 (Washington, DC: The Brookings Institution, 1987).

[52] Schultze, "Economic Effects of the Defense Budget," *The Brookings Bulletin* 18 (Fall 1981), 2. In the end, Thurow acknowledges this point by saying: "It is technically feasible for America to spend more on defense than Japan and still have a world-class economy if we are willing to pay for it by raising taxes to cut civilian consumption." Thurow (fn. 45), 124.

[53] "Defense spending is a form of consumption" (*ibid.*, 122).

[54] In 1987, the federal government spent over $40 billion or almost 14% of the military budget on defense R & D. *National Patterns of Science and Technology Resources: 1987* NSF 88–305 (Washington: National Science Foundation, 1988), 15.

however, that the percentage has actually declined significantly during the seventies and eighties. The same study also found no indication of a shortage in scientists and engineers, even at the peak of the Reagan buildup, and no evidence that the "best and the brightest" were being drawn from civilian to defense work, whether by higher salaries or the promise of greater intellectual stimulation.[59] In fact, judging by some recent reports, it is government rather than industry that is now most concerned about attracting first-rate technical personnel, thanks largely to limits on salaries imposed by the pay system of the civil service.[60]

If a shortage of talented labor for nondefense projects did exist, a reduction in the military budget would not be the only way of dealing with the problem. Instead of cutting defense R & D (thereby freeing researchers to take on work in the civilian sector that is presumably going undone), the federal government might try to expand the total skilled manpower pool by providing more support for education and technical training.[61] Increasing the supply of scientists and engineers could make it possible for more defense *and* nondefense research to be done in the United States.

The third variant of the argument linking defense, investment, and growth focuses on "spinoffs" and "tradeoffs." Since the end of World War II, the United States government has spent a great deal of money on research and development. In 1987, federal R & D expenditures were around $60 billion, roughly half the combined national total of government and private sector spending on research.[62] Of this sum, 69 percent went to defense-related projects—18 percent more than in 1977.[63] Some observers believe that these expenditures, whatever their impact on American military strength, produce little of value for the economy as

neers worked primarily on defense projects, with another 3.8% concentrating most heavily on work connected with the space program. DeGrasse (fn. 15), 102. Other analysts put the figure close to 50%. For a range of estimates, see Adams and Gold (fn. 37), 50–51. For a 1981 breakdown by specialty of skilled personnel involved in defense work, see John P. Holdren and F. Bailey Green, "Military Spending, The SDI and Government Support of Research and Development: Effects on the Economy and the Health of American Science," *Journal of the Federation of American Scientists* 39 (September 1986), 7.

[59] Drawing on N.S.F. survey data, a National Research Council report finds that, between 1972 and 1984, the fraction of scientists and engineers with bachelor's degrees working on projects sponsored by the Defense Department fell from 18.6% to 15.5%. The figures for researchers with master's and doctoral degrees fell from 23.8% to 19.9% and from 10.5% to 8.5%, respectively. National Research Council, *The Impact of Defense Spending on Nondefense Engineering Labor Markets: A Report to the National Academy of Engineering* (Washington, DC: National Academy Press, 1986), 74–76, 9–10, and 91.

[60] For example, a 1987 report by the Defense Science Board found that, at one government laboratory, mean salaries were $14,000 less than at a facility operated by private contractors. The best researchers at the government lab could be paid no more than $72,000 a year; their private-sector counterparts sometimes made over twice as much. Defense Science Board, *Technology Base Management* (Washington, DC: G.P.O., December 1987), 16–17.

[61] For recommendations along these lines aimed at satisfying "both national security and commercial needs," see U.S. Congress, Office of Technology Assessment, *The Defense Technology Base: Introduction and Overview—A Special Report,* OTA-ISC-374 (Washington, DC: G.P.O., March 1988), 18.

[62] Total R & D expenditures in the U.S. now equal 2.7% of GNP, around the same as in West Germany and Japan. When defense-related R & D is excluded, however, the U.S. total falls to 1.8% of GNP. By contrast, less than 10% of research in Japan and Germany is defense-related. Although the dollar amounts spent are smaller, these two countries have for over fifteen years been devoting more of their GNP to civilian research than the United States. *National Patterns* (fn. 54), 19–20.

[63] *Economic Report of the President* (fn. 11), 179–80.

a whole.[64] If money were transferred from defense to civilian R & D, enhanced productivity, greater competitiveness, and faster economic growth would result.

The question of how much spins off, spills over, or trickles down from military R & D to civilian industry is a contentious one.[65] Even many skeptics acknowledge, however, that defense-related research has often produced indirect and sometimes unintended commercial benefits.[66] If the federal government were to eliminate spending for defense research, and

if the funds freed up as a result did not find their way into other forms of R & D, the net impact on the U.S. economy would probably be negative. On the other hand, there is little reason to think that spending on military R & D is the most efficient way of promoting progress in nondefense sectors. In the words of one noted authority on science policy, "if economic spin-off is what is desired, it is better to stimulate it directly than to try to derive it indirectly from military spending."[67]

Even if government-funded defense research produced no spin-offs at all, it would not necessarily be doing any harm to the economy as a whole. The real concern about military R & D is, therefore, that it has opportunity costs—that it must somehow be displacing either nongovernment research on civilian projects or government-funded nondefense research, or both. As has already been discussed, defense R & D could conceivably cut into the civilian sector by drawing away skilled manpower and driving up research costs. Although there appears to be little direct evidence, it is possible that this may have happened in the past and that, if the government had supported less military research, more work would have been done by industry on purely civilian projects.

It is also at least conceivable that if the federal government had spent less over the years on defense R & D, it could have devoted more of its own funds to work with direct commercial applications. In view of the pressures of the strategic competition with the Soviet Union and the traditional American aversion to central planning and economic intervention by the government, such a shift in priorities was not likely. Similar, although possibly less stringent, constraints will no doubt continue to apply for some time to

[64] One author asserts, for example, that the much vaunted "spinoff" or "spillover" argument that military-oriented technological development produces massive improvements in areas of civilian application and thus does not retard civilian technological progress, makes very little conceptual sense, and more to the point, is massively contradicted by straightforward empirical observation.
See Lloyd J. Dumas, "Military Spending and Economic Decay," in Dumas, ed., *The Political Economy of Arms Reduction* (Boulder, CO: Westview Press, 1982), 13. For the opposite viewpoint, see Hitch and McKean (fn. 49), 82–83.

[65] Kennedy (p. 532) points out that there are "technical spinoffs from weapons research," but he does not consider them sufficient to offset the other, negative consequences of defense spending.

[66] One proponent of considerable cuts in defense spending argues:
Clearly, military research has yielded a large number of commercially viable products—including many of the breakthroughs in electronics, recombinant DNA, jet engines, fiberglass and other composite materials, and a major portion of communications technologies. Indeed, many of the inventions that have most altered the postwar world economy have evolved from military-related research.
Ann Markusen, "The Militarized Economy," *World Policy Journal* 3 (Summer 1986), 503. For a useful survey of the military's role in the development of American technology, see Merritt Roe Smith, ed., *Military Enterprise and Technological Change* (Cambridge: MIT Press, 1987).

[67] Brooks (fn. 56), 183.

come.[68] A one-for-one transfer of defense R & D dollars to carefully chosen government-sponsored projects aimed at commercial innovation might well have a beneficial impact on American economic performance; but any sharp move in this direction would certainly arouse concerns and political opposition on both national security and economic grounds.

Without necessarily cutting defense R & D or adopting a full-fledged national industrial policy aimed at picking commercial winners and losers, the federal government could spend more on supporting basic science and on promoting certain research projects intended to have widespread and immediate civilian application. In addition to whatever it did directly in these areas, the government might also take steps designed to encourage private industry to invest more heavily in its own R & D programs.[69] Finally, assuming that some military research will continue into the foreseeable future, that work might be conducted in ways aimed at maximizing civilian spin-offs.[70] The question must remain open whether such spin-offs have, on balance, outweighed the opportunity

costs of government-sponsored defense research in the past. Regardless of the answer, there are no grounds for asserting that such research must inevitably be a net drain on the economy.

To sum up: although Kennedy does not offer any direct judgment as to their significance, it is possible that large peacetime defense expenditures, combined with a range of other factors (including relatively high levels of consumption and, perhaps, an inadequate supply of skilled scientific manpower and insufficient spending on civilian R & D) may have helped to retard and distort postwar American economic growth. It also seems probable that factors having little or nothing to do with defense have had an equal and possibly far greater role in shaping the events of the past four decades.[71] Military expenditures alone did not cause

---

[68] For these reasons, Harvey Brooks concluded in 1986 that "any viable U.S. industrial policy is likely to derive from military policy for many years to come if only because of the traditional reluctance of Americans to accept government intervention in the market economy" (*ibid.*). There is now some evidence of movement in precisely this direction. See "Bigger Role Urged for Defense Department in Economic Policy," *New York Times,* October 19, 1988, p. A1.

[69] Measures of this sort could include changes in the tax laws and selective relaxations in antitrust restrictions prohibiting collaboration by major producers in the same industrial sector. See Report to the Secretary of Defense by the Under Secretary of Defense (Acquisition), *Bolstering Defense Industrial Competitiveness* (Washington, DC: Department of Defense, July 1988), 16–18.

[70] Jacques S. Gansler has suggested, for example, that the Defense Department could in-

vest more heavily in developing certain kinds of manufacturing technology instead of focusing its R & D efforts so heavily on particular full-scale weapons systems. According to Gansler, "these manufacturing technologies could contribute significantly to the nation's ability to produce high-quality, low-cost military equipment, in addition to contributing to the long-term competitiveness of the nation's industrial base." Gansler, "Needed: A U.S. Defense Industrial Strategy," *International Security* 12 (Fall 1987), 55–56.

[71] The list of suspects includes, but is by no means limited to, the following: systematically misguided management practices, poor labor-management relations, insufficient incentives for productive domestic investment, fluctuating government macroeconomic policies, a poorly designed tax code, a chronically overvalued dollar, and expanding government regulations. For entry into the vast literature on these subjects, see Bruce R. Scott, "U.S. Competitiveness: Concepts, Performance, and Implications," in Bruce R. Scott and George C. Lodge, eds., *U.S. Competitiveness in the World Economy* (Boston: Harvard Business School Press, 1985), 13–70; Otto Eckstein et al., *The DRI Report on U.S. Manufacturing Industries* (New York: McGraw Hill, 1984); and Seymour Zucker et al., *The Reindustrialization of America* (New York: McGraw-Hill, 1982).

that portion of America's relative decline which may have been, in some sense, avoidable. Defense cuts, by themselves, can also not be expected to produce dramatic improvements in the future economic performance of the United States.

Even if, in the past, the United States hindered itself by spending between 5 and 10 percent of its GNP on defense, attempts to continue a similar level of effort may not inescapably lead to equivalent harm. If the federal government were to adopt policies aimed at promoting savings, productive investment, education, and scientific research, there is no apparent reason why moderate defense budgets could not be combined with rising productivity, steadier growth, and enhanced international competitiveness.

CONCLUSIONS

The foregoing analysis suggests three sets of conclusions; they are discussed briefly in ascending order of generality. First, the United States can continue to support something resembling its present military posture without running enormous deficits or accelerating its relative economic decline. Doing so will have costs, however. These might include, for example, higher taxes, lower levels of private consumption, and fewer entitlements for some members of the middle class. Whether or not these costs are worth paying and who, precisely, should pay them are political decisions: they are conditioned but not determined by economic factors. How they are made will strongly influence both the coming shape of U.S. society and the future extent of the country's involvement in world politics.

Second, concerning the economic impact of defense spending, much remains to be understood. Future work might usefully focus, not only on the search for universal generalizations, but on what David Greenwood has called the "disaggregated" approach—the

> elucidation of how, in the actual circumstances of the individual case, a particular hypothetical change in the scale and/or pattern of military outlays may plausibly be expected—on given, explicitly stated assumptions—to impinge on the rate of growth of aggregate income and output or on some specific aspect of economic performance.[72]

As applied to the United States, for example, such an approach might involve an investigation of the impact of fluctuating defense expenditures on the evolution, over four decades, of key industrial sectors such as machine tools, steel, electronic equipment, and semiconductors.

Finally, more thought must be given to developing a political economy of national strategy. How and how well do states manage, over long periods of time, to direct the flow of national resources so as to achieve both internal wealth and external power? Such problems continue to be on the minds, not only of American statesmen, but of their counterparts in the Soviet Union, China, and Japan. They ought to be central to the concerns of students of international politics.

[72] Greenwood (fn. 37), 103.

CHAPTER 2

The American Budget Deficit

The readings in this section consider the nature of American budget deficits. Richard Darman, Director of the Office of Management and Budget in the Bush administration, contends that the federal budget is an out-of-control "Cookie Monster," made worse by future claims on the budget (such as retirement programs, credit guarantees, and insurance obligations). He argues for deficit reduction, incentives for private savings, investment in human capital, enterprise zones, and reform of the congressional budget process.

The next selection analyzes the political economy of America's foreign debt. Gerald Epstein notes that "the United States, once the world's largest creditor nation, is now the world's largest debtor, owing more to foreigners than it is owed by them." Epstein's argument is that analyses of America's foreign debt should not ignore "the role that the globalization of U.S. corporations has played in the creation of the country's foreign debt problem." According to Epstein, the United States is the world's largest debtor, in part, because "it is also the world's largest overseas investor and home to many of the world's largest multinational corporations. In an age of globalized production," he says, "these corporations have progressively abandoned their commitment to the United States, with negative consequences not only for America's balance of payments but also for the U.S. standard of living."

4. Director's Introduction to the New Budget

Richard G. Darman

GREEN EYESHADES AND THE COOKIE MONSTER

If anything were meant for viewing through proverbial green eyeshades, it would seem to be the Federal budget. The

SOURCE: *Budget of the United States Government, Fiscal Year 1991.*

typeface is small. The text is tedious. Tables are seemingly endless.

The sheer size of the budget makes it seem like a monster. It contains almost 190,000 accounts. At the rate of one per minute, eight hours per day, it would take over a year to reflect upon these! The budget's annual outlays are larger than all countries' economies except those of the

United States, Japan, and the Soviet Union. (The Federal budget is roughly the size of the entire West German economy.) Clearly, at some point, green eyeshades must be put aside. Detail must be considered; but the capacity to abstract should not be lost.

Of course, with or without green eyeshades, monsters do not naturally invite examination. Still, if a monster is present, one might address certain threshold questions: Is it threatening or potentially helpful, and how is one to tell? The answers are not always as obvious as the questions.

On "Sesame Street," the children's educational television program, there is a wonderful character known as Cookie Monster. As all monsters are, Cookie Monster is initially intimidating. His manner is gruff. His clumsiness occasionally causes damage.

But quickly, Cookie Monster comes to be seen as benign—indeed, downright friendly. He has a few bad habits. He cannot resist gobbling up anything and everything that might be consumed—especially cookies. And he cannot quite control the way in which he spews forth crumbs. He is the quintessential consumer. Yet clearly, he means no harm.

The budget, for all its intimidating detail, might be seen similarly: as the *Ultimate Cookie Monster.* Its excessive tendencies toward consumption are not exactly ennobling. (It does not ordinarily present itself as seriously concerned with investment.) But at the same time, its underlying motivation is clearly not malevolent. What harm it may cause is largely unintended. Its massive presence might be understood as little more than a compilation of cookies received, cookies crumbled, and crumbs spewed forth.

Yet apt though the Cookie Monster perspective may be, it does not suffice. It is not quite fair to either Cookie Monster or the budget. In reality, a budget is not just a monstrous mass of cookies and crumbs.

It is more: an implicit statement of values and expectations for the future. Inescapably, it is headed somewhere—or other. To gain a meaningful sense of the whole, and where it may be headed, one must look beyond green eyeshades and the Cookie Monster. One must frame the budget from several broader (and more serious) perspectives. This introduction tries to help do that.

Among the additional perspectives are these: a global historical perspective; a conventional deficit-eliminating perspective; a capital budgeting perspective; a perspective that gives greater weight to future liabilities; another that attends to investment in the future; and finally, a congressional perspective. These are discussed (sequentially) below.

AND THE WALL CAME A'TUMBLIN' DOWN . . .

Looking a bit beyond Cookie Monster to the television news, one is struck with a rare impression: there may be a compelling pattern to the flow of current events. It is not represented in the budget detail by any quantitative "baseline," nor any conventional statistical measure. It was captured visually by a single dramatic symbol, beamed around the world, and etched in the mind of people everywhere: the fall of the Berlin wall.

To put the symbolic fact more clinically: State-centered, command-and-control systems seem to be decomposing. The Soviet Union has been forced to explore the virtues of restructuring, decentralization, and openness. Communist regimes in Eastern Europe have been falling like dominoes. The Iron Curtain has been opened. And the drama has not been confined to Eastern Europe. Just as liberated celebrants have cheered the opening of the Berlin wall and the decline of communist dictators, so too have liberated Panamanians celebrated the fall of the dictator in near-by Panama.

While it would be naively euphoric to consider this pattern "the end of history" (even in the limited Hegelian sense), clearly the sudden and dramatic shift toward pluralist democracy has far more than the ordinary historical significance. The events of 1989, and what they will have unleashed, may one day rise to a place with those of 1688, 1776, or 1789. This is not small stuff. It is another giant leap of the human spirit yearning to breathe free.

Yet this great historical shift has been almost trivialized in its translation into public debate about the budget. The issue has been framed as: "How big is the 'peace dividend'?"—and, in effect, "How can I get mine?" These are issues that the budget and the political system must treat. They are discussed further in the budget. But they are second-order issues at best.

Ahead of them in line, surely, ought to be these points:

- The favorable pattern of recent events has not been caused exclusively by the political and economic bankruptcy of particular state-centered regimes. It has also resulted from U.S. (and allied) military and economic strength. These, in turn, have resulted from market-oriented economic policies and sound public and private investment policies. It would be a highly unfortunate irony if—just as the world were affirming more market-oriented and investment-oriented principles—the United States were to do anything other than strengthen its commitment to these very principles.
- As the world moves away (at whatever pace) from an emphasis on the risk of traditional military superpower conflict, the relative importance of U.S. economic strength only increases. Increased economic strength is essential to inspire and to assist evolving lesser powers. And it is fundamental to suc-

cess in the global competition with rising economic superpowers.

- Thus, there is a first-order issue for the budget (and the economic policy it represents): How can it best preserve and build on America's strengths, while advancing the American economy toward even greater capacities for leadership and growth? If the "dividend" metaphor must be applied to the budget: How can policy best assure that there is a continuing *growth dividend?*

HOW BIG IS THE DEFICIT?—LET ME COUNT THE WAYS

In considering this issue, many traditional analysts turn first to the size of the budget deficit. This is not necessarily as relevant a starting point as many argue. But it is relevant.

Unfortunately, a meaningful answer to the question—How big is the deficit?—is not quite as simple as the question. This budget attempts to answer the question from a wide range of relevant perspectives.

- *The "Gramm-Rudman-Hollings (G-R-H) Baseline Deficit"*—This perspective is flawed. It biases analysis toward excessive outlay growth. But it is required by law. It constructs an estimate that uses the Administration's economic and technical assumptions; assumes entitlements grow with the beneficiary population and with prescribed benefit changes; and assumes discretionary programs grow with inflation (in effect, treating them as permanent entitlements). It assumes *no change in current law.* From this perspective, the estimated deficit for the current fiscal year (1990) is $122 billion; and for the coming budget year, 1991, it drops to $84.7 billion. It moves to surplus in fiscal year 1994.
- *"Adjusted G-R-H baseline deficit"*—The G-R-H baseline, an artificial con-

struct, is used by some for reference purposes. Even for its advocates, it can be misleading. This year, for example, the Food Stamp authorization for appropriations expires. It will almost certainly be extended in some form, but G-R-H does not assume that. Conversely, the decennial census of 1990 will not be repeated in 1991. But G-R-H implicitly assumes that it will be. If one adjusts for these anomalies, the adjusted G-R-H baseline deficit for 1991–95 would be as in Figure 4.1.

This suggests that without major legislative action—but *assuming continued economic growth*—the deficit would move toward surplus in 1995. This would mark a steady, although slow, pattern of correction from the deficit high of $221.2 billion reached in 1986.

• *The "President's policy deficit"*—[President Bush's] investment-oriented proposals would help assure that the economic growth assumed in the baseline is actually achieved. Other policy proposals would further improve the rate of deficit reduction by reducing spending on low-return programs, reforming selected mandatory programs, and charging appropriate fees. These additional program savings (relative to the G-R-H baseline) are discussed further in Parts V and VII. Their total contribution is $36.5 billion for 1991, rising to $95.8 billion for 1995.

As a result, the Administration estimates that implementation of the President's budget would meet (and slightly surpass) the legally required G-R-H deficit targets of $64 billion in 1991 and zero

Figure 4.1
Adjusted G-R-H Baseline Estimate (in billions of dollars)

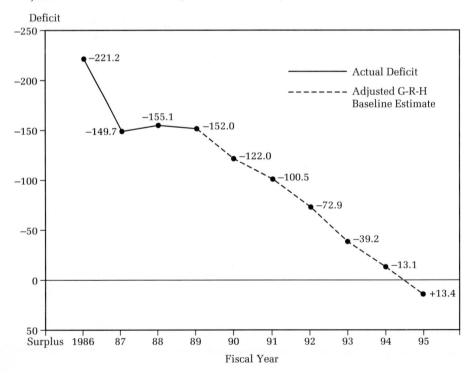

in 1993. The President's Policy deficit would be $63.1 billion in 1991, moving to surplus for 1993–95 (even after adjusting to assure Social Security integrity). (See Table 4.1.)

Overall spending for 1991 would still *increase*—by about 3.0 percent. Almost every Department of the government would have higher budget outlays than it did the previous year. But the deficit would be reduced because estimated receipts would increase even more—by $96.8 billion or 9.0 percent (without "ducks"). *This reflects the "flexible freeze" at work:* spending growth is held at a level slightly below the inflation rate; while revenues increase at a higher rate on the strength of economic growth. This is summarized in Table 4.1.

- *The treatment of Social Security*—Current law defines Social Security as "off-budget," but requires its inclusion for purposes of G-R-H deficit calculations. Social Security is also included in traditional "consolidated" or "unified" deficit estimates. There are many good and important reasons to continue to include Social Security in these calculations.

  But in recent years a problem has arisen. The increasing annual Social Security operating surpluses have masked the true size of the underlying non-Social Security operating deficit. In effect, the surpluses have allowed more non-Social Security spending than might otherwise have been the case. If this were long to continue, it would result in an excessive burden of debt for future generations. It would thus undermine the effect of the build-up of reserves intended for retiring baby-boomers.

  To address this problem, without doing violence to the traditional concept of a consolidated budget, the [Bush] Administration proposes to establish a "Social Security Integrity and Debt Reduction Fund." It would receive each year, as outlays, an amount equivalent to an increasing portion of the projected Social Security operating surplus (reaching 100 percent in 1996). It would be obliged to use these outlays to reduce Federal debt and thus leave a more manageable financing burden for future generations. This Fund would be linked with a continuing obligation to meet a G-R-H deficit target of zero (i.e., a permanent balanced budget) starting in 1993. Thus, the proposal *would effectively prevent the government from spending Social Security receipts on*

Table 4.1   President's Policy: Outlays, Receipts, and Deficit Improvement for 1991
(In Billions of Dollars)

	1990	1991	Change Amount	Change Percent
Outlays:				
Department of Defense	286.8	292.1	+5.4	+1.9%
Non–Department of Defense	910.4	941.2	+30.7	+3.4%
Total Outlays	1,197.2	1,233.3	+36.1	+3.0%
Receipts:				
Current Law	1,072.8	1,156.3	+83.5	+7.8%
New Measures	0.6	13.9	+13.3	+1.2%
Total Receipts	1,073.5	1,170.2	+96.8	+9.0%
Deficit	123.8	63.1	−60.7	−49.0%

Table 4.2 Deficit/Surplus—Under Selected Definitions
(In Billions of Dollars)

	1990	1991	1992	1993	1994	1995
"G-R-H Baseline Deficit/Surplus"	−122.0	−84.7	−55.5	−20.1	7.9	36.3
Adjust for outlay anomalies:						
Food Stamps	—	−16.2	−17.0	−17.7	−18.6	−19.5
Census	—	1.0	1.3	1.3	1.5	1.5
Debt service	—	−0.6	−1.7	−2.6	−3.9	−5.0
Total "Adjusted G-R-H Baseline Deficit/Surplus"	−122.0	−100.5	−72.9	−39.2	−13.1	13.4
Adjust for policy recommendations	0.6	36.5	46.9	57.5	75.6	95.8
Adjust for "Social Security Integrity and Debt Reduction Fund"	—	—	—	−14.1	−53.6	−101.8
Total "President's Policy Deficit/ Surplus" excluding "gimmicks" (speed-ups)	−121.4	−64.0	−26.0	4.2	8.9	7.4
Adjust for on–off budget:						
Exclude Social Security	−62.0	−80.3	−93.1	−107.4	−124.2	−137.2
Total "On–Budget Policy Deficit/ Surplus"	−183.4	−144.3	−119.1	−103.2	−115.3	−129.8
Adjust for G-R-H and speed-ups:						
Include Social Security	62.0	80.3	93.1	107.4	124.2	137.2
Include withholding and other speed-ups	—	1.0	—	—	—	—
Total "President's Policy Deficit/ Surplus" including speed-ups	−121.4	−63.0	−26.0	4.2	8.9	7.4
Adjust for "Consolidated Budget":						
Include asset sales	—	1.6	1.6	1.6	1.6	1.6
Include Postal Service	−2.4	−1.7	−0.7	−0.1	0.1	0.4
Remove nondefense spendout adjustment	—	0.1	—	—	—	—
Total "Consolidated Budget Deficit/ Surplus"	−123.8	−63.1	−25.1	5.7	10.7	9.4

non-Social Security purposes. The proposal is discussed further in Parts VI–A and VII–A. Its effects on the deficit are displayed along with the other ways of looking at the deficit in Table 4.2.

- *The effect of alternative economic scenarios*—In considering the deficit—by whatever definition—it is important to consider its sensitivity to economic variables. For a discussion of these sensitivities, see Section Two, Part I: "Note on Economic Assumptions and Sensitivities." The single most important variable affecting the size of the deficit

is probably the real economic growth rate. As a practical matter, the net-deficit-reducing effects of economic growth (or its absence) are likely to be far greater than the effects of a so-called peace dividend.

As a general rule of thumb, a sustained one percent additional increase in real GNP growth—with all else equal—would reduce the deficit by an additional $18 billion in 1991 and an additional $98 billion in 1995. (A sustained one percent lesser increase in real GNP growth—all else equal—

would have roughly the equivalent numerical effect, but with the sign changed.) For those seriously interested in either achieving greater deficit reduction or freeing up resources for greater spending, this underlines the importance of pursuing policies likely to maximize the *growth dividend.*

The economic assumptions used by the Administration are toward the optimistic end of the credible range. But the Administration's assumptions are plausible and achievable.

The Administration first presented its own economic assumptions in July 1989—at which point they were also judged to be at the optimistic end of the credible range. Intervening performance has, in fact, been highly consistent with the Administration's forecast. But that does not mean either that macroeconomic science has improved substantially, or that the Administration will always be so fortunate as to be correct.

In developing the budget, the Administration formally considered several alternative economic scenarios. Two of these are discussed in the "Note" in Section Two, Part I. Both of these are also plausible. One is slightly more optimistic, and one more pessimistic, than the scenario actually adopted. These alternative scenarios are specifically described in the Note. If the President's Policy deficit were presented with either the higher growth or the lower growth assumptions, the deficit (or surplus) would appear as shown in Table 4.3 (after adjustment to assure

Social Security integrity).
• *Deficits as a share of GNP*—Meeting the G-R-H deficit target for 1991, as proposed by the President, would reduce the consolidated deficit to about 1 percent of GNP. The deficit would thus fall clearly within the "normal" range for most of America's major trading partners. In any case, it would mark a significant improvement from the 5.2 percent level of 1983 (6.3 percent for the fiscal year). The pattern is suggested by Figure 4.2. While the trend is favorable, however, it should not be given excessive weight. The United Kingdom and Japan are both running surpluses—but with very different real growth rates. *As with all measures of the deficit, it is necessary to get beyond this somewhat superficial measure, to an examination of the underlying economic policies and their relation to the future.*
• *Deficit effects of capital budgets*—The current budget concept—essentially a "cash" budget—was developed to conform with the President's Commission on Budget Concepts (1967). The "cash" perspective is especially useful for determining needs for financing in the public debt market. Indeed, it is essential. That is why, regardless of whether trust funds are treated as "on" or "off" budget, there must be some consolidated accounting that shows the total governmental cash position. *But if one is seriously interested in the effects of budget policy on the future, one must get beyond the cash budget frame of reference represented by the G-R-H and consolidated deficit calculations.* One needs a better sense of future liabilities

Table 4.3   Deficit (−)/Surplus (+) Under Alternative Assumptions
(In Billions of Dollars)

	1991	1992	1993	1994	1995
Higher growth scenario	− 54.6	− 16.9	+ 15.1	+ 24.7	+ 31.6
Lower growth scenario	− 77.5	− 48.4	− 27.2	− 32.9	− 42.4

Percent
of GNP

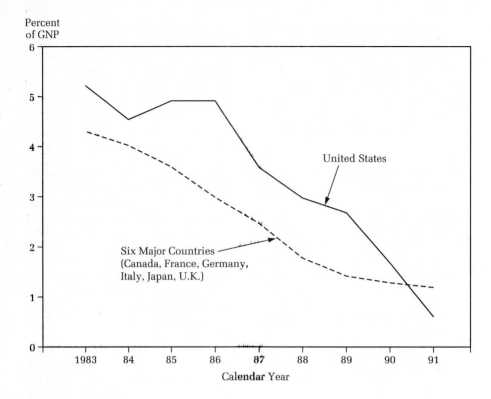

Figure 4.2
Deficits as a Share of GNP: U.S. vs. Major Trading Partners

and of the extent to which current income and borrowing are financing investment for the future (as opposed to current consumption and transfers).

With this perspective in view, many have criticized the Federal Government's "cash" budget. Some have argued that the Federal Government should adopt one form or another of capital budget and/or a budget that better distinguishes between trust funds, governmental operating needs, and activities conducted by Government-sponsored enterprises.

In order to begin to address this thoroughly appropriate interest in getting beyond cash budgeting, the President's budget is re-configured as it might appear under the conceptual approach suggested by the General Accounting Office and the approach used by the state of California. These approaches are strictly illustrative—and are presented in Section Two, Part II: "Note on Alternate Approaches to Budget Presentation." They are not intended—now, or in the future—to displace the cash budget; but rather, they are intended to supplement it.

While these additional perspectives are useful, it is clear that they, too, are not fully satisfactory. In going only as far as they do, they tend to do little more than confirm what is now generally accepted wisdom: that the Federal Government invests a relatively small percent of its annual expenditures in capital; and that there is a sharp dichotomy between the operating surpluses in certain trust funds and the operating deficits that characterize the rest of government. They necessarily suggest, but do not satisfactorily settle, many difficult issues of definition as to what is and is not investment. They do not adequately treat "intellectual capital" and "human capital," for example. And they do not provide a dynamic picture of expected future liabilities and future returns.

Stepping back from this surfeit of deficits—all differently conceived and defined—one might summarize where the collection of different deficit pictures suggests things may be, and where they may be headed.

- *First,* by several different deficit measures, *the consolidated Federal deficit seems, at worst, to have stabilized.* If the President's policies were adopted, this pattern of stabilization would obtain, in the near term, even if Social Security were excluded from deficit calculation. *The pattern of continuous erosion that characterized the early- and mid-1980s seems to have been broken.* By many measures, the deficit is headed toward improvement—*assuming that economic growth continues.* Although further progress is not guaranteed, the change in the underlying pattern must be viewed as welcome. See Figure 4.3.

  The proviso concerning the necessity for continued economic growth is fundamental, however. The economy is in its eighth consecutive year of growth. This is the second-longest period of continuous growth in America's history. (Post-War Japan has enjoyed two longer periods of growth: one of 20 years, 1953–73 and one of 15 years, 1975 to the present.) There is reason to suggest that the traditional notion of the inevitability of a tight business cycle

may be overtaken. But, to underline the obvious: Growth is not automatic. It depends on growth-oriented policies being pursued not only by the Administration, but also by Congress and the Federal Reserve.

- *But second, stabilization of the underlying deficit should not lead to complacency.* Complacency would lead to a loss of fiscal discipline. And even with stabilization, deficits mean rising debt. America's recorded Federal debt is already approaching three trillion dollars. (See Parts III–A and VI–A.) That is not necessarily bad per se. It depends on whether or not the debt is being used in conjunction with policies that will increase future productivity, growth, and capacities for debt service—and whether future hidden liabilities are being kept within reasonable bounds. Here, unfortunately, is where conventional Federal deficit accounting and budget presentation have been woefully inadequate. And here is where there is legitimate cause for concern—as is discussed further below.

HIDDEN PACMEN

The problem with relying solely on the consolidated cash budget—or even on that plus a capital budget—is that it does not give a full picture of the Federal "balance sheet." There is a host of technical reasons why it is not now possible to present a complete and valid Federal balance sheet—not to mention a valid projection of the future balance sheet. But it is possible to do a better job of highlighting potential liabilities, as well as important areas of investment, which have significant future effects. This budget presentation attempts to move in that direction.

One curious thing about future Federal liabilities is that many of them are not yet fully visible. Their particular nature varies. But each is like a hidden PACMAN,

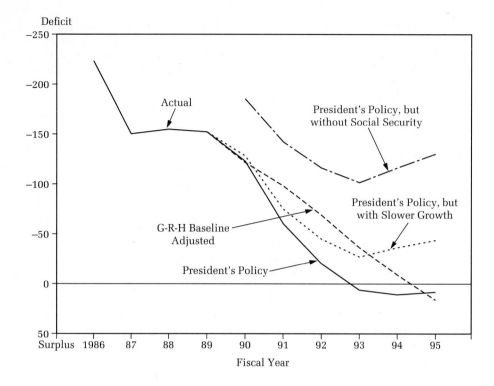

Figure 4.3
Alternative Deficit Paths (in billions of dollars)

waiting to spring forward and consume another line of resource dots in the budget maze. These hidden PACMEN are discussed in some detail in Parts VI–A and VI–B. A few introductory points may help outline the problem:

- *Rising costs of health care*—A quarter of a century ago, health care expenditures consumed about 6 percent of America's GNP. Now, that share has almost doubled, to 12 percent. Within the growing Federal budget, the share has risen even more rapidly, from less than 5 percent in 1970 to a projected 15 percent in the early 1990s. Obviously, this is a trend that cannot be sustained forever—or health care costs would drive out all else. There are, nonetheless, increasing demands to assure health in-

surance coverage for those not now covered, and to provide better financing for long term care. Each of these could entail an additional multi-billion dollar annual bill. Yet the projected health expenditure obligations of current law are not fully covered by projected future receipts. The estimated present value of unfunded liabilities (the actuarial deficiency) for Medicare hospital insurance alone could be over *$250 billion.* (See Parts V and VI–A.)
- *Rising budgetary claims of mandatory programs*—In President Kennedy's Administration, transfer payments to individuals comprised about a quarter of the Federal budget. Now they consume almost half. So-called "mandatory" programs—selected payments to individuals (entitlements) and other auto-

matic spending programs—have grown from 34 percent of the budget in 1970 to roughly half the 1991 budget—and will reach a projected 57 percent for 1995. (Mandatory programs plus net interest expenditures account for almost 62 percent of the budget.) Since these programs generally have broad-based and well-represented beneficiary populations, they tend to have a powerful claim on resources, and grow faster than the economy as a whole. Yet again: It would seem obvious that this pattern of more rapid growth cannot be extended indefinitely. (See Part V.)

- *Unfunded retirement program liabilities*—There is much talk about the projected build-up of Social Security reserves to cover the anticipated obligations to the baby-boom generation when it reaches retirement. The medium term build-up intended by (and projected under) current law is, indeed, enormous. But even so, over the long term, under some assumptions, the present value of current-law obligations minus projected receipts could be a negative number. This is a speculative matter with a high degree of uncertainty. (See Part VI–A.) Somewhat less speculatively, there are clearly identifiable major shortfalls in unfunded Federal employee retirement programs—although these should be able to be serviced by future contributions. And the Railroad Retirement System, although not fully a Federal responsibility, is substantially underfunded—with a reported actuarial deficiency of *$14 billion.*

- *Obligations to clean up federal facilities*—For a variety of reasons, the Federal Government historically has not been prompt in attending to environmental clean-up at many of its facilities. For reasons of both law and policy, the pattern of the past is now changing. But the bills are yet to be fully paid. The present-value cost of already-iden-

tified future clean-up obligations and waste management improvements at Federal facilities over the next 30 years is on the order of *$140–200 billion.* (See Part VI–C.)

- *Contingent risks of federal credit programs and government-sponsored enterprises (GSEs)*—The Federal Government's direct and indirect credit subsidies are far more extensive than is commonly appreciated. In housing, over a trillion dollars in outstanding mortgages have been guaranteed by Federal agencies or securitized by GSEs. In agriculture, the Farmers Home Administration has accounted for 15 percent of all farm debt outstanding, and the Farm Credit System has financed another 26 percent—for a combined total of about $55 billion. In education, nearly all student loans are Federally guaranteed. The government helps provide credit for export finance, rural utilities, small businesses, and minority-owned businesses. The purposes of all this credit support are generally worthy. But there can be no denying that there is an enormous and increasing Federal exposure—approaching one trillion dollars in direct and federally guaranteed loans alone. This necessarily involves a risk of substantial future claims against the government. These claims are virtually certain to be in the *tens of billions of dollars.* Without continued economic growth, and the credit reforms proposed by the President, the claims would be substantially higher. (See Part VI–B.)

- *Contingent risks of federal insurance programs*—The Federal Government funds programs that directly insure individuals and firms against many hazards not covered by private insurance. These formal insurance programs cover bank deposits, pensions, veterans life insurance, crops, floods, overseas private investment, nuclear risks, and war risks. The total face value of this insurance coverage (excluding Medicare) exceeds four trillion dollars. Deposit insurance accounts for about 70 percent of this total. But the remainder is still over one *trillion* dollars. Clearly, the Federal government is not at risk for the entire face value of the insurance. But again: The likely future claims are virtually certain to be in the *tens of billions of dollars.* (See Part VI–B.)

When one adds up all these likely future claims—unfunded health and retirement programs, environmental clean-up obligations, credit risks, and insurance risks—one can produce a rather intimidating total. (See especially Parts VI–A and VI–B.) But it is important to put this, too, in perspective. The claims do not come due all at once. Indeed, they come due over an extended period of time. If one assumed that the likely range of unfunded claims were spread smoothly over the extensive time period in which they are to come due, one would reduce the total to a much less intimidating—indeed, a *manageable*—level.

This is not to say that there is not a built-in shortfall. There is. (See Part VI.) *It is to say, rather, that the "amortized" annual amount of the projected shortfall may be on the order of one-half to one percent of GNP—assuming the problem is managed on an orderly basis.*

Over the long term, there are five ways this shortfall could be handled:

- by reducing the growth of future obligations—through "mandatory" program reforms, credit reforms, and insurance reforms (these are discussed in Parts V, VI–A, and VI–B);
- by reducing spending on other Federal programs where returns on investment are judged to be of lower relative value (these are discussed in Part VII—B–1);
- by increasing the government's managerial integrity and efficiency (this is discussed in Part VII);
- by pursuing growth-oriented economic

and budgetary policies—investing in the future—so that future economic productivity and Federal receipts are higher than otherwise projected (this is the principal area of emphasis in Section One, the Overview, and is discussed especially in Part III); or
- by increasing the relative burden of debt and/or new taxes (these latter approaches are not a part of the President's program).

INVESTING IN THE FUTURE

As noted, "Investing in the Future" is a theme given special emphasis in the Budget Overview. It was first introduced to the presentation of the budget by the President, last year, in *Building a Better America.*

The emphasis is consistent with three fundamental points: First, a budget must be viewed as more than a static snapshot; it necessarily influences the future, and the nature of that influence must be examined. Second, there is a generally accepted moral obligation to try to leave future generations in a better position than their predecessors. Third, the obligations for future expenditures and debt service are more manageable insofar as current expenditures and tax policy contribute to increased growth. Together, these three points argue compellingly for attention to the extent to which a budget (and its associated economic policy) encourage *investment*—investment in the future.

The President's budget encourages investment in a host of ways that are discussed in greater detail in the Overview. These are outlined here—with references to appropriate Parts of the Overview noted parenthetically:

- *Deficit reduction*—By reducing the deficit, meeting the G-R-H targets, and then buying down debt, the President's budget policy would improve the U.S. savings rate and reduce the cost of capital. (This is discussed further in Part III–A.)

- *Incentives for private savings and long-term investment*—The President's program would improve the incentives for saving and investment through *Individual Retirement Accounts* (IRAs); create a new all-purpose savings incentive through *Family Savings Accounts*; and encourage growth-oriented, job-creating investment through a new long-term *capital gains incentive.* (These are discussed further in Part III–A.)
- *Research and development*—The President's budget funds initiatives to expand human frontiers in space—NASA would grow 24 percent over 1990 to a record $15.2 billion—and in biotechnology; to advance the development of the superconductive supercollider and to increase investment across the full range of basic research ($12.3 billion—up almost $1 billion); to advance applied research in areas as diverse as defense and health, agriculture and high speed rail transportation, semiconductor development and materials processing. The President also proposes to enact and extend major tax incentives to encourage greater investment in R&D by the private sector. Total proposed governmental expenditures for R&D would exceed $70 billion. (These are discussed in Parts III–B and III–C.) In the design and implementation of Government programs, the President's budget also recognizes and encourages the innovative role of "States as Laboratories" (discussed in Part IV).
- *Investment in human capital*—Although Federal money is not the key to solving the nation's serious education problems, the President does propose to increase the discretionary budget authority of the Department of Education by $1.2 billion—bringing the Departmental total to a record $24.6 billion. Program increases are principally in areas of investment that are consistent with the Federal Government's role and

responsibilities—reflecting the basic understanding that true solutions must depend heavily on states, localities, parents, and a system that promotes greater innovation, flexibility, and accountability. The budget re-proposes the President's child care initiative—on which the Congress failed to act last year. And the President proposes not only to reauthorize Head Start, but to increase it by half a billion dollars in a single year—bringing Head Start to an unprecedented $1.9 billion. (These and other investments in human capital are discussed in Part III–D.)

- *Drug control strategy*—Clearly, it makes little sense to invest in human capital only to have drug abuse undermine that investment and, indeed, destroy the very social fabric that makes human growth and investment worthwhile. Drug abuse negates investment. It is fundamentally destructive. It must be stopped. Like education, drug abuse is a problem that cannot be solved by Federal funds alone—or by funds alone whatever their source. Nonetheless, the 1991 budget proposes $10.6 billion in budget authority and $9.7 billion in outlays to combat drug abuse. These levels represent increases of 12 percent in budget authority and $2.8 billion (41 percent) in outlays relative to 1990. They are necessary to advance the next stage of the comprehensive National Drug Control Strategy (and are discussed further in the Strategy, which is published separately, and in Part III–E).
- *HOPE and enterprise zones*—The problems of economically distressed areas will be alleviated some by the job-creating effects of continued economic growth. The problems will be mitigated also by the President's anti-drug abuse strategy. But more needs to be done to bring hope and opportunity to severely distressed areas. Thus, the President is re-proposing his initiative to stimulate growth through the creation of special incentives for investment and job cre-

ation in *Enterprise Zones*—a proposal on which the Congress has failed to act. And he is introducing legislation to advance project HOPE—Homeownership and Opportunity for People Everywhere. (These proposals are discussed further in Part III–H.)

- *Transportation infrastructure*—Improving the U.S. transportation system is essential to economic efficiency and growth. It is a shared responsibility involving the private sector, Federal, state, and local government. The Federal contribution is substantial. For example, the President proposes a record $8.6 billion for aviation in 1991 to help keep the U.S. commercial aviation system the best in the world. Of this, $2.5 billion—an increase of 45 percent—is proposed to modernize the FAA's air traffic control system. (These and related transportation issues are discussed in Part III–G.)
- *Environmental protection*—The emphasis on the importance of economic growth must, of course, be accompanied by a responsible concern for the protection and preservation of the environment. The President proposes over $2 billion in new spending to fund: "America the Beautiful," a new program to improve the stewardship of public lands and natural resources, and to promote reforestation; a major increase in the U.S. Global Change Research Program; an acceleration of hazardous waste clean-up; and a 12 percent increase in the EPA operating budget. (These are discussed in Part III–F.)
- *The American heritage*—To the extent that investment tends to emphasize rapid technological advance, there is need for a complementary emphasis on aesthetic values, history, and the traditional cultural values that have made America uniquely strong. Although the Federal role in this area must be limited—for important reasons of plural-

istic philosophy—it must not be overlooked. America's progress in the future will be the greater for building on its diverse cultural strengths. Thus programs to foster and preserve the American Heritage are treated as themselves an issue of investment. (These are discussed in Part III–J.)

- *National security*—None of the foregoing would be worth very much if the budget failed to provide for the protection of U.S. national security. Though responsible analysts may differ about the best means of protecting it, national security holds a fundamental claim on governmental investment. Without adequate investment in national security, ultimately, all that America holds dear could be lost. There is, further, an obligation that America has long championed: the advancement of pluralistic, market-oriented democracy throughout the world. These fundamental interests and obligations are dependent upon U.S. economic growth. But they are also, in some respects, preconditional to it. (They are discussed in Part III–I.)
- *Management oversight*—Federal investments in the future will only achieve their objectives if they are effectively managed. Improved returns on investment require a better budget process and more effective management oversight. Americans are entitled to greater assurance that their tax dollars are being invested wisely and managed with efficiency and integrity. Proposals to manage America's government better are discussed in Part VII below.

WONDERLAND REVISITED—THE CURRENT CONGRESSIONAL PATH

In the presentation of the first Bush Administration budget, a critique of "Wonderland" budgeting was offered. It focused on the curious Washington habit (indeed, legal requirement) of "current services baseline" budgeting. Under this system, a "cut" may really be an increase; and a deficit said to be going "down" may really be going up. With "current services" built-in bias toward increasing expenditures, it should be little wonder that the system has failed to bring the deficit under satisfactory control.

In the Mid-session Review of the Budget, OMB introduced a new budget projection: the "Current Congressional Path." This was done in order to underline what some might think an obvious point. That is, the deficit is not determined, in the end, by either "current services" projections or by mathematical extensions of a "President's Policy." Forecasts based on such projections are almost always bound to be wrong. Budgets are legislated. Congressional action (or inaction) is, therefore, a fundamental determinant of actual deficits. In trying to forecast realistically, it is important to have some sense of the "Current Congressional Path."

Unfortunately, however, the Current Congressional Path is not entirely clear. Indeed, Wonderland seems to be running wild with attractive fantasies, but without yet having established coherent direction. One might consider, for example, the two big games now in play—and a third that is soon to be:

• *The spend-the-peace-dividend-game*— This is a new game, premised on the assumption of a substantial, near-term "peace dividend." It starts by over-estimating the dividend. Then each player plans to spend the dividend in his or her preferred way. The sum of all such planned expenditures totals about ten times the over-estimated dividend, which is itself perhaps five times the actual dividend. Thus, Washington entertains the notion of spending fifty times a dividend that has not yet defin-

itively materialized—a true Wonderland phenomenon.

In reality, the *near-term* peace dividend is likely to be smaller than is commonly assumed for three reasons: First, the true cost of the previously planned and Congressionally-approved defense program is substantially higher than the current DoD funding levels (and higher than "current services"). Much of the dividend will have to be used just to adjust the previous program downward toward current levels. Second, this adjustment—while politically popular in the abstract—will not be politically popular in all its particulars. Third, any tendency to cut further would likely focus on reducing U.S. troop strength abroad at a more rapid rate than proposed by the President—a more rapid rate than consistent with preserving a strong alliance and negotiating equitable and enforceable agreements with the Soviet Union. Presumably, these countervailing interests will be better appreciated as the debate about the "peace dividend" unfolds.

• *The cut-Social-Security game*—This is ordinarily a very dangerous game politically. But in its most recent form, it has started with a superficially attractive proposal: to cut Social Security taxes. Clearly, that would be desirable if it could be done without significant cost to the people paying the taxes and to the economy as a whole. Unfortunately, the most recent proposal to attract significant attention fails that test.

It is ironic in three respects. First, some of its advocates have argued, until recently, that the government was under-financed (and under-taxed) *not over*-financed. Yet few, in fact, can seriously argue that the government as a whole is over-financed. Second, the emerging conventional wisdom had been that one needed to do more to protect the capacity to pay future Social Security benefits, *not less*. Cutting Social Security taxes now would mean giving up on that objective—giving up on the bipartisan commitment to build up reserves for the future retirement needs of the baby boom generation. Third, and perhaps most telling: Cutting Social Security taxes now would likely hurt the very people it is ostensibly intended to benefit, today's workers. It would either force an increase in their non-Social Security taxes (to compensate for the enormous revenue loss—$55 billion in 1991 alone); or it would force a reduction in their future retirement benefits. (See Part VI–A.)

The President's proposal to establish a "Social Security Integrity and Debt Reduction Fund" is a responsible way to protect the future interests of today's workers. But Social Security is a notoriously volatile subject when it enters the political domain; and whether rationality will prevail remains to be determined.

- *The Beat-the-Budget game*—This is the game that begins with the reaction to the President's budget. It has become an annual ritual. At the start, it is predictably partisan. Priorities are judged to be incorrect. Economic assumptions are ridiculed (but later adopted). Gimmicks are scorned (but later outdone). The failure of the budget process is lamented (but ideas for evasion proliferate). The refusal to raise "new taxes" is condemned (as proposals to cut taxes are advanced). Incentives for savings and investment are criticized for their alleged adverse effects on the deficit (as alternative proposals to increase the deficit are advocated). Stalemates are followed by "heroic compromises" that earn the parties self-congratulation, but somehow manage to leave much of the serious job to the future. And the public, understandably, grows more skeptical.

It may be apt to view all this metaphorically as a set of children's games: the Budget as Cookie Monster; its future threatened by hidden PACMEN; its path a journey through Wonderland. But at some point, it is appropriate to put games aside—at least for a while. *At some point, there is an obligation to be serious.* At some point, partisan posturing must yield to the responsibility to govern.

Sooner or later, the American political system will rise to the responsibility to be serious: to complete the job of fiscal policy correction. It may do this in small steps or large. It cannot do it with sidesteps.

This year's budget meets the responsibility to be serious. It is seriously presented—giving a more complete and balanced perspective on both the present and the future than has previously been characteristic. Its emphasis on investment and growth-oriented policies and its realistic attention to long-term liabilities should be welcome. Its economic assumptions are not outside the credible range. It meets the Gramm-Rudman-Hollings deficit targets with specific and defensible deficit-reduction measures—and without gimmicks. It seeks to preserve a meaningful consolidated budget, while tightening the budget process. If implemented, it would reach balance in 1993 (as required by law), and would therefore begin the process of reducing Federal debt.

This, of course, is not to assert that the budget will be treated seriously in the very next round of the Beat-the-Budget game. It is simply to suggest that it should be.

5.   Mortgaging America

Gerald Epstein

The United States, once the world's largest creditor nation, is now the world's largest debtor, owing more money to foreigners than it is owed by them. This turnabout has come swiftly. As recently as 1985 the United States was in the black; four years later U.S. foreign debt stood at more than $650 billion—roughly 12 percent of its gross national product (GNP). And in the next few years, most economists agree, U.S. foreign indebtedness could reach $1 trillion.

While no one disputes America's increased dependence on foreign capital, what all of this borrowing means for the United States and the world is less obvious, as the range of "expert" opinion on the subject suggests. To investment banker Felix Rohatyn, it represents a loss of U.S. "economic independence." America's international debt, he contends, has made us more vulnerable to the vagaries of foreign capital and less able to influence world events. Harvard economist Benjamin Friedman warns of a "day of reckoning" when we, our children, or our grandchildren will have to pay for our sins of profligacy. And according to William Cline and C. Fred Bergsten of the Institute for International Economics, we will pay either by fire (a financial panic as foreigners lose confidence and abruptly withdraw their funds) or by ice (a long, slow, painful decline in our standard of living as we hand over more and more of our earnings to foreigners in debt payments). For these analysts, it is time to face the music and

tighten our belts—to cut government spending, raise taxes, and end our national "consumption binge."

Keynesian economist Robert Eisner disagrees. We're not really that much in debt, he argues. And besides, a little debt is a useful thing, since it provides demand for goods and services that keeps the economy—ours and the rest of the world's—growing and prospering. In fact, says supply-sider Arthur Laffer, we should celebrate. Foreigners want to invest here because our brand of supply-side capitalism, which is now being embraced by converts from behind the former Iron Curtain, has been so profitable. Foreign investments, Laffer contends, will make our economy even more productive and profitable.

Each of these views has its supporters, but despite their popularity they provide at best only a partial explanation of America's international debt position. What is missing from all of these views is an understanding of the role that the globalization of U.S. corporations has played in the creation of the country's foreign debt problem. Paradoxically, the United States is today the world's largest debtor in part because it is also the world's largest overseas investor and home to many of the world's largest multinational corporations. In an age of globalized production, these corporations have progressively abandoned their commitment to the United States, with negative consequences not only for America's balance of payments but also for the U.S. standard of living.

In many ways America's international debt problem is thus a symptom of a larger and more serious problem—the mobility of capital. By failing to come to grips with this problem, all of the cur-

SOURCE: Reprinted with permission from *World Policy Journal*, vol. 8, no. 1, Winter 1990–1991, pp. 27–59. The author would like to thank Arthur MacEwan and Trish Kelley for their research assistance.

rently popular responses to our foreign debt problem—which range from cutting the budget deficit to curbing foreign investment in the United States—can only make matters worse.

U.S. FOREIGN DEBT: AN OVERVIEW

Each year billions of dollars enter and leave the United States in search of a profitable return. These flows of investment cumulate in stocks of U.S. assets held abroad and foreign assets held in the United States. When the stock of assets held by Americans abroad is larger than the stock of assets held by foreigners here, the United States is said to be in a net creditor position. Conversely, when the stock of assets held by foreigners in the United States is greater than that held by Americans abroad, the United States is in a net debtor position—as it has been since 1985.[1]

Foreign investment here and U.S. investment abroad can take several forms. Most foreign investment involves buying financial assets, either stocks or bonds.[2] The main distinction between different types of financial investments is whether or not they confer "control" over the company in question. Those that do are called direct investments; those that do not are called portfolio investments. Since it is extremely difficult to determine whether a particular investment confers actual control, an arbitrary figure is chosen for statistical purposes. Thus if an investor buys 10 percent or more of the stock of a company, it is regarded as a direct investment; ownership of bonds or less than 10 percent of a company's stock constitutes a portfolio investment. Currently, foreign investment in the United States consists largely of portfolio investments—government securities held by foreign governments and portfolio investments held by private interests. Together these made up 79 percent of all

foreign investment in 1988; foreign direct investment, on the other hand, made up 18 percent.

Even though direct investment constitutes a small portion of total foreign investment, there is little doubt that the share of foreign direct investment in the United States relative to the size of the economy has increased. From 1977 to 1988, foreign direct investment in the United States grew threefold, from controlling less than 2.5 percent of the economy's capital stock to around 7.5 percent. The proportion of manufacturing assets controlled by foreign companies is even greater, having risen from 5 percent in 1977 to 12.5 percent in 1987. As a result, by 1987 foreign-owned companies provided about 5.4 percent of all manufacturing jobs in the United States.

Who are the leading foreign investors? When many Americans think of foreign investment in the United States, they think of Japan. A look at the data, however, suggests that concern about Japanese investment is exaggerated. True, since 1980 the Japanese share of total foreign direct investment has grown threefold and at a faster rate than that of the other major investor countries. But it is important to realize that the Japanese, relative newcomers, started with a small share—about 7 percent. And while their share of foreign investment has grown quickly, so too has that of Great Britain, making up in part for the declining share of Dutch and Canadian investment. Indeed, Britain's share of foreign direct investment is almost twice that of Japan's (30 percent versus 16 percent in 1988), yet since the Beatles arrived one has not heard much talk about a British invasion.

There are three competing images that economists employ to explain America's foreign debt situation. In the first, the United States is a "rising corporation," revitalized by Ronald Reagan's supply-side magic. In this view, the rising corporation is so profitable and so competitive that other corporations naturally want to get a piece of the action. They invest in the corporation to get a share of its spectacular profits. Far from being a sign of decline, therefore, foreign investment in the United States is a sign of success. By implication, America's net debtor status is nothing to worry about.

Appealing though this image is, it fails to provide a satisfactory explanation. First of all, if the United States were truly a rising corporation, one would expect most foreign investment to be direct investment—the better to profit from the extraordinary strength of U.S. business. But most foreign investment in the United States, we have seen, is portfolio investment; indeed, a good 20 percent has been in government securities. In their purchase of these securities, foreigners have simply been following the example of their rich American cousins. Attracted by the high U.S. interest rates— to some extent brought about by the tight monetary policies of the Federal Reserve—these investors have sought the same relatively risk-free yields that have allowed wealthy Americans to further enrich themselves. This same logic, of course, applies to money-market funds, certificates of deposit, and other financial assets that respond to high interest rates.

Moreover, what direct foreign investment there has been has not been used to build new plants here, as one would also expect if the United States were truly a rising corporation. Instead, most of this investment has been used to acquire already existing plants. In 1989, for example, foreign companies spent $64 billion to acquire U.S. companies but only $9 billion to establish new ones.[3] As economists Edward Graham and Paul Krugman aptly describe it, "One should think of Campeau's purchase of Federated Department Stores, not Honda's opening of its Marysville plant, as the characteristic way in which foreign investment has grown."

A further weakness of this explanation is apparent if one looks at returns on investment in the United States. Estimates of the rate of profit on real investments in plant and equipment in the United States relative to those abroad are not higher than elsewhere. Yet one would expect a significant difference if the United States had indeed become an unusually profitable place to invest.

A final flaw of this explanation concerns chronology. While there has been a surge in foreign direct investment in the United States, that surge occurred in the late 1970s, before Ronald Reagan and his supply-siders took office. Since that time, there has been no significant increase in foreign direct investment relative to total foreign investment. What's more, by 1988 foreign direct investment had not even reached the level achieved in 1951, when it represented 19 percent of total foreign investment. What this means is that the country is witnessing a return to an earlier (and perhaps more normal) level of foreign direct investment.

These flaws in the rising corporation argument are amply illustrated by recent developments. Over the past year, America's reputation as a haven for relatively risk-free investment has been shaken by what one analyst calls "the triple whammy of the savings and loan crisis, weakness in the U.S. banking system, and the decline in the real estate market."[4] As a result of these developments and the decline in U.S. interest rates (relative to those in Europe and Japan), foreign investors have been fleeing the U.S. market. Thus while in 1989 the United States attracted a net inflow of $72 billion in foreign direct investment, the tide is now turning and a net outflow of $22 billion is projected for 1990.[5]

The second image used to explain America's indebtedness is that of the United States as one big family working to earn a living and spending money to consume. There are two kinds of families according to this view: the Good Thrifty Family that never spends more than it earns and saves the rest for the future, and the Bad Spendthrift Family that spends more than it earns and has to go into debt to support its profligate habits. It is not hard to see what kind of family the United States has been. Living well beyond its means, it has had to borrow substantially from foreigners.

By this logic there are two main culprits. The first is the American consumer, who, we are told, has been on a consumption binge. The second is the U.S. government, which has also overspent and may have undertaxed as well. To make up the difference between its spending and its earnings, the United States has had to borrow.

While these arguments have some basis in fact—more so than the first explanation—they are still misleading. First, take the idea that "we" have been consuming too much. On the face of it this appears to be true.[6] In the 1970s, consumption accounted for 89.6 percent of disposable income on average. In the early 1980s that figure rose to 91.8 percent, and in the latter half of the decade to 93.1 percent. But averages deceive. A closer look at the figures makes clear that one group in particular was largely responsible for the increase in consumption—the wealthy. The wealthiest 20 percent of the population increased their consumption 11.2 percent *annually* from 1981 to 1987, accounting for approximately 80 percent of the overall increase in U.S. consumption during that period, while the poorest 20 percent of the population increased their consumption by only 1.6 percent in the first half of the 1980s, and the next 20 percent decreased their consumption by 3.5 percent. Hence, it was not Americans as a whole who were on a consumption binge, but rather, the richest Americans.

It comes as no surprise that the wealthy increased their consumption as much as

they did, given the dramatic increase in income they experienced. Before taxes, the real income of the wealthiest 10 percent of the nation's families rose, on average, 21 percent from 1979 to 1987, while that of the poorest 10 percent fell by 12 percent. It is estimated that the fraction of Americans who are "rich" nearly doubled from 1979 to 1987; meanwhile, the fraction of families living below the poverty line increased by 15 percent.[7] Census figures confirm this trend. Between 1980 and 1988, the wealthiest 20 percent of the population saw their share of income rise from 41.6 percent to 44 percent—the highest their share has been since the Census Bureau began measuring these figures in 1949.[8] The share of the top 1 percent of the population increased from 9 percent to over 11 percent during the same period.

Wealthy Americans were able to go on a spending spree in part because of changes in government policy. Thanks to Reagan's tax cuts, the average tax rate for the wealthiest 1 percent of Americans fell by 6 percent between 1977 and 1988, and for the wealthiest 5 percent by 2.6 percent. Meanwhile the burden on the poorest 10 percent increased by 1.6 percent, and on the poorer 50 percent by an average of 0.6 percent.[9] Contrary to supply-side claims, the tax cuts contributed to the federal budget deficit, and because the wealthy favored consumption over saving, the tax cuts led to a reduction in private savings as well.

Partisans of the Spendthrift Family explanation lay much of the blame for the buildup in U.S. foreign debt not just on private consumption; they blame large increases in public consumption—the budget deficit—as well. The logic is simple: the more the U.S. government spends in relation to what it earns in taxes, the more it has to borrow. And because of the country's low private savings rate, more and more of that borrowing is from abroad. The Reagan-era tax cuts contributed greatly to the budget deficit, but they represent only one side of the ledger. On the other side were enormous increases in government spending, in particular the big ticket item of the 1980s: military spending. The increases alone in military expenditures from 1981 to 1987—close to $600 billion—amount to 90 percent of America's debt accumulation in those years.[10]

Thus the Spendthrift Family explanation contains some elements of truth. A few members of the family—namely, America's wealthy—indeed went on a consumption binge in the 1980s. And government expenditure did increase, particularly in unproductive areas such as the military and debt servicing. These trends reduced national savings and contributed to increased borrowing from abroad—but not in a way that would justify the standard prescription of austerity for the average American and cuts in nonmilitary spending that adherents of the Spendthrift Family view put forward.

The third image used by economists to illustrate America's debt situation is that of a "declining corporation." According to this view, U.S. industry is no longer competitive in world markets. As a consequence, the United States is running a large trade deficit that can only be financed by borrowing from abroad.

This argument, too, contains some important element of truth. The United States has fallen behind its competitors in many key sectors and product areas. From 1980 to 1988, for example, the U.S. share of world automobile exports dropped 46 percent, computer exports 36 percent, microelectronic exports 26 percent, and machine-tool exports 17 percent.[11] As a result, the U.S. trade imbalance widened significantly in manufactures, and the high-tech sector registered a deficit for the first time ever.

The solution, according to proponents of this view, is to restore U.S. competitiveness. What this means varies depending on the political stripes of the proponent. For some it means cutting the budget deficit to lower the cost of capital, maintaining a low rate of corporate taxation, and keeping regulations to an unobtrusive minimum. For others it entails improving education and worker training, increasing civilian research and development, and revitalizing public infrastructure.

Leaving aside for now the question of what an appropriate competitiveness strategy would look like, the essential problem with this position is that it does not distinguish between the competitiveness of U.S.-based industry and that of U.S. corporations producing overseas. The latter remain highly competitive, the former less so. This is evident from the fact that while the U.S. share of world manufacturing exports fell from 17.1 percent in 1966 to 11.7 percent in 1986—a drop of more than two-thirds—U.S. multinationals essentially maintained their share of the world market, and the foreign affiliates of U.S. multinationals actually *increased* their share from 8.0 percent to 9.8 percent in the same period.[12] It is an oversimplification, therefore, to suggest that America's debt problem derives from declining U.S. competitiveness. With a few exceptions, U.S. manufacturers have maintained their competitiveness, but not from their factories in the United States.

This basic fact helps to explain why the U.S. trade deficit has been so resistant to correction by traditional exchange-rate measures. To enhance U.S. competitiveness and to redress America's trade imbalance, the Reagan and Bush administrations have sought to force down the dollar and thus make U.S. exports less expensive. But with U.S. companies having moved production abroad, the lower dollar has brought only marginal improvement to the U.S. trade deficit.

While some adherents of the declining corporation explanation acknowledge this fact, others have erroneously seized on the low-dollar strategy as the principal cause for what, in their view, is a worrisome surge of foreign investment into the United States. The lower dollar, these critics charge, has had the effect of making U.S. assets—American companies as well as national landmarks—available to foreigners at "fire sale" prices. But, in fact, the surge of foreign direct investment preceded the great borrowing spree of the 1980s. If there was a fire sale at all, it occurred in the late 1970s as the dollar was depreciating. Since that time, there has been no general increase in foreign direct investment relative to borrowing. Investors have not favored real assets over financial assets during this period; they have bought both at about the same rate.

While the effects of the low dollar have certainly not been negligible, the flow of foreign direct investment into the United States in the 1980s can be more plausibly explained in terms of the competition among major global corporations for market share and profits. The United States consumes nearly one-third of the world's goods. The desire to be close to this market and the fear of future tariff restrictions are powerful motivating forces. At a time when international sales are increasingly important to foreign firms, these companies simply cannot afford to take the chance of being closed out of the U.S. market by tariffs or quotas, or of failing to anticipate changing fashions and tastes that might be hard to discern from afar. In short, it is strategic business decisions, not bargains, that have prompted foreign companies to purchase U.S. firms.

Each of the images presented above—especially the last two—contains important elements of truth. The United States is spending more than it produces; it is becoming less competitive than certain other nations; and its tax and monetary policies have drawn some foreign direct investment into the country. But the picture is far from complete, for what is needed is an understanding of what caused the government deficit, the consumption binge of the wealthy, and the loss of competitiveness. To understand the reasons for these trends, one needs also to understand the role that the multinationalization of U.S. corporations has played in generating U.S. debt and in making it so costly and difficult to control.

U.S. MULTINATIONALS AND U.S. FOREIGN DEBT

While foreign direct investment in the United States has raised concern in many circles, it is, paradoxically, U.S. direct investment abroad that provides a better explanation of America's growing international debt problem. To be sure, foreign direct investment in the United States has grown rapidly in the past decade, but U.S. direct investment abroad has been growing at an even faster rate since the mid-1980s. Indeed, for much of the past 25 years U.S. investment abroad has outpaced investment at home, reflecting an apparent decision by many large American corporations to reduce their commitment to the United States as a production site. Moving production abroad may have helped U.S. multinationals maintain their competitive edge, but it has also had far-reaching and detrimental consequences for the country and its balance of payments.

To begin with, the multinationalization of U.S. business has, as suggested earlier, exacerbated the U.S. trade deficit. Increased production and exports on the part of U.S. corporations outside the United States have meant reduced production and exports for companies within the United States. In some cases this has also resulted in increased U.S. imports from foreign-based U.S. multinationals.

Thus while the United States now runs

sizeable trade deficits each year with countries such as Japan, Taiwan, and Singapore, it is U.S. multinationals based in these countries that are often the leading contributors to this trend.[13] IBM-Japan, for instance, employs 18,000 Japanese workers and is one of the country's largest exporters of computers. Texas Instruments employs over 5,000 people in Japan to make advanced semiconductors; almost half of these semiconductors are exported, many to the United States. In Taiwan, U.S. multinationals—AT&T, RCA, and Texas Instruments—figure among the largest exporters; U.S. corporate production there is responsible for more than one-third of Taiwan's trade surplus with the United States. And Singapore's largest private employer is a U.S. multinational—General Electric—which accounts for a large share of the country's exports.

These are not isolated examples. In fact, the production and sourcing practices of U.S. multinationals account for a substantial share of the U.S. trade imbalance not only with Taiwan and Singapore but also with Mexico, South Korea, and other newly industrializing countries. According to a recent study, by 1986 U.S. multinational corporations were exporting more goods from their overseas affiliates than they were from the United States.[14]

Not only are U.S. companies producing more goods abroad and exporting them back to the United States, but they are also shifting more and more of their research and development (R & D) activities abroad. According to National Science Foundation figures, U.S. corporations increased their overseas R & D spending by 33 percent between 1986 and 1988, compared with a 6 percent increase in the United States. This can only contribute to the further erosion of U.S. competitiveness in the long run and to the loss of high-wage jobs.

Of course, it is conceivable that moving production abroad would not necessarily result in the loss of production and jobs at home, as defenders of U.S. corporate practices argue. It is possible, for example, that foreign-based U.S. firms would import inputs from their U.S. affiliates, thus boosting production and employment at home. However true these arguments might have been in the 1960s and 1970s, they have no basis in fact in the 1980s. Recent studies suggest a decline in U.S. exports to countries experiencing increases in U.S. multinational production.[15] These same studies also indicate that as U.S. multinational corporations increase employment in their foreign subsidiaries, they draw down the number of workers in their U.S.-based operations. Moreover, U.S. multinationals tend to reduce their investment at home as they increase their investment abroad.[16] This lack of investment, economists of all stripes agree, is one of the principal causes of America's trade and competitiveness problem.

It is relatively easy to see, then, that by weakening America's trade position the multinationalization of U.S. business has contributed to the U.S. accumulation of debt. The United States now exports less than it imports and thus must borrow the difference from abroad, at least in part because U.S. multinationals have moved production overseas. If U.S. corporations had invested more in production at home over the past decade, the U.S. trade deficit today would be smaller. So would America's borrowing needs.

But the movement of production abroad is only one aspect of the multinationalization of U.S. business that has contributed to the debt problem. The other aspect relates to the globalization of U.S. banking and the effect this has had on international demand for U.S.-produced goods in the 1980s—especially in those areas, such as agriculture, where the United States remains competitive.

In the 1970s large U.S. commercial

banks went abroad with a vengeance, lending almost $300 billion to less developed countries over the course of a decade. This unregulated flow of U.S. capital abroad, particularly to Latin America, may have improved the trade position of the United States for a short period, but as these countries became unable to service their debts, it began to have the opposite effect. In the interest of maintaining the solvency and profitability of the large commercial banks, the U.S. government, in conjunction with the International Monetary Fund and the World Bank, pressured Third World debtor countries to adopt austerity adjustment programs so that these countries could increase exports and reduce imports, thus allowing them to earn enough foreign exchange to service their debts. The effect of such programs, however, has been to undermine America's traditional export markets in Latin America. It has been estimated that between 25 and 40 percent of the increase in the U.S. current account deficit—and therefore in U.S. foreign borrowing—over this period can be attributed to the Third World debt crisis.[17]

The multinationalization of U.S. business has also exacerbated America's debtor status by helping to increase the federal budget deficit. While the causal relationship among the budget deficit, the trade deficit, and foreign borrowing may have been exaggerated in the past, there can be little doubt at this point that the federal budget is contributing to our international debt problem. What is not appreciated is the fact that U.S. multinational corporations have contributed to the budget deficit on both the revenue and expenditure sides of the equation.

On the revenue side, for every dollar invested abroad that would have been invested at home, the United States loses employment and tax income. It is estimated that 3.4 million U.S. jobs were lost in the 1977–86 period as a result of U.S.

foreign direct investment abroad. This translates today into a tax loss of about $30 billion a year.[18] To this figure, however, one needs to add the quite considerable tax losses that arise as a result of the various tax advantages that U.S. multinationals enjoy.

U.S. tax laws—riddled with loopholes despite recent reform efforts—give U.S. multinational corporations numerous opportunities to reduce their liabilities to the U.S. government. To begin with, U.S. multinational corporations do not always have to pay U.S. taxes on their earnings abroad; the law grants foreign countries the opportunity to tax these firms first. Only if the foreign tax rate is lower than the U.S. rate do U.S. multinationals have to pay U.S. taxes (in which case they pay the difference between the two rates). In other words, firms get a foreign tax credit for taxes paid to foreign governments—to the tune of $21.5 billion in 1986, the latest year for which data are available.[19] This is a far more generous provision than would be the case if corporations were allowed simply to deduct the taxes paid from their gross income, as they do with any other business cost.

Often, however, U.S. firms are able to avoid paying even those taxes. This is because U.S. law allows a U.S. firm to defer tax payments until it repatriates its profits back to the United States. As a result, firms can simply reinvest their overseas profits in foreign countries, thereby avoiding U.S. taxes indefinitely. The countries that host U.S. firms are not necessarily any richer as a result, for U.S. multinationals often seek to further avoid taxes by shifting profits to foreign countries that have low tax rates.

One of the most common ways of shifting profits is through transfer pricing. Transfer prices are what firms charge themselves for inputs bought from their subsidiaries. By manipulating these prices, multinational corporations can spirit their profits to low-tax havens. A firm may have its subsidiary in a low-tax country overcharge for an input, for instance, thus lowering the recorded profits in the high-tax country and raising the recorded profits in the low-tax country.

The opportunities for such tax evasion are clearly not hypothetical. In a recent study of more than 12,000 foreign subsidiaries of 453 U.S. firms, it was found that 8,277, or 69 percent of them, paid no dividends, interest, rent, or royalties to their U.S. parent corporations in 1984 and therefore had to pay no U.S. taxes at all on their foreign earnings. Or, to put it another way, 433 of the 453 parent U.S. corporations had at least one foreign entity that made no payments to its parent and therefore generated no U.S. tax liabilities.[20]

The ability of U.S. multinationals abroad to protect their profits from taxation has serious repercussions for the U.S. fiscal balance. Consider that in 1984 the United States netted only $6.4 billion in taxes on foreign-source income totaling $64 billion. That represents an effective tax rate of 10 percent. With the changes stemming from the 1986 tax reforms, this figure is likely to fall to about 4 percent. This is a good deal for U.S. multinationals, which are now earning over 25 percent of their income abroad. But for the U.S. government, which is highly dependent on corporate income tax as a source of revenue, the consequences are quite damaging—more so than for other advanced capitalist countries because these rely to a greater extent on progressive income taxes and value-added taxes, which are harder for companies to evade.

How much tax revenue could be generated if the tax laws were changed? In particular, what would be the effect of eliminating deferral and substituting tax deductions for the foreign tax credit? According to analysts at the Treasury Department, eliminating deferral would have increased taxes by $4.2 billion in

1984, the latest year for which such estimates are available. While this may not seem like very much in dollar terms, it nonetheless represents a 65 percent increase in tax payments on foreign-source income for that year.[21] If, in addition, the United States had substituted deductions for foreign tax credits, there would have been a further increase of nearly $21 billion in tax revenue.[22] The total increase— roughly $60 billion in 1989 dollars if one also factors in the $30 billion in taxes lost by U.S. direct investment abroad—represents about 40 percent of the $150 billion federal budget deficit for that year or 55 percent of the $106 billion borrowed from abroad.

Naturally these estimates are very rough and assume, among other things, that firms do not resort to other ways of avoiding taxes.[23] But the fact remains that for many firms these changes would remove a very large incentive to produce abroad. And if companies can be induced to shift production back to the United States, the benefits will be considerable: more jobs, more income, and, of course, more tax revenue.

The loss of tax revenue from these forms of tax evasion and reduction is in some ways less serious than the indirect costs associated with the shift of U.S. multinational production abroad. Most striking among these is the change in attitude that the management of U.S. multinational corporations has undergone. Since World War II, as U.S. firms have shifted more and more of their operations overseas, their sense of identity has ceased to be closely associated with their country of origin. This is reflected in remarks by Charles Exley, the head of National Cash Register, who told the *New York Times* last year, "National Cash Register is not a U.S. corporation. It is a world corporation that happens to be headquartered in the United States."

There are practical consequences that follow from this change in attitude. As

U.S. multinational corporations feel less tied to the United States, they are less willing to pay to maintain the quality of domestic productive factors that in the past would have been necessary to the success of their operations—an educated workforce and a sound infrastructure. They are less willing to support U.S. public investment because they no longer see themselves as directly benefiting from it.

An economist might argue that the market will correct this problem. By this reasoning, U.S. or Japanese multinational corporations may not wish to pay taxes back home, but they can be expected to support taxes in countries where they do produce—not for reasons of altruism but because of their need for skilled technicians, modern communication systems, efficient transportation facilities, and the like. In reality, however, it does not work this way. A corporation can always threaten to move to another country if taxes get too high—an option that each corporation knows is available to all other corporations. In classic free-rider fashion, each corporation benefits from the effect that other firms' propensity for flight has on the host government. Collectively, corporations are thus able to cow governments into maintaining low rates of taxation. In the end, all nations and even the corporations themselves suffer as a result, since revenue is simply not available for needed investments in physical and human infrastructure. The invisible hand of perfect capital mobility, far from solving the problem, only aggravates it.

At the same time that U.S. multinationals have become less dependent on domestic infrastructure, they have become more concerned with maintaining a hospitable international environment for trade and investment and with preserving their competitive position in key markets abroad. They have thus tended to be supportive of increased U.S. military spending, which they see not only as contributing to a secure environment for their investments but also as strengthening their bargaining position with countries dependent on the United States for military security—countries such as South Korea, Saudi Arabia, and the members of the European Community.[24] The days when U.S. multinationals could expect the U.S. military to intervene to protect their investments in banana republics may be over, but still one cannot deny the indirect benefits that a strong U.S. military posture abroad has tended to accord U.S. multinationals. It is no accident that Western Europe has tended to treat U.S. investment more favorably than that from Japan, or that Japan grants U.S. multinationals greater access than it does European firms. Of course, now that the Cold War is over it remains to be seen whether U.S. multinationals will remain as supportive of a strong military since the United States is not likely to enjoy the same leverage with its friends and allies in the absence of the Soviet threat.

As a result of this change in orientation, one would expect U.S. corporations to support a strong U.S. military and diplomatic posture abroad while showing less willingness to pay taxes to finance domestic education and infrastructure programs. This is precisely what one has seen for the past two decades and particularly during the Reagan years, when U.S. multinationals lobbied hard not only for lower taxes but also for increased military spending. As Thomas Ferguson and Joel Rogers document in their book, *Right Turn,* the U.S. multinational corporate community contributed heavily to candidates and political organizations favoring increased military spending in the 1978–82 period—the incipient years of America's largest peacetime military buildup ever.[25] Although the ideological right took this military expansion further than many in the business community thought· prudent, corporate America's support was clearly critical to the formation of a consensus that sanctioned the buildup in the first place.

The lobbying efforts paid off. Corporate taxes, as a share of federal, state, and local revenue, have declined sharply from a high of 45 percent in 1945 to roughly 10 percent in 1988. Meanwhile, there has been a dramatic increase in military expenditures relative to total expenditures, and especially relative to expenditures on domestic infrastructure. U.S. military stock grew by 700 percent from 1973 to 1987, while the ratio of public capital to employed worker actually fell in the same period.[26]

In these ways, then—through diminished tax contributions and support for increased military spending—U.S. corporate activity abroad bears substantial responsibility for the budget deficit. And to the extent that the U.S. budget deficit is linked to U.S. net foreign borrowing, as is widely believed, the operations of U.S. multinationals have contributed directly to the accumulation of U.S. foreign debt.

Moreover, the change in public spending priorities that U.S. multinationals have helped to bring about threatens to exacerbate the consequences of that borrowing. The lack of U.S. multinationals' support for spending on public infrastructure, in general, and their unwillingness to pay taxes, in particular, have resulted, as we have seen, in declining rates of public capital investment. Yet as recent studies demonstrate, adequate public infrastructure is critical to the productivity of private investments. Lower public capital investment means lower productivity growth. And that, in turn, means that future foreign debt-servicing burdens will be more onerous than they would be otherwise.

The globalization of U.S. capital or, more specifically, its flight from the United States, diminishes America's ability to handle its international debt burden in another way: it makes it more dif-

ficult to reap the benefits of foreign investment in the United States. Such investment, in theory, could help revive U.S. communities by providing badly needed tax revenues, jobs, and training. Yet while foreign investment has certainly yielded important benefits in some cases, overall its contribution to date has been limited. In part this is because most foreign investment in the United States involves takeovers of existing plants rather than the construction of new plants. But even when foreign investors build new plants, the benefits to the community are often fewer than one might expect. To attract investment, many communities feel they must offer generous tax abatements to foreign firms, sometimes engaging in bidding wars with other communities. According to the findings of one study, the state of Kentucky paid more than $100,000 per job to attract a Toyota plant to Scott County in 1988.[27] And yet, there is no evidence to suggest that tax inducements are a significant factor in attracting investment. More important considerations, from a company's point of view, are the cost of labor, the level of union activity, the proximity to markets, and even the weather. Tax incentives, in other words, often amount to pure giveaways.

Another reason the United States does not always reap gains from foreign investment is because many foreign multinational companies operating in the United States—especially Japanese firms—tend to import more inputs from abroad than do U.S. companies, especially in their start-up phase. As a result, their overall impact on the U.S. trade balance may be neutral or even negative in some cases, even though they are producing in the United States. Also, foreign multinational companies operating in the United States turn out to be just as adept at avoiding taxes as are U.S. multinationals operating abroad. A congressional study of 36 U.S. affiliates of foreign corporations concluded that more than half paid little or no U.S. tax over a 10-year period. Japanese companies increased their sales by nearly 50 percent in 1987, yet the reported income on which they paid taxes fell by two thirds.[28] A House Ways and Means subcommittee, which held hearings on the matter last summer, estimates that the United States is losing as much as $35 billion a year as a result of foreign-owned U.S. companies using transfer pricing and other schemes to avoid U.S. taxation.

In principle, the United States could step up its tax enforcement efforts with respect to foreign multinationals. Indeed, Dan Rostentowski (D-IL), chairman of the House Ways and Means Committee, has proposed a measure that would make it more difficult for foreign-owned corporations to understate their tax liabilities. Foreign corporations that sell goods through a U.S. subsidiary would as a matter of course be required to pay taxes on 50 percent of the profits earned on sales in the United States unless they could justify additional deductions to the Treasury Department. This would reduce the incentive for foreign companies to conceal profits behind inflated transfer prices and other spurious expenditures.

The U.S. government could also impose performance requirements on foreign companies operating in the United States to ensure that they operate in the interest of the community. Other advanced industrial countries—among them Canada, Sweden, Great Britain, and West Germany—have at various times imposed performance requirements on foreign multinational corporations operating in their countries. Such requirements could include labor regulations in addition to tax-payment requirements and environmental regulations. Organized labor has lobbied for the adoption of legislation along these lines in the United States since the early 1970s, but without success.

This raises the question of foreign cor-porate influence on the U.S. political process—an issue that figures prominently in the debate over foreign investment. Many fear that foreign corporations use their political influence to promote policies that are at odds with the interests of the U.S. public. And at times these corporations do. Efforts by Sony, for instance, along with Canadian, Dutch, British, and other foreign investors, are thought to have been responsible for the 1986 repeal of California's unitary tax. (Unitary taxes are calculated on the basis of a company's worldwide earnings rather than its local earnings and thus make it more difficult to reduce tax liabilities through income-shifting schemes.) But while it is true that a number of foreign business interests have strong lobbies in the United States and at times seek to use their clout to shape federal and state legislation,[29] their effectiveness is actually quite limited. So great is the suspicion with which foreign influence is viewed on Capitol Hill that legislators often go to lengths to avoid even the appearance that their votes have been bought.

A far greater influence has been exerted on national and local policy—and often against the interests of the U.S. public—by U.S. multinational corporations. The history of U.S. tax reform contains numerous failed attempts by Congress, the Treasury Department, and organized labor to close loopholes that have allowed multinational corporations to reap enormous profits at the taxpayer's expense. When in 1962, President John Kennedy's Treasury Department urged Congress to eliminate deferral, U.S. multinationals frustrated the effort.[30] Similarly, in the early 1960s Congress tried to curb abuses of transfer pricing through adoption of a unitary tax scheme, but U.S. multinationals again managed through intense lobbying to undermine the effort. The Burke-Hartke Bill, which sought to eliminate deferral and replace the foreign tax credit with a tax deduction, met the same fate and for the same reasons—intense lob-bying on the part of U.S. multinational corporations.[31] Tax reform is not the only area where the interests of U.S. multina-tionals have often prevailed. Over the years they have also been successful in defeating plant-closing and local-content legislation.

The lobbying efforts of U.S. multina-tionals are not always limited to matters that bear on them directly. U.S. multina-tionals, in fact, have been among the more vigorous opponents of U.S. legisla-tion aimed at *foreign* companies operat-ing in this country. In 1988, for example, Rep. John Bryant (D-TX) introduced an amendment to the Omnibus Trade Bill calling for stricter reporting requirements on foreign companies investing in the United States. The reporting require-ments were extremely modest, very sim-ilar to the information requirements of other advanced capitalist countries, and within the guidelines established by the Organization for Economic Cooperation and Development (OECD). Nevertheless, the House amendment, and its Senate version sponsored by Sen. Tom Harkin (D-IA), provoked intense opposition from U.S. multinational corporations, which clearly undercut it.[32]

Although this opposition may seem strange, it is not hard to understand the basis of it. U.S. multinationals worry that foreign countries may retaliate and take action against the substantial invest-ments these firms have abroad. Moreover, since U.S. multinationals themselves ex-port heavily to the United States, they too might be affected by any efforts to restrict the activities of firms operating overseas. Ironically, then, U.S. multinational cor-porations, out of concern for their invest-ments abroad, end up defending the interests of foreign multinational corporations here at the expense of America's communities, taxpayers, and workers.

It should be clear from the preceding discussion that the real problem is not the nationality of corporations but the lack of correspondence between the interests of multinational corporations and the com-munities in which they operate. Capital and production, able to move freely around the globe, have turned the multi-national corporation—regardless of na-tional origin—into a "foreign" entity in relation to the community in which it op-erates.[33] In this age of international cap-ital mobility, it seems that Adam Smith's invisible hand—which has always been imperfect in translating self-interest into common good—has developed severe ar-thritis.

AMERICA'S FOREIGN DEBT: THE REAL DANGERS

Just as it is important to establish clearly the sources of America's foreign debt, so is it important to appreciate the true dan-gers of that debt. The conventional wis-dom argues that the United States has been borrowing excessively and that as a result the country has become vulnerable to the whims of its foreign creditors. But the real problem is not so much the level of foreign debt, high though it may be. Rather, the real problem is that the United States has essentially been squan-dering the large sums it has been borrow-ing while, at the same time, its public policies have failed to respond to the ef-fect that the globalization of U.S. corpo-rations has had on investment and in-come patterns in the United States. The net result is that the United States has been investing insufficiently in its pro-ductive capacity—a trend that, if un-checked, will lead to accelerating eco-nomic decline, an increasing burden on middle- and working-class Americans, and a loss of economic control.

By historical standards, the United States is by no means an excessive bor-rower. At the moment, America's net for-eign debt stands at 10 percent of its gross national product (GNP). This is compa-rable to the level of debt the country sustained for nearly 50 years beginning in the early 19th century. Of course if current trends continue, the U.S. debt will approach 30 percent of GNP by 2000; this would certainly represent an unprecedented degree of indebtedness.

More serious than the current level of debt, however, is the fact that the United States has not been investing what it has been borrowing. On average during the 1980s, the United States borrowed about 2.6 percent of its net national product (NNP) from abroad and invested less than 5 percent. (See Figure 5.1.) Compared with other large debtors this is a disturbing pattern indeed. By contrast, in the 19th century the United States borrowed about 1 percent of its NNP and invested 14 percent. Moreover, it invested this capital in railways, canals, factories, and other productive resources as opposed to the wasteful ends to which borrowed funds are put today. Productive capacity expanded as a consequence and the

United States had no trouble servicing its foreign debt in the decades that followed.[34]

The experience of the past decade could not be more different. The money the United States borrowed from abroad was not used for productive investment—for automating our factories or for upgrading the skills of our workforce. Rather, it went into leveraged buy-outs, real estate speculation, unnecessary and exotic military systems, luxury consumer imports, and runaway plants—none of which added to the nation's economic strength. Thus the United States accumulated major financial liabilities without adding real assets to the nation's productive capacity that would enable it to service and pay off these liabilities in the future.

The United States, in short, has been operating like a huge and irresponsible savings and loan. By borrowing as much as we have without investing in our pro-

Figure 5.1
Net Investment and Net Foreign Borrowing Relative to Net National Product

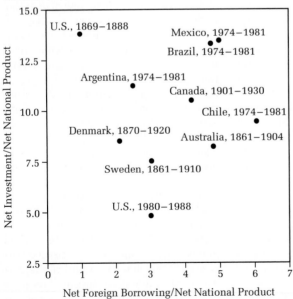

ductive capacity, we have condemned ourselves and our children to a lower standard of living in the future and our nation to a slow economic decline.

There are, of course, a number of reasons why net investment rates have not increased as foreign borrowing has climbed—slow economic growth, high interest rates stemming from tight monetary policy, and the short-term investment horizons of money managers, among others. But the increased globalization of U.S. business, as I have argued, must also bear part of the responsibility for our nation's poor investment record. By favoring private investment abroad and increased military spending over investment at home, and by eroding the tax base necessary to finance public investment, U.S. multinationals have contributed to America's lost decade.

In addition to hastening the nation's economic decline, the process of multinationalization and the concomitant lack of investment in productive capacity also exacerbate inequality in the United States. On the one hand, multinational investment abroad has reduced the number of good jobs at good wages in the United States. This has forced an increasing number of Americans to accept lower paying jobs, which explains why the average real income of the bottom 60 percent of Americans has declined during this period. On the other hand, the multinationalization of U.S. business, by allowing companies to increase their profit margins, has tended to increase the wages and income of the upper-income groups, who either own stock in U.S. multinationals or who provide services to the multinational business community—as investment bankers, lawyers, accountants, and engineers. In the 1980s, the average real income of the top five percent of the population increased by nearly 30 percent in real terms.

In an advanced industrial society, one would expect a nation's taxation and

spending policies to correct this growing inequality. But up to this point, the U.S. government has sought to service America's international debt obligations by policies that only worsen inequality: it has increased the tax burden on the lower 60 percent of the population through increased payroll and sales taxes while lowering the burden for those who have benefited most from globalization and the accumulation of international debt.

There is, of course, a question of how much of a burden the country's international debt actually poses. After all, the United States is not like other debtors historically. Because of the key currency role of the dollar, the United States can borrow in its own currency. This privilege allows the country to continue to borrow during crises and to devalue, in effect, its foreign obligations by paying back foreign creditors with cheaper dollars over time. Yet, as the increasing talk of yen-denominated Treasury bills suggests, there are limits to this privilege that relate to investor confidence and world demand for dollars. Ironically, the very process of the globalization of U.S. corporations that is in part responsible for our debtor position is also undermining the key currency role of the dollar. For world confidence in and world demand for the dollar ultimately derive from the underlying strength of the U.S. economy itself. The more competitive is U.S. industry, the greater will be the international demand for dollars to buy U.S. products and to invest in U.S. industry. Without sufficient private and public investment, however, the industrial foundation of the dollar's international role is eroded. Only higher interest rates can then generate demand for U.S. dollars and U.S. debt.[35] But higher interest rates only accelerate decline by raising investment costs and increasing our debt-service burden. Moreover, higher interest rates worsen inequality by shifting the distribution of income from lower- and middle-income groups dependent on debt to finance the necessities of life, to wealthy bond holders, both foreign and domestic.

A mistaken sense of danger leads, naturally enough, to mistaken prescriptions. Currently there are three popular, though wrongheaded, policy responses to the U.S. international debt position. The first is to cut the U.S. budget deficit by cutting spending and raising taxes. The second, under the guise of enhancing U.S. competitiveness, is to use U.S. diplomatic and political clout to open other countries to U.S. foreign investment. The third is to place curbs on foreign investment into the United States. Partly because they ignore the problems associated with the multinationalization of U.S. business, all of these responses misdiagnose the underlying causes of the U.S. debt problem and therefore ignore the real dangers associated with the problem. What is more serious, they prescribe medicine that is likely to make the problems worse.

Cutting the U.S. Budget Deficit

Analysts contend that cutting the budget deficit is necessary to reduce international borrowing. This was one of the main concerns that prompted the recent round of federal tax increases and budget cuts. According to conventional wisdom, U.S. budget deficits and foreign borrowing raise U.S. and world interest rates, which in turn lower U.S. investment.[36] Cutting the budget deficit, the argument goes, will therefore lower interest rates and increase U.S. investment. And since it would reduce borrowing from abroad as well, cutting the budget deficit is also expected to lower the possibility of a foreign run on the dollar that could force interest rates even higher. The plan seems tailor-made to redress the problems of decline and inequality. The question is, can it succeed?

First, consider the matter of interest rates. For a claim that is perhaps the most widely repeated "economic fact" on Capitol Hill and in the media, there is very little evidence that the high budget deficits have raised interest rates.[37] What has kept interest rates from rising thus far is the fact that the United States has been able to draw on excess world savings, particularly from Germany and Japan. Now, however, with the demands of German unification absorbing German surpluses and with Japan cutting back on overseas lending as a result of greater domestic needs, continued U.S. borrowing may begin to put upward pressure on world interest rates. Yet, it is by no means clear that reducing the budget deficit will necessarily lower interest rates. That, in part, depends on the actions of the Federal Reserve and the decisions taken by the central banks of Japan and Germany.

Moreover, even if cutting the budget deficit were to lower interest rates, there is nothing to suggest that this would necessarily lead to increased investment in the United States, as the conventional wisdom promises. For one thing, declines in interest rates will do little or nothing to stimulate public investment—at least in the current political climate. To be sure, declines in interest rates would lessen the government's debt obligations and thus free up money for public investment. But the recent budget agreement indicates that the government clearly prefers to spend on deficit reduction and a large military. Lower interest rates will not necessarily produce greater private investment either. While U.S. corporations are more likely to borrow when interest rates decline, they may not invest in the United States. If recent history is any guide, they will use the money to expand production elsewhere. (U.S. direct investment abroad has increased over the past nine months as interest rates have come down.) Or if these corporations do invest in the United States, they may very well favor speculative over productive investments, especially if demand is stagnant and public investment remains inadequate to restore the nation's deteriorating infrastructure.

Thus, cutting the budget deficit is not likely to expand public and private investment. Nor is it likely to promote greater equity. For while lowering interest rates would improve the distribution of income, since most interest income goes to the wealthiest Americans and foreigners, the way in which deficit reduction has been achieved—by raising taxes on poor and middle-income Americans and cutting their services—only worsens an already badly skewed income distribution.

A more equitable and economically desirable approach to budget deficit reduction is, of course, conceivable, but it would require significant tax increases for the wealthy and major cuts in the military as well as more spending on public investment to increase productivity. Yet, despite the end of the Cold War and growing concern about the fairness of the tax system, this budget-deficit package remains off the political agenda.

Still, it is argued, budget-deficit reduction is critical to avoid a run on the dollar, which America's large foreign borrowing has made more likely. For years, many economists have warned of such a danger. The resulting panic would drive up interest rates, cause a fall of asset prices, and bring on a recession—or worse. The result would be a "hard landing" for the U.S. economy. Claiming that this is no idle possibility, William Cline of the Institute for International Economics points out, "There have already been storm warnings that the hard-landing scenario could occur, as two episodes of rising U.S. interest rates in 1987 [when foreign private finance began to dry up and central banks had to finance most of the U.S. external deficit] provoked first a bond market collapse and then the stock market crash of October."[38]

While not entirely implausible, this view tends to overstate the significance of America's net debtor position. Being a net debtor is neither a necessary nor a sufficient condition for an international financial panic. In 1979, there was a flight from dollar assets, yet the United States was a net creditor at the time. And the Japanese stock market crash of February 1990 struck the world's largest creditor nation. Creditor status, therefore, is no guarantee against a run on the dollar. Cutting the budget deficit to improve the U.S. international debtor status, then, does not buy protection.

Rather than forestall a run on the dollar, cutting the budget deficit could actually produce such an outcome in the long run, especially if Congress continues to favor a combination of regressive tax increases and cuts in public investment. As suggested earlier, the steady erosion of the country's productive base will only undermine the dollar's international role. This will bring the "day of reckoning" that much closer—the day when foreigners prefer to hold the currencies of countries that have been maintaining superior rates of public and private investment, such as the European Community's deutsche mark (in whatever guise) or Japan's yen. Under these circumstances, foreign (and even domestic) investors will demand higher and higher rates of interest from the United States, unless the United States is willing to denominate its debt in truly "hard" currencies—the deutsche mark or the yen.

Indeed, some foreign investors are already registering their concern. Recently, there have been some signs that foreigners, in particular the Japanese and Germans, have been pulling away from investments in the United States. This reluctance, interestingly enough, has occurred as the government has finally taken steps to cut the budget deficit. Evidently this form of deficit reduction has done nothing to improve the economy's outlook. The inability of the United States to enhance its industrial competitiveness, the potential of continued unproductive military expenditure associated with the Gulf crisis, and fears of a recession-induced financial crisis worsened by budget cutting may be driving away foreign investment. In the short run, who wants to hold U.S. paper when a recession might lead to a large-scale financial blowout? And in the long run, who wants to hold paper denominated in a currency that is based on an increasingly fragile foundation?

Enhancing U.S. Competitiveness by Opening the World to U.S. Investment

If current methods of budget cutting will only exacerbate the real dangers associated with U.S. foreign debt, what about making the United States more competitive? This, of course, has become the clarion call of virtually all policymakers and economists. Yet the United States, unlike many of its rivals, has no real policy to make its industry more competitive. While the country needs a coherent, large-scale program that supports investments in education, research and development, and other infrastructure, the U.S. government is presently investing very little in public capital. Its "industrial policy" consists of cutting budget deficits, hoping that interest rates will fall and that private investment, in response, will increase. This, I have suggested, amounts to no more than wishful thinking.

It may be no accident that the United States lacks a government strategy to make its home-based businesses more competitive, for it seems instead to prefer to pressure the rest of the world to open its doors to U.S. corporate investment. In trade negotiations with Japan in recent years, for instance, the United States has expended much diplomatic capital petitioning Japan to lower barriers to investment by U.S. banks, securities firms, and insurance companies. Similarly, it lobbied Ottawa hard to reduce restrictions on U.S. companies operating in Canada as part of the free-trade agreement between the two countries. Negotiations with Brazil, Mexico, and even India involve a similar U.S. government preoccupation with facilitating U.S. foreign investment abroad.

Yet it is hard to see how a strategy of encouraging more U.S. direct investment abroad will do anything to correct the fundamental economic weaknesses that are at the heart of America's debt problem. True, more U.S. investment abroad may improve America's balance sheet for a short period of time. But, as we have seen, investment abroad also entails the loss of investment and jobs at home, which to date have not been offset by corrective government policies. Thus, under current circumstances, a strategy of more direct foreign investment will only accelerate economic decline in the United States, worsen our distribution of income, and further erode control over our communities.

Placing Curbs on Foreign Investment

If neither cutting the budget deficit nor trying to promote U.S. investment abroad is a sensible approach to the problems associated with foreign borrowing, perhaps it makes sense to limit foreign investment into the United States, as some members of Congress, journalists, businesspeople, and academics suggest. New York investment banker Felix Rohatyn, for instance, has proposed a review process for foreign investment. "No other major industrial power in the world . . . allows foreign control of strategic companies to be acquired without government approval," he says.[39] In a similar vein, the late publisher Malcolm Forbes proposed the creation of a Board of Knowledgeables that would approve all foreign purchases regardless of size. Likewise, regional planners Norman Glickman and Douglas Woodward propose the creation of a federal Multinational Investment Review Agency and Department of Research to review inward investment.[40]

From time to time similar proposals emanate from Congress. Responding to fears of Arab takeovers following OPEC oil-price increases, Congress entertained more than 70 bills in the 1970s to limit foreign investment in the United States. In an attempt to head off these restrictionist impulses, President Gerald Ford signed a bill that established the Committee on Foreign Investment in the United States to monitor investment by non-nationals. Congress also approved the Exon-Florio Amendment to the 1988 Omnibus Trade Bill, giving the president the power to block certain foreign takeovers and mergers that may "impede national security." More recently, some members of Congress are taking aim at foreign (especially Japanese) companies suspected of making large profits without paying their fair share of taxes. Already new penalties have been adopted for understating income and there is interest in tightening the tax loopholes that foreign multinationals exploit.

Will placing additional curbs on foreign investment in the United States solve the problems we face? The short answer is no, for reasons that by now should be evident. The problem is not *foreign* investment per se; it is the destructive effects of unregulated international investment—both domestic and foreign—that are undermining our economy. Focusing attention on investment only by foreigners merely diverts attention from the real issues. To be sure, there is clear value to some of these efforts. Regulating foreign investment to minimize the destructive effects of specula-

tive mergers and acquisitions on the U.S. industrial base; ensuring that foreign multinational corporations operating in the United States pay their fair share of taxes; insisting that foreign multinational corporations abide by environmental, labor, and antidiscrimination standards; and reducing the power of the foreign corporate lobby through campaign finance reform are all steps in the right direction. But if these efforts are directed only at Japanese and other foreign corporations—to the exclusion of U.S. multinational corporations—they will not succeed in redressing the real problems associated with America's foreign debt.

RESTORING CONTROL, REVERSING DECLINE

The United States clearly lacks a fair and economically coherent strategy for managing its international debt problem. The Bush administration's approach—cutting the budget deficit and opening other countries to U.S. investment—amounts to nothing more than a program of squeezing America's poor and middle class to free up savings and investment capital for U.S. corporations to invest abroad. And calls by Congress to curb foreign investment, while they may appeal to certain xenophobic impulses, are no more promising.

The obvious alternative to these simplistic solutions is a long-term strategy of strengthening the productive capacity of the U.S. economy so that we can begin to earn at least as much as we spend and thus be able to reduce our debt relative to the size of our economy. Many of the elements of such a strategy have gained currency over the years—for instance, major increases in public and social investment, expanded research and development, improved education and worker retraining, progressive taxes on the wealthy and speculative activities, dramatic cuts in military spending, and international debt relief to revive U.S. export markets in the developing world. As important as these various measures are, however, they will not add up to a coherent strategy unless we come to grips with the basic problem of capital mobility and the globalization of U.S. corporations. How to maintain adequate levels of public and private investment and at the same time ensure rising wages and environmental standards in an age of global corporations and international capital mobility is the dominant question of the 1990s.

There are, of course, no easy answers to this question. But it is an issue that can no longer be ignored or wished away. And it is a matter of concern not just for the United States. Eastern Europe, which faces a capital shortage yet lacks the political infrastructure to regulate investment, is especially vulnerable to the vicissitudes of foreign investment. So is Latin America, many of whose countries are now under pressure from the United States to further relax restrictions on capital flows. Even Western Europe has reason for concern, as the lowering of barriers to multinational investment in 1992 will bring new problems in addition to competitive advantages. As communities in these and other regions around the globe search for job- and tax-revenue–creating investment, they need to be able to exert greater control over multinational corporate activity so that the human and natural resources they possess are not merely exploited for the benefit of others.

In today's interdependent world economy, where the mobility of capital threatens to ratchet down living standards for the great majority, what is needed is a global regulatory framework for multinational corporations—a set of common standards for labor rights, tax and wage rates, and environmental protection, as well as the means—both national and international—to enforce them. Such a regulatory framework, it is clear, will not

emerge, at least not initially, from the lengthy and often empty exercises that have characterized treatment of this issue to date, including the effort begun in the 1970s under the auspices of the United Nations to establish a code of conduct for multinational corporations. Little will be accomplished until nations and communities take it upon themselves to exert more control over multinational corporations.

But what control can communities possibly exercise over today's global corporations? In isolation, of course, small communities are virtually powerless; yet large communities or collectives of smaller ones operating in unison have considerable power at their disposal. The establishment of an integrated European economy in 1992, for example, creates the opportunity for these nations to exercise significant control over multinational corporations. The United States, too, is large enough to wield such control. And if it were to pursue negotiations with its neighbors leading to common policies governing the regulation of multinational investments, instead of its current efforts to form a free-trade zone with Canada and Mexico, the interests of the United States would yet be better served.

In each of these cases, the source of control lies with access to the market. In markets characterized by oligopolistic competition—as most manufacturing markets are—profits are intimately tied up with market share. Large corporations gain huge economic rents by having access to markets.[41] These are rents that a government can threaten to reduce if corporations are not willing to invest in a nation's well-being. The United States, for instance, could alter the terms of access to its market that corporations (domestic and foreign) now enjoy. In this way, corporations could be induced to help realize, rather than undermine, national and community goals.[42]

The purpose of such regulation would not be to shift more investment from one country to another, for this would only fuel investment wars among nations. Rather, the idea is to reduce the power the multinational corporation now has to pit one country against another. In this way a more level playing field would emerge, and multinational corporations would find it more difficult to ratchet down tax rates, public investment, wages, and environmental standards.

One way to accomplish these goals would be through the use of social tariffs.[43] If the United States were to adopt a social tariff system, for instance, companies that reap a cost advantage by producing under labor, environmental, or other conditions that are below certain international standards would have to pay a compensating tax or tariff to bring their costs and prices up to the levels faced by companies not violating these standards. The imposition of social tariffs would help level the playing field among firms since those corporations that do not meet international standards would no longer have cost advantages over those that do. The revenue collected from social tariffs could then be channeled back into public investment or international development assistance to ensure that everyone gained in the process.

Critics no doubt will argue that social tariffs are protectionist. However, unlike traditional protectionist measures, social tariffs do not discriminate against foreign producers in favor of U.S. companies. All goods, regardless of nationality, would be similarly affected. Nor do social tariffs reward inefficient industries the way traditional protectionist measures do. Companies in fact would have an additional incentive to innovate and develop less costly ways of producing, since they would no longer be able to rely on the usual "externalities" to achieve cost advantages. But perhaps most important, the benefits of social tariffs would be more universally shared than those of traditional protectionist measures, which are usually designed to protect a single

industry or firm and thus tend to be costly for a community, not truly protective of it.

While social tariffs may seem like a radical idea, there is a precedent for them. The general idea of social tariffs is already used to some extent in the Generalized System of Preferences, which authorizes the president to deny benefits (i.e., reduced tariffs) to countries that do not respect internationally recognized labor rights. And some communities have already made access to their market contingent on meeting production requirements. In the early 1960s, for instance, auto manufacturers wishing to sell cars in California were required to meet tough emission standards adopted by the state. Rather than forgo California's lucrative market, automakers developed the technologies necessary to satisfy the new requirements. Soon after, those standards were adopted by the United States as a whole.

The same principle has been employed at the international level as well. Several years ago, the U.S. Federal Reserve wished to increase the capital requirements of banks operating in the United States so that they would be less vulnerable to failure. The central banks of the other major industrial countries, concerned about maintaining access to the U.S. banking market, agreed to these increases.[44] More recently, when members of Congress and the Treasury Department attempted to close tax loopholes on foreign multinational corporations operating in the United States, they found officials in Great Britain and other European Community countries receptive to a unified negotiated closing of tax loopholes on *all* multinational corporations.[45] In sum, the United States has the power not only to exercise control over multinationals, but also to induce other countries to cooperate on this issue as well.

Of course, social tariffs by themselves will not solve all the problems associated with the U.S. international debt. As suggested earlier, to protect against further economic decline and to restore fairness to its economic system, the United States must also be willing to increase its investment in public infrastructure and to finance that increase by taxing the wealthy. But here, too, social tariffs can help. While current budget-cutting measures reduce public investment and raise taxes for the lower 60 percent of the population, social tariffs would generate revenue for public investment and would fall on the owners of multinational corporations. Moreover, by removing the cost advantages of relocating production, social tariffs would help tie multinational corporations to the communities in which they operate, making them more likely to support public investment in those communities.

In short, social tariffs would be a much more effective way of increasing public and private investment, reducing the budget deficit, and maintaining U.S. competitiveness than the budget cutting we have witnessed in Washington. The tax revenue generated by social tariffs could be augmented by changes in the U.S. tax code that govern U.S. corporations abroad. Congress, in fact, made some progress toward closing loopholes as part of the tax package it passed in November. It increased the penalties for transfer price abuse and adopted stiffer reporting requirements. Admittedly these are small steps, but they at least suggest that the current climate is not hostile to reforms that harness the power of the multinational corporation.[46]

Ultimately the problem is one of political will. It is certainly within the power of Congress and the president to establish conditions in which multinational corporations can operate profitably while at the same time better serving community interests. Yet as long as our elected representatives remain beholden to the "special interests" of the wealthy or fail to see, for lack of political courage, the problems posed by the hypermobility of U.S. capi-

tal, the bold action that is required to revitalize the country will not be forthcoming. The sources of America's decline are no mystery. What we need to do is muster the resolve to reverse it.

NOTES

1. These stocks, and therefore the country's net-debtor and net-creditor position, are difficult to measure accurately because their value depends on the rate at which old holdings appreciate or depreciate, the effects of changes in exchange rates, bankruptcies and defaults, and the like. These valuation problems can create rather large discrepancies among estimates. Robert Eisner and Paul Pieper have argued that because U.S. foreign direct investment abroad is undervalued in official statistics, the U.S. net debt position is much less than it seems. A main point of this article, however, is that the U.S. people as a whole benefit little from U.S. foreign direct investment abroad and therefore its true value is much less than its accounting value. Eisner and Pieper's point thus loses much of its force since U.S. foreign direct investment abroad, as an asset to offset the debt side of the balance sheet, is actually of much less value than it appears.

2. The main exception is the direct purchase of real estate (as opposed to the stock or bonds of a real estate company).

3. *Survey of Current Business,* May 1990, p. 23. These figures are based on preliminary data.

4. Glenn Frankel, "Europe Views U.S. Crisis as Sign of Economic Ills," *Washington Post,* October 7, 1990.

5. According to data compiled by Salomon Brothers. Cited in Frankel (fn. 4).

6. For the data in this and the next paragraph, see the interesting work by

Robert A. Blecker, *Are We on a Consumption Binge?: The Evidence Reconsidered* (Washington, DC: Economic Policy Institute, 1990).

7. Reported by Paul Krugman, "The Income Distribution Disparity," *Challenge,* July/August 1990, pp. 4–6.
8. Kevin Phillips, *The Politics of Rich and Poor* (New York: Random House, 1990), p. 12.
9. Data are from the Congressional Budget Office, *The Changing Distribution of Federal Taxes: 1975–1990,* October 1987, Table 8, p. 48, as reported in Phillips (fn. 8), p. 83.
10. Of course, I am not suggesting that increases in military spending *caused* 90 percent of the increase in the net debtor position. I am simply suggesting that the increases in military spending had a significant bearing on the U.S. net debtor position.
11. These figures are taken from John Judis, "Goodbye to All That," *In These Times,* November 7–13, 1990.
12. Irving B. Kravis and Robert E. Lipsey, "Technological Characteristics of Industries and the Competitiveness of the U.S. and Its Multinational Firms," National Bureau of Economic Research, Working Paper No. 2933, 1989.
13. For most of the data in the following few paragraphs, see Robert Reich, "Who is Us?" *Harvard Business Review,* January/February 1990, pp. 53–64.
14. Kravis and Lipsey (fn. 12).
15. Irving B. Kravis and Robert E. Lipsey, "The Effect of Multinational Firms' Foreign Operations on their Domestic Employment," National Bureau of Economic Research, Working Paper No. 2760, 1988.
16. In a study of the foreign and domestic investment behavior of a small sample of U.S. multinational corporations, Guy V. G. Stevens and Robert E. Lipsey found that investment abroad and domestic investment tended to be negatively correlated. If this small sample is representative of the behavior of U.S. multinational corporations generally, it implies that expansion abroad by U.S. multinationals tends to reduce investment at home. See Stevens and Lipsey, "Interactions Between Domestic and Foreign Investment," National Bureau of Economic Research, Working Paper No. 2714, 1988.

17. See Gerald Epstein, "The Triple Debt Crisis," *World Policy Journal,* Vol. 2, No. 4 (Fall 1985); and Arthur MacEwan, *Debt & Disorder: International Economic Instability and U.S. Imperial Decline* (New York: Monthly Review Press, 1990).
18. The job loss estimates are from Norman J. Glickman and Douglas P. Woodward, *The New Competitors: How Foreign Investors Are Changing the U.S. Economy* (New York: Basic Books, 1989). My estimate of the tax loss is a crude one because it assumes that the net job loss remained 3.4 million. Since some of those 3.4 million no doubt found other jobs, my estimate may exaggerate the tax loss. On the other hand, since others subsequently lost jobs, and, moreover, the jobs lost tended to pay higher-than-average wages, my estimate perhaps understates the tax loss. Also, I only take into account the effects of job loss on federal revenue, not state and local revenue, which further minimizes the impact of tax loss.
19. U.S. Treasury Department, *Statistics of Income Bulletin,* 1989, Table 13.
20. James R. Hines, Jr. and R. Glenn Hubbard, "Coming Home to America: Dividend Repatriations By U.S. Multinationals," National Bureau of Economic Research, Working Paper No. 2931, 1989.
21. Timothy Goodspeed and Daniel Frish, "U.S. Tax Policy and the Overseas Activities of U.S. Multinational

Corporations: A Quantitative Assessment," mimeo, U.S. Treasury Department, Office of Tax Analysis, 1989, Table 11 and p. 41. These numbers assume the pre-1986 46 percent corporate rate. The 1986 tax reforms lowered the rate to 34 percent, which would have reduced collections in 1984 to only $2.6 billion on $64 billion of foreign income. The elimination of deferral would have increased collections to $4.5 billion—an increase of almost 75 percent.

22. These estimates are based on extrapolating Hufbauer's figures to the current period. They should be seen as very rough estimates. See G. C. Hufbauer, "A Guide to Law and Policy," in G. C. Hufbauer, et al., *U.S. Taxation of American Business Abroad* (Washington, DC: American Enterprise Institute, Policy Study 16, September 1975).

23. See *Ibid.,* p. 6; also C. Fred Bergsten, Thomas Horst, and Theodore H. Moran, *American Multinationals and American Interests* (Washington, DC: Brookings Institution, 1978); ch. 6.

24. For an analysis of the use of military and other sanctions in protecting foreign investment, see Gerald Epstein and Herbert Gintis, "International Capital Markets and the Limits of National Economic Policy," in Tariq Banuri and Juliet Schor, eds., *Financial Openness and National Autonomy* (New York: Oxford University Press, forthcoming).

25. Thomas Ferguson and Joel Rogers, *Right Turn: The Decline of the Democrats and the Future of American Politics* (New York: Hill & Wang, 1986).

26. Alicia H. Munnell, "Why Has Productivity Growth Declined? Productivity and Public Investment," *New England Economic Review,* January/February 1990, pp. 3–22.

27. Glickman and Woodward (fn. 18), p. 230.

28. "Higher Taxes, Stricter Audits Lie in Wait," *Financial Times,* August 22, 1990, p. 15.

29. See Martin and Susan Tolchin, *Buying Into America: How Foreign Money is Changing the Face of Our Nation* (New York: New York Times Books, 1988).

30. Bergsten, et al. (fn. 23), p. 170.

31. *Ibid.,* pp. 111–112. There have been some modifications in these tax laws over time, but there has been no fundamental change in them since the early 1920s. See *Ibid.,* ch. 6 and, for a more recent treatment, Hugh J. Ault and David Bradford, "Taxing International Income: An Analysis of the U.S. System and its Economic Premises," National Bureau of Economic Research, Working Paper No. 3056, 1989.

32. Glickman and Woodward (fn. 18), p. 281.

33. I am not arguing that U.S. corporations in an earlier time were more altruistic and for that reason might have been more willing to invest in education, infrastructure, etc. The point is that in previous periods the interests of U.S. corporations were more organically connected to those of the communities in which they operated. Of course, in other respects U.S. corporate interests have been in conflict with community interests, as the numerous violations of environmental and labor laws on the part of U.S. businesses attest.

34. The data for the figure were compiled from a large number of sources. A primary source is Simon Kuznets, "International Differences In Capital Formation and Financing," in M. Abromovitz, ed., *Capital Formation and Economic Growth: A Conference* (Princeton: Princeton University Press, 1955), pp. 19–107. For more

information on the data sources for any figures, readers may contact the author.

35. See below for a possible qualification of this point.

36. C. Fred Bergsten, *America in the World Economy: A Strategy for the 1990's* (Washington, DC: Institute for International Economics, 1988); William R. Cline, *United States External Adjustment and the World Economy* (Washington, DC: Institute for International Economics, 1989); Benjamin M. Friedman, *Day of Reckoning: The Consequences of American Economic Policy Under Reagan and After* (New York: Random House, 1988); Stephen Marris, *Deficits and the Dollar: The World Economy at Risk* (Washington, DC: Institute for International Economics, 1987).

37. See Paul Evans, "Do Budget Deficits Raise Nominal Interest Rates? Evidence From Six Countries," *Journal of Monetary Economics,* September 20, 1987, pp. 281–300; C. I. Plosser, "Fiscal Policy and the Term Structure," *Journal of Monetary Economics,* September 20, 1987, pp. 343–367; Robert J. Barro and Xavier Sala i Martin, "World Real Interest Rates," National Bureau of Economic Research, Working Paper No. 3317, 1990.

38. Cline (fn. 36), p. 3.

39. Third World countries can use an analogous strategy. Low wage/high productivity countries may have to seek control over multinational corporations on the basis of access to labor rather than to the market, while resource-rich countries may do so on the basis of access to primary materials. Here again, small countries operating alone will not have much success.

40. Quoted in Glickman and Woodward (fn. 18).

41. On the existence of such rents see Epstein and Gintis (fn. 24).

42. On the use of such threats to rents to enforce desirable social outcomes, see Peter Dorman, "Worker Rights and International Trade Policy," mimeo, Smith College, Northampton, MA, 1989; and Kiarin Honderich, "Rent Seekers' Revenge: The Use of Rents to Control International Trade," mimeo, University of Massachusetts, 1989.

43. See Dorman (fn. 42).

44. Federal Reserve Bank of New York, "The Risk-Based Capital Agreement: A Further Step Toward Policy Convergence," *Quarterly Review,* Vol. 12, No. 4 (Winter 1987–88), pp. 26–34.

45. *Financial Times,* August 1, 1990, p. 1.

46. *New York Times,* October 30, 1990, p. A23.

CHAPTER 3

The Structural Basis of the American Economy

This section looks to internal policies as an explanation for American economic performance. The first article, from a report by the congressional Office of Technology Assessment, investigates the problem of financing long-term investment. The report contrasts U.S. and Japanese savings rates, financial market structures, and industrial policies. It also considers the effects of mergers, acquisitions, and leveraged buyouts on the American economy.

Economist David Alan Aschauer then examines the state of American public works. He contends that declining American public investment is a significant cause of reductions in productivity and capital formation.

In the next selection, political economists Barry Bluestone and Bennett Harrison maintain that the "deindustrialization of America" has ushered in a period of lower wages and greater income inequality. They assert that the contrast between the Upper West Side and the South Bronx is becoming a metaphor for America. They call for a technology- and education-led competitive strategy.

Finally, economists Rudiger Dornbusch, James Poterba, and Lawrence Summers argue that a strong industrial base is the driving force behind technical progress and high wage rates. They claim that the American economy can be strengthened by reducing the federal budget deficit, encouraging savings and investment, curtailing protectionism, reaching trade agreements with NICs, creating a hospitable environment for foreign direct investment, and foregoing efforts to stabilize exchange rates at current values.

6.   Financing Long-Term Investments
Office of Technology Assessment

Developing improved technology requires long-term investment. This is true of all the activities involved in technological advance—research, development, commercialization, and acquisition of new capital equipment. All these undertakings have a better chance of success when there is a steady commitment of money, often for several years before the investment begins to pay off.

Much has been said about the short planning horizons of American business managers compared with the longer term view taken by foreign competitors, especially the Japanese. Because Japan's economic success shows most clearly what long-term investment can accomplish, this section concentrates mostly on Japan, although examples from other countries (e.g., Germany and South Korea) would be equally appropriate.

Several explanations have been offered for the Japanese propensity to take the long-term view, and for the American focus on shorter term returns. One is, simply, national culture and, by extension, business culture. But this is less an explanation than an observation. A factor with more explanatory power is the remarkable growth of the Japanese economy since World War II, and the comparatively sluggish growth, on average, of the post-1960s American economy. American firms, doing most of their business domestically, faced potential growth rates whose mean was close to overall economic growth—3 percent per year or so, in real terms. Japanese manufacturers,

however, were also looking outward, and had not only their own rapidly growing market to expand into, but the U.S. market as well. When markets are expanding at a rapid clip, investment for greater market share over the long term can reap more rewards than playing for short-term gains. Conversely, economic stagnation, recession, or even sluggish growth can work to the detriment of long-term investors and make winners out of short-term profit takers.

Japan's rapid economic growth in the postwar period and its government's effectiveness in promoting swift recovery from the oil shocks and recessions of the 1970s and 1980s partially explain the penchant of Japanese managers to focus on the long term. Likewise, sluggish growth explains some, but not all, of America's managerial myopia. Another determining factor is the financial environment. If a focus on short-term returns and profits is hurting American firms in competition with Japanese and German firms—and this is widely accepted as true—then it follows either that U.S. managers persist in ill-judged strategies in the face of evidence to the contrary, or that there is something about such strategies that is rational, viewed from the perspective of the managers. To achieve any long-lasting changes in the strategic behavior of American firms, it is necessary to understand how the American financial environment fosters short-term strategies, and how the Japanese financial environment resists such pressures.

A major part of the answer lies in the terms on which capital is provided, which includes, but is not limited to, its cost. By common consent, Japanese firms have deep pockets and patient capital. Patient capital is, almost by definition,

SOURCE: U.S. Congress, Office of Technology Assessment, *Making Things Better: Competing in Manufacturing,* OTA-ITE-443 (Washington, DC: U.S. Government Printing Office, February 1990), pp. 93–112.

low-cost capital, or it behaves like low-cost capital. And there is substantial evidence that Japanese businesses have enjoyed lower cost capital than American firms over most of the postwar period. Moreover, the financial climate has encouraged relatively heavy investment in things like R&D and fixed capital to an even greater extent than differences in simple cost of capital suggest. The question is why.

Today, when Japanese national income per capita is among the world's highest and Japanese corporations are swimming in profits, it may be hard to remember that, not so long ago, capital was relatively scarce in Japan. The Japanese personal savings rate has been extraordinarily high throughout the postwar period. But initially, incomes were low, so the total amount saved was not very great. On the other side of the ledger, demands for capital were high, mainly to feed the appetite for investment capital of a rapidly industrializing economy but also to finance frequent deficits in the national government budget. The workings of free capital markets do not explain the low cost of capital to Japanese firms during those years. The wide gap between American and Japanese capital costs, through the mid-1970s at least, was a result of government regulation of the Japanese financial market.

Today, after years of deregulation, Japanese financial markets have become more open, and real interest rates, many suggest, have converged somewhat with American ones. Yet even if interest rates were the same, the risks to business in making long-term investments might still be lower in Japan. That is, in large part, because both debt and equity financing are provided on a less risky, more long-term basis in Japan (and Germany) than in the United States, in effect lowering the cost of capital to Japanese firms even if the cost of funds (interest rate paid on debt capital, for example) were the same as America's.

INTERNATIONAL CAPITAL COSTS

An often-repeated argument holds that if money flows freely between nations there should be no difference in the cost of capital based on the national identity of firms. Investment capital, regardless of its origin, will seek investments that are expected to yield the highest return, and investors will seek the best terms from creditors. If there are enough of both (that is, if no investor or creditor has inordinate market power), capital flows should be sensitive only to risk. This argument presumes, logically, that there is no difference in risk based on nationality. And indeed, one study concludes that there is no persistent difference in real short-term interest rates between the United States and Japan (the nation most often alleged to enjoy favorable terms on capital provision).[1]

There are many flaws in this kind of argument. Short-term interest rates are not a very relevant basis for comparison, and comparisons of other real rates do show a difference between Japan and the United States. For instance, the real lending rate in the United States in the 1980s was higher than that of Japan by 1.1 to 4.8 percentage points, averaging 2.6 percentage points.[2] But a more fundamental flaw is the failure to take into account the difference between cost of funds—inter-

[1] National Science Foundation, *The Semiconductor Industry,* Report of a Federal Interagency Staff Working Group (Washington, DC: Nov. 16, 1987), p. 36. This point is quite debatable, even on short-term rates. The NSF study does not mention which short-term rates were compared, and other studies have concluded that there are substantial differences in short-term interest rates.

[2] The prime lending rate in the United States, and the lending rate in Japan, according to *International Financial Statistics.* The rates were deflated using GDP deflators, from the Organization for Economic Cooperation and Development.

est rates or the cost of equity—and the cost of capital, which is influenced by corporate tax rates, the economic depreciation of the investment and its tax treatment, and other fiscal incentives for investment.[3] Numerous studies have documented the gap—sometimes several percentage points—between Japanese and American capital costs over the past two or more decades.[4] Jorgenson and Kuroda, for example, estimate that Japan's lower capital costs have been a very important contributor to the increasing international competitiveness of Japanese firms over the postwar period, excepting the years 1973, 1978, and 1989 (Figure 6.1).[5]

The most thorough study, comparing capital costs of the United States, Japan, West Germany, and the United Kingdom, calculated capital costs for various types of investment, including research and development, new plants, and machinery and equipment. The study concluded that American and British capital costs for all types of investment were substantially higher than those of Japan and West Germany over the period 1977 to 1988 (Figures 6.2 to 6.4). Specifically, each year from 1977 to 1988, the cost of capital in America averaged 3.4 percentage points higher than the cost of capital in Japan for investments in machinery and equipment with a physical life of 20 years; 4.9 percentage points higher for a factory with a physical life of 40 years; and 8 percentage points higher for a research and development project with a 10-year payoff lag.[6]

The impact of differences this great is profound. Even small disparities can be important and have long-lasting effects. A 1-percentage-point difference in the after-tax cost of capital can result in differences in capital stock of 7 to 13 percent in the long run.[7] Even if American and Japanese capital costs were the same today—which they are not—markedly lower costs in previous decades in Japan would still favor the Japanese firms.

Sustained differences in capital costs of the magnitudes shown by McCauley and Zimmer are not likely under free market conditions in international finance.[8] Based on evidence of capital-cost

[3] Robert N. McCauley and Steven A. Zimmer, "Explaining International Differences in the Cost of Capital," *Federal Reserve Bank of New York Quarterly Review,* summer 1989, pp. 7–28.

[4] For example, see "U.S. and Japanese Semiconductor Industries: A Financial Comparison," Chase Financial Policy for the Semiconductor Industry Association, June 9, 1980; George N. Hatsopoulos and Stephen H. Brooks, "The Gap in the Cost of Capital: Causes, Effects, and Remedies," *Technology and Economic Policy,* Ralph Landau and Dale Jorgenson (eds.) (Cambridge, MA: Ballinger Publishing Co., 1986); Albert Ando and Alan J. Auerbach, "The Cost of Capital in the U.S. and Japan: A Comparison," Working Paper No. 2286, National Bureau of Economic Research, Inc., June 1987; and Dale W. Jorgenson and Masahiro Kuroda, "Productivity and International Competitiveness in Japan and the United States, 1960–1985," paper presented at the Social Science Research Council Conference on International Productivity and Competitiveness, Stanford, CA, Oct. 28–30, 1988.

[5] Dale W. Jorgenson and Masahiro Kuroda, "Productivity and International Competitiveness in Japan and the United States, 1960–1985," paper presented at the Social Science Research Council Conference on International Productivity and Competitiveness, Stanford, CA, Oct. 28–30, 1988.

[6] McCauley and Zimmer, op. cit., p. 16.

[7] M. Fukao and M. Hanazaki, "Internationalization of Financial Markets: Some Implications for Macroeconomic Policy and for the Allocation of Capital," OECD Working Paper, No. 3, November 1986.

[8] It is quite possible, however, that smaller differences could be sustained simply by different calculations of investment risk based on currency fluctuations, even if capital moves across national borders without restriction. A Japanese investor, for example, might insist on a higher return on a foreign investment than on a comparable domestic one simply to cover the risk of losses induced solely by changes in currency value.

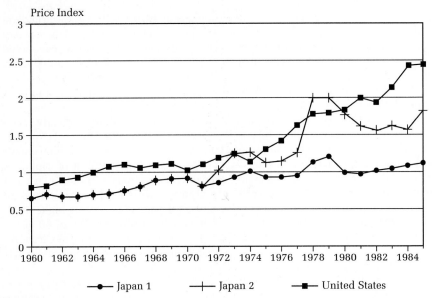

Figure 6.1

Capital Input Prices, United States and Japan

SOURCE: Dale W. Jorgenson and Masahiro Kuroda, "Productivity and International Competitiveness in Japan and the United States, 1960–85," paper presented at the Social Science Research Council Conference on International Productivity, Stanford, CA, Oct. 28–30, 1988.

Figure 6.2

Comparative Capital Costs: Equipment and Machinery, 20-Year Life

SOURCE: Robert N. McCauley and Steven A. Zimmer, "Explaining International Differences in the Cost of Capital," *Federal Reserve Bank of New York Quarterly Review,* summer 1989, table 2.

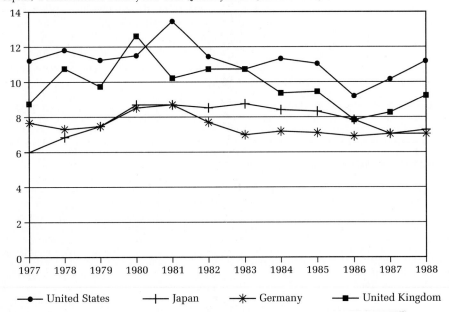

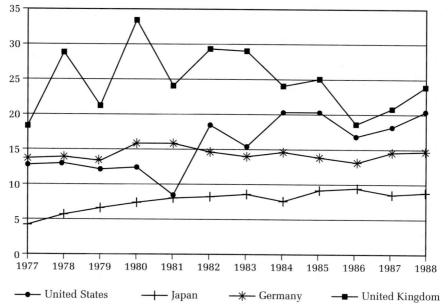

Figure 6.3
Comparative Capital Costs: R&D, 10-Year Payoff
SOURCE: Robert N. McCauley and Steven A. Zimmer, "Explaining International Differences in the Cost of Capital," *Federal Reserve Bank of New York Quarterly Review,* summer 1989, table 2.

Figure 6.4
Comparative Capital Costs: Factory, 40-Year Life
SOURCE: Robert N. McCauley and Steven A. Zimmer, "Explaining International Differences in the Cost of Capital," *Federal Reserve Bank of New York Quarterly Review,* summer 1989, table 2.

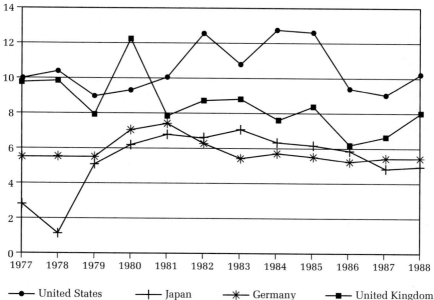

differences alone, we would conclude that the financial market of either the United States or Japan is not free to seek its own equilibrium. Since the American financial market is known to be relatively open internationally, and interest rates are higher here, the hypothesis is that the Japanese financial market has been controlled. That is in fact the case.

Moreover, regulated financial markets are not the only influence on capital investment or formation. Tax incentives and exemptions are widely used to promote capital investment in Japan, often for quite specific purposes. The Japanese main-bank system has also played a crucial part in lowering capital costs and reducing the risk of investment in Japan.[9] So, too, has the Japanese network of stable shareholding, designed to help managers resist pressure from equity owners to concentrate on short-term profits and dividends at the expense of market share.

The American financial environment is markedly dissimilar. Not only are there fewer provisions, public and private, to promote investment, but the government gives less effort to maintaining overall macroeconomic stability, shareholders demand much greater accountability, and relationships between banks and companies they lend to are more distant. Moreover, the pressure exerted by the financial environment to focus on short-term payoff, or simply to invest less compared with Japan, is growing.

The Japanese Financial Market: Sharing the Risk

Capital costs are based on risk. Riskier investments must promise higher returns to induce investors to provide capital. There is evidence based on the likely future earnings potential of American and Japanese firms in 1989 that the interna-

tional Japanese manufacturing firms could now be better bets than the American ones. While they were often satisfied with lower profits in the past, many international Japanese firms are earning handsome profits now; their reputations are sounder, and their capital spending plans are lavish. A 26.3 percent real increase is anticipated in Japanese capital spending in manufacturing in fiscal year 1989, and 11.8 percent overall,[10] compared with a 12.1 percent increase planned expenditures on new plant and equipment on the part of U.S. manufacturers.[11] A stable prosperous future for Japanese manufacturers is a recent development, at least in the eyes of international investors. In the 1960s and even in the 1970s, large, long-term investments by Japanese companies in markets dominated by European and American corporate giants must have been viewed with much more skepticism than comparable large investments in Japan now. Yet this higher degree of risk was not perceived in the same way in Japan, nor was it reflected in the costs of capital for large Japanese manufacturing concerns.

The regulation of many facets of the financial system of Japan made it possible for these companies to get low-cost capital. According to Abegglen and Stalk, "[t]he policy of the Japanese government is, and long has been, to hold interest rates to industry at as low a level as prudent monetary policy management al-

[9] Y. Kurosawa, op. cit.

[10] The Japan Development Bank, "The Japan Development Bank Reports on Capital Spending: Survey for Fiscal Year 1988–90," mimeo, September 1989, pp. 2–3. Mr. Nobuyuki Arai, Deputy Manager and Economist of the Economic and Industrial Research Department of JDB expects these planned targets to be met. Personal communication with Mr. Arai, November 1988.

[11] U. S. Department of Commerce, Bureau of Economic Analysis, "Plant and Equipment Expenditures, the Four Quarters of 1988," *Survey of Current Business,* September 1988, p. 19.

lows."[12] Until the 1980s, Japan's financial market was effectively closed to outsiders, and Japanese investors had few options for investment outside Japan.[13] Moreover, Japan's financial system spread the risks of long-term investments in industrial development widely among banks, savers, consumers, and corporations. This was done through controlled interest rates; tax policies that limited consumer spending, encouraged saving and transferred household savings to businesses on very favorable terms; and a variety of tax incentives that reduced the cost of investment. In America, much more of the risk of long-term investment is borne by the corporation itself.[14] In addition, Japan's high rate of savings and rapidly rising income levels have provided an increasingly generous pool of capital for investment. Since World War II, net savings as a percent of GNP averaged well above 20 percent in Japan through the late 1970s, and have declined only modestly since. Net savings as a percent of GNP have rarely approached as much as 15 percent in other advanced

industrial democracies.[15] America is the worst performer among the most advanced OECD nations; net saving hovered at just below 10 percent of GNP through the end of the 1970s, and then plummeted, reaching a low of 2.4 percent in 1987, and then recovered slightly (Figure 6.5). Capital formation, as a percent of GDP, has also been higher in Japan than in the United States or OECD Europe (Figure 6.6). Finally, Japanese lenders—stockholders and large city banks—tend to have much closer and more influential relationships with their corporate debtors than is the case in the United States.[16]

Although some of the conditions described above are slowly changing as the Japanese financial system is deregulated, their combined influence over the postwar period was to give Japanese firms substantially more freedom to make riskier, long-term investments at lower cost than American (or probably European) firms enjoyed. From this perspective, Japan's much-touted long-term vision—and correspondingly, the much remarked myopia of American managers—becomes understandable. Rational managers, operating under the rules and conditions of financing in both countries, could be expected to behave quite differently. This view is persuasive even if the numerical difference in interest rates—as low as 1 to 3 percentage points, according to some analyses—is modest.

The sharing of risk in Japan is not the result of any single action or actor, but rather of a variety of institutions and laws. Moreover, the risk-sharing that lowers the cost of capital to corporations

---

[12] James C. Abeggen and George Stalk, Jr., *Kaisha, the Japanese Corporation* (New York, NY: Basic Books, Inc., 1985), p. 178.
[13] The following discussion draws heavily from the following sources: M. Therese Flaherty and Hiroyuki Itami, "Finance," *Competitive Edge: The Semiconductor Industry in the U.S. and Japan,* Okimoto, Sugano and Weinstein (eds.) (Stanford, CA: Stanford University Press, 1984), pp. 136–76. Philip A. Wellons, "Competitiveness in the World Economy: The Role of the U.S. Financial System," *U.S. Competitiveness in the World Economy,* Bruce R. Scott and George C. Lodge (eds.) (Boston, MA: Harvard Business School Press, 1985), pp. 357–394.
[14] The developed economies of Western Europe, except West Germany, more closely approximate the American model than the Japanese, at least in terms of capital costs, according to available evidence. See, for example, Y. Suzuki, *Money and Banking in Contemporary Japan* (New Haven, CT: Yale University Press, 1980).

[15] Flaherty and Itami, op. cit., p. 137.
[16] For example, Corbett makes the point that Japanese banks probably monitor the companies they lend heavily to more actively than is the case in other countries. See Jenny Corbett, "International Perspectives on Financing: Evidence from Japan," *Oxford Review of Economic Policy,* vol. 3, No. 4, 1987, p. 45.

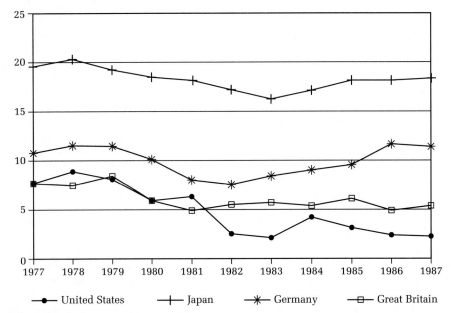

Figure 6.5
Net Savings, Percentages of Gross Domestic Product
SOURCE: Organization of Economic Cooperation and Development, *Historical Statistics 1960–87* (Paris, France: 1989), table 6.16.

does not apply to consumers. The factors that spread the risk of business investment include closed or controlled financial markets, channeling of funds to businesses and away from consumer loans, a large pool of savings for investment, and close relationships between companies and capital providers (banks, affiliated financial institutions, government institutions, and stockholders). For targeted industries—those viewed as having most promise for development—there are other mechanisms as well, some of them explicit (subsidies for R&D and capital investment, for example) and some implicit or consensual, such as protection from the threat of hostile takeovers.[17]

Controlled Financial Markets   The history of the Japanese financial system is a study in control and fragmentation. Although recent market-opening moves have gained widespread attention, it is only in the 1980s, under intense internal and external pressure, that real liberalization has occurred, and even so, Japan's financial market remains one of the world's more controlled.[18]   Between World War II and the early 1980s, a dominant purpose of the Japanese financial system was to revive and strengthen Japanese industry, often at the expense of consumers. Guidance of the financial system had two aims, subsumed under the single purpose of promoting Japan's reconstruction and economic develop-

---

[17] Personal communication with Ronald Dore, Imperial College, University of London; and Edward J. Lincoln, The Brookings Institution, March 1989.

[18] Aron Viner, *Japanese Financial Markets* (Homewood, IL: Dow Jones-Irwin, 1988).

Percent of GDP

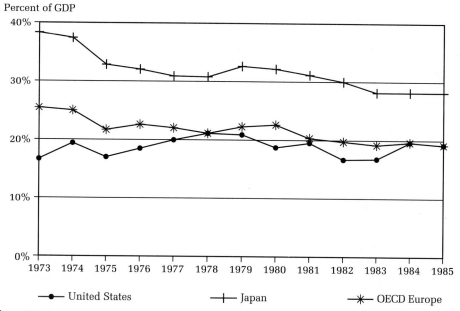

Figure 6.6
Capital Formation in the United States, Japan, and OECD Europe
SOURCE: Organization for Economic Cooperation and Development, *National Accounts 1960–1984* (Paris, France: 1986).

ment. First, the system was designed to favor business investment instead of current consumption, or, in the words of an official of the Ministry of Finance, "to prepare the ground for industry to walk on."[19] Second, the government selectively promoted heavier investment in certain sectors as a part of Japan's industrial policy, and also helped non-targeted industries cope with the costs of adjustment.

Preparing the Ground Japan was a poor country after World War II. Its needs for capital were enormous. Much of its industry had been devastated by or dismantled after the war, and the *zaibatsu*, family-controlled bank-holding compa-

nies that were major providers of capital pre-war, were dismantled during the occupation.[20] To rebuild industrial production—and then, beginning in the 1950s and 1960s, to accelerate development of targeted industries like machinery, motor vehicles, and electronics—required what capital there was in Japan to be preferentially provided to utilities and manufacturing. Several things made this transfusion possible.

[19] Personal communication, OTA staff with Mr. Kitamura, Financial Bureau, Ministry of Finance, Tokyo, Japan, Mar. 13, 1989.

[20] The following discussion of Japan's financial system depends heavily on the following sources: Viner, op. cit.; Andreas R. Prindl, *Japanese Finance: A Guide to Banking in Japan* (New York, NY: John Wiley & Sons, 1981); Philip A. Wellons, "Competitiveness in the World Economy: The Role of the U.S. Financial System," in Bruce R. Scott and George C. Lodge, *U.S. Competitiveness in the World Economy* (Boston, MA: Harvard Business School Press, 1984).

Japan's financial institutions were compartmentalized and fragmented, each with its own rather narrow purpose and with many proscriptions on its behavior. Briefly, the institutions worked together to increase savings rates (generating capital for investment) and pass them on to industrial users without high costs. They also worked to reduce the risk associated with financial downturns and the costs of financial distress to the firms.[21] The institutions that promoted high savings rates in Japan included a lump-sum payment at retirement (rather than a lifetime annuity) and a marginal system of social security (though this is changing to become more generous); large required downpayments on houses; the absence of scholarships at universities; a system of postal savings banks authorized to pay interest rates higher than rates available elsewhere on deposits, and tax exemptions on interest on postal savings up to a certain level (14 million yen in the early 1980s); a bonus-pay system of compensation in Japanese corporations; and very high interest rates (with no tax deductibility of interest paid) on consumer loans.[22]

Together, these measures discouraged consumption and encouraged saving. In addition to providing a large pool of capital, the system also controlled the cost of raising it. Households were paid low rates of interest on the savings they put into banks,[23] but rewarded by the tax benefits, or "maruyu," for doing so. Securities markets were tightly controlled so as to concentrate household savings in postal savings and in banks, so that banks, with their controlled interest rates, did not have to compete for savings by paying high rates of interest to depositors, and thus narrow their profit margins. Interbank transfers of funds were also handled so as to minimize the eventual interest rate that industry paid. The result of all this control was that money was channeled from households through several banks to corporations, at rates that greatly favored industrial investment and expansion at the expense of consumption. The extent of the transfer was huge. According to one estimate, if these measures lowered the interest rate to business by 2 percentage points in 1971, 800 billion yen was transferred from households to businesses in that year— money that, under free market conditions, would not have gone to the corporate sector.[24]

Both commercial and governmental banks lend money to Japanese corporations, but the distinction between them is rather more blurred than is the case in most other industrialized nations. The commercial banks include the large city banks, which specialized in lending to

---

[21] Wellons, op. cit., p. 361. Another set of institutions, equally important, gave Japanese firms preferential access to the domestic market, helping to assure a demand for the products of Japanese industry without ruinous competition from (at that time) abler foreign competitors. Japan's trade policies and their relation to industry policy will be discussed in the final report of this assessment of Technology, Innovation, and U.S. Trade.

[22] To be specific, a change in the rules governing consumer finance companies—known as *sarakin*—in 1985 reduced the maximum rate on consumer loans from 109.5 percent per annum to 73 percent, and set a maximum of 10 percent of annual salary of 500,000 yen to the amount one customer could borrow. Source: Viner, op. cit., p. 339. For an explanation of how the bonus-pay system promotes savings, see Abegglen and Stalk, op. cit., p. 196.

[23] Banks did not pay as high interest rates as postal savings, but the upper limit on the amount of any one postal savings account, the trouble of keeping several accounts, and the fact that company employees are often encouraged to use the company's main bank or an affiliate, kept some household savings accounts in banks.

[24] Y. Kurosawa, op. cit., p. 13.

large, blue chip corporations during the high growth period;[25] regional banks, which tend to lend to small and medium-sized companies; the Bank of Tokyo, technically a city bank, but the only one that could make foreign exchange transactions until World War II, and is still a specialist in foreign trade financing and foreign exchange; trust banks, which specialize in managing pension funds; specialized banks; the postal savings system; and long-term credit banks created in the 1950s and 1960s by government to make long-term funds available for industrialization. These last (which include the Industrial Bank of Japan and the Long Term Credit Bank) were able to provide funding to companies even when there were severe liquidity shortages, thus reducing the vulnerability of Japanese firms to ordinary fluctuations in economic conditions.

The government exercises control over and through the banks in many ways. First, interest rates have been tightly regulated since 1947, when the Temporary Interest Rate Adjustment Law was passed.[26] By 1986, after 2 years of steps toward deregulation, about 80 percent of deposits in Japan still came under fixed interest rate regulations.[27] Interest rates have historically been negotiated by the Ministry of Finance, the Bank of Japan, and long-term credit banks, the financial institutions most concerned with the

competitiveness of Japan's industry. Equity-to-asset ratios have also been extremely low by international standards; they averaged 2.19 percent for the city banks as of March 1986, compared with 5 to 6 percent for U.S. banks.[28] This allows Japanese banks to make low-interest loans both domestically and (lately) abroad.

There are informal controls as well. The Ministry of Finance exercises enormous (though waning) control over all aspects of Japanese finance. Much of this is through so-called administrative guidance, which takes a variety of forms, and can affect behavior at the level of the individual firm or bank. MoF's instructions and desires are not often ignored, even when they are not backed by force of law. Its staff are "the most gifted graduates of the best universities."[29] Like many other powerful Japanese institutions, MoF operates through frequent contact and consensus building; it holds regular meetings with the management of main Japanese banks, influencing the actions of Japanese branch banks in foreign nations as well as at home. When its senior staff retire,[30] many of them accept positions at the long-term credit banks, which were privatized decades ago. According to Viner, ". . . it is neither accurate nor meaningful to describe the three long-term credit banks as private institutions. Their ties with the government are so close that in many respects they resemble auxiliary components of the Ministry of Finance."

---

[25] Both deregulation and the financial success of the large corporations of Japan have encouraged the city banks to look for new kinds of business. Now, with many large businesses financed mainly by bonds, depreciation, and retained earnings, the city banks are turning increasingly to medium-sized businesses for customers. Personal communication with Mr. Tatsuo Takahashi, Manager, Public Relations Division, Japan Development Bank, March 1989.

[26] The word "temporary" is misleading; the law is still in effect.

[27] Viner, op. cit., pp. 306–307.

[28] Viner, op. cit., p. 202. This low equity-to-asset ratio is typical, despite the fact that the 1954 Banking Act required a ratio of 10 percent. According to Viner, "this level was considered absurdly high by banks and was ignored."

[29] Prindl, op. cit., p. 9.

[30] The term for this is *amakudari,* or "descent from heaven"—which by itself connotes a status of civil servants that is very different from American experience.

Industrial Policy Formal and informal controls can be used both systemwide—to advance capital relatively cheaply to firms and away from personal consumption, for example—and in pursuit of more industry-specific goals. The government acts both as a direct lender and as a bellwether for other private sector lenders. Its direct role is small—in 1980, only 5.6 percent of all funds placed in financial institutions in Japan reached business directly from governmental institutions,[31] and long-term credit banks provided another 5.2 percent. But this governmental role is more powerful than its modest funding would suggest. According to Wellons, "few dispute that private lenders in Japan treat this lending as a sign that the firm or project has government support, which would reduce the risk of the credit." Many Japanese sources agree. According to Kurosawa,

> The government also helped to reduce risk; MITI established specific goals and initiated investment for companies, and when necessary, adjusted the order [of] which group of companies should invest first and which next *(Rinban Toshi).*[32]

One way the Japanese Government primes the private lending pump is through the Japan Development Bank (JDB). When motor vehicles were chosen for rapid development in the 1950s, and electronics in the 1960s and 1970s, the Japanese companies were generally far behind American and European companies in technology, and financial returns from heavy investments in those industries were therefore quite uncertain. City

banks, with much of the lendable capital, might have been wary of making heavy investments in such industries, but were reassured by JDB's lending. Throughout the postwar period, JDB loans have been among the most important sources of funds for new equipment acquisition in manufacturing. In fact, even in the 1980s, long after the end of any real capital scarcity in Japan, about one-fourth of JDB's funds still go to manufacturing.[33] Where JDB lends is, in turn, decided by a variety of government departments, with strong participation from MITI, and its lending is meant to help major strategic industries directly.[34]

Financial support for both industry as a whole and strategic industries in particular has been a crucial element of Japanese industrial policy, but it is by no means the only one. Government support takes a variety of forms, including preferential access to the Japanese market,[35] support for research and development, market segmentation among domestic firms, and control of foreign investment.

---

[31] These institutions include the Japan Development Bank, the Japan Export-Import Bank, and agencies to finance small and medium-sized business. Source: Wellons, op. cit., p. 380.

[32] Y. Kurosawa, op. cit., p. 16.

[33] Robert J. Ballon and Iwao Tomita, *The Financial Behavior of Japanese Corporations* (Tokyo: Kodansha International, 1988), p. 37.

[34] Personal communication with Mr. Kitamura, Ministry of Finance, op. cit., and Ballon and Tomita, op. cit.

[35] This is not total market protection, as is sometimes claimed; however, access to Japan's markets in targeted industries is carefully controlled and limited, as are opportunities for direct foreign investment and direct investment abroad. Preferential access allows Japanese producers to sell goods in Japan at higher prices or of lower quality than they could if foreign products were allowed unlimited access. Barriers to foreign competition are usually phased out once the Japanese industries have grown to be formidable competitors. However, we are now beginning to see Japan resorting to voluntary restraint agreements in industries that are under pressure with the rise of the yen and the growing competence of other Asian competitors. A more complete discussion of these mechanisms will appear in the next and final report in this OTA assessment.

With such a panoply of tools at hand, and the demonstrated willingness to use them to support development of industries, government can pack a powerful punch with a relatively modest direct financial role.[36] Also, the variety of available tools helps to make up for weaknesses in the use of any one. For example, pump priming alone would not have induced Japanese banks to invest in certain sectors where the expected returns were especially low; it was decisive, however, where both expected returns and risks were high.[37]

The government's control over the financial markets is lessening. Many Japanese financial institutions see narrowing opportunities for growth domestically, as prosperous Japanese firms are increasingly able to finance themselves, or have more freedom to choose among domestic and foreign financing options. International pressure has also been a factor forcing liberalization of Japanese financial markets. However, it would be a mistake to regard Japan's financial market as open—the deregulation is proceeding deliberately, so as to avoid major shocks—or to discount the advantage that tight

controls gave to Japanese industry during the postwar period through the early 1980s. Without the deliberate channeling of capital away from personal consumption and towards industry—particularly those that were targeted—it is unlikely that so many Japanese industries would be so prominent on the international scene as they are now. It is also prudent to assume that, if Japanese manufacturing comes under increasing international pressure, the financial system is capable of mobilizing quickly in response.

Corporate Finance It is well established that Japanese firms rely more heavily on external financing—both debt and equity—than American firms, and that the reliance was greater in the past than it is now. Debt financing in particular has played a greater part in corporate finance in Japan than in the United States (until very recently) and other western industrialized nations, and it still does so today, even though the percentage of equity financing is growing in Japan.

Precise figures are somewhat deceptive, as many critics have pointed out. The gearing ratios[38] reported are based on the book value of companies' assets, which are reported at historic cost. Inflation, especially the run-up in the value of property and land in Japan, tends to understate asset value and thus overstate gearing ratios. However, even when the figures are corrected to reflect more realistic measures of Japanese (and American) firms' asset values, gearing ratios in Japan were still roughly twice as high as those in the United States only a few years ago. In 1981, for example, Japanese gearing ratios were estimated at 0.56 to 0.62; American at 0.28 to 0.30.[39] Japanese

---

[36] Although their number is declining, there are experts who dispute the degree to which Japan's industrial policies have been responsible for the postwar success of her industries. Clearly, other nations have used tools similar to Japan's without the same results, and Japan herself has demonstrated remarkable ability to develop industries in earlier periods when policies were quite different, as in the decades following the Meiji Restoration in the late 19th century. Thus, more than industrial policy is responsible for Japan's recent performance. However, industrial policy has been and remains a critical factor in Japan's development, as will be explained more fully in the next and final report in this OTA assessment.

[37] Sakakibara Eisuke, Robert Feldman, and Yuzo Harada, *The Japanese Financial System in Comparative Perspective,* study prepared for the Use of the Joint Economic Committee (Washington, DC: U.S. Government Printing Office, 1982).

[38] Gearing ratio is defined as the sum of short- and long-term liabilities divided by total assets.

[39] Figures reported in Jenny Corbett, "International Perspectives on Financing: Evidence

dependence on bank financing is also high compared with that of European nations. American companies have depended much more heavily on retained earnings (internal financing) and equity. This remains true even with modest moves away from debt as a source of new funds in Japan and increases in debt in America,[40] the latter resulting mostly from takeovers and leveraged buyouts to defend against the possibility of takeovers.

Japanese reliance on bank financing, particularly when capital was much less available there than it is now, underlines the importance of low interest rates in Japan. It also means that firms' relationships with banks are more important than their relationships with shareholders, compared with the United States (and much of Europe). As long as Japanese banks are sympathetic to the need to make long-term investments with little immediate return, firms are more likely to make such investments. This would be true even if Japanese firms' relationships with their shareholders were the same as those of American firms; however, Japanese shareholders are also more sympathetic to the long-term interests and performance of Japanese firms than in short-term financial gains, compared with American shareholders.[41] In short, while the structure and regulation of Japanese finance would alone lead to the conclusion that Japanese firms are better able to make long-term, relatively heavy investments than American firms, the nature of the relationships between capital providers and firms supports this conclusion as well.

Japanese banks—including both commercial banks like city and regional banks, and government institutions like the Japan Development Bank—are more involved with their clients than are American banks. This is true at every step of the process, from screening to monitoring of firm performance.[42] To begin with, Japanese firms usually have a special relationship with one bank, a system known as the main-bank system, and this relationship is an important part of the risk-sharing that allows Japanese firms to enjoy or act like they have lower capital costs. Kurosawa characterizes the main bank system this way:

> The main bank almost always has the largest share in such business relationships as lending, shareholding, trusteeship of bonds, deposits, and so on. It gives special priority to the client firms in credit rationing, and in the case of a severe slump or bankruptcy crisis, coordinates the responses of other lending financial institutions and acts as a mediator and supporter for the clients' survival. Consequently, it is essential for the main bank to monitor the firm, and for the other banks the actions of the main bank act as a signal. If the actions of the main bank remain unchanged, there are no problems in the firm. The main bank's additional loans in effect guarantee the security of the other banks' loans.[43]

Differences begin with the way they screen potential borrowers. For example, city banks are less concerned about debt/equity ratios and are more sensitive to the firm as a going concern (rather than as a

---

from Japan," *Oxford Review of Economic Policy,* vol. 3, No. 4., p. 34.

[40] Ben Bernanke, "Testimony on corporate debt," mimeo, May 25, 1989.

[41] This is largely due to the institution of stable shareholding, as is explained later in this chapter.

[42] This conclusion, and much of the following discussion about banks' relationships with firms, depends heavily on Corbett, op. cit., passim.

[43] Y. Kurosawa, op. cit., p. 18.

default risk) than are non-Japanese banks. The screening is extensive, so when a city bank takes on a client it is generally considered a good credit risk by others. Part of the screening is done by the city banks, but they are also able to rely on extensive screening by the Japan Development Bank and the Industrial Bank of Japan (IBJ).[44] There is some genial disagreement between these two institutions as to which developed the screening procedures both employ—both lay claim to it—but in any case, it is thorough. According to IBJ, the screen consists of increasingly smaller sieves. First, the Industrial Research Department (IRD) develops information on specific industries, examining in detail possibilities for growth and international competition. The IRD also examines new sectors and technologies, such as biotechnology and superconductivity, for their eventual commercial possibilities. Once industry prospects are understood, the Credit Department screens individual companies. If IBJ accepts a company, that is a powerful signal to other financial institutions of the company's creditworthiness, and a pattern of heavy lending to any particular industry or sector is also a bellwether.

There are several reasons why the close ties between main banks and their corporate customers could lead to a longer term outlook on the part of businesses, and possibly even to better decisionmaking than in countries like the United States or England, where ties between banks and the companies they lend to are more frequently arm's-length. As noted above, the close relationships between city banks and their customers are based on massive amounts of information, always a good basis for sound advice and decisionmaking. The city banks, along with other major Japanese financial institutions like JDB, have become powerful information brokers, and their ability to gather and process information about businesses and business conditions in a variety of industries around the globe probably exceeds that of all but the very largest corporations. Banks can therefore serve as important sources of information for strategic and operating decisions for their closest customers. This assistance on the part of banks is influential in encouraging companies to focus on longer term goals in Japan and Germany.

Another difference between Japanese and American bank lending is that loans from city banks are much more likely to be long term. According to the Bank of Japan, about 40 percent of Japanese corporate borrowing had a maturity of more than a year, compared with only 19 percent in the United States, as of 1985. However, the longer maturities of many Japanese loans are not exceptional compared with France and the United Kingdom (where about 40 percent of loans are classified as being long or medium term) or Germany (where about 60 percent of corporate loans are long term).[45]

Finally, it is well established that the conditions of loans are changed when economic conditions change in Japan. Although this practice is also common in western industrialized nations, the kinds of changes made are different. Corbett points out that a shortening of the term of a loan would be expected if a firm gets into trouble; yet in Japan loan maturities have lengthened at the same time that bankruptcies increased. With heavy investments of both capital and prestige in the success or failure of their clients, Jap-

---

[44] The Industrial Bank of Japan is one of Japan's three long-term credit banks, and it is usually described as the most prestigious of all Japanese private banks. Its purpose is to provide long-term capital to private corporations, with priority given to industries that are part of the government's industrial policy.

[45] Bank of Japan, *Economic Statistics Annual,* various years; and Corbett, op. cit., p. 42.

anese (and also German) banks are far more likely, in a crisis, to extend additional financing and assistance before pulling the plug than an American or a British bank.[46] Japanese banks often forgive payments on debt principal during tough economic times, or restructure debt in order to allow firms additional options to overcome their problems.[47] While some firms do eventually go bankrupt or are forced to restructure severely, banks explore many other options with their clients (often at great cost to themselves) before declaring loans in default. Prindl tells the story of Ataka, the fourth largest Japanese trading company in the early 1970s.[48] It got into trouble over excessive credit extended to a refinery in Canada, and eventually had to merge with another firm, C. Itoh. However, $370 million in uncollectable receivables were absorbed by its house banks, Sumitomo and Kyowa. This was possible, in part, because of the widespread belief that no large bank would be allowed to fail. Indeed, in 1986, Japan had its first bank failure since World War II, and that was a result of "massive, long-term corruption." This situation is changing, like so much of Japanese business. According to Viner, "banks have been informed that they can no longer expect central bank rescue in the event of a liquidity crisis."[49] So far, this new policy has not been tested.

Even the promise of government support does not seem adequate to explain why Japanese banks are more willing to go the distance with their clients, as long as there is some chance of maintaining the company in business. In part, it is because the main bank's relationship with a client company goes far beyond a loan. Companies generally encourage their employees to deposit their savings in their main bank, and deal with the main bank or its affiliates for life insurance and managing the pension fund. In addition, the main banks, in return for bearing some of the risk of the company's long-term investment, are privy to a great deal of information about the company, and are allowed to take part in its management should it get into trouble. Main banks often accept deferment of payment on principal and interest if a client gets into trouble,[50] and will coordinate rescue funds from other banks. In addition, however, they investigate whether the company can be restructured to get it out of trouble, and often draw up the restructuring plan.[51] Corbett points out that exchanges of personnel at both senior and junior levels between banks and large firms (and government ministries) are common.[52] Banks sometime suggest changes in strategy when evaluating a customer's request for a loan, and make more forceful suggestions of strategic changes when a firm gets into trouble.

The kind of involvement that large banks maintain with their customers resembles that of preferred stockholders more than creditors, according to Kurosawa. Preferred stock may have a fixed dividend, but if profits are insufficient to support it, the rate will be reduced and carried over.[53]

But what about actual equity holders? Here, too, there are different relationships in Japan. Most large Japanese firms

---

[46] Corbett, op. cit.

[47] Personal communication with David Hugh Whittaker, 1988; Flaherty and Itami, op. cit., p. 144; Corbett, pp. 46–51 passim.

[48] Prindl, op. cit., p. 64.

[49] Viner, op. cit., p. 196.

[50] This should not be regarded as a distant possibility. Ballon and Tomita point out that, "more often than not, [the] bank at some point in time has had to stage a rescue operation for its major clients with the cooperation of other parties concerned." Ballon and Tomita, op. cit., p. 60.

[51] Y. Kurosawa, op. cit., pp. 19–20.

[52] Corbett, op. cit., p. 45.

[53] Y. Kurosawa, op. cit., p. 20.

belong to groups known as keiretsu, which translates as "group arranged in order." These are companies that have primarily been associated with one city bank, and hold relatively large amounts of each other's stock—1 to 3 percent, typically, of the stock of each other member of the group. The result is that a majority of shares of all members are held by other members of the same keiretsu.[54] Japanese city banks also typically hold stock in the companies they provide credit to, with the maximum amount now limited to 5 percent. Finally, although intra-keiretsu shareholding is decreasing, a majority of stock in Japanese corporations is still typically held by corporate and other institutional investors, rather than by individual shareholders. As of 1988, 69 percent of all shares listed on the Tokyo exchange were held by domestic institutional investors—19 percent by banks, 13 percent by life insurance companies, and 26 percent by other corporations—while 25 percent was held by individual Japanese stockholders and 6 percent by nonresidents.[55] In contrast, 57 percent of U.S. equities were held by individuals as of mid-1989.[56]

More important than the pattern itself is the character of equityholding in Japan. Until the early 1970s, it was virtually impossible for more than a tiny trickle of foreign capital to find a way into Japan without the express permission—indeed, sponsorship—of government. In 1971, the door was opened a crack through revision of the Securities Exchange Law, and along with the liberalization came mounting concern that foreign compa-

nies would take over Japanese corporations. To prevent that, Japanese companies—at the urging of government—resorted to a system known as stable shareholding.

Stable shareholders are Japanese nationals who can be counted on to keep their shares, no matter what happens to their price. It is a primary duty of financial officers of corporations to find stable shareholders. According to Ballon and Tomita,

> When a capital increase is planned, financial executives usually visit the major shareholders who might be willing to subscribe to new shares and request their cooperation in purchasing the new shares at par while retaining both old and new shares. However, a request for further subscription of shares frequently implies a favor in return . . . the firm may at this time confirm its friendly relationship with the bank by promising (albeit unwillingly) to buy more bank shares.[57]

Stable shareholding has had the direct result of permitting companies to keep a longer term view in their capital investment. Stable shareholders prefer retaining earnings to receiving high dividends, permitting the company that issued the stock to reinvest its earnings. This reinvestment, in turn, is viewed as directly contributing to higher share prices. Since stocks are carried on their owners' books at purchase price, rather than market value, the rapid increase in share value has allowed Japanese banks and corporations to carry substantial hidden reserves. These hidden reserves are the utility infielders of Japanese accounting: they can be used to manipulate the reported levels of profit, and thereby, taxes and dividends. For example, if the company has a loss and needs to show a small

[54] Viner, op. cit., p. 2.

[55] Hideo Ishihara, "Japan's Compliant Shareholders," *The Asian Wall Street Journal Weekly*, June 13, 1988, p. 17.

[56] Securities Industry Association data, compiled from *Flow of Funds Accounts*, Federal Reserve Board. This total is down from 65 percent in 1985 and 85 percent in 1965.

[57] Ballon and Tomita, op. cit., p. 52.

profit, it can sell a portion of its investment securities, whose book value is usually significantly underreported. Often, it sells these to an affiliate or another stable shareholder, and expects in its turn to pay the same consideration to its affiliates when needed.[58] The amount of hidden reserves is staggering: at the end of March 1988, the hidden reserves of securities of the 13 city banks alone totaled $229 billion.[59]

Stable shareholding has served the needs of the Japanese economy admirably. It permitted long-term investment at a time when Japan's companies were much more vulnerable to foreign competition than they are now. It has helped Japanese companies to continue expansion and market share-building during the various economic upheavals that paralyzed their competitors—through energy shocks of the 1970s, the recessions of 1974 and 1982, and through *endaka* in 1985-86. Most observers expect stable shareholding to continue for the foreseeable future, although it will face increasing challenges in the years ahead. Financial liberalization in Japan and the expansion of Japan's business and financial ties around the world have made it more vulnerable to outside economic uncertainties. While its recovery during the postwar period has been robust, this new international exposure could well reduce its power in the future. The high yen, too, has put the whole economy on a more precarious footing. Some of the advantages Japanese firms receive have narrowed or disappeared, and strong competition from a new set of industrializing nations has left Japanese manufacturers with less ability to ride out a prolonged downturn. In a downturn, stable shareholding might start to unravel, as companies in trouble draw down their hidden reserves. The demise of their institution is unlikely without a major recession, and not certain even with one; however, if it does happen, the system is likely to come apart rapidly.[60] That, according to Ballon and Tomita, "would have profound repercussions on the stock market and the Japanese economy as a whole."[61] It would tend to shorten the perspectives of Japanese managers and firms, making them more like American firms. However, given the pervasive effect of administrative guidance from the Ministry of Finance, it seems unlikely that the Japanese financial market will behave a great deal like that of the United States anytime soon.

In sum, a network of policies, practices, and relationships acts to support heavy investment in long-term performance in Japanese industry by spreading risk. In contrast, American firms must carry more of the risk of such investments by themselves. While changes are occurring in the Japanese financial market, the backlog of more than three decades of such advantages has been highly effective in putting Japanese firms in the secure positions they now hold, relative to American and European competitors. Even if the changes were dramatic and rapid (which they are not) these advantages would not disappear quickly. It may well be that alterations in the way American managers are *taught* to think about business could foster a more positive attitude toward long-term investment, particularly in improved technology. But it is the rules under which they must operate rather than their education that is the principal influence on how U.S. managers view long-term investment.

Even with changes in the rules, however, there will be outliers. High capital

---

[58] Ballon and Tomita, op. cit., p. 202.
[59] Y. Kurosawa, op. cit., p. 20.

[60] Personal communication, OTA staff with Kimihide Takano, Senior Analyst, Corporate Division, The Nikko Research Center, Ltd., Tokyo, Mar. 22, 1989.
[61] Ballon and Tomita, op. cit., p. 53.

costs have hobbled but not crippled American firms in international competition; some firms are able to make substantial investments in technology development for many years. If a firm exploits its R&D effectively, such investments are rewarded, not penalized, by equity holders. But now, with increasing competition, more firms are forced to choose between supporting profit margins or stock prices and postponable expenditures like R&D.

Some long-term investments pay off, and some don't. We should not expect that risk-sharing will necessarily result in longer term investment across the board in America, or that every long-term investment will be successful. However, without some changes in the financial rules of the game, American companies will continue to focus mostly on short-term profit, to their detriment in international competition.

THE AMERICAN FINANCIAL MARKET

The problem for America is not only that Japan's capital costs are lower than those of the United States, or that Japan's providers of debt and equity capital are content to take more of their rewards as capital gains rather than as cash payments. Among the developed nations, Japan goes unusually far down these paths. America is, for the most part, at the other end of the scale. Our capital costs are high not only relative to Japan's, but relative to those of many European countries as well, and they are high in real terms, compared to what they were in the 1960s and 1970s. Institutional investors are, if anything, more insistent on receiving short-term financial gains than they have been, and they have powerful tools to use if their interests are not addressed. Rather than mobilizing its resources to support American manufacturing during its difficulties, the United States often

seems indifferent to or contemptuous of the nation's manufacturers. The problems of manufacturers, we often say, are self-generated; manufacturing is badly managed, and badly managed firms ought to fail, or change hands. The contrasts with Japan, and with Europe as well, are great.

Some—not all—of what we attribute to bad management is simply a matter of intelligent people playing by the rules. If our interest rates are such that American managers can prudently invest $0.37 in return for $1.00 in 6 years, while a Japanese manager could invest $0.66 for the same return,[62] we would expect to see about half as much long-term investment in America as in Japan. If stockholders evaluate a company's performance on the basis of quarterly or half-yearly reports of profit, we would expect managers to emphasize short-term profits, even when it raises possible conflicts with longer term investment. And if showing a profit for shareholders is one of the most important factors in the survival of a business, we should expect to see financial specialists wielding more power in companies than in nations where share price is a less pressing daily concern to company managers. The preoccupation with finance and short-term share price performance was reinforced by the wave of mergers and acquisitions American business experienced in the 1980s. Rather than moving toward an environment more conducive to long-term investment in the development and use of outstanding technology, the U.S. system raised the hurdles.

Another complicating factor is insta-

[62] These figures reflect the actual cost-of-capital difference of Japan and America, according to one calculation. See James M. Poterba, "The Cost of Capital Consequences of Curbing Corporate Borrowing," Testimony before the Committee on Ways and Means, U.S. House of Representatives, May 16, 1989.

bility in the financial environment. Federal decisions affecting the value of the dollar and interest rates take business competitiveness into account only tangentially, if at all; yet such changes can have profound effects on the ability of businesses to make prudent long-term investments. Again, Japanese policies contrast sharply. U.S. Government support for long-term research, development and investment has also been somewhat shaky, leaving businesses that invest in such projects vulnerable. For example, the Administration sent confusing signals about its support for technology development in semiconductors and high definition television in 1989. Even if the modest support for R&D in these areas is continued, the unreliability of Federal commitment to such programs could make industry wary of such ventures.[63] Another example of the inconstancy of Federal efforts to promote technology development and diffusion is the impermanence of tax measures that favor capital spending or R&D.

In short, America's financial environment is generally unfavorable to long-term investments in technology development and diffusion, and government actions that mitigate the effects of this unfavorable environment have lacked commitment.

---

[63] In late 1989, rumors of an Administration proposal to kill funding for Sematech in the fiscal year 1991 budget surfaced. The rumor arose concurrently with Administration proposals to shut down the Defense Manufacturing Board, and an OMB proposal to reduce DARPA funding for HDTV. While the Administration eventually denied any plan to kill funding, the rumor was widely believed and taken seriously by much of the electronics industry. See "Administration Charged With Seeking Funding Cuts for Sematech, Other Projects," *International Trade Reporter*, Nov. 15, 1989, pp. 1481–1482; and Lucy Reilly, "Death Knell for Sematech?" *New Technology Week*, Nov. 6, 1989, p. 1.

The Decline in Savings

Nations must continuously invest in productive assets—plant and equipment, people, and technology development—to sustain investment and living standards. Investment funds come from saving, domestic and foreign. In the 1980s, an increasing proportion of U.S. investment has come from foreign saving, because U.S. savings rates have fallen.

In the 1970s, net national saving (the percent of national income saved by business, government, and households) averaged 7.9 percent. Of this, 96 percent was invested domestically, and 4 percent was invested abroad. In the 1980s, savings rates dropped, and by the middle of the decade—1985 to 1987—net national saving dipped to 2.1 percent before rising to just above 5 percent in 1989. Net domestic investment (the percent of national income invested) dropped to 5.7 percent, lower than in the 1970s but greater than the amount of investable capital provided domestically. The United States made up the difference by becoming a net importer of investment funds, borrowing $417 billion from abroad over the 1985-87 period.[64] To attract savings from abroad, the United States has had to raise interest rates, or the return to investors. Importing capital allowed the United States to invest more than its own savings would permit, but it also raised the price of domestic investment. This means that improving and replacing productive assets and technology for U.S. firms became more expensive in the 1980s. A nation trying to keep pace with well-financed and technologically

---

[64] George N. Hatsopoulos, Paul R. Krugman, and James M. Poterba, *Overconsumption: The Challenge to U.S. Economic Policy* (New York, NY and Washington, DC: American Business Conference and Thermo Electron Corp., 1989), pp. 6–7.

sophisticated competition can ill afford this.

The decline in savings occurred across the board. The sharpest change in the 1980s was a decline in government saving, manifested by budget deficits at the federal level. Falling household and business savings contributed to the decline as well. The Federal budget deficit resulted from a tax cut, which slowed the growth of revenue, and from increased outlays, principally for defense.

The reasons behind falling household savings are less obvious. Many explanations have been advanced for this drop—and conversely, the rise in consumption as a percent of national income—but there is little consensus on which are most significant. Some analyses attribute part of the decline to high interest rates, which made it possible for corporations to decrease contributions to pension funds (these are included in household savings). The jury is out on the effect of demographics. Some think the baby boom was a major factor in increasing consumption rates: since young people typically save less than the middle-aged, they expect personal savings rates to rise as the baby boomers mature. Other dismiss demographics as having little explanatory power. Another often-cited argument is that gains in wealth in the 1980s—capital gains on corporate equities and homes—encouraged consumption. If people feel richer because their assets are increasing, goes the argument, they feel less need to save. On the other hand, since real wages and salaries dropped during the 1980s, falling savings may reflect attempts to keep up consumption patterns in the face of (for most families) declining incomes.[65] Another theory is that the propensity to consume

may have been fueled by the easy availability of consumer credit.[66]

The enormous increase in Federal Government debt and the fall in household savings rates were enough by themselves to force a curtailment of capital formation, or a switch to capital imports, or both. The decline in business saving has been less remarked, but is important for two reasons. Between the mid-1960s and the late 1970s, business saving—measured in national accounts by the retained earnings of corporations—fell from 4.5 percent of GNP to 2.75 percent. By the mid-1980s, business saving fell still further, to 1 percent of GNP.[67] Unlike the ballooning Federal deficit and falling household savings, the decline of business savings is long-standing, and cannot be fully understood in terms of the events of the 1980s alone. Nonetheless, the depression of business savings to the lows of the 1980s is part of another change in the financial environment—that is, mergers and acquisitions—that limits the willingness of American companies to make long-term investments.

Mergers and Acquisitions

Mergers and acquisitions are a normal feature of the U.S. financial landscape, and ordinarily not a controversial one. Occasionally, though, merger and acqui-

---

[65] Katherine Gillman and Joy Dunkerley, "Is the Middle Class Shrinking?" *Futures,* April 1988.

[66] The following sources discuss reasons for falling savings rates: Barry P. Bosworth, "There's No Simple Explanation for the Collapse in Saving," *Challenge,* July-August 1989, pp. 27-32; George N. Hatsopoulos, Paul R. Krugman, and James M. Poterba. *Overconsumption: The Challenge to U.S. Economic Policy* (Washington, DC: American Business Conference, 1989); David E. Bloom and Todd P. Steen, "Living on Credit," *American Demographics,* October 1987, pp. 22-29; and William D. Nordhaus, "What's Wrong With a Declining National Saving Rate?" *Challenge,* July-August 1989, pp. 22-26.

[67] Nordhaus, op. cit., p. 23.

sition (M&A) activity heats up, as it did in the 1980s, provoking debate and examination. M&A activity has raised many questions including those of basic efficacy (are mergers and acquisitions really an effective managerial disciplinary force, for example) and effect (do mergers and acquisitions generally improve long-term productivity, or produce outcomes as desirable from society's standpoint as from target shareholders'?). None of the questions are resolved. Even questions that are somewhat peripheral to the whole debate—such as the effect on managers' willingness to undertake longer term investments in technology development and diffusion—are hotly debated. While there is a growing body of research and empirical evidence on the causes and consequences of M&A, there are few points of consensus in the argument. But it is clear that the takeover wave of the 1980s is a special feature of the American financial environment, much more prominent here than in any other nation. The length of the following discussion is not meant to imply that M&A is the only, or even the major, factor that causes American managers to focus strongly on short-term profit, but M&A does intensify the pressures of the American financial environment, characterized by high interest rates and capital costs and macroeconomic instability.[68]

Briefly, the argument goes as follows. One point of view—often articulated by businessmen—is that corporate raiders have forced a preoccupation with short run performance that has disrupted business planning. With access to new capital instruments (junk bonds), acquirers can afford to pay inflated prices to get controlling interest in their targets. The first

defense against potential raiders, therefore, is to keep the stock price high enough to fend them off. Since stock prices can fall significantly on disappointing quarterly profit performance, business managers must focus on keeping short term profits at acceptable levels. This, in turn, exaggerates the already short-term planning horizons of American business.[69]

In some cases, more drastic steps may be taken to fend off a potential takeover, such as taking the company private by means of a leveraged buyout (LBO), or implementing some kind of "poison pill" defense. While these strategies can keep the company from changing hands, the effects on planning horizons can, ironically, be no friendlier to long-term investment and planning. In the case of a defensive LBO, the company exchanges equity for debt, making it safer from raiders but harder pressed to maintain cash flows. Debt payments must be made, while dividends can be postponed during thin times. Cash flows that could have been invested in research and development, plant and equipment, or other long-term projects must be at least partly dedicated to paying interest and debt retirement; so companies may defer long-term projects in favor of meeting their short-run obligations.[70]

Current concern is spurred by the fact that the availability of high-risk, high-re-

---

[68] The United States is not unstable compared to most countries, but the American financial environment for business is less stable than that of either Japan and West Germany, our premier international competitors.

[69] John C. Coffee, Jr., Louis Lowenstein, and Susan Rose-Ackerman, *Knights, Raiders and Targets* (New York, NY: Oxford University Press, 1988), pp. 3–4.

[70] For a brief summary of the arguments on both sides of the controversy, see Robert R. Miller, "The Impact of Merger and Acquisition Activity on Research and Development in U.S.-Based Companies," contractor report to OTA, November 1989. The report is a summary of interviews with R&D directors of 19 firms with a variety of M&A experiences. Some had undergone friendly mergers, some hostile takeovers, some leveraged buyouts, and a couple had no recent experience with M&A.

turn bonds has subjected many more companies to the threat of a takeover than in the past. Junk bond financing can turn even relatively small operators into potential raiders, and even large companies are not immune from the possibility of a takeover. Any company that appears undervalued may be fair game.[71] Moreover, a company's value to a raider can seem inordinately high to many business managers;[72] company managers feel pressed to keep their stock price above even inflated asset value.

The foregoing argument raises two questions. First, it is difficult to accept at face value the contention that a price can be too high if a willing buyer agrees to pay it. The difference between managers' estimation of the real value of their companies and that of potential acquirers may therefore be that outsiders can see higher yielding opportunities for managing companies' assets than managers do. Experts hold divided opinions on whether acquisition prices are too high.

The concern implicit in the arguments of many businessmen is that equity markets consistently undervalue long-term investments. If the resulting stock prices do not fully reflect the companies' investments in future output, then perhaps acquisition prices are *not* too high, but represent a more realistic appraisal of long-term company value. Here, too, there is no consensus of expert opinion, but it should be pointed out that there is no necessary inconsistency here: while ordinary stock prices may be too low, acquisition prices may be too high.[73]

The opponents in the debate view debt very differently. Those who see takeovers and mergers as a necessary disciplinary force on management see the higher debt levels that result from much of the current takeover activity as keeping managers from squandering corporate assets on less productive ventures.[74] Others regard the high debt that often results from a hostile takeover, or a defense against one, as a ball and chain hampering companies' abilities to invest, particularly in long-term ventures like R&D. The pressure of high debt load is expected to cause many defaults or bankruptcies in a recession. Even without a recession, however, the junk bond market is troubled; in 1989, corporate bond defaults were up 136 percent over 1987, largely due to defaults on junk bonds.[75]

Most of the evidence indicates that the *direct* effect of all kinds of M&A activity on R&D expenditures or intensity (R&D as a percent of sales) is small or negligible. Bronwyn Hall, examining approximately 250 manufacturing acquisitions between 1977 and 1986, concludes that the post-acquisition R&D intensity of the firms was about the same as pre-acquisition; moreover, the R&D intensity of the post-acquisition firms was not different from the R&D intensity of all manufacturing firms during the same period.[76] In addition, there is a broad consensus that R&D-intensive firms are unlikely to be attractive takeover targets, and that the majority of M&A happens in firms that do

[71] Miller, op. cit., p. 3.

[72] Warren E. Buffett, Michael D. Dingman, and Harry J. Gray, with Louis Lowenstein, Moderator, "Hostile Takeovers and Junk Bond Financing: A Panel Discussion," in Coffee, et al., op. cit., pp. 10–27.

[73] Coffee, et. al., op. cit., p. 4.

[74] Miller, op. cit., p. 6.

[75] Richard D. Hylton, "Corporate Bond Defaults Up Sharply in '89," *The New York Times,* Jan. 11, 1990.

[76] These results are summarized in "Testimony of Bronwyn Hall in Hearings on Corporate Restructuring and its Effects on R&D Before the Science, Research and Technology Subcommittee of the House Committee on Science, Space and Technology, July 13, 1989"; and Bronwyn Hall, "Effect of Takeover Activity on Corporate Research and Development," Alan J. Auerbach (ed.), *Corporate Takeovers: Causes and Consequences* (Chicago, IL: University of Chicago Press, 1988), pp. 69–96.

relatively little research and development.[77]

Some use this kind of evidence to dismiss the possibility that M&A is having corrosive effects on R&D in particular or long-term investment in particular.[78] Yet there is reason for skepticism. First, while much of the evidence supports the contention that the effect of M&A on R&D is small, it is not unanimous. The National Science Foundation examined the R&D spending and intensity of the 200 largest industrial R&D performing companies in 1984-86.[79] These companies account for almost 90 percent of all U.S. industrial research and development. Among the 200 firms were 24 firms that had either merged or undergone an LBO during the period; these 24 accounted for nearly 20 percent of the R&D spending of the entire group of 200 in 1987. The firms that did not undergo restructuring increased real spending on R&D by 5.4 percent, while the 24 firms that were restructured through M&A reduced their R&D spending by 8.3 percent in real (deflated) terms from 1986 to 1987. These overall findings were consistent with comparisons of restructured and unrestructured firms at the industry level as well.[80] The NSF data should be interpreted cau-

tiously—the study spans only 3 years, and some of the reductions in R&D might be elimination of redundant programs in newly merged companies—but they indicate a need for equal caution towards studies that show negligible impacts of restructuring.

One possible reason for inconsistencies between the studies cited above is that not all restructurings are alike. One of the few points of consensus in the debate is that M&A in the 1980s is unlike earlier waves of M&A activity, and is certainly different from the background level of restructuring. Different kinds of restructuring—friendly mergers, hostile takeovers, defensive LBOs, and other management buyouts, for example— would be expected to have different effects on managers' abilities and incentives to invest in R&D and other activities considered discretionary in the short run.

The last wave of M&A activity, which occurred in the 1960s, was characterized by diversification and agglomeration. The 1980s, in contrast, are characterized by so-called bustup takeovers of diversified companies with subsequent selloffs of the components.[81] Hall's study includes many mergers from what could be considered another era—the late 1970s— which may blur the effects observed by the NSF study which focused on the mid-1980s. High debt is closely associated with the bustup takeover. Friendly mergers often have little or no effect on overall corporate debt levels, while hostile takeovers and defensive LBOs, in particular, often leave very highly leveraged companies in their wake. One of the striking effects of the 1980s wave of M&A is the

[77] See, for example, Lawrence Summers, "LBO Debt and Taxes," *Across the Board,* April 1989; Hall, op. cit.; and Abbie Smith, "Corporate Ownership Structure and Performance: The Case of Management Buyouts," *Leveraged Buyouts and Corporate Debt,* Hearing Before the Committee on Finance, United States Senate, Jan. 24, 1989.

[78] For example, see Joseph A. Grundfest, "M&A and R&D: Is Corporate Restructuring Stifling Research and Development?" Address to National Academies of Sciences and Engineering, Academy Industry Program of the National Research Council, Oct. 11, 1989.

[79] The term "industrial" refers to companies in mining, construction, and manufacturing. The vast majority are in manufacturing.

[80] Testimony of Mr. William L. Stewart, National Science Foundation, before the Committee on Science Space and Technology, Sub-

committee on Science, Research and Technology, House of Representatives, July 13, 1989.

[81] Lynn E. Browne and Eric S. Rosengren, "The Merger Boom: An Overview," *New England Economic Review,* March/April 1988, p. 23.

substantial increase in corporate debt attributed to it. According to one estimate, the corporate debt burden was 20 percent higher in 1988 than it would have been without the effects of corporate restructuring.[82]

It is quite possible that high-debt restructuring has a greater impact than friendly mergers on R&D. This proved to be the case in OTA's interviews with 19 manufacturing companies representing a variety of different restructuring experiences. Although the sample was not a statistically valid sample of M&A as a whole, the firms that had increased debt as the result of a takeover or as a defense against a takeover consistently reduced R&D following the event. The reductions may not prove permanent—companies may rebuild R&D as they pay down their debt—but most of the R&D managers of the firms that had cut back also believed their firms' future ability to compete was compromised as a result.[83] Hall downplays the overall importance of R&D cutbacks following LBOs (which invariably results in much higher leverage), citing evidence that most firms that undergo LBOs do no R&D. Also, Hall points out that in her sample of 200 manufacturing acquisitions, 30 were LBOs. Those 30 had very low R&D intensity—on average, 0.4 percent of sales—and accounted for only 1 percent of the R&D done in the private sector in the years 1984-86.[84]

What all this seemingly conflicting evidence may mean is that LBOs as a whole have not directly affected R&D overall by a measurable amount, but that LBOs in large manufacturing firms have resulted in reduced R&D, at least in the short run, because of the pressures of high debt. Indirect support for this conclusion comes from another study. Abbie Smith found that R&D intensity declined in firms that reported R&D expenditures before their LBO, and that sold assets after the LBO. Smith warns against any conclusory interpretation of this result, however, because so few of the firms in the population of LBOs studied reported any R&D at all.[85]

Another complicating factor is firm size. Most service firms and small manufacturing firms perform very little or no R&D. The fact that NSF's top 200 R&D spenders accounted for 90 percent of all industrial R&D is telling. Summers points out that many LBOs occur when the owner-manager of a small establishment approaches retirement, and that these are "almost certainly benign."[86] In another common LBO situation, a company finds that a certain line of business no longer fits into its overall strategy, and makes amicable arrangements with the managers of a division for the sale. Again, these buyouts could be expected to have little or no effect on R&D, either because many of the firms involved do little or none, or because amicable transfer of ownership of a division to its current managers can often be accomplished without the high acquisition prices often associated with LBOs.

Analysts have concentrated more on the effects of M&A on research and development than on its effects on other discretionary expenditures. But R&D isn't the only kind of discretionary expenditure that affects a firm's technology;

[82] Goldman Sachs, *Financial Market Perspectives,* December 1988, quoted in Lawrence Summers, "Taxation and Corporate Debt," in U.S. Congress, House of Representatives, *Leveraged Buyouts and Corporate Debt,* Hearing Before the Committee on Finance, U.S. Senate, Jan. 25, 1989. The Goldman-Sachs analysis shows the outstanding debt of nonfinancial corporations as a percent of the gross domestic product of those corporations at 66 percent in 1988, compared with an estimated 55 percent without restructuring.

[83] Miller, op. cit., p. 14.

[84] Hall, op. cit., p. 3.

[85] Smith, op. cit., p. 71.

[86] Summers, op. cit., p. 187.

the other is capital expenditure. There are no clear and consistent answers to questions about the effects of corporate restructuring. Capital expenditure is necessary if firms are to keep up with and advance technology, but like R&D, capital expenditure may be postponed for a short time without long-term material damage to a firm's technological base. The duration and depth of sustainable cuts varies by industry and by firm, but even so, available evidence gives some cause for concern. Smith reports a substantial and significant reduction in capital expenditures as a percentage of sales that occurred in 58 management buyouts between 1977 and 1986.[87] This finding is consistent with anecdotal evidence. For example, consider Houdaille, a machine-tool maker that underwent an LBO in 1979. Pressured by foreign competition and (later) the effects of the 1982 recession as well as its high debt burden, Houdaille cut capital spending as a percent of revenues in half following its post-buyout restructuring.[88] One owner of a machine-tool making business states, "When we hear LBO, we know they're not going to be buying anything."[89]

Most analyses of the consequences of M&A have been confined to measurable direct effects—spending on various activities or overall performance of companies that have undergone restructuring. Two others should also be considered. First, there are qualitative effects, not readily measurable, on R&D or firm activities. Again, we would expect (and find, according to the limited evidence) that different kinds of restructuring have different qualitative effects. In OTA's interviews, [for] firms that mounted successful defenses against hostile takeovers (leaving the companies with high debt) long-term R&D had invariably been significantly cut back in favor of projects with promise of quicker payoff.[90] Some analysts interpret this kind of cutback as making R&D more efficient, and this is indeed possible in the short run. R&D is by its nature a long-term process, and firms can cut back on new long-term projects without impairing their ability to exploit the results of projects undertaken in the past. So a shift in emphasis toward shorter term projects would be unlikely to show up as detrimental for at least a year or two. But in the long run, it seems unlikely that increasing the focus on short-term projects on the part of American firms will permit them to maintain even their current level of competitiveness.

Friendly mergers, on the other hand, had either little impact on R&D, or effects that would be generally accepted as positive. One example is the purchase of Celanese Corp. by the West German chemical firm Hoechst. Hoechst was interested in expanding its U.S. operations through the purchase of an American firm with strong R&D, and after the acquisition increased Celanese's R&D expenditures by 10 percent annually. Significantly, the new German managers were also more willing to commit substantial resources to long-term projects with less certain payoffs.[91] A similar story was told by the president of Materials Research Corp., a semiconductor equipment and materials company recently acquired by Sony. After the deal was completed, the president was told by Akio Morita, the president of Sony, that he had "essentially unlimited capital," and was no longer obliged to concern himself with quarterly profits. "I

[87] Smith, op. cit., p. 47.
[88] Max Holland, "How to Kill a Company," *The Washington Post,* Apr. 23, 1989.
[89] Howard Greis, President, Kinefac, personal communication, Nov. 16, 1989.

[90] Miller, op. cit., p. 18.
[91] Miller, op. cit., p. 31.

can think of projects that take two years,'' said Dr. Sheldon Weinig, the president. "It's a wonderful way to live."[92]

It is difficult to make a few cases add up to a strong finding, but the anecdotes about the qualitative effects on manufacturing R&D of different kinds of M&A activity are consistent with quantitative evidence, if the focus is adjusted correctly. In other words, both the qualitative and quantitative evidence suggest the following: in manufacturing firms that have appreciable amounts of R&D, restructurings that result in high debt levels depress R&D spending or intensity, or both, and often shorten the allowable time for completion of R&D projects. Because such restructurings are not common—most happen in firms that do little R&D, and many of them are in service firms—the overall direct effects of M&A on overall national R&D are not yet large, and may never be, particularly as hostile takeover/LBO activity seems to be winding down for now. This does not justify complacency about M&A. NSF's data are disturbing, and will be more so if the highly leveraged companies continue to lag in R&D spending or long-term planning. Additional depression of discretionary expenditures on capital equipment or R&D could well occur in the event of a recession, or perhaps even when growth is less than robust. Such cutbacks, normal in recessions, are more likely when companies are highly leveraged.

Finally, the indirect effects of M&A must be considered. The 1980s added a new wrinkle to the takeover enterprise: the expansion of the pool of potential raiders. In the past, in most takeovers, large firms acquired smaller ones. In the 1980s, junk bonds made it possible for "individuals, smaller entities, and investment banking firms" to take part.[93] In another contrast to past takeover waves (and ordinary M&A activity), these new players often intended to dismantle the acquired company rather than to assimilate it. Both factors—the increase in number of raiders, and the consequences of a successful takeover—have apparently increased managers' fears of takeovers markedly, and may also have depressed discretionary expenditures. Managers, feeling that an unwelcome takeover bid might come at any time, might take steps that approximate what they would do to defend against a real hostile takeover bid, with the same effects on spending for R&D and capital equipment. In mid-1989, for example, Honeywell acted to discourage potential raiders by cutting out certain lines of business (reducing the breakup value of its assets), eliminating 4,000 jobs, repurchasing up to 10 million shares of its own stock, and increasing its annual dividend to shareholders by 31 percent.[94] There had been speculation that Honeywell might be a takeover target, but no actual bid.

Few companies make moves as dramatic as Honeywell's, but many members of corporate boards and senior managers report that hostile takeovers came to dominate corporate board meetings and decisionmaking to an unprecedented extent in the 1980s. The effect on overall business planning, almost certainly, was to increase the emphasis on distributing profits to shareholders in preference to reinvesting in the company.

Hostile takeover activity seems to be winding down, although not crashing;

[92] Andrew Pollack, "The Challenge of Keeping U.S. Technology At Home," *The New York Times,* Dec. 10, 1989.

[93] John C. Coffee, Jr., "Shareholders Versus Managers: The Strain in the Corporate Web," in Coffee, et al., op. cit., p. 77.

[94] Tony Kennedy, "Honeywell Acts Against Potential Raiders," *The Washington Post,* July 25, 1989.

the number of deals completed in the first 9 months of 1989 was smaller, according to a preliminary estimate, than the number in the first 9 months of any of the preceding 3 years. The first three quarters of 1989 saw 2,298 completed acquisitions, compared to 2,790 in 1988, 2,851 in 1987, and 2,707 in 1986. However, the value of these deals in 1989 was $144 billion, just below the peak of $144.7 billion in 1988. The story is different for LBOs: there were slightly fewer completed in the first 9 months of 1989 (214) than in a similar period of 1988 (221), but the total value of those LBOs in 1989—$47 billion—was quite a bit higher than the previous high of $29.1 billion in 1988.[95] The numbers aren't the only story. There is a widespread perception that the market has grown pickier about the kind of deals that can be approved, and there has been a flight from junk bonds.[96] Acquisitions continue, but many believe that the wave of highly leveraged, bustup takeovers is on the wane. If this is true, it could provide time to examine how much of the negative effects of M&A is associated with this particular type of financial activity, and time for policymakers to evaluate how to tailor possible regulation to the real problems.

FOR FURTHER READING

KENNETH J. ARROW AND MORDECAI KURZ, *Public Investment, the Rate of Return, and Optimal Fiscal Policy,* Johns Hopkins Press, Baltimore, 1970.

DAVID A. ASHAUER, "Is Public Expenditure Productive?" *Journal of Monetary Economics,* Vol. 23, 1989a.

———, "Public Investment and Productivity Growth in the Group of Seven," *Economic Perspectives,* Vol. 13, No. 5, 1989b.

———, "Why Is Infrastructure Important?" in *The Third Deficit: The Shortfall in Public Capital Investment,* Federal Reserve Bank of Boston, Conference Series, No. 34, 1991 (forthcoming).

DAVID A. ASHAUER AND JEREMY GREENWOOD, "Macroeconomic Effects of Fiscal Policy," in Karl Brunner and Allan H. Meltzer, eds., *The "New Monetary Economics," Fiscal Issues and Unemployment,* North-Holland, Amsterdam, 1985.

MICHAEL R. DARBY, "The U.S. Productivity Slowdown: A Case of Statistical Myopia?" *American Economic Review,* Vol. 74, 1984.

KEVIN T. DENO, "The Effect of Public Capital on U.S. Manufacturing Activity: 1970 to 1978," *Southern Economic Journal,* Vol. 55, No. 2, 1988.

STANLEY FISCHER, "Symposium on the Slowdown in Productivity Growth," *Journal of Economic Perspectives,* Vol. 2, No. 4, 1988.

LAWRENCE MISHEL AND DAVID M. FRANKEL, *The State of Working America, 1990–91 Edition,* Economic Policy Institute, Washington, D.C., 1991.

ALICIA H. MUNNELL, "Why Has Productivity Growth Declined?" *New England Economic Review,* January/February, 1990.

———, "How Does Public Infrastructure Affect Regional Economic Performance?" in *The Third Deficit: The Shortfall in Public Capital Investment,* Federal Reserve Bank of Boston, Conference Series, No. 34, 1991 (forthcoming).

[95] Judith H. Dobryzinski, "Deals, Yes. Maniac Deals, No," *Business Week,* Oct. 30, 1989.
[96] Christopher Farrell, with Leah J. Nathans, "The Bills Are Coming Due," *Business Week,* Oct. 30, 1989.

7. Infrastructure: America's Third Deficit
David Alan Aschauer

In the past few years, a number of tragic incidents have focused attention on the disrepair of the nation's public infrastructure:

- a bridge collapses on the NY State Thruway, taking the lives of ten motorists;
- a dam bursts in Georgia, flooding a bible school and drowning school-aged children;
- medical debris washes up on the shores of Long Island, posing a health risk to millions of people.

Concern has also grown over the less dramatic but pervasive congestion of our streets, highways, and air routes. Delays proliferate in a transportation network that is apparently insufficient to meet the needs of a growing economy. The U.S. Department of Transportation has estimated that in 1985, total vehicle delays on the highways exceeded 722 million hours; it is projected that this alarming number will skyrocket to 3.9 billion hours by the year 2005 if improvements to the nation's freeway system are not forthcoming. While these cars and trucks sat in traffic, they wasted nearly 3 billion gallons of gasoline, almost 4 percent of annual consumption in the United States. The total cost of this congestion was estimated at $9 billion.

According to the Federal Aviation Administration, air travel delays in 1986 resulted in $1.8 billion in additional airline operating expenses and $3.2 billion in time lost by travelers.

Underlying these headlines, anecdotes, and cost estimates is a larger question: To

SOURCE: Reprinted with permission of M. E. Sharpe, Inc., Armonk, New York 10504, from *Challenge*, March–April 1991, pp. 39–45.

what extent has the decline of investment in public infrastructure affected the performance of the U.S. economy as a whole?

This article will show that the reduction of public investment spending in the United States over the past twenty-five years played a central role in a number of our long-term economic ills. If the United States had continued to invest in public capital after 1970 at the rate maintained for the previous two decades, we could have benefited in the following ways:

- Our chronically low rate of productivity growth could have been up to 50 percent higher—2.1 percent per year, rather than the actual rate of 1.4 percent;
- Our depressed rate of profit on nonfinancial corporate capital could have averaged 9.6 percent instead of 7.9 percent;
- Private investment in plants and equipment could have increased from the sluggish historical rate of 3.1 percent, to 3.7 percent of the private capital stock.

These results indicate that close attention should be paid to the critical role played by public infrastructure in augmenting overall economic performance.

U.S. PRODUCTIVITY SLUMP

A number of signs indicate that the United States' economy has not performed as well in recent years as in the so-called "golden age" of the 1950s and 1960s. For two decades the economy has experienced a *continuing slump in the growth rate of economic productivity*, measured either conventionally as output per labor hour (labor productivity) or alternatively as output per unit of combined private labor and private capital services (called total factor or multifactor productivity). Beginning sometime in the early 1970s—the specific date is much debated—productivity growth fell by some 1.4 percent per year. In the case of labor productivity, the drop was from 2.8 percent to a much lower 1.4 percent. This was clearly an important development. It meant that labor productivity would no longer double every twenty-six years; under the new trend we could only expect labor productivity to double once every fifty-one years. This implies that on a per capita basis, our future income must rise much more slowly, thereby generating a wide variety of concerns on issues such as the viability of our national social insurance programs and our national security.

Low productivity growth was reflected in a 3.3 percent decrease in the real average hourly wage between 1979 and 1987. Annual average wages and salaries only held up in this period because people were working 5.8 percent more hours per year. The typical worker in the factory, on the construction site, and behind the check-out counter increasingly feels the bite as wages fail to keep up with inflation.

Not only has productivity growth fallen over time in the United States, it has been low for the past three decades relative to our major international competitors. For example, from 1965 to 1985, Japan and West Germany achieved labor productivity growth rates in excess of 3 and 2 percent per year, respectively. One reflection of our low productivity growth, when coupled with persistently high consumption growth, is the yawning trade deficit and the switch, during the 1980s, from our nation's position as the world's largest creditor to the world's largest debtor.

A second dimension of poor economic performance which is related to low productivity growth is a *low profit rate.* During the 1970s and 1980s, the profit rate was depressed to a considerable amount below its level in the 1950s and 1960s—from about 11 percent to about 8 percent.

A third indicator of poor economic performance which is closely linked to the fall-off in the profit rate is a *low rate of net private investment.* For instance, the growth rate of the private capital stock (the value of capital assets) has been about 3 percent per year in recent years, down from about 4 percent in the 1950s and 1960s. Of course, there is much controversy about the validity of these facts as well as about their appropriate interpretation. For instance, some argue that no true productivity slowdown has occurred; instead, what we have in this regard is "a case of statistical myopia." Others, such as Martin Feldstein and Lawrence Summers, argue that there is really no long-term downtrend in the corporate profit rate. And there is much controversy about whether investment really has been depressed during the 1980s. Paul Craig Roberts, for example, chooses to emphasize gross, as opposed to net, investment rates, and gross investment has been relatively stable during recent years. Finally, it is necessary to be careful about interpreting movements in productivity, profit rates, and investment—or, for that matter, other variables such as the current account deficit—as indicators of economic *malaise.* The appropriate, or optimal, rates of national savings, investment, and productivity growth are inherently unobservable and may well be changing over time. It seems clear, nevertheless, that the economy has not been performing well of late and that the typical person in the street is rightly concerned about our long-term economic prospects. (See Michael Darby in For Further Reading.)

FALL-OFF IN PUBLIC INVESTMENT

The reasons for our low productivity growth, our low profit rate, and our low net investment rate—in general, our state of economic *malaise*—have so far resisted explanation by economists. Many obvious culprits have been brought to trial in the economics literature and, for one reason or another, all have been found largely innocent.

For example, the Bureau of Labor Statistics came to the conclusion that at most one-half of the total fall-off in productivity growth can be explained by obvious suspects such as oil price hikes during the 1970s, a decline in research and development spending after the mid-1960s, and mismeasurement of labor input.

This article brings another suspect before the bench: public infrastructure capital. What role did movements in the amount of public infrastructure capital play in the evolution of the macroeconomy over the past forty years?

To be potentially important for explaining shifts in the performance of the aggregate economy, the public capital stock must be large relative to the private capital stock, and it must display variable trends over time. Table 7.1 provides 1987 data on the levels of total, private, and public stocks of fixed reproducible capital. It can be seen that of the total physical capital stock of $6.5 trillion, $2.3 trillion (36 percent) is held by the public sector. For every $2 of private capital, there is $1 of public capital.

While military capital makes up the bulk of the federal capital stock, it only amounts to 7 percent of the nation's total (public and private) stock of capital. Nonmilitary capital accounts for 29 percent of the national stock of tangible capital. Finally, the stock of "core infrastructure capital" (streets and highways, water and sewer systems, mass transit, airports, and electrical and gas facilities) comprises nearly 20 percent of the nation's stock of physical capital. Moreover, because the elements of core infrastructure are intrinsic to almost every sector of private production, they are especially influential in the determination of total national economic output. Clearly, the public capital stock has sufficient magnitude to influence the behavior of the private economy in a meaningful way.

Table 7.1   Private and Public Capital Stock, 1987

Capital Stock	Billions of Dollars	Percent of Totals
Total	$6,487.3	100
Total Private	4,142.8	64
Nonfarm Business	3,974.6	61
Farm	168.2	3
Total Public	2,344.5	36
Military	457.7	7
Nonmilitary	1,886.8	29
Core Infrastructure	1,195.7	18
Education, Hospital, & Other Buildings	535.9	8
Conservation & Development	155.2	2

Source: Bureau of Economic Analysis.

Setting military spending to one side, the bulk of the public capital stock resides in the state and local government sector. For instance, in 1985 the total federal net stock of public capital, excluding military equipment and facilities, was $247.1 billion in 1985 dollars. But the state and local counterpart to this amount was $1,518.7 billion. Thus, the state-local component of total civilian public capital was roughly 86 percent (Bureau of Economic Analysis, 1987).

Not only is the public capital stock large, but it also has evolved in a marked pattern over the post-World War II period, as shown in Figure 1. The level of nonmilitary public investment generally rose during the 1950s and 1960s, reaching some 3.9 percent of GNP in the latter decade. It then fell during the 1970s and the early 1980s. While in recent years public investment has rebounded slightly, it remains far below levels attained during the mid-1960s. This striking pattern prevails for nearly all functional categories of public capital investment. Relative to output, the level of investment in core infrastructure peaked within a year of the peak in nonmilitary public capital spending, and it has risen only modestly in the last half-decade. Nonmilitary public investment minus spending on educational structures and highways displays similar trend behavior.

Note that the levels depicted in Figure 7.1 pertain to gross investment in nonmilitary capital; no deduction has been made for the physical wear and tear on the nation's total stock of public capital. Once the public stock is adjusted for depreciation, the negative trend becomes even more disturbing. As shown in Figure 7.2, by 1982 *net* public investment in core infrastructure had nearly ground to a halt in the United States, coming in at less than 0.5 percent of total output. This means that the United States was doing little more than replacing the existing public capital stock; almost nothing was

Figure 7.1

Trends in Public Investment Relative to GNP 1950 to 1987

SOURCE: Bureau of Economic Analysis

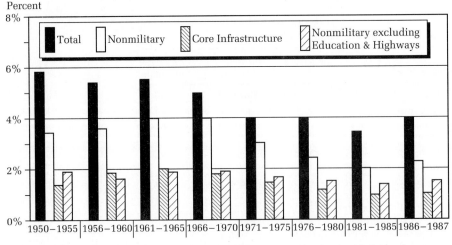

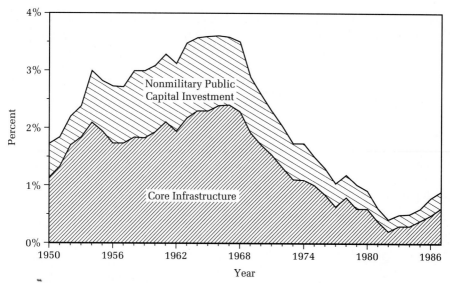

Figure 7.2
Net Public Investment Relative to GNP 1950 to 1987
SOURCE: Bureau of Economic Analysis

being added, despite the needs of the growing private economy.

This fall-off in public investment is reflected in a similar fall-off in the amount of infrastructure capital available to each worker in the economy. After climbing from around $8,500 per worker in 1950 to $15,000 per worker in the early 1970s, the public capital stock tumbled to some $13,000 per worker by the end of 1987.

At the same time, the dollar value of private plants and equipment per worker has continued to climb throughout the post-World War II period, from about $16,000 in 1950 to roughly $34,000 by the end of 1987. Thus, while the *private* sector has largely, though not completely, been doing its job in equipping workers with adequate tools and work environments, the public sector has been negligent in providing the appropriate amount of infrastructure, the necessary foundation to the private economy.

U.S. ECONOMY'S THIRD DEFICIT

It is common for economists to talk about the "twin deficits" of the 1980s: the federal government budget deficit; and the trade or current account deficit. But in a sense, the last decade has also witnessed a third deficit: a deficit in spending on vitally needed public works. Indeed, the fundamental thesis of this article is that this third deficit is central to some of our most important long-term economic difficulties: our declining private profit rate on machinery and structures; our overall failure to invest adequately in our future; and our sluggish growth in productive efficiency.

Recent empirical evidence indicates that the public capital stock is an important factor of production; the slowdown in public investment can help explain a significant portion of the slump in productivity growth in the past two decades. Historical statistical (time series) evidence for the post-World War II period in the United States demonstrates that the "core infrastructure" bears a substantially positive and statistically significant relationship to both labor productivity and multifactor productivity. (See Aschauer [1989a] in For Further Reading.) The core infrastructure category is the most statistically significant of the various categories of public capital. By these estimates, a one percent increase in the stock of infrastructure capital will raise productivity by 0.24 of one percent.

Figure 7.3 illustrates the close relationship estimated between total factor productivity and the nonmilitary public capital stock. To highlight the link between longer-term movements in total factor productivity and the public capital stock, the measures have been adjusted for business cycle effects.

The graph shows how that portion of total factor productivity which *cannot* be explained by technological progress (proxied by time) or by the state of the

business cycle (proxied by the capacity utilization rate) *can* be explained by movements in the public capital stock. One can see the close association between changes in productivity and public capital; indeed, the empirical estimates in my paper (1989a) suggest that of the total 1.4 percent annual fall-off in productivity growth during the 1970s and 1980s, fully 57 percent—or 0.8 percent per year—can be attributed to the downturn in public investment spending. The levels of productivity and public capital stock peaked in the late 1960s to the early 1970s and during the mid-1960s, respectively.

Certain refinements of my paper (1989a) by Munnell (1990) entailed adjusting the standard Bureau of Labor Statistics measure of labor input to account for changes in the age/sex composition of the labor force and updating the sample period to 1987. Munnell obtained strong parallel results on the importance of public capital in private sector production.

Figure 7.3
Public Capital and Productivity 1950 to 1985
SOURCE: Author's calculations.

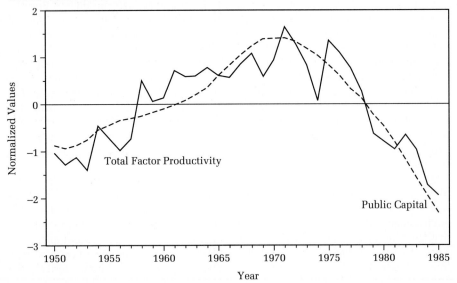

Munnell also computed adjusted measures of multifactor productivity growth, and found that after accounting for changes in the quality of the labor force and for changes in the growth rate of the core infrastructure capital stock, the falloff in multifactor productivity growth during the 1970s and 1980s relative to the 1950s and 1960s was "much more in line with expectations . . . [Much] of the drop in published multifactor productivity numbers may reflect the omission of public capital from the calculations of inputs rather than a decline in technological innovation." (See Munnell [1990] in For Further Reading.)

Of course, from a policy standpoint it would not be prudent to rest such strong conclusions solely on the basis of aggregate historical data from one country. It should be very instructive to examine cross-sectional evidence by comparing states, industries, or countries. In fact, additional empirical results buttressing the case for expanded public spending on infrastructure are available.

Analysis shows that public investment in streets, highways, and water and sewer systems is an important factor in explaining the variation in levels of productivity across states. Also, the level of such public spending is lower than would be chosen by optimizing governmental bodies. Indeed, the inefficiency of our existing allocation of investment resources is underlined by the finding that increases in GNP resulting from increased public infrastructure spending are estimated to exceed those from private investment by a factor of between two and five. This means that a shift from private to public investment would increase GNP substantially; it reflects the dearth of resources presently committed to infrastructure. Munnell estimates the sizes of state-area public capital stocks and finds that public infrastructure capital is an important factor of production determining the level of state-area productivity. The categories of public capital bearing the most importance for private productivity turn out to be streets and highways and water and sewer systems; other public capital facilities have little or no explanatory power in private sector output regressions. (See Aschauer [1991]; Munnell [1991] in For Further Reading.)

Further substantiation of these findings emerges in studies using comparative historical (pooled time series) data from national comparisons for the Group of Seven nations (Canada, France, Germany, Italy, Japan, Great Britain, and the United States) over the period 1965 to 1985. Upon controlling for private investment and employment growth, public nonmilitary investment bears a significantly positive relationship to growth in gross domestic product per employed person. This is a noteworthy result because a number of researchers have pointed out that the productivity slump was not a disease unique to the United States; on the contrary, it had epidemic-like proportions, affecting nearly all industrialized economies. The explanation for the productivity slowdown "is unlikely to lie in the special circumstances of a single country" (see Stanley Fischer in For Further Reading). In that regard, it is interesting to note that public investment spending as a share of gross domestic product fell during the late 1960s and early 1970s in five of the seven countries in the Group of Seven. Furthermore, the ratio of public investment to total government spending declined during this period in all the Group of Seven countries.

Clearly, the size of the public capital stock is an inescapable feature of the explanation for national productivity trends. This conclusion holds when considering the evolution over time of productivity in the United States; it holds when comparing disparate productivity levels in the states; and it holds when comparing the productivity performance of major industrial nations.

Furthermore, changes in the *public* capital stock may influence the marginal productivity of *private* factors of production. For example, a better transportation network would allow Federal Express to make better use of additional trucks and airplanes which, in turn, would raise profit rates on such private capital goods. Historical statistical analysis (aggregate time series) suggests that the rate of return to private capital in the nonfinancial corporate sector is positively affected by changes in the stock of public capital per worker. Data on manufacturing firms over the period 1970 to 1978 show similarly strong effects from public capital (highways, sewers, water facilities) as well as the total of these. In particular, there is evidence of a complementary relationship between public and private capital. In short, public capital is "profitable" because it boosts the returns to private capital. (See Kevin T. Deno in For Further Reading.)

PUBLIC CAPITAL PROMOTES PRIVATE GROWTH

The evidence appears to support overwhelmingly the proposal that investing in public infrastructure directly augments private sector production. Therefore, a valid case can be made for a significant increase in public investment spending. But what impact would an increase in public capital spending have on private investment? If the public investments merely displace private investments in plant and machinery—economists call this a complete "crowding out" of private capital accumulation—then national investment (private plus public) would be left unchanged and relatively minor productivity gains could be expected.

An increase in public investment can be expected to have two basic effects on private investment activity. One is the positive effect on the profitability or the rate of return to private capital. The theory of the firm suggests that firms will respond to heightened profit rates by expanding the pace of capital investment. But if we assume that the private sector profit rate remains constant, the second effect of greater public capital investment would be to reduce private investment as national investment (private plus public) is pushed beyond the level which optimizing agents would choose.

Historical data for the United States suggest that both types of effects may well be operative. More specifically, results indicate a nearly one-to-one "crowding out" of private by public investment (holding fixed the rate of return to private capital) as well as a "crowding in" of private by public investment—as the rate of return to capital responds over time to the increases in the public capital stock which are brought about by higher public investment. In the long run—in this case four or five years—the "crowding in" effect dominates and overall private investment is stimulated; *indeed, for every dollar increase in public investment, private investment rises by approximately 45 cents.*

SIMULATION DATA

It is instructive to bring together some of these empirical results to consider how large an effect public investment has on crucial dimensions of economic performance: investment, profits, and productivity. This is accomplished by utilizing empirical estimates to construct a minimal model capable of simulating the effect of higher public investment on the aggregate economy. The increase in public investment hypothesized for the purpose of the simulation is consistent with what the United States would have experienced if the actual historical rate of public investment from roughly 1950 to 1970 had held up for the following two decades, rather than falling off as it did.

The simulation exercise conducted below depicts an increase in the level of public nonmilitary investment by one percent of the private capital stock during the period from 1970 to 1986, an amount 125 percent greater than the actual level of public investment in this time period, so that the rate of public investment since 1970 is comparable to that of the 1950s and 1960s.

The actual data document that between 1970 and 1988, inferior economic performance was experienced relative to the 1953-1969 period, along with a lower rate of return to private capital (7.9 percent as opposed to 10.7 percent), lower private investment (3.1 percent of the private capital stock rather than 3.8 percent), and lower labor productivity growth (1.4 percent per annum as opposed to 2.8 percent).

The simulation data also reveal relationships between public nonmilitary investment, private profitability, private investment, and private sector productivity growth. In the first five years of the hypothetical expansion in public investment, the rate of return to capital rises by 2 percentage points over its actual level, remaining at its 1953-1969 level of 10.7 percent instead of falling to 8.7 percent. This is due to the cumulative positive effect of the rising public capital stock on the productivity of private capital. During the same period, the private investment rate averages 3.9 percent of the private capital stock, the same as in the actual data. This reflects two offsetting forces: In the first three years of the higher public investment, private investment is pushed lower due to the direct crowding out effect of higher public investment, while in the next two years private investment is brought above its historical level by the higher rate of return to private capital. In the same period, private sector productivity growth is enhanced by 1.5 to 1.9 percent per year. As the private investment rate (as a percent of the

capital stock) is seen to remain steady, this enhancement of productivity growth reflects the direct, positive effect of a growing public capital stock on the productivity of labor.

In the later years of increased public investment, the simulation results show that the rate of return to private capital could have held up to between one and two percentage points more than the historical levels. At the same time, productivity growth would then rise by a more substantial amount (nearly one percent per year above historical values) because the direct effect of growth in the public capital stock is augmented by the indirect effect of a higher return to capital, raising private investment which, in turn, stimulates productivity growth.

On the whole, the simulation exercise suggests the possibility that the performance of the economy might have been greatly improved by an increased investment in public facilities. Comparing the 1970-1988 period to the 1953-1969 period, the rate of return to private capital could have been only 1.1 percentage points lower (instead of 2.8 percentage points); private investment could have been only 0.1 percentage points lower (rather than 0.7 percentage points lower); and annual productivity growth could have been 0.7 percent per year lower (instead of 1.4 percent lower).

PRESENT POLICY

President George Bush, Secretary of Transportation Samuel Skinner, Budget Director Richard Darman, and Council of Economic Advisers Chairman Michael Boskin are all well aware of these arguments for the importance of a sound infrastructure to our economic vitality. In his introduction to Secretary Skinner's recent report on the nation's transportation needs, President Bush said that "our competitive success in the global economy depends [on preparing] our transportation system to meet the needs of the 21st Century." Similarly, in the President's proposed Fiscal 1991 Budget, Richard Darman wrote that "it is intuitively apparent that some public investments—particularly those of infrastructure such as streets, highways, airports, and water and sewer systems—provide direct productive services and are complementary with private capital. Comparisons over time and across countries seem to indicate that some relationship may exist between additions to such capital and growth." In the 1990 *Economic Report of the President,* Michael Boskin asserted that "inadequate government infrastructure can impede improvements in productivity growth" and that "taking advantage of productive opportunities to maintain and improve the infrastructure is an important part of federal, state, and local government policies to raise economic growth."

These sentiments notwithstanding, the Administration's FY 1991 budget involved a level of spending on nonmilitary equipment and structures, relative to total output, 26 percent below the 1960 level and 24 percent below the 1980 level. Grants to state and local governments for physical investment purposes, relative to total output, were 40 percent under the 1960 level and 43 percent below the level in 1980. Likewise, the level of total federal investment (in physical capital, as well as in research and development, and education) lay 33 percent below its 1960 level and 10 percent under its 1980 level.

Of course, it is highly unlikely that the mix and level of public investment spending which was chosen over the past forty years will be preferred in the future. Even if, for instance, it were established beyond a shadow of doubt that the Interstate Highway System was a key determinant of productivity growth in the 1960s and 1970s, such a discovery would not necessarily imply that a similar effect

on productivity would be obtained from the construction of another 40,000 miles of controlled access highways. We live in a dynamic economy which changes constantly in response to technological progress, foreign competitive pressures, and alterations in the demographic characteristics of the domestic workforce. In the future, infrastructure needs may well shift from surface to air transportation, from the transport of goods to that of ideas, and from a national to an international focus. Potentially large efficiency gains are best to be expected, therefore, from improved air and seaport facilities and from telecommunications networking, among other things.

The evidence surveyed in this article, along with the related simulation results, suggest that the neglect of the quality and quantity of our nation's infrastructure facilities will act as a severe drag on our overall economic performance. Unless we address our public capital needs immediately, we can expect a continuation of lackluster productivity growth, low profit rates on the existing private capital stock, stagnant real wages, and sluggish private net investment.

The United States should directly augment its public capital stock through a stepped-up rate of infrastructure investment. Following this course will help equip the nation to compete effectively in the international arena and, at a minimum, it offers some hope for a partial reversal of our sliding economic fortunes.

FOR FURTHER READING

KENNETH J. ARROW AND MORDECAI KURZ, *Public Investment, the Rate of Return, and Optimal Fiscal Policy,* Johns Hopkins Press, Baltimore, 1970.

DAVID A. ASHAUER, "Is Public Expenditure Productive?" *Journal of Monetary Economics,* Vol. 23, 1989a.

———, "Public Investment and Productivity Growth in the Group of Seven,"

Economic Perspectives, Vol. 13, No. 5, 1989b.

——, "Why Is Infrastructure Important?" in *The Third Deficit: The Shortfall in Public Capital Investment,* Federal Reserve Bank of Boston, Conference Series, No. 34, 1991 (forthcoming).

DAVID A. ASHAUER AND JEREMY GREENWOOD, "Macroeconomic Effects of Fiscal Policy," in Karl Brunner and Allan H. Meltzer, eds., *The "New Monetary Economics," Fiscal Issues and Unemployment,* North-Holland, Amsterdam, 1985.

MICHAEL R. DARBY, "The U.S. Productivity Slowdown: A Case of Statistical Myopia?" *American Economic Review,* Vol. 74, 1984.

KEVIN T. DENO, "The Effect of Public Capital on U.S. Manufacturing Activity: 1970 to 1978," *Southern Economic Journal,* Vol. 55, No. 2, 1988.

STANLEY FISCHER, "Symposium on the Slowdown in Productivity Growth," *Journal of Economic Perspectives,* Vol. 2, No. 4, 1988.

LAWRENCE MISHEL AND DAVID M. FRANKEL, *The State of Working America, 1990–91 Edition,* Economic Policy Institute, Washington, D.C., 1991.

ALICIA H. MUNNELL, "Why Has Productivity Growth Declined?" *New England Economic Review,* January/February, 1990.

——, "How Does Public Infrastructure Affect Regional Economic Performance?" in *The Third Deficit: The Shortfall in Public Capital Investment,* Federal Reserve Bank of Boston, Conference Series, No. 34, 1991 (forthcoming).

8.   America's Great U-Turn

Barry Bluestone and Bennett Harrison

In the 1970s and eighties, America began making a U-turn from the path of higher wages and greater equality in earnings and family incomes to lower wages and to income inequality that rivals that of the Great Depression era.

During this U-turn, average wages stagnated or actually declined; the low-wage share of the total employment pie expanded, particularly among workers who work year-round and full-time; and earnings became more polarized—more low-wage jobs, paying $12,000 or less in today's dollars; more high-wage jobs, paying $48,000 or more; and a shrinking middle.

America was certainly creating more than just hamburger flippers and security guards, but nearly three out of five, or 58 percent, of the new jobs created between 1979 and 1984 paid $7,400 or less a year (in 1984 dollars). In contrast, less than one in five of the additional jobs generated between 1963 and 1979 had paid such low wages.

Many critics suggested that the wage trends we forecast would not stand the test of time, particularly as the post-1982 economic recovery continued into its fifth and sixth years. We now have additional data, which have persuaded even some of the most skeptical observers to admit that the trends have still not reversed: In both 1987 and 1988, real average weekly earnings continued to decline, maintaining a trend that began in 1973. In fact, by 1988, inflation adjusted weekly earnings were lower than at any time since 1960. Further, wage inequality went up in 1986 and again in 1987.

SOURCE: Reprinted with permission from *New Perspectives Quarterly,* vol. 6, no. 3, Fall 1989, pp. 35–37.

For families, real median income rose slightly in 1987, but just enough to finally return to its 1973 level. At the same time, however, family income was continuing to become more unequally distributed, setting for the fifth year in a row a new post-World War II record for inequality: In 1986, the average annual income of the poorest fifth of all families was $8,033—more than $1,740 less than they would have received had their share of national income remained the same as in 1968. By contrast, the wealthiest fifth of all families were the prime beneficiaries of growing inequality. By 1986, they were receiving nearly $5,600 more per year (on top of an average $71,700 income) than they would have received under the 1968 distribution.

Our findings on family income were confirmed in a detailed study carefully prepared by the House Ways and Means Committee of the US Congress and released in 1988. According to the Ways and Means study, from 1979 to 1987, the standard of living for the poorest fifth of the population fell by nine percent, despite a growing economy during the last five years of the period. The living standard of the top fifth rose by 19 percent. The Committee report reflects author Tom Wolfe's theme in *Bonfire of the Vanities:* The Upper West Side vs. the South Bronx is becoming the metaphor for where America is going.

MAPPING AMERICA'S U-TURN

There are several different theories as to what caused the growth in low-wage job creation and in overall wage inequality, but the most convincing evidence points to a complex of factors that include stagnation, deindustrialization, deunionization, growing education differentials, and growing global competition.

The stagnation hypothesis argues that what happened during the 1970s and continued into the eighties was stagnation in productivity. There is no doubt that productivity declined during the 1970s, and, while there has been some recovery in manufacturing, overall productivity increases have been weak in the eighties. In the long run, the level of real wages must reflect the level of productivity. If there is stagnation in productivity, there will be stagnation in wages.

The premise of the deindustrialization theory is that the U-turns in real wages and wage dispersion can be explained by the shift in the economy from manufacturing to services. Accordingly, the displacement of workers from the manufacturing sector and the restructuring of the wage bargain within industry has resulted in the destruction of a disproportionate number of higher wage jobs. In their place, the service and retail trade sectors of the economy have generated millions of new jobs but these tend to be associated with a polarized earnings distribution, with more low-wage employment being created than high-wage positions.

Deunionization, as well as the declining value of the minimum wage are also important factors in explaining the U-turns in wages and wage inequality.

In addition to these factors, educational differentials have also played a key role in the growth of the wage gap. We have found that the degree of wage erosion over time—measured as the ratio of mean real annual earnings in 1987 to those in 1973—is directly related to the level of schooling completed. By 1987, the real average wage for workers who did not complete high school had dropped to 77 percent of its 1973 value and for those with a high school degree, 89 percent. Only those with education beyond the high school diploma have

been able to maintain their real mean earnings—at 97 percent of their 1973 value.

SHORT-SIGHTED SOLUTIONS

Some argue that the American U-turn in wages and equality is the price we must pay for creating enough jobs to put the baby-boom generation, and the benefactors of the women's movement, to work. We don't agree. We believe that, in addition to the factors already mentioned, the recent stagnation of American incomes and the rise of inequality originated in the growth of global competition and, more specifically, in a distinctive array of "lean and mean" business strategies adopted by American corporate managers to cope with the ensuing decline in corporate profitability.

As foreign competition intensified toward the end of the Vietnam era, and as workers and communities continued to bid for better working and environmental conditions, the leaders of American industry inevitably faced a crucial strategic choice. They could attempt to relieve the squeeze on profits through a short-term fix, by attacking labor costs and regulation, or they could join in the difficult and largely uncharted search for new forms of organization, new product development, and new relationships with civil society that might restore long-term productivity growth and rebuild the competitive position of American goods and services.

Unfortunately, the path many corporate strategists chose in order to cope with international competition during the late 1970s and throughout the eighties was the "lean and mean" approach.

Profit rates—net after tax rate of return on all private, non-financial corporations—which had been falling since the middle of the 1960s, rebounded strongly after the 1981-82 recession. But the cost to America of pursuing this particular set of strategies was immense: average wages fell, low-wage employment increased, and earnings and incomes polarized.

If we had had more rapid productivity growth, if we had remained more competitive in terms of international markets, we would have been able to expand our market share, both in manufacturing and to a lesser extent in services, so that higher wages would have been possible.

REGAINING THE COMPETITIVE EDGE

What continues to be troubling is that the "lean and mean" strategies adopted by business have rebuilt profits, but not necessarily the competitiveness of the US economy. Productivity in the manufacturing sector is somewhat higher today than it was during the 1970s, but this gain was accomplished more by reducing the work force and lopping off older capacity than by making significant new investments in advanced technology: Total employment in the manufacturing sector was reduced by nearly two million workers between 1979 and 1987.

Europe, in general, has followed a different wage and employment policy than the US. Americans have emphasized job creation at the apparent cost of stagnating living standards, while the Europeans have chosen a higher productivity, higher wage road and have accepted higher unemployment rates if necessary. Essentially, the Europeans have main-

tained higher wages in both manufacturing and services. As a consequence, they have introduced more capital into their production processes, driving up productivity but also unemployment. The Japanese, on the other hand, appear to have been able to achieve both wage growth and full employment, based on their strong export performance.

During the 1990s, America can decide to choose either of two paths back to global competitiveness. The low road is based on low wages and is basically the strategy we have followed for the past 15 years. We can attempt to compete in the world on South Korea's and Mexico's terms—low wages for less skilled workers. This may help us a bit in the short run, but as other countries gain "newly industrialized country" status, we will be forced to constantly maintain low wages to meet the challenge of even "newer" low-wage competitors.

The alternative is the high road of a technology and education-led competitive strategy. We must work not cheaper, but smarter, with smarter machines. The high road suggests that as a nation we must undertake enormous new investments in science and technology, in applied research and development efforts, in new capital formation, in education, training and retraining, and in new forms of labor-management practices that foster economic democracy and teamwork. If we are successful, we shall be able to reverse the tragic U-turns we have taken since the early 1970s.

9.   The Case for Manufacturing in America's Future

Rudiger W. Dornbusch, James Poterba, and Lawrence H. Summers

MANUFACTURING

Spurring Technical Progress

The manufacturing sector is crucial to technical innovation. (See Table 9.1.)

While manufacturing accounts for about one-fifth of annual gross domestic product, it performs 95 percent of private research and development. Manufacturing firms spend an average of nine percent of their revenues on research and development, compared to less than one-tenth of one percent for non-manufacturing firms.

Investment in technology has contributed to higher productivity in manufacturing. The productivity growth rate for manufacturing has averaged 3.5 percent since 1970, while non-manufacturing has managed only a 0.3 percent growth rate.

America's performance in world markets depends upon the technological innovation of manufacturing companies.

Better Wages

Men and women in manufacturing consistently earn greater than 20 percent more than those employed in non-manufacturing jobs, and nearly 30 percent more than employees in the service sector. (See Table 9.2.)

Manufacturing firms pay employees better for several key reasons. First, the integrated nature of production puts a premium on a stable and motivated

SOURCE: Eastman Kodak Company, Communications & Public Affairs, 343 State Street, Rochester, NY 14650.

workforce—a workforce maintained by top pay and benefits. Second, advanced skills are required in many manufacturing jobs, justifying higher wages. Third, greater productivity in manufacturing may enable firms to pay more.

High-wage jobs and a higher standard of living are more likely to result from expansion of the manufacturing sector than from expansion of other sectors.

Driving Overall Growth

Manufacturing is a powerful source of demand for the output of other industries. In 1986, manufacturing directly contributed over one-fifth of America's gross national product, yet shipments by manufacturing companies equaled almost 60 percent of the GNP. The difference, equaling nearly 40 percent of the GNP, reveals the extent of manufacturing's purchases from other sectors of the economy. (See Table 9.3.)

Ironically, many services that are featured in "post-industrial economy" scenarios depend on the demand created by manufacturing. Education, banking and communications are among the services for which manufacturing provides a significant portion of the demand.

Unemployment rates offer another striking example of manufacturing's tight bond to the overall economy. A rise in manufacturing unemployment of one percentage point results in unemployment increases of 3.2 percent in construction, 2.4 percent in service and 1.5 percent in retail trade. When manufacturing suffers, so does the rest of the economy.

Table 9.1   The Importance of Manufacturing to Research & Development

	Manufacturing	Non-Manufacturing
R&D Expenditures ($ billion, 1984)	69.0	2.6
R&D/Employee ($ thousands, 1984)	3.610	.035

Source: National Science Foundation, Bureau of Labor Statistics.

Dramatic Impact of Changes in the U.S. Economy

The peaks and troughs of American business cycles are amplified in the manufacturing sector. During expansions, manufacturing output increases about 26 percent, while non-manufacturing output increases just 16 percent. During downturns, manufacturing output typically declines about 7 percent, compared to a 1 percent decline for non-manufacturing. (See Table 9.4.)

Manufacturing also bears the brunt of trade imbalances created by economic policies. Manufacturing trade dwarfs trade in services. Thus, the trade deficits in recent years are accounted for almost entirely by a shift in the manufacturing trade balance.

Fluctuations in defense spending also dramatically affect manufacturing. The U.S. defense build-up has greatly helped many manufacturing firms. Nearly 60 percent of all private jobs generated by defense spending are in manufacturing firms. Between 1980 and 1986, when manufacturing jobs shrank by 1.29 million, defense-related jobs actually increased by .74 million. Without this build-up, manufacturing employment in 1987 would have been at its lowest level since 1965. While future levels of defense spending are not established, it seems clear that the major jobs stimulus of increased defense spending has passed. Thus, alternatives for growth in manufacturing jobs will need to be created.

How Does the U.S. Compare?

American manufacturers in many industrial sectors have lost market share at home and in export markets. While manufacturing in many other countries has enjoyed substantial growth, the manufacturing contribution to the U.S. economy has been stagnant and U.S. manufacturing jobs have declined. (See Table 9.5.)

The loss of markets is clearly seen in the world trade picture. In a recent 15-year period, U.S. exports grew at an an-

Table 9.2   Hourly Compensation in Manufacturing and Other Sectors
(1986 $ per Hour)

	Manufacturing	Services	Trade	Total Non-Manufacturing
1950–86	$12.26	8.47	9.72	8.85
1987 (March)	$14.79	11.73	9.51	12.08

Source: Department of Commerce, Bureau of Labor Statistics.

Table 9.3   Spillover Effects of Manufacturing Unemployment

Sector	Increase in Sector Unemployment Rate from One Point of Manufacturing Unemployment
Construction	3.2
Wholesale Trade	1.4
Retail Trade	1.5
Finance, Insurance, Real Estate	0.7
Services	2.4
Professional	−0.1
Government	1.0
Weighted Sum	2.0

Source: Kevin J. Murphy and Robert Topel, "Unemployment in the United States," in *NBER Macroeconomics Manual, 1987.* Stanley Fischer, ed.

nual rate three percent below that of other industrialized nations. Over such an extended period, that difference becomes substantial. Electronic goods offer a typical example of the declines. Between 1979 and 1985, the U.S. share of exports dropped by 6.3 percent in electronic parts, 4.3 percent in automatic processing equipment and 2.8 percent in business electronics, figures that translate into billions of dollars of lost business.

The relative decline of U.S. manufacturing is due in part to a lower rate of manufacturing productivity than other nations. Between 1960 and 1979, U.S.

Table 9.4   Percentage Change in Output, Manufacturing and Non-Manufacturing

	Manufacturing	Non-Manufacturing
Economic Upturns:		
1954 to 1957	12.1%	8.6%
1958 to 1960	11.6%	7.3%
1961 to 1969	58.1%	37.8%
1970 to 1973	22.6%	10.5%
1975 to 1980	21.5%	16.4%
1982 to 1986	28.0%	15.8%
Economic Downturns:		
1953 to 1954	7.3%	0.3%
1957 to 1958	− 8.7%	1.6%
1960 to 1961	0.2%	3.2%
1969 to 1970	− 5.6%	1.2%
1973 to 1975	−11.9%	1.3%
1981 to 1982	− 6.1%	− 1.5%

Source: Commerce Department. Turning point years based on National Bureau of Economic Research dating of business cycle.

Table 9.5 Volume of Manufacturer's Exports
(Index 1980 = 100)

	1970	1980	1986	Avg. Growth Rate 1970–86 (%)
U.S.	49	100	81	3.2
Japan	39	100	142	8.4
Europe	56	100	124	5.0
Developing Countries	30	100	184	12.0
World Exports	51	100	129	6.0

Source: United Nations.

productivity grew at one-third the rate in Japan. Lower productivity growth hampers cost competitiveness and facilitates greater market penetration by foreign producers. A particularly startling example is provided by the capital goods market, where imports today account for nearly 40 percent of the U.S. market, versus 14 percent as recently as 1980.

If the U.S. continues to yield markets abroad and our own markets to foreign suppliers, the country's standard of living will markedly decline. The notion that this decline is inevitable or desirable must be firmly rejected.

SUMMARY

Recommendations for a Healthy Economic Future

The primary reason for the difficulties of American manufacturers is national economic policies that have given rise to huge budget and trade deficits, favored consumption over saving and investment and been insufficiently sensitive to the need for free markets at home and abroad. Following are policy recommendations for each of these areas.

Fiscal Policy *Reduce federal deficits* Federal deficit reduction should be the overriding priority of national economic policy. Over two-thirds of private saving in recent years has been absorbed by these deficits. Low national saving reduces the supply and increases the cost of capital, choking off investment needed to increase productivity in manufacturing. Reducing federal deficits will require spending cuts and tax increases. Cuts must be considered in all areas of the budget.

Encourage savings and investment Structural tax policies should be redirected towards the goals of promoting saving and investment rather than consumption. A crucial long-run policy priority is finding ways to raise the anemic American private saving rate.

Structural Trade Policies *Stop the trend toward protectionism* U.S. restrictions on trade are increasing faster than those of any other industrialized country—and at a time when such restrictions are most damaging. While an individual firm or industrial sector competing against imports may temporarily benefit from protectionism, manufacturing and the economy in general suffer. For its temporary benefits, protectionism is very expensive, since costs increase for intermediate goods required by manufacturers and for goods sold to consumers. Further, retaliation is likely and foreign markets may close to successful exporters. Even without retaliation, protectionism would strengthen the dollar and hurt exports.

Realize the opportunities of newly industrialized countries (NICs) U.S. manufacturing must realize the opportunities of, rather than seek protection from, the growing role of NICs as competitive production centers. The U.S. must consider bilateral free trade agreements with major NICs like Mexico, Brazil, and Korea, where large but mostly protected new markets are emerging. This approach would put the U.S. ahead of Japanese firms who are now entering these markets, offset the increasingly inward focus of the European market, and offer more leeway in convincing the developing countries that trade is a two-way street.

Remain open to direct foreign investment in the U.S. An outward-looking manufacturing sector must hold an open view of foreign investment in the U.S. Foreign investment means competition for managers, but it also means good jobs and increased manufacturing activity. Foreign investment is likely to benefit the economy, even though in some cases it might hurt entrenched American firms.

Exchange Rate Policy *Efforts to stabilize exchange rates at current levels are misguided* They run very serious risks of throwing the economy into recession and making an eventual financial collapse more likely. American monetary policy should be directed at insuring continued economic growth as the budget deficit declines, not at arbitrary exchange rate targets. Policy-makers should take a "hands-off" approach, recognizing that a continued dollar decline is both likely and desirable to allow the economy to make a "soft landing."

Rapid growth in the world economy and the expanding markets that it brings about are crucial to the health of the manufacturing sector Easing monetary policy to sustain growth in the face of budget cuts assures that part of the adjustment takes place via dollar depreciation and net exports. Other nations should be encouraged to stimulate their domestic demand, instead of relying on exports to the U.S. for growth.

CHAPTER 4
U.S./Japanese Economic Relations

The theme of this chapter is economic conflict between the United States and Japan. The first article is excerpted from the best-selling book, *The Japan That Can Say No*. Shintara Ishihara, a member of the Japanese Diet, argues that Japan should be responsible for its own defense. He holds out the threat that Japan could alter the balance of military power by refusing to sell critical microchip technology to the United States. He also claims that America is a land of low savings rates, a poor educational system, and an ill-trained work force.

The next article, by Clyde Prestowitz, is excerpted from another best-selling book, *Trading Places: How We Allowed Japan to Take the Lead*. Prestowitz claims that much of Japan's economic success is due to "buy Japan" government purchasing policies, industrial cartels, a technically oriented education system, government-business cooperation, infant industry protection, and an emphasis on the needs of producers.

The following article, "Japan and the United States in the New World Economy," is by C. Fred Bergsten, Director of the Institute for International Economics. Bergsten argues that the 1990s are witnessing three global transformations of historic importance: the end of the Cold War, the reduced significance of international security issues, and the movement toward a tripolar world economy. He warns that a U.S.-European coalition against Japan, or a U.S.-Japanese coalition against Europe, or a European-Japanese coalition against the United States "would be extremely destabilizing for both global politics and economic affairs." He calls on "The Big Three" to create a new international monetary regime to replace Bretton Woods, and to push for trade liberalization within GATT.

The final article in this chapter is a report by the U.S. Special Trade Representative regarding the Structural Impediments Initiative Agreement with Japan. This compact commits the United States and Japan to "structural" changes to balance their bilateral trade account. Japan pledged to increase spending on infrastructure, to rationalize land use, and to reduce exclusionary business practices. The United States pledged to reduce the federal budget deficit, to promote private savings, and to improve the quality of its work force.

10.   A Japan That Can Say No

Shintaro Ishihara

Thirty years have passed since the renewal of the US-Japan Security Treaty. Now it's time for a change.

The *raison d'etre* of the Treaty—that Japan would provide the front line of defense for the American-led postwar order in Asia against expanding communism—has collapsed.

Consequently, the US-Japan Security Treaty is gradually losing its significance and will eventually become totally obsolete.

Although it would be hasty, even careless, at this time to call for the abolition of the treaty, it should be dramatically changed from a one-sided arrangement that supports only the US strategic objectives to one that enables Japan to provide for its own defense and pursue its own interests.

Despite the illusory protection of Japan by the strategic US nuclear umbrella, Japan cannot tactically defend itself under the present terms of the treaty—as even Germany can do as a member of the NATO Alliance.

As top ranking officials of the Japan Defense Agency continually point out, only one division of the US forces stationed in Japan is devoted to the defense of Japanese territory. The rest are assigned to a strategic mission that encompasses the defense of an area West of Hawaii all the way to Capetown, South Africa—in other words, half the world! Why is it in the interest of Japan to defend Australia or New Zealand and the whole Southern Hemisphere? I don't really think that the Japanese people are very interested in defending Africa.

Although we have spent much money revamping our maritime self-defense force, it comprises just a single division of the American Seventh Fleet under whose command it is integrated. It functions only to monitor submarines in the seas around Japan, not as a means of defending Japanese territory.

The situation is similar with respect to ground forces. The northern-most island of the Japanese archipelago, Hokkaido, is the first most likely place for an invasion of Japanese territory. Yet, there is not a single American soldier stationed on this island.

From the Japanese standpoint, one is obliged to ask two questions about these ridiculous arrangements: Aside from the US strategic agenda, why are American forces stationed in Japan if not for the defense of Japan? And, if they are not defending Japan, why are we constantly being pressured by the US to pay more for them?

Answers to the first question can readily be found in Pentagon planning documents, where the Soviet Union is listed as enemy number one, China as enemy number two and Japan as enemy number three. Recently, a commander of the US Marine Corps, in testimony before the US Congress, frankly admitted that the reason US troops are in Japan is to ensure that we cannot enhance our military capabilities and once again become a major military power.

Yet, we are expected to foot the bill so America will, supposedly, save us from ourselves. Already, Japan is shouldering 40 percent of the necessary expenses of maintaining American forces stationed here. This amounts to about eight million yen per soldier, or the average annual pay of a typical *salaryman,* as the price we

SOURCE: Reprinted with permission from *New Perspectives Quarterly,* vol. 7, no. 3, Summer 1990, pp. 10–13.

must pay for forces not directly defending Japan.

Talk of Japan's enjoying a "free ride" of military protection at the expense of the US taxpayer is thus obviously unfounded. We in Japan are really fed up with such nonsense. As it is, the Japanese are prohibited from using either their brains or their hands to defend their homeland.

It is time for this to change. While staying well within the constraints of the Japanese Constitution—both its one percent of GNP cap on military spending and its restriction against offensive weapons—Japan can reorganize its forces under the terms of the Treaty so that we are tactically capable of defending our territory by ourselves.

First, we could defend our own coastline with high-speed cruisers that possess ship-to-air missiles: We must be able to close Japan's three most vital sea straits in the event of foreign attack. Secondly, we need our own jet fighter, the FSX. Thirdly, we can dispense with the ridiculously out-of-place tank defense of an island nation that is mainly mountainous and forested.

Additionally, we should seek the return of at least one of the three large US air bases on the outskirts of Tokyo. The Yakota Air Base, in particular, is not used to any great extent, while the air control situation around Tokyo is dangerous due to very heavy congestion at both Narita and Haneda airports. If I were prime minister of Japan, or governor of the Tokyo metropolitan government, I would demand the return of Yakota immediately. We need it desperately and the US hardly uses it.

I do not oppose cooperation with the US and even the maintenance of US forces on Japanese soil. To the extent they help defend Japan, our own forces must be capable of defending the US bases from attack. But, to the extent the strategic mission of US forces is beyond direct Japanese interests, they should not be based here rent free.

By reconfiguring our forces in this way, we can improve Japan's defense fourfold while remaining within the one percent of GNP constraint. It would not go unnoticed, of course, that because of the size of Japan's GNP our nation would then have the third largest expenditures for defense after the USSR and the US.

The importance of the size of Japanese military spending, however, should not be exaggerated. At the end of the 20th century, civilization is entering a new era where economic and technological might outweighs the importance of military power.

Japan is the nation most strongly positioned to play a major role in this new era, especially with our mass-production capabilities in semiconductors. Indeed, as the Pentagon's own Very High Speed Integrated Circuit Committee Report of 1986 made alarmingly clear, the weaponry upon which the US world strategy relies already depends fundamentally on Japanese mass production of high-quality semiconductors.

It is precisely this vital technological role that gives us the leverage that will allow us to chart an independent course in which Japan designs its own contribution to the world order.

For example, the US will not allow the sale of reconnaissance satellites to Japan. Yet, without reconnaissance satellites of our own, how can we obtain the information that will allow us to independently and accurately assess not only military threats, but also the ecological and development problems that we are called upon to help alleviate? Under present arrangements, if a developing country wants aid from Japan, they must first go to Washington for approval—then Washington calls on us. Japan is not willing to continue such stupid efforts. Our money just disappears down a hole with no measurable effect.

I think it is time for Japan to consider the possibility of playing our microchip card in order to bring the US to its senses over arrogantly and arbitrarily constraining our capacity for initiative in the world.

Japan's technological prowess, however, is not only a negative lever, but also a positive asset. In fact, it is the basis for the global ideal of the "dynamics of Japanese aid," which I believe can be Japan's chief contribution to the new international order.

Information and resource-efficient technologies are central to modernizing the developing world. More than anything else, these countries need an information and renewable-energy infrastructure if they are not going to be left out of the 21st century.

In all these areas—from consumer electronics such as VCRs and TVs to the most sophisticated microchip, optical fibers and flat display, to solar batteries—Japan has the most advanced technologies. Since all of these technologies were developed commercially rather than for military purposes, they are both cost efficient and nonthreatening. Other countries may be able to provide the infrastructure of the past, such as highways, railroads and huge power stations, but only Japan can mass produce the communications and energy infrastructure of the new age at a low cost.

The "dynamics of Japanese aid" could make an even more powerful contribution to countries with a higher level of skills and education, such as Hungary or Czechoslovakia. I am convinced that if a concerted multilateral effort supported this idea of Japanese-style aid, we could turn those two countries around within five years. And, no doubt, Great Britain and France would welcome our efforts, since they would provide a counterweight to German economic domination of Eastern Europe.

Thirty years after the signing of US-Japan Security Treaty, which subordinated Japan to the strategic objectives of the US, Japan is capable of going its own way. We are capable of devising a global strategy and should do so.

A Japan that can say no to US orders is a Japan that has recovered its full sovereignty, just like any other nation.

11.   Japanese vs. Western Economics
Why Each Side Is a Mystery to the Other

Clyde Prestowitz

Under great pressure from the United States as a result of rising trade frictions, in 1981 Nippon Telegraph and Telephone (NTT), the Japanese telecommunication company, agreed to open its annual procurement of $6 billion to foreign bidders. However, NTT's chairman at the time maintained that the only thing his company could buy from foreign firms would be buckets, mops, and telephone poles. Indeed, in the next two years, the firm purchased only about $30 million of U.S. goods, mostly in the bucket-and-mop category. In 1983, again under pressure from the United States, NTT finally decided to buy something significant from a U.S. manufacturer. Thus, on July 23 a delegation from the company arrived at Hughes Aerospace Corp. in El Segundo, Calif. Its stated mission was to buy software.

The Japanese and U.S. accounts of this meeting differ as night and day. As counselor to Secretary of Commerce Malcolm Baldrige, I received an irate telephone call from a Hughes executive that evening. Did I know, he asked, that the Japanese group, which the U.S. government had encouraged him to receive, was trying to obtain the technology for constructing its own telecommunications satellite? No, I responded, I understood they were looking for software. "Well," said the executive, "they described the software and it essentially involves teaching them how to build a satellite." Furthermore, he said, "We know they're in the market for a satellite, and when we asked if we could bid, they told us that they couldn't buy an American satellite because it is Japanese government policy to develop one of their own."

NTT later expressed surprise at Hughes's reaction, maintaining that it was interested only in software that would make satellites work better.

Whatever the truth of the situation, the subsequent facts are not in doubt. News of the meeting sent a shock wave through Washington. The U.S. government immediately asked the Japanese government to explain its policy. If, in fact, NTT could not buy a satellite, all the praise the government had earlier heaped on Japan for opening its telecommunications market would be shown to have been misplaced. More important, the incident would support the belief of many Americans that Japan's important markets remain closed because its leaders target certain industries for development.

After several months of crashing silence, the Japanese finally admitted that they did have an "infant industry" policy

aimed at promoting indigenous satellite production. Long, hard negotiations ensued, at the end of which Japan agreed to buy two U.S. satellites. But the most interesting aspect of the talks was that despite the obvious contradiction with free-trade doctrine, Japan did not abandon its infant-industry policy. All government users of satellites had to continue to buy Japanese, and other users were directed to "consider the national interest" in their purchases.

These events exemplify some of the strategies that the Japanese have used to gain a foothold in many key industries. The basis of these strategies was spelled out in 1983, when MITI officials told U.S. negotiators that in key technologies the government must intervene to make its firms competitive, thereby assuring the security of the country's economy. Nor are the Japanese policies limited to encouraging new industries. Companies beset by the problems common to mature industries are often directed to set certain production levels and to engage in joint buying, marketing, and stockpiling.

Many U.S. commentators deny the efficacy of these policies and argue that the Japanese simply do the things that create business success better than Americans or other Westerners. They point to Japan's high savings rates, well-educated labor force, and large population, and say that Japan would have achieved success with or without its industrial strategies. The fallacy of this view is evidenced by the fact that no Japanese hold it. As the economist Hiroya Ueno has noted, the Japanese government has always intervened to obtain a specific economic order viewed as favorable to the national interest. Few Americans understand these wide-ranging efforts or how directly they contradict Western economic doctrine and expose its weaknesses.

Western economic doctrine holds that consumption is the main purpose of economic activity. The demands of consumers are reflected in the unseen hand of the free market, which allocates resources most efficiently. Many firms, having no market power, compete on prices until they drop to a level that covers only costs. Internationally, the theory goes, nations should specialize in the goods they are best endowed to produce and trade for the rest. According to this doctrine of "comparative advantage," if a nation has a large unskilled labor force, for example, it should concentrate on making textiles or other labor-intensive goods. It should buy technologically advanced items such as airplanes from the United States, say, which has a resource base better-suited to making them.

The whole point of free trade is to enable an entrepreneur or a firm to exploit its particular capability worldwide. Free-trade doctrine says this is a benefit, not a threat, because it allows consumers everywhere to enjoy the fruits of efficiency and discovery. It is on this hallowed thinking that the international trade system rests.

The Japanese have difficulties with this theory. Since it assumes that a nation's products are determined by its resource endowment, the theory implies that national economic activity will remain relatively static. And because profits are driven down by extreme price competition, there is no return to invest in R&D. This means that advanced countries will always retain their position and formalizes a kind of colonial relationship with less developed nations. Indeed, based on the writings of the British economists, Adam Smith and David Ricardo, the theory justified England's dominance of world trade during the Industrial Revolution.

Joseph Schumpeter, an Austrian economist and Harvard professor who wrote in the 1940s, formulated an alternative view of capitalist dynamics often ignored in the West. In his theory, what matters

is not price competition or resource endowment but the competition arising from new technology, sources of supply, and industrial organization. An example of what Schumpeter meant is the Toyota just-in-time manufacturing system, which has led to a doubling and even tripling of productivity. The severe price competition of perfectly free markets may actually retard the R&D necessary for this kind of advance because a company will not have the profits to invest.

Schumpeter's concept of dynamic competition suggests that less industrialized nations can catch up, and that governments can legitimately intervene to make this happen. This is music to Japanese ears. As Naohiro Amaya, a former vice-minister of the Ministry of International Trade and Industry (MITI), indicated to me, "Businessmen are risk averse. Therefore, if the invisible hand cannot drive the enterprise to R&D, the visible hand must."

U.S. observers usually describe such an industrial policy as one of picking winners and losers, and most firmly believe that bureaucrats never do anything except pick losers. But the Japanese, aiming to attain as much autonomy as possible, attempt to foster development of as many industries as possible. According to Myohei Shinohara, a longtime member of Japan's Industrial Structure Council, it is especially desirable to encourage industries with high technology content, in which costs decline rapidly with increases in production. It is also important to promote industries that have ripple effects on other sectors. Semiconductors, for example, both have high technology content and are used in key products such as computers. These criteria seem simple and straightforward to the Japanese, whose bureaucrats do not feel that they rely on a mystical laying on of hands and do not claim any special clairvoyance.

All of Japan's domestic policies serve

the goal of building its industrial strength. The education system provides an example. The Confucian tradition that Japan inherited from China emphasizes education, but technology never loomed large in this system. The thousands of engineers pouring out of Japanese universities today result from policies that deliberately encourage students to pursue engineering. This is borne out by the fact that Japan graduates relatively few chemists and physicists.

Japan's economic policies also serve its industrial policy. Japan maintains low interest rates for industry, but consumer loans, if available at all, usually carry high interest charges. Japan sets energy prices relatively high for consumers but keeps them low for industry. Everything is structured with one objective: to achieve industrial strength. This is the opposite of the U.S. approach where the consumer is king; in Japan, the consumer comes last.

Such an outlook accords well with the Samurai ethic of the Japanese, who cannot accept that their country will remain behind in any area of endeavor. It also reflects their view of economic health as national security. Since the time of Perry, the Japanese have seen foreign economic intrusion as a form of colonialism. Their dependence on the United States for defense makes them especially anxious to avoid economic domination. In lieu of a significant military establishment, an industrial policy aimed at achieving economic "security," by which they mean autonomy, has become Japan's strategy and its only assurance of some degree of independence on the international stage. Japan formulates its economic policies with an eye not only to their economic effect but also toward its overall power.

Japan puts these tenets into practice through an extraordinary domestic network that extends well beyond the efforts of the well-known MITI. Some of the main tools are the Industrial Structure Council, the Telecommunications Advisory Council, and other similar councils, which constantly study key industries and their relationships with others. These councils—which usually consist of members chosen from among leaders in business, consumer groups, labor unions, academia, government, and the press—issue a steady stream of white papers, often termed "visions," which form the basis for legislation for promoting or restructuring industries and encouraging R&D. MITI and other ministries also develop "elevation plans," which specify production levels for export, as well as R&D spending for specific projects from the visions. The elevation plans look much like the two- or three-year plans of major corporations and are in fact drawn up with industry representatives.

Many U.S. observers dismiss the plans as mere exhortation. But in Japan's group-oriented hierarchy, these procedures create a powerful consensus for achieving the objectives. The violent reaction to U.S. proposals in 1984 for placing Japanese nationals working for the Japanese subsidiaries of U.S. companies on the councils is strong evidence of their importance. Many Americans viewed as hyperbole the Japanese comparison of the Industrial Structure Council, which advises MITI, to the National Security Council. In fact, it was apt.

Japanese ministries have many tools at their disposal to achieve the goals established in the visions. They can set up companies such as the Japan Electronic Computer Corp., the government-backed leasing company established by MITI in the early 1960s to promote the Japanese computer industry in its battles with IBM. The Japan Electronic Computer Corp. provided immediate cash payments for computers manufactured by the financially strapped Japanese producers, and the company then leased the computers to customers.

MITI also often sets standards for industrial products that differ from those of other nations, automatically protecting the Japanese market from invasion by outsiders. And the Japan Development Bank makes low-interest loans to specific projects. Western economists often dismiss these loans as unimportant because they are usually just below the market rate, and because they fund only a small part of any R&D project. What outsiders do not realize is that by long tradition the loans are a signal to the financial community that it should give preference to targeted industries. The banks are willing to do so because the government backing reduces their risk. Companies can also draw up legal agreements to cooperate in cartels on deciding what goods to produce. Japanese machine-tool manufacturers have used such an agreement for the past 30 years to determine what sorts of machine tools each would make, as well as what direction the industry should take.

All these devices are important because they encourage investment and reduce risk. Even though Japan is a conformist, risk-averse society, it nevertheless produces business leaders lauded the world over for their long-term strategic thinking. The solution to the paradox is that the government socializes the risk, removing it from individual firms. In such circumstances, it is easy to be a long-term thinker.

GAINING THE ADVANTAGE IN FIBER OPTICS

The fiber-optics industry provides an example of how the Japanese have used these tools to capture markets in which U.S. companies once had a clear advantage. Optical fiber was invented in the 1960s by Corning Glassworks using private funds. Corning obtained U.S. patents on its inventions in the mid-1970s. But Japan did not grant many of the key pat-

ents for more than 10 years, leaving Corning's technology unprotected in this major market.

When Corning attempted to sell its fiber and cable in Japan, NTT, the monopoly buyer, told the company that Japan would develop its own technology. NTT then launched a fiber-optic R&D project with three firms, each of which contributed to the costs. NTT agreed to pay a high price for the optical fibers they developed, and to make purchases in proportion to each company's share of R&D costs—a procedure similar to U.S. defense contracting. These measures reduced risk every step of the way.

At the same time, NTT suggested that Corning consider a joint venture with a Japanese company. Corning invited Japanese representatives to its plants and laboratories and provided them with much useful information during discussions of possible joint ventures. After long negotiations, Corning was informed that the Japanese company could not establish a joint venture because NTT would not buy from such an entity. With Corning thus locked out, the Japanese developed a process so similar to Corning's that the U.S. International Trade Commission, Canadian courts, and finally U.S. courts found that the American company's patents had been infringed. NTT meanwhile began buying optical fibers at inflated prices from the three Japanese companies.

The story does not end there. In 1980 to 1981, Siecor, a company producing cable from Corning's fibers, offered to sell its products to NTT after the latter had agreed to open its procurement to foreign bids. Siecor's cable performed better than that produced by Japanese companies and cost only one-third as much. But to submit a formal bid for supplying the cable, Siecor needed a copy of NTT's specifications. Only after months of haggling and pressure from the U.S. government did NTT provide this information. Meanwhile, procurement from Japanese manufacturers was expanding rapidly.

NTT insisted that Siecor not only meet its specifications but provide the same cable design as the Japanese manufacturers. On its face this seemed a reasonable request, and Siecor was criticized for not trying hard enough. Yet some NTT executives later told me that the real problem was simply that NTT believed it had to support its own industry. The Japanese knew that Siecor's cost advantage was related to its design, and that Siecor would have to install an expensive new plant to change it. The U.S. firm did finally offer to build the plant if it was guaranteed a share of the market, as its competitors had been, but the Japanese denied the request as not being in accord with free trade.

These maneuvers—as well as the designation of fiber optics as an industry of the future—enabled the Japanese firms to build enough capacity to fill their own market three times over. The companies then inevitably began the search for export markets—and, as always, the biggest was the United States. By 1983, Japanese manufacturers were selling optical fiber in the United States at prices well below the market. Corning brought suit in U.S. federal court and won in 1987, but by then its patents had almost expired.

This was promotion policy at work. While the Japanese government was reducing risk for its companies, the U.S. government was ignoring American firms, assuming that the free play of the market would allow the best to win. Japan became a powerful competitor, and U.S. observers congratulated it for its diligence and foresight while criticizing the rigidity of American business. Similar events have occurred in virtually every industry, from supercomputers to aircraft—the latter being two key areas where the Japanese now threaten the significant U.S. advantage.

THE JAPANESE BUILD A SUPERCOMPUTER INDUSTRY

Supercomputers flared into the headlines just a year ago, in the spring of 1987, when a secret cable from the U.S. embassy in Tokyo to the State Department was leaked to the press. The cable reported Makota Kuroda, a top MITI official, as saying that the United States might have to consider nationalizing Cray, the dominant player in the world supercomputer market, to save it from Japanese competition. The cable concluded in a shocked tone that Japan is intent upon dominating the industry.

U.S. officials should not have been surprised. Kuroda was only telling them what had been obvious for some time. Cray had entered Japan in the 1970s and sold two machines in 1980. With no Japanese supercomputers on the market, the Americans indisputably had the best and least expensive machines. In 1981, MITI announced a program to develop a supercomputer. From that time, Cray's prospective customers in Japan seemed to disappear. Government research institutes, a major market, told Cray it was a waste of time even to send representatives because the ministries that controlled their budgets would not allocate funds for foreign machines. Cray's sense of unfairness deepened when it learned that U.S. government laboratories, including Lawrence Livermore, were helping the Japanese companies with the design of their machines.

In response to U.S. inquiries, the Japanese government explained that its research institutes were too small to make use of such large machines. Two years later, however, when Japanese manufacturers finally introduced their products, many of the small institutes placed orders. Today, supercomputer sales in Japan are booming. Cray has managed to sell a few machines after enormous pressure from the U.S. government, but its share of the market remains small. Meanwhile, Japanese computer makers have already begun an export drive based on extremely low prices. In November 1987, M.I.T. canceled plans to buy a supercomputer from the Nippon Electric Co. at about one-third the normal price only after being warned of a possible antidumping investigation by the Commerce Department.

BATTLES OVER THE AIRCRAFT INDUSTRY

The Japanese are also moving vigorously into aviation—the one remaining area where the United States has a definite advantage. In 1981, the question of who would produce Japan's next generation jet fighter, the FSX, became a major trade issue. In the past, Japan's fighters had been versions of U.S. aircraft. At first, these planes had been made in the United States, but the Japanese had gradually insisted on building more and more under license from U.S. producers. Now strong forces in Japan were urging that it build the FSX entirely on its own, despite the fact that doing so would cost substantially more than buying from the United States or continuing with licensed production.

U.S. officials were dismayed. With the bilateral trade deficit approaching $60 billion, it seemed logical that Japan should buy its planes from the United States, which could build them for half the price of the Japanese producers. In the past, when Japan had insisted that it had to manufacture the planes in Japan, the United States had agreed to allow Japanese co-production of aircraft to assure the interoperability of the two nations' forces. The Americans had even relaxed the traditional ceiling on the percentage of the planes that the Japanese could build. Now, however, Japan was proposing to build a whole new plane itself in spite of the higher cost and the trade deficit.

In the end, under enormous pressure from the United States, Japan agreed to "jointly develop" a modified version of the F-16 with General Dynamics. But the fact that Japan chose to fight this battle at a time of bitter trade disputes with the United States is a measure of its dedication to self-development and autonomy. This has been confirmed by subsequent developments. The United States and Japan have recently been negotiating over the meaning of "joint development." The Japanese plans, as now revealed to the United States, seem to entail building the original FSX and calling it an F-16.

In fact, the Aircraft and Machinery Industries Council decided in the 1960s that Japan had to have a modern aircraft industry to be a technologically advanced nation. MITI promoted this goal by pledging $1 billion to $2 billion for a consortium of Japanese companies to become 25 percent equity partners in Boeing's new 757 jet liner. MITI also promoted development of industries in avionics, flight control, engines, and fuel systems.

Military co-production with the United States has made significant contributions to this technology base and Japan's emergence as a world-class aircraft builder. Some U.S. military personnel have been leery of this information transfer: after concluding the co-production agreement on the F-15, air force specialists drew up a detailed list of technologies considered too sensitive to give Japan because of the danger that they would fall into Soviet hands. Yet when Japanese officials indignantly confronted U.S. officials with the list, arguing that it would be too difficult to make repairs, the department released much of the technology.

Japan was especially adamant about obtaining the technology for making the carbon composites that compose the speed brake of the F-15. The air force strongly opposed this transfer but was overriden by the secretary of defense. By 1981 Japan could reproduce the technology, and Japanese executives later acknowledged that it had been valuable in several key commercial projects.

U.S. officials, in contrast, have been frustrated in trying to transfer Japanese "dual-use" technology—used for both military and commercial products—to U.S. defense manufacturers. Years of negotiation produced an agreement in 1983 that Japan would permit such transfers. However, virtually no technology has been forthcoming, despite Japan's dependence on the United States for defense. Thus, while the United States has sought security by giving away technology, Japan has sought it by hoarding technology, even from the United States. Ironically, the United States, Japan's defender, has now become its target.

USING CARTELS TO RESTRUCTURE INDUSTRIES

As mature Japanese industries begin to decline, the other major component of the nation's industrial policy—restructuring—comes into play. This is especially necessary since Japan's promotion policies tend to create excess production capacity, which can lead to severe price cutting and financial losses. The United States sees such price cutting as a boon to consumers, but Japan thinks that excessive competition can damage companies that may be critical for the long-term health of the economy. Moreover, Japan does not believe that the merger and acquisition activity so popular in the United States enhances productivity.

Japan has therefore developed an elaborate set of tools to restrain competition, including allowing companies to form cartels to jointly restrict production and

capacity. An important characteristic of the cartels is that they reduce production in relation to each company's market share. This virtually guarantees market dominance in perpetuity to those who dominate at maturity. Companies thus tend to overinvest in an attempt to gain dominance. The risk is low even for the eventual losers because they know every effort will be made to keep them alive.

Moves to jointly reduce production require even greater cooperation between government and business than efforts to promote specific industries. The steel industry provides perhaps the best example of this policy. In 1977 MITI directed 52 electric-furnace steel producers to cut production by 35 percent or face a fine. They complied. Then in mid-1982, MITI issued a "guideline" to reduce steel production while raising prices, in an effort to restore profitability. Japan's Fair Trade Commission investigated from time to time but took no action.

The mechanics of the guidelines to the steel industry reveal the close coordination between industry and government. Every Monday at noon, black limousines swarm around the Iron and Steel Building in Tokyo. From them emerge men from Japan's eight major steel companies. They go to room 704, where a sign reads "Regular Monday Club Meeting." The men take their places at a large, rectangular table, at whose head is the chief of MITI's Iron and Steel section. This group has met every Monday since 1958 to iron out a consensus on the MITI guideline for appropriate levels of investment and production. During this time, and even today, Japan's steel industry has been the world's most powerful.

To the rest of the world, Japan insists that it is winding down such depressed industries to make room for imports. Not surprisingly, in view of the wide-ranging MITI efforts at revitalization, the reverse has occurred. Frank Upham, an economist at New York University, found that of 14 officially depressed industries in Japan, only 2 saw increases in imports.

Even if imports in mature industries do rise, they tend to be under Japanese control. The aluminum-smelting industry provides an example. With the highest energy costs in the industrial world, Japan's smelting industry languished after the oil crises of the 1970s. MITI gave it preferential electric rates, special loans, and other aids. When in 1982 the world price was half that in Japan, both MITI and the industry, concluding that it could not be revived, set in motion a plan to move it to Indonesia and Brazil. Instead of simply allowing its companies to contract with foreign producers, the Japanese government consciously set out to ensure that half the domestic supply of aluminum would come from Japanese installations overseas, which were thought to be more reliable than those of other suppliers.

Japanese investment in the United States also reflects Japan's style of retaining as much control as possible in Japanese hands. For example, Toyota's new plant in Georgetown, Ky., is not being built by U.S. contractors, but by Ohbayashi Gumi Corp. Topy Industries, a supplier in Japan, plans to set up shop nearby to make wheels for the new factory. Hitachi, too, is building a plant in the area, and just down the road Trinity (Japanese also, despite the name) has set up an auto-painting facility. The Mitsui Bank is providing the financing.

U.S. observers such as the journalist Fletcher Knebel have noticed similar phenomena elsewhere. Living in Honolulu, Knebel observed that Japanese tourists arrive on Japan Airlines, take Japanese tour buses downtown to Japanese-owned hotels, and dine at Japanese-owned restaurants. In San Francisco, this practice is known as the "closed circle," and local

travel agencies have brought suit on antitrust grounds.

Some analysts glibly say that the United States retains negotiating leverage in dealing with Japan because it needs the U.S. market. But America's debtor status makes its need for Japanese money much more powerful, and this need is already having portentous political effects. Indeed, Tennessee Governor Lamar Alexander told me in 1987 that he had been to Tokyo more often than to Washington during the past four years since "that's where we can get some real help." Kentucky Governor Martha Layne Collins remarked that during one of her trips to Japan, she met 14 other governors there as well.

DEALING WITH RESENTFUL PARTNERS

The result of Japan's policies has been one of the strongest sustained economic performances of all time—along with a rising tide of resentment from its trading partners. The Japanese have not been able to understand this and believe it is due to misperception. A major task of Japan's leaders is therefore to explain their industrial policies in a way that reconciles them with the free-trade system. Such explanations are difficult: having rejected the economic theories of the West, Japan nevertheless tries to show that its policies do not conflict with them.

MITI officials modestly maintain that their power to coerce private industry is limited. MITI, they say, simply studies industries carefully, writes reports, and makes forecasts. The officials liken these to the *U.S. Industrial Outlook,* an annual forecast of business activity published by the Commerce Department. They point out that the Japanese government supports only about 30 percent of Japan's total R&D budget, while the U.S. government supports over 50 percent of the American total. These officials neglect to mention that one reason for the large U.S. figure is a defense burden Japan does not bear.

MITI officials stress their belief that huge U.S. defense expenditures stimulate U.S. technological development and enhance the competitive power of major companies such as IBM and Texas Instruments. They acknowledge that these programs are aimed at military, not commercial, development but say they still result in spin-offs. The Japanese clearly take for granted the necessity for governments to intervene to assure economic leadership.

American officials react with surprise to such statements. They understand the need to ward off threats to national security in the traditional military sense. But they are only beginning to grasp that Japan feels threatened if foreign countries move ahead in commercial areas.

The Japanese view of defense spending as an engine of technological progress is particularly significant. To the extent that the U.S. technological lead derives from defense spending, the Japanese government feels it must intervene to offset this effect. Thus, the supreme irony: the United States is spending partly to defend Japan, while Japan feels compelled to help its industry overcome the results.

RECONCILING THE DIFFERENCES

Both the United States and Japan need to make significant changes. The Japanese policies are beginning to foster tremendous resentment worldwide. Other countries, as well as the United States, are tired of the fact that Japan only sells and never buys. Japanese officials looking at long-term security have to wonder about survival in such a world. They should create a foreign presence in their industries by promoting acquisition of Japanese firms by foreign investors and imports from foreign countries. Since Japan

has maintained a distance from foreigners for the last 100 years, this won't happen naturally, and a version of affirmative action may be necessary.

Japan should also bear more of the cost of maintaining the free-world system. The United States spends some 8 percent of its GNP for this purpose, while the Japanese spend only 1 percent. They should reasonably be expected to attain European levels of 4 to 5 percent of GNP, or $100 to $150 billion a year. This could be used to support the U.S. military presence in the Pacific, provide debt relief for developing nations, and furnish international aid.

Internally, Japan needs to temper its self-sacrificing, non-consumerist orientation, which deprives its citizens of access to the fruits of their labor and deprives trading partners of the ability to sell to Japanese markets.

Several factors discourage consumption and increase prices—Japanese televisions, cameras, and other goods cost more in Tokyo than in New York. Laws protecting thousands of "mom and pop" shops severely limit the number of large retail outlets. This creates the need for a multi-tiered distribution system, which adds to the cost of everything. Moreover, major industrial groups such as Sumitomo and Mitsui—which have assets of some half a trillion dollars and sell everything from glass products to telecommunications satellites and real estate to semiconductors—exert enormous control over this distribution system. Consumer-credit interest rates are as high as 60 percent. The restrictions on large retail outlets should be loosened, major manufacturers' control over the system should be reduced by strictly enforcing antitrust laws, and consumer interest rates should be lowered.

Overly strict land-use regulations are another problem. To protect farmers, half of Japan's scarce land is reserved for agriculture, while the 94 percent of Japanese who are not farmers make do with the other half. Tight zoning restrictions impede office and apartment construction. As a result, Japan has both the world's highest food prices—rice sells at five to ten times the world price—and its highest land prices. A two-bedroom condominium an hour and a half by train from Tokyo costs nearly $600,000, and apartments are so small that consumers have no place to put products they might buy. Japan should let agricultural land be sold for other purposes and revise building codes to allow construction of more houses and apartments.

However, the Japanese may not do everything the United States might like them to. Reducing land prices would require a shift of political power away from farmers. And even though there might seem to be a natural incentive to increase the size of dwellings and reduce the cost of products, the Japanese live better today than they did 10 years ago. Moreover, it is the United States that has the problem with remaining competitive. Thus, this nation needs to seek solutions that do not depend on Japan.

The United States must deal with its swollen budget deficit and boost its low savings rate if it hopes to provide industries with crucial investment capital. A cabinet-level entity that evaluates all forms of government investment, including those of the military, for their effect on the health of the U.S. economy would go a long way toward revitalizing the nation's industries.

Ventures such as Sematech, the government-industry effort to revitalize semiconductor production, are another important step. In a grudging 1987 editorial supporting Sematech as a lesser evil than protectionism, the *Washington Post* offered three excellent criteria for setting up such projects: the industry of concern should be crucial to the economy, it should be able to draw up its own research agenda, and it should contribute half the cost. It is clearly more important to encourage industries that contribute disproportionately to economic growth and productivity than, for example, the real-estate industry, which has been favored for years.

The United States must also realize that the primary basis for international trade—the General Agreement on Tariffs and Trade—is no longer adequate for doing business with Japan, if it ever was. The first step is to discard the belief that the Japanese market is like that of the United States, and that it can be made to operate similarly if only the Japanese will stop being unfair. In situations where the United States concludes that free trade is unlikely, it should bargain for specific conditions.

International airline negotiations provide a model. Most countries' airlines are regulated, and many are state-owned, since nations consider them a symbol of power. The United States knows that negotiating for free trade in this area would be useless, so instead it works out reciprocal deals. We give a certain number of flights a week to Japan, and they give us a similar number of flights in return. It is not an open market, but a great deal of competition occurs within a limited framework.

The United States has also been pressing for more open financial markets abroad as it has deregulated its own banking system over the past several years. But when Japanese and other countries' banks quickly gained major positions in the U.S. market, the U.S. Treasury did not call for free trade. Instead, recognizing that banking is a key industry, it persuaded foreign banks operating in the United States to increase their capital reserves to the levels required of U.S. banks. Imagine the outcry against protectionism had the United States demanded that Japan's semiconductor companies saddle themselves with the same cost of capital as the U.S. companies. But what is the difference? Only that Treasury thinks banking has a significance that semiconductors lack.

Even if the two societies do change, confrontation will undoubtedly continue. To avoid an increasingly rancorous relationship, the next president should convene a high-level conference of executive and legislative leaders from both Japan and the United States to create a new framework for mutual relations. The conference should deal not only with trade matters but also with guidelines for investment, the sharing of military and aid costs, and future political dealings. Only in this way can America's most important bilateral relationship be maintained in a healthy state.

12.   Japan and the United States in the New World Economy

C. Fred Bergsten

Three global transformations of historic dimension are well underway as we enter the 1990s. First, the reforms in the Soviet Union and Eastern Europe, if carried through successfully, will end most components of the Cold War and the most direct elements of East-West confrontation. Substantial reductions in military arsenals will ensue in the NATO and Warsaw Pact countries.

Second, as a result, the importance of security issues will decline sharply. Economics will move much closer to the top of the global agenda. The international position of individual countries will derive increasingly from their economic prowess rather than their military capability. The status of a uniting Europe and, especially, Japan will rise. The relative power of the United States and, especially, the Soviet Union will fall.

Third, the world economy will complete its evolution from the America-dominated regime of the first postwar

SOURCE: Delivered to the Commemorative Symposium for the First Anniversary of the Founding of the Taisho Research Institute, Tokyo, Japan, May 21, 1990. *Vital Speeches of the Day* 56:21 (August 15, 1990).

generation to tripolarity. An economically united Europe will be the world's largest market and largest trader. Japan is already the world's largest creditor and leader in many key technologies, and its GNP will exceed three quarters of America's by 2000 at growth rates and exchange rates that now seem likely.

The United States will remain the only superpower in both military and economic terms. It alone will remain in the top rank as the nature of world affairs changes. But the United States is the power in relative economic decline, caught in a scissors movement between its increasing dependence on external economic, especially financial, forces and its declining capacity to influence those forces.

In the short to medium run, the international economic positions of the Big Three are likely to converge further. Growth seems likely to continue at 4 percent or so in Asia and Europe but only 2-2 1/2 percent in America. Productivity increases in Japan and most other Asian countries are considerably higher than in the United States. Europe will be buoyed by "completion of the internal market" by 1992 or so, by Economic and Monetary Union (EMU) by the mid-1990s, and by economic revival in Eastern Europe. By 2000, the Big Three economies will be more alike than different on most key counts: levels of GNP and external trade, and their dependence on international trade and financial flows.

Indeed, Europe may become the chief magnet for international capital flows in the 1990s. Europe held such a position in the 1960s when the Common Market was initially formed and extensive immigration helped to fuel a prolonged boom. Latin America was the chief target for foreign investment in the 1970s. The United States acceded to that role in the 1980s. But Europe, fueled by elements similar to the 1960s, may become the most attractive site for global capital in the period ahead—with Japan rather than the United States as the main supplier.

International relations will look very different by 2000 as a result of these transformations. Economics will play a central role. There will be three economic superpowers. The hierarchy of nations will shift to a considerable degree. The Big Three of economics will supplant the Big Two of nuclear weaponry on the issues that will shape much of the early twenty-first century. Japan, a uniting Europe and the United States will need to become full partners in managing the world economy.

A central global question for the 1990s and beyond is whether the new international framework will produce conflict over economic issues, or a healthy combination of competition and cooperation. History suggests that there is considerable risk of conflict, even spilling over from the economic sphere to create political rivalries. Such a pattern contributed to the breakdown of global order prior to 1914 and again in the interwar period.

The world would have to adjust to the fundamental shift in economic relationships among the major countries whether or not security arrangements had

changed as well. But the end of the Cold War could sharply heighten the prospect of trade war. Throughout the postwar period, the overriding security imperative has blunted trans-Atlantic and trans-Pacific economic disputes. The United States and its allies, including Japan, have frequently made economic concessions to avoid jeopardizing their global security structures. Cold War politics in fact sheltered the economic recoveries of Europe and Japan, and America's support for them. The United States seldom employed its security leverage in pursuing its economic goals; indeed, security and economic issues remained largely compartmentalized in all of the industrial democracies.

Removal of the security blanket could erode this segmentation. Indeed, it could tempt the United States (and perhaps others) to use security issues to seek economic advantage. This would make it considerably harder to maintain cooperation in both the economic and security dimensions. At the same time, since East-West confrontation has provided the rationale for much of America's international engagement throughout the postwar period, an end to the Cold War may suggest to some Americans that the country should largely withdraw from such engagement, including in the economic domain.

There is intimate two-way interaction between the current political and economic transformations: removal of the security blanket increases the risk of economic conflict, while economic conflict would erode security ties. The ultimate paradox of the twentieth century would be a realization of the Marxist prophecy of inevitable conflict among the capitalist nations just as the political conflict spurred by Marxist ideology was waning.

The risk of economic conflict is already acute. Shintaro Ishihara has predicted that "the twenty-first century will be a century of economic warfare." Such conflict would be most likely to surface between the United States and Japan.

Japan is clearly changing. Its global current account surplus fell from $87 billion in 1987 to $57 billion in 1989, less than 2 percent of GNP. The growth of Japan's imports from the United States has been six times greater than its export growth to the United States over that period. Manufactured goods now comprise more than half of total Japanese imports. Japanese investors, supported on occasion by the monetary authorities, have displayed a willingness to continue financing a large portion of America's deficits, even while the dollar was falling steadily during 1985-87, and to contribute substantially to global funding needs elsewhere (Third World debtors, aid recipients, even Eastern Europe). The image of an omnipotent "Japan, Inc." has eroded considerably in early 1990 with the sharp decline of Tokyo stocks and the yen, and the apparent inability of the Japanese authorities to stop it. The initial results of the Structural Impediments Initiative (SSI) talks are encouraging.

But American frustration with Japan continues. The bilateral imbalance between the countries remains large, and may start rising again because of the weakening of the yen over the past two years and slower Japanese growth. There remains much exasperation over Japan's seemingly impenetrable markets for many imports and most foreign direct investment. A major concern is Japan's pursuit of superiority in a wide range of strategic high-technology industries, including many in which the United States retains a substantial competitive advantage.

The debate is taking an ominous new direction in both countries. In America, many "liberal internationalists"—including many mainstream economists—have come to agree that "Japan is different" and should be treated differently. The latest negotiating effort between the two countries, the Structural Impedi-

ments Initiative, addresses some of these differences but is unlikely to produce rapid results—strengthening the view that a new tack is required.

Attitudes are of course changing in Japan as well. Dismay bordering on disdain appears to increasingly characterize Japanese reactions to America's continued failure to correct its budget and trade deficits, raise national saving, improve the educational system and boost competitiveness at the company level. The fragility of Japan's political system and the redirection of Japanese policy to the improvement of domestic living standards generate pressure for turning inward. Hence Japan may not accept any renewed "bashing" from America in its traditional docile fashion.

On the other side of the Pacific, America's self-confidence in its international economic position has been shaken by continuing large trade deficits, the resultant buildup in external debt and dependence on foreign capital, losses of technological leadership in key sectors, growing reliance on Japan and others to deal with such problems as Eastern Europe and Third World debt, and frustration over its inability to achieve needed changes in both national economic policy (especially the budget) and firm-specific competitiveness. "Trade hawks" argue that the reduction in the security imperative now opens the way for much "tougher" action on economic issues. And it is true that the United States can now be less solicitous of its allies—American leverage is enhanced to an extent by the declining need to place overriding priority on political cohesion and thus to mute its economic demands.

In this environment, U.S.-Japan economic tension is already high. U.S.-European economic confrontation could erupt as well if "Europe 1992" or EMU turn out to be protectionist, or even inward looking. Any significant downturn of the U.S. economy could trigger an outbreak of protection. Renewed growth in the external deficit could discredit the strategy crafted by then-Secretary of the Treasury James Baker and the Group of Seven in 1985-87 to respond to trade pressures primarily through currency changes and macroeconomic policy co-operation—particularly since such co-operation has virtually disappeared and the yen-dollar exchange note has been moving in the wrong direction for over two years. A new financial crisis or failure of the several ongoing trade negotiations, bilateral or multilateral, would intensify the proclivity in Washington to "blame the foreigners."

A key question surrounding potential economic conflict in the future is how each of the Big Three will line up vis-a-vis the others. At present, the countries frequently find themselves arrayed with different partners on different issues: America and Europe seek to open Japan's markets for manufactured goods, America and Japan confront Europe on its rules for foreign investors, Europe and Japan criticize the United States on its budget deficit and trade unilateralism. Shifting coalitions of this type generally provide a healthy basis for systemic stability, especially if they occur within a framework of agreed international rules and institutional arrangements.

However, "almost all (students of international relations) agree that a tripolar system is the most unstable configuration." History and game theory both suggest a strong tendency for each of the three parties to fear that the other two will line up against it permanently. Moreover, given the inevitable self-perception of vulnerability on the part of each of the three parties, two *will* tend to ally against the third under conditions of rough tripolar equality—perhaps in an effort to create their own "bipolar" dominance.

In the real world, all three theoretical pairings could in fact eventuate. The most widespread view, especially in the United States, is that conflict among the Big Three would soon evolve into an alliance between America and Europe against Japan. Japan's "differentness" would brand it as an outlier on both trade and investment issues, and thus a target for the other industrial (and perhaps many developing) countries.

A second possibility is that the United States and Japan would band together against uniting Europe. If Europe is the only true bloc, and has thereby become the world's largest and most powerful economic entity, the other global actors might tend to coalesce against it for traditional balance-of-power reasons. If Europe turns inward and begins to discriminate overtly against outsiders, or pursues a "Europe, Inc." strategy, that motivation would be enhanced.

In addition, interdependence between the United States and Japan has grown enormously. Japan's bilateral surplus represented almost half of America's deficit in 1989, and inclusion of the Asian NICs brought the ratio to about 70 percent. Correspondingly, Japan and other Asians are financing much of America's twin deficits. A plethora of U.S.-Japan corporate and financial alliances are binding the two nations ever more closely together.

Europeans argue that Germany's surpluses and Britain's (or Spain's) deficits are no longer a legitimate global concern, because Germany finances Britain (and Spain) and Europe as a whole is in balance with the outside world. A similar concept for the Pacific Rim region would suggest that Japan, Taiwan and other Asians could keep running surpluses with the United States (and perhaps the rest of the Western Hemisphere) as long as they were ready to go on financing the imbalances. America's emergence as the world's largest debtor country is mirrored to a considerable extent by Japan's emergence as the world's largest creditor, and their financial symbiosis is certain to rise much further before either imbalance could possibly level off. This is the economic rationale for more formal linkages among the nations of the Pacific Rim, centered on a U.S.-Japan economic alliance.

A third possibility is a Europe-Japan nexus. As noted, these regions are likely to enjoy higher growth rates than America during this critical transitional period—perhaps by a substantial margin. Their economic policies, especially toward international issues, have tended to be more stable and predictable. They will thus offer attractive markets and business partners for interpenetration, via both trade and investment, as reflected in the recent linkage between Mitsubishi and Daimler-Benz.

In addition, there are doubts about America's future dynamism in Europe and Japan (and other parts of Asia). They may come to feel that the United States will reform its domestic policies only if they join together to provide external pressure on it to do so—*gaiatsu* for America. Any major protectionist steps by the United States would feed these doubts and drive the two together. Helmut Schmidt and Giscard d'Estaing created the European Monetary System in the late 1970s partly as a buffer against economic instability emanating from America, and similar linkups between Asia and Europe are clearly possible in the 1990s and beyond.

Emergence of any of these configurations on a lasting basis would be extremely destabilizing for both global politics and economic affairs. The region targeted by such an "alliance" would almost certainly turn inward as the external pressures strengthened internal forces which sought such a course anyway: protectionists in America, regionalists in Europe, traditionalists in Japan. The target would probably seek to form (or expand) its bloc of nearby supporters,

and the other areas would respond in kind. All economies would suffer, and risks of trade warfare would become real.

The good news is that today's global economic competitors enter the new era as political allies with strong security ties and democratic governments. Their cooperation over the past four decades, while uneven, has largely avoided major crises and has proven superior to all historical antecedents. Moreover, the extensive trade and financial interpenetration among their economies would cause substantial costs for each to result from serious conflict among them. Thus there is hope that the interaction between economies and security can be very different from the interwar and pre-1914 periods, when the struggle for world economic leadership coincided with political hostility (and eventual conflagration).

The bad news is that the world economy has enjoyed prolonged periods of stable prosperity only under the hegemonic leadership of a single country—the United Kingdom in the latter part of the nineteenth century and the United States in the first postwar generation. There will be no new hegemon to supplant the United States, however. Neither Japan nor even a fully united Europe could achieve the global dominance, even in the economic sphere alone, that is needed to support such a role.

Hence effective international economic cooperation will depend on the achievement of joint leadership by the Big Three economic superpowers, just as nuclear deterrence was maintained by the Big Two military superpowers. There is simply no alternative. But the world has never experienced successful "management by committee." The construction and subsequent maintenance of a stable regime in such circumstances is a daunting task. Even more daunting is the transition to such a regime; the historical precedents, particularly in the interwar period, failed miserably and led to disaster.

Systemic economic reforms are most essential when there are basic changes in the underlying relationship among the capabilities of the major countries. In the late nineteenth and early twentieth centuries, the United Kingdom resisted sharing its economic leadership with the rising powers—mainly France, Germany and the United States. Skirmishes among these countries dotted the period and intensified the political rivalries which eventually led to the First World War. In the interwar period, Germany and Japan rose to economic prominence but were not accommodated. This again escalated tensions and added to the disintegration of the global system.

Under reasonably consistent American leadership, the postwar economic regime succeeded impressively through its first generation. The contrast is particularly striking with the interwar period when few institutional arrangements existed, the challenging powers (notably Germany and Japan) remained outside those which did, and America was unwilling to take over leadership from Britain.

But the postwar regime was eroding by the early 1970s. American economic hegemony declined. Unintegrated Europe and reticent Japan could not fill much of the void. The institutions began to lose credibility and even relevance. Largely as a result, currency misalignments and instability have become endemic. Large trade imbalances persist. Protectionism and neomercantilism continue. Third World debt remains unresolved. Policy cooperation is *ad hoc* and fragile.

The major countries have proved exceedingly adept at responding to crises with sufficient skill to avoid lasting economic effects. But there have been a number of close calls: American leadership nearly faltered in responding to the Mexican debt crisis in 1982, enormous pro-

tectionist momentum was permitted to build in the United States before dollar adjustment and credible trade policies were launched in 1985, and extensive financial disruption resulted from the plunge of the dollar in 1987. Moreover, the globalization of world financial markets could now overwhelm individual governments or even their collective responses. And new sources of conflict among nations could well result from the contemporary changes in global politics and economic capabilities.

The system no longer provides strong defenses against such threats. To restore these defenses, a uniting Europe, Japan and America must join together to provide collective leadership. The United States must accept, welcome and actively promote a true sharing of responsibilities as well as burdens. Japan and Europe must become willing to accept leadership responsibility as well as pay the bills. The Big Three need to start acting as an informal steering committee for the world economy—reinvigorating the existing institutional structures, creating new ones and initiating concrete steps to utilize them.

Such international leadership must rest on firm internal foundations in each area. The United States, which has to make the difficult adjustment from hegemon to partner, can do so only with full restoration of its international competitive position and, at a minimum, cessation of further buildup of its foreign debt.

This will require some combination of sharp cuts in the Federal budget deficit and increased private saving. It calls for changes in a number of underlying fundamentals including the education system and far greater export orientation on the part of American companies. It may also require structural changes in America's system of governance, such as institution of a "fast track" procedure for fiscal policy commitments made as part of international bargains, to permit it to deal more effectively with the parliamentary governments of Europe and Japan where the executive branch can speak authoritatively for the country as a whole.

Changes of this nature can eventuate only on the basis of fundamental alterations in American attitudes. The traditional mindset in the United States, derived from nearly a century of global dominance and a virtually self-sufficient continental economy, has been to adopt whatever public policies and corporate strategies fit the domestic environment. The rest of the world was largely ignored. But American public policies and corporate strategies must increasingly be framed in a global context. Americans will have to start viewing themselves as part of an integrated global economy, and pushing their government and firms to behave accordingly, if they are to prosper and remain world leaders into the twenty-first century.

Japan faces the opposite problem. As in the United States, a small minority recognizes the basic change in the country's international position and seeks new policies (per especially the Maekawa Commission reports). For Japan, this requires adopting the mindset of a huge creditor country that is confident of its ability to compete throughout the world. It means dropping the self-perception of a vulnerable island that must "export or die," and protect its own market and firms against "powerful outsiders." Indeed, participation as an equal partner in effective tripolar management of the world economy might provide a unifying concept for Japanese foreign policy that has been conspicuously lacking to date, and would seem to offer considerable appeal to Japan as it would play to the country's obvious comparative advantage.

As noted above, Japan has already begun to change impressively. But much more is needed quickly: further increases in imports of both manufactured (including high technology) products and agricultural goods, a conspicuous expansion in the presence of foreign investors, eschewal of infant industry protection and industrial policies, additional reductions in its surpluses both globally and with the United States. Japan has repeatedly demonstrated an enormous aptitude for reform, as in its responses to the two oil shocks and the doubling of the yen in 1985-87. It can clearly do so again *if* convinced that such change is a national imperative, although the historical record suggests that continued outside pressure will be needed to galvanize such a strategy.

The result of these internal changes, along with successful completion of "Europe 1992" and EMU, would be a considerably different Big Three: a newly competitive America, a newly internationalized Japan, and an economically integrated Europe. Absent such internal developments, each area will lack the internal self-confidence or the international respect needed to play its part in global leadership. But achievement of these crucial changes within each of the Big Three can be promoted, perhaps decisively, by the active pursuit of tripolar economic leadership itself. Adoption of commitments to that end would underline the need for domestic reforms and outward orientation in each area, and strengthen those groups within each that support such a focus. Internal and external policy measures can reinforce each other as part of comprehensive national strategies.

Political leaders of the Big Three first need to recognize publicly the dramatic changes in the global environment and declare their intention to construct and maintain a stable international economic order based on shared leadership and mutual responsibility. Such a commitment should be enunciated at the Houston summit in July, the first of the 1990s, to set the essential political framework and begin to define the needed initiatives.

The commitment would obviously be credible only if it encompassed effective follow-through to translate principle into practice. Several major areas must be addressed: monetary arrangements and economic policy cooperation, trade, the entry of Eastern Europe and the Soviet Union into the world economy and its institutions, the environment, energy and the needs of the Third World. Money and trade are the most essential components of the package.

The Big Three should start the process by launching the construction of a new international monetary regime to replace the Bretton Woods system that collapsed in 1971-73. No system worthy of the name has existed since that time, with enormous costs for the world economy. But stable and effective monetary arrangements are as crucial to the world economy as is national monetary stability to each individual country.

The preferred course is to build in evolutionary fashion on the "reference ranges," initially adopted by the United States and Japan in the Baker-Miyazawa Agreement of October 1986 and subsequently generalized in the Louvre Accord of February 1987, and on the "economic indicators" adopted at the Tokyo summit in 1986 to guide coordination of national economic policies. The key countries would agree to set target zones for their currencies which, given reasonable consistency of domestic policies, would avoid large current account imbalances (and thus limit both financial risks and protectionist pressures). The zones would be shifted in response to differences in national inflation rates and to major changes in the world economic environment, such as large jumps in oil prices, but the countries would otherwise pledge to adopt new policies as needed to preserve them. Over time, the zones could be narrowed if experience with the

system suggested the feasibility of doing so, perhaps leading ultimately to a regime similar to Bretton Woods or the EMS. Other policy instruments would be adjusted if necessary to achieve internal economic goals.

This new regime should be implemented as soon as actions have been taken that promise to correct today's continuing large imbalances. The monetary officials, in addition to launching the systemic reform effort, therefore need to work out firm commitments for definitive fiscal adjustment in the United States, for continued expansion of domestic demand and structural liberalization in Japan and Europe, and for further exchange rate changes among the Big Three.

On trade, the immediate key is a successful Uruguay Round that would convincingly resume market liberalization and refurbish the credibility of the GATT. A strong push from the Houston summit is essential to achieve this result, just as the summits of the late 1970s were decisive in galvanizing a successful conclusion to the Tokyo Round.

Much more is needed, however, to make the needed leap in the effectiveness of global trade arrangements. The Big Three should thus agree to push for the implementation of four sweeping reforms by 2000: elimination of all tariffs on all industrial trade, as proposed by Japan at an early stage of the Uruguay Round; a complete ban on all quantitative trade barriers including "voluntary export restraint agreements"; a sharp expansion in the independence and mandate given the GATT to police the system; and creation of a "GATT for Investment" to provide a stable framework for international corporate activities (and help resist protectionist pressures in this area, notably in the United States).

These proposals should be taken up promptly after the conclusion of the Uruguay Round. The "bicycle theory" posits that trade policy either moves steadily forward toward liberalization or topples in the face of protectionist pressures; launching a new negotiation toward such major steps would keep the bicycle moving forward without delay, avoiding the post-negotiation malaise which permitted substantial protectionist pressures to flourish after the conclusion of both the Kennedy and Tokyo Rounds.

Initiatives by the Big Three to reform and dramatically improve the international monetary trade regimes along these lines, on the basis of substantial changes in their internal economic structures, would clearly mark the beginning of a new era of collective leadership of the world economy. It would indicate that each could adopt new mindsets: a willingness to share power with others for America, an acceptance of international responsibility for Japan, acting jointly on the global economic and monetary (as well as trade) scene for Europe.

Through such steps, the Big Three would assert control of an issue-area that will inexorably emerge as central to world events as the Cold War dissipates. They would preempt the risk that removal of the security blanket and economic rivalry itself would generate severe international conflict. They would create an orderly framework for managing some of the elements that will dominate relations among them in the years ahead. They would provide a new global role for Japan, and through it a new global framework within which overall relations between the United States and Japan could flourish.

13.   Structural Impediments Initiative Agreement

U.S. Special Trade Representative

- We have reached agreement today with the Japanese Government on a Joint Report on the Structural Impediments Initiative [SII].
- The SII is an unprecedented cooperative effort to identify and solve structural problems in both countries that stand as impediments to trade and to balance of payments adjustment, with the goal of contributing to the reduction of payments imbalances.
- A year ago we were asked by our heads of government to submit this report to President Bush and Prime Minister Kaifu by the time of the Houston Summit, a goal we have met.

SOURCE: United States Special Trade Representative; "Structural Impediments Initiative Agreement," June 28, 1990.

- Our talks this week have been lengthy and intensive, taking us beyond the originally scheduled two days. This reflects the complexity of the subject and seriousness with which both sides view this exercise.
- We have reviewed a range of U.S. structural impediments, including saving and investment patterns, competitiveness, corporate behavior, government deregulation, research and development promotion, and workforce training and education. We have also reviewed an equally broad range of structural problems in the Japanese economy, including public investment, land use, distribution, exclusionary business practices, keiretsu relationships, and pricing mechanisms. In all of these areas, progress has been made.

- We believe that this report is an historic document that contains wide-ranging commitments and actions with significant benefits for both economies. It also represents substantial progress since the Interim Report which the Working Group released in the beginning of April.
- We believe that the commitments and actions spelled out in the report should help to reduce payments imbalances, lead to more efficient, open and competitive markets, promote sustained economic growth and enhance the quality of life in both Japan and the United States.
- Both governments are firmly determined to achieving these goals.

We have agreed, therefore, on a follow-up mechanism, involving a number of meetings, to:

- review progress achieved regarding issues identified in the Final Report;
- discuss matters relevant to problem areas already identified in the SII and the need for actions to address them; and
- produce in spring of each year a written report respectively on the progress made by each country toward solving its structural problems thereby contributing to the reduction of external imbalances, review the reports together, and issue them with a joint press release.

KEY ELEMENTS OF SII JOINT REPORT

The U.S.-Japan Working Group on the Structural Impediments Initiative ... reached agreement on an SII Joint Report during talks on June 25-28. This follows an Interim Report issued on April 5, 1990.

These talks have involved a unique effort by the U.S. and Japan to identify and solve structural impediments in both economies that stand as impediments to trade and balance of payments adjustment. During this year, both sides have made commitments and taken action designed to address these problems. The measures contained in the Joint Report should contribute to the promotion of open and competitive markets, the reduction of trade and current account imbalances, and an improved quality of life. In order to review jointly the implementation of its commitments in the Joint Report and to discuss the need for further actions, the SII Working Group agreed to establish an open, flexible follow-up process, which will include regular meetings, a review of progress, and an annual report with a joint press release.

Attached is an informal summary list of the policy commitments made by the Japanese and U.S. Governments, as contained in the Joint Report.

Japanese Commitments

I. Saving and Investment Patterns A principal objective of the SII talks is a further reduction in the current account imbalances of Japan and the United States. Reducing the gap between domestic saving and investment in Japan is important for the further reduction of the Japanese current account imbalance. The appropriate way to close the gap is not by reducing Japanese savings, but through increased investment. Japan also has an acknowledged need for a substantial increase in public infrastructure investment to improve the quality of life in Japan.

Therefore, an important component of Japan's efforts to reduce its current account surplus is a substantial new long term public investment program. Specifically, Japan has agreed to the following commitments and statement:

- A clear recognition of the need to continue to reduce Japan's current account surplus and a strong reaffirmation of its commitment to work actively toward that end.
- A recognition that a further reduction of the Japanese current account surplus is compatible with Japan's ability to continue to export long-term capital.
- The launching of a 430 trillion yen (about \$2.8 trillion) comprehensive public infrastructure plan for the years FY1991-2000 plus an expected 25 trillion yen in investment by Nippon Telephone and Telegraph and Japan Railways, which should also make a meaningful contribution to Japanese current account adjustment.
- A major increase in public investment over the previous decade from these actions.
- The preparation on a fast track basis of eight new larger, long term sectoral plans in key infrastructure areas such as housing, airports and port facilities, parks and sewers, with these larger yen values to be fixed by March 31, 1991.
- A Government of Japan intention to prepare large long-term plans for certain other key areas, such as roads, when the current plans expire, on a scale similar to that for the eight new plans.
- A major contribution from these plans to addressing the needs of the Japanese people for improved infrastructure to facilitate a higher level of imports.
- A more effective utilization of public investment financing procedures such as through multiyear budget funding and intermediation by public bodies, for example, the Fiscal Investment and Loan Program (FILP) in order to implement the new plans.

II. Land Use   Recent sharp rises in land prices have made home ownership increasingly difficult in Japan, and have widened the gap between those who own land and those who do not. High land prices also discourage business entrants, including foreign businesses, while the rise in land values has improved incumbent businesses' ability to borrow. At the same time, a substantial amount of metropolitan land in Japan is used inefficiently, or is held idle. More neutral land policies would increase the supply of land available for residential, commercial and public investment, and slow the rise in land prices. The Government of Japan recognizes that this is one of the most serious domestic problems it faces, and has committed to implement a wide range of measures designed to increase the supply of land and public and commercial facilities, including:

- Expeditious rationalization of assessments for inheritance tax, bringing the assessment closer to market value.
- Enactment of legislation to deregulate zoning limits on building heights and housing density and promote more efficient use of urban land.
- Comprehensive review and reform of the system of land taxation, in accordance with the principles of the recently enacted Basic Land Law, with the objective of making taxes more equitable, neutral and simple.

    This review began in April 1990 and is expected to be completed in November 1990, with a view toward submitting legislation to the Diet by the end of FY1990.

    The Sub-Commission on Land Taxation issued opinions in May containing useful suggestions on the possibility of ending the deferral system on inheritance tax and the fixed assets tax, and increasing the special land holding tax on idle land.
- Review of Land Lease Law and House Lease Laws to improve the legal rela-

tionship between lessors and lessees, taking into account the desirability of greater availability of housing. Any subsequent changes in these laws are expected to increase in the supply of housing for lease.

- Improvement and increase of infrastructure necessary to facilitate an increase in the supply of housing and residential land.
- Review of divisions between Urban Promotion Areas and Urbanization Control Areas, and changes in zoning designations in order to facilitate planned conversion of agricultural land in urban areas.
- Establishment of a new system for identifying and promoting the utilization for housing, business, and commercial purposes, etc., of idle land. Commitment to encourage local authorities to utilize actively and expeditiously this new system.
- Identification of idle and underutilized state-owned land by end FY-1990, with the goal of converting idle and underutilized state-owned land to productive use by the end of FY-1991.
- Commitment to encourage more vigorous utilization of eminent domain. Commitment to encourage more effective use of subterranean property.

III. Distribution Greater access to the Japanese market is a central objective in SII. Reform of the Japanese distribution system through deregulation, strengthened antitrust enforcement, and the improvement of import-related infrastructure will ease entry for new firms and allow imports to penetrate the Japanese market with more speed and less cost. Government of Japan commitments include:

- Concrete steps to implement the goal of "24 hour" import clearance, e.g., establishing an integrated import processing system among customs and other agencies, initiating pre-arrival processing and improving cargo processing infrastructure and systems.
- Improved infrastructure for imports, including a substantial increase in airport capacity to meet rapidly growing demand and a high priority on import-related harbor facilities.
- Creation of an Import Board to present concerns of importers and foreign business to the Prime Minister and his Trade Council.
- Review of standards, certification and testing, including industry associations standards, to ensure they are transparent and performance based.
- Easing of restrictions in the distribution area, including liquor licensing, trucking, commercial "800" toll calls, and general pharmaceutical goods.
- Substantial liberalization of the Large Scale Retail Store Law in May, including shortening the approval period to 18 months and introduction of legislation in the next Diet session to shorten the period further to 12 months and increase the transparency of the approval process, with emphasis on concerns of consumers rather than competitors.
- Strengthened antitrust enforcement against anticompetitive practices in the distribution sector and JFTC issuance of specific Antimonopoly Act guidelines on unlawful practices in distribution by the end of FY-1990.
- Issuance of MITI guidelines on fair trading practices.
- JFTC pledge to enforce premium restrictions so that they do not impede foreign entry, and to review all industry "fair competition codes" to ensure they do not restrict imports or investment.

IV. Exclusionary Business Practices Elimination of exclusionary business practices is essential to ensuring an open Japanese market. Vigorous antimonopoly enforcement, encouragement of non-discriminatory corporate procurement, faster processing of patent applications and more transparent and pro-competitive government interaction with business will benefit Japanese consumers and provide enhanced market opportunities for foreign and domestic firms. Commitments by the Government of Japan include:

- Increased staff and investigatory resources of the Fair Trade Commission (FTC);
- More vigorous enforcement of the Antimonopoly Act (AMA), including formal (rather than informal) FTC actions against price fixing, supply restraints, market allocation agreements, bidrigging and group boycotts.

   Much stronger criminal enforcement of the AMA, including vigorous pursuit of criminal sanctions against price-fixing, supply restraints, market allocations, bidrigging and group boycotts and formal coordination between the FTC, Ministry of Justice and prosecutors.
- Increased AMA penalties to levels that effectively deter violations through new legislation to be submitted in the next Diet session.
- Making private remedies for AMA violations effective, including strong FTC actions to facilitate successful private damage actions and a study of possible changes in filing fees.
- Greater efforts to eliminate bidrigging on government-funded projects, including increased vigilance by procuring agencies, strengthened administrative penalties and commitments to report bidrigging information to enforcement authorities.
- A reduction of the patent examination period to 24 months within 5 years (down from 37 months) with significant and continuous increases in the number of patent examiners.

- Minimizing exemptions to the Antimonopoly Law and preventing the use of recession cartels to impede imports.
- More transparent and fair administrative guidance by ensuring that administrative guidance does not restrict market access or undermine fair competition; publication of written administrative guidance except in special situations like national security or divulgence of trade secrets.
- More open and inclusive advisory committees and study groups including commitments to publish results; consider consumer and foreign interests; permit foreign participation; prohibit discussion of anticompetitive measures; place emphasis on imports in "visions" involving trade matters; and prohibit the use of "visions" to favor particular companies.
- Encouragement of transparent and non-discriminatory procurement by private Japanese companies, including support of guidelines adopted by the Japan Federation of Economic Organizations (Keidanren) and the conducting of annual surveys of private procurement procedures.

V. Keiretsu Relationships and Foreign Direct Investment   The network of formal and informal ties among Japanese companies known in Japan as *keiretsu* can promote preferential group trade, negatively affect foreign direct investment in Japan, and give rise to anticompetitive business practices. Loosening keiretsu relationships and making them more transparent would facilitate the entry of foreign goods, services, and investment into the Japanese market. The Government of Japan's commitments include:

- Commitment to make keiretsu more open and transparent and take necessary steps toward that end.
- Issuance of a policy statement affirming

that the Government of Japan will implement measures to ensure that keiretsu relationships do not hinder fair competition and calling on the cooperation of keiretsu firms toward that end.

- Commitment to restrict cross shareholding or require divestiture of shares where the FTC finds that such cross shareholding may lead to certain Antimonopoly Act violations.
- Strengthened enforcement of the Antimonopoly Act and FTC monitoring of transactions within keiretsu, including regular FTC analyses of various aspects of keiretsu groups, with a special emphasis on the role of trading companies.
- Enhanced public disclosure requirements for related-party transactions in line with FASB Standard No. 57 in the U.S., and enhanced consolidated and segmented reporting requirements.
- Liberalization of Japan's policies on foreign direct investment, including amending the Foreign Exchange and Foreign Trade Control Law to:
  abolish the broad authority of the Government of Japan to block foreign direct investment on broad economic grounds; and
  relax or abolish the prior notification requirement for foreign direct investment and importation of technology into Japan.
- Review the Commercial Code with a view to enhancing shareholders' rights and public disclosure requirements.

Pricing Mechanism

The joint U.S. Department of Commerce-MITI price survey established the existence of substantially higher prices for both foreign and domestic products in the Japanese market. These may be regarded as indicators of the existence of structural barriers to import competition; changes in the pattern and level of price

differentials will serve as a barometer of the effectiveness of overall SII reforms. In addition to actions in other areas which are expected to impact price differences, the Government of Japan has also undertaken the following commitments:

- Publication in July 1990 of a report by the Joint Government-LDP Price Headquarters on implementation of 52 measures to eliminate price differentials, as well as a clearer schedule for further implementation.
- Establishment of a Third Administrative Reform Council to pursue implementation of Second Administrative Reform Council recommendations, and identify new areas for deregulation.
- Recognition that changes in prices are significantly related to structural issues, and agreement to submit price surveys to the SII follow-up for senior level discussions.
- Agreement that methodology, analysis, and identification of price differentials for SII-related price surveys will be transparent and discussed by both sides.
- Commitment that price surveys will not be mandatory, will not compel disclosure of trade secrets.
- Agreement to conduct future joint price surveys for use in the SII process.

U.S. COMMITMENTS IN THE STRUCTURAL IMPEDIMENTS INITIATIVE

Below is a list of the principal commitments made by the U.S. Government during the Structural Impediments Initiative (SII) talks.

1. Saving and Investment Patterns:

Federal budget deficit

- The Administration's top priority is to eliminate the Federal budget deficit and to reduce the Government's outstanding debt. President Bush has reaffirmed his commitment to achieving these aims by initiating bi-partisan negotiations with Congressional leaders to develop a responsible and lasting solution to Federal budgetary imbalances.

• These budget negotiations are intended to reach an agreement that would reduce the deficit substantially on a multi-year basis, allow the economy to continue to grow, strengthen the budget process, and avoid the adverse economic and programmatic effects of a budget stalemate. President Bush outlined the key elements of an acceptable deficit reduction agreement in a statement issued on June 26, 1990. Reviewing the status of these negotiations, he said:

It is clear to me that both the size of the deficit problem and the need for a package that can be enacted require all of the following: entitlement and mandatory program reform; tax revenue increases; growth incentives; discretionary spending reductions; orderly reductions in defense expenditures; and budget process reform—to assure that any Bipartisan agreement is enforceable and that the deficit problem is brought under responsible control. The Bipartisan leadership agree with me on these points.

• Building upon the 1989 legislation enacted to remedy problems in the savings and loan industry, the Administration is committed to reducing the Government's exposure to potential risks posed by Federal credit programs. Work is being done to ensure the financial safety and soundness of the Government Sponsored Enterprises and the Federal deposit insurance system.

Promoting private saving

• The Administration is strongly urging the Congress to enact the Savings and Economic Growth Act of 1990, which is designed to stimulate private saving and investment. The Act would create new Family Savings Accounts, enhance existing Individual Retirement Accounts, and cut effective tax rates on capital gains.

• These proposals would serve to expand the pool of available savings and would be particularly beneficial for long-term investment.

II. Corporate Investment Activities and Supply Capacity: Improvement of U.S. Competitiveness

Antitrust reform

• The Administration will strongly support enactment of the Cooperative Production Act of 1990, which would reduce uncertainty about antitrust law treatment of those joint production ventures that enhance competition, while retaining appropriate safeguards for consumers.

Product liability reform

• The Administration strongly endorses the Product Liability Coordinating Committee (PLCC) Act that would reform product liability laws by contributing to uniformity among the states and limiting damage awards.

Openness to foreign direct investment

• The Administration will issue a detailed policy statement reaffirming its strong commitment to an open and non-discriminatory direct investment policy. This statement will be issued as soon as possible following the release of the SII Joint Report.

Tax treatment of foreign investors

- The Administration will seek to ensure that Japanese investors will be given non-discriminatory treatment under the U.S.-Japan Tax Treaty.
- The Treasury Department will continue to make clear to Congress its opposition to pending legislation which would tax certain foreign shareholders on capital gains from the sale of stock in U.S. corporations.

III. Corporate Behavior

- The Administration is supporting policies to lower the cost of capital such as reducing effective tax rates on capital gains, promoting private saving and eliminating Federal dis-saving. A lower cost of capital would facilitate long-term investment and long-term planning by companies in the United States.
- As a part of its review of factors influencing U.S. corporate competitiveness, the Treasury is analyzing what governmental barriers exist, if any, that detract from a constructive relationship between shareholders and corporate management.

IV. Government Deregulation

Export deregulation

- In accordance with COCOM agreed guidelines, the Administration plans to implement a new system this summer that would eliminate most licensing requirements for trade among COCOM nations.
- The Administration will review improvements in the ability of the Government of Japan and other cooperating governments to screen and verify exports and will consider eliminating U.S. reexport controls accordingly.

Energy exports

- The Administration supports a recommendation in a Commerce Department study which called for a partial relaxation of the ban on exports of California heavy crude oil.

V. Research and Development

Support for research and development

- The Administration supports a substantial increase for the FY-1991 Federal funding for research and development (civilian—12%; defense—4%), civil space activities (22%), and the National Science Foundation (14%).
- The Administration seeks to make permanent the Research and Experimentation (R&E) credit, and to revise the R&E allocation rules.

Adoption of the metric system

- An updated "Metric Conversion Policy for Federal Agencies," including stronger guidance for Federal metric implementation and agency reporting requirements to Congress, will be published in July 1990.
- The Interagency Committee on Metric Policy will develop a timetable for actions in carrying out the objectives of metrication.

VI. Export Promotion

- President Bush has directed the Economic Policy Council to undertake a Commercial Opportunities Initiative to assist U.S. exporters. The cornerstone of this initiative will be the Trade Promotion Coordinating Committee (TPCC), to be chaired by the Secretary of Commerce. The TPCC will, for the first time, unify and streamline Federal trade promotion activities.

- The Department of Commerce is implementing a special Japan export promotion program aimed specifically at increasing exports to the Japanese market.

VII. Work Force Education and Training

Work force education

- The President and the Nation's governors agreed on national education goals that stress excellence in education and scholastic achievement. These goals are to be reached by the year 2000.
- President Bush has proposed a variety of measures to improve science and math education, including increased Federal funding.

Work force training

- The Secretary of Labor has launched a seven-point action plan to improve the quality of the work force. The plan will draw on and reinforce the growing commitment of the private sector to work force training.
- The Japanese Ministry of Labor and the U.S. Department of Labor will cohost a symposium in November 1990, which will highlight Japanese human resource development policies. This conference, to be held in Washington, will allow human resource executives of more than 200 corporations to learn how Japanese business, government and labor work together to build a quality work force.

CHAPTER 5

The Distribution of International Economic Power

This section is concerned with the changing international economic environment. The first article, by Georgetown University political scientist Robert Lieber, considers the implications of the Persian Gulf war for the world oil market and for global energy security. Lieber notes three reasons for a sanguine conclusion. First, Iraq's devastating military defeat should discourage further military threats in the region. Second, oil-producing and oil-consuming countries absorbed the oil-related problems of the Gulf crisis. Third, "elasticities of both supply and demand appear to insure that world energy markets can and will cope with potential disruptions." However, Lieber remarks that "avoidance of serious upheaval was by no means inevitable." He recommends three policy measures: First, "maintain some mix of forces capable of intervening effectively in the Gulf." Second, work with international agencies to reduce the threat of chemical and nuclear weapons in the Gulf. Third, strengthen the international strategic petroleum reserve.

The second article is the final communique of the London Economic Summit in 1991. The leaders of the advanced industrialized countries pledged to coordinate their economic policies, to reverse trade protectionism, to stabilize global energy supplies, to integrate Eastern Europe and Russia into the world economy, to increase aid to developing countries, to protect the international environment, and to strengthen the U.N.

The next article reviews the state of the post-Soviet economy. The author, Howard Wachtel, asserts that post-Soviet economic reform has been paralyzed for many reasons: Gorbachev's lack of commitment to reforms, the magnitude of the problem, and the power of the state bureaucracy. Wachtel then argues that the $100 billion "grand-bargain" concept is doomed to failure because of its excessive cost and its limited prospects for improving everyday life for ordinary citizens. He concludes that the former Soviet economy needs to earn hard currency, to encourage intermediate economic institutions (such as small independent banks), to import massive shipments of food, and to sell off state enterprises.

The transition from a socialist economy to a market-oriented economy is also the topic of the next article, "Economic Reforms in Eastern Europe." The author, a World Bank economist, reviews the efforts of Eastern European nations to convert centrally planned economies to market economies. He argues that Eastern European countries must control inflation, adopt appropriate exchange rate policies, reform financial institutions, and dismantle their public enterprises. He also contends that the countries of Eastern Europe must reverse environmental degradation and renovate their physical infrastructures.

The fifth article in this section examines the politics of economic growth in the NICs of East Asia (Taiwan, South Korea, Hong Kong, and Singapore). The author, Stephan Haggard, notes various factors which may be responsible for the growth of these economies: expanding world trade, pressure from the United States for reform, import-substitution policies, meritocratic governmental bureaucracies, and the lack of interest group pressures. Haggard concludes that economic growth in the East Asian NICs "did not spring from a blind faith in the market."

The next article, by Jeffrey Schott, concerns the role of trading blocs in the world trading system. Schott notes the fear that international trade will become increasingly regionalized. He examines recent developments in three potential trading blocs: the EC, North America, and East Asia. He concludes that "a European trading bloc is clearly in existence and developing further; a North American bloc is evolving, although with a distinct outward orientation; and an East Asian bloc remains a remote prospect."

The final selection concerns recent economic behavior in China. Roger Gordon and Wei Li review the economic reforms introduced by the Chinese government between 1979 and 1989, including decentralization, relaxation of price controls, and allowing firms to retain a larger portion of profits. The Chinese government also "made it easier for local governments, collectives, and even private households to set up their own firms outside of the state planning structure." The authors conclude that decentralized decision making caused rapid increases in output and productivity. However, they note that rapid rates of inflation have created price distortions and "growing opportunities for tax evasion."

14.   Oil and Power after the Gulf War

Robert J. Lieber

What are the implications of the Gulf War for the world oil market and for global energy security? On initial examination, there would seem to be little cause for concern, and no fewer than three separate factors contribute to such a conclusion. First, the devastating defeat suffered by Iraq suggests that both past and future military threats can be minimized. Second, the success with which producing and consuming countries managed to cope with the purely oil-related components of the Gulf crisis suggests that both the supply and the price of petroleum are manageable. Third, regardless of policy choices made by these countries, elasticities of both supply and demand appear to insure that world energy markets can and will cope with potential disruptions.

However, an assessment of oil and power in the aftermath of the Gulf War provides evidence for concluding that the risks were in fact very substantial and that avoidance of serious upheaval was by no means inevitable. This interpretation rests not only on analysis of the Gulf crisis itself, but also on the lessons of the two oil shocks of the 1970s, as well as on experience from the following decade. In this light, each of the three arguments above proves less reassuring.

In the military realm, the extraordinary victory of the American-led coalition in an air war lasting just over five weeks and

a ground war of 100 hours has given rise to a virtual consensus on both the invincibility of the coalition and the inevitability of its triumph. However, cases both old (the debacle of Australian and other British Empire forces at Gallipoli against the Ottoman Turks in 1915[1]) and more contemporary (the failure of Desert One, the American effort to rescue the Iranian-held hostages in April 1980[2]), and even the ambiguous consequences of Israel's 1982 war in Lebanon,[3] suggest that the triumph of the forces of modern or Western powers over those of less technically-advanced Middle Eastern regimes cannot simply be taken for granted.

Moreover, timing proves to have been crucial. Had Saddam Hussein's forces promptly followed their August 2, 1990, invasion and occupation of Kuwait by a drive into Saudi Arabia, the Saudis and Americans would have lacked the military means to stop the hundreds of thousands of troops and the thousands of armored vehicles under the command of the Iraqi dictator. At best, this might have triggered a longer, less successful, and far

[1] A brief account of the Gallipoli expedition and debacle can be found in David Fromkin, *A Peace to End All Peace: The Fall of the Ottoman Empire and the Creation of the Modern Middle East* (New York: Avon, 1990), pp. 150–187. For a comprehensive treatment, see Alan Moorehead, *Gallipoli* (New York: Harper and Brothers, 1956).

[2] See, for example, Gary Sick, *All Fall Down: America's Tragic Encounter with Iran* (New York: Random House, 1985), pp. 296–302.

[3] In particular, see Avner Yaniv's assessment of what he terms a "Pyrrhic victory," as well as the unforeseen domestic and international political reverberations, in Yaniv, *Dilemmas of Security: Politics, Strategy and the Israeli Experience in Lebanon* (New York: Oxford University Press, 1987), pp. 117ff and 216–284.

SOURCE: Reprinted from *International Security,* vol. 17, no. 1, Summer 1992, pp. 155–176 by permission of The MIT Press, Cambridge, Massachusetts. Copyright © 1992 by the President and Fellows of Harvard College and the Massachusetts Institute of Technology.

An earlier draft of this paper was presented at a conference on "Iraq Under the Ba'ath," Haifa University, May 27, 1981. I would like to thank the participants there for comments.

more costly war. At worst, Saddam might have controlled the Saudi Gulf Coast ports and major Saudi oilfields, leaving the United States with two unwelcome options: to mount a military campaign without the benefit of the Saudi ports and facilities and to risk the kind of destruction later seen in Kuwait on a still vaster scale against the oilfields of Saudi Arabia, or to acquiesce in Iraq's control of almost half the world's proved oil reserves, as well as the likelihood of Saddam's domination of the remainder of the Gulf oil producers.

The cutoff of Kuwaiti and Iraqi oil from world oil markets was managed, but with a costly volatility in world oil prices. Saudi Arabia increased its own oil production by more than 3 million barrels per day (mbd), approximately the amount previously supplied by Iraq, and other countries more than made up the shortfall caused by the loss of Kuwait's production. On the demand side, the countries of the International Energy Agency (IEA), led by the United States, eventually took measures to signal both their ability and their will to reduce demand and subsequently to release oil from their strategic stocks. Nonetheless, the United States and the IEA countries were slow to announce their intent to draw down stocks, and these delays appear to have been costly.

While markets did work, the temporary run-up of prices proved costly in terms of inflation and in tipping a weakening American economy into a serious recession.[4] Moreover, one lesson of the 1973–

[4] The annual "Economic Report of the President" subsequently concluded that the rapid rise in oil prices and uncertainties accompanying the crisis with Iraq were among the factors that tipped the U.S. economy, then only barely growing, into recession in the third quarter of 1990. See John M. Barry, "Administration's Annual Economic Report Presents Lower Expectations," *Washington Post,* February 6, 1992, p. A14.

74 and 1979–80 oil shocks is that markets often over-shoot, and that inelasticities of both supply and demand for energy can make the adjustment process long and very costly. Indeed, even with the supply and demand effects largely under control, initial uncertainties and market psychology caused oil prices to triple. These surged from a pre-crisis level of $13 per barrel in May 1990, to a peak of over $40 per barrel in the early autumn, before falling back to the $20 per barrel range.

In sum, the experience of the Gulf crisis—as well as the evidence of the past two decades—leaves little reason for complacency, and the case thus deserves careful examination. The remainder of this article attempts to do so, first, by assessing oil as a problem in international politics and political economy, in terms of the need for integrating both economic and political dimensions of analysis. It then considers the status of oil from Iraq and the Persian Gulf along with problems posed by the fact that two-thirds of proved world petroleum reserves are located in the Gulf region. Next, the article turns to specific consideration of Iraqi and Saudi oil, and the way in which the global oil system reacted to the crisis. Finally, a number of policy implications are examined.

OIL AS A PROBLEM IN POLITICAL ECONOMY

A reliable understanding of the role of oil in international politics and international political economy has proven elusive. A principal reason for this is that too many observers approach the subject through perspectives that are narrowly economic or, conversely, mostly political. These interpretations, in their most pristine forms, can be considered as "ideal types."

From the vantage point of the exclusively economic perspective, it is simply assumed that the market mechanism will provide an eventual equilibrium for supply and demand.[5] Thus if shortages of oil develop, prices will rise until the available supply matches demand. Higher prices will have the effect of causing additional supplies of oil and other forms of energy to be developed and brought to market. At the same time, higher prices will result in reduced demand as buyers seek to economize by conserving or by switching to other forms of energy.

From the economic perspective, policies aimed at protecting energy security or incorporating externalities are seen as largely irrelevant, and the risks of energy crises are seen as minimal.[6] Moreover, the economic perspective points to both the unintended consequences and to the failure of deliberate governmental policies. For example during the 1970s, price regulation and allocation policies for oil and natural gas did not prevent, and may even have fostered, spot shortages, gas lines, congressional stalemate, and polit-

ical recrimination, and they were ultimately discarded. Also unsuccessful and later abandoned was the expensive synthetic fuels program initiated by the Carter administration.

However, the economic perspective itself remains seriously deficient when used in isolation. For one thing, it tends either to minimize the importance of the Organization of Petroleum Exporting Countries (OPEC) in shaping the world oil system, or else to suggest that long-term market factors make it largely impossible for OPEC to have a lasting impact. Moreover, this approach tends to overlook the implications of geography, particularly the fact that no less than 67 percent of proved world oil reserves are located in the Persian Gulf area, one of the most politically unstable regions on earth. In addition, market imperfections and barriers to market entry, in terms both of cost and time, are disregarded. Yet, regardless of market signals, it costs many billions of dollars and takes many years to find and develop a new oil field or develop particular energy sources. Finally, an exclusively economic perspective does not successfully meet an historical reality test. That is, given the costly and disruptive cases of the 1973–74 and 1979–80 oil shocks, it fails to provide a convincing explanation for why such disruptions may not be repeated.

Conversely, analyses of oil which are essentially—or even exclusively—political also provide only a one-dimensional perspective. These approaches tend to minimize the role of market phenomena. They thus have overstated the threat of oil embargoes, exaggerated the relationship between world oil supply and the Arab-Israeli conflict, and inflated the fundamental power of individual oil-producing countries. After each of the 1970s oil shocks, the political approach tended to assume that oil prices would continue to rise indefinitely.

To be sure, many of the prevailing eco-

[5] For example, the initial National Energy Policy Plan of the Reagan administration held that market forces could increase petroleum investment and production, and it also held that this approach should be applied in times of crisis: "In the event of an emergency, preparedness plans call for relying primarily on market forces to allocate energy supplies." Summary of National Energy Policy Plan, U.S. Department of Energy, *Energy Insider,* Washington, D.C., August 3, 1981, p. 3.

[6] For example, the Reagan administration initially made clear that it would not use governmental action or resources to reduce oil imports or oil consumption. And, despite the previous decade of experience with international energy instability, it held the view that, "Achieving a low level of oil imports at any cost is not a major criterion for the nation's energy security and economic health. Even at its current high price, imported oil is substantially less expensive than available alternatives." Quoted in *Energy Insider,* August 3, 1981, p. 3. Moreover, as late as 1985, the administration advocated a "moratorium" on filling the Strategic Petroleum Reserve during the 1986 fiscal year. *New York Times,* February 5, 1986.

nomic (or political) interpretations are more complex than these ideal types convey. For example, one of the more sophisticated market-oriented interpretations, which sees economic forces tending to push oil prices lower over the long term and tends to downplay the risk of future oil shocks, nonetheless incorporates policy recommendations for the United States that go well beyond merely letting the market take its own course.[7] Thus, Eliyahu Kanovsky urges that the United States take steps to limit its vulnerability to Middle East supply disruptions through actions such as incentives for Third World states to pursue oil exploration and development, as well as the introduction of American fiscal and regulatory policies to encourage domestic energy efficiency and conservation.

In reality, oil can be understood most effectively through integrating insights from both economics and politics. Without this synthesis, there exists the kind of problem identified by Robert Gilpin, in which political scientists tend to overlook the role of markets, while economists often neglect the importance of power and the political context of events.[8]

[7] See Eliyahu Kanovsky, *OPEC Ascendant? Another Case of Crying Wolf,* Policy Papers No. 20 (Washington, D.C.: Washington Institute for Near East Policy, 1990), pp. x and 53–56. An earlier paper by the same author argued that competition for market share and revenue needs of oil exporters, along with advances in oil exploration and production, energy efficiency, and the conclusion of the Iran-Iraq war, would hold down the price of oil for the foreseeable future. Kanovsky, *Another Oil Shock in the 1990s? A Dissenting View,* Policy Papers No. 6 (Washington, D.C.: Washington Institute for Near East Policy, 1987.) See also the discussion of Kanovsky's approach by Hobart Rowen, *Washington Post,* May 12, 1991, p. H16.

[8] Robert Gilpin, *U.S. Power and the Multinational Corporation: The Political Economy of Direct Foreign Investment* (New York: Basic Books, 1975), pp. 4–5.

Oil issues in the Middle East take on a broad significance because they encompass both political and economic dimensions and because they often have consequences that spread far beyond regional confines. Under certain very specific circumstances, events occurring in the Gulf can reverberate halfway around the world, and do so almost instantaneously. The most dramatic (though least common) pattern is that of an oil shock, defined as a profound disruption of the existing supply and price system. However, two major phenomena must be present simultaneously for such an event to take place. One is the existence of a tight or precarious balance between supply and demand, in which available world oil supplies only just manage to satisfy world oil demand and there is little or no additional unused production capacity. The second component is some major event (war or revolution being the most pertinent) that triggers a disturbance in existing supply patterns. When these two circumstances intersect, and only then, the result is an oil shock.

The political economy of world oil thus involves an integrated world system. All countries that import or export petroleum are linked to it. Developments occurring anywhere in the system that have a bearing on the demand or supply for oil, whether political or economic in nature, affect the overall balance of that system. Hence, when a serious disequilibrium occurs, the effects are felt globally. For example, even if the United States imported little or no Middle East oil, the fact that it imports any oil—and that its oil imports provide nearly 50 percent of its total petroleum supplies—means that it is almost instantly affected.

IRAQ AND PERSIAN GULF OIL

Prior to the outbreak of the Gulf crisis and war, Iraq was producing 3.4 million barrels of crude oil per day.[9] This represented a 20 percent increase over average output for 1989 and meant that Iraq had regained its level of peak production set in 1979, the last full year prior to the Iran-Iraq war. Even at the July 1990 figure, however, Iraq's oil output accounted for just 5.7 percent of world production.[10]

By another measure, however, Iraq's importance to the world oil system is significantly greater. In terms of proved oil reserves, Iraq is second only to Saudi Arabia. (See Table 14.1.) Set against a world total of just under one thousand billion barrels, the Saudis, with 260 billion barrels, hold approximately 26 percent of the world total. Iraq has 100 billion barrels, equivalent to 10 percent, and is followed closely by the United Arab Emirates (98 billion barrels), Kuwait (97 billion barrels), and Iran (93 billion barrels). By contrast, the next largest group of producers, Venezuela, the Soviet Union, and Mexico, fall in the 51–59 billion barrel range. For its part, the United States has just 26 billion barrels, or the equivalent of only 2.6 percent of world proved reserves.

The significance of Iraq's position, par-

[9] *Monthly Energy Review* (Washington, D.C.: U.S. Department of Energy, Energy Information Administration, March 1991), Table 10.1a, p. 118.

[10] Percentage calculations throughout this paper are those of the author. World crude oil production in 1990 amounted to 60.072 mbd; *Monthly Energy Review,* March 1991, Table 10.1b, p. 119.

Table 14.1   Proved Oil Reserves

Country	Billion Barrels	Percent of World
Saudi Arabia	260.3	26.3
Iraq	100.0	10.1
United Arab Emirates	98.1	9.9
Kuwait	96.5	9.7
Iran	92.9	9.4
Venezuela	59.1	6.0
USSR	57.0	5.8
Mexico	51.3	5.2
United States	26.3	2.7
China	24.0	2.4
Libya	22.8	2.3
Nigeria	17.9	1.8
Algeria	9.2	0.9
Norway	7.6	0.8
Indonesia	6.6	0.7
India	6.1	0.6
Canada	5.6	0.6
Egypt	4.5	0.5
Oman	4.3	0.4
Yemen	4.0	0.4
United Kingdom	4.0	0.4
Others	32.9	3.1
World Totals	991.0	100.0

Notes: Based on data from *Oil and Gas Journal,* December 30, 1991, for reserves recoverable with present technology and prices. Data for Saudi Arabia and Kuwait include half of the Neutral Zone. UAE includes Abu Dhabi, Dubai, Ras al-Khaimah, and Sharjah. Figure for USSR is "explored reserves," including proved, probable and some possible. Author's calculations for "others" and percentages. Due to rounding, sum of percentages exceeds 100.0.

ticularly in the crisis, thus becomes more evident. As of August 2, 1990, not only did the regime of Saddam Hussein control both its own reserves and those of Kuwait—and thus some 20 percent of the world figure—but it directly menaced Saudi Arabia. Iraq thus was in position to dominate—either directly or indirectly—56 percent of all proved reserves, when oil of the rich but militarily inconsequential United Arab Emirates is counted.

To grasp the implications of this, it is essential to understand the importance of Gulf oil—and of OPEC more broadly—along with the reasons why this importance seems to wax and wane at various intervals. In brief, the volatility is due to a phenomenon which one analyst has called "the OPEC multiplier."[11] Oil-importing countries, due to a combination of political and economic reasons, have tended to rely on OPEC oil as a last resort. They prefer, where possible, to utilize domestic oil and energy resources. If they must resort to imports, they next seek supplies from non-OPEC countries. But when these other avenues are no longer available or are full utilized, they must turn to OPEC suppliers. As a consequence, changes in the demand for OPEC oil can be disproportionate to overall changes in world oil demand.

When world demand falls, the reductions thus affect OPEC to a greater extent than other suppliers. In the case of the United States, where total oil demand fell by more than 3.6 mbd—or almost 20 percent—between 1978 and 1983, domestic oil production continued at levels near full capacity, and imports of non-OPEC oil actually increased. At the same time, U.S. imports of OPEC oil fell sharply,

dropping from 5.7 to 1.8 mbd (a reduction of 68 percent).[12]

However, the OPEC multiplier works in the opposite direction as well. During the last half of the 1980s, a combination of economic growth, cheaper oil prices, and gradual decreases in American oil output caused an upsurge in world oil demand. At the time, most of the non-OPEC suppliers were producing at or near capacity, and so demand for OPEC oil rose rapidly. U.S. imports of OPEC oil increased by 2.5 mbd, to a level of 4.3 mbd. Global demand for OPEC oil surged from a low point of 16.6 mbd in 1985 to 24.3 mbd by the spring of 1990. At the time, OPEC still possessed several mbd of unused capacity, but much of this was concentrated within Saudi Arabia and other nearby areas in the Gulf.

IRAQI AND SAUDI OIL IN THE GULF CRISIS

In the weeks following the Iraqi invasion of Kuwait, the United Nations embargo against Iraq's oil exports had the effect of removing approximately 4.0 to 4.3 mbd from world supplies of crude oil.[13] World crude oil markets, reacting initially to the threat of war in the Gulf and then to the loss of oil from Iraq and Kuwait, saw a dramatic run-up in prices. As a result of growing tensions in the region, prices which had been as low as $13 per barrel

---

[11] For elaboration of the concept, see Bijan Mossavar-Rahmani, "The OPEC Multiplier," *Foreign Policy,* No. 52 (Fall 1982), pp. 136-148.

[12] In 1978, "petroleum products supplied" (i.e., total demand for petroleum) in the United States amounted to 18,847 mbd. By 1983 the figure had declined to 15.231. *Monthly Energy Review,* March 1991, p. 17.

[13] As of December 1989, Iraq had been producing 3.0 mbd and Kuwait 2.1. By December 1990, these figures had fallen to 0.425 for Iraq and a mere 0.075 for Kuwait. Counting domestic uses of various kinds, the combined reduction of nearly 4.6 mbd was greater than the two countries' net exports, together estimated in the range of 4.0 to 4.3 mbd.

for Saudi light crude oil in June 1990 had already climbed to $20 by mid-July. By August 2, the day of the invasion, oil reached $24 per barrel. Not surprisingly, prices moved steeply higher in the following weeks, peaking at $40.42 on October 11.[14]

Set against world oil production of some 60 million barrels per day, Iraqi and Kuwaiti oil exports before the crisis amounted to approximately 7 percent of the global total. A shortfall of this magnitude, had it not been offset by production increases elsewhere, would have been in the same range as the one that triggered the 1973–74 oil crisis, and would have been larger than the 4 percent shortfall experienced during the second oil crisis in early 1979.[15]

Moreover, even though a supply shortage did not materialize, the economic impacts of sharply higher oil prices threatened to be significant. Thus, had oil remained at an average price of $30 per barrel for all of 1991, instead of receding to $20 by late January, the industrial democracies of the Organization for Economic Cooperation and Development (OECD) would have seen 2 percent additional inflation, 0.5 percent reduction in gross national product (GNP) growth, and an adverse $90 billion shift in the balance of trade.[16] By themselves, these effects would have been less damaging than the results of the 1970s oil shocks (the numbers for inflation and balance of

trade, for example, were only one-third those of the earlier period[17]), but they could nonetheless have been significant factors in tilting the world economy into recession. Moreover, even the relatively brief price "spike" that did occur exacerbated economic problems in Eastern Europe and parts of the Third World, and damaged certain industries (e.g., aviation, automobiles) in the more prosperous Western countries.

In reality, despite the loss of Iraqi and Kuwaiti crude oil, and fears that terrorism or war could further reduce supplies of oil from the Gulf, sufficient oil production increases became available to offset the potential shortfall. Almost 80 percent of this production came from Persian Gulf states and from other member countries of OPEC, with smaller amounts from producers elsewhere around the world. However, Saudi Arabia proved to be the greatest source of increased production.

Between December 1989 and December 1990, Saudi production of crude oil rose by nearly 2.9 mbd, to a level of almost 8.6 million barrels per day. (See Table 14.2.) In other words, although a great deal of additional activity took place elsewhere, including not only production increases, efforts to curtail or defer demand, and a January 17, 1991, pledge by the twenty-one states of the International Energy Agency to make available 2 mbd

[14] With the exception of the June figure, all prices are for light sweet crude oil quoted on the New York Mercantile Exchange; see *New York Times,* October 12, 1990, and March 1, 1991.

[15] See Robert J. Lieber, *The Oil Decade: Conflict and Cooperation in the West* (Lanham, Md.: University Press of America, 1986), especially pp. 13–43.

[16] Data from "The World Economy: Third Time Lucky," *The Economist* (London), August 11, 1990, p. 23.

[17] The increased wealth transfer at $30 per barrel from the OECD countries would have been on the order of 0.6 percent of GNP, whereas in each of the 1970s oil shocks, the figure was 2.0 percent. In addition, compared with a hypothetical OECD inflation increase of 2 percent for 1991, the actual net increase for the Group of Seven leading industrial countries ("G7") in the 1974 shock was 6.1 percent (i.e., rising from 7.9 percent in 1973 to 14.0 percent in 1974). In the second oil shock, the inflation rate of the G7 increased by almost 6 percentage points. See "The World Economy: Third Time Lucky."

Table 14.2   Production of Crude Oil

Producers	December 1989	December 1990	Change	
Iraq	3.000 mbd	0.425 mbd	− 2.575 mbd	
Kuwait	2.090	0.075	− 2.015	
Total loss:				− 4.590
Estimated Global Loss (net of domestic consumption):				− 4.0 to 4.3
Saudi Arabia	5.696	8.570	+ 2.874	
Iran	2.900	3.300	+ 0.400	
Libya	1.201	1.500	+ 0.299	
Algeria	1.110	1.210	+ 0.100	
Qatar	0.395	0.370	− 0.025	
UAE	2.406	2.400	− 0.006	
Net Additions from Persian Gulf:				+ 3.642
Venezuela	1.977	2.340	+ 0.363	
Mexico	2.476	2.660	+ 0.184	
Indonesia	1.434	1.550	+ 0.116	
Nigeria	1.854	1.950	+ 0.096	
Total of Other Major Net Additions				+ 0.759
Other Totals:				
Arab OPEC	15.897	14.550	− 1.347	
Persian Gulf	16.529	15.182	− 1.347	
Total OPEC	24.605	24.280	− 0.325	
World	61.320	60.449	− 0.871	

NOTE: Numbers are given in millions of barrels per day (mbd).
SOURCE: Author's calculations from data in *Monthly Energy Review* (Washington, D.C.: U.S. Department of Energy, Energy Information Administration, March 1991), pp. 118–119.

from their reserves,[18] more than two-thirds of the reduction in oil from the Gulf was made up by Saudi Arabia alone,

[18] With the aim of reducing market volatility related to the Gulf War, the IEA countries agreed to make available approximately two million barrels per day from their governmental reserves and to take conservation measures to reduce demand by an additional 500,000 barrels per day. However, in implementing the plan at the end of January, 1991, Agency officials noted that oil would only be sold if oil companies indicated a need to buy it. See Steven Greenhouse, "International Energy Agency Affirms Plan to Tap Stocks," *New York Times,* January 29, 1991. This represented the first time since the IEA's creation in 1974 that its emergency draw-down system was put into effect. Shortly after the end of the war, on March 6, the IEA ended emergency sales of oil.

with less than 20 percent coming from outside the Middle East.[19]

Elsewhere, net additions to world supplies came from Iran (0.4 mbd), Venezuela (0.36), Libya (0.3), Indonesia (0.1), Algeria (0.1), Nigeria (0.1), with lesser amounts from a variety of other producers around the world. One important fac-

For details, see Steven Greenhouse, "International Energy Agency Ends Emergency Oil Sales," *New York Times,* March 7, 1991.
[19] Note that figures for oil supply from the Gulf and OPEC, as well as world figures, often vary depending on the particular source quoted, differing time periods, and other factors. For reasons of consistency, except when otherwise noted, data used in this paper comes from the *Monthly Energy Review* of the Energy Information Administration, U.S. Department of Energy.

tor worked in the opposite direction, however; due to a continuing decline in Soviet production, between December 1989 and December 1990, the reduction there came to more than 1 mbd. In total, world oil production in December 1990 was 60.4 mbd. Despite the Gulf crisis, this was just 0.9 mbd below the figure of a year earlier. With a reduction in world demand of some 1 mbd in response to the sharply higher price of crude oil, as well as the subsequent decision by the United States and other IEA countries to make available additional oil from stocks,[20] world oil supplies remained adequate.

In sum, no real oil crisis developed. The shortfalls from Iraq and Kuwait were effectively offset. By mid-January of 1991, oil prices fell below $20 per barrel, thus returning close to their pre-invasion levels and then fluctuating in a narrow range around that figure during the Gulf War and its aftermath.

Given this result, as well as the post-crisis commitment of the Saudis to maintaining high levels of oil production, the gradually increasing flow of Kuwaiti oil, and the prospect that some amounts of Iraqi oil will eventually be exported again, there might appear to be grounds for complacency: a potentially destabilizing loss of supply from two major producing countries was absorbed with no major crisis, while the accompanying surge in oil prices subsided within five months.

However, a closer look suggests reasons why the ability to experience a potential crisis without severe disruption cannot be taken for granted. The single most important factor here remains the role of Saudi Arabia. Had the Saudis been unable or unwilling to respond as they

did, the history of the Gulf crisis would have been far different. First, an Iraqi invasion of Saudi Arabia during the earliest days of the crisis would have been beyond the ability of the Saudis themselves—or of the American forces in their initial deployments—to repel. Saudi oil fields are concentrated in the vicinity of Ras Tanura, less than 200 miles from the Kuwaiti border, and these could have been seized by a determined Iraqi assault. In such circumstances, even had the Saudis retained any kind of nominal independence, it is unlikely they could have been in a position to do anything except acquiesce in whatever demands Saddam would have placed upon them and their resources.

Initially, on August 4, the U.S. Central Intelligence Agency (CIA) reported that Saddam's forces already numbered more than 100,000 men, and that the only obstacle between the Iraqis and the Saudi oil fields was a Saudi National Guard battalion of less than 1000 men.[21] At that moment, the U.S. ability to mount a military operation was extremely problematic. In the event, the American deployments succeeded because they had the full cooperation of the Saudi government, access to Saudi ports, and the use of a vast infrastructure of modern airbases. Without these requisites, an American military effort aimed at driving the Iraqi invaders out of both Saudi Arabia and Kuwait would have been exceptionally difficult and costly, if the Bush administration had even opted to attempt it. The widespread diplomatic, political,

[20] OECD stocks would have been sufficient to provide 2 mbd for an additional 4.5 years. Data on stocks from International Energy Agency, reported in *The Economist,* August 11, 1990, p. 21.

[21] Bob Woodward, *The Commanders* (New York: Simon and Schuster, 1991), p. 248. Moreover, during the first two weeks of American force deployments, the situation remained precarious, and both U.S. Chief of Staff General Colin Powell and Secretary of Defense Dick Cheney are reported to have believed that Saddam Hussein's forces would have had the upper hand. Ibid., pp. 278, 282–285.

and military support that the American-led coalition enjoyed would also have been far more difficult to assemble under circumstances in which Saddam's triumph looked self-evident and the costs of reversing it unsustainable.[22]

The subsequent Iraqi destruction and torching of Kuwait's oil wells in the midst of the allied military triumph also suggest that even a successful American assault on the Iraqi forces in Saudi Arabia would have resulted in unprecedented destruction of oil facilities. The threatened reduction, or actual disappearance, of 8.5 million barrels in oil supply (as measured against Saudi Arabia's December 1990 oil production) would have triggered a disastrous crisis in world oil supplies. Its consequences in shortfalls of petroleum for the world economy, staggering price increases, alliance disarray, and political blackmail can only be imagined.

As a consequence, by mid-August 1990, Saddam Hussein would have been in a position to exercise control over the oil resources of Kuwait and Saudi Arabia, along with those of Iraq. With 46 percent of the world's proved reserves of crude oil subject to his direct dictate, and with his Gulf neighbors painfully aware of his ability to use any means at his disposal, the Iraqi president would have gained access to a vast source of present and future wealth. Moreover, based on the record of the past two decades, there is every reason to believe that these resources would have permitted him to purchase the most modern forms of technology and arms, including missiles and nuclear weapons technology.

The sobering conclusion of this scenario is that oil-importing countries and Iraq's Middle Eastern and even European neighbors have been fortunate in what did *not* happen after August 2, 1990. Despite the shattering military defeat of Iraq and the destruction of much of its most dangerous weaponry, the avoidance of disaster was by no means inevitable.

IRAQ AND WORLD OIL: PAST AND FUTURE PATTERNS

Saddam Hussein's seizure of Kuwait had multiple causes, not least the Iraqi leader's characteristic over-reaching with its disastrous consequences. Nonetheless, important economic considerations are quite evident as well. During the decade of the 1980s, Iraq spent approximately $100 billion on its military. By mid-1990 the country had accumulated an international debt of approximately $90 billion,[23] on which interest payments

---

[22] A counterargument is that a more powerful and threatening Iraq might make it easier to muster support from other regional powers such as Iran and Syria, which might be expected to balance rather than bandwagon in their behavior. Moreover, Stephen Walt's work provides evidence of alliance formation in the Middle East in which state behavior is driven by reaction to threat. See Walt, *The Origins of Alliances* (Ithaca: Cornell University Press, 1987). However, practical—indeed brutal—regional realities work to minimize balancing. Saddam would have achieved a *fait accompli*. Moreover, against his demonstrated willingness to use violence with extreme ruthlessness against his internal and external adversaries, as well as his ability to wield both bribery and blackmail, the ability of his neighbors to effectively align themselves with the United States would have been highly problematic. In particular, having been militarily defeated after an eight-year war in which their cities were exposed to demoralizing Scud attacks, the Iranians' willingness and ability to play an active role in an anti-Saddam coalition, let alone balance by aligning themselves with America (the "Great Satan"), would have been improbable.

[23] Laurie Mylroie cites this figure, noting that it represented a $10 billion increase over the previous two years, i.e., from the time of the ceasefire with Iran. See Mylroie, *The Future of Iraq,* Policy Papers No. 24 (Washington, D.C.: Washington Institute for Near East Policy, 1991), p. 29.

amounted to some $8–10 billion per year. With world oil prices at $20 per barrel, exports of 3 mbd would generate less than $20 billion per year in revenues. Moreover, by June 1990, with both Iran's and Iraq's oil exports having increased following the end of their bloody war in 1988, oil prices had slipped to as low as $13 per barrel. At that figure, Iraq would earn approximately $14 billion per year, barely enough to cover debt service and imports of necessities. Given the costs of reconstruction following the Iran-Iraq war, the demands of the Iraqi economy and popular expectations, and Saddam's continuing and grandiose military spending predilections, the Iraqi leader sought means of increasing his country's revenues. Thus the resources and income afforded by the seizure of Kuwait, as well as the prospect of exerting leverage over Saudi Arabia and hence influence over world oil prices, offered a tempting target for the Iraqi leader.

In the aftermath of the Gulf War and continuing United Nations sanctions on oil exports, Iraq's economy has had an acute need for oil revenues. This reality provides some opportunity for external actors to influence that country's conduct. Sooner or later, however, Iraq will resume oil exports. When it does, the amounts involved can grow rather quickly. Indeed, just two months after the war ended, a CIA estimate concluded that within three months after restrictions were lifted, Iraq could be producing 1 mbd. And, with the investment of an additional $1.5 billion to repair pumping facilities, output could have reached 2.7 mbd by the end of 1992.[24]

Given Iraq's indebtedness, estimated costs of $30 billion to repair destruction caused by the latest war, and UN-mandated reparations of as much as $50 billion to pay for the destruction and looting in Kuwait,[25] Iraq will continue to have a pressing long-term need for export revenues. This provides motivation for Saddam, or his eventual successors, to seek ways of encouraging higher world oil prices. Moreover, it also suggests an underlying danger. It is that, barring major changes in existing circumstances, Iraq will have its own reasons for seeking to intimidate its neighbors. Apart from efforts to shape oil production and pricing policies, the aims of such pressure could also include obtaining financial assistance (in less polite terms, blackmail), influencing other countries' defense and foreign policies, and causing changes in the internal regime structure of adjacent states.

As long as the United States remains committed to regional security, whether in terms of troop presence or via longer-term security arrangements with an unambiguous American commitment, this potential intimidation from Iraq will not have much effect. The role played by the United States was unique in opposing the Iraqi takeover of Kuwait, in orchestrating UN condemnation and sanctions, and finally in leading an international coalition in a brief, devastating war against Iraq. However, if the United States proves unable to sustain a long-term commitment, or if regional states are unwilling or unable to collaborate in the maintenance of it, then Iraq will eventually find ways to reassert strength within the region. Under such circumstances, the regime of Saddam Hussein (or a successor regime with

[24] These calculations assumed that mutual agreement on lifting the sanctions would have been achieved, and that Western countries would have agreed to sell oil equipment to the Iraqis. However, Iraq rejected the UN terms for resuming initial limited oil exports and as of April 1992 no agreement had yet been

reached. The CIA report is described in Patrick E. Tyler, "Hussein's Ouster is U.S. Goal, But at What Cost to the Iraqis?" *New York Times,* April 28, 1991.
[25] *New York Times,* May 15, 1991, p. A16.

comparable interests and values) will continue to threaten both longer-term regional stability and the prevailing Persian Gulf oil regime. Although even in the absence of this threat there would remain internal and external sources of instability, for example Islamic fundamentalism and the uncertain nature of Iran's role, nonetheless Saddam and Iraq represent a demonstrably significant danger to their neighbors.

The oil dimension of this incorporates two distinct elements. One is that Iraq—having previously attacked four of its neighbors (Iran, Kuwait, Saudi Arabia, and Israel) and having bitter quarrels (Syria) or uneasy relations with others (Turkey)—could again find itself in a conflict or war. If so, the danger to oil facilities, whether intentional or not, is present. Alternatively, if Iraq succeeds in regaining regional power and influence, this may lead to an attempt to manipulate oil production for the purpose of increasing world prices. To be sure, the economic and market dimensions of the political economy of oil make it uncertain whether Iraq could ever succeed in these efforts. The experience of the OPEC countries in the 1980s suggests that this is a difficult task. On the other hand, if Iraq ultimately did manage to exert control over its neighbors, or succeed in intimidating them, the results could be quite different.

The interplay among politics and economics also means that if Iraq finds ways to regain a measure of economic strength and to loosen the sanctions upon itself, oil revenues can again be translated into offensive military power which once more could jeopardize the security of the region. Unless a UN embargo on weapons exports can be sustained and rigorously enforced, at least some arms manufacturing countries will seek markets for their exports of tanks, aircraft, missiles, chemical weapons, and nuclear weapons tech-

nology. The pressing financial predicament of the emergent East European economies, the problems of Latin American manufacturers such as Brazil and Argentina, and the behavior of China make this a long-term problem. Indeed, post-Gulf War accounts of a Czech decision to supply T-72 tanks to Syria, of China's shipment of M-9 missiles to Syria and construction of a nuclear "research" reactor in Algeria, and of an Argentine Condor II surface-to-surface missile program financed by Iraq[26] provide evidence that any sustained effort to control the export of advanced offensive weapons to the region will face great difficulties. Moreover, even with an embargo, the capability of Iraq's existing defense industrial base, coupled with the leakage of technology from outside sources, particularly from the former Soviet Union, presents an additional problem.

SUMMING UP

The principal developments in world oil over the past two decades have come largely as surprises, and many of these have run directly counter to conventional wisdom among policymakers, analysts, and scholars. Such cases include the tightening world oil market after 1970, the oil shocks of 1973–74 and 1979–80, the oil gluts (and accompanying price reductions) of 1976–78 and especially of

[26] The Condor II project was a secret program organized by the Argentine air force, over which government officials had little control. After his election as president, Carlos Menem initially found himself in a bureaucratic battle with the air force over the program, which had become a sensitive issue in relations with the United States in the aftermath of the war with Iraq because Argentina had aided Iraq's missile development program. See Nathaniel C. Nash, "Argentine's President Battles His Own Air Force on Missile," New York Times, May 13, 1991, p. 1. Subsequently the program was halted.

the mid-1980s, and Iraq's August 1990 invasion of Kuwait.

The long-term pattern of oil supply and price, along with the broader stability of the Middle East, depends on a complex interplay of elements that are economic, political, and military. Such factors as the fate of the Ba'athist regime of Saddam Hussein, the availability of oil revenues to finance a rearming of Iraq, the durability of the U.S. commitment to regional security, the role of Saudi Arabia and the stability of its regime, the pattern of long-term oil and energy demand outside the region, declining Russian oil production, the inability of the United States to implement an energy policy to reverse its rising dependence on imported oil, and the risk of renewed warfare within the region can all interact. In other words, economic and energy variables partially determine political and military outcomes and vice versa.

In sum, the fact that the first great crisis of the post-Cold War era did not produce a severe oil shock should not be grounds for complacency. A reconsideration of the three optimistic but widely shared notions cited at the start of this article suggests grounds for caution.

First, despite the crushing defeat of Iraq and the destruction of much of its military infrastructure, Saddam Hussein has survived the initial aftermath and managed a bloody suppression of uprisings by Shi'ites in Southern Iraq and Kurds in the North. Although he has been subjected to a continuing oil and weapons embargo, the durability of these restraints is problematic over the long term. Absent a change of regime, Saddam and his Ba'athist leadership could eventually pose a renewed regional threat. Moreover, the crisis that began in August 1990 could have had a far more dangerous outcome if Saddam had sent his forces into Saudi Arabia immediately or the U.S. administration had been less effective in

gaining United Nations support, assembling an unprecedented international coalition, and ultimately gaining congressional approval for its actions.

Second, the ability of oil producers and consumers to weather the crisis owed a great deal to the willingness and ability of Saudi Arabia to increase production. However, had Saudi oil facilities been disrupted by the crisis, or had its leaders decided not to boost production (or had they been prevented from doing so), the economic and political consequences of the crisis would have been far more serious.

Third, while the market mechanism functioned successfully, both in the recent crisis and in moderating the policies of OPEC countries during the past decade, the market does have its limits. For example, markets tend to overshoot. Thus, in the aftermath of Iraq's seizure of Kuwait, and despite the factors that allowed producing and consuming countries to avoid serious disruption, panic buying resulted in a price spike to more than $40 per barrel. Moreover, markets by themselves cannot change geography, in this case the concentration of two-thirds of the world's proved oil reserves in the Gulf area. These supplies remain potentially vulnerable to military or political events that have nothing to do with markets, but which can have an enormous impact on oil supply and price.

Indeed, even though markets can and do have benign effects in regulating supply and demand for oil and energy, market imperfections have consequences as well. These include the role of OPEC in influencing (though by no means determining) world oil supply and price, and time delays before markets regain equilibrium. While it is true that the price spikes of 1973–74 and 1979–80 ultimately proved reversible, the damage done to Western and developing country economies during these two shocks was quite serious. By one estimate the Group of Seven industrial counties lost $1.2 trillion in economic growth as a result of the two oil shocks.[27] In addition, the developing countries' grave problems of indebtedness, which have plagued their economies and societies during the 1980s and early 1990s, are in part a legacy of these "temporary" oil price disturbances.

While the picture that emerges of Iraq and the world oil system in the aftermath of the Gulf crisis and war can provide reassurance, at the same time it gives reason for caution. An awareness of the interrelated political and economic dimensions of the problem, and a willingness to draw lessons from the 1990–91 crisis, as well as those of 1973–74 and 1978–79, is essential if future threats to energy security are to be avoided as well.

POLICY IMPLICATIONS

Comprehension of a problem does not automatically dictate the response. Moreover, the urgency of the problem will vary due to factors which may be only modestly influenced by policy choices. In the present case, these include future levels of oil and energy production outside the Persian Gulf, the global supply and demand balance for oil, and the degree of instability and conflict which actually take place within the Gulf area. Nonetheless, the broad outlines of an appropriate U.S. policy can be suggested.

Iraq's invasion of Kuwait and the subsequent crisis and war suggest continuing need for the United States to maintain some mix of forces capable of intervening effectively in the Gulf. Obtaining international collaboration also appears important, to achieve legitimacy, effective-

ness, and funding. In the specific case of Iraq, the ability of the United States to organize and lead a coalition with the support of the UN Security Council was not only important internationally, it was also a prerequisite for obtaining congressional authorization for the use of force. The alternative to American leadership in the crisis would have been international inaction.

In retrospect, the postwar survival of Saddam Hussein, and the resistance of his regime to compliance with UN Security Council resolutions requiring identification and destruction of facilities for production of nuclear and chemical weapons and missiles, provide reason to conclude that the war was brought to a close too early. Key units of the Republican Guard which sustains the Ba'athist regime should have been destroyed. Moreover, allowing Saddam's forces to use attack helicopters against uprisings by Shi'ites in the south and Kurds in the north was also short-sighted. As long as Saddam Hussein's regime endures, the stability of the Gulf area will remain particularly vulnerable.

The role of Saudi Arabia is central. Indeed, the Saudis' importance to the world oil system is even greater than previously suggested. While the most commonly reported numbers, including those officially used by the Saudis themselves, credit the kingdom with 260 billion barrels of proved reserves, the actual figure is much more likely to be in the range of 320–330 billion barrels.[28] This represents approximately one-third of the global total.

After a long period of internal evolution and debate following the oil shocks of the 1970s, the Saudi political system

---

[27] Daniel Yergin, "Crisis and Adjustment: An Overview," in Yergin and Martin Hillenbrand, eds., *Global Insecurity: A Strategy for Energy and Economic Renewal* (Boston: Houghton Mifflin, 1982), p. 5.

[28] From interviews by the author with officials in Saudi Arabia, October 8–14, 1991. The official figure of 260 billion barrels does not include 30 billion barrels of light sweet crude oil in the more recently discovered al-Hawta field.

has managed to demonstrate a much greater durability than might have been expected. Although the long-term stability of the Saudi system and its political evolution remain imponderables, the Saudi leadership has made a series of choices which commit it to energy, economic, and security policies aligning its own future with that of the United States and the other industrial democracies. It has also displayed a certain degree of pragmatism toward other regional issues and the Arab-Israeli conflict. But the war and the unprecedented deployment of American forces in the kingdom do not mean that the Saudis have chosen to embrace a substantial and on-going U.S. force deployment. From their standpoint, the fact that the United States was willing to lead a world-wide coalition and to deploy a half-million troops even without having a formal treaty or large permanent bases in Kuwait or Saudi Arabia leads them to conclude that they can retain this commitment with only modest additional steps involving force deployments or signed agreements. For both Saudi Arabia and the United States, dealing with the long-term development of this security relationship will be a complex task.

More broadly, American and international efforts to reduce the proliferation of missiles and of chemical, biological, and nuclear weapons in the Gulf region may contribute to stability, or at least reduce the scope of destruction in the event of future wars there.

The United States must cooperate with International Energy Agency countries for dealing with a future crisis. However, the United States should seek agreement on earlier use of strategic stocks in the event of a potential crisis. Both the United States and the IEA were slow to commit themselves to announcing stock draw-downs in the 1990–91 crisis. By acting earlier, they could have alleviated the kind of market panic that drove prices to over $40 per barrel. Their announcement of willingness to use the strategic reserve in August or September 1990 could have blunted the price spike significantly, and thus reduced its negative economic effects.[29]

The criterion for judging domestic policies is not the unattainable goal of energy independence. Instead, it is the reduction of oil consumption and imports and thus the lessening of U.S. vulnerability in the event that some kind of serious disruption arises in the future. The United States should adopt a more coherent and sustained program to encourage energy efficiency and conservation, including the use of tax policies to encourage more efficient use of gasoline.[30] It should strive for a robust, diverse energy mix with incentives for domestic production of oil and natural gas, encouragement of clean-burning coal technologies, maintaining a viable nuclear power option, pursuing more ambitious policies for research and development of new technologies (including solar energy), and increasing the Strategic Petroleum Reserve to its originally intended target of one billion barrels.

---

[29] The case for early release of the SPR has been made, for example, by the Chairman of the Energy and Power Subcommittee of the House Committee on Energy and Commerce, Congressman Philip Sharp. See Sharp, "How Bush Made the Recession Worse," *Washington Post*, December 29, 1991, p. C7. Also see Sharp's exchange of letters with Deputy Energy Secretary Henson Moore, *Washington Post*, January 23 and February 10, 1992.

[30] The OECD has noted that energy prices and energy taxes are far lower in the United States than in Western Europe and Japan; gasoline sells in the United States for one-third its price in Italy and France. The OECD annual report on the American economy concludes that higher U.S. energy taxes would be consistent with enhanced energy security and with environmental goals. See Steven Greenhouse, "OECD Forecasts Slow U.S. Recovery From Recession," *New York Times*, November 26, 1991.

Finally, there remains the question of whether the need for policy can correspond with the capacity for policymaking, or whether this intersection represents a very "small set." The years since the first oil crisis in October 1973 do not provide a great deal of encouragement. While there do exist elements of effective policy response (e.g., creation of the International Energy Agency, passage of the Corporate Average Fuel Economy (CAFE) standards for automobile fuel efficiency, and establishment of the Strategic Petroleum Reserve), these tend to be exceptions. Thus the Carter administration found itself in a long policy stalemate in 1977–78 over a series of energy issues, particularly natural gas, until the oil crisis brought on by the fall of the shah in early 1979. During the 1980s, the Reagan administration largely de-emphasized energy policy and dismantled much of what had existed.[31] The Bush administra-

tion began by seeking development of a National Energy Strategy (NES) with the aim of reducing dependence on imported oil, but the Department of Energy recommendations were watered down by the White House before their release in early 1991. The remaining proposals became stalled in Congress until the issue of drilling for oil in the Alaskan National Wildlife Refuge (ANWR) was finally removed.

This experience suggests a sobering conclusion. It is that while the United States generally has an impressive capacity for responding to crisis, its policy process is far less effective in providing coherent policy responses in non-crisis situations. This is especially true for issues such as energy security which are themselves complex, involve huge resource allocation choices, tend to engage the attention of tenacious advocates and institutions on opposite sides, and rarely attract strong executive branch leadership. It thus may be the case that while the broad elements of an effective policy are more or less evident, their implementation may await the time of some future crisis in energy security.

[31] For an evaluation of Reagan administration energy policy, see Robert J. Lieber, "International Energy Policy and the Reagan Administration: Avoiding the Next Oil Shock?" in Kenneth A. Oye, Robert J. Lieber and Donald Rothchild, eds., *Eagle Resurgent? The Reagan Era in American Foreign Policy* (Boston: Little, Brown, 1987), pp. 167–189.

15.   Group of Seven Summit Declarations

U. S. Department of State

Following are the texts of the economic, political and arms control declarations issued at the close of the London Economic Summit, London, England, July 17, 1991.

SOURCE: U.S. Department of State Dispatch, July 22, 1991, pp. 519–527.

BUILDING WORLD PARTNERSHIP

1. We, the Heads of State and Government of the seven major industrial democracies and the representatives of the European Community, met in London for our 17th annual Summit.
2. The spread of freedom and democ-

racy which we celebrated at Houston has gathered pace over the last year. Together the international community has overcome a major threat to world peace in the Gulf. But new challenges and new opportunities confront us.

3. We seek to build world partnership, based on common values, and to strengthen the international order. Our aim is to underpin democracy, human rights, the rule of law and sound economic management, which together provide the key to prosperity. To achieve this aim, we will promote a truly multilateral system, which is secure and adaptable and in which responsibility is shared widely and equitably. Central to our aim is the need for a stronger, more effective UN system, and for greater attention to the proliferation and transfer of weapons.

Economic Policy

4. Over the last year, some of our economies have maintained good growth, while most have slowed down and some gone into recession. But a global recession has been avoided. The uncertainty created by the Gulf crisis is behind us. We welcome the fact that there are now increasing signs of economic recovery. Progress has been made too in reducing the largest trade and current account imbalances.

5. Our shared objectives are a sustained recovery and price stability. To this end, we are determined to maintain, including through our economic policy coordination process, the medium-term strategy endorsed by earlier Summits. This strategy has contained inflationary expectations and created the conditions for sustainable growth and new jobs.

6. We therefore commit ourselves to implement fiscal and monetary policies, which, while reflecting the different situations in our countries, provide the basis for lower real interest rates. In this connection, continued progress in reducing budget deficits is essential. This, together with the efforts being made to reduce impediments to private saving, will help generate the increase in global savings needed to meet demands for investment. We also welcome the close cooperation on exchange markets and the work to improve the functioning of the international monetary system.

7. We will also, with the help of the Organization for Economic Cooperation and Development (OECD) and other institutions, pursue reforms to improve economic efficiency and thus the potential for growth. These include:

a) greater competition in our economies, including regulatory reform. This can enhance consumer choice, reduce prices and ease burdens on business.

b) greater transparency, elimination or enhanced discipline in subsidies that have distorting effects, since such subsidies lead to inefficient allocation of resources and inflate public expenditure.

c) improved education and training, to enhance the skills and improve the opportunities of those both in and out of employment, as well as policies contributing to greater flexibility in the employment system.

d) a more efficient public sector, for example through higher standards of management and including possibilities for privatisation and contracting out.

e) the wide and rapid diffusion of advances in science and technology.

f) essential investment, both private and public, in infrastructure.

8. We will encourage work nationally and internationally to develop cost-effective economic instruments for protecting the environment, such as taxes, charges and tradeable permits.

International Trade

9. No issue has more far-reaching implications for the future prospects of the world economy than the successful conclusion of the Uruguay Round. It will stimulate non-inflationary growth by bolstering confidence, reversing protectionism and increasing trade flows. It will be essential to encourage the integration of developing countries and Central and East European nations into the multilateral trading system. All these benefits will be lost if we cannot conclude the Round.

10. We therefore commit ourselves to an ambitious, global and balanced package of results from the Round, with the widest possible participation by both developed and developing countries. The aim of all contracting parties should be to complete the Round before the end of 1991. We shall each remain personally involved in this process, ready to intervene with one another if differences can only be resolved at the highest level.

11. To achieve our objectives, sustained progress will be needed in the negotiations at Geneva in all areas over the rest of this year. The principal requirement is to move forward urgently in the following areas taken together:

a) market access, where it is necessary, in particular, to cut tariff peaks for some products while moving to zero tariffs for others, as part of a substantial reduction of tariffs and parallel action against non-tariff barriers.

b) agriculture, where a framework must be decided upon to provide for specific binding commitments in domestic support, market access and export competition, so that substantial progressive reductions of support and protection may be agreed in each area, taking into account non-trade concerns.

c) services, where accord on a general agreement on trade in services should be reinforced by substantial and binding initial commitments to reduce or remove existing restrictions on services trade and not to impose new ones.

d) intellectual property, where clear and enforceable rules and obligations to protect all property rights are necessary to encourage investment and the spread of technology.

12. Progress on these issues will encourage final agreement in areas already close to conclusion, such as textiles, tropical products, safeguards and dispute settlement. Agreement to an improved dispute settlement mechanism should lead to a commitment to operate only under the multilateral rules. Taken all together, these and the other elements of the negotiations, including GATT rule-making, should amount to the substantial, wide-ranging package which we seek.

13. We will seek to ensure that regional integration is compatible with the multilateral trading system.

14. As we noted at Houston, a successful

outcome of the Uruguay Round will also call for the institutional reinforcement of the multilateral trading system. The concept of an international trade organization should be addressed in this context.

15. Open markets help to create the resources needed to protect the environment. We therefore commend the OECD's pioneering work in ensuring that trade and environment policies are mutually supporting. We look to the General Agreement on Tariffs and Trade (GATT) to define how trade measures can properly be used for environmental purposes.

16. We are convinced that OECD members must overcome in the near future and, in any case, by the end of the year, remaining obstacles to an agreement on reducing the distortions that result from the use of subsidized export credits and of tied aid credits. We welcome the initiative of the OECD in studying export credit premium systems and structures and look forward to an early report.

Energy

17. As the Gulf crisis showed, the supply and price of oil remain vulnerable to political shocks, which disturb the world economy. But these shocks have been contained by the effective operation of the market, by the welcome increase in supplies by certain oil-exporting countries and by the actions coordinated by the International Energy Agency (IEA), particularly the use of stocks. We are committed to strengthen the IEA's emergency preparedness and its supporting measures. Since the crisis has led to improved relations between producers and consumers, contacts among all market participants could be further developed to

promote communication, transparency and the efficient working of market forces.

18. We will work to secure stable worldwide energy supplies, to remove barriers to energy trade and investment, to encourage high environmental and safety standards and to promote international cooperation on research and development in all these areas. We will also seek to improve energy efficiency and to price energy from all sources so as to reflect costs fully, including environmental costs.

19. In this context, nuclear power generation contributes to diversifying energy sources and reducing greenhouse gas emissions. In developing nuclear power as an economic energy source, it is essential to achieve and maintain the highest available standards of safety, including in waste management, and to encourage cooperation to this end throughout the world. The safety situation in Central and Eastern Europe and the Soviet Union deserves particular attention. This is an urgent problem and we call upon the international community to develop an effective means of coordinating its responses.

20. The commercial development of renewable energy sources and their integration with general energy systems should also be encouraged, because of the advantages these sources offer for environmental protection and energy security.

21. We all intend to take a full part in the initiative of the European Community for the establishment of a European Energy Charter on the basis of equal rights and obligations of signatory countries. The aim is to promote free and undistorted energy trade, to enhance security of supply, to protect the environment and to as-

G-7 AGREEMENT ON MULTILATERAL ISSUES

Opening statement during a press briefing, London, England, July 16, 1991.

On behalf of President Bush and the entire American delegation, let me begin by thanking [British] Prime Minister [John] Major, Foreign Minister [Douglas] Hurd, and all of their colleagues for the fine hospitality and excellent work that has gone into putting together this series of very productive meetings.

Foreign Minister Hurd, of course, has already released the political and nonproliferation declarations, and he has presented to you the Chairman's statement in some detail. But let me highlight just a couple of points.

First, we have issued separately a declaration on non-proliferation. As the world's continuing problems with Iraqi weapons programs remind us daily, the proliferation of weapons is a problem that we must all work together to solve. We think that today's statement builds constructively on President Bush's initiative and builds constructively on what was a very successful meeting last week in Paris.

Second, the seven [Group of 7 (G-7)] made clear that they attach overriding importance to launching a process designed to bring comprehensive, just, and lasting peace and reconciliation between Israel, the Arab states, and the Palestinians. The declaration supports the concept of a peace conference, starting parallel and direct negotiations between Israel and representative Palestinians on the one hand, and Israel and the Arab states on the other. Our G-7 partners have confirmed their continuing support for our current initiative to advance the peace process which we collectively believe offers the best hope of progress toward a settlement.

Third, the seven are agreed on the need for a high-level official to direct and coordinate UN emergency and disaster relief efforts. With the recent tragedies in Bangladesh, in Iraq, and the Horn of Africa, we hope that such a streamlined mechanism will greatly facilitate the international community's efforts not only to cope with but, indeed, to prevent such tragedies.

Fourth, as you know, tomorrow the leaders will meet with [Soviet] President [Mikhail] Gorbachev. Our common aim is to support the political and economic transformation of the Soviet Union in their effort to build multiparty democracy and a free market economy. That transformation, as we have said before, will take time, and it will be difficult. So we see tomorrow's meeting not as a one-shot event but as another step in an engagement that will extend far into the future.

sist economic reform in Central and East European countries and the Soviet Union, especially by creating an open, non-discriminatory regime for commercial energy investment.

Central and Eastern Europe

22. We salute the courage and determination of the countries of Central and Eastern Europe in building democ-

racy and moving to market economies, despite formidable obstacles. We welcome the spread of political and economic reform throughout the region. These changes are of great historical importance. Bulgaria and Romania are now following the pioneering advances of Poland, Hungary and Czechoslovakia. Albania is emerging from its long isolation.

23. Recognizing that successful reform depends principally on the continuing efforts of the countries concerned, we renew our own firm commitment to support their reform efforts, to forge closer ties with them and to encourage their integration into the international economic system. Regional initiatives reinforce our ability to cooperate.

24. All the Central and East European countries except Albania are now members of the International Monetary Fund (IMF) and the World Bank. We welcome the steps being taken by those countries that are implementing IMF-supported programmes of macroeconomic stabilization. It is crucial that these programmes are complemented by structural reforms, such as privatizing and restructuring state-owned enterprises, increasing competition and strengthening property rights. We welcome the establishment of the European Bank for Reconstruction and Development (EBRD), which has a mandate to foster the transition to open, market-oriented economies and to promote private initiative in Central and East European countries committed to democracy.

25. A favourable environment for private investment, both foreign and domestic, is crucial for sustained growth and for avoiding dependence on external assistance from governments. In this respect, technical assistance from our private sectors and governments, the European Community and international institutions should concentrate on helping this essential market-based transformation. In this context, we emphasize the importance of integrating environmental considerations into the economic restructuring process in Central and Eastern Europe.

26. Expanding markets for their exports are vital for the Central and East European countries. We welcome the substantial increases already made in exports to market economies and we undertake to improve further their access to our markets for their products and services, including in areas such as steel, textiles and agricultural produce. In this context, we welcome the progress made in negotiating Association Agreements between the European Community and Poland, Hungary and Czechoslovakia, as well as the Presidential Trade Enhancement Initiative announced by the United States, all of which will be in accordance with GATT principles. We will support the work of the OECD to identify restrictions to East/West trade and to facilitate their removal.

27. The Group of Twenty-four (G24) process, inaugurated by the Arch Summit and chaired by the European Commission, has mobilised $31 billion in bilateral support for these countries, including balance of payments finance to underpin IMF-supported programmes. Such programmes are in place for Poland, Hungary and Czechoslovakia. We welcome the contributions already made for Bulgaria and Romania. We are intensifying the G24 coordination process and we reaffirm our shared willingness to play our fair part in the global assistance effort.

The Soviet Union

28. We support the moves towards political and economic transformation in the Soviet Union and are ready to assist the integration of the Soviet Union into the world economy.
29. Reform to develop the market economy is essential to create incentives for change and enable the Soviet people to mobilise their own substantial natural and human resources. A clear and agreed framework within which the centre and the republics exercise their respective responsibilities is fundamental for the success of political and economic reform.
30. We have invited President Gorbachev to meet us for a discussion of reform policies and their implementation, as well as ways in which we can encourage this process.
31. We commend the IMF, World Bank, OECD and EBRD for their study of the Soviet economy produced, in close consultation with the European Commission, in response to the request we made at Houston. This study sets out many of the elements necessary for successful economic reform, which include fiscal and monetary discipline and creating the framework of a market economy.
32. We are sensitive to the overall political context in which reforms are being conducted, including the "New Thinking" in Soviet foreign policy around the world. We are sensitive also to the importance of shifting resources from military to civilian use.
33. We are concerned about the deterioration of the Soviet economy, which creates severe hardship not only within the Soviet Union but also for the countries of Central and Eastern Europe.

The Middle East

34. Many countries have suffered economically as a result of the Gulf crisis. We welcome the success of the Gulf Crisis Financial Coordination Group in mobilising nearly $16 billion of assistance for those countries suffering the most direct economic impact of the Gulf crisis and urge all donors to complete disbursements rapidly.
    Extensive assistance is being provided by Summit participants for the Mediterranean and the Middle East, as well as by the IMF and World Bank.
35. We believe that enhanced economic cooperation in this area, on the basis of the principles of non-discrimination and open trade, could help repair the damage and reinforce political stability. We welcome the plans of major oil exporting countries for providing financial assistance to others in the region and their decision to establish a Gulf Development Fund. We support closer links between the international financial institutions and Arab and other donors. We believe this would encourage necessary economic reforms, promote efficient use of financial flows, foster private sector investment, stimulate trade liberalization and facilitate joint projects e.g., in water management, which would draw on our technical skills and expertise.

Developing Countries and Debt

36. Developing countries are playing an increasingly constructive role in the international economic system, including the Uruguay Round. Many have introduced radical policy re-

forms and are adopting the following principles:

   a) respect for human rights and for the law, which encourages individuals to contribute to development;
   b) democratic pluralism and open systems of administration, accountable to the public;
   c) sound, market-based economic policies to sustain development and bring people out of poverty;

We commend these countries and urge others to follow their example. Good governance not only promotes development at home, but helps to attract external finance and investment from all sources.

37. Our steadfast commitment to helping developing countries, in conjunction with a durable non-inflationary recovery of our economies and the opening of our markets, will be the most effective way we have of enhancing prosperity in the developing world.

38. Many of these countries, especially the poorest, need our financial and technical assistance to buttress their own development endeavours. Additional aid efforts are required, to enhance both the quantity and the quality of our support for priority development issues. These include alleviating poverty, improving health, education and training and enhancing the environmental quality of our aid. We endorse the increasing attention being given to population issues in devising strategies for sustainable progress.

39. Africa deserves our special attention. Progress by African governments towards sound economic policies, democracy and accountability is improving their prospects for growth. This is being helped by our contin-

ued support, focused on stimulating development of the private sector, encouraging regional integration, providing concessional flows and reducing debt burdens. The special Programme of Assistance for Africa, coordinated by the World Bank and providing support for economic reform in over 20 African countries, is proving its worth. We will provide humanitarian assistance to those parts of Africa facing severe famine and encourage the reform of United Nations structures in order to make this assistance more effective. We will also work to help the countries concerned remove the underlying causes of famine and other emergencies, whether these are natural or provoked by civil strife.

40. In the Asia-Pacific region, many economies, including members of the Association of South-East Asian Nations (ASEAN) and the Asia-Pacific Economic Cooperation (APEC), continue to achieve dynamic growth. We welcome the efforts by those economies of the region which are assuming new international responsibilities. Other Asian countries, which are strengthening their reform efforts, continue to need external assistance.

41. In Latin America we are encouraged by the progress being made in carrying out genuine economic reforms and by developments in regional integration. We welcome the continuing discussions on the Multilateral Investment Fund, under the Enterprise for the Americas Initiative which, together with other efforts, is helping to create the right climate for direct investment, freer trade and a reversal of capital flight.

42. We recognize with satisfaction the progress being made under the strengthened debt strategy. Some

countries have already benefited from the combination of strong adjustment with commercial bank debt reduction or equivalent measures. We encourage other countries with heavy debts to banks to negotiate similar packages.

43. We note:

  a) the agreement reached by the Paris Club on debt reduction or equivalent measures for Poland and Egypt, which should be treated as exceptional cases;
  b) the Paris Club's continued examination of the special situation of some lower middle-income countries on a case by case basis.

44. The poorest, most indebted countries need very special terms. We agree on the need for additional debt relief measures, on a case by case basis; for these countries, going well beyond the relief already granted under the Toronto terms. We therefore call on the Paris Club to continue its discussions on how these measures can best be implemented promptly.

45. We recognize the need for appropriate new financial flows to developing countries. We believe the appropriate way to avoid unsustainable levels of debt is for developing countries to adopt strengthened policies to attract direct investment and the return of flight capital.

46. We note the key role of the IMF, whose resources should be strengthened by the early implementation of the quota increase under the Ninth General Review and the associated Third Amendment to the Articles of Agreement.

Environment

47. The international community will face formidable environmental challenges in the coming decade. Managing the environment continues to be a priority issue for us. Our economic policies should ensure that the use of this planet's resources is sustainable and safeguards the interests of both present and future generations. Growing market economies can best mobilise the means for protecting the environment, while democratic systems ensure proper accountability.

48. Environmental considerations should be integrated into the full range of government policies, in a way which reflects their economic costs. We support the valuable work in this field being undertaken by the OECD. This includes the systematic review of member countries' environmental performance and the development of environmental indicators for use in decision-making.

49. Internationally, we must develop a cooperative approach for tackling environmental issues. Industrial countries should set an example and thus encourage developing countries and Central and East European nations to play their part. Cooperation is also required on regional problems. In this context, we welcome the consensus reached on the Environmental Protocol of the Antarctic Treaty, aimed at reinforcing the environmental preservation of this continent. We note the good progress of the Sahara and Sahel Observatory as well as the Budapest Environmental Centre.

50. The UN Conference on Environment and Development (UNCED) in June 1992 will be a landmark event. It will mark the climax of many international environmental negotiations. We commit ourselves to work for a successful Conference and to give the necessary political impetus to its preparation.

51. We aim to achieve the following by the time of UNCED:

   a) an effective framework convention on climate change, containing appropriate commitments and addressing all sources and sinks for greenhouse gases. We will seek to expedite work on implementing protocols to reinforce the convention. All participants should be committed to design and implement concrete strategies to limit net emissions of greenhouse gases, with measures to facilitate adaptation. Significant actions by industrial countries will encourage the participation of developing and East European countries, which is essential to the negotiations.

   b) agreement on principles for the management, conservation and sustainable development of all types of forest, leading to a framework convention. This should be in a form both acceptable to the developing countries where tropical forests grow and consistent with the objective of a global forest convention or agreement which we set at Houston.

52. We will seek to promote, in the context of UNCED:

   a) mobilisation of financial resources to help developing countries tackle environmental problems. We support the use of existing mechanisms for this purpose, in particular the Global Environment Facility (GEF). The GEF could become the comprehensive funding mechanism to help developing countries meet their obligations under the new environmental conventions.

   b) encouragement of an improved

flow of beneficial technology to developing countries, making use of commercial mechanisms.

   c) a comprehensive approach to the oceans, including regional seas. The environmental and economic importance of oceans and seas means that they must be protected and sustainably managed.

   d) further development of international law of the environment, drawing inter alia on the results of the Siena Forum.

   e) the reinforcement of international institutions concerned with the environment, including the United Nations Environment Programme (UNEP), for the decade ahead.

53. We support the negotiation, under the auspices of UNEP, of an acceptable framework convention on biodiversity, if possible to be concluded next year. It should concentrate on protecting ecosystems, particularly in species-rich areas, without impeding positive developments in biotechnology.

54. We remain concerned about the destruction of tropical forests. We welcome the progress made in developing the pilot programme for the conservation of the Brazilian tropical forest, which has been prepared by the Government of Brazil in consultation with the World Bank and the European Commission, in response to the offer of cooperation extended following the Houston Summit. We call for further urgent work under the auspices of the World Bank, in cooperation with the European Commission, in the framework of appropriate policies and with careful attention to economic, technical and social issues. We will financially support the implementation of the

preliminary stage of the pilot program utilising all potential sources, including the private sector, non-governmental organisations, the multilateral development banks, and the Global Environmental Facility. When details of the programme have been resolved, we will consider supplementing these resources with bilateral assistance, so that progress can be made on the ground. We believe that good progress with this project will have a beneficial impact on the treatment of forests at UNCED. We also welcome the spread of debt for nature exchanges, with an emphasis on forests.

55. The burning oil wells and polluted seas in the Gulf have shown that we need greater international capacity to prevent and respond to environmental disasters. All international and regional agreements for this purpose, including those of the International Maritime Organisation (IMO), should be fully implemented. We welcome the decision by UNEP to establish an experimental centre for urgent environmental assistance. In the light of the recent storm damage in Bangladesh, we encourage the work on flood alleviation under the auspices of the World Bank, which we called for at the Arch Summit.

56. Living marine resources threatened by over-fishing and other harmful practices should be protected by the implementation of measures in accordance with international law. We urge control of marine pollution and compliance with the regimes established by regional fisheries organisations through effective monitoring and enforcement measures.

57. We call for greater efforts in cooperation in environmental science and technology, in particular:
    a) scientific research into the global climate, including satellite monitoring and ocean observation. All countries, including developing countries, should be involved in this research effort. We welcome the development of information services for users of earth observation data since the Houston Summit.
    b) the development and diffusion of energy and environment technologies, including proposals for innovative technology programmes.

Drugs

58. We note with satisfaction progress made in this field since our Houston meeting, notably the entry into force of the 1988 United Nations Convention Against Illicit Traffic in Narcotic Drugs and Psychiatric [sic] Substances. We welcome the formation of the United Nations International Drugs Control Programme (UNDCP).

59. We will increase our efforts to reduce the demand for drugs as a part of overall anti-drug action programmes. We maintain our efforts to combat the scourge of cocaine and will match these by increased attention to heroin, still the principal hard drug in Europe and Asia. Enhanced cooperation is needed both to reduce production of heroin in Asia and to check its flow into Europe. Political changes in Central and Eastern Europe and the opening of frontiers there have increased the threat of drug misuse and facilitated illicit trafficking, but have also given greater scope for concerted Europe-wide action against drugs.

60. We applaud the efforts of the "Dublin Group" of European, North American and Asian governments to focus attention and resources on the problems of narcotics production and trafficking.

61. We commend the achievements of the task-forces initiated by previous Summits and supported by an increasing number of countries:

   a) We urge all countries to take part in the international fight against money laundering and to cooperate with the activities of the Financial Action Task Force (FATF). We strongly support the agreement on a mutual evaluation process of each participating country's progress in implementing the FATF recommendations on money laundering. We endorse the recommendation of the FATF that it should operate on a continuing basis with a secretariat supplied by the OECD.

   b) We welcome the report of the Chemical Action Task Force (CATF) and endorse the measures it recommends for countering chemical diversion, building on the 1988 UN Convention against drug trafficking. We look forward to the special meeting in Asia, concentrating on heroin, and the CATF meeting due in March 1992, which should consider the institutional future of this work.

62. We are concerned to improve the capacity of law enforcement agencies to target illicit drug movements without hindering the legitimate circulation of persons and goods. We invite the Customs Cooperation Council to strengthen its cooperation with associations of international traders and carriers for this purpose and to produce a report before our next Summit.

Migration

63. Migration has made and can make a valuable contribution to economic and social development, under appropriate conditions, although there is a growing concern about worldwide migratory pressures, which are due to a variety of political, social and economic factors. We welcome the increased attention being given these issues by the OECD and may wish to return to them at a future Summit.

Next Meeting

64. We have accepted an invitation from Chancellor Kohl to hold our next Summit in Munich, Germany in July 1992.

STRENGTHENING THE INTERNATIONAL ORDER

1. We, the leaders of our seven countries and the representatives of the European Community, renew our firm commitment to the ideal of a peaceful, just, democratic and prosperous world. The international community faces enormous challenges. But there is also reason for hope. We must reinforce the multilateral approach to the solution of common problems and work to strengthen the international system of which the United Nations, based on its charter, remains so central a part. We call on the leaders of other nations to join us in that cause.

2. It is a matter for hope and encouragement that the UN Security Council, with the backing of the international community, showed during the Gulf crisis that it could fulfill its role of acting to restore international peace and security and to resolve conflict. With the East-West confrontation of the last four decades behind us, the international community must now build on this new spirit of cooperation not only in the Middle East but wherever danger and conflict

threaten or other challenges must be met.

3. We believe the conditions now exist for the United Nations to fulfill completely the promise and the vision of its founders. A revitalized United Nations will have a central role in strengthening the international order. We commit ourselves to making the United Nations stronger, more efficient and more effective in order to protect human rights, to maintain peace and security for all and to deter aggression. We will make preventive diplomacy a top priority to help avert future conflicts by making clear to potential aggressors the consequences of their actions. The UN's role in peacekeeping should be reinforced and we are prepared to support this strongly.

4. We note that the urgent and overwhelming nature of the humanitarian problem in Iraq caused by violent oppression by the government required exceptional action by the international community, following UNSCR 688. We urge the United Nations and its affiliated agencies to be ready to consider similar action in the future if the circumstances require it. The international community cannot stand idly by in cases where widespread human suffering from famine, war, oppression, refugee flows, disease or flood reaches urgent and overwhelming proportions.

5. The recent tragedies in Bangladesh, Iraq, and the Horn of Africa demonstrate the need to reinforce UN relief in coping with emergencies. We call on all Member States to respond to the secretary general's appeal for voluntary contributions. We would like to see moves to strengthen the coordination, and to accelerate the effective delivery, of all UN relief for major disasters. Such initiatives, as part of an overall effort to make the United Nations more effective could include:

a) the designation of a high level official, answerable only to the UN Secretary General, who would be responsible for directing a prompt and well-integrated international response to emergencies, and for coordinating the relevant UN appeals; and

b) improvements in the arrangements whereby resources from within the UN system and support from donor countries and NGOs can be mobilised to meet urgent humanitarian needs in time of crisis.

The United Nations would then be able to take the early action that has sometimes been missing in the past. The United Nations should also make full use of its early warning capacity to alert the international community to coming crises and to work on the preparation of contingency plans, to include the question of prior earmarking of resources and material that would be available to meet these contingencies.

6. Since we last met the world has witnessed the invasion, occupation and subsequent liberation of Kuwait. The overwhelming response of the international community in reversing the forcible annexation of one small nation was evidence of the widespread preference for:

- taking collective measures against threats to the peace and to suppress aggression,
- settling disputes peacefully,
- upholding the rule of law, and
- protecting human rights.

These principles are essential to the civilised conduct of relations between states.

7. We express our support for what the countries of the Gulf and their neighbours are doing to ensure their security in future. We intend to maintain sanctions against Iraq until all the relevant resolutions of the Security Council have been implemented in full and the people of Iraq, as well as their neighbours, can live without fear of intimidation, repression or attack. As for the Iraqi people, they deserve the opportunity to choose their leadership openly and democratically. We look forward to the forthcoming elections in Kuwait and to an improvement of the human rights situation there and in the region.

8. We attach overriding importance to the launching of a process designed to bring comprehensive, just and lasting peace between Israel and her Arab neighbours, including the Palestinians. Such a peace should be based on UN SCRs 242 and 338 and the principle of territory for peace. We support the concept of a peace conference starting parallel and direct negotiations between Israel and representative Palestinians on the one hand and Israel and the Arab states on the other. We confirm our continuing support for the current American initiative to advance the peace process, which we believe offers the best hope of progress towards a settlement. We urge all the parties to the dispute to adopt reciprocal and balanced confidence-building measures and to show the flexibility necessary to allow a peace conference to be convened on the basis set out in this initiative. In that connection we believe that the Arab boycott should be suspended as should the Israeli policy of building settlements in the occupied territories.

9. We take note with satisfaction of the prospects opened by the restoration of security in Lebanon. We continue to support efforts by the Lebanese authorities to achieve the implementation of the Taif process, which will lead to the departure of all foreign forces and the holding of free elections.

10. We express our willingness to support the development of economic cooperation among the countries of the Middle East on the basis of liberal policies designed to encourage the repatriation of capital, an increase in investment and a decrease in obstacles to trade. Such policies should be accompanied by comprehensive long-term efforts to bring about more stability for the Middle East and the Mediterranean.

11. We welcome the further substantial progress in reform, both political and economic, achieved in the countries of Central and Eastern Europe during the last year and recognise that these gains will need to be maintained through a difficult period of economic transition, including through regional initiatives. We have a strong interest in the success of market reforms and democracy in Central and Eastern Europe and we commit ourselves to full support for these reforms. We also take note of the progress of Albania towards joining the democratic community of nations.

12. Our support for the process of fundamental reform in the Soviet Union remains as strong as ever. We believe that new thinking in Soviet foreign policy, which has done so much to reduce East/West tension and strengthen the multilateral peace and security system, should be applied on a global basis. We hope that this new spirit of international cooperation will be as fully reflected in Asia as in Europe. We welcome efforts to create a new union, based on consent not coercion, which genuinely responds to the wishes of the peoples

of the Soviet Union. The scale of this undertaking is enormous: an open and democratic Soviet Union able to play its full part in building stability and trust in the world. We reiterate our commitment to working with the Soviet Union to support their efforts to create an open society, a pluralistic democracy and a market economy. We hope the negotiations between the USSR and the elected governments of the Baltic countries will resolve their future democratically and in accordance with the legitimate aspirations of the people.

13. It is for the peoples of Yugoslavia themselves to decide upon their future. However the situation in Yugoslavia continues to cause great concern. Military force and bloodshed cannot lead to a lasting settlement and will only put at risk wider stability. We call for a halt to violence, the deactivation and return of military forces to barracks and a permanent cease-fire. We urge all parties to comply with the provisions of the Brioni agreement as it stands. We welcome the efforts of the European Community and its member states in assisting in the resolution of the Yugoslav crisis. We therefore support the dispatch of EC monitors to Yugoslavia, within the framework of the CSCE emergency mechanism. We will do whatever we can, with others in the international community, to encourage and support the process of dialogue and negotiation in accordance with the principles enshrined in the Helsinki Final Act and the Paris Charter for a new Europe, in particular respect for human rights, including rights of minorities and the right of peoples to self-determination in conformity with the Charter of the United Nations and with the relevant norms of international law, including those relating to territorial integ-

rity of states. The normalization of the present situation will allow us to contribute to the indispensable economic recovery of the country.

14. We welcome the positive developments in South Africa, where the legislative pillars of apartheid have at last been dismantled. We hope that these important steps will be followed by the de facto elimination of apartheid and improvement in the situation of the most impoverished among the population of South Africa. We hope that negotiations on a new Constitution leading to non-racial democracy will begin shortly and will not be disrupted by the tragic upsurge of violence. All parties must do all that is in their power to resolve the problem of violence. We are concerned that the foundation for a new non-racial South Africa will be undermined by mounting social problems and declining economic prospects for the majority of the population, which have contributed to the violence. There is an urgent need to restore growth to the economy to help reduce inequalities of wealth and opportunity. South Africa needs to pursue new economic, investment and other policies that permit normal access to all sources of foreign borrowing. In addition to its own domestic efforts, South Africa also needs the help of the international community, especially in those areas where the majority have long suffered deprivation: education, health, housing and social welfare. We will direct our aid for these purposes.

15. Finally, we look for further strengthening of the international order by continued vigorous efforts to deter terrorism and hostage taking. We call for the immediate and unconditional release of all hostages wherever they may be held and for an accounting of

all persons taken hostage who may have died while being held. We welcome the undertakings given by governments with an influence over hostage holders to work for the release of hostages and urge them to intensify their efforts to this end. We extend our sympathy to the friends and relations of those held. We reaffirm our condemnation of all forms of terrorism. We will work together to deter and combat terrorism by all possible means within the framework of international law and national legislation, particularly in the fields of international civil aviation security and the marking of plastic explosives for the purpose of detection.

16. This forum continues to provide an invaluable opportunity for representatives from Europe, Japan and North America to discuss the critical challenges of the coming years. But we cannot succeed alone. We call on the leaders of the other nations to join us in our efforts to make a practical and sustained contribution to the cause of peace, security, freedom and the rule of law, which are the preconditions for trying to bring about greater justice and prosperity throughout the world.

DECLARATION ON CONVENTIONAL ARMS TRANSFERS AND NBC NON-PROLIFERATION

1. At our meeting in Houston last year, we, the Heads of State and Government and the representatives of the European Community, underlined the threats to international security posed by the proliferation of nuclear, biological and chemical weapons and of associated missile delivery systems. The Gulf crisis has highlighted the dangers posed by the unchecked spread of these weapons and by excessive holdings of conventional weapons. The responsibility to prevent the re-emergence of such dangers is to be shared by both arms suppliers and recipient countries as well as the international community as a whole. As is clear from the various initiatives which several of us have proposed jointly and individually, we are each determined to tackle, in appropriate fora, these dangers both in the Middle East and elsewhere.

Conventional Arms Transfers

2. We accept that many states depend on arms imports to assure a reasonable level of security and the inherent right of self-defence is recognized in the UN Charter. Tensions will persist in international relations so long as underlying conflicts of interest are not tackled and resolved. But the Gulf conflict showed the way in which peace and stability can be undermined when a country is able to acquire a massive arsenal that goes far beyond the needs of self defence and threatens its neighbours. We are determined to ensure such abuse should not happen again. We believe that progress can be made if all states apply the three principles of transparency, consultation and action.

3. The principle of *transparency* should be extended to international transfers of conventional weapons and associated military technology. As a step in this direction we support the proposal for a universal register of arms transfers under the auspices of the United Nations, and will work for its early adoption. Such a register would alert the international community to an attempt by a state to build up holdings of conventional weapons beyond a reasonable level. Information should be provided by

all states on a regular basis after transfers have taken place. We also urge greater openness about overall holdings of conventional weapons. We believe the provision of such data, and a procedure for seeking clarification, would be a valuable confidence and security building measure.

4. The principle of *consultation* should now be strengthened through the rapid implementation of recent initiatives for discussions among leading arms exporters with the aim of agreeing a common approach to the guidelines which are applied in the transfer of conventional weapons. We welcome the recent opening of discussions on this subject. These include the encouraging talks in Paris among the Permanent Members of the UN Security Council on 8/9 July; as well as ongoing discussions within the framework of the European Community and its Member States. Each of us will continue to play a constructive part in this important process, in these and other appropriate fora.

5. The principle of *action* requires all of us to take steps to prevent the building up of disproportionate arsenals. To that end all countries should refrain from arms transfers which would be destabilising or would exacerbate existing tensions. Special restraint should be exercised in the transfer of advanced technology weapons and in sales to countries and areas of particular concern. A special effort should be made to define sensitive items and production capacity for advanced weapons, to the transfer of which similar restraints could be applied. All states should take steps to ensure that these criteria are strictly enforced. We intend to give these issues our continuing close attention.

6. Iraqi aggression and the ensuing Gulf war illustrate the huge costs to the international community of military conflict. We believe that moderation in the level of military expenditure is a key aspect of sound economic policy and good government. While all countries are struggling with competing claims on scarce resources, excessive spending on arms of all kinds diverts resources from the overriding need to tackle economic development. It can also build up large debts without creating the means by which these may be serviced. We note with favor the recent report issued by the United Nations Development Programme (UNDP) and the recent decisions by several donor countries to take account of military expenditure where it is disproportionate when setting up aid programmes and encourage all other donor countries to take similar action. We welcome the attention which the managing director of the International Monetary Fund (IMF) and the President of the World Bank have recently given to excessive military spending, in the context of reducing unproductive public expenditure.

Non-Proliferation

7. We are deeply concerned about the proliferation of nuclear, biological and chemical weapons and missile delivery systems. We are determined to combat this menace by strengthening and expanding the non-proliferation regimes.

8. Iraq must fully abide by Security Council Resolution 687, which sets out requirements for the destruction, removal or rendering harmless under international supervision of its nuclear, biological, and chemical warfare and missile capabilities; as well as for verification and long-term

monitoring to ensure that Iraq's capability for such weapon systems is not developed in the future. Consistent with the relevant UN resolutions, we will provide every assistance to the United Nations Special Commission and the International Atomic Energy Agency (IAEA) so that they can fully carry out their tasks.

9. In the nuclear field, we:

- Re-affirm our will to work to establish the widest possible consensus in favor of an equitable and stable non-proliferation regime based on a balance between nuclear non-proliferation and the development of peaceful uses of nuclear energy.
- Reaffirm the importance of the nuclear Non-Proliferation Treaty (NPT) and call on all other non-signatory states to subscribe to this agreement;
- Call on all non-nuclear weapon states to submit all their nuclear activities to IAEA safeguards, which are the cornerstone of the international non-proliferation regime;
- Urge all supplier states to adopt and implement the Nuclear Suppliers Group guidelines;

We welcome the decision of Brazil and Argentina to conclude a full-scope safeguard agreement with the IAEA and to take steps to bring the Treaty of Tlatelolco into force, as well as the accession of South Africa to the NPT.

10. Each of us will also work to achieve:

- Our common purpose of maintaining and reinforcing the NPT regime beyond 1995;
- A strengthened and improved IAEA safeguards system;
- New measures in the Nuclear Suppliers Group to ensure adequate export controls on dual-use items.

11. We anticipate that the Biological Weapons Review Conference in September will succeed in strengthening implementation of the convention's existing provisions by reinforcing and extending its confidence-building measures and exploring the scope for effective verification measures. Each of us will encourage accession to the convention by other states and urge all parties strictly to fulfill their obligations under the convention. We each believe that a successful Review Conference leading to strengthened implementation of the BWC, would make an important contribution to preventing the proliferation of biological weapons.

12. The successful negotiation of a strong, comprehensive, and effectively verifiable convention banning chemical weapons, to which all states subscribe, is the best way to prevent the spread of chemical weapons. We welcome recent announcements by the United States which we believe will contribute the swift conclusion of such a convention. We hope that the negotiation will be successfully concluded as soon as possible. We reaffirm our intention to become original parties to the convention. We urge others to become parties at the earliest opportunity so that it can enter into force as soon as possible.

13. We must also strengthen controls on exports which could contribute to the proliferation of biological and chemical weapons. We welcome the measures taken by members of the Australia Group and by other states on the control of exports of chemical weapons precursors and related equipment. We seek to achieve increasingly close convergence of prac-

tice between all exporting states. We urge all states to support these efforts.

14. Our aim is a total and effective ban on chemical and biological weapons. Use of such weapons is an outrage against humanity. In the event that a state uses such weapons each of us agrees to give immediate consideration to imposing severe measures against it both in the UN Security Council and elsewhere.

15. The spread of missile delivery systems has added a new dimension of instability to international security in many regions of the world. As the founders of the Missile Technology Control Regime (MTCR), we welcome its extension to many other states in the last two years. We endorse the joint appeal issued at the Tokyo MTCR meeting in March 1991 for all countries to adopt these guidelines. These are not intended to inhibit cooperation in the use of space for peaceful and scientific purposes.

16. We can make an important contribution to reducing the dangers of proliferation and conventional arms transfers. Our efforts and consultations on these issues, including with other supplier countries, will be continued in all appropriate fora so as to establish a new climate of global restraint. We will only succeed if others, including recipient countries, support us and if the international community unites in a new effort to remove these threats which can imperil the safety of all our peoples.

16.   Post-Soviet Economic Reforms

Howard M. Wachtel

The ongoing chit-chat about reforms for the post-Soviet economy, accompanied by limited action, is all the more demoralizing for the citizens of that troubled region, because their economy, since 1952, has perpetually been in the process of reform. The Gorbachev era produced little that is substantively different from the Krushchev or Brezhnev past, except for the collapse of the economy in the wake of the removal of the threat system inherent in their command economy.

GRAND SCHEMES AND PARALYSIS

Soviet and post-Soviet economic reform has been and is paralyzed—even after the unsuccessful coup—for many reasons: earlier lack of commitment by Gorbachev to reforms, the seeming enormity of the problem, a population not ready for a market economy, and the power of a bureaucracy that was Gorbachev's natural political constituency. Reform has also been paralyzed because it has fixated on grand schemes that are "Stalinesque" in their proportions. The most recent one—the $100-billion plan put together between Harvard and the Center for Economic and Political Research (EPCenter) of the USSR—is no exception. (Launched as a trial balloon before the Summer 1991 G-7 Summit, the $100-billion figure was publicly withdrawn on the advice of Chancellor Helmut Kohl to Gorbachev after it received a cold reception in Washington.)

This plan was to start in June 1991 and complete its first phase in 1993, has thirty-four separate actions spread over three stages, followed by seven additional Soviet steps to be taken in a second phase between 1994 and 1997. The project, called "Window of Opportunity," was codirected by Graham Allison of the Kennedy School and Grigory Yavlinsky, a Yeltsinite who has bounced in and out of favor depending upon the pro- or anti-reform cycles of Gorbachev. Rehabilitated following the failed coup—after being discredited in the wake of the G-7 summer summit—Yavlinsky led the Soviet team in Bangkok, at the October 1991 meetings of the World Bank and International Monetary Fund.

Stage 1 of Phase 1 in the report is "institution-building," including small-scale privatization, freeze on new social spending, reduction of enterprise subsidies, and so on through nine additional measures. Stage 2, to be completed in 1992, is about macrostabilization and market reforms (fourteen measures); stage 3 (1993), called "Consolidation of Stabilization, Large-Scale Privatization and Beginning of Structural Reforms," has eight separate parts. Calibrated to each stage are "western responses." The vague document lacks a core, and reads like other Soviet reform plans written by, of, and for the bureaucracy.

These forty-one measures over six-and-a-half years never show how an additional loaf of bread will be produced in the post-Soviet Union, or how ordinary retail transactions we are accustomed to will replace the maddening three-part transaction in a Soviet store, or how incomes will increase. The market system in these proposals is an abstraction—a

SOURCE: Reprinted with permission of M. E. Sharpe, Inc., Armonk, New York 10504 from *Challenge,* January–February 1992, pp. 46–48.

mantra composed by western economists for recitation by elites in countries targeted for reform. Promising a new utopia to replace an earlier one, the free market plans stumble on their own magisterial pretensions.

ENDGAME THINKING

The Harvard-EPCenter plan is the most recent in a lineage of IMF stabilization programs that since 1976 have been implanted in some fifty Third World countries. It follows on the IMF-inspired Polish Big Bang of 1990 but is sketched on a larger canvas. These programs are designed to achieve financial and monetary stability and integrate more countries into the global financial order. They frequently succeed with these important yet narrow objectives, but they do not generate economic revival and growth. Stability is achieved at the expense of employment growth and improvements in living standards that remain stuck at a post-stabilization trough that usually is lower than the position the economy was in before it went through the stabilization-wringer.

The key to understanding the $100-billion Harvard plan is private foreign capital investment that is supposed to move in and buy the antiquated assets of the former Soviet state enterprises, once financial stability and a convertible ruble is in place. Everything follows from this end-game position:

- to attract foreign capital, the ruble must be made convertible so companies have the assurance they can repatriate their profits.
- to make the ruble convertible, financial and monetary stability must be achieved: inflation brought down below 10 percent; the budget in near balance; the rate of growth of the money supply reduced to 10 percent.

- to achieve financial stability there must be: short-run hyperinflation to sop up excess purchasing power; unemployment as budget subsidies to the state enterprises are cut; sharp devaluations in the ruble until it achieves stability.

There are two problems with this strategy: (1) the cost; and (2) the prospects for improving the life of the ordinary citizen of the post-Soviet Union.

One cost is imposed on the population that is asked to endure extraordinary adjustment pains. The other cost is on the taxpayers in industrial countries who are being asked to ante up $100 billion for a hard currency fund to defend the ruble as it moves toward stability and convertibility. The prospects for economic revival, however, even with a successful stabilization outcome are gloomy. Evidence from nearly fifty experiments in Third World countries over fifteen years shows that monetary stability can be attained but economic revival rarely, if ever, occurs.

REALISTIC, POSITIVE STEPS

The problem of post-Soviet economic reform should not be underestimated, but it should also avoid abstractions that make it seem all the more insurmountable. Breaking it down into pieces makes the reform process more manageable:

- The former Soviet economy now needs to earn hard currency. It turns out the country has vast potential for doing this rather quickly. It has more oil and gas reserves than Saudi Arabia—more than any country in the world. It is using 1930s technology that is archaic and decrepit. Here is where foreign investment can easily be mobilized and show results within a year. A convertible ruble is not needed to attract the foreign investment, because there are well-established ways to compensate foreign investors with oil and gas instead of cash. The former Soviet Union is also rich in other natural resources and has anywhere from $3 to $15 billion of mined gold—and much more un-mined—depending on which estimate you believe. So the hard currency prob-lem can be solved for the next three years without the need for a convertible ruble, thereby sparing the Soviet pop-ulation from a difficult and politically treacherous austerity regime.

- The Soviet financial problem has two sources: inflation and an out-of-control monetary expansion that is required to subsidize state enterprises. On the first problem—inflation—there is an imbal-ance between purchasing power and supplies of products to buy. This so-called "ruble overhang" represents cash in the hands of consumers that for-age for products it cannot find. The $100-billion Harvard plan treats this by obliterating purchasing power through a Polish Big Bang hyperinflation. This is one of the silliest schemes concocted by economists in recent years. Why not accomplish the same result by expand-ing supplies of products so people have something to buy with their rubles and do not feel cheated out of their hard-won earnings?

- You do this by starting a small-scale private sector and supporting it through the creation of intermediate in-stitutions, such as small independent banks. These new small banks, regu-lated and limited in size, do what banks do: they accumulate savings of deposi-tors, provide loans to the embryonic small enterprises, and remove some ru-bles from the street. Excess rubles can be mobilized for employment and growth instead of thinking about how to confiscate them within a regime of economic austerity. It avoids the utter irrationality of deliberately inducing a hyperinflation, as was done in Poland, solely to confiscate people's earnings. Imagine the anger of a population that worked hard for earnings that couldn't buy anything and now has those earn-ings "taxed away" by the very state that deprived it of commodities in the first instance.

- Food this year is a major problem and there is no way to avoid massive for-eign shipments. This should be accom-panied, however, by a concerted effort to target market reforms and privatiza-tion to the food-producing capacity of the Soviet economy. One possibility is to sell off military trucks, for example, to demobilized soldiers and others who would be offered low-interest loans to set up the mediating distribution insti-tutions that are so lacking in the Soviet economy. Other creative ways to estab-lish the middle sectors of the economy should be explored using the new in-dependent banking system's cache of ruble savings from Soviet citizens. This way the positive results of a market economy are there for everyone to see and do not require the abstract meta-physical apparatus of the economist.

- Finally there is the problem of the state enterprises and their budget-busting subsidies. No matter what is said in whatever report, this remains an in-tractable problem that will not be solved easily and certainly not simply by making the ruble convertible, as the Poles have discovered. Some may be sold off to foreigners, others can be auc-tioned off with scrip distributed to the population, as is being done in Poland, but most will remain as museum pieces that have to be subsidized a little longer while employment growth occurs in the newly-born private enterprises. I would establish a "social contract" with the population that calibrates the reduction of subsidies and employment in the state sector to growth in the new independent sectors of the economy. One typical problem of a market economy does not exist in the post-Soviet Union: everything produced there can be sold.

"CIVIL" ECONOMIC CHANGE

The one exception to this gloomy assessment is the cooperatives—a nascent private sector that was legalized under Gorbachev. But even here the authorities take back with one hand what they promise with the other. The coops have not been given adequate access to raw materials and intermediate inputs that remain monopolized in state enterprises. There are no independent banks they can go to for loans and credit. The bureaucracy thwarts them at every stage in their efforts to attain benefits legally available for their employees. In short, the coops face obstacles at every turn from a bureaucracy that Gorbachev has not taken on. When legal avenues for survival are cut off, the coops have resorted to the black market—much as they did before they

were legalized. This has opened them to the charge of doing business with gangsters and being part of organized crime. Some of this no doubt goes on but when you are cut off from economic requirements and travel into the murky world of the black market, this is what happens.

Gorbachev opened up space for a new civil society as soon as he took office, and it saved his skin. He did not do this in the economy. What would the Soviet economy look like today if there had been five years of development of the "civil" economic institutions that interpose themselves between producer and consumer, comparable to the civil society in politics? This is the image that economic reform must hold out: the creation of new independent economic institutions in the middle sectors of the economy that were banished by central planning ideology. If Soviet citizens are being asked to have faith in the market, it should not be presented as a new secular religion but as concrete measures that produce observable results.

17.   Economic Reforms in Eastern Europe

Willi Wapenhans

The historic changes in the countries of Eastern Europe pose new challenges to their governments and the international community. Following a long period of slow growth, these countries—Bulgaria, Czechoslovakia, Hungary, Poland, Romania, and Yugoslavia—are dismantling the old centrally planned system and starting to create the environment needed for a market economy. These massive reforms often must be carried out at the same time as countries address large fis-

SOURCE: *Finance & Development,* December 1990, pp. 2–5.

cal and balance of payments deficits and heavy debt burdens. Systemic reform and stabilization, in turn, give rise to large social costs, for which the existing social support systems were not designed. All this is taking place in parallel with, and it could be argued, is only possible because of, radical internal political transformation and changes in global power relations.

Since macroeconomic stabilization and systemic reform are needed more or less simultaneously, everything on the reform agenda of Eastern Europe could be considered urgent. This raises serious questions about how to best manage the transition. At issue are the speed, the combination, and the sequence of measures that would lead to a strong and sustainable market-based supply response and rekindle growth. In addition, the long-term development issues—the prime concern of the Bank—must be tackled. Five broad areas are critical: reforming the enterprise system, developing new institutions of economic governance, modernizing infrastructure, strengthening the social safety net, and rehabilitating the environment. Given the daunting nature of this agenda, substantial external support will be needed, requiring the coordinated efforts of bilateral donors and regional institutions (such as the newly founded European Bank for Reconstruction and Development), as well as the World Bank Group and the IMF.

THE TRANSITION

To provide an appropriate framework of relative prices for market-oriented reform, macroeconomic stability must be assured and, in particular, inflationary tendencies controlled, through fiscal and monetary discipline. In addition, an appropriate exchange rate policy must be followed. But stabilization programs alone will not be enough. Experience, for example from Yugoslavia, suggests that such programs fail in the absence of significant reform of the old public enterprise structures and financial institutions.

During the initial stages of reform, price liberalization tends to lead to price increases, as competition does not exist and the pent-up demand for all types of goods brings suppressed inflation into the open. In many cases, both inflation and inefficiency have been fed by subsidies to enterprises, through direct operational support and unrestrained access to credit at negative real interest rates.

This has enabled enterprises to increase wages and fuel inflation without concern about efficiency or their survival. But in an economic context marked by severe rigidities (i.e., where production is still dominated by monopolistic state firms and very limited mobility of both labor and capital), stabilization measures are likely to have a short-term negative impact on output and employment. In Poland, for example, the government's recent reform program involves a significant hardening of firms' budget constraints and a tightening of demand through monetary and fiscal stringency. This has already resulted in a sharp reduction in production and rising unemployment levels.

The best approach is to rapidly implement policy reform packages that increase both competition and supply through, for example, import liberalization, private sector development, and antimonopoly actions. But experience tells us that most components of such reforms require institutional and behavioral changes—and these tend to be slow. At the same time, the question of social resilience and adaptation must be faced, as social protection and the provision of safety nets ranks as a critical component of transition management (see article by Julian Schweitzer in this issue). Two issues arise in this context: First, programs of unemployment compensation or income maintenance are needed to provide short-term relief without impairing labor mobility; however, adequate institutions for the provision of such relief do not exist and social security entitlements are often tied to the place of work, without necessarily being transferable. Second, such programs quickly become political and fiscal liabilities, unless accompanied by early measures that both genuinely widen work opportunities and speed the adjustment of the real economy to market conditions.

The strategic challenge thus becomes

how to design a short-run reform that sets a demanding pace for market-oriented change, while avoiding the main risks of (1) being politically and economically undermined by the failure of the real economy to respond adequately and quickly to large macroeconomic changes, or (2) having the reform slowed down by the erosive effects of the old and entrenched system.

But the implied degree of some central control during the transition naturally raises the difficult issue of how to ensure that controls are sharply different in kind from those of the old system and are genuinely transitional and supportive of the process of transformation. Unfortunately, experience offers little guidance on the appropriate make-up of this "minimum" package of reforms, their appropriate sequencing, and the size of related social costs. Then, too, given the speed of changes these days, decisions often have to be made before options can be properly researched and analyzed.

SYSTEMIC TRANSFORMATION

The reform agenda, of course, extends well beyond the issues of stabilization and transition management. For all of the Eastern European countries, the task is not merely to dismantle the discarded command system but to fashion—virtually from scratch—the overall structure and core components of modern market economies.

Enterprise Reform

The state enterprise system is the heart of the command economy, and its successful transformation is central to the overall success of reform in industry, agriculture, and services. The scale of reform called for is colossal: the process involves stimulating private sector development, breaking up monopolies, closing nonvi-

able units, restructuring the financial sector, and introducing proper accounting systems and modern managerial expertise. Experience has also shown that reform of the financial sector is especially important in order to support enterprise restructuring and provide a sound basis for future private sector growth. For most of the countries, it is clear that private investment will, in time, emerge as the leading force for growth. To stimulate and accelerate the process, however, privatization of existing productive structures is essential, so that the private sector is spurred to quickly supplant the state as the main economic actor in the productive sectors.

In the short term, enterprise reform stands to play a pivotal role by stimulating supply and production, and in the long term, it holds the key to improved resource allocation. But the supply response will not be forthcoming, and resources will not be reallocated, unless capital and labor mobility is enhanced. A variety of measures would contribute to increasing factor mobility, including establishing retraining programs and reducing the housing constraints. However, the critical factor is ownership, as without clear ownership rights, capital cannot move and resources can only be reallocated at the margin. Moreover, clear accountability of management to ownership is critically important for enhanced incentives and efficiency.

The actual shape and pace of enterprise reform in these countries will also be influenced by the changes underway in the Council for Mutual Economic Assistance (CMEA, or Comecon), which has governed their regional trade and payments arrangements for the past 40 years (see "Whither Comecon?" by Martin Schrenk, *Finance & Development*, September 1990). The importance of this trade varies among members, but all Eastern European countries must contend with a substantial restructuring problem—both to increase trade in convertible currencies and to overcome the inefficiencies and inferior quality production that have developed within the CMEA system. Unraveling this situation will not be easy, owing to distorted prices and an elaborate system of cross-border, joint production arrangements, as well as trade links. Enterprises sheltered by this trade regime have enjoyed an inherently large measure of protection that once removed will threaten their survival. At the same time, changing over to settling international accounts with the Union of Soviet Socialist Republics in convertible currencies would result in significant terms-of-trade losses.

Economic Governance

The macroeconomic objectives of reform include the establishment of trade, monetary, financial, and fiscal and prudential regimes, which will provide a stable basis for markets to operate and a radical extension of the role of market-determined prices in governing economic activity. For these objectives to be fully realized, countries will have to build new institutions of economic governance.

In the narrower sense, the institutions of economic management have to be established or greatly strengthened: a diversified banking and finance system, in which the functions of the central bank are distinct from those of the commercial banks and the government; a properly functioning tax system, trade and customs administrations appropriate to a liberal regime, and so on. The basic tools of a modern information and management system are not present, and the statistical, accounting, and auditing standards and capacities need upgrading urgently.

More broadly, a framework of law, economic regulation, and public and private institutions will have to evolve to underwrite the new social contract now emerging in these countries. The role of law is especially important in establishing a secure basis for private economic activity. The establishment of a regulatory framework in place of direct control is likely to be a difficult process, but essential both for the accountability of newly autonomous state enterprises and for reorienting government institutions toward new roles. The establishment of a new set of institutional relations between individuals, groups, and the government will also underscore the need for a new framework in the area of public administration. Individuals at the local level must be adequately represented, and decentralized autonomous structures at the municipal and provincial levels must be set up.

Infrastructure Development

The modernization and renovation of the physical infrastructure—especially in the areas of transport and communications—will require massive efforts. At this point, much of the infrastructure is outdated, seriously rundown, and inefficient, and major investments in this area would serve as an essential underpinning for development of the private sector. In addition, Eastern European countries will have to reassess their energy use. Energy efficiency is low, too much energy is generated, and little attention has been given to industry's role as a source of massive environmental pollution.

Social Protection and Human Resource Development

The challenge here is to develop a modern system of responsibilities and relationships among the government, enterprises, and individuals. Social benefits should be financially affordable and leave economic incentives undistorted, while providing adequate support and protection to the most vulnerable population groups. Tasks in this area include the need to scale back and target the system of pervasive consumer subsidies, reform health and education services, develop an efficient housing system that allows for labor mobility, provide unemployment compensation, and establish social security systems compatible with the need for labor mobility in a market economy.

Environmental Rehabilitation

The environment is integral to system reform, as it relates directly to the quality of life and to the political perception of social progress under reform. A large part of the catastrophic environmental damage in Eastern Europe was in effect inflicted by "the system" itself—a good example of where the market (and political accountability) is more benign environmentally than is a command system. This occurred through unbridled investments, gross inefficiencies in the use of physical resources—especially energy, and the emphasis on meeting physical output targets, regardless of costs or side effects. The severity of environmental degradation means that environmentally benign incentives and behavior must be built into the reformed economic system from the start (e.g., into pricing policy in energy and transport), and the costs of rehabilitation must be regarded as an integral part of the costs of system reform.

ROLE OF EXTERNAL SUPPORT

Faced with these formidable challenges, Eastern European countries will require a great deal of outside help if they are to accomplish this transformation and restore sustained growth. The needs will vary from country to country, as well as over time—the key variables being debt loads, creditworthiness, the nature of the reform policies implemented, the supply response to such policies, the external economic picture, and access to foreign markets (especially the European Community). But throughout, support will be needed in several critical areas.

All Eastern European countries need infusions of modern technology to raise the productivity of their industry and agriculture, and greatly expand and improve the efficiency of their service sectors (including communications, banking, insurance, finance, and trade). These countries also face enormous shortages of knowhow in business management, as well as in the design and administration of institutions in accounting, auditing, tax collection, and social security, and in the legal framework needed for the operation of competitive markets. Finally, they could use advice and counsel in the design and administration of instruments of economic policy and economic governance.

Private direct investment stands to make a unique contribution to the development of Eastern Europe. Besides facilitating the transfer of technology and managerial knowhow, it could help accelerate the process of privatization and market development. But for foreign private investment flows on the requisite scale to materialize, there will have to be political stability, as well as an hospitable domestic, legal, regulatory, and macroeconomic environment, reflecting a public consensus generally supportive of private ownership of capital. Moreover, huge investments will be needed in sectors and activities that either are not likely to attract much private foreign capital, or may only attract sufficient quantities once reforms begin to show signs of success. It cannot be expected that these additional resources will be generated solely from increases in already substantial domestic savings rates or from inflows of private finance. Clearly, public financial assistance will be needed, and in the early days, may even have to shoulder a large share of the overall financial burden in several countries.

COUNTRY SCENARIOS

At this stage, future economic developments and financial assistance needs are still shrouded in uncertainty for all Eastern European countries, but it is likely that most of them will be adversely affected by the recent Middle East conflict. Already, output has fallen throughout the region, as the oil shock has exacerbated an already reduced internal demand, the unraveling of CMEA trading arrangements, and the inevitable disruptions that have accompanied the political revolutions. Then, too, there has been a growing vacuum created by the dissolution of economic command structures, while steps are being taken to set up a new institutional order geared toward the needs of a market economy.

These countries have been so vulnerable to the latest oil developments, because their economies are highly energy intensive, and the price paid for oil from the USSR has typically been below international prices, reflecting distortions arising from CMEA arrangements. Increases in the international oil price will result in significant rises in domestic costs and a substantial terms-of-trade deterioration. Moreover, disruption of trade with Iraq—with which a number of them have bilateral trade arrangements—will force them to turn elsewhere. The USSR has already run into difficulties in supplying oil to Eastern Europe, and securing oil from the open market would require payment in hard currencies, which would not be easy to obtain. Thus greater efforts must now be made to conserve energy, adjust energy prices, and make other necessary structural adjustments. At the same time, recent events, including changes within the CMEA, will raise their external financing requirements.

To date, Hungary and Poland have had the lengthiest experience with reform efforts, whereas Bulgaria, Czechoslovakia, and Romania are just starting down this path. Yugoslavia constitutes a special case, as it long took a somewhat unconventional approach. Shunning the concept of a centrally planned economy decades ago, it has let many prices be freely determined. However, strong regional centrifugal tendencies, an accelerating debt burden in the 1980s, easy bank financing, and continued financing of loss-making enterprises under the complex arrangements of worker self-management have imparted considerable macro instability. This prompted Yugoslavia to adopt a stabilization and reform program in early 1990. The focus is on supporting bank and enterprise restructuring through a fiscal adjustment, and facilitating privatization through the introduction of a new system of property rights.

The next country in the region to undertake reforms was Hungary, with the introduction of a "New Economic Mechanism" in 1968. By and large, the verdict on these reforms, however, has not been laudatory, as central planning—although abolished in one stroke—was replaced by a complex system of bargaining between enterprise managers and bureaucrats (on such items as prices, interest rates, credit, and subsidies). These multiple, numerous, ad hoc interventions have vitiated the positive impact of the original reform impulse, leading many observers, particularly within the country, to conclude that "partial" reforms cannot work.

Hungary's approach to reform has concentrated upon the building of institutions—the first Eastern European country to install a value-added tax and an income tax, and the first (not counting Yugoslavia) to introduce a two-tier banking system, comprising a fully fledged central bank and a set of commercial banks. Over the last year, the pace of reform has accelerated, with a discernible speed-up in price and trade liberalization, and privatization. A stringent stabilization program has been adopted to contain inflationary pressures and prevent the

THE ROLE OF THE WORLD BANK GROUP

The World Bank has responded to the increasing demands from Eastern Europe for assistance by mobilizing additional resources for priority areas—such as enterprise and financial sector reform, modernization of industry and infrastructure, protection of the environment, the setting up of adequate social safety nets, and the support of macroeconomic adjustment programs. The International Finance Corporation, the affiliate charged with promoting private sector development, has also been actively financing projects and providing advice and technical assistance so far to Hungary, Poland, and Yugoslavia. And the Multilateral Investment Guarantee Agency, the affiliate that encourages investment flows to developing countries, has started working with its members in the region, currently Czechoslovakia, Hungary, and Poland.

World Bank lending to Hungary, Poland, and Yugoslavia in fiscal year 1990 totaled about $1.8 billion, a rise of over $1 billion from the previous year. The bulk of the increase was channeled to Poland, where the Bank was able to quickly mount a large program based on earlier discussions with the Polish authorities. These projects included two loans totaling $360 million aimed at improving export capacities of enterprises in manufacturing and agroindustries, as well as a modest ($18 million), but innovative, operation that provides technical assistance to the Government on dealing with the serious environmental problems. In Hungary, a $66 million loan was extended to modernize the financial system and support institutional development. In Yugoslavia, a $292 million loan supports efficiency improvements, as well as additional investment in the highway sector. Project activities planned for fiscal year 1991 include an employment services loan to Poland, designed to strengthen the institutions providing social support to the unemployed, and a loan to Hungary aimed at modernizing the antiquated telecommunications system.

Bank lending to Eastern Europe also includes structural adjustment loans

balance of payments from veering into unsustainable deficit, particularly given the large external debt.

For Poland, the reform efforts began in the 1980s, as it progressively phased down central allocation, freed a number of prices, and experimented with providing incentives to enterprises, albeit in a setting of unreformed property rights. But growing debt difficulties and lax monetary policies (in the form of accommodating worker demands for higher wages and enterprise demands for sub-sidies) led to an accelerating inflation—bordering on hyperinflation—at the end of the decade. Since then, Poland has engaged in a courageous, bold effort to change direction. The "Big Bang" of January 1, 1990, liberalized most prices, instituted a unified and devalued exchange rate, established a balanced budget, and imposed strict controls on the money supply growth. As a result, inflation has dramatically fallen and exports have grown rapidly. At the same time, slow but steady progress has been made in re-for Hungary ($200 million), Yugoslavia ($400 million), and Poland ($300 million). These loans are intended to support the implementation of structural adjustment measures within the context of the reform programs launched by these countries, particularly in the areas of enterprise restructuring and privatization, financial sector development, and the creation of adequate social safety nets.

The strategic challenge now facing the World Bank Group stems from recent developments in Eastern Europe that have resulted in the acceleration of the pace of reforms—as well as increases in their scope and complexity—and the emergence of new countries as potential claimants for assistance. The new governments have confirmed their desire to obtain increasing support from the World Bank Group for two broad reasons: the Group's multinational character provides it with an objective, impartial view of their problems and issues; it is also perceived as having the capacity to help marshal diverse kinds of assistance, including policy-based lending.

In providing such assistance, the Group will be collaborating with other agencies, such as the European Investment Bank, the European Bank for Reconstruction and Development, the European Community, the IMF, and bilateral donors. The time required for the transformation process will vary from country to country, but could well last a decade or more. Over the longer term, the Group's involvement will be oriented toward assisting these countries make the transition to improved creditworthiness and complete reliance on private capital markets for capital inflows.

The Group will need to focus on the priority development issues relating to systemic reform. But in light of the links between systemic transformation and macroeconomic stability, the Group—in collaboration with the IMF—will also need to ensure that the macroeconomic and financial policies support programs in these areas. To implement this strategy in the region, the Group aims to (1) expand its capacity for policy advice, technical assistance, and training; (2) build a balanced portfolio of lending, which includes policy-based and project loans, with a special emphasis on projects; and (3) strengthen private sector development and foreign private direct investment.

forming the financial system, instituting unemployment compensation, and crafting privatization legislation. However, domestic output has also fallen and the unemployment rolls have lengthened, as enterprises have begun their long journey toward efficiency and competitiveness.

CONCLUSIONS

The commitment of Eastern European countries to a fundamental transformation of their societies poses challenges to the design of economic reforms that go beyond those typically encountered in promoting economic stabilization and structural adjustment, as they also involve simultaneous and unprecedented political and social change. In addition, reforming governments are likely to face difficult implementation issues, because adjustment and stabilization policies usually entail substantial economic and social costs early on, while the benefits, in terms of growth and income, may only emerge in the long term.

Particularly troublesome problems arise in building the institutions needed to support market reforms, in redefining the role of the public sector in the new economic environment, and in the sequencing and phasing of economic reforms. While there are several common policy reform problems—whose resolu-

tion could be assisted by experience elsewhere in the region—and some issues that could benefit from region-wide approaches (e.g., trade with other CMEA countries), international assistance and support should be tailored to the circumstances and needs of individual countries.

18.   The East Asian NICs in Comparative Perspective

Stephan Haggard

ABSTRACT: Purely economic analyses of the East Asian newly industrializing countries have overlooked the politics of their growth. Why were these countries able to pursue strategies that combined rapid growth with a relatively equitable distribution of income? The reason lies partly in external conditions, including expanding world trade, and, in the case of Taiwan and Korea, pressure from the United States for policy reform. Domestic social and political conditions were also auspicious, however. Export-led growth was facilitated by weak labor movements and the absence of leftist or populist parties. A relatively brief period of import-substitution policies prevented the development of strong protectionist business interests. Equity was advanced by land reforms in Korea and Taiwan and by the absence of a rural sector in Hong Kong and Singapore. No explanation is complete, however, without reference to the strength of the East Asian states, including their insulation from interest-group pressures and their cohesive, mer-

itocratic bureaucracies. These political institutions facilitated coherent, decisive, yet flexible policy.

Economic analyses of the East Asian newly industrializing countries (NICs)—Korea, Taiwan, Hong Kong, and Singapore—have foundered on a simple puzzle. Export-oriented development clearly contributed to their rapid growth. Yet if such a strategy is superior, why have so few developing countries successfully replicated it? The development experience of the East Asian NICs certainly have lessons for other countries, but it would be misleading to overlook the factors that explain why the East Asian countries opted for growth-oriented policies. This article explores why political leaders choose the development strategies they do, comparing the East Asian NICs with countries that have pursued more inward-looking policies, particularly Brazil and Mexico.[1]

SOURCE: Reprinted with permission of Sage Publications, Inc. from *Annals of the American Academy of Political and Social Science,* vol. 505, September 1989, pp. 126–141.

[1] For further reading, see Stephan Haggard, "The Newly Industrializing Countries in the International System," *World Politics,* (38)2 (Jan. 1986); Stephan Haggard with Tun-jen Cheng, "State and Foreign Capital in the East Asian NICs," in *The Political Economy of the New Asian Industrialism,* ed. Fred Deyo (Ith-

Three historical patterns of Third World industrialization can be distinguished, each linked with important policy choices: an import-substitution trajectory, characteristic of Mexico, Brazil, Turkey, India, and other large less developed countries; an export-led growth pattern, of which Korea and Taiwan are the most successful cases; and an entrepôt path, of which Singapore and Hong Kong are examples.

Virtually all developing countries began their contact with the world economy as primary-product exporters; many remain dependent on commodity exports. In this stage of growth, the primary sector produces food for local consumption—the traditional sector—and raw materials or foodstuffs for export—the enclave sector. Exports generate local purchasing power and finance the import of consumer goods. In the typical colonial economy, government policy supported this pattern. Trade was relatively free and exchange rates were fixed. The nonprimary sector consisted mainly of commercial services and craft production.

One transition from an economy based on primary exports is usually toward import-substituting industrialization (ISI). In the first stage of ISI, the earnings from primary-product exports, supplemented with foreign borrowing and aid, finance the import of producer goods. These provide the foundation for local production of consumer goods, such as textiles. ISI may occur naturally, as the result of balance-of-payment problems or as a by-

product of trade and exchange controls designed to manage them. ISI can also result from explicit policies designed to support manufacturing, such as protection and subsidized finance.

There is debate as to whether primary import substitution naturally reaches some point of exhaustion, when the domestic market for import substitutes is saturated.[2] Size is crucial here. Large internal markets present the temptation to forge backward linkages into intermediate and capital goods industries in which scale economies are important. The move into heavy industries raises policy choices about the appropriateness of different leading sectors and the role of foreign and state-owned firms, which are likely to be important in this new phase of growth.

A final stage of this growth path, seen in the 1970s and 1980s in Latin America, has been to supplement import substitution with the expansion of manufactured exports. Exports were pushed out by special incentives, but these efforts did not solve chronic payment imbalances and were accompanied by an expansion of foreign borrowing. With the evaporation of foreign credit in the 1980s and the need to repay past obligations, export efforts intensified.

The industrialization of countries pursuing export-led growth also began with a period of primary-product export and was similarly followed by a period of import substitution. The limitations of the first phase of ISI were met in part by continued import substitution in selected sectors, but primarily through a shift in incentives to favor the export of labor-intensive manufactures. This involved stable macroeconomic policies; devalua-

aca, NY: Cornell University Press, 1987); Stephan Haggard, *Newly Industrializing Asia in Transition: Policy Reform and American Response* (Berkeley: University of California, Institute of International Studies, 1987). The discussion of alternative development strategies is summarized in Bela Balassa, "The Process of Industrial Development and Alternative Development Strategies," in *The Newly Industrialized Countries in the World Economy,* by Balassa (Elmsford, NY: Pergamon Press, 1981).

[2] See Albert Hirschman. "The Political Economy of Import-Substituting Industrialization in Latin America," in *A Bias for Hope,* by Hirschman (New Haven, CT: Yale University Press, 1971).

tion, which signaled to domestic firms their comparative advantage; and selective import liberalization to give exporters access to needed inputs. It also entailed more targeted and discretionary supports to exporters. A third economic transition came in the 1970s and 1980s in the effort to promote the development of more technology- and capital-intensive sectors. Both Korea and Taiwan targeted particular industries for support, and the second phase of export-led growth thus bears some resemblance to the third stage of import substitution. The East Asian economies were more sensitive to developments in world markets, however, and this put limits on the pursuit of such industrial deepening.

Entrepôts, finally, have large service and commercial sectors to support their function as intermediaries between primary-product-exporting hinterlands and the world economy. Because entrepôts have no rural sector of their own, both food and labor are pulled from the hinterland. The first important transition is the diversification from purely commercial activities into manufacturing. With restricted domestic markets, trade is free, though the extent of direct government involvement in production varies between laissez-faire Hong Kong and Singapore's dirigism. The second transition, similar to that in the model of export-led growth, is toward industrial diversification, but with commercial and entrepôt functions continuing in importance.

EXPLAINING DEVELOPMENT STRATEGIES

Four sets of political factors can affect the choice of national strategies: pressures emanating from the international system, domestic political coalitions, domestic political institutions, and the influence of ideology.

International Constraints: Shocks, Size, and Major Power Influence

The international system can constrain policy either through economic shocks and pressures or through the direct influence of dominant states. One would predict a shift from a model of primary-product export to ISI when commodity producers face price shocks or when access to markets, supplies, and capital is severed. Price shocks change the relative rates of return between agriculture and manufacturing activities. Incentives to substitute for imports will also increase when foreign exchange earnings and capital inflows dwindle and needed inputs become scarce.

Historical evidence supports these generalizations. The 1930s were a period of accelerated industrialization and increased government intervention across Latin America.[3] The two world wars also disrupted traditional trade and capital flows and were important catalysts to industrialization in Latin America. In Korea and Taiwan, severe balance-of-payments crises associated with war and reconstruction forced import substitution. In Hong Kong, the Chinese Revolution and the strategic embargo associated with the Korean War reoriented traditional trade patterns. In Singapore, the breakdown of association with Malaysia in 1965 forced a reorientation of growth strategy toward world markets.

Negative shocks have much stronger effects than positive ones. A positive shock of expanding world trade will not provide a sufficient incentive to launch export-oriented policies. Once the strategy of protection is chosen, it entrenches the interests of policymakers and busi-

[3] See Fernando Enrique Cardoso and Enzo Faletto, *Dependency and Development in Latin America* (Berkeley: University of California Press, 1979).

ness in the domestic market. Once manufactured export-oriented growth is launched, by contrast, firms acquire a stake in the outward-looking strategy.

This strategy exposes firms to new international pressures, though. The East Asian NICs all faced problems of adjustment in the 1970s and 1980s as a result of shifting comparative advantage, protectionism, and slowed growth in their major markets. The response to these pressures varied, however. Korea responded with an aggressive, state-directed push into heavy industries; Hong Kong barely budged from its tradition of laissez-faire. These differences cannot be explained with reference to the external environment alone.

The second way in which the international system acts on state choice is through direct political pressures. The greatest influence is exercised by formal empire or military occupation, since control of the colony's economic activity is directly in the hands of the metropole. A lesser but still significant degree of influence is exercised by an alliance leader that can link military and economic support to policy reform. Finally, the least degree of political influence can be expected where there are asymmetrical economic relations but no imperial controls, security links, or aid ties.

This distinction between formal empire, military alliance, and economic hegemony is useful in distinguishing the degree of influence exercised by the major powers in East Asia and Latin America. The United States controlled an informal empire in the Caribbean and Central America, but by the 1930s, the large Latin American countries had been independent for over a century and frequently adopted policies at odds with U.S. preferences. Security considerations had some role in economic developments in Mexico and Brazil in the late 1930s and during World War II, but these

worked to increase the freedom of maneuver of the large Latin American states. The United States was more concerned about their stance in the global conflict than the Latin American nations were dependent on the United States for their security.

The East Asian NICs, by contrast, have all been colonies in this century. The early development of Singapore's and Hong Kong's economic policy to this day has been overseen by the British. The early stages of Korean and Taiwanese development were shaped by Japan's conception of regional autarky that combined production of raw materials and foodstuffs with investment in infrastructure and industry in its colonies. The defeat of Japan in World War II was followed by the occupation of Korea, war, and the emergence of separate regimes in north and south. The Chinese Revolution pushed the Nationalist Party, or Kuomintang (KMT), to Taiwan. By 1950, the divided Republics of China and Korea were integrated into a U.S. security complex in Asia. U.S. aid was important not only materially but also because of the political support it rendered to the two new regimes. In both cases, the United States financed ISI based on a significant array of state controls. The United States did have a significant tool for influencing policy in the threat to terminate aid. It was not wielded until aid policy was reassessed in the late 1950s and under the Kennedy administration. The move to reduce aid commitments increased the influence of American advisers, who became important transnational allies of domestic economic reformers.

Society as an Explanation

A societal approach rests on several simple assumptions. Policies have distributional consequences. Groups will mobilize to advance their interests. Politicians will respond to these pressures to achieve their own personal and political aims. Policies will thus be exchanged for support and will reflect the interests of dominant coalitions, whether seen as ruling parties, sectors, classes, or interest groups. The state is seen as the arena in which coalitional battles are waged.[4]

There are problems establishing the connection between coalitions and public policies in the NICs. The easily identifiable electoral and legislative coalitions that influence public policy in the advanced industrial states are not relevant in the authoritarian NICs. Even during democratic periods in Singapore, Korea, and Brazil, the link between electoral politics and economic policy is weak. Are the relevant groupings, therefore, those based on sector, class, factors of production, firms, or interest groups? One approach is to begin with some simple expectations about how the power and interests of agriculture, the industrial working class, and business affect national strategy. These sectors correspond roughly to the factors of land, labor, and capital, though it is clear that none of these groups constitute a homogeneous set of interests.

The Legacy of the Countryside

The trade and exchange-rate policies supporting ISI are biased against agriculture, and the cheap-food policies favor-

able to industrialization are detrimental to the countryside. One might therefore expect more balanced trade, exchange-rate, and pricing policies where agricultural interests are strong or where political elites have a concern about the allegiance of the peasantry.[5] There is no evidence in either Korea or Taiwan that concern with the rural sector was a direct influence in the transition to an outward-oriented strategy, however. More important was the absence of a natural resource base generating export earnings. This, coupled with the impending decline in U.S. aid, left few options for financing a costly ISI strategy.

As colonies, Korea and Taiwan were agricultural appendages to Japan, though Japan invested heavily in agricultural modernization in both cases. Decolonization was followed by land reform, motivated in Taiwan by the debacle on the mainland and in Korea by the political pressures associated with the division of the peninsula. Hong Kong and Singapore did not have to contend with the thorny problem of agricultural transformation. Gauging the importance of the land reforms—and the absence of an agricultural sector in the entrepôts—for subsequent industrialization demands posing some hypotheticals. The reforms enhanced the state's freedom of maneuver by eliminating a potential source of opposition to industrial initiatives.

The redistribution of assets in land had a broadly equalizing effect on development in Korea and Taiwan.[6] The absence

[4] Among prominent societal approaches to development strategies are Markos Mamalakis, "The Theory of Sectoral Clashes," *Latin American Research Review*, 4(3) (1969); Robert Kaufman, "Industrial Change and Authoritarian Rule in Latin America: A Concrete Review of the Bureaucratic Authoritarian Model," in *The New Authoritarianism in Latin America*, ed. David Collier (Princeton, NJ: Princeton University Press, 1979); Michael Lipton, *Why Poor People Stay Poor: The Urban Bias in World Development* (Cambridge, MA: Harvard University Press, 1977).

[5] See Jeffrey Sachs, "External Debt and Macroeconomic Performance in Latin America and East Asia," *Brookings Papers on Economic Activity*, no. 2 (1985). On the role of agriculture in East Asian development, see Kym Anderson and Yujiro Hayami, *The Political Economy of Agricultural Protection: East Asia in Comparative Perspective* (Winchester, MA: George Allen & Unwin, 1988).

[6] For comparative analyses of the equity issue, see Joel Bergsman, *Growth and Equity in*

of a rural sector in Singapore and Hong Kong had the same effect, since agricultural productivity and incomes tend to be lower than those in the modern sector. This, in turn, had political consequences. Despite the squeeze on agriculture that followed the reforms in Korea and Taiwan, they created at least tacit rural support for both regimes.

The shock to the agriculture- and mining-based economies of Latin America in the 1930s strengthened the political and economic position of manufacturing interests. The political transition to a national strategy favoring industry showed a wide variation of coalitional patterns, however.[7] In Brazil, the transition was accompanied by political compromises with rural elites, and the state's penetration of the countryside remains limited. Mexico's social revolution legitimated redistribution of land. This project was pursued under Cárdenas in the 1930s but faltered as a result of a variety of political pressures, including the creation of new landed interests out of the "revolutionary family" itself. Despite recurrent pressures for redistribution of land, ownership remains highly skewed. The Cárdenas period had an unexpected political consequence, however: the creation of a party organization that ensured political support from, and control over, the peasantry.

ISI may be disadvantageous to the rural sector as a whole, but the importance of agriculture in generating foreign ex-

change resulted in support of export-oriented and modern agriculture in both countries. A new stratum of commercial agricultural interests was created through the extension of irrigation, infrastructure, and credit, but at the expense of the peasantry.[8]

In both the East Asian and Latin American NICs, the pursuit of industrialization was accompanied by a relative political weakening of agricultural interests, but it is difficult to tie industrial policy to the outcome of an overt sectoral clash. Nor is there evidence that the strength of, or concern for, rural interests was important in the transition to export-led growth. The transformation of agriculture is of significance in explaining the consequences of different industrial strategies, however, particularly the high levels of inequality characteristic of Latin American industrialization. Neither Mexico nor Brazil experienced the equalizing reforms of Korean and Taiwanese development, and ISI further skewed the unequal distribution of income.

Labor

The political weakness of the industrial working class appears common to all the NICs. Analysts of Brazilian and Mexican labor have stressed the importance of state and party corporatist controls. While there are differences in the political organization of labor in the East Asian NICs, labor movements have either been weak—Taiwan and Hong Kong—or where active, either drawn under state corporatist control—Singapore—or repressed, as in Korea. The organization of labor occurred at a relatively early stage of Latin America's development and was

---

Semi-Industrialized Countries, World Bank Staff Working Paper no. 351 (Washington, DC: World Bank, 1979); Gary S. Fields, "Employment, Income Distribution and Economic Growth in Seven Small Open Economies," *Economic Journal,* vol. 94 (Mar. 1984). See, however, Hagen Koo's skeptical view, "The Political Economy of Income Distribution in South Korea," *World Development,* 12(10) (1984).

[7] Kaufman, "Industrial Change and Authoritarian Rule in Latin America."

[8] See Merilee Grindle, *State and Countryside: Development Policy and Agrarian Politics in Latin America* (Baltimore, MD: Johns Hopkins University Press, 1986).

tied to the development of leftist parties and ideologies that supported an economically nationalist project. Despite a variety of subsequent controls and struggles between capital, the state, and labor, organized labor benefited from ISI. The longer ISI was pursued, the greater the constraining weight of its urban political constituency, of which labor was a part.

Drawing primarily on the Argentine and Brazilian cases, Guillermo O'Donnell has argued that the second phase of ISI "demanded" new controls on labor.[9] There is no compelling reason why this should be so, and the argument sits poorly with historical fact. In Mexico, government organization of labor predates the self-conscious adoption of ISI. In Brazil, secondary ISI was part of a populist political project that antedates the military coup in 1964.

Variations in the political organization of labor in Brazil and Mexico do help explain differences in the way ISI was pursued. In Mexico, corporatist control over labor allowed the Institutional Revolutionary Party to weather a sharp and painful devaluation in 1954, beginning the period of so-called stabilizing development that remained intact until populist pressures resurfaced in the 1970s. In Brazil, the competitive bidding for support associated with a multiparty system contributed to inflationary pressures over the 1950s and early 1960s. The repression of the labor movement that followed the military coup in 1964 resulted from political considerations as much as economic strategy, but the new political order granted market-oriented technocrats a new degree of freedom. Over the last 1970s, the effort to compress wages in both Brazil and Mexico had another

source: the effort to adjust to huge external debt burdens.[10]

A plausible connection can be said to exist between the pursuit of a strategy based on exports of labor-intensive manufactures and labor weakness.[11] The weak form of the argument is that the absence of a mobilized labor movement expanded the freedom of government and business. Weak labor movements help explain the absence of leftist and nationalist coalitions and allowed the state to impose relatively free labor markets, keeping wage pressures down and increasing profits and managerial flexibility. A stronger form of the argument asserts that labor was controlled for the purpose of pursuing export-led growth. This hypothesis cannot be sustained. In Taiwan and Korea, labor controls had political roots, and in Hong Kong a steady stream of refugees and peculiar features of the union structure kept labor weak. Only in Singapore does control of labor appear to be tied directly to economic strategy, though during the last 1970s, this meant allowing wages to rise to force firms to adopt more technology-intensive practices.

Despite extensive controls on trade union activity in Taiwan, Korea, and Singapore, export-led growth contributed to a relatively egalitarian distribution of income. The East Asian NICs have seen a decline in poverty, increases in real wages, and sustained state interest in the development of human capital. Real wages have lagged increases in productivity, and there is clearly urban marginalism in all of the NICs. Overall, however, East Asian labor markets do not appear

---

[9] Guillermo O'Donnell, *Modernization and Bureaucratic Authoritarianism* (Berkeley: University of California, Institute for International Studies, 1973); Collier, ed., *New Authoritarianism in Latin America.*

[10] Robert Kaufman, "Democratic and Authoritarian Responses to Stabilization in Latin America," *International Organization,* vol. 39 (Summer 1985).

[11] See Fred Deyo, *East Asian Labor in Comparative Perspective* (Berkeley: University of California Press, forthcoming).

to be characterized by the same degree of dualism visible under ISI in Latin America.[12]

The Interests of Business

In both East Asia and Latin America, the protectionist policies associated with the first stages of ISI favored local entrepreneurs, but when these policies were launched the domestic industrial bourgeoisie was politically and economically weak. In Taiwan, and to a lesser extent Korea, it might be more accurate to say that protection fostered the local bourgeoisie rather than the other way around. In Mexico and Brazil, the adoption of a coherent policy toward industrial development was very slow in coming and, while the evidence is controversial, resulted as much from state interest and adjustment to international shocks as from business influence.

Explaining the shift to secondary ISI, and particularly to export-led growth, in terms of business interests is particularly difficult. Export-led growth poses a threat to firms oriented toward the domestic market. There is no evidence in Korea or Taiwan that local industry was the driving force behind export-oriented policies. In Singapore, local manufacturing was particularly weak and was further marginalized by a strategy based largely around multinational corporations. In Hong Kong, there is a more plausible case that business influence mattered, but it was not the influence of manufacturing interests that was important but rather the commercial and financial establishment, which pushed laissez-faire.

There were characteristics of local business that favored the adoption of export-oriented policies in Korea and Tai-

[12] See Alejandro Portes, "Latin American Class Structures: Their Composition and Change during the Last Decades," *Latin American Research Review,* 20(3):7–39 (1985).

wan. With relatively small internal markets, surplus capacity in light manufacturing could be turned to production for international markets. The period of ISI was relatively short, and the state was able to both force and ease the transition into international markets. Rather than reflecting business interests, however, the ability to shift policy toward a more outward-looking growth strategy rested on a certain political autonomy from the short-term interests of the private sector.

This does not mean that government was oblivious to business concerns. The risk and uncertainty associated with an export-oriented course helps explain the extensive state intervention characteristic of economic growth in Korea, Taiwan, and Singapore. The turn to export-led growth in the larger Asian NICs was a two-tiered process. At one level, the state shifted incentives to promote exports, signaling potentially competitive firms of their advantages. This incentive reform was supplemented by state interventions through targeted loans, selective protection, the provision of information, and the organization of business itself. These institutional reforms reduced the risks associated with the transition.

In the large Latin American NICs, the longer duration of ISI produced entrenched protectionist interests that constrained the freedom of government maneuver. As protection was extended upstream into new industries, the coalition supporting inward-looking policies broadened. Domestic end users of protected intermediates and capital goods were naturally disadvantaged in efforts to penetrate foreign markets. When the Latin American NICs did adopt liberal policies—after 1964 in Brazil and in the 1970s in Argentina and Chile—the experiments came under authoritarian regimes with significant independence from local manufacturing interests.

One hypothesis common to recent studies of Latin America is that multinationals have been key actors in determining patterns of industrialization.[13] The incentives associated with secondary ISI and export-led growth certainly provided new opportunities for multinationals, adding them to the coalitions favoring the new policy courses. Two caveats are important, however. First, multinational corporations seeking to exploit the new incentives, whether export oriented or import substituting, generally entered after the change in policy. Second, the positive and negative effects attributed to foreign investment can also frequently be attributed to the nature of policies themselves.

In all cases except Singapore, where the local private sector was weak, export-led policies provided opportunities for national firms. Given their external orientation and rapid world trade growth, multinationals and local firms could coexist side by side without the threat of denationalization. In Latin America, the role of foreign direct investment involved greater potential for political conflict. The shift to a secondary phase of ISI demanded an opening to foreign firms, which quickly came to occupy a dominant position in the new ISI industries, such as the automobile industry.

The State as Actor and Organization

A third perspective on policy reform focuses on the legal and institutional setting in which social forces operate. Changes in strategy are generally accompanied by broader institutional changes, and as Douglass North has noted, "insti-

tutional innovation will come from rulers rather than constituents since the latter would always face the free rider problem."[14] While a coalitional approach to policy looks at the interests and organization of social actors, an institutionalist approach explains policy in terms of the preferences and organizational power of state actors.

Three aspects of the state affect the ability of political elites to realize their goals. First, different political arrangements can increase political elites' insulation from societal groups seeking particularistic benefits, thus expanding their leeway to act.[15] Second, the coherence of policy is affected by the internal cohesiveness and centralization of decision-making authority. Finally, the ability of government leaders to achieve their objectives, and the way in which they pursue them, is affected by the range of policy instruments they have at their disposal.

The economic history of the NICs suggests repeatedly that state-society linkages limiting the level of independent organization of interests were crucial for policy reform, including the move from the primary-product phase to ISI in Latin America, the move to so-called stabilizing development in Mexico after 1954, and the move toward market-oriented policies in Brazil after 1964 and in the Southern Cone in the 1970s. Insulated political leaderships also help explain the turn to export-led growth in the East Asian NICs. In Korea, crucial economic policy changes were launched following the military coup in 1961 that brought

---

[13] Peter Evans, *Dependent Development: The Alliance of Multinational, State and Local Capital in Brazil* (Princeton, NJ: Princeton University Press, 1979); Richard Newfarmer, *Profits, Progress and Poverty* (Notre Dame, IN: Notre Dame University Press, 1985); Stephan Haggard, "The Political Economy of Foreign Direct Investment in Latin America," *Latin American Research Review*, 29(1) (1989).

[14] Douglass North, *Structure and Change in Economic History* (New York: Norton, 1981), p. 32.

[15] This is an unstated implication of Mancur Olson, *The Rise and Decline of Nations* (New Haven, CT: Yale University Press, 1982). See the discussion of "soft" and "hard" states in Gunnar Myrdal, *The Challenge of World Poverty* (New York: Vintage Books, 1970).

Park Chung Hee to power. Park was able to cut through the rent-seeking that had characterized the presidency of his predecessor, Syngman Rhee. Chiang Kai-shek's KMT enjoyed virtually complete political autonomy through its extensive penetration of Taiwanese society. Singapore's pursuit of a strategy based on multinationals came after Lee Kuan Yew consolidated one-party rule. Even Hong Kong fits the East Asian political pattern. Economic policy remains in the hands of a powerful financial secretary.

The cohesiveness and centralization of decision making will also affect the ability of the state to inaugurate reforms. Factions in an internally divided state are more likely to seek clients and pursue their independent visions of the public good. An internally cohesive state, by contrast, is more likely to pursue consistent and credible policies. Brazil and Mexico have experienced periods of relatively coherent policy—in Mexico from 1954 through 1970 and in Brazil following the coup in 1964—that reflected such internal bureaucratic consistency. On the whole, however, the larger states of Latin America have had greater difficulty maintaining their internal coherence.

Korea in the 1950s also provides a case study in internal fragmentation. This was reversed following the military coup of 1961, however. While intrabureaucratic conflict is certainly not absent from the East Asian NICs, the period of export-led growth in all four has been characterized by a relatively centralized and concentrated economic decision-making apparatus.

Finally, political elites view the solutions to particular problems through the lens of the instruments available to them. Their options are limited or expanded by the tools they have at hand. This fact is important in explaining the way particular strategies are pursued. In Brazil, Mexico, Korea, and Taiwan, the turn to import substitution corresponded with a

period of state building and the accretion of new policy instruments. A number of variations in national policy can be traced to this early period of national consolidation. For example, strong and conservative central banks developed early in Mexico and Taiwan, compared to Korea and Brazil, where central banks have been subordinated to finance and planning ministries.

An interesting example of the importance of the instruments available to state elites is provided by the way the East Asian NICs adjusted to the shocks of the 1970s and 1980s. The Korean leadership turned to its control over the financial system to direct a second round of import substitution. Taiwan relied to a greater extent on fiscal measures and particularly on state-owned enterprises, which had been a feature of the KMT's management of the economy since its rule on the mainland. Lee Kuan Yew's consolidation of political power hinged critically on wooing key segments of the labor movement into state-affiliated unions. Ever since, Singapore's development strategy was hinged centrally on the control of wages. Hong Kong, by contrast, developed few instruments of intervention and has consistently relied on a market-oriented system of adjustment.

Policy must always be viewed through the lens of what Barry Ames has called the "survival interests" of politicians.[16] Policies will reflect the effort to build and sustain coalitions. But the ability to do so also rests on characteristics of the state as an institution: the degree of autonomy from social forces; the cohesion of the policy-making apparatus, and the instruments state elites have at their disposal.

[16] Barry Ames, *Political Survival: Politicians and Public Policy in Latin America* (Berkeley: University of California Press, 1987).

Ideas: The Transmission of Policy-Relevant Knowledge

If international constraints, societal interests, and state capacities could be shown to determine policy choice, an ideational perspective would be superfluous. Yet the range of options open during a time of crisis is not entirely determined by these factors. The economic ideologies available to political elites often loom large as an explanation of state action. By "economic ideologies" I mean more or less coherent frameworks of policy-relevant knowledge. These ideas originate among professional economists and policy analysts and are transmitted through international organizations, bilateral aid missions, the training of professional economists, universities, research centers, and think tanks.

The ideas of the United Nations Economic Commission on Latin America in the 1950s and 1960s and various forms of thinking that grew out of it provided a theoretically elaborated rationale for inward-looking policies. It is plausible that these ideological currents shaped the direction of economic policy in a number of Latin American countries, but since size, external shocks, and domestic political interests also pushed in the same direction, it is difficult to establish the independent role of ideas. The shift to export-oriented growth in East Asia, by contrast, provides a somewhat better testing ground since the structural constraints appear somewhat less binding, at least for the two larger NICs. Both faced declining U.S. aid commitments, but various ideas existed about how to respond. In the mid-1950s, more conservative KMT members championed a statist adjustment strategy, while young colonels in the Korean junta in 1962 and 1963 were advocating so-called self-reliant policies. In both cases, the American Agency for International Development had influence on development thinking.

Similarly, Hong Kong's economic orientation has been institutionally entrenched in a succession of financial secretaries for whom laissez-faire constituted a virtual article of faith.

CONCLUSION

I began by tracing three growth trajectories and identifying critical transitions within them. Policy played an important role in these transitions. I outlined a series of causal variables aimed at explaining the salient differences between the Latin American and East Asian development paths. External shocks, whether from war or depression, played a critical role in the development of local manufacturing capabilities. Outside the entrepôts, the controls instituted to manage balance-of-payment crises strengthened local manufacturing interests both politically and economically.

The crucial puzzle is why the East Asian NICs abandoned the strategy of import substitution to launch a new industrial course. Part of the answer is that they did not wholly abandon ISI; protection remained in place and the government played a role in developing new industries. Yet in comparative perspective, East Asian development does differ sharply from that of other developing countries. A second explanation is size and resource endowment. The East Asian NICs were too small and too poor in resources to rely on the domestic market. Market size helps account for the lure of continuing import substitution in the larger Latin American NICs, but a number of developing countries have pursued policies quite at odds with their comparative advantage. The deeper question is why these countries pursued growth-oriented policies at all.

There are a number of factors that have not been considered here: the emphasis East Asian societies place on education; the role of Confucian culture; the proximity of Japan and the Japanese model. I have stressed three different pieces of the puzzle, however. First, all of the East Asian NICs adopted a manufacturing-oriented growth strategy in the wake of external pressures: aid cuts for Korea and Taiwan, the severing of political relations with Malaysia for Singapore, and the interruption of trade with China for Hong Kong. Second, government institutions granted political elites a high degree of autonomy in pursuing their developing goals. Freed to some extent from short-run political pressures, and controlling strong bureaucracies and decision-making structures, state elites could formulate and implement coherent strategy. Finally, some attention must be paid to the diffusion of ideas through transnational networks, even though they were ultimately filtered through distinctive national institutions.

This analysis suggests the need for some caution in drawing lessons from the East Asian cases. Some factors, such as external shocks, are beyond control, though their importance has hardly waned. The debt crisis is currently producing profound changes in economic policy and political structures throughout the developing world. Strong states cannot be created overnight, nor should we forget the underside of authoritarian rule in East Asia. Political development has clearly lagged economic growth.

Yet there are also some lessons to be learned. It is worth underlining that East Asian success did not spring from a blind faith in the market. While Hong Kong pursued a laissez-faire course, this was but one route to rapid growth. In the other NICs, state and market were viewed as complementary. Second, economists give particular attention to specific policy reforms, such as devaluation or trade liberalization. My account suggests that equal weight must be given to institutional development. The NICs' success is attributable in no small measure to bureaucracies and decision-making structures that generated consistent and credible policy. In supporting policy reform, aid donors and international agencies could pay greater attention to creating the institutional infrastructure that would generate informed, even if politically constrained, policy decisions in the future.

19.   Trading Blocs and the World Trading System *

Jeffrey J. Schott

1. INTRODUCTION

While the current Uruguay Round of multilateral trade negotiations holds the promise of trade reforms, the failure of the Brussels ministerial in December 1990 brought those talks to near collapse. The Brussels outcome lowered expectations of what eventually could be achieved in GATT talks, and revived concerns about the future of the GATT system itself. Critics suggested that the GATT had become *depassé, and that the multilateral trading system was devolving, de facto* if not *de jure,* into regional trading blocs.

This paper seeks to test that contention by analyzing developments in the European Community, North America,[1] and East Asia.[2] Each region will be examined to determine whether it is moving toward

SOURCE: Reprinted with permission from *The World Economy,* vol. 14, no. 1, March 1991, pp. 1–17.
   * This article is a substantially revised version of a paper originally given at a conference in Hamburg in November 1989. The author benefitted greatly from extensive comments on earlier drafts by Bela Balassa, Thomas O. Bayard, C. Fred Bergsten, Kimberly A. Elliott, and Marcus Noland, and from the able research assistance of Lee Remick.
   [1] North America comprises the United States, Canada, and Mexico.
   [2] The East Asian region is comprised of Australia, Hong Kong, Indonesia, Japan, Korea, Malaysia, New Zealand, the Philippines, Singapore, Taiwan, and Thailand. This grouping covers all the Asian members participating in the Asian Pacific Economic Cooperation initiative except Brunei, plus Hong Kong and Taiwan (which are key economic players in the region but have not yet been included for political reasons).

regional trading arrangements, and, if so, whether such movement is seen as a complement to, or at the expense of, the multilateral trading system. But first a few words about trading blocs.

2. WHAT IS A TRADING BLOC?

In brief, one can define a trading bloc as an association of countries that reduces intra-regional barriers to trade in goods (and sometimes services, investment and capital as well). The purpose is to "give smaller economies the large region and market they need to create the 'critical mass' of production and sales needed to be competitive" (Drucker 1989, p. 131). Trading blocs seek to (1) generate welfare gains through income and efficiency effects and trade creation; (2) augment negotiating leverage with third countries; and (3) sometimes promote regional political cooperation.

The effect of bloc formation can be either trade-creating or trade-diverting. The liberalization of trade barriers reduces transaction costs and trade policy irritants within the bloc, thus encouraging intra- and inter-industry specialization and promoting economic efficiency and growth. Increased intra-regional trade results from both new trade creation generated by the income and efficiency effects, and third-country import substitution (that is, trade diverted by the bloc preferences). If the latter effect is stronger than the former, the bloc may be on balance trade-diverting from the point of view of world welfare.

Theoretically, the most desirable trading bloc is one that is the most trade-creating, and that bloc is global. Such a bloc comprises countries with the most diverse range of comparative advantage, which affords the greatest scope for trade creation and the least scope for trade diversion. In practice, however, successful blocs—i.e., those that hold together over time and that increase the welfare of their members—usually exhibit four basic characteristics:

- similar levels of per capita GNP,
- geographic proximity,
- similar or compatible trading regimes,
- political commitment to regional organization.

The first factor pertains to the ability of the member countries to accommodate the redistribution of income and employment within the region resulting from the adjustments in trade flows. Blocs with wide disparities in national incomes face difficulties because producers in the richer countries are invariably seen as swamping those in the poorer countries (while the reverse is seen to occur with regard to labor). As Wonnacott and Lutz conclude from their examination of free trade areas and other regional preference schemes, "the division of gains is a major economic and political problem of almost any association that includes developing countries, whether these countries join with other developing nations or with developed nations" (Schott, 1989b, p. 71).

A second factor is geographic proximity. This is often a key factor because of the importance of transportation and communications, and because it may explain complementarities in the structures of the member economies that increase the benefits of bloc formation. Proximity is not a ticket to success, however. While most successful blocs have been among neighbors, many FTAs and customs unions among contiguous states also

have foundered (particularly among developing countries).[3]

The third and fourth factors pertain to the durability of the trading bloc and the sustainability of the trading relationships among the member countries. Compatible trading regimes indicate similar, if not common, laws and regulations governing trade flows among members and between members and third countries. The administration of such policies, or the coordination of national trade policies, will require some regional organization to manage the plurilateral trade relationship and to mediate disputes. For such a regional body to work usually requires a political commitment to dilute national sovereignty in favor of broader regional policies (though this commitment can sometimes be weak, as in the case of the European Free Trade Association and the Canada-US FTA).

While liberalization in GATT generally is applied on a most-favored-nation (MFN) basis, trading blocs explicitly discriminate against outsiders by according trade preferences only to the partner countries. Even so, regional trading blocs are not inconsistent with the GATT because Article XXIV of the GATT allows exceptions to MFN obligation for bilateral and regional arrangements that remove barriers to substantially all trade among the partner countries and that do not raise barriers to third country trade. These requirements are designed to preclude ad hoc discrimination through sectoral trade preferences that are likely to promote trade diversion instead of trade creation.

In practice, however, the discipline of Article XXIV has fallen into disuse since the notification of the formation of the EC, which was not contested in large part

---

[3] For a broader discussion of this issue, see the chapter by Wonnacott and Lutz in Schott (1989b).

due to US interest in fostering a stronger and more united Western Europe.[4] Since then, countries frequently have derogated from their MFN obligations without meeting the requirements of Article XXIV and without fear of retaliation.[5] In most cases, GATT members hold their criticism of preferential trading arrangements lest their own pacts become subject to censure.[6] The lax enforcement of Article XXIV exceptions has "set a dangerous precedent for further special deals, fragmentation of the trading system, and damage to the trade interests of non-participants" (Leutwiler et al., 1985, p. 41).

While this has not been a major problem because multilateral trade liberalization has reduced over time the value of bilateral preferences, the potential for trouble exists. Failure to keep up the pace of multilateral trade liberalization in the Uruguay Round could create new trade frictions between the major trading countries in the 1990s.

3. THE EUROPEAN COMMUNITY

The concept of a European trading bloc is the easiest to explore since it has been in existence since the Treaty of Rome of 1957. The enlargement of the Community to 12 countries, along with the internal market reforms that are being implemented pursuant to the Single European Act of 1987, has created a cohesive and continental trading regime.

Moreover, the EC bloc is both broadening its geographic scope and deepening its level of integration toward the creation of a continent-wide European Economic Space. This process has proceeded in several steps during the past 20 years: the enlargement of the EC to 12 members; the conclusion of industrial FTAs between the EC and members of the European Free Trade Association (EFTA); the growth of the network of association and preferential trading arrangements with 66 countries in Africa, the Caribbean, and the Pacific under the Lomé Agreement; the possible further expansion of the Community to include Austria, Sweden, and possibly others during the 1990s (or the expansion of the EC-EFTA arrangements into a customs union);[7] and the elaboration of association arrangements with the emerging democracies in Eastern Europe (not to mention the reunification of East and West Germany).

During its three decades, the EC has substantially succeeded in promoting the integration of its member economies. The growth of intra-EC trade has far outpaced the growth of exports to third markets. In 1963, intra-EC trade was less important than exports to the rest of the world; by 1979, intra-EC trade was 20 per cent higher than exports to the rest of the world. This ratio dropped during the early to mid 1980s due to the prolonged recession in Europe (and the more rapid

---

[4] By placing political considerations above concerns about conformity with GATT rules, this case set a precedent for GATT inaction that has been difficult to reverse.

[5] More than 50 FTAs, customs unions, and preferential trading arrangements have run the gauntlet of Article XXIV reviews since the GATT came into force. In almost every case, however, the GATT Council has neither approved nor disapproved granting an exception under Article XXIV because of disagreements among members of the GATT working party relating to third-country trade effects, trade coverage, and timing and implementation of the agreement. For a list of the agreements notified to the GATT, see Schott (1989b, annex A).

[6] Indeed, most countries participate in some type of preferential trade agreement. The main exceptions are in Asia. See Stoeckel, Pearce and Banks (1990, p. 24).

[7] Austria and Sweden have already applied for accession to the EC. However, EC President Delors stated that no membership application will be considered until after the 1992 process has been completed (*Financial Times,* 18 January 1989, p. 1).

recovery in the United States), higher oil prices, and dollar overvaluation. However, since the integration of the EC economies began to accelerate in 1985, both internal EC trade and exports to the rest of the world have grown substantially. From 1985 to 1989, intra-EC trade rose from $337 billion to $678 billion, an increase of more than 100 per cent; exports to the rest of the world rose by 46 per cent from $313 billion to $456 billion.[8]

The EC has also strengthened its trade ties with its proximate neighbors in Europe, the members of EFTA, with which it has had industrial FTAs since the 1970s. While almost half the growth in EC exports to the rest of the world since 1980 has gone to North America, the EFTA countries have been the fastest growing export market since 1985. Again, the dollar misalignment and differences in relative growth rates in Europe and North America during the 1980s explain a good deal of these patterns.

From 1985 to 1989, EC exports to EFTA grew by 84 per cent from $64.3 billion to $118.2 billion (compared to an export growth of 34 per cent to North America during this period). Exports to EFTA members now account for more than 26 per cent of total shipments to non-EC countries; in turn, exports to the EC account for almost two-thirds of total EFTA exports to non-members. Their strong dependence on the EC market requires EFTA members to adopt trade regulations and product standards that are consistent with EC norms, which in turn strengthens the integration of the EC and EFTA economies. This process has effectively increased the size and geographic reach of the European trading bloc, and created the conditions for negotiations on a European Economic Space.

Of the three regions, the EC best meets the four characteristics of an economic bloc cited above. The countries are at relatively similar levels of development (though the recent inclusion of Portugal and Greece has increased the variance); the national markets are, if not wholly contiguous, then quite proximate to each other; external trade policy is more or less coordinated in Brussels (more on tariffs, less on services), which in turn promotes the convergence of national laws and regulations; and all members share by treaty a political commitment to the Community (though differences exist regarding the extension of EC jurisdiction into some new economic areas and the degree of political cooperation). Each of these factors is discussed below.

First, since the inception of the EC, the member economies have maintained a relatively homogeneous level of development. In 1958, the average EC per capita income was about $975, with almost two-thirds the total EC population above that level. By 1988, more than 80 per cent of the EC had per capita income above $12,800. Although Greece and Portugal were well below the average EC per capita GDP of about $13,500 and Spain and Ireland only slightly more than half that amount, the combined population of these four low-income countries was less than 20 per cent of the EC total. The EC has a 'North-South' income imbalance generally favoring the northern members over the Mediterranean members (which is reflected *within* Italy as well), but it involves only a small share of the overall Community and creates problems mainly with regard to agricultural issues, state subsidies, and trade in textiles and apparel.[9]

Second, the EC is comprised of geographically proximate, if not always con-

---

[9] The 80/20 split makes it easier for Brussels to subsidize structural adjustment in the low-income countries through income support retraining and other assistance programs.

[8] Data are from IMF, *Direction of Trade Statistics Yearbook,* various issues; and Table 1.

tiguous, states. The addition of new members has expanded the geographic reach of the bloc, which now encompasses a greater share of the broader European Economic Space. The noncontiguous members (the United Kingdom, Ireland, and Greece) are separated by only narrow stretches of sea, which often pose fewer problems for internal transport than the Alps. Nonetheless, EC enlargement has focused attention on the need to reduce internal transport barriers, a key part of the 1992 agenda.

The third and fourth factors—involving complementary trading regimes and regional organization—were evident prior to the Treaty of Rome and now are fulfilled almost by definition by the EC Commission, Council, and Parliament. In the 1950s, complementary trade regimes were forged by membership in the Organization for European Economic Cooperation and the European Coal and Steel Community. Since the formation of the customs union in 1957, the EC has erected a common external tariff and jurisdiction over trade policy rests in Brussels. While some non-tariff barriers have been maintained on a national basis, these controls are supposed to be harmonized on an EC-wide basis or eliminated by the internal market reforms.

In sum, the EC's internal market reforms are contributing to the further integration of the European market and the evolution of a strong regional trading bloc. To date, the multilateral trading system has been able to accommodate this development. Indeed, because of the desire of the United States and other countries to reduce external EC trade barriers and thus the preferences among EC members, the evolving EC bloc actually became a catalyst for launching and concluding both the Kennedy and Tokyo Rounds of GATT negotiations.

But has the evolution of a regional European trading bloc now made the EC less dependent on the GATT system? In the Uruguay Round, the EC seems to have been distracted by its internal market reforms, and initiatives on monetary and political union, to the detriment of the GATT negotiations. Reluctance to accept reform of its agricultural programs—which contributed importantly to the collapse of the Brussels ministerial in December 1990—is widely cited as evidence of this preoccupation.[10]

What goes on in Brussels seems to be more important for EC firms than what goes on in Geneva. The fact that EC and EFTA markets account for about 70 per cent of the total trade (intra-EC plus trade with non-EC countries) of the EC-12 members feeds fears that Europe may be quite content to settle for minimal results in the GATT talks, leaving its barriers to third-country trade intact. On the other hand, as Victoria Curzon Price (1988) has argued, the 1992 process has been driven by the need of EC firms to become more efficient and productive to compete in *world* markets since the ratio of total EC trade with third countries to EC-12 GDP is about 20 per cent.

What these two arguments suggest is that there is an important *intersection* between the EC 1992 process and the Uruguay Round of GATT negotiations. Whether there is an *interaction* between the two processes will determine in large part whether the focus of EC trade policy will be inward looking and concerned about adjustment pressures generated by the internal market reforms, or outward oriented and guided by GATT rights and obligations. The outcome will depend importantly on whether the 1992 process is trade creating or trade diverting.

[10] However, reacting to domestic budgetary constraints as well as international pressures, the EC initiated a comprehensive review of its farm policies in January 1991, which could open the door for a GATT agreement later in 1991.

4. NORTH AMERICA

In North America there has also long been a trading bloc that encompasses the world's largest integrated market: the United States of America. It, too, is expanding.

During the past five years, the United States has negotiated a series of bilateral agreements with Canada and Mexico, its largest and third largest trading partners respectively (see Schott and Smith, 1988; and Schott, 1989b). A US-Canada FTA was signed in January 1988; in the Spring of 1991 negotiations will likely begin on a North American FTA, including Mexico in a pact based closely on the US-Canada model.[11]

Successful trilateral negotiations would create a North American trading bloc that encompasses a market about the same size and with the same population as the EC and EFTA countries combined.[12] Would such a bloc be successful and sustainable, given the criteria set out in this paper?

Political interest and support for a prospective North American bloc derives importantly from the fact that the three economies are already integrated to a significant extent. Business enterprises have already taken advantage of the close proximity of the three markets to forge substantial trade and investment ties between the three countries. The support of the business community in each country

is an important factor behind the political commitment to a regional arrangement.

Both Canada and Mexico conduct about two-thirds of their trade with the United States, and each benefits from substantial US direct investment in their economies. US trade with its North American neighbors accounts for about 26 per cent of total US trade, but is more diversified than that of its neighbors (about one-third with East Asia and one-fifth with the EC in 1989).

Another factor contributing to a shared interest in the development of a North American trading bloc is the fact that each country in the region runs a large current account deficit. Each needs to increase its exports to help redress these imbalances—which effectively means that total regional exports to third markets need to increase substantially. Closer economic integration of the three countries could help promote economies of scale of production, increase productivity, and thus enable regional industries to compete more effectively in world markets. This is particularly important for Mexico and Canada, which benefit more than the United States from the income effects of market integration.

Despite their shared interest in export-led growth, the complexities of integrating economies at very different levels of development as well as Mexican and Canadian concerns about political and cultural sovereignty will complicate the negotiation of the North American trading bloc. Mexico's per capita GNP is only one-tenth that of the United States and one-eighth that of Canada, but its population is 30 per cent of its northern neighbors. Mexican labor productivity and wage levels are far below those in the United States and Canada. Such disparities exacerbate fears that the burden of adjustment to an FTA will fall disproportionately on Mexican industry and US and Canadian unskilled labor.

[11] In addition, the United States launched in June 1990 an "Enterprise for the Americas" initiative, which seeks to create over time a Western Hemisphere free trade zone. To date, however, discussions have been limited to strengthening bilateral consultative mechanisms, including new framework agreements on trade and investment issues.

[12] In 1989, the EC and EFTA combined had a GNP of $5,971 billion and a population of 358 million. The three countries of North America combined had a GNP of $5,943 billion and a population of 359 million.

256   Jeffrey J. Schott

To be sure, there are fewer precedents of successful FTAs between developed and developing countries. This could be due, however, in large part to the high protectionist walls insulating the poorer economies that make adjustment to free trade with an industrialized economy difficult and politically unsustainable. During the past five years, Mexico unilaterally has undertaken very significant trade and economic reforms that have substantially opened up most sectors of the economy to foreign competition. Today, Mexico's trade regime fits the Canadian and US mould more than that of most other countries (except Chile) in Latin America.

In sum, despite the disparity in the level of economic development between Mexico and its northern neighbors, the North American trading bloc exhibits most of the basic characteristics of a successful trading bloc. The members meet the geographic proximity test, have a strong political commitment to regionalization, and, because of the rapid pace of Mexican economic reform, differences in trade regulatory systems are rapidly fading.

The evolution of a North American bloc is unlikely to diminish support in the region for the multilateral trading system. All three countries regard the regional relationship as a complement to

Table 19.1   Emerging Trading Blocs?
(Billion Dollars and Percentage)

	1980		1986		1989	
EC-12						
Total Exports	691.2	100	796.5	100	1,133.7	100
of which: Intra-regional Trade	369.1	53	451.3	57	677.8	60
Exports to ROW	322.2	47	345.2	43	455.9	40
to East Asia	25.8	4	36.0	5	66.2	6
to North America	46.8	7	84.9	11	100.8	9
North America*						
Total Exports	304.1	100	323.6	100	509.2	100
of which: Intra-regional Trade	99.5	33	129.0	40	205.3	40
Exports to ROW	204.6	67	194.6	60	303.9	60
to East Asia	52.1	17	58.9	18	115.8	23
to EC-12	67.4	22	58.5	18	100.3	20
East Asia						
Total Exports	283.1	100	414.6	100	641.4	100
of which: Intra-regional Trade	96.4	34	116.4	28	223.6	35
Exports to ROW	186.8	66	298.2	72	417.8	65
to North America	68.1	24	153.3	37	206.8	32
to EC-12	41.6	15	58.5	14	100.1	16

ROW = Rest of World
* United States, Canada, and Mexico
Source: GATT, *International Trade 87-88, 88-89:* Volume II, Table AA10, Geneva 1988; Volume II, Table A3, Geneva 1989; IMF, *Direction of Trade Statistics Yearbook 1990; 1987;* Ministry of Economic Affairs, *Foreign Trade Development of The Republic of China 1987.*

Table 19.2   Emerging Trading Blocs?
(Billion Dollars and Percentage)

	1980		1986		1989	
EC-12						
Total Imports	826.5	100	781.4	100	1,165.8	100
of which: Intra-regional Trade	399.5	48	445.4	57	677.2	57
Imports to ROW	427.0	52	336.0	43	498.6	43
from East Asia	49.0	6	63.9	8	104.5	9
from North America	85.8	10	66.0	8	104.2	9
North America*						
Total Imports	335.7	100	481.9	100	635.9	100
of which: Intra-regional Trade	107.5	32	150.5	31	210.4	33
Imports to ROW	228.2	68	331.4	69	425.5	67
from East Asia	64.2	19	159.4	33	202.0	32
from EC-12	50.1	15	90.6	19	105.8	17
East Asia						
Total Imports	294.5	100	308.7	100	558.2	100
of which: Intra-regional Trade	92.8	32	117.9	38	224.5	40
Imports to ROW	201.7	68	190.8	62	333.7	60
from North America	59.6	20	69.9	23	123.8	22
from EC-12	29.2	10	40.4	13	77.0	14

ROW = Rest of World
* United States, Canada, and Mexico
Source: IMF, *Direction of Trade Statistics Yearbook.* Ministry of Economic Affairs, Foreign Trade Development of The Republic of China 1987.

their multilateral trade relations. Each country has an important stake in the multilateral system, for several reasons.

First, as shown in Tables 19.1 and 19.2 and unlike the EC, intra-regional trade accounts for only 36 per cent of the combined total trade of the United States, Canada, and Mexico (up only 32 per cent in 1980). Trade with East Asia accounts for 28 per cent of total trade (up from 18 per cent in 1980); the total is 18 per cent for the EC (unchanged from 1980). The importance (notably for the dominant US economy) of exports to third markets accounts for the strong support by the members of the North American bloc for the multilateral system.

Second, as noted above, all the coun-

tries in the region need export-led growth beyond North America, and thus benefit from GATT rules and procedures that safeguard their access to overseas markets. In this regard, all three countries are seeking substantial trade liberalization in the Uruguay Round to increase their export opportunities.[13]

Third, Canada and Mexico find that the GATT system affords them some protection and added leverage in dealing with their powerful neighbor.[14] For its part,

[13] For a fuller discussion of this point, see Bergsten (1988, chap. 6) and Schott (1989a and 1990).

[14] For example, Canada has challenged the U.S. imposition of a customs' user fee, and

the United States also needs the GATT to deal with problems relating to subsidies and agricultural protection that have not been amenable to solution on a bilateral or regional level.

In sum, the three countries in the region maintain their outward orientation and dependence on a strong multilateral trading system. Indeed, a successful Uruguay Round could greatly facilitate the negotiation and ratification of the North American FTA. Problems in sensitive areas such as textiles, agriculture, and steel could be resolved, or at least partly mitigated, by GATT agreements, and in so doing deflect much of the potential political opposition to the emerging North American accord.

5. EAST ASIA

During the 1980s, East Asia experienced the strongest export growth of the three regions. The region's total trade more than doubled; much of the growth was generated by sales to the North American market. Because of the strong growth in exports to third countries, East Asia has been the only region in which the relative share of intra-regional trade to total exports remained basically the same in the 1980s, fluctuating from 34 per cent in 1980 to 28 per cent in 1986 and back to 35 per cent in 1989 (see Tables 19.1 and 19.2). Its focus has been primarily outward-oriented, particularly to the US market on which most of the countries in the region are highly dependent.[15]

The concept of a potential East Asian trading bloc has been advanced in two somewhat related forms. Some see such a bloc emerging because the countries of the region seem to be coalescing around the region's dominant economy, Japan. Others regard the growing interest in Pacific Basin initiatives as the catalyst for a new trading bloc, with the United States and Japan at the core (so that the United States blocks Japanese economic dominance in the region). Prospects for each are discussed below.

An East Asian economy centered on Japan is not a new idea; however, the sharp memory of the historical precedents of such a regional bloc (or "Co-Prosperity Sphere") have long deterred formal initiatives to that end. However, some analysis suggests that such a bloc may be developing on a *de facto* basis as countries in the region expand their trade and investment ties with Japan.[16]

Japanese trade and investment in East Asia has grown dramatically over the past decade, *but so has Japanese trade and investment in North America and Europe.* As shown in Table 19.3, Japanese trade with North America has been larger, and grown faster, than trade with East Asian countries (excluding the People's Republic of China) during the 1980s. Japanese trade with East Asian countries rose from 25 to 29 per cent of

---

both Canada and Mexico have protested the discriminatory US oil import tax included in the 1986 Superfund amendments. GATT panels have ruled against the United States in each case and recommended that the programs be revised.

[15] For example, in 1987, exports to the United States accounted for 37 to 44 per cent of the total exports of Taiwan, Korea, and Japan, and 21 per cent for the ASEAN countries. Australia and New Zealand were the outliers

at 11 per cent and 15 per cent respectively. See Schott (1989a, pp. 30–31).

[16] For example, *The Economist* (1989) cites four reasons for the emergence of a Japan-centered trading bloc: Japanese trade with other Asian countries has grown larger than its trade with the United States (though not with the North America region); Japanese imports of manufactured exports from Asian countries have grown dramatically; the growing internationalization of the yen (although this reflects more Japan's huge savings surplus, and thus its massive capital exports, plus the related rapid development of the Tokyo money markets); and Japanese foreign direct investment in Asia has grown substantially.

Table 19.3   Japanese Trade with East Asia, North America, and the EC
(Billion Dollars and Percentage)

	East Asia		US/Canada/Mexico		EC	
	X + M	Percentage of Total Trade	X + M	Percentage of Total Trade	X + M	Percentage of Total Trade
1980	67.5	25.0	65.8	24.3	24.5	9.1
1981	70.9	24.0	75.1	25.4	27.4	9.3
1983	68.2	25.0	78.7	28.8	26.6	9.7
1985	71.6	23.5	105.0	34.4	28.9	9.5
1987	100.2	26.5	131.8	34.8	55.4	14.6
1988	126.6	28.0	150.6	33.3	70.9	15.7
1989	140.0	28.8	161.2	33.2	76.1	15.7
1990*	142.3	28.8	157.6	31.9	85.7	17.3

* Data for January–September at an annualized rate.
X = exports; M = imports.
Source: IMF, *Direction of Trade Statistics Yearbook*; OECD, *Monthly Statistics of Foreign Trade* (December 1990); Bank of Japan, *Balance of Payments Monthly* (October 1990).

total Japanese trade during the 1980s; however, trade with North America rose from 24 to 32 per cent (after peaking at 34.8 per cent in 1987). In addition, the EC share of total Japanese trade almost doubled to 17 per cent during the same period.

To be sure, Japanese trade with East Asia since 1985 has increased twice as fast as trade with North America (and three times as fast since 1987). This recent surge has been taken as a bellwether for future trends. However, since the first quarter of 1988, this trend has moderated, with Japanese imports from East Asia growing at about the same rate as total trade.

Japanese foreign direct investment (FDI) in East Asia has shown similar growth in recent years, albeit from a relatively low base (see Table 19.4). Outward investment to that region quadrupled from $2 billion to $8.2 billion during the period FY 1985 through FY 1988, matching the growth rate of overall Japanese FDI in North America. However, more money was invested in Europe during this period, a cumulative total of $21.1 billion in Europe versus $19.8 billion in East Asia (including the PRC).

Unlike the trade flows, FDI in East Asia accounts for only a small share of cumulative Japanese FDI. As of 31 March 1989, the East Asian region (including the PRC) accounted for only 22.3 per cent of cumulative Japanese FDI, compared to 40.3 per cent for North America and 16.2 per cent for Europe.

About one-half of cumulative Japanese FDI has been in manufacturing and financial services. The composition differs by region. For example, FDI in manufacturing accounts for 34 per cent of the total in East Asia, 32 per cent in North America, and only 16 per cent in Europe (though this figure has undoubtedly risen in the past two years); in financial services, the regional breakdown is 49 per cent in Europe, 16 per cent in North America, and 8 per cent in East Asia.[17]

The trade and investment data point to

[17] Data from the Japanese Ministry of Finance. For a detailed analysis of Japanese FDI in the United States, see Graham and Krugman (1989) and Balassa and Noland (1988).

260 Jeffrey J. Schott

Table 19.4 Japanese Foreign Direct Investment, by Region and Composition
(Billion Dollars and Percentage)

	Total	To East Asia[a]		To North America[b]		To EC[c]	
		Value	Percentage of Total	Value	Percentage of Total	Value	Percentage of Total
FY 1985	12.2	2.0	16.4	5.5	45.1	1.9	15.6
FY 1986	22.3	3.3	14.8	10.4	46.6	3.5	15.7
FY 1987	33.4	6.3	18.9	15.4	46.1	6.6	19.8
FY 1988	47.0	8.2	17.4	22.3	47.4	9.1	19.4
Cumulative FDI (as of 31/3/89) of which:	186.4	41.5	22.3	75.1	40.3	30.2	16.2
Manufacturing (%)	26.7	34.0		31.9		16.1	
Financial Services (%)	22.5	8.5		16.5		49.2	
Real Estate (%)	11.1	7.7		21.0		4.6	

[a] Includes PRC.
[b] Excludes Mexico. Cumulative Japanese FDI in Mexico totaled $1.7 billion as of March 1989.
[c] Includes Switzerland.
Source: Ministry of Finance, Japan.

a growing inter-nationalization of the Japanese economy, but not with the East Asian region alone or with East Asia more than other regions. The United States remains the primary focus for Japanese trade and investment, and Europe—especially since the advent of the 1992 process—has become an increasingly important market. Japanese trade with the EC almost tripled from 1985 to 1989 (albeit from a lower base than trade with East Asia and North America), and more than half of Japan's cumulative $30 billion in FDI in Europe took place in FY 1987–88.

The growing internationalization of the Japanese economy, coupled with ongoing political and cultural concerns in the East Asian region about Japanese hegemony, have spurred interest in a broad regional grouping involving both Pacific economic powers, Japan and the United States. From an Asian perspective, the logic of such a grouping would be to have the United States shield the smaller Asian economies from Japanese domination. Such considerations seem to be at

least partially behind the initiative of Prime Minister Hawke of Australia on Asia Pacific Economic Cooperation (APEC), in which the United States and Canada now participate.[18] Similar broad-based Pacific Basic arrangements also were proposed by the Japanese Ministry of International Trade and Industry, which have now been dovetailed into the APEC initiative (MITI 1989).

The APEC initiative establishes a broader regional grouping in the Pacific Basin that encompasses Australia, New Zealand, Japan, Korea, and the ASEAN, as well as the United States and Canada. Hawke stated that the aim is not to create a regional trading bloc, but rather to establish a mechanism by which the countries in the region could "best take advantage of the possible economic complementarities . . . in the region" and "through closer economic cooperation . . . to also be a force within the world for

[18] Originally, the Hawke proposal excluded the United States, and generated little support in the region as a result.

arguing the case for a freer international trading environment" (*Financial Times,* 14 June, 1989, p. 6). The process is designed to be complementary rather than competitive with existing multilateral fora, and in particular the GATT.[19]

Could the APEC initiative lead over the medium term to the evolution of a regional trading bloc? A combination of economic and political factors argues to the contrary.

First, the countries in the Pacific Basin (as defined by the APEC membership) are widely dispersed geographically and have diverse levels of economic development. Distances between markets in the region are quite large, even if one excludes the North American countries. Per capita incomes range from poor (Indonesia and the Philippines) to moderate (Korea) to comfortable (Australia, Hong Kong, Singapore, and New Zealand) to wealthy (United States, Canada, and Japan). Integrating such a diverse and expansive region would pose enormous physical and adjustment problems.

Second, the last two characteristics of successful trading blocs postulated at the start of the paper also seem to be lacking. Trade policies and regulatory regimes differ markedly from country to country, and there seems to be little political commitment to an evolving regional organization.[20] For example, the ASEAN countries have long been wary of economic arrangements in the region to the extent that, after twenty years, they have not yet even established a free trade area among themselves. It is unlikely that the ASEAN would be interested in the development of a regional trading bloc, as long as multilateralism remains a viable alternative.

Finally, the dependence of East Asian economies on the US market argues against the evolution of an East Asian bloc, for two reasons. First, it is more important for the East Asian countries to maintain access to the US market—arrangements with the United States thus take precedence over regional trading initiatives (as evidenced by the strong interest of these countries in potential FTAs with the United States along the lines of the Canada-US FTA).[21] Second, and related to the first, these countries have a vested interest in the strengthening of GATT disciplines, which they believe provide the best safeguards against further encroachments on their access to the US and European markets.

6. ARE TRADING BLOCS EVOLVING?

The short answer to the main question posed by this paper is: yes, maybe, and no. A European trading bloc is clearly in existence and developing further; a North American bloc is evolving, although with a distinct outward orientation; and an East Asian bloc remains a remote prospect.

In Europe, intra-EC trade as well as trade with EFTA countries has been booming since 1985. Intra-regional trade among the EC-12 is almost 50 per cent greater than exports to the rest of the world. As a result of the 1992 process, and for a variety of other political and economic reasons, the EC-12 bloc is

[19] For a discussion of the Canberra meeting that initiated the APEC, see the chairman's summary statement of Gareth Evans, Minister for Foreign Affairs and Trade of Australia, Canberra, 7, November 1989.

[20] However, it has been suggested that existing bodies such as the Pacific Economic Cooperation Council or the Pacific Basin Economic Council could provide the institutional structure for APEC, if it evolves from a consultative to contractual organization. See Preeg (1990).

[21] For these countries, bilateral trade pacts with the United States are seen as a defensive strategy against the potential increase in US protectionism and wavering in US support for the GATT. See Schott (1989a).

likely to evolve and expand throughout the 1990s.

In North America, the Canada-US FTA is being expanded to include Mexico in a North American FTA. Further down the road, other countries in the Western Hemisphere may also join in some form pursuant to the Enterprise for the Americas initiative. Trade with third countries, and reliance on GATT rights and obligations, will remain a priority, since each member needs to increase its exports to help redress its large current account imbalance—total regional exports to the rest of the world thus will need to expand significantly.

In East Asia, the evidence of an evolving trading bloc seems to have been predicated at least in part on exaggerated claims regarding the increasing importance of intra-regional trade. While intra-regional trade has grown substantially, so too has trade with third countries. Indeed, many countries in the region have become increasingly reliant on access to the US market; their trade policy priority is thus to secure that access through international treaty. GATT provides the best means to do so.

To date, there is little evidence that regionalism is replacing multilateralism on a broad scale in the trade policy of the leading trading nations. The successful conclusion of the Uruguay Round remains the number one priority of US trade policy; the North American FTA is designed to build on and reinforce existing multilateral rights and obligations in the GATT.[22] Similarly, the dynamic economies of East Asia regard multilateralism as the best safeguard of access to their primary markets in North America (and to a lesser extent in Europe); bilateral or regional arrangements with the United States are being explored by some

of these countries primarily as a defensive strategy in case the multilateral process stalls, or the United States turns protectionist.[23]

In both regions, the evolution of a regional trading bloc has been considered only a second or third-best alternative, in the event the Uruguay Round falters. Only in Europe is there some ambiguity about the priority of GATT talks vis-à-vis the ongoing 1992 process.

Will these trends continue? Much depends on the results of the Uruguay Round. The multilateral trading system is still considered the "first-best" option for international trade relations by a growing number of trading nations. Success in the GATT will reinforce the multilateral process, as well as the outward orientation of the North American region even as movement toward regional integration continues.

If the Uruguay Round achieves only modest results, countries will likely focus on a "second best" option to supplement the GATT outcome. Such an approach could lead to a "GATT-Plus" negotiation, in which "like-minded" countries would seek to negotiate an open-ended FTA to supplement GATT disciplines and achieve further liberalisation among themselves in an effort to buttress the multilateral system. A more ambitious variant of this approach would be the negotiation of a "Free Trade and Investment Area" among the OECD countries as suggested by Gary Hufbauer (see Hufbauer, 1989).[24]

A complete breakdown in the Geneva

[23] The exception to this rule is Taiwan, which has actively sought an FTA with the United States to shore up the bilateral *political* relationship. However, Taiwan also has applied recently for accession to the GATT.

[24] However, Hufbauer's approach would need to be a complement to a GATT accord; if the GATT talks broke down, the same problems that plagued the negotiators in Geneva would lead the EC and others to balk at an OECD-wide compact.

[22] Indeed, a movement away from the GATT system would greatly complicate the negotiation and ratification of a North American pact. See Hufbauer and Schott (1991).

talks could change the focus of these regions away from multilateralism and toward the further elaboration of bilateral and regional trading arrangements (and in the United States this would be coupled with more aggressive use of unilateral trade measures). This would not mark the end of the GATT, but it would unleash a series of actions which would have a debilitating effect on the multilateral process. In short, regional blocs would provide only a "third-best," and distinctly suboptimal, option for world trade.

However, in such a "third best" world, one would likely witness the evolution of two rather than three regional trading blocs, reflecting the trend of trade and investment flows of the past decade. Such a bipolar world would likely pit the European bloc against a Pacific Basin bloc, in which North America forges special relations with Japan, Korea, ASEAN, and others. Europe would come out on the short end of that competition in terms of economic size, population, and technological prowess; but the real losers would be the developing countries that gain the most from a strong multilateral trading system.

REFERENCES

BALASSA, B. AND M. NOLAND (1988), *Japan in the World Economy,* Washington: Institute for International Economics.

BERGSTEN, C. F. (1988), *America in the World Economy: A Strategy for the 1990s,* Washington: Institute for International Economics.

CURZON PRICE, V. (1988). *1992: Europe's Last Chance? From Common Market to Single Market,* Occasional Paper 81, London: Institute for Economic Affairs for the Wincott Foundation.

DRUCKER, P. F. (1989), *The New Realities,* New York: Harper and Row.

GRAHAM, E. M. AND P. KRUGMAN (1989), *Foreign Direct Investment in the United States,* Washington: Institute for International Economics.

HUFBAUER, G. C. (1989), "Beyond GATT," 77, *Foreign Policy* (Winter 1989–90), 64–76.

HUFBAUER, G. C. AND J. J. SCHOTT (1991), *Prospects for North American Free Trade,* Washington: Institute for International Economics, forthcoming.

LEUTWILER, F. ET AL. (1985), *Trade Policies for a Better Future: Proposals for Action,* Geneva: GATT Independent Study Group, March.

MINISTRY OF INTERNATIONAL TRADE AND INDUSTRY (MITI), Japan (1989), "Report of the Council for the Promotion of Asian-Pacific Cooperation: Toward an Era of Development through Outward-looking Cooperation," (English language summary), June.

PREEG, H. (1990), "Rationale, Objectives, and Modalities," in Grant, Jordan, Preeg, and Wanandi, *Asia Pacific Economic Cooperation: The Challenge Ahead,* Washington: Center for Strategic and International Studies.

SCHOTT, J. J., ED. (1990), *Completing the Uruguay Round: A Results-oriented Approach to the GATT Trade Negotiations,* Washington: Institute for International Economics.

SCHOTT, J. J. (1989a), *More Free Trade Areas?* Policy Analyses in International Economics 27, Washington: Institute for International Economics, May.

SCHOTT, J. J., ED. (1989b), *Free Trade Areas and US Trade Policy,* Washington: Institute for International Economics.

SCHOTT, J. J. AND M. G. SMITH, EDS. (1988), *The Canada-United States Free Trade Agreement: The Global Impact,* Washington: Institute for International Economics, and Halifax: Institute for Research on Public Policy.

STOECKEL, A., D. PEARCE AND G. BANKS (1990), *Western Trade Blocs: Game, Set or Match for Asia-Pacific and the World Economy?* Report for the Confederation of Asia-Pacific Chambers of Commerce and Industry. Canberra, Australia: Centre for International Economics.

THE ECONOMIST (1989), "A Survey of the Yen Block: A New Balance in Asia?" 15 July.

20. Chinese Enterprise Behavior under the Reforms

*Roger H. Gordon and Wei Li**

During the recent decade of economic reforms from 1979 to 1989, the Chinese government adopted a series of policy and institutional changes aimed at increasing the productivity of the economy. While the initial efforts focused on agriculture, the government also tried to improve the performance of the nonagricultural sectors. Prior to the reforms, these sectors were heavily dominated by state-owned firms operating under central planning. The reforms decentralized many decisions to the firm level, or at least to the local government level. By 1985 most firms, for example, could change output quantity and variety, production technology, and the timing of production. To improve incentives, firms were allowed to retain a much larger fraction of profits. While the central planning apparatus remained in place, planned inputs and outputs became increasingly small fractions of the total inputs and outputs of firms. In principle they should not have affected marginal incentives. Outside-of-plan inputs and outputs could be traded freely among firms. While prices for goods allocated through the plan were tightly controlled, there were increasing attempts to relax control over the prices at which trade took place outside the plan. This type of dual-pricing system directly imitated the structure of the "responsibility system," which had proved so successful in agriculture.

Little attempt was made, however, to introduce factor markets in the state-enterprise sector. Even at the end of the period, firms continued to complain about being compelled to employ excess workers and workers could not quit without permission, though firms were given the discretion to hire temporary workers under contract. While the People's Construction Bank was set up to handle credit for new capital investment, proposed projects still needed to be approved at some level of government, and in practice investment decisions continued to be made primarily by the government planning ministries or by local governments.

Another key aspect of the economic reforms was to make it easier for local governments, collectives, and even private households to set up their own firms outside of the state planning structure. There

SOURCE: Reprinted with permission from *Papers and Proceedings of the Hundred and Third Annual Meeting of the American Economic Association* (Washington, D.C., December 28–30, 1990), vol. 81, no. 2, May 1991, pp. 202–206. Copyright © American Economic Association, 1991.

   * Department of Economics, University of Michigan, Ann Arbor, MI 48109. We thank Michael Orszag, Michelle White, and Zhong Zhang for comments on an earlier draft. Some of the results reported in this paper come from a survey of 403 Chinese state enterprises conducted as part of a joint research project with the Chinese Academy of Social Sciences, funded by the Ford Foundation.

was rapid growth in the number and output of such firms in response to the new flexibility. For example, the output of township firms grew dramatically from 8.6 percent of national nonagricultural output in 1979 to 26.6 percent in 1988. (See State Statistics Bureau, 1989, pp. 44; 248.)

The objective of this paper is to examine more closely the incentives created by these reforms, in order to better understand the causes of their success and failure. We start by discussing the state-owned sector, then examine the private and collective sectors.

I. STATE-OWNED ENTERPRISES

Prior to the economic reforms, managers of state-owned enterprises in China were rewarded primarily based on their success in meeting physical output targets set by the government. With the reforms, rewards were instead based much more heavily on the firms' tax payments and accounting profits. While the tax rate on firms remained high by Western standards, in practice more than three-quarters of retained profits went to the firms' managers and workers. The link between accounting profits and manager/employee compensation might if anything have been stronger than in Western firms. These strong financial incentives, along with the decentralization of decision making, in theory should have led to a sizable increase in efficiency.

The story was not quite so simple, however. Given the large differences between accounting prices and market prices, accounting profits could well provide a poor approximation to true economic profits. When existing goods prices differ from market prices and allocation decisions are decentralized, barter trade should commonly arise at implicit prices for each type of good, which together are sufficient to clear all markets. What impact does barter trade

have on firms' accounting profits and marginal incentives? If underpriced output is exchanged for a combination of cash plus a sufficient amount of underpriced input, then the two errors in the accounts should just offset, leaving pre-tax accounting profits unaffected. However, firms often sell underpriced output for underpriced consumer goods, or even for under-the-table cash payments. According to the evidence reported in our 1990 paper, sellers appear not to report receiving these extra payments, while buyers do report making them. The most compelling evidence was that firms reported that the inflation rate in the output price of machinery and industrial materials was very low, consistent with sales at official prices, whereas firms reported that the prices they paid when buying machinery and industrial materials grew at a rate roughly approximating the inflation rate in market prices. Since the responsibility for auditing a firm's accounts often rests with the firm itself, this evasion should not be surprising. This tax evasion increases the fraction of economic profits retained by the firm, reinforcing the incentives to raise efficiency. The amount of such evasion increased quickly during the period as market prices grew with inflation while official prices remained relatively constant.

The resulting loss in tax revenue led the government in 1986–87 to shift to a contract system in which each firm signed a contract with the government, typically for 5 years, agreeing to minimum tax payments during each year of the contract. But firms could still evade any tax on sales and profits above that necessary to justify the minimum tax payments, and in any case the inflation rate was high enough that real tax payments continued to fall.[1]

---

[1] In a sample of 361 firms with available data (see our 1990 paper), the annual growth rates of total tax payments from 1984 to 1987

Barter trade was not possible in all markets, however. Unless barter is costless, distorted official prices lead directly to distorted incentives. Often these distortions were sufficiently large that the government continued to intervene, either directly ordering decisions or else offering enough cheap credit or subsidized inputs to make the decisions it desired profitable from the firm's perspective. For example, the pay structure within firms remained highly egalitarian, so not surprisingly firms reported having an excess number of unskilled workers and a shortage of skilled workers. Given this pressure, the government continued to assign workers to firms and virtually forbade layoffs.

The interest rate on bank loans was also kept far below a market-clearing level. Not only was the interest rate low, but both interest *and* principal payments were normally tax deductible. Allowing these deductions is equivalent to allowing expensing of debt-financed new investments for tax purposes. In theory, under expensing no tax is collected in present value on a marginal investment—the cash flow to the government is proportional to that received by the firm, so when the firm breaks even so does the government. Therefore as a result of the below-market interest rate, debt-financed investments were subsidized on net.[2] Demand for loans exceeded the supply of funds, and increasingly so during the period as the rising inflation rate caused the real interest rate on loans to drop. Gov-

ernment intervention was necessary to ration credit.

When making allocation decisions, the government could not rely on the information available in a firm's financial accounts to judge the merit of any given project. That left the government with the option either of correcting the accounts for the distortions created by mispricing, or of continuing to plan directly the desired allocation of resources. Given the importance of the distortions, most importantly in interest rates, energy prices, foreign exchange rates, and the cost of skilled workers, and the pervasive way that these distortions filtered through the entire pricing structure, correcting the financial accounts would be virtually impossible.[3] It is no wonder that the government was loathe to rely on such accounting figures to determine which firms to push into bankruptcy.

In spite of the problems with the financial accounting figures, they were still used heavily in determining the allocation of new investment, if only by requiring firms to invest a given fraction of their net-of-tax accounting profits. These reinvestment requirements were not self-enforcing, however—given the high tax rates on future profits, a firm's employees should much prefer the money now to receiving a fraction of the flow of net-of-tax profits resulting from investing the money in new capital. In practice, reinvestment rates were far below the levels required by regulation.

Even basing pay on a correct measure of economic profits would still create anomalous incentives if employees do not remain with the firm throughout the period affected by any given economic decision, or if employees fear a change in the compensation rule in the future. For

---

were 10.48, 3.31, 1.47, and −1.35 percent, respectively, while the official annual retail price inflation in the same years were 2.8, 8.8, 6.0, and 7.3 percent, respectively. See State Statistics Bureau, p. 689.

[2] In fact, depreciation deductions were allowed as well, but during much of the period 40–50 percent of these deductions had to be handed over to the government, thereby mostly offsetting the gain from the tax deduction.

[3] See, for example, the complicated discussion in I. M. D. Little and James Mirrlees (1974) concerning how to correct appropriately for such distortions in cost-benefit analyses.

example, managers might have an incentive to sell off existing capital in order to generate current profits and current bonuses, hoping that by the time the future losses show up they have been promoted or retired. Western firms try to avoid these incentives by basing the compensation of managers on changes in share values rather than on current profits. Chinese officials did recognize this problem. One experimental solution, known as the Asset Management Responsibility System, involved auctioning the job of manager every 5 years. The departing manager would receive a bonus based on the bid price of the new manager, thereby tying his compensation to the future prospects of the firm.

What happened in response to all these policy changes? In our earlier paper, we found in a sample of 403 state-owned enterprises that total factor productivity in the sample grew between 1983 and 1987 at a rate of 4 percent per year, while real output grew on average at 8 percent per year. Thus, decentralized decision making, even with badly distorted incentives, raised productivity in the state sector.

II. THE PRIVATE AND COLLECTIVE SECTOR

The planning system in China, similar to that in the Soviet Union, favored heavy industry and highly capital-intensive technologies, resulting in a very different allocation of resources than is seen in market economies. For example, in 1986, 5 percent of workers were employed in the commercial trade sector in China, compared with 15 percent in Indonesia, 11 percent in Brazil, and 21 percent in the United States. (See State Statistics Bureau, p. 997.) Therefore, it should not be surprising that opening the economy to the entry of new firms would lead to rapid changes.

Private and collective enterprises responded swiftly to the economic liberal-

ization. The former quickly expanded in the retail sector, while the latter become much more important in the industrial sector.[4] Not only did these firms produce badly needed goods and services, but they also introduced competitive pressures into the economy, undermining the monopoly power of state-owned firms.

While the proliferation of private firms should not be surprising to Western economists, one should keep in mind that this occurred despite arbitrary taxes and erratic government interference, limiting, for example, their scope of trade, employment, and access to credit and scarce resources. Until 1985, for example, private firms could employ no more than seven workers. They also faced the risk of being shut down by the government at any point. Nonetheless, they grew and prospered.

The rapid growth of collectives, especially township enterprises, cannot be explained so simply. The local government normally controlled the access of collectives to workers, scarce inputs, and credits, and had to approve the appointment of managers, investment decisions, and even production plans. In addition, however, the local government kept most of the taxes paid by collectives in its jurisdiction,[5] and had some control over the allocation of retained earnings. Since the local government effectively owned and controlled these firms, and operated in competition with many other local jurisdictions, the resulting allocation deci-

[4] The market share of retail sales by private enterprise rose from 0.24 percent in 1979 to 17.8 percent in 1988, while the share of industrial output of the collectives rose from 21.53 percent in 1979 to 36.38 percent in 1988. See State Statistics Bureau, pp. 601; 267.

[5] Under the fiscal system adopted in 1985, all profit taxes from locally controlled firms including all collectives and some state firms go to the local government treasury, while other tax payments, such as the product tax and the value-added tax, were still shared with the national government.

sions should have been relatively efficient. Each local government was small enough to take as given the implicit market prices for factors as well as goods—mobility across jurisdictions increased substantially during this period. The local government, by increasing efficiency, increased the resources under its control. Local government incentives remained distorted, however, to the degree to which some of the taxes paid by collectives had to be transferred to higher levels of government. In contrast, the national government's allocation decisions for state-owned firms would not be so constrained by market pressures. Thus, decentralization, even within the government, brought increased prosperity to the economy.

These improved incentives required decentralizing both control of tax revenue and control of the operations of firms to the same level of government. This was done not only for collectives but also for many smaller state-owned firms, implying the same improvement in incentives. Occasionally, however, control of the operations of larger state-owned firms was also delegated to local governments even though the bulk of the tax revenue went to the national government. The high national tax rates on these firms discouraged local investment in them, particularly when they were competing against locally owned firms whose tax revenue stayed within the jurisdiction.

Due to local taxes and distorted prices, locally controlled firms themselves faced different incentives than the local governments. As a result, local governments felt compelled to intervene regularly. This intervention often took the form of restrictions on trade with other jurisdictions. For example, when the implicit market price for a good exceeded the local opportunity cost of producing it, then the local government had an incentive to force local firms to buy the locally pro-

duced good, even if its price exceeded the implicit market price. Similarly, when the consumer price of a good exceeded its implicit market price, the local government had an incentive to prevent outside firms and individuals from selling directly to local consumers, to keep the profits from the price differential within the community.

III. LESSONS FOR THE FUTURE

The shift towards decentralized decision making during the reform period in China resulted in a rapid increase in output and in productivity. Yet in spite of these successes, the economic situation was very bleak by the end of the reform period. The problems arose mainly from the growing inflation rate. Official prices did not keep up with inflation, resulting in increasing price distortions and growing opportunities for tax evasion. The right to buy at official prices became increasingly valuable, resulting in growing corruption and growing rent-seeking behavior, which undermined political support for the reforms. In addition, the increasing distortions to the measure of financial profits made oversight by the government of firm behavior, and even of the behavior of the economy as a whole, more and more tenuous.

REFERENCES

GORDON, ROGER H. AND WEI LI, "The Change in Productivity of Chinese State Enterprises, 1983–1987," mimeo., University of Michigan, 1990.

LITTLE, I. M. D. AND JAMES MIRRLEES, *Project Appraisal and Planning for Developing Countries.* London: Heinemann, 1974.

STATE STATISTICS BUREAU, *China Statistics Yearbook 1989.* Beijing: China Statistics Press, 1989.

CHAPTER 6

The American Economy and International Trade

This section deals with the role of the United States in world trade. In the first article, Robert Baldwin notes that in the 1970s and 1980s the United States pursued an aggressive trade strategy "oriented toward domestic economic interests and particular regional political objectives." He reviews the main features of American trade policy: nontariff barriers, voluntary export restraints, countervailing duty laws, and antidumping laws.

The second article outlines American proposals for changes in international rules governing agriculture. The recommendations of the U.S. Department of Agriculture (USDA) seek to make "major reforms in import access, export competition, and internal support policies." The USDA suggestions are intended to produce higher world market prices, reduce taxpayer costs, and lower consumer prices.

The third article, "Trading Places: Industries for Free Trade," examines the political economy of protectionism. Helen Milner, a political scientist, notes that the world economy did not witness rapidly rising protectionism and international trade wars in the 1970s (unlike the 1920s), despite the fact that the world experienced a major recession. The difference in outcomes, she argues, is due to "the increased economic interdependence of the post-World War II period." She provides evidence for the hypothesis that "firms with greater international ties in the form of exports, multinationality, and global intrafirm trade will be less interested in protection than firms that are more domestically oriented."

The next article, "The Uruguay Round," chronicles the issues currently facing international trade negotiators: market access issues, such as agriculture and textiles; rules, including safeguards, antidumping, subsidies, and dispute settlement; and new areas, such as trade-related investment measures, intellectual property rights, and services. The authors, H. B. Jung and Clemens Boonekamp, warn that failure to resolve these issues might accelerate the trend toward bilateral and regional trading arrangements, thereby slowing the growth of global trade.

21.   U.S. Trade Policy
Recent Changes and Future U.S. Interests

Robert E. Baldwin

There have been major changes in recent years in the trade policy strategy used by the United States in promoting its economic and political goals. In contrast to the benevolent multilateral approach from the early 1940s through the 1960s in which international cooperation aimed at strengthening the free world was emphasized, the United States in the 1970s and 1980s has increasingly pursued an aggressive bilateral strategy oriented toward domestic economic interests and particular regional political objectives.

One manifestation of this policy shift is the increased use of bilateral negotiations in which the United States threatens to restrict access to its domestic market in order to force open a trading partner's markets for more U.S. exports or to curtail market-disrupting imports from the country. Negotiating free-trade agreements with the Caribbean basin, Israel, and Canada is another. Other indicators of this strategy shift are an increased emphasis on "fair" trade, the greater use of the antidumping and countervailing duty laws to restrict imports, and a willingness to give up the most-favored-nation principle in limiting imports even when injury to a domestic industry is not due to unfair foreign trade practices. The United States has not abandoned the multilateral approach, as its participation in the Uruguay Round negotiations demonstrates, but even here the United States seems less willing than in the past to compromise for the purpose

of achieving a consensus among the participants.

This paper briefly analyzes the reasons for this shift in trade policy strategy and considers its usefulness for promoting U.S. interests in the future.

I. FROM HEGEMON TO OLIGOPSONIST

During and shortly after World War II, plans were formulated for establishing an international economic order in which the major nations would share the responsibility for promoting full employment and economic development through a system of open trade and stable exchange rates. Though most of the planned institutional structure was put in place, this concept of shared power and responsibility failed to become a reality. The task of restoring prewar production levels in Western Europe and Japan and increasing growth rates in the developing countries turned out to be much more difficult than anticipated. Consequently, the noncommunist nations turned to the United States for the economic assistance needed to implement the goals of the new international economic order.

While the United States responded generously to this challenge in the first few years after the war, it was a political event, namely, the expansionist efforts of the Soviet Union in Western Europe, that led U.S. political leaders to accept fully the role and responsibilities of the hegemon in the free world. U.S. international economic policies became instruments of U.S. foreign policy as trade liberalization and foreign aid were used to strengthen noncommunist countries in the hope of

SOURCE: Reprinted with permission from *American Economic Review*, May 1989, pp. 128–133.

increasing their resistance to Soviet expansionary efforts.

These policies also promoted the economic interests of key domestic groups. The U.S. share of industrial country exports rose from 25.6 percent in 1938 to 35.2 percent in 1952, while the combined export share of Germany and Japan fell from 24.0 to 11.4 percent between these years (see my 1958 paper). The export surplus that prevailed in almost every major industry helped to maintain high employment and profit levels during the early postwar years. Although the widespread existence of exchange controls reduced the immediate benefits from the tariff concessions obtained during the GATT-sponsored trade liberalizing negotiations, U.S. industry was able to establish important market positions in Europe and elsewhere by exporting and undertaking direct foreign investment.

The hegemonic actions of the United States aimed at maintaining a liberal international economic framework and strengthening the noncommunist countries succeeded very well. By 1960, production in most of the war-damaged industrial countries had reached or exceeded prewar levels. As would be expected, this return to peacetime production levels meant that the exceptionally high market shares of the United States declined. In manufacturing, for example, the U.S. world market share declined sharply from 29.4 percent in 1953 to 18.7 percent by 1959 (see William Branson, 1980, for these and other data on shares in this paragraph). Stiff foreign competition was evident in the cotton textile and oil industries as well as in some agricultural sectors by the late 1950s and, aggravated by a progressively overvalued dollar, spread to such industries as footwear, radios and television sets, tires and inner tubes, semiconductors, earthenware table and kitchen articles, jewelry, and some steel items by the late 1960s. By 1971, the U.S. share of world exports of

manufactures had fallen to 13.4 percent. In contrast, Western Europe's share of world manufacturing exports increased from 48.6 percent in 1953 to 52.3 percent in 1959, and then to 55.1 percent in 1971, while Japan's share rose from 3.9 to 6.8 to 10.7 percent over these years.

Thus, it became apparent by the late 1960s that the American economic position of the early postwar years had eroded to the point where the United States became one of a small group of countries whose individual actions significantly influenced, but did not dominate, the international economic order. The U.S. international economic status became similar to that of an oligopsonist in a product market; its trade policy actions were strategically linked to those of the other major trading nations and, in selecting its best policies, it could no longer largely ignore the reactions of these other nations.

II. THE U.S. TRADE POLICY RESPONSE

In failing to pass the Burke-Hartke bill in 1971, Congress rejected a general protectionist approach as the means of dealing with the increased import competition. But members of Congress and the administration became increasingly receptive to the claim of many import-competing and export-oriented producers that unfair trade practices by foreign firms and governments were a major cause of their competitive problems. Consequently, in the Trade Act of 1974, Congress gave the president broad powers to eliminate "unjustifiable and unreasonable" foreign import restrictions and also directed the president to seek a tightening of GATT rules on unfair trading practices during the Tokyo Round of multilateral trade negotiations.

While the U.S. share of world manufacturing markets was relatively stable in the 1970s as the country's international competitiveness benefited from the dollar depreciation in the early part of the decade, certain politically powerful industries such as steel, automobiles, and machine tools faced increasingly intense import and export competition. Moreover, after the Tokyo Round was concluded in 1979, it quickly became clear that the newly negotiated GATT codes of "good" behavior were too general to be effective in meeting the concerns of such industries about unfair trade practices.

It was, however, the sharp increase in the U.S. trade deficit in the early 1980s that gave the greatest impetus to the acceptance of the view that a major cause of U.S. competitive problems was unfair trade actions by foreign governments and firms. As has been explained by economists many times, the jump in the trade deficit was caused by several factors: the increase in federal government spending relative to tax collections, the tight monetary policy of the Federal Reserve, a drop in private U.S. savings, the attractiveness of investment opportunities in the United States compared to those in other developed and developing countries, and the Japanese government's removal of certain controls over foreign investment. These developments led to a large inflow of foreign funds and return of U.S. funds invested abroad, thereby resulting in a very significant appreciation of the U.S. dollar.

The appreciation of the dollar not only exacerbated the profitability difficulties of such industries as textiles and apparel, footwear, steel, and automobiles, but caused significant international competitive problems for many traditionally vigorous export-oriented and import-competing industries. The resulting political pressure to rectify this situation caused the trade deficit to become a matter of concern to almost all members of Congress and most parts of the executive branch.

But both Congress and the administration faced difficult political problems in trying to correct the conditions causing both the budget and trade deficits. President Reagan had pledged not to raise taxes and was also committed to large defense expenditures. Cutting social spending was the administration's proposal for solving the problem, but most members of Congress rejected this approach both on ideological grounds and for fear of disapproval by their constituents. Voting for an increase in taxes, especially when the president was likely to veto such a bill, also was not a politically feasible alternative for Congress. Instead, more and more members began to adopt the view that the unwillingness of foreign governments to open their domestic markets to the extent that the United States had already done was a major cause of the U.S. trade problem. Blaming foreigners did not involve the risk of voter disapproval that raising taxes or cutting social or defense expenditures did. The fact that the administration had not made widespread use of this argument also made it attractive as a way of shifting blame for the trade deficit problem from Congress to the president. Consequently, Congress took various steps in the late 1970s and 1980s to make it easier for domestic firms to gain protection under U.S. antidumping and countervailing duty laws, and to increase further the powers of the president to act against unfair trade practices.

Under prodding by the Congress, the Reagan Administration began to use bilateral negotiations to an increasing extent to pressure foreign governments into opening their markets and modifying certain of their export-increasing practices. A greater willingness to utilize country-selective quantitative restrictions, even though import injury was not caused by traditional unfair trade practices, also was related to the new views about fair trade. It came to be regarded as unfair for foreign producers to increase their exports so rapidly that they caused injury to U.S. producers, no matter what the reason for the export increase.

III. THE NEW STRATEGY AND FUTURE U.S. INTERESTS

One of the most significant economic relationships demonstrated with a high degree of consistency over the last forty years is the greater rate of economic growth enjoyed by outward-looking countries pursuing liberal, market-oriented policies than by countries whose governments interfere extensively with domestic and foreign trade. An impressive body of evidence from both developed and developing nations supports this conclusion.

In America's hegemonic period, U.S. government leaders had little difficulty politically in following outward-looking, liberal policies, and U.S. experience supported the hypothesis that procompetitive policies promote high growth rates. However, as the preceding section has indicated, the adjustment problems associated with the country's new international position led to significant changes in U.S. trade policy strategy. While most leaders in the public and private sectors still favor an open international trading system, an obvious question is whether these new policies facilitate the maintenance of such a regime.

The greater use of bilateral negotiations and free-trade arrangements has both merits and drawbacks as means of promoting an open trading order. To the extent that other countries reduce or eliminate import barriers, bilateral pressures obviously contribute to openness. But, in opening their markets for U.S. goods, these countries may simply restrict imports from third countries. This not only tends to offset the initial world welfare gains, but can lead to a disruptive diversion of exports to the United States. As a

U.S. trade surplus becomes necessary to service the growing foreign debt resulting from the trade deficit, countries may also use the general U.S. arguments about fair trade to block this needed increase in exports. Furthermore, American pressures on Japan and the newly industrializing countries to be less export oriented may lead to import-substituting policies in these economies that restrict export market opportunities for the United States and other nations.

It would clearly be more desirable to achieve a greater opening of world markets through multilateral negotiations in the GATT. But certain liberalizing actions, such as significant reductions in the high levels of protection in developing countries, greater protection of intellectual property rights, the elimination of trade-restricting investment policies, and liberalization in agriculture and textiles are very difficult to achieve via the GATT route, since they require either changes in existing GATT rules or are not presently covered by these rules. Domestic economic interests that lose from liberalization are often able to persuade their governments to block meaningful liberalization in the GATT, a 96-member organization that reaches agreements by consensus. Consequently, bilateral pressure by a large country like the United States, backed by the threat to restrict access to its own markets or to conclude special regional agreements with other countries, may be the only way to achieve greater liberalization on the part of some countries. However, some form of multilateral monitoring over such bilateral actions seems necessary to ensure that the end result really contributes to an open and fair trading system.

The greater emphasis by the United States on preventing unfair trade also has both positive and negative effects in promoting an open trading order. For example, careful scrutiny of a country's subsidy programs by another country with a view toward possible countervailing duty actions can serve to reduce the likelihood that special interest groups within the first country will be successful in getting subsidies that not only reduce the country's own welfare but slow down growth in other countries. Similarly, predatory dumping restricts competition in the long run and thereby slows growth. The protection of intellectual property rights is also necessary for maintaining high rates of technological progress.

Unfortunately, the fair trade laws are currently being used by some as anticompetitive, growth-retarding instruments. There is considerable evidence (see J. Thomas Prusa, 1988, and Patrick Messerlin, 1988, for example) indicating that American and European firms are using the antidumping laws as a means of pressuring their foreign competitors into agreements that raise prices and reduce general welfare. The U.S. position that government subsidies are bad, no matter what the circumstances, is another example of the inappropriate use of the fair trade laws. There is an extensive literature in international economics demonstrating that, when certain domestic distortions and market imperfections exist, domestic subsidies can increase world welfare. Temporary subsidies to aid injured export industries and trade-displaced workers are also as justifiable as temporary protection for injured import-competing industries. There is, of course, the danger that political pressures from special interest groups will result in many welfare-reducing subsidies, but this possibility should not in itself rule out efforts by GATT members to develop a sensible set of rules on subsidies. The U.S. antidumping and countervailing duty laws are based on the simplistic and unrealistic economics of the pre-1930s and need to be modified to reflect modern economics and the current world international commerce.

The recent willingness to restrict imports selectively from countries whose export success is not due to unfair trade practices undermines the fundamental principle of international competitiveness, and represents a major step toward a system of managed trade that is not in the long-run economic interests of the United States. Furthermore, imposing quantitative restrictions on a country-selective basis is often ineffective in providing protection to domestic producers, as the U.S. experience in the late 1970s with selective import controls on color TV sets and shoes demonstrated. Quality upgrading by the controlled exporters and increases in supply from noncontrolled sources tend to negate the domestic output-increasing effect of selective quantitative restrictions. In addition, the expansion of capacity by noncontrolled producers makes the import competition problem worse than ever for domestic producers, once controls are lifted on all suppliers.

This does not mean, however, that governments should automatically restrict all the items in a particular tariff classification from all sources, even though some of the items are poor substitutes for each other. Small planes for two or three passengers are not good substitutes for large commercial aircraft, nor are small inexpensive cars very good substitutes for large luxury cars. Raising import duties on small cars such as the Honda Civic and Volkswagen Rabbit and on luxury cars like the Mercedes, even though increased imports of the former type of car is the cause of the import injury, is just as unfair as raising the tariff on Honda Civics and not on Volkswagen Rabbits. Econometric techniques for estimating appropriate demand elasticities are now available (see James Levinsohn, 1988) to determine if some items can be removed from a tariff line without undermining the efficacy of Article XIX actions nor unfairly discriminating against particular countries. Of course, the GATT dispute-settlement procedures must operate effectively to prevent abuses of this x-ing-out procedure.

An important reason for the abandonment of the MFN principle and the misuse of the antidumping provisions is the inadequacy of existing U.S. import-injury law. The part relating to the cause of injury needs to be modified to prevent such outcomes as the rejection of the petition by the automobile industry in 1980 on the grounds that the recession was a more important cause of serious injury than increased imports, even though it was generally agreed that increased imports also caused serious injury. More effective provisions are also needed to retrain and relocate workers in injured industries as well as those who have already lost their jobs. Recent experiments with various types of temporary wage subsidies indicate the feasibility of adjustment assistance schemes that do not have the drawback of lengthening the period of unemployment. These changes in the import-injury law coupled with changes in the antidumping law should make use of the escape clause route more attractive to firms and workers. However, to provide a better balance between producer and consumer interests, an agency such as the International Trade Commission or the Council of Economic Advisers should inform the public of the expected welfare costs of any protection that is proposed.

The increased use of nontariff measures (NTMs) in recent years also undermines the benefits of an open trading system. By not being as transparent as tariffs, NTMs are more difficult to eliminate, once in place. Moreover, in the case of one of the most widely used NTMs, voluntary export-restraint agreements (VERs), it has been estimated that the U.S. government annually loses about $5 billion in revenue that could be reclaimed by shifting back to tariffs or to a system of quota auctions.

There are many other international and domestic policies that affect the nature of the world trading system, but this is not the place for a general examination of U.S. economic policies. Yet, one issue that significantly influences the medium-term prospects for moving toward a more open regime, namely, the trade deficit, must be mentioned. Unless this deficit is reduced to a level perceived by most to represent an equilibrium position, political pressures for anticompetitive, anti-growth trade policies will remain high and continue to endanger the achievement of a stable, open trading system. The complex macroeconomic policy issues involved in trying to reduce this deficit as well as the federal government's budget deficit are discussed in William Cline's paper in this session. This paper has assumed that the twin deficits ease sufficiently for policymakers to begin to evaluate the usefulness of recent trade policy changes in promoting the economic goals of the United States in the 1990s and beyond.

REFERENCES

BALDWIN, ROBERT E., "The Commodity Composition of Trade: Selected Industrial Countries, 1900–1954," *Review of Economics and Statistics,* February 1958, *40,* 50–68.

BRANSON, WILLIAM H., "Trends in United States International Trade and Investment since World War II, " in Martin Feldstein, ed., *The American Economy in Transition,* NBER, Chicago: University of Chicago Press, 1980.

LEVINSOHN, JAMES, "Empirics of Taxes on Differentiated Products: The Case of Tariffs in the U.S. Automobile Industry," in Robert Baldwin, ed., *Trade Policy Issues and Empirical Analysis,* NBER, Chicago: University of Chicago Press, 1988.

MESSERLIN, PATRICK A., "The EC Antidumping Regulations: A First Economic Appraisal, 1980–85," paper presented at the International Seminar in International Trade sponsored by the Centre for Economic Policy Research and the NBER, St. Catherine's College, Oxford, August 24–25, 1988.

PRUSA, J. THOMAS, "Why Are So Many Dumping Cases Withdrawn?" paper presented at a conference sponsored by the Institute for Governmental Affairs, University of California-Davis on Designing Policies to Open Trade, November 18–19, 1988.

22.   GATT Trade Liberalization
The U.S. Proposal

U.S. Department of Agriculture

After 3 1/2 years, the Uruguay Round of the General Agreement on Tariffs and Trade (GATT) is moving into its final stages. The United States and several other nations have presented separate proposals for comprehensive agricultural trade reform. The U.S. proposal seeks to make major reforms in import access, export competition, internal support policies, and sanitary and phytosanitary measures. If implemented, this proposal would produce higher world market prices, lower taxpayer costs, and, in some key countries, significantly lower consumer prices.

Current multilateral GATT negotiations offer a historic opportunity to restructure agricultural policies around the world. Such a restructuring could free up the world's agriculture to respond to market signals rather than the artificial demands

SOURCE: U.S. Department of Agriculture, Economic Research Service, Agriculture Research Service, Agriculture Information Bulletin No. 596, March 1990.

based on government policies. Such artificial demands distort trade relationships among countries by taking trade away from the more efficient producers and marketers. Removal of the significant trade distortions would lead to some adjustments in production and consumption patterns around the world, but the longer term effects would include a more efficient environment for the world's farmers.

The U.S. proposal, calling for a 10-year phased reduction in trade-distorting interventions, would greatly facilitate world adjustment to longrun comparative advantage, where each country exports that which it produces most efficiently. The proposal allows many types of programs to continue. Other programs now distorting trade could be redesigned to be less distorting. Thus, even in the transition period, it is possible to design policies that would maintain farmers' income.

Many groups in the United States and elsewhere ask why existing programs should be changed when farmers have done so well under them. The answer begins with a consideration of the changing nature of the world economy. Given the fundamental changes that have occurred, policies that once worked when the world's economies were more independent do not work so well with growing interdependence. Furthermore, highly inefficient agricultural policies which demand large budget outlays cannot coexist with the mounting public pressure to reduce government spending.

Also, maintenance of the status quo is probably no longer possible in the arena of international politics. The likely alternative to a successful GATT Round is not a continuation of the past conditions, but pressure for increasing protectionism. Such protectionism has proved to be extremely costly. Indeed, after the Smoot-Hawley Act of 1930, the successively increasing protectionism which moved around the world led to a general collapse of trade and was a major factor in the global depression of the 1930's.

TRADE TALKS REEXAMINE 50 YEARS' WORTH OF AGRICULTURAL POLICIES

Growing interdependence among nations and mounting government outlays force a new look at agricultural policy. More efficient farm production, reduced tax burdens, and lower consumer prices are among the anticipated effects of agricultural trade liberalization.

In the current Uruguay Round of GATT negotiations, the major agricultural trading nations are reexamining the nature of the agricultural policies they have formulated over the last 50 years. This reexamination is motivated by depressed commodity markets in the mid-1980's, budgetary pressures in a time of government deficits, and stronger macroeconomic linkages drawing countries closer together. Because the agricultural policies of one country can affect producers and consumers in other countries and because the rate of intervention in agricul-

ture is so much higher than in industry, enough pressure built up for agriculture to be included in a significant way for the first time in the current GATT multilateral trade negotiations. These negotiations offer major trading nations an opportunity to improve commodity markets and reduce taxpayer costs by multilaterally reformulating their agricultural policies to reduce market distortions.

Agricultural trade has not been a significant part of the post-World War II trade-liberalizing trend. Agricultural policies have been largely exempt from GATT rules, while tariffs on industrial countries' manufactured goods declined from a 40-percent level in the mid-1960's to 6–8 percent by 1974. After the GATT Tokyo Round (1974–79), those tariffs were reduced to 4–6 percent, representing a reduction of another 30 percent or more. Meanwhile, nominal protection rates for agricultural commodities in industrial countries rose from 21 percent to 28 percent between 1965 and 1974 and reached 40 percent in 1988.

World trade of agricultural commodities grew rapidly in the 1970's, induced by strong demand in developing countries and changes in the policy posture of centrally planned countries. Rapidly increasing commodity prices accompanied this surge in trade. In the 1980's, however, growth in global commodity markets was nearly halted by global recession, the debt crisis, and fluctuations in exchange rates. Agricultural production sectors, distorted by both import protection and strong support inducements, were geared up to produce, and surpluses piled up in the face of stagnant or declining trade. As global prices fell, those governments that could afford to do so further increased subsidies to agriculture. It was not until the 1988 drought in North America that global demand exceeded production and commodity prices began to return to the higher 1970 levels.

Growing Interdependence

Macroeconomic factors increasingly affect world agricultural markets. Institutional developments outside of agriculture have fundamentally altered the environment in which agricultural trade operates. These developments have illuminated issues that have been largely neglected or ignored in the past. Growing integration of the world economy, the development of a well-integrated world capital market, and the movement to flexible exchange rates have important implications for the agricultural sector. Macroeconomic policies now often work through variations in exchange rates more than through changes in interest rates. These policies have a greater effect on trade-intensive sectors such as agriculture.

The agricultural and macroeconomic policies of one nation increasingly affect agricultural sectors of others. The current set of world agricultural policies was developed at a time when the structure of world trade and economic interdependence was very different than it is now. Under conditions in which capital flows and trade were not as important, it was easier for nations to ignore the international effects of their policies. But the current world with instantaneous communications and transfers of assets does not allow us to ignore the international consequences of domestically focused policies.

For example, the EC's Common Agricultural Policy (CAP) was designed to stimulate domestic production and generate revenue when EC countries were net agricultural importers. Now the policy contributes to surpluses. In addition to becoming a surplus producer, the EC has also become a major subsidizing exporter, helping to drive world prices down. Export restitutions now make up about 39 percent of the total EC budget.

The United States, on the other hand, saw itself as a major supplier of grains and oilseeds to the world market. With the trends of the late 1970's in mind, U.S. legislators designed an agricultural policy in the 1981 farm bill that would be consistent with assumptions of strong global demand and continued inflation. But neither assumption proved to be correct. So in practice, the legislation reduced U.S. competitiveness in world markets and generated record stocks and farm subsidy payments.

The Japanese have achieved rice self-sufficiency by providing producers with support prices that exceed by fivefold the world market prices for wheat and rice. By holding domestic prices far above world prices, Japan has substantially lowered wheat and livestock imports from what they otherwise would be. The Japanese consumer, however, pays dearly for this intervention.

Unforeseen consequences are not the only result of the current panoply of agricultural policies. The other result is policies that have been added to defend policies that did not achieve what was intended in the first place. Thus, to defend the CAP which was instituted to further European integration, the EC has had to institute separate exchange rates for agriculture (the so-called "green rates"), set variable levies, pay export restitutions, and develop a set of administratively complicated policies.

Expenses Mount

While many agricultural policies have been successful in achieving some of the objectives, such as production increases, the success has often come at great cost. Budget expenditures on agricultural support programs in industrial countries in 1986 amounted to approximately $100 billion, while the total transfer from taxpayers and consumers was a much higher

---

TRADE LIBERALIZATION: WHAT IT ACTUALLY MEANS

- World market prices for highly supported agricultural commodities would be higher after trade liberalization. Larger share of farm income would come from the marketplace.
- Farmers would be more efficient . . . subject to less government intervention and better able to respond to market signals. These gains in efficiency would benefit the general economies of countries.
- Production would shift from those areas with current high support levels to those with lower levels of sup-

port. To the degree that U.S. agriculture has a natural comparative advantage in production, this would work to the advantage of the United States.
- Taxpayers would be better off. Reduced tax burdens could save more than $80 billion a year around the world, based on 1986 levels of support.
- In several key countries, especially the EC and Japan, consumers would pay lower prices.

$271 billion. Because of both distorted prices and the expense of operating government programs, only about 70 percent of government budget outlays and consumer expenditures above free market levels get passed on to farmers in the form of higher farm incomes in the industrial countries. The bulk of U.S. direct farm income support (deficiency payments) is borne by the taxpayer rather than the consumer, in stark contrast to the EC and Japan, where the hidden cost of agricultural policies is in the form of much higher consumer prices.

Budget outlays averaged around $25 billion in the mid-1980's in the United States and are projected to decline in the 1990's. EC budget outlays amounted to $35 billion, and consumer costs exceeded the direct budget costs. In Japan, actual budget outlays have been relatively small. Most of the cost of the farm program is born by the consumer, with consumer costs averaging about $50 billion (an average of more than $1,000 per nonfarm family in 1986).

THE GATT AND PAST AGRICULTURAL TRADE NEGOTIATIONS

The GATT is a multilateral agreement establishing the code of rules governing international trade. GATT also serves as an institutional forum for negotiating reductions of trade barriers and other trade-distorting measures. The overall aim of the GATT is to encourage economic growth and development by liberalizing world trade and placing it on a more secure basis.

The GATT's importance in influencing world trade has grown over time. The GATT was first established in 1948, with 23 original signatories. The 97 current signatories together account for approximately 90 percent of total world trade. An additional 28 countries apply GATT rules on a de facto basis.

The GATT is based on a few general principles. Most important is the "most-favored nation" (MFN) clause stating that trade must be conducted on a nondiscriminatory basis. That is, concessions to one country must be given to all other GATT signatories with few exceptions. Another principle is that imported goods should be treated no less favorably than domestically produced goods. And, protection to domestic industry should be assured by use of tariffs rather than by use of nontariff barriers.

The GATT includes certain exceptions from general rules for agricultural or primary products. For example, Article XI of the GATT bans the use of quantitative restrictions in general, but paragraph 2(c) of that article allows such restrictions to be imposed on agricultural or fisheries products if the domestic production or marketing of these products is also restricted. In 1957, the GATT adopted a rule to prohibit export subsidies. However, this was not extended to cover primary products, including agricultural products.

Many countries have taken additional measures to exempt agriculture from GATT rules. The United States sought and received in 1955 a waiver from GATT obligations for action taken under Section 22 of the Agricultural Adjustment Act of 1933, as amended in more recent U.S. legislation, which could require restrictions on the quantity of imported commodities. Other countries have also contributed to the proliferation of nontariff barriers. A significant example here is the EC's variable levy which blocks most agricultural imports. Other GATT exemptions affecting agricultural products relate to export subsidies.

There were seven negotiation rounds before the Uruguay Round. "The substantial reduction of tariffs and other barriers to trade" was established as a principal aim of GATT. The earlier rounds focused primarily on tariff cuts. They also focused on manufactured products. Attempts to bring agricultural trade into the talks in a significant way generally were unsuccessful.

The Tokyo Round, from 1974 to 1979, was much more ambitious than earlier rounds. There were substantive changes for agriculture in the Tokyo Round, but overall effects were small. In the Tokyo Round, tariffs on manufactured products were cut with the use of a formula while tariffs on agricultural products were cut in response to specific requests. Commodity agreements on beef and dairy were also negotiated. The agreement reached on bovine meat was weak and mainly provided an opportunity for regular consultations on world supply and demand and matters affecting international trade. The International Dairy Ar-

---

GATT ROUNDS

• Geneva	1947	
• Annecy	1949	
• Torquay	1951	First seven rounds focused on tariff cuts on
• Geneva	1956	manufactured goods
• Dillon	1960—61	
• Kennedy	1964—67	
• Tokyo	1974—79	
• Uruguay	1986—90	First to focus on agriculture

rangement was negotiated with minimum price provisions. However, the United States pulled out of the agreement in 1984 when the EC violated it by selling below the minimum price. The United States also took the lead in fashioning a new International Wheat Agreement, but, in the end, participants failed to agree on the fundamental points and no agreement was reached.

In addition, five specific agreements on nontariff barriers called "codes" were adopted to define more explicitly the rules governing the use of these nontariff barriers. These codes related to dumping, subsidies, standards, government procurement, customs valuation, and import licensing procedures. However, those codes most significant to agriculture proved generally unsuccessful in stopping the proliferation of subsidies and trade barriers.

HISTORY OF THE URUGUAY ROUND

The need for comprehensive negotiations for major reform in agricultural domestic and trade policies became evident to the United States and other major exporters by the mid-1980's. Piecemeal approaches to trade problems had either failed or been offset by other policies.

The Punta del Este Declaration, signed in September 1986, launched the Uruguay Round and affirmed a comprehensive approach to trade liberalization. The declaration noted the urgent need to bring discipline and predictability to agricultural trade by preventing distortions, thereby reducing uncertainty, imbalances, and instability in world agricultural markets. The declaration also stated that the aim of the negotiations was "to bring all measures affecting import access and export competition under strengthened and more operationally effective rules and disciplines" through re-

ducing import barriers, increasing disciplines on subsidies, and minimizing the adverse effects of sanitary and phytosanitary regulations on trade.

In July 1987, the United States submitted a proposal for agricultural trade reform to GATT, designating three areas for comprehensive reform: (1) 10-year phaseout of all agricultural subsidies which directly or indirectly affect trade, (2) phaseout of import barriers over 10 years, and (3) harmonization of health and sanitary regulations on the basis of internationally agreed standards. Reductions were to be based on an aggregate measure of support and all agricultural commodities including food, beverages, forest products, and fish and fish products would be included. Income payments not based on production and bona fide food aid would be allowed. Several other contracting parties also submitted proposals.

In November 1988, the United States submitted a "Framework Proposal" specifically written as a framework for future negotiations and as a guide for GATT's Mid-Term Review. The Mid-Term Review was to assess the progress made in the first 2 years of the negotiations and to lay out a work plan for the following 2 years. Among other things, the U.S. proposal stated the United States would be willing to freeze support, subsidies, and protection during 1989 and 1990. The paper also introduced "tariffication," which is the conversion of nontariff barriers to tariffs, and called for a phased reduction of tariffs resulting in elimination.

The contracting parties were not able to agree on the objectives of the agricultural negotiations at the Mid-Term Review in December 1988. The United States and the Cairns group (Argentina, Australia, Brazil, Canada, Chile, Colombia, Fiji, Hungary, Indonesia, Malaysia, New Zealand, the Philippines, Thailand, and Uruguay) sought agreement on language calling for a barrier-free, market-oriented agricultural trading system. This would effectively require the EC, as well as most other industrialized countries, to substantially alter their support policies. But, the EC continued to promote the objective that the negotiations should arrive at a disciplined market-sharing arrangement. Negotiations then broke down over whether or not to include language calling for "elimination" of trade distortions.

The Mid-Term Agreement eventually reached in April 1989 was a compromise document. It maintained the fundamental objectives agreed to in the Punta del Este Declaration and also acknowledged the concerns of several groups of participants. The objective agreed to reflected the market-oriented approach of the United States and the Cairns group and stated that the "long-term objective of the agricultural negotiations is to establish a fair and market-oriented agricultural trading system." The controversial language calling for elimination of trade distortions was replaced by a phrase calling for "substantial, progressive reductions in agricultural support and protection sustained over an agreed period of time." The agreement also called for strengthened rules and established a work plan for 1989. In addition to the basic issues of market access and subsidies, participants were to advance proposals on a variety of topics, including food security concerns, special and differential treatment for developing countries, and ways to counter the possible negative effects of the reform process on net food importing countries. Thus, the food security concerns of Japan and others as well as the concerns of the developing countries and net food importing countries were incorporated. Finally, the Mid-Term Agreement states that by the end of 1990 participants would agree on a long-term reform program and the period for its implementation.

In keeping with the program established in the Mid-Term Agreement, the United States submitted a paper in July 1989 outlining a procedure to convert all nontariff barriers to tariffs with the understanding that tariffs would then be substantially and progressively reduced. The reason for this approach is that tariffs are the preferred means of protection under the GATT. In 1989, several countries and groups of countries, including the United States, submitted proposals. . . .

THE U.S. PROPOSAL AIMS AT MARKET-ORIENTED AGRICULTURE

The U.S. proposal would move global agricultural markets and trade of the GATT nations toward a more market-oriented trading environment. All countries would be able to compete on relatively equal terms, according to their natural comparative advantage instead of their level of government support. Trade liberalization would reduce trade barriers and eliminate artificially low prices caused by subsidized overproduction.

The U.S. comprehensive proposal submitted in October 1989 has four main sections: (1) import access, (2) export competition, (3) internal support, and (4) sanitary and phytosanitary measures. Since reforms in one area can be counteracted by policies in another area, the proposal is an integral proposal, not four separate components. There is also a separate section on special and differential treatment for developing countries. The proposal concludes with three annexes dealing with product coverage, types of export subsidies to be prohibited, and classification of internal policies.

Import Access

Import access would be improved by converting all nontariff import barriers to their tariff equivalents, then reducing all tariffs over time. Use of "tariff rate quotas" would be allowed during the transition to ease the transition to tariffs and maintain some minimum import access. Safeguard measures, which would allow tariffs to "snap back" to some higher level, would be used to guard against sudden import surges.

As a first step in the tariffication process, no new nontariff barriers would be permitted and existing nontariff barriers would be replaced with tariffs on January 1, 1991. So-called "tariff rate quotas" would be established wherein initial quotas would be set at a level equal to either the level of imports that existed in 1990 (or in another recent historical period) or at a negotiated level. Tariffs within the quota would be established at agreed-upon rates. Tariffs would be the only form of protection outside the quota, although the initial tariff rates might be high enough in some cases to effectively preclude additional imports at first. The tariff rates outside the quota would be calculated using the price gap that existed between an established domestic price and a world reference price. The tariff rates could be expressed either as an ad valorem or a specific tariff using average prices for 1986–88. Over time, the quota would expand while the tariff on overquota imports would decline until, at the end of the transition, a modest (or zero) tariff would remain as the only import barrier.

Export Competition

Fundamental changes in export competition would occur under the U.S. proposal. Export subsidies would be phased out over a 5-year period, with either the level of government expenditures on subsidies or the quantities of commodities receiving subsidies used as the basis for this phaseout. Bona fide food aid would be exempt from the prohibition of export subsidies, but because of existing ambiguities, new rules would have to be developed to clarify when exports would be considered food aid. Export prohibitions and restrictions, which are sometimes applied in cases of short-supply situations, would be prohibited beginning in 1991. This would require a change in GATT Article XI 2(a), which allows nations to restrict or prohibit exports when domestic supplies are short. Differential export taxes, sometimes used by countries to discourage exports of raw commodities and to encourage exports of processed or secondary products, must be progressively reduced. Elimination of the differentials would take place over a 5-year period.

Internal Support

A major objective of the proposal is to orient domestic agricultural policies to market forces. Fundamental changes in internal support policies would be required. All policies transferring funds to agricultural sectors would be classified into one of three categories based on the degree of their trade-distorting effects. Those policies judged to be the most trade-distorting would be phased out over 10 years. These policies include administered price policies, income support policies linked to production or marketing, input and investment subsidies not available to all producers or processors of agricultural commodities on an equal basis, and certain marketing programs. Countries would have some freedom in choosing how to phase out these policies. For example, a country using administered price policies could either progressively reduce the administered prices, or the amount of production eligible for price supports, or both. Nevertheless, the reduction would have to be in equal annual steps over the 10-year period.

Less trade-distorting policies, such as input subsidies generally available to all producers within an agricultural sector, would be brought under new GATT disciplines. New GATT disciplines would be designed to prevent use of these policies in ways that would injure another country. Reductions in such policy transfers would be based on an aggregate measure of support (AMS) and would be scheduled for a 10-year period of implementation. An AMS measures the percentage of price received by the farmer that is due to government subsidy. The producer subsidy equivalent (PSE) developed by the OECD could be used, but the U.S. proposal also states that other AMS's could be developed.

No new GATT disciplines would be necessary for policies with minimal trade-distorting effects. These policies include income support policies not linked to production or marketing, as well as environmental and conservation programs, bona fide disaster programs, bona fide domestic food aid, certain domestic marketing programs, general services such as research and extension, resource retirement programs, and certain programs for food reserves.

Sanitary and Phytosanitary Regulations

Sanitary and phytosanitary (S&P) regulations are measures that provide for food safety and plant and animal health. Such regulations have a straightforward and important role to play in protecting the food consumed by a nation's consumers, but they have often been misused as implicit trade barriers. Because of this, the proposal seeks to establish an agreed-upon process for settling trade disputes involving food safety, animal and plant health issues, and harmonization of standards. GATT rules relating to such issues would be amended so that measures to protect human, animal, or plant health would be undertaken on the basis of sound scientific evidence and on the principle of equivalency. Equivalency simply means that measures that are not identical but have the same effect in en-

suring a given level of protection shall be deemed to be equivalent.

The new GATT process would include provisions for notification, consultation, and dispute settlement. Notification would be handled through the GATT Secretariat, with each contracting party required to notify the GATT Secretariat of any proposed S&P regulation which could have a significant effect on the trade of other contracting parties. The country that proposes the new regulation would respond promptly to requests for consultations and attempt to bilaterally resolve disputes. Where informal consultations cannot resolve a dispute, recourse to a formal dispute settlement process would be possible. Here again, contracting parties would be encouraged to make use of the appropriate international organizations such as the Codex Alimentarius, the International Plant Protection Convention, and the International Office of Epizootics.

The United States recognizes that the proposal may pose some difficulties for developing countries. The proposal therefore encourages the contracting parties to consider the effects of enhanced GATT sanitary and phytosanitary procedures on developing countries. Technical assistance through the United Nations' Food and Agriculture Organization might be provided.

Developing Countries

The United States also proposed special consideration for developing countries. Developing nations with relatively advanced economies and/or well-developed agricultural sectors would be expected to comply with the implementation mechanisms outlined in the U.S. proposal. But the U.S. proposal recognizes that some developing nations have distinctive problems making compliance difficult. This is especially true because of problems caused by underdeveloped infrastructures, which could pose prob-

---

U.S. COMPREHENSIVE PROPOSAL AT GATT

Import Access

- Nontariff barriers to be converted to tariffs
- Tariff rate quotas to be used as a transition mechanism
- Tariffs to be reduced and quotas expanded over 10 years
- Tariff "snapback" allowed as a safeguard mechanism during transition

Export Competition

- Export subsidies to be phased out over 5 years
- Bona fide food aid allowed to continue

Internal Measures of Support

- Most trade-distorting policies to be phased out over 10 years
- Policies with minimal trade distortions can continue
- New GATT disciplines for other policies

Sanitary & Phytosanitary (S&P) Measures

- S&P standards to be harmonized across nations
- S&P trade disputes to be settled with input from existing international organizations

Special & Differential (S&D) Treatment for Developing Countries

- Recognizes some need for S&D treatment affecting some tariffs and subsidies

---

lems in implementing the parts of the proposal with respect to import access and internal support. The proposal thus suggests that deviations from implementation could be considered if a nation could demonstrate need for exceptional treatment. But exceptions would not be permanent.

REMAINING SCHEDULE OF THE ROUND: OTHER PROPOSALS

Several other countries and groups of countries have also submitted proposals. Some, like that of the Cairns group, are similar to the U.S. proposal in arguing for major trade reforms. The proposals from Japan and several other countries have a strong emphasis on food security. The developing countries propose continued special and differential treatment to address the specific concerns of these countries.

Although the United States was the first country to submit a comprehensive proposal, the Cairns group, the EC, and Japan each submitted comprehensive proposals by the end of 1989. Additional proposals also were presented by the Net Food Importing Developing Countries group, Austria, Switzerland, the Nordic countries, South Korea, and jointly by Brazil and Colombia.

Japan

The Japanese proposal emphasizes food security, with food security defined in terms of self-sufficiency in "basic foodstuffs." Proposals from South Korea, Austria, Switzerland, and the Nordic countries expressed concerns similar to those in the Japanese proposal. The Swiss, Austrians, and Japanese each had presented earlier papers focusing on the "noncommercial objectives" of agriculture. Their basic premise remains that subsidies used to achieve food security, environmental goals, territorial settlement, and other social policies should be allowed under the new rules established by GATT since producing for world trade is not the main goal of these programs. The United States agrees that these are important objectives, but thinks that they can be better met by the use of direct income payments which are not linked to production and thus do not distort trade in the process of achieving other goals.

Cairns Group

The Cairns group is generally aligned with the United States on the issue of long-term reform of trade. These countries have played an important role in the negotiations up to this point because of their combined share of world trade and because they represent a coalition of developed and developing countries. The Cairns group countries indicate that their combined market share has decreased as a direct result of U.S. and EC export subsidies, and their primary goal is to ensure that both these major players agree to disciplines in this area. In addition, they would like to see a reduction in domestic subsidies and import access barriers. Overall, the comprehensive paper of the Cairns group is very similar to the U.S. comprehensive paper.

EC

The EC proposal sees a structural imbalance between supply and demand in world agriculture as the main problem and would address it by reducing support slowly until "balanced markets" are achieved. The EC would reduce support mainly through lower administered prices. The proposal would leave in place the current basic policy structure and mechanisms. In addition, the EC is promoting a "readjustment" in external protection to reduce distortions in the market. It has become clear that by "readjustment," currently referred to as "rebalancing," the EC would actually increase import barriers on oilseeds and corn gluten feed, while reducing import barriers on selected other commodities. The U.S. position is that the status quo or marginal changes in existing policies would result only in the continuation of the current problems facing world agricultural trade to the detriment of producers around the world.

Developing Countries

The two proposals put forward by the Net Food Importing Developing Countries group and by Brazil and Colombia focus on the need for developed countries to grant developing countries special and differential treatment. Many developing countries indicate that they have not contributed to the current world problem of overproduction and should therefore not be subjected to the strict disciplines which might be agreed to by developed countries. They want to be granted longer timeframes for adjustment as well as smaller cuts in tariffs, nontariff barriers, and trade-distorting support measures. The first of these proposals also strongly focuses on what might be done to alleviate the burden of increased prices on food import bills and enhance the capacity of these countries to increase agricultural production.

REFERENCES

BALLENGER, NICOLE, JOHN DUNMORE, AND THOMAS LEDERER. *Trade Liberalization in World Farm Markets.* AIB-516, U.S. Dept. Agr., Econ. Res. Serv., May 1987.

RONINGEN, VERNON O. AND PRAVEEN DIXIT. *How Level is the Playing Field? An Economic Analysis of Agricultural Policy Reforms in Industrial Market Economies.* FAER-239, U.S. Dept. Agr., Econ. Res. Serv., Dec. 1989.

U.S. DEPARTMENT OF AGRICULTURE, ECONOMIC RESEARCH SERVICE. *Agriculture in the Uruguay Round: Analyses of Government Support.* Staff Report AGES880802. Dec. 1988.

————. *Agricultural-Food Policy Review: U.S. Agricultural Policies in a Changing World.* AER-620. Nov. 1989.

————. *Estimates of Producer and Consumer Subsidy Equivalents: Government Intervention in Agriculture, 1982–86.* Staff Report AGES880127. Apr. 1988.

————. *GATT & Agriculture: The Concepts of PSE's and CSE's.* MP-1468. Apr. 1989.

23. Trading Places
Industries for Free Trade

*Helen Milner**

INTRODUCTION

Today, protectionism is once again a central political issue in the United States. Pressures for protectionism have captured the national attention several times during the 20th century. In the 1920s, U.S. trade policy made a U-turn. Protectionism had declined from the Dingley tariff bill in 1897 until the Fordney-McCumber tariff law of 1922, as the average value of tariffs on dutiable goods fell from 45 percent to 28 percent.[1] But this downward trend was reversed during the 1920s: between 1922 and 1930, the United States closed its market dramatically, with tariffs attaining an ad valorem average of 53 percent.[2] This level, set by the 1930 Smoot-Hawley tariff, was one of the highest ever, and the highest so far in the 20th century.

Beginning in the 1930s, protectionism in the U.S. once again abated. The Reciprocal Trade Agreements Act (R.T.A.A.), which was introduced in 1934 and

SOURCE: Reprinted with permission of the publisher, The Johns Hopkins University Press, from *World Politics,* vol. 40, no. 3, April 1988, pp. 350–376.

* I would like to thank David Baldwin, Jeffrey Frieden, Stephen Haggard, Robert Keohane, and the participants at the Ford Foundation Conference on Blending Political and Economic Analysis of International Trade Policies for their helpful comments.

[1] Robert Pastor, *Congress and the Politics of U.S. Foreign Economic Policy* (Berkeley: University of California Press, 1980), Table 3, p. 78; David Lake, "International Economic Structures and American Foreign Economic Policy, 1887–1934," *World Politics* 35 (July 1983), 517–43, Table 2, p. 534.

[2] *Ibid.*

served as a model for future trade acts, initiated the opening of the American market. Between 1934 and 1972, average U.S. tariff levels declined by some 70 percent.[3] By 1972, tariffs averaged a mere 9.9 percent.[4]

In the early 1970s, the course of U.S. trade policy again became a source of heated debate. Among the questions that were raised about the future of American trade policy was what direction trade policy would take in the 1970s and beyond. Many observers and scholars feared a resurgence of rapidly rising protectionism and international trade wars.[5] Extrapolating from previous historical periods of rising and falling protectionism, these analysts expected the 1970s and 1980s to look much more like the 1920s than like the period between 1934 and 1970. In fact, the 1920s were offered frequently as the example for the decade after 1973. For many, the threat of a significant closure of the U.S. market evoked a repetition of the dismal interwar years.

In this article, I challenge that view of the current period. There were sizable differences in trade policy outcomes between the 1920s and the 1970s; these differences are puzzling because they belie the predictions of other theories. I maintain that a primary reason for these different policy outcomes was the growth of international economic interdependence after World War II. By the 1970s, the expansion of these international economic ties helped to dampen pressures for trade barriers as the preferences of industries turned against protectionism. Using evidence from a number of industries in the 1920s and the 1970s, I shall show how the internationalization of firms reduced their interest in protection even in difficult economic times, and thus helped the United States to resist protectionism in the 1970s.

THE PUZZLE

Two common elements, which distinguish the 1920s and the 1970s from the intervening years, seem central in this comparison between their trade policies. First, both the 1920s and the 1970s were times of serious economic distress and instability. Such difficult conditions have been seen as a key precondition for rising protectionist activity. One economist noted:

It is generally agreed that in a modern industrial economy the cyclical state of the economy and the country's competitive position internationally are the principal determinants of the degree of protectionist pressure. Low levels of economic activity, high unemployment, unused capacity, trade deficits, rapid increases in imports, and increases in import penetration all operate to increase the temptation to protect

---

[3] U.S. Tariff Commission, *Trade Barriers: An Overview*, No. 665 (Washington, DC: G.P.O., 1974), 81–82.

[4] Pastor (fn. 1), Table 6, p. 119.

[5] Harald Malmgren, "Coming Trade Wars?" *Foreign Policy* I (Winter 1970), 115–43; C. Fred Bergsten, "The Crisis in US Trade Policy," *Foreign Affairs* 49 (July 1971), 619–35; June Kronholz, "Trade and Currency Wars Deepen the Depression," *Wall Street Journal,* October 23, 1979, p. 1.

Hegemonic stability theorists have also predicted such a resurgence. See Charles Kindleberger, *The World in Depression, 1929–1939* (Berkeley: University of California Press, 1973), esp. 307–8; Robert Gilpin, *U.S. Power and the Multinational Corporation* (New York: Basic Books, 1975), esp. 258–62. For more skeptical views, see Stephen Krasner, "State Power and the Structure of International Trade," *World Politics* 28 (April 1976), 317–47; Robert O. Keohane, "The Theory of Hegemonic Stability and Changes in International Economic Regimes," in Ole Holsti, Randolph Siverson, and Alexander George, eds., *Change in the International System* (Boulder, CO: Westview Press, 1980), 131–62.

Table 23.1   Averages for Three Major Economic Indicators
(Percent)

	1923–1929	1973–1979
Average annual growth in real GNP	3.1	2.3
Average mean value of unemployment rate	3.5	6.8
Average value of non-residential fixed investment to GNP	11.2	10.2

SOURCE: All data from Feldstein (fn. 7), 104–5.

domestic industries from import competition.[6]

Economic difficulties were similar in the two periods, which were marked by relatively high unemployment rates and sizable agricultural and industrial overcapacity. In the 1920s and early 1930s, the U.S. economy suffered two major downturns—one in 1920–1923 and one in 1929–1933. Price deflation, labor unrest, and international monetary problems created further economic instability.[7] In the 1970s, the U.S. economy experienced deep recessions during 1973–1975 and 1978–1982. Sparked by the oil shocks, these recessions were aggravated by rapidly shifting trade patterns, price instability, and a confused international monetary situation. These high levels of economic distress and instability that were felt in the 1920s and 1970s might be expected to generate similar widespread protection.

Indeed, in view of the absolute levels of economic distress during the two periods, the 1970s might have generated even greater levels of market closure than the 1920s.[8] The averages for three major economic indicators all are worse in the 1970s than in the 1920s, as Table 23.1 indicates. Since the U.S. economy performed more poorly in the 1970s, one might expect that, if economic difficulty were a precursor to protectionism, this period should have experienced protectionism with a vengeance.

A second similarity between the 1920s and 1970s that has been linked to protectionism is the declining power of the world's hegemonic state. This change in the international distribution of power has been cited as a major factor leading

[6] Wendy Takacs, "Pressures for Protectionism: An Empirical Analysis," *Economic Inquiry* 19 (October 1981), 687–93, at 687. In general, see Timothy McKeown, "Firms and Tariff Regime Change: Explaining the Demand for Protectionism," *World Politics* 36 (January 1984), 215–33; Giulio Gallarotti, "Toward a Business Cycle Model of Tariffs," *International Organization* 39 (Winter 1985), 155–87; Susan Strange and Roger Tooze, eds., *The International Politics of Surplus Capacity* (London: Butterworths, 1980).

[7] W. Arthur Lewis, *Economic Survey, 1919–1939* (London: Allen & Unwin, 1949); U.S. Department of Commerce, *Survey of Current Business,* various issues, 1919–1930 (Washington, DC: G.P.O.); U.S. Census Bureau, *Historical Statistics of the U.S., Colonial Times to the Present* (Washington, DC: G.P.O., 1975); Kindleberger (fn. 5), esp. chaps. 5–8; League of Nations, *Economic Fluctuations in the U.S. and U.K., 1918–1942* (Geneva: League of Nations, 1942); Martin Feldstein, ed., *The American Economy in Transition* (Chicago: National Bureau of Economic Research, 1980), 12.

[8] Sidney Ratner, James Soltow, and Richard Sylla, *The Evolution of the American Economy* (New York: Basic Books, 1979), 482, 502–3. The worst economic difficulties of the Great Depression followed (rather than preceded) the tariff increases, occurring in the early 1930s: unemployment averaged 3% in 1930, the year Smoot-Hawley was passed, but rose to 25% by 1933, the year before the Reciprocal Trade Agreements Act.

to the closure of the world's markets. Robert Gilpin has stated that

> Today, . . . the dominant economy is itself in relative decline and is being challenged by rising centers of economic power. With the decline of the dominant economic power, the world economy may be following the pattern of the late nineteenth century and of the 1930s: it may be fragmenting into regional trading blocs, exclusive economic alliances, and economic nationalism.[9]

In the 1920s, Great Britain, the hegemon of the 19th century, was losing its status. From a peak of 24 percent in 1870, Great Britain's share of world trade had fallen to 14 percent before World War I.[10] Furthermore, its share of the world's manufacturing output tumbled from a dominant 32 percent in 1870 to a third-rate level of 14 percent in 1913.[11] Germany and the United States overtook it in industrial competitiveness in certain critical, advanced sectors.[12] In addition, Britain's control over the international monetary system was declining. Its problems in returning to and maintaining the gold standard in the 1920s and its final abandonment of that system in 1931 signaled this loss of influence.[13] By the 1920s, then, Britain's hegemony had seriously eroded.

The situation was fairly similar in the 1970s. By the early part of the decade, the global dominance that the United States had exercised in the 1950s and 1960s had been reduced as other nations mounted a challenge. America's share of world trade dropped from 18.4 percent in 1950 to 13.4 percent in 1977.[14] More tellingly, its share of the world's manufactured exports plummeted from nearly 30 percent in 1953 to about 13 percent in the late 1970s.[15] Its share of the world's manufacturing output also lost ground, dropping from 62 percent in 1950 to 44 percent in 1977.[16] Many U.S. industries had lost their economic advantage and faced bitter competition both at home and abroad. In addition, the United States was no longer as dominant in the international monetary system. By 1973, it had scuttled the monetary system it had created and found itself unable to fashion a new, stable one. American hegemony in monetary relations in the 1970s, however, was not as reduced as Britain's had been in the 1920s and early 1930s.[17] But it had declined substantially, especially in trade and production, leaving the international distribution of power in the 1970s more closely resembling that of the

[9] Gilpin (fn. 5), 258–59. Also see Kindleberger (fn. 5), esp. 307–8; Krasner (fn. 5), 317–47; Keohane (fn. 5), 131–62; David Lake, "Structure and Strategy: The International Sources of American Trade Policy, 1887–1939" (Ph.D. diss., Cornell University, 1983); Charles Kindleberger, "Dominance and Leadership in the International Economy," *International Studies Quarterly* 25 (June 1981), 242–54; Robert Gilpin, *War and Change in World Politics* (Cambridge: Cambridge University Press, 1981).
[10] Lake (fn. 1), Table 1, p. 525.
[11] Ratner, Soltow, and Sylla (fn. 8), 385.
[12] Lake (fn. 1); Alexander Gerschenkron, *Economic Backwardness in Historical Perspective* (Cambridge: Harvard University Press, 1962), chaps. 1 and 2; Samuel Hays, *The Response to Industrialism, 1885–1914* (Chicago: University of Chicago Press, 1957), chaps. 1, 7, 8.

[13] Robert O. Keohane and Joseph S. Nye, Jr., *Power and Interdependence: World Politics in Transition* (Boston: Little, Brown, 1977), 70; Kindleberger (fn. 5), 63–68, 146–70.
[14] Lake (fn. 1), Table 3, p. 541; Keohane and Nye (fn. 13), 141.
[15] Feldstein (fn. 7), 193, 196.
[16] *Ibid.,* 191.
[17] U.S. hegemony in money was diminished less than in trade. Its ending of the Bretton Woods system was more an act of power than of weakness, according to many analysts. See Keohane and Nye (fn. 13), 141, 165–86; John Odell, *U.S. International Monetary Policy: Markets, Power, and Ideas as Sources of Change* (Princeton: Princeton University Press, 1982), chap. 4, esp. p. 219.

interwar period than that of the immediate post-World War II period. This eclipse of hegemony might have been expected to produce widespread protectionism, as it had in the 1920s.

Although both periods experienced the decline of a hegemon, this may be less important to American policy than the relative position of the United States. The striking fact is how similar the relative international position of the U.S. appears to be in the late 1920s and the late 1970s, and how different it was in the 1950s and 1960s. America's share of the world's manufacturing output reached 42 percent in 1929 and had leveled off at 44 percent in 1977. In contrast, the U.S. had dominated in the 1950s and 1960s, with 62 percent in 1950 and 51 percent in 1960. In the trade area, the United States was more dominant in the 1920s than in the 1970s, but nowhere near as dominant as in the 1950s. In the 1920s, it was the world's largest exporter and biggest foreign investor, and ranked second only to Britain in its imports.[18] By the late 1970s, it had become the world's second-largest exporter of manufactures—West Germany led with almost 16 percent compared to America's 13 percent—and was being challenged for that spot by Japan (11 percent). In 1953, by contrast, the U.S. had reigned supreme in trade, controlling nearly 30 percent of all manufactured exports.[19]

A similar story is told by changes in relative economic size and productivity. According to Lake, who uses these two measures in his analysis of international economic structures, the position of the United States was almost identical in 1929 and 1977.[20] This contrasts with its clear predominance in 1950. Moreover,

in both 1929 and 1977, the U.S. appeared similarly situated relative to its nearest rivals. In 1929, it led all countries on these two indicators, barely edging out Britain while retaining a substantial lead over France and Germany. In 1977, its relative position was comparable: it was almost even with West Germany, but still outdistanced Japan and France.

Hence, two strong similarities in the international distribution of economic power existed in the 1920s and 1970s. In both, a hegemon was in decline, and in both the relative position of the United States was slightly superior to all others—but, most importantly, was being challenged by several nations. These conditions in the international economic structure have been linked to rising protectionism, and thus might have been expected to engender similar protectionist responses in the two periods.[21]

The argument here is *not* that the 1920s and the 1970s were alike in all respects. Two important differences, at least, may attenuate the comparison. First, the United States was a rising hegemon in the 1920s and a declining one in the 1970s. Although hegemonic stability arguments provide no theoretical reason to expect this difference to affect a hegemon's trade policy, the notion of a lag has been introduced to account for this.[22] A rising hegemon may fail to appreciate its own significance, while a declining one may fail to understand its weakness and need for closure. This difference may account for dissimilarities between the two periods. But the reason for such a lag is obscure.

Second, there was a difference in the monetary systems operating at the two times. In the 1920s, a shift occurred from the controlled flexible exchange-rate system that had been in effect before 1925, to a fixed gold-standard system which

---

[18] Ratner, Soltow, and Sylla (fn. 8), 464; Feldstein (fn. 7), 191.

[19] Feldstein (fn. 7), 196.

[20] David Lake, "Beneath the Commerce of Nations," *International Studies Quarterly* 28 (June 1984), Figs. 5 and 6, pp. 143–70.

[21] I do not agree with Lake's interpretation of these two structures and their differences; see fn. 20.

[22] Kindleberger (fn. 5); Krasner (fn. 5).

was in effect until 1931. In the 1970s, the movement was in the opposite direction: from a fixed, dollar-gold standard to a managed flexible rate system after 1973. The consequences of these two different systems for trade policy are unclear, however; the effects of different exchange-rate systems on trade are not well understood. It has been asserted by some that flexible rates should hinder protectionism because such barriers are nullified by exchange-rate changes.[23] Others maintain that flexible rates augment protectionist pressures by increasing risk, and that fixed rates are best for ensuring free trade.[24] It seems fair to say that the exchange-rate systems operating in both periods did little to provide a stable environment for international trade.

A related issue is whether the value of U.S. exchange rates had a different effect on trade policy in the two periods. The argument is that the level of exchange rates was driving trade policy, especially in the 1970s. Thus, the relative undervaluation of the dollar in the late 1970s weakened protectionist pressures, while its overvaluation in the early 1980s led to new pressures for barriers.[25] The problem with this argument is that the 1920s look similar: after World War I, the U.S. dollar appeared to be undervalued, supposedly mitigating protectionist pressures. But later in the decade, the dollar seemed overvalued relative to the mark, lira, franc, and gold, although undervalued relative

to sterling.[26] Differences in exchange-rate levels, then, do *not* seem to distinguish the two periods.

Despite these differences, the similarities between the 1920s and 1970s in terms of economic difficulties and the relative economic position of the United States might lead one to expect that U.S. trade policy in the 1970s would look like that of the 1920s. The 1970s, however, were not marked by the extensive closure of the U.S. market that occurred in the 1920s. American trade policy remained oriented toward a relatively open market. Although it is commonly believed that protectionism grew substantially in the 1970s and the early 1980s, U.S. trade policy actually had mixed currents. Overall, there was probably a small net increase in trade barriers relative to the 1960s, but these new barriers never reached levels near those attained in the 1920s. Moreover, unlike in the 1930s, these barriers had little effect on the volume of trade: global and U.S. trade continued to grow throughout the decade of the 1970s, and to grow faster than production. In addition, tariffs had been reduced to their lowest levels, about 5 percent on average, through the GATT Tokyo Round negotiations.[27]

On the other hand, some non-tariff barriers (NTBs) were growing. These are difficult to measure (and were generally not measured while tariffs remained high), but their relative importance increased in the late 1970s. By that time, nearly 30 percent of all categories (not values) of American manufactured imports were affected by them.[28] One empirical study concludes, however, that these new NTBs have had only limited protectionist

[23] Herbert Grubel, *International Economics* (Homewood, IL: Irwin, 1977), chap. 22; Charles Kindleberger and Peter Lindert, *International Economics,* 6th ed. (Homewood, IL: Irwin, 1978), chap. 21; Robert Baldwin and J. David Richardson, *International Trade and Finance,* 3rd ed. (Boston: Little, Brown, 1986), chap. 21.

[24] C. Fred Bergsten and William Cline, "Overview," in William Cline, ed., *Trade Policy in the 1980s* (Washington, DC: Institute for International Economics, 1983).

[25] Kindleberger and Lindert (fn. 23), chap. 21, esp. Fig. 21.5.

[26] *Ibid.,* chap. 21, Fig. 21.3. Note how all other currencies rise in value against the dollar after the change in 1931.

[27] U.S. Tariff Commission (fn. 3), 81–82.

[28] Robert Reich, "Beyond Free Trade," *Foreign Affairs* 61 (Spring 1983), 773–804, at 786.

effects; as the authors point out, "on average over a full range of manufactured products, the protection given by NTBs that may limit or reduce imports . . . is not nearly as large as the protection afforded by tariffs . . . or natural barriers to trade. . . ."[29] They project that, "if the United States continues on its present policy course, the U.S. economy will be considerably more open in 1985 than it was in 1976."[30] Thus the erection of NTBs in the 1970s and 1980s may have produced a small net increase in protection. But this increase did not approach the levels of the 1920s even though two key preconditions—serious economic distress and declining hegemony—characterized both periods. Given the fertile ground of the late 1970s, protectionism could have grown rampantly, as it did in the 1920s. For some reason, it did not.

OTHER EXPLANATIONS

The question, then, is why trade policy was different in the 1920s and 1970s even though key pressures influencing it were similar. This puzzle has been addressed by a number of studies. Three answers, all of which focus on aspects of the international or domestic system that are different from the one central to this study, require examination. They should be seen less as competing than as being pitched at different levels of analysis. I maintain that the argument developed in this study has been neglected and that it is more basic than these others.

One type of explanation looks at the international distribution of power, usually in terms of economic capabilities. It involves modifications of the hegemonic stability thesis, which, as has been shown, cannot in its original form explain the differences in policy outcomes between the 1920s and the 1970s.[31] Three modified arguments have been presented. First, it has been asserted that American hegemony has not declined enough to set off the expected protectionist response.[32] Even though other countries have caught up with the United States, it still remains the strongest, especially when its military might is considered. Thus, this argument depends on military capabilities being an important factor in trade policy considerations. However, the fungibility of these power resources is questionable.[33] In fact, the second type of hegemonic stability argument denies this fungibility. Considering only trade-related power resources, it suggests that U.S. hegemony has not declined enough to evoke extensive protectionism.[34] But in comparison to its trade position in the 1920s, the U.S. held a similar, or even less dominant, position in the 1970s. One explanation for this disparity is the lag phenomenon discussed earlier. A third argument modifying the thesis of hegemonic stability holds that different configurations of states in terms of their relative economic power lead to

---

[29] Peter Morici and Laura Megna, *U.S. Economic Policies Affecting Industrial Trade: A Quantitative Assessment* (Washington, DC: National Planning Association, 1983), 11.

[30] *Ibid.,* 103.

[31] Krasner (fn. 5).

[32] Bruce Russett, "The Mysterious Case of Vanishing Hegemony; or, Is Mark Twain Really Dead?" *International Organization* 39 (Spring 1985), 207–32; Susan Strange, "Still An Extraordinary Power," in Raymond Lombra and Willard Witte, eds., *Political Economy of International and Domestic Monetary Relations* (Ames: Iowa State University, 1982).

[33] David Baldwin, "Power Analysis and World Politics: New Trends Versus Old Politics," *World Politics* 31 (January 1979), 161–94; Keohane and Nye (fn. 13), chap. 2.

[34] *Ibid.,* chap. 3; Robert O. Keohane, *After Hegemony: Cooperation and Discord in the World Political Economy* (Princeton: Princeton University Press, 1984), chaps. 4, 9; Vinod Aggarwal, *Liberal Protectionism: The International Politics of Organized Textile Trade* (Berkeley: University of California Press, 1985), chaps. 2, 7.

different outcomes in trade policy. But this argument is not able to explain the differences between the 1920s and 1970s, since the configuration of states at those two points (1929 and 1977) was very similar.[35]

A second type of explanation focuses on the existence of an international regime in trade. In this view, the creation of the GATT system after World War II and its continued functioning have been partially responsible for the maintenance of a relatively open international economy. In the 1920s, the lack of any such regime helped to spread protectionism. GATT is seen as working against protectionism in numerous ways. Some analysts argue that it operates through the externalization of a norm—i.e., "embedded liberalism"—which promotes trade but also minimizes its domestic costs and, with it, protectionist demands.[36] Others suggest that the regime and its norms are embodied in domestic policies and practices and that it is effective through constraining and shaping domestic behavior.[37] Still others see the re-

gime as encouraging international commerce by increasing its efficiency.[38] Differences thus exist over exactly how the GATT has worked to abate protectionism, but generally it is seen as exerting a brake on domestic pressures for protection.

In all of these views, however, regimes play only an intermediate role. They are acknowledged as an intervening variable, influencing the preferences, pressures, and practices already established at the domestic and international levels.[39] In order to judge the effect of the regime, it is necessary to examine these pre-existing factors. Regime analysis thus needs to be supplemented with analyses of other domestic and international forces, which this study provides.

A third type of explanation focuses on the structure of the domestic policy-making system. The argument here is that, despite the pressures for protection in the 1970s, a different policy structure existed which helped defuse these pressures. This structure insulated political actors, especially Congress, from societal pressures for protection. Hence, the state was able to resist such pressures in the 1970s, but not in the 1920s. Explanations differ on the specific way this insulation occurred. Most scholars acknowledge the importance of the shift in tariff-making authority from Congress to the President as being central.[40] Others point to the nature of the relationship between Congress and the executive;[41] some to the way trade policy is made within the executive

---

[35] Lake (fns. 1, 9, and 20). To overcome this difficulty, Lake makes two points: first, that due to the disruption caused by World War I, much greater uncertainty existed in the 1920s, which prompted more protectionist activity. Second, he implies that the height of protectionism globally was in the 1930s, not the 1920s, when the structure was somewhat different. Protectionism, however, was rising world-wide throughout the 1920s; it hit its peak in the U.S. by 1930 and elsewhere by 1933 or 1934. This explanation of trade policy outcomes is more sophisticated and perhaps more accurate than other hegemonic stability arguments, but it still has difficulty accounting for the differences between the 1920s and the 1970s.

[36] John Ruggie, "International Regimes, Transactions, and Change," *International Organization* 36 (Spring 1982), 379–415.

[37] Charles Lipson, "The Transformation of Trade," *International Organization* 36 (Spring 1982), 417–56; Stephanie Lenway, *The Politics of U.S. International Trade* (Boston: Pitman, 1985).

[38] Lipson (fn. 37).

[39] See *International Organization* 36 (Spring 1982), esp. the introduction by Stephen Krasner.

[40] Pastor (fn. 1); Judith Goldstein, "The Political Economy of Trade," *American Political Science Review* 80 (March 1986), 161–84; I. M. Destler, *American Trade Politics: System Under Stress* (Washington, DC: Institute for International Economics, 1986).

[41] Pastor (fn. 1).

branch;[42] some to the lessons of the 1930s and the norms and ideology now surrounding those lessons;[43] and yet others to the way Congress functions and responds to societal pressures.[44]

This proliferation of domestic policy "structures" indicates that trade policy is not made within one structure. Many economic actors are involved, and they bring their complaints and pressures to bear on different political actors. Moreover, no single, coherent national trade policy exists. The policy relating to one sector of the economy may differ completely from that concerning another. Thus, the policy for automobiles may differ greatly from the policies for wheat, textiles, or telecommunications equipment. Moreover, for each of these industries, the influence of Congress, the executive, and the International Trade Commission varies. A knowledge of the relevant domestic actors and their trade preferences is essential to understanding the influence of the particular policy structure for that sector on the policy outcome.

THE ARGUMENT

My argument operates on a different level of analysis. I maintain that the increased international economic interdependence of the post-World War II period has been a major reason why protectionism did not

spread widely in the 1970s and early 1980s. By altering domestic actors' preferences, aspects of America's greater integration into the international economy worked against recourse to protectionism. Specifically, while increased interdependence has subjected some areas of the economy to new foreign competition, it has also greatly augmented international economic ties for some firms in the form of exports, imports of critical inputs, multinational production, and global intrafirm trade. Despite pressures for closure, the growth of these international ties is a major reason for the maintenance of a relatively open market in the 1970s.

Evidence of the growth of these international ties is abundant. American trade grew phenomenally between the 1920s and the 1980s.[45] More goods and more different types of goods were traded. Specifically, America's trade dependence grew substantially. U.S. export dependence (exports as a percentage of total domestic production) rose from about 2 percent in 1923 to 9 percent in 1960, and to about 20 percent by the late 1970s. Likewise, imports climbed from 2.5 percent of total domestic consumption in 1921 to 5 percent in 1960, and to over 20 percent in 1980.[46] The multinationality of American firms also rose substantially over these five decades. The total of American direct foreign investment abroad grew from about $5.5 billion in 1923 to $11.8 billion in 1950, and to over $86 billion in 1970.[47] Moreover, the in-

[42] Roger Porter, *Presidential Decision-Making* (New York: Cambridge University Press, 1980); Gilbert Winham, "Robert Strauss, The MTN, and the Control of Faction," *Journal of World Trade Law* 14 (September-October, 1980), 377–97.
[43] Goldstein (fn. 40); Judith Goldstein, "A Reexamination of American Commercial Policy" (Ph.D. diss., UCLA, 1983).
[44] E. E. Schattschneider, *Politics, Pressures and the Tariff* (Englewood Cliffs, NJ: Prentice-Hall, 1935); Raymond Bauer, Ithiel de Sola Pool, and Lewis Dexter, *American Business and Public Policy* (Chicago: Aldine-Atherton, 1972).

[45] Ratner, Soltow, and Sylla (fn. 8), 463–66.
[46] For the 1920s, see Robert Lipsey, *Price and Quantity Trends in the Foreign Trade of the U.S.* (Princeton: Princeton University Press, 1963), 434–35; for the period from 1960 on, see Report of the President's Commission on Industrial Competitiveness, *Global Competition: The New Reality,* Vol. I (Washington, DC: G.P.O., 1985), 36.
[47] Robert Dunn, *American Foreign Investments* (New York: Viking, 1926), 182; Kent

ternationalization of American industry grew in relative terms. Foreign assets of U.S. industry accounted for only 2.5 percent of total industrial assets in 1929, but for over 20 percent in the 1970s.[48] In addition, the global operations of these firms intensified, leading to the creation of webs of international trade flows within firms. Exports by American multinationals from foreign production sites back to the U.S. market have grown immensely. This practice was almost unknown before the 1940s; at present, these types of transfers account for somewhere between 15 and 50 percent of all U.S. industrial imports.[49] In sum, the integration of the United States into the international economy through both trade and multinationality has deepened considerably since the 1920s.

This aspect of increased interdependence has lessened pressures for protec-

---

Hughes, *Trade, Taxes, and Transnationals* (New York: Praeger, 1979), 94. Ratner, Soltow, and Sylla (fn. 8), 464, show it grew to $17.2 billion in the 1920s and then retreated to $11.5 billion by the end of the 1930s. According to Robert Pollard, *Economic Security and the Origins of the Cold War* (New York: Columbia University Press, 1985), 205, U.S. direct foreign investments dropped to their lowest point in the century so far in 1946.

[48] For the 1920s, see U.S. Congress, Senate, *American Branch Factories Abroad*, S. Doc. No. 258, 71st Cong., 3rd sess., 1931, p. 27, on the value of U.S. direct foreign investment in manufacturing, and Lipsey (fn. 46), 424, on the value of U.S. manufacturing GNP. For the 1970s, see U.S. Department of Commerce, *1977 Enterprise Statistics* (Washington, DC: G.P.O., 1981).

[49] The figures vary widely. See Joseph Grunwald and Kenneth Flamm, *Global Factory* (Washington, DC: Brookings Institution, 1985), 7; Gerald Helleiner and Real Lavergne, "Intrafirm Trade and Industrial Exports to the U.S.," *Oxford Bulletin of Economics and Statistics* 41 (November 1979), 297–312; Gerald Helleiner, "Transnational Corporations and the Trade Structure," in Herbert Giersch, *On the Economics of Intra-Firm Trade* (Tübingen: Mohr, 1979), 159–84.

tion in domestic industries. I hypothesize that firms with greater international ties in the form of exports, multinationality, and global intrafirm trade will be less interested in protection than firms that are more domestically oriented. The former will view protection as undesirable, since it will be more costly for them than for the latter, for five reasons. First, firms that export or produce abroad will be concerned about foreign retaliation and its costs. Demanding protection at home may prompt greater protection abroad, which may lead to a reduction of exports or to new restrictions on foreign operations and their trade flows, thus reducing profitability. Second, protection in one market may hurt a firm's exports to third markets as other exporters divert their products to these markets to compensate for market closure elsewhere.

Third, firms with a global web of production and trade will view trade barriers, even at home, as a new cost—one that may undermine their competitiveness. For these firms, protection will be disruptive and costly. Fourth, for firms dependent on imports—whether from subsidiaries, subcontractors, or foreign firms—new trade barriers will increase costs and thus erode competitiveness. Finally, intra-industry rivalries will create opposition to protectionism. Trade barriers will put internationally oriented firms at a disadvantage relative to their domestically oriented competitors. Such barriers impose new costs on international firms while providing benefits to domestic ones. These different relative costs and benefits within an industry may lead international firms to oppose protection. For all these reasons, firms with strong international ties will find protection of the home market very costly and will be likely to resist appeals for it, even when faced with severe import competition.

While containing an international element, this argument is similar to those concerning domestic interest groups. Most interest-group analyses, however, focus on the forces pushing *for* protection.[50] One reason is the assumption of a collective action problem in trade politics. Small groups of producers (management and labor) facing import competition are seen as more likely to press actively for help since it will bring them concentrated and substantial benefits, while larger groups (other industries, consumers) opposing protection will be less likely to act since the benefits of openness will be diffuse and less tangible.[51] But some small groups may also suffer from the high costs of protection and receive important tangible benefits from openness.

Increasingly, the interest-group literature has focused on the variables examined here. Several aggregate-level studies of U.S. industries have shown that high levels of export dependence reduce industries' preferences for protection and lead to lower trade barriers for these industries.[52] Other studies reveal that, even

in the 1920s, the growth of an export sector contributed to attempts to open American and foreign markets.[53] Some have also linked the adoption of the R.T.A.A. in 1934, with its antiprotectionist bent, to the influence of American exporters and multinationals.[54] These studies have lent credence to the idea that export-dependent industries may not prefer protection and may even advocate the dismantling of trade barriers.

Scholars have also examined how multinationality and its related intrafirm trade affect trade policy. On the one hand, the idea that the spread of multinational firms would reduce trade barriers has been challenged because these firms often enter a market to circumvent such barriers, and thus come to see them as a brake against other foreign competitors; on the other hand, the growth of global intrafirm trading has led to the idea that firms with such trade would be adverse to protection in their markets.[55] Analysis at the aggregate industry level has produced mixed evidence for both of these arguments.[56]

[50] Examples are Richard Caves, "Economic Models of Political Choice: Canada's Tariff Structure," *Canadian Journal of Economics* 9 (May 1976), 278–300; William Brock and Stephen Magee, "The Economics of Special Interest Politics: Case of the Tariff," *American Economic Review, Papers and Proceedings* 68 (May 1978), 246–50; Robert Baldwin, *The Political Economy of U.S. Import Policy* (Cambridge: MIT Press, 1986); Jonathan Pincus, *Pressure Groups and Politics in Antebellum Tariffs* (New York: Columbia University Press, 1977); Edward Ray, "Determinants of Tariff and Nontariff Trade Restrictions in the U.S.," *Journal of Political Economy* 81 (No. 1, 1981), 105–21; Real Lavergne, *The Political Economy of U.S. Tariffs* (Toronto: Academic Press, 1983).
[51] Mancur Olson, *The Logic of Collective Action* (Cambridge: Harvard University Press, 1965), for the classic treatment; also see Brock and Magee (fn. 50).
[52] Glenn Fong, "Export Dependence and the New Protectionism" (Ph.D. diss., Cornell University, 1982) supports this contention. So does Robert Baldwin (fn. 50). Lavergne (fn. 50)

and Goldstein (fn. 43) provide mixed evidence for this assertion.
[53] Joan H. Wilson, *American Business and Foreign Policy, 1920–33* (Boston: Beacon, 1971); William Becker, *The Dynamics of Business-Government Relations* (Chicago: University of Chicago Press, 1982).
[54] Thomas Ferguson, "From Normalcy to New Deal," *International Organization* 38 (Winter 1984), 40–94.
[55] Gerald Helleiner, "Transnational Enterprise and the New Political Economy of U.S. Trade Policy," *Oxford Economic Papers* 29 (March 1977), 102–16; also Helleiner (fn. 49). See Lipson (fn. 37) for a discussion of the effect of intra-industry trade on industry trade preferences.
[56] Baldwin (fn. 50) and Lavergne (fn. 50) do not find much influence exercised by these variables, but Thomas Pugel and Ingo Walter, "U.S. Corporate Interests and the Political Economy of Trade Policy," *Review of Economics and Statistics* 67 (August 1985), 465–73, do find multinationality to be an important brake on protectionist preferences.

In this study, I do not adopt an aggregate approach; rather, I examine a set of industries and their firms in detail. This method permits the consideration of firms who are the chief actors experiencing the particular costs and benefits of protection. It thus overcomes a central problem of aggregate studies; that is, that they mask the distribution of international ties within an industry, and with it the intra-industry divisions over protectionism. The poor results of aggregate analyses concerning export dependence and multinationality are partly due to these divisions within industries. An industry that is highly multinational may actually contain only one or two large multinational firms, who may or may not be able to impose their preferences against protection on the industry and/or on state actors. These intra-industry differences and their effects on trade policy will be examined in the present study.

This focus corrects for another problem. Unlike arguments based on international systems, regimes, or domestic structures, my argument can account for differences in trade policy outcomes among industries during the same period. Why some industries demand and receive protection, while at the same time others do not, is hard to explain parsimoniously with these other arguments. For example, the fact that 60 percent of all imports entered the U.S. duty-free in the 1920s is not easily explicable if one asserts that the international structure, the lack of any regime, or the domestic political structure encouraged the adoption of widespread protectionism at that time.[57] The argument here is better able to address such differences among industries at any one time and to account for differences over time. It should not be seen, however, as directly competing with the other explanations, which operate at different levels of analysis and

may all have some validity. The point is that examinations of trade politics have missed antiprotectionist interests, and that a domestic politics view of the pressures for and against trade barriers is the place where one should start to understand trade policy.

THE CASE STUDIES

The industries examined were those experiencing the greatest growth in import penetration among those already having high levels of import penetration in the two decades.[58] In addition, these industries showed evidence of other economic difficulties: unemployment, profit problems, overcapacity, and so forth. Since studies have demonstrated that high levels of import penetration are strongly associated with demands for protection and high actual levels of protection, the industries selected should be the least likely to confirm my argument;[59] they should have been most likely to desire protection. Indeed, it would be surprising to find that these import-threatened industries did *not* prefer new trade barriers.

Once these "hard" cases were chosen, I explored the extent of their integration into the international economy and their trade policy preferences. To measure their integration, data on their export dependence, import requirements, multinationality, and global intrafirm trade were collected for both the industry and its firms. In order to understand their

[57] Lake (fn. 9), chap. 5, p. 8 and Table 5–1.

[58] Eighteen industries were examined in detail; see Helen Milner, "Resisting the Protectionist Temptation: Industry Politics and Trade Policy in France and the US in the 1920s and 1970s" (Ph.D. diss., Harvard University, 1986).

[59] Many studies have found that high levels or high rates of increase in import penetration are strongly correlated with high levels of demand for protection and high actual levels of protection. See, for example, Baldwin (fn. 50); Lavergne (fn. 50); Goldstein (fn. 43).

preferences, I surveyed their activities in a number of political arenas. In the 1920s, these were (1) the U.S. Congress, which handled most issues related to tariff levels; (2) the U.S. Tariff Commission, which investigated industry complaints about trade matters; and (3) industry trade associations, whose internal deliberations over trade issues were reported in various newspapers and industry trade journals. For the 1970s, the arenas were slightly different: (1) the U.S Congress, which authorized general tariff level changes and introduced bills to help particular industries; (2) the U.S. International Trade Commission (I.T.C.), which investigated industry trade complaints; (3) the U.S. Special Trade Representative (S.T.R.) and other executive agencies, who decided on and implemented solutions to industry trade complaints while also managing U.S. activities in the GATT negotiations; and (4) the industry trade associations, which developed industry-wide positions on trade.

The investigation of the industries chosen revealed a strong correlation between their firms' international ties and their trade policy preferences. (See Table 23.2.) In the face of mounting import competition, firms that lacked ties to the international economy voiced rising demands for extensive protection. By contrast, firms with well-developed multinational operations, *including integrated global production and trade flows,* and strong exports did *not* seek protection even when imports rose to high levels. In fact, these firms often desired that markets at home and abroad be opened further still. Firms with substantial export dependence but no multinational production also did not desire protection as long as import competition did not swamp their exports. Finally, firms with some foreign production but no U.S. exports or intrafirm trade often resorted to limited protectionism when facing import competition. These firms sometimes

sought selective protection; that is, they attempted to curb their strongest competitors through limited protection against a particular country or product line while leaving undisturbed the main foreign markets in which they were involved. Overall, the cases revealed that the more integrated a firm was into the international economy, the less likely it was to seek import restraints even when imports rose significantly.

U.S. manufacturers of woolen goods in the 1920s and producers of footwear in the 1970s were typical of industries lacking international economic ties. Most firms in the woolen goods sector were domestically oriented, with few exports and no multinationality. After World War I, when import competition resumed and other difficulties set in, the majority of firms in this industry began lobbying for closure of the U.S. market.[60] They demanded and received increased tariffs through the 1921 Emergency Tariff bill; later, during the Fordney-McCumber tariff hearings, they called for a 130 percent rise in their duties and were granted a sizable increase. They lobbied for even higher tariffs before and during the Smoot-Hawley hearings after problems arose in the late 1920s. Success with Congress did not satisfy them, however: they fought against changes in tariff-making rules that could have made tariff reductions easier. They also pressured the U.S. Tariff Commission for greater protection. Thus, the woolens manufacturers' demands were voiced in all possible political arenas and were focused on obtaining global protection for all segments of the industry. In view of their economic problems and lack of international ties, their intense and unified advocacy for closure of the home market was not surprising.

Like the woolen goods manufacturers,

---

[60] For the full story, see Milner (fn. 58), 138–63.

Table 23.2   The Industries, Their Preferences, and Policy Outcomes

International Ties		Industry	Expected Preferences	Actual Preferences	Policy Outcomes
Export Dependence	Multinational and Global Intrafirm Trade				
Low	Low	Woolens, 1920s	Protectionist	Protectionist	High, increasing tariffs
		Watches and Clocks, 1920s	Protectionist	Protectionist	High, rising tariffs
		Footwear, 1970s	Protectionist	Protectionist	Some protection via voluntary export restraints in mid-1970s
High	Low	Textile Machinery, 1920s	Open markets, esp. abroad	Divided; some free trade and some moderate protection	Low tariffs in early 1920s; some increases later
		Machine Tools, 1970s	Open markets, esp. abroad	Free trade in 1970s; Protectionist in early 1980s	Tariff reductions in 1970s; voluntary export restraints in mid-1980s
Low	High	Newsprint, 1920s	Selective protection, if any	Free trade	Duty-free
		Tires, 1970s	Selective protection, if any	Free trade, some complaints of unfair trade	Tariff reductions
		Watches & Clocks, 1970s	Selective protection, if any	Divided; some free trade, some selective protection	Some tariff reductions
		Radios & Television sets, 1970s	Selective protection	Some selective protection; some free trade	Some tariff reductions; voluntary export restraints in mid-1970s
High	High	Fertilizer, 1920s	Free trade	Free trade	Duty-free
		Photo Equipment, 1920s	Free trade	Moderate protection; increasing free trade	Some tariff increases in early 1920s; some decreases in late 1920s
		Semiconductors, 1970s	Free trade	Free trade in 1970s; strategic trade demands in 1980s	Tariff reductions, but export pricing agreement with Japan in mid-1980s

the American (non-rubber) footwear producers had largely domestic operations in the 1970s. Beginning in the late 1960s, when shoe imports began flooding the U.S. market, the industry association—backed by almost all of the producers—launched a campaign to obtain tariff protection.[61] After the early 1970s, the association and the firms pursued this goal with increasing intensity. The association filed numerous trade complaints with the I.T.C.; it lobbied Congress for help and formed a coalition of congressmen to promote the industry's cause; and it launched a public relations campaign to generate public support. These activities forced President Carter to negotiate voluntary export restraints with several East Asian competitors; even those restraints were not restrictive enough for many of the firms who sought global quotas. By the early 1980s, however, the industry's unity over trade matters began to decline. A growing number of producers started to oppose renewed protection as they began importing or producing offshore. This opposition weakened the association's appeals for help and contributed to its more limited political success since then. Overall, the firms' waxing and waning protectionist demands were related to the level of their international economic ties.

By contrast, large multinationals with extensive international trade flows and exports from the United States avoided protection as a solution to their import problems largely because of the costly effects it would have on the firms' global operations. U.S. fertilizer producers in the 1920s and the semiconductor producers in the 1970s were characteristic. By the early 1920s, for example, the large fertilizer producers were highly export-dependent and multinational. Despite their economic problems, they preferred

freer trade.[62] In the 1921 tariff hearings, they requested and received the retention of the duty-free status of their products. During the Smoot-Hawley hearings, this preference prevailed among most of the firms, although certain producers advocated demanding protection on certain goods if they did not receive tariff reductions on others. This strategy was aimed at, and resulted in, greater openness of the U.S. market, since no tariffs were imposed on fertilizers, and some were reduced. Finally, throughout the 1920s, the major producers—i.e., those with international operations—opposed the demands of some small domestic producers for higher tariffs on various fertilizer products. In general, the internationally oriented fertilizer manufacturers wanted to preserve the U.S. market's openness and, despite mounting foreign competition, opposed attempts to erect new barriers around it.

During the 1970s, the American semiconductor industry faced serious competition for the first time. The largest firms in this industry—I.B.M., Texas Instruments, and Motorola—had widespread foreign operations and intrafirm trade flows, while the remainder were more domestically oriented. Most of the firms favored trade liberalization throughout the 1970s; despite rising foreign competition, demands for aid or protection were nonexistent before the late 1970s.[63] Later in the decade, the smaller firms, united in the new Semiconductor Industry Association (S.I.A.), began formulating a trade complaint against Japan. Due to the opposition of the large firms—mainly I.B.M. and T.I.—this complaint was not formalized at the time. Instead, I.B.M. joined the S.I.A. and helped turn its attention toward negotiations with Japan over further tariff *reductions*. These

[61] *Ibid.*, 300–19.

[62] *Ibid.*, 244–70.
[63] *Ibid.*, 343–71.

negotiations, impelled by the industry, resulted in lower tariffs for semiconductors; other negotiations, to open the Japanese market further, continued as well. In the early 1980s, however, the S.I.A. and some firms within the industry filed several trade complaints against the Japanese, as did the Reagan administration itself.[64] These complaints resulted in intensified efforts to open the Japanese market and in a pact to regulate export prices of Japanese semiconductors, which was intended to alleviate illegal dumping. On the whole, however, American firms resisted the strong pressures for protection; their international economic ties made protection less desirable than the further opening of markets at home and abroad.

Like these trade-oriented multinationals, firms with extensive export dependence (but not multinationality) tended to avoid protectionist demands in times of difficulty. Examples are the U.S. textile machinery builders in the 1920s and machine tool manufacturers in the 1970s. The former, while having significant export dependence in the aggregate, were divided: the producers of cotton machinery had become substantial exporters since World War I, while those of woolen machinery were still domestically oriented.[65] This division, as well as the novelty and volatility of the producers' exports, rendered the industry unable to develop a unified trade policy preference. In the early 1920s, when exports were most significant, the producers did not lobby Congress for any change in their tariffs despite severe economic distress and rising imports. Over the decade, the export interests of some firms declined, and so did the capacity of these firms to forestall protectionist demands.

In the 1929 Smoot-Hawley hearings, firms from the woolen machinery sector pressed for and received moderate tariff increases on their machines; the more export-oriented firms remained silent. Even though they were besieged by imports, these exporters refrained from demanding protection for much of the decade and remained moderate and divided in their later requests.

The American machine tool builders were sizable although declining exporters in the 1970s. During this decade, these producers lost major market shares to imports and experienced other economic difficulties. Their response, however, was not a resort to demands for protection; rather, the industry association— backed by most producers—favored tariff reductions during the GATT negotiations and lobbied Congress to obtain aid for their exports.[66] In particular, the builders wanted to open major foreign markets— especially those of the Soviet Union and other Eastern bloc countries. By the late 1970s, the failure of these export initiatives, the continuing decline of the industry's export trade, and the rising import tide pushed some in the industry to seek relief from imports. Pressure for protection rose in the late 1970s; but it was not formalized into a public complaint until the early 1980s, when the tide of imports overwhelmed the firms' exports. The Reagan administration responded to this trade complaint against several countries' imports—mainly Japan's—by negotiating a set of voluntary export restraints.[67] The case of the machine tool builders thus shows how sizable export dependence may promote an interest in freer trade and dampen pressures for protection even when imports surge. But, when the firms' export orientation de-

---

[64] *Boston Globe,* April 13, 1986, Business section, pp. A-1, A-9; *Wall Street Journal,* March 12, 1986, p. 7; *Wall Street Journal,* March 31, 1986, p. 2.
[65] Milner (fn. 58), 190–215.

[66] *Ibid.,* 320–42.
[67] *New York Times,* February 3, 1986, p. D-2; *New York Times,* March 6, 1986, p. D-3.

clined, their trade preferences shifted as well.

Industries with firms that had foreign production but no intrafirm or export trade showed some resistance to protection when imports grew, but it was often weaker than that of export-oriented industries. In many of these industries, growing foreign competition was met by calls for limited protection because the costs of this protection could be minimized. Two examples are the American newsprint producers in the 1920s and U.S. television makers in the 1970s. Newsprint producers in the 1920s were multinational but had only minor U.S. exports. Their foreign operations were concentrated almost exclusively in Canada; from there, they exported heavily back to the United States. The industry thus had substantial intrafirm trade. Throughout the 1920s, the newsprint producers actively supported freer trade of their products, and did not try to have the duty-free status of newsprint altered in either the 1921 or the 1929 tariff revisions.[68] In 1921, several manufacturers did attempt to make their status conditional on other countries' treatment of imports and exports. But this strategic maneuver was distasteful to many firms and was never adopted as part of U.S. policy. As their trade between Canada and the U.S. grew in the 1920s, interest in protection waned even more. During the Smoot-Hawley tariff revision, when most tariffs reached their highest levels ever, the newsprint manufacturers uniformly supported the continuing duty-free status of their products. Not even rising imports could induce these international producers to think about protection.

American television makers had some foreign operations in the 1970s; but, unlike the newsprint producers, they were not very trade-oriented. The industry was, in fact, divided in two: the largest producers, RCA and General Electric, were multinationals with global trading operations, while the rest, including Zenith, Magnavox, and GTE-Sylvania, were domestic producers. In the 1970s, imports started pouring into the United States, and the domestically oriented firms, led by Zenith, initiated a series of trade complaints on several specific products, targeted against a few East Asian countries.[69] These complaints met with varying success, but they were opposed by RCA, the industry's giant multinational. By the late 1970s and early 1980s, much of this protectionist activity had abated as the domestically oriented American firms moved production abroad, left the industry, or were bought by foreign interests. This international adjustment process eroded support for even the limited, selective protection that some had desired earlier.

In all of these cases, then, the existence or creation of extensive international economic ties prompted firms to resist seeking protection even in times of severe import competition. Conversely, the lack or loss of these ties was associated with rising demands for protection. This pattern occurred both in the 1920s and the 1970s. In both decades, increased integration into the international economy was experienced similarly by firms in spite of their different historical contexts. This pattern helps to explain the varied nature of trade policy *within* each time period. At each point, industries that were dominated by firms with extensive international ties were less protectionist than those that were not.

In addition to accounting for variation in preferences *within* each period, the argument and the cases suggest why trade policy varied *between* the two periods.

[68] Milner (fn. 58), 271–97.

[69] *Ibid.*, 372–96.

On a macro level, the evidence implies that in periods like the 1970s, when such international economic ties are widespread and well-developed, pressure for protection by industries will be reduced.

Although the growth of international ties contributed to the maintenance of free trade in the 1970s and early 1980s, it must be noted that the internationalization of U.S. industry went hand in hand with trade liberalization in the postwar period. The liberalization of trade in the 1950s and 1960s was one factor promoting the growth of these international ties. But much of this expansion had occurred before the two most significant reductions in trade barriers. U.S. export dependence, and especially U.S. multinationality, had grown significantly before the phasing in of the Kennedy Round tariff cuts in the early 1970s. America's industrial export dependence (exports as a percent of total domestic production) rose 33 percent between 1960 and 1970, while the value of U.S. direct foreign investment in manufacturing increased nearly 800 percent between 1950 and 1970.[70] The growth of these international ties cannot be separated from the liberalization of trade occurring at the same time. But, since industries with international ties were in place prior to the 1970s, they probably contributed to the liberalization that occurred during that decade. In any case, by the 1970s there were many more firms that were willing to resist protectionist pressures. Despite higher levels of import penetration, demands for protection were less widespread than they had been in the 1920s. This provides a partial answer to our central puzzle.

[70] Consistent data series on export dependence and multinationality as a percent of GNP from 1945 on are not available. The export dependence data come from Report of the President's Commission (fn. 46), 36. The data on direct foreign investment come from Feldstein (fn. 7), Table 3.30, p. 240.

INDUSTRY DIVISIONS, CONTEXT, AND POLICY OUTCOMES

The argument raises three further issues. The first deals with intra-industry divisions on trade issues. One notable feature of the growing internalization of U.S. industries has been its uneven character. Within an industry, some firms—usually the largest—have become international, while the smaller ones have often remained dependent on the domestic market. This difference has tended to divide industries on trade politics: a pattern of large multinationals opposing the more numerous but smaller domestic-centered firms is evident in the cases.

Two consequences of this political division stand out. First, it makes developing an industry-wide stand difficult. As seen in the textile machinery case, internal divisions created by different international interests can leave an industry without the capacity to develop a political position on trade. Second, the attempt to create an "industry" position in a divided industry may lead to the fashioning of compromises that are not as protectionist as the majority of firms may prefer, as was evidence in the semiconductor case. Both results may reduce protectionist demands even more than the extent of internationalization of the industry would suggest. Thus, the creation of these intra-industry divisions through unevenly rising interdependence may further reduce pressures for protection.

In the 1920s, these internal divisions were less apparent than in the 1970s, because internationalization was less widespread.[71] Moreover, existing divisions tended to be only the initial breach in an industry's unity—a consequence of recent internationalization. The textile machinery industry is a good example. Thus, intra-industry divisions, another

[71] Milner (fn. 58), chap. 8.

counterweight to protectionist pressures, were also weaker in the 1920s.

Second, contextual differences between the two periods have been alleged to undercut any comparison between them.[72] But contextual differences did not override the powerful influence that a firm's international position exerted on its trade preferences. In both periods, internationally oriented firms opposed protectionist solutions to their problems. This finding suggests that the broad differences between the two periods—e.g., in macroeconomic circumstances, political structures, and economic ideology— did not greatly affect the way firms calculated their preferences. The similarities in preferences in the two periods imply that factors differentiating the two times may have only a minor impact on demands for protection by industries at any time.

Moreover, firms often did not take these contextual features as given. In both periods, some firms worked to alter domestic political structures responsible for trade policy. In the 1920s, for example, several industries attempted to make U.S. procedures more free-trade oriented, opposing the American valuation plan and supporting flexible tariff provisions; other industries, including the domestically oriented woolen goods one, took the opposite stance.[73] In the 1970s, those footwear and television manufacturers who pursued protection lobbied to change U.S. procedures in order to make them more open to protectionist outcomes. This involved efforts—most of which were successful—to loosen U.S. trade laws and to shift their enforcement to agencies more favorable to domestic

industry.[74] Certain contextual features, such as the domestic political process for trade issues, may thus not be exogenous; rather, the structures in which firms are assumed to operate may be responsive to the influence of firms.

A final issue involves the question of trade policy outcomes. I have focused more on explaining firms' preferences than on policy decisions. The influence of such preferences on policy outcomes has been largely assumed. The cases presented here provide support for this assumption. In almost all of the cases, the industries' demands for protection or for freer trade had some effect upon policy.[75] (See Table 23.2.) First, in none of the cases were industries accorded protection when they did not demand it. This suggests that the issue of protection was usually placed on the political agenda by the industries themselves. Second, industries desiring the maintenance of low trade barriers or reductions of restraints were successful in all the cases, as the fertilizer, newsprint, and semiconductor industries show. Thus, no systematic bias against low or reduced trade barriers appears to have existed even in the 1920s.

Finally, industries seeking increases in trade barriers also tended to be successful. Where an industry was divided, however, its capacity for effective political influence was reduced, as exemplified by the limited success of the domestically oriented television makers in the 1970s. In contrast, where industries were united in favor of protection, they generally received it. This was true for all cases in the 1920s and for all but two in the 1970s. Although the footwear producers failed throughout the early 1970s to have new trade barriers erected, their efforts met with some success in the late 1970s, when the Carter administration negoti-

---

[72] For example, see Kenneth A. Oye, "The Sterling-Dollar-Franc Triangle: Monetary Diplomacy 1929–1937," *World Politics* 38 (October 1985), 173–99, at 199.

[73] Milner (fn. 58), chap. 4.

[74] *Ibid.*, chap. 5.

[75] *Ibid.*, see cases and chap. 8.

ated voluntary export restraints for them. Likewise, the early efforts of the machine tool builders in the late 1970s and early 1980s failed to produce any response from the government. By the mid-1980s, however, the Reagan administration was pressing the industry's case and negotiating export restraints with foreign governments.

In neither period did industries always get exactly what they wanted when they wanted it. But their demands tended in time to move policy in the desired direction. The greater difficulty that industries experienced in attaining their demands for protection in the 1970s may reflect both the greater awareness among industry and government officials of the international problems caused by protection and the more limited responsiveness to domestic pressures of the executive (now in control of more trade issues) as opposed to Congress (which played a larger role in the 1920s). Some bias in the trade policy system against protection appears evident in the 1970s. Unlike firms' preferences then, trade policy outcomes may depend more on factors that differed in the two contexts, such as policymaking structures and ideology.

In both periods, industries were able over time to realize trade policies close to the ones they desired. Thus, their preferences seemed to count in the policy process. Other influences on trade policy, such as the interests of labor or the ideologies of decision makers, were also likely to be important. The evidence presented here simply shows that, by itself, reduced interest in protection by internationally oriented industries in the 1970s was one important reason for the resistance to protectionism in the United States.

CONCLUSION

Why did trade policy outcomes differ between the 1920s and the 1970s when a number of conditions influencing trade politics were similar? Why was protectionism resisted in the 1970s when economic difficulties were severe and U.S. hegemony was in decline? While noting other answers to this puzzle—such as the influence of the international distribution of power, international regimes, and domestic political structures—I maintain that aspects of rising international economic interdependence in the post–World War II period led to changes in the trade policy preferences of domestic actors. Rising interdependence meant, in part, the growth of firms' ties to the international economy through exports, multinationality, and global intrafirm trade; because of these ties, protectionism had become a more costly policy. The new interdependence made protectionism a less viable option for many firms facing serious import competition. Consequently, it dampened the demand for protection.

Examination of a set of industries from the 1920s and 1970s supports the contention that internationally oriented firms were less likely to demand protection than were domestically oriented ones, even if both faced high levels of import penetration. The cases also pointed to the importance of firm-level analysis. International ties conditioned firms' preferences, and divergences in these ties *within* the industry created important political divisions over trade. These intra-industry divisions also helped to dampen pressures for protectionism.

Differences in the historical context between the 1920s and 1970s did not override the argument. Despite differences in the international and domestic structures, internationally oriented firms in both periods were less protectionist than their domestic counterparts. In fact, features often considered contextual were responsive to influence by firms. Moreover, trade preferences among the firms examined mattered. Policy outcomes often reflected the desires of firms. Thus, reduced demand for protection in the 1970s may be one important, but not the only, reason why U.S. trade policy differed in the two periods.

24.   The Uruguay Round

H. B. Junz and Clemens Boonekamp

In late February 1991, the Uruguay Round of multilateral trade talks was relaunched, as a result of an understanding among the participants that the critical agricultural issues would be addressed explicitly and with reasonable flexibility. The much troubled talks—rather than concluding as scheduled in Brussels in December 1990—had been suspended over this issue. But even if agriculture had not been a sticking point, it would not have been easy to achieve consensus on a number of other outstanding issues. Hence the decision to resume the four-year trade round without setting a specific time frame for a conclusion. Indeed, the recognition was widespread that for the 108 participating nations to reach agreement, it would require months, not weeks.

At stake is an agreement that would bring a material increase in world trade and, thereby, growth. In Brussels, a package appeared in sight that would (1) reduce tariffs significantly, including those on higher value-added production; (2) gradually bring trade that had moved outside the multilateral framework, including textiles and clothing, back into the GATT; (3) bring discipline to the trade-related aspects of intellectual property; (4) improve the rules and dispute settlement system of the GATT; and (5) provide, at least, a framework for trade in services. Other questions, such as those on trade-related investment measures (discussed below) and the functioning of the GATT system—including the GATT's relationship with the IMF and the World Bank in achieving greater coherence in policy formulation probably could have fallen into place with agreement elsewhere. In fact, this package would have gone a considerable way toward meeting the objectives set at Punta del Este, Uruguay, in September 1986 (see "The Uruguay Round: Revitalizing the Global Trading System," by Naheed Kirmani, in *Finance & Development,* March 1989).

But achieving these objectives involves confronting and solving deep-seated political and economic problems that beset most participating countries, large and small, developed and developing—a challenge that policymakers in many countries have found most difficult. Not to do so, however, raises the risk of yet another breakdown in the talks, and some doubt that the Uruguay Round could survive another stoppage. This article (based on a longer background paper by the authors and Grant Taplin) looks at the underlying problems and the progress up to early 1991 on key negotiating issues, as well as the prospects for success and the dangers of failure.

UNDERLYING PROBLEMS

From the very beginning of the Uruguay Round, there have been signs that many countries were not yet ready to address the problems that had given rise to a network of subsidies and noneconomic production in farming, managed trade in var-

SOURCE: *Finance and Development,* vol. 28, June 1991, pp. 11–15.

ious sectors, defensive attitudes toward the establishment of foreign firms, and a host of other distorting policies. This difficulty, in fact, was behind the numerous setbacks: it caused a four-year interval between initial efforts to get agreement on the need for a Round in 1982 and the adoption of its terms of reference in 1986; it brought the negotiations to a four-month halt at the time of the mid-term review—from December 1988 to April 1989; and it derailed them in Brussels in late 1990.

These economic and political problems find a focal point in agriculture, where policies in many countries involve the whole complex of basic reasons that drive departures from market solutions—such as social, political, and cultural concerns, and more recently, environmental ones. . . . Some, or all, of these considerations also play into other areas of the negotiations, particularly where there have been large changes in the size and location of production capability. At root are internal market rigidities that stem from delays in dealing with changing economic realities.

In recent years, however, developed and developing countries alike have begun to reappraise their economic strategies, increasingly opting for a basic policy stance that looks to market signals for guidance and seeks to reduce, if not eliminate, government intervention. In keeping with this outlook, many governments have included market opening and trade liberalization as a major element in their economic programs, although in many industrialized countries, the emphasis was more on domestic deregulation. This shift should have greatly enhanced the trade negotiating environment, but countries have found it extremely difficult to bring these attitudes into the Uruguay Round, where each liberalizing measure is viewed as a "concession" requiring a counterconcession. This has led to the question whether the agenda was too ambitious, and therefore, an impossible task from the outset. The answer then and now is that the Round's ambition sprang from necessity—a necessity to reverse trade policy trends that tended to export the effects of delays in difficult policy decisions.

Paradoxically, however, despite the danger signals of increasing defensive actions in some sectors and concentration of economic power or market management in others, domestic and international markets remained dynamic during the 1980s. This dynamism can be traced, in part, to the vigorous development of trade sectors that have benefited from deregulation of domestic markets coupled with technological advances that tended to globalize business activity, particularly in services. Consequently, part of the support for the Round may be related to the extension and preservation of these dynamics. In this respect, while there is broad support for eliminating barriers and expanding trade opportunities, there remain basic tensions between the interests of "sunrise" and "sunset" (or emerging and declining) industries, and it is often the latter that capture the greatest attention. Thus, the Round's issues are integral to the domestic policy debate—and this sets it apart from previous trade talks, which addressed mainly levels of broader protection and its rules.

Further complicating matters have been the numerous links—both tactical and functional—between issues, reflecting their complexity, the breadth of the Round's objectives, and the array of special interests. The decision early on to create 15 separate negotiating groups met the need for various negotiating aspects to have their own forum, but now, in moving to concrete results, the linkages again dominate (the 15 groups were reduced to seven in late April, 1991). At the tactical level, negotiating a balanced package means that each negotiator will agree to some points contingent upon agreement in other areas. For example, some more efficient agricultural producers have held back agreement in some areas awaiting an agricultural package. Functional linkages relate, for example, progress in product-based groups, such as textiles, to improving those rules that, for lack of clarity and difficulty of application, have pushed these sectors outside the GATT to begin with.

MARKET ACCESS ISSUES

Agriculture

The need for reform of agricultural trading policies is not in question in the Round. This sector is riddled with economic distortions that have achieved a life of their own, with some farmers being paid not to produce, and others stimulated to increase production, sometimes within the same region. The result has been rising agricultural support costs, which burdened taxpayers and consumers in the Organization for Economic Cooperation and Development (OECD) countries alone to the tune of almost $300 billion in 1988, equivalent to about 3 percent of OECD consumption expenditure and 10 percent of savings in that year. Not surprisingly, direct and indirect import barriers proliferated under these policies and export subsidies skyrocketed. But reform moves meet serious political obstacles, in part because the subsidies enable efficient producers to reap large economic rents, while the inefficient ones enjoy political leverage well beyond their numbers, owing largely to cultural and social reasons.

The United States—supported in the main by the Cairns Group of agricultural exporters (Argentina, Australia, Brazil, Canada, Chile, Colombia, Fiji, Hungary, Indonesia, Malaysia, New Zealand, the Philippines, Thailand, and Uruguay)—

has sought large reductions in export subsidies (phasing them down by 90 percent by the year 2000), with accompanying commitments to reduce internal price supports and import barriers. They argue that improved market access and better world market conditions require both direct remedies and a substantial, continuing effort. Trade developments of the past two decades seem to support this view: for example, the EC's share of world exports of agricultural products rose from 24 percent in 1970 to 36 percent in 1988, just below the almost 38 percent held by the Cairns Group and the United States together over that period. Although it is not possible to quantify the effects on the structure of trade of lower levels of EC protection, it is still illuminating that a stable export share for the EC between 1970 and 1988 would have implied an increase in the exports of other suppliers of some $43 billion.

The EC's original offer—supported in part by Japan, the Nordic countries, and Switzerland—was based on a reduction in the level of total assistance (by 30 percent over a ten-year period from its 1986 level). This would narrow the gap between world and domestic prices, but the latter would continue to be cushioned by a fixed margin of Community preference and a variable buffer to protect against exchange rate fluctuations and world market price changes. Within the overall level of assistance, protection would be "rebalanced" by raising import barriers for certain products (e.g., oilseeds), as barriers are lowered on others.

Although some flexibility in negotiating approaches emerged in Brussels, including the possibility of a specific commitment on export subsidies, the absence of a dynamic that would assure permanence of reductions in export support and of increases in market access beyond 1995 was a major element in the suspension of the negotiations in December. The basis for resumption was provided by confirmation that specific commitments in each of the areas of agricultural support—domestic support, market access, and export subsidies—would be part of the negotiations. At the same time, EC efforts to review fundamentally the workings of its internal support system, even if unrelated to the trade talks, has helped provide a better basis for a longer view. Nevertheless, a complicating factor may well be the lengthy nature of such a review process.

Textiles and Clothing

For the past three decades, trade in this area has been subject to special restrictions as the main importers (industrial countries) have asserted the need for protection against "market disruption" by lower-cost suppliers (usually developing countries). Thus, under the current Multifibre Agreement (MFA), some 50 percent of textiles and clothing trade is regulated through bilateral quotas in a continued breach of the GATT's nondiscrimination principle. With developing and Eastern European countries relying on these goods for almost 40 percent of their manufactured exports, and with potential higher value-added production hampered by fears that successful investment would lead to a broadening of quotas, developing countries, in particular, insist that integration of the sector into GATT be based on a phase-out of the MFA.

Under the draft text, the MFA would be phased out in three stages over a ten-year period. But only 45 percent of covered products would be liberalized before the final stage, and countries could choose the timing for bringing specific products under the GATT. Consequently, liberalization of the most sensitive products could be left to the end, raising doubts about achieving full integration into the GATT by the specified terminal date. Further, during the phase-out,

countries could introduce discriminatory restrictions on those products not already made subject to the GATT, or on which they do not have existing bilateral arrangements.

All these elements, which reflect strong vested interests in the status quo, especially in the United States, make it unclear that the phase-out will be trade-expanding, particularly in the initial stage; but bringing MFA trade back under GATT means *de facto* acceptance that bilateral sectoral management of trade is at odds with multilateral rules, thereby halting the drift in that direction. The latter, however, as well as implementation of the phase-out, critically depends on strengthened GATT rules, particularly on antidumping and trade in counterfeit goods, and on the readiness of developing countries to open their own markets.

Traditional Market Access Issues

Progress in other market access areas—tariffs, nontariff measures (NTMs), and natural resource-based and tropical products—is closely connected to progress in agriculture. As it is the overall incidence of border protection that matters, few countries are ready to commit to lower NTMs until they have a clearer view of the outcome in tariffs, and vice versa. Willingness to reduce NTMs also depends on the results in the rule-making areas (e.g., safeguards).

Negotiations on tariffs have proved difficult, in part because previous trade rounds reduced average tariff rates on manufactures in industrial countries to about 5 percent, leaving most industrial participants with tariffs concentrated in sensitive areas. Moreover, the low averages frequently disguise both tariff peaks and tariff escalation (where tariff rates for a commodity rise with the degree of processing)—both key issues for developing countries. A substantial package may be within sight, however, especially if it incorporates the US offer of a so-called "zero-for-zero" option, under which industrial countries would reduce some 2,000 industrial tariff lines to zero or very low rates. This still presents problems in some sensitive areas, but could well be accepted in others, including chemicals, pharmaceuticals, and, perhaps, steel. A positive outcome could also result in a sizable increase in bindings (a legal commitment not to raise a specific tariff above a given level) by developing countries and in significant reductions in their tariffs. This would support the permanency of the recent trade liberalization in many developing countries and be a major step toward the active partnership sought by the industrial countries.

RULES

In recent years, trade expansion and, consequently, investment, has been deterred not so much by tariffs as by numerous measures that were largely of a unilateral and bilateral nature, of dubious GATT legality, and implemented with little predictability. Bringing clarity and consistency to trading rules, along with a credible dispute settlement mechanism, therefore, is key to achieving the objectives of the Round. But the need to balance the rights and obligations of signatories, and the imperative of not losing the objectives of consistency and appropriate tightness in the process, has created great difficulty. Thus, in the search for compromise in the important areas—safeguards, antidumping, and subsidies—the price for bringing all trade back into the GATT may turn out to be high in terms of allowing relatively easy access to defensive action. The limited effect of the commitment not to use measures inconsistent with the GATT during the negotiations and, indeed, to roll them back so that they could be eliminated by the Round's end, point in that direction. By contrast, there has been progress toward a more credible dispute settlement mechanism.

Safeguards

The need to incorporate temporary protection of industries injured by import competition into the system is evident. Since the mid-1970s, the perceived inadequacy of the safeguard rules has led to their being increasingly by-passed through recourse to bilateral actions, such as voluntary export restraints, that restrict imports of a product from selected sources. Re-establishing GATT control over such actions has been central to the safeguards negotiations, with the key issue being whether actions should be applied selectively. The EC has argued for selectivity, while smaller industrial and developing countries prefer nondiscrimination, as they fear that selective measures both increase their vulnerability to pressure from major traders and can lead to market-sharing arrangements. Recently, the EC proposed a modified form of selectivity—"modulated" quotas—covering all suppliers, but the degree of restraint would vary according to the perceived contribution of individual suppliers to disruption of domestic industry.

The other elements of a safeguards agreement seem clear, although their implications are less so. The critical points include the following: (1) countries could assert injury to domestic producers and take measures, initially largely beyond multilateral questioning; (2) measures could be in place for five to eight years, and trading partners could not initiate compensation or retaliation procedures during the first three years at least; (3) measures would be price-based, in principle, but "modulated" quotas could change this; and (4) measures would be eased progressively and subject to multilateral monitoring and dispute settlement procedures. In return, participants would rule out non-GATT specified measures and phase out existing ones over a three- to four-year period. However, the relatively easy access to safeguards could open the danger of first-resort use. The main benefits would lie in the increased transparency in the use of safeguard measures, the progressiveness of their phase-out, and their being subject to multilateral surveillance.

Antidumping

Abuse is central to the negotiations on antidumping. These actions are meant to protect domestic producers against predatorily priced imports, but they may now have become a preferred protective instrument in some countries. For example, since 1980, the four leading users of antidumping measures (Australia, Canada, the EC, and the United States) have initiated over 1,000 investigations, of which some 50 percent have led to action. As a result, the countries that are often subject to such actions—led by Japan and other Asian exporters—want clear rules to prevent unpredictability; they suggest an agreed methodology for calculating dumping margins and strict limits for the period between initiation and definitive findings of antidumping actions. On the other side, the EC and the United States want the rules to cover circumvention (e.g., assembly of dumped inputs in the domestic or third markets). But the framing of rules to determine "intent" in investment decisions is difficult in the face of internationalization of production that can make exporting via third countries, or moving assembly operations into markets, an economically sensible undertaking. There is also the danger of loss of consistency in dealing with local content rules (see section on TRIMs). The need to find a solution is the more pressing as failure to do so could well delay imple-

mentation of, if not agreement to, the phasing out of the MFA.

Subsidies

Although there is virtually a worldwide move toward reduction of subsidies, these efforts have taken on Herculean aspects, as they involve difficult internal policy dilemmas of which trade distortion is only one aspect. Addressing them primarily in the context of trading rules has created basic difficulties, especially for the EC, which has to balance the domestic priorities of its member states while retaining sufficient flexibility vis-à-vis other participants. In this respect, moves by the EC to limit sector-specific subsidies, in the context of completing its internal market integration by 1992, may assist its Uruguay Round position.

The central point concerns outright prohibition of subsidies. The United States would go furthest, prohibiting all export subsidies and those domestic subsidies that distort trade. The EC, Japan, Korea, the Nordic countries, and Switzerland would treat agricultural export subsidies within agriculture, but would prohibit others, including those that relate to export performance. However, neither Japan nor the EC would prohibit domestic subsidies; the EC would deal with these on a case-by-case basis, depending on clearly demonstrated negative trade effects, and would rely on tightened countervailing measures. Most developing countries resist outright prohibition, arguing that subsidies are an essential development instrument. But given domestic budgetary pressures and the need to fend off domestic vested interests, a number might well agree to limitation on industrial export subsidies.

Dispute Settlement

A major problem in this area has been the painfully slow process of adopting and implementing findings of GATT panels. However, negotiators now are close to an agreement that could improve this situation materially. The agreement provides that, unless the GATT Council decides to the contrary, panel findings would be adopted automatically. Moreover, retaliation would be possible if the findings were not implemented within defined time limits. This contrasts with present procedures, which require an explicit Council decision for adoption of findings, normally on a consensus basis. Even this improvement, however, does not provide small traders with appropriate leverage in case of non-implementation, given that it is based on retaliation. In return for injecting some automaticity into dispute settlement procedures, countries would renounce the use of unilateral measures inconsistent with GATT rules. At issue is the operation of Section 301 of US trade law and the tendency of other countries to emulate that law. But many countries, including the United States, would not undertake such a commitment without appropriate results on dispute settlement and elsewhere in the Round. Thus, material improvement in the dispute settlement mechanism could be lost if other elements of the package lag.

NEW AREAS

Trade-Related Investment Measures (TRIMs)

As with subsidies, many participants regard certain TRIMs as a form of protection in that they divert trade and encourage inefficient production. Most industrial countries hold that certain TRIMs—such as local content and trade balancing requirements—should be prohibited as they are contrary to present GATT Articles (on national treatment and the elimination of quantitative re-strictions, respectively); further, prohibition also should include export performance requirements, which are not currently covered by the GATT. By contrast, many developing countries maintain that TRIMs are necessary for development purposes and opt for a case-by-case approach that addresses only clearly identified adverse trade effects. A further question is whether disciplines should apply only to requirements that are to be met by investors, or also, as argued by many OECD countries, to measures that offer or withdraw incentives, such as subsidies or tax advantages, and that, therefore, could become TRIMs as well. Despite the basic questions, a compromise appeared possible in Brussels, with many developing countries indicating a willingness to accept the prohibition of those TRIMs that would be regarded as running counter to GATT rules.

Trade-Related Aspects of Intellectual Property Rights (TRIPs)

National sovereignty concerns also dominated the early discussions on TRIPs—an area where the United States, for example, estimates it is losing tens of billions of dollars. However, developing countries now agree on the need to deal with trade in counterfeit goods, estimated to have grown to 3–6 percent of world trade. The debate on intellectual property rights has generally sought to balance protection for the holders of these rights with the national objectives of developing countries, including technology transfers and avoidance of high charges for patent rights, at least in certain socially sensitive areas (e.g., pharmaceuticals). Basic agreement seems possible on substantive norms to protect these rights and on multilateral disciplines to enforce the norms. There remains a question on where to lodge enforcement of rules and disciplines on TRIPs—in GATT, including its dispute settlement mechanism, or elsewhere.

Services

Bringing this area—which covers some 20 percent of world trade—under multi-lateral rules is a major element in a strong Uruguay Round package. Negotiating difficulties include the problems associated both with bringing under one framework a "supersector" comprising very diverse subsectors and the tendency to carry over existing language, some of which is under negotiation, from the GATT into the agreement—meaning that the emerging framework may well include some GATT ambiguities.

The main issues are threefold:

- devising appropriate rules for trade in services, especially as delivery of a service frequently depends on the right of establishment (e.g., a subsidiary in a foreign market). Negotiation of the latter falls outside the limits of the traditional GATT and, therefore, is being challenged by some. An important point of debate is whether, in case of disputes, countries could retaliate across services sectors—a particular concern in financial services—and across services and goods, as well;
- formulating coverage, as a number of sectors are managed by bilateral treaties (civil aviation), and others are effectively closed to genuine competition—either to accommodate strong domestic and cartel-type interests (maritime services, especially in the United States), or because they are in the hands of government monopolies (telecommunications in most countries); and
- confronting the "free-rider" issue, which springs from the fact that in a number of areas and in a number of countries, market access has been

largely unregulated, if not relatively free. This raises the question of how to bring along those who are reluctant to liberalize access. The US proposal to make most-favored-nation (MFN) treatment conditional, based on the degree of access participants are willing to bind, was opposed as compromising a basic principle of the GATT; the EC's sectoral nonapplication approach, based on a participant's liberalization commitments for a particular sector, creates problems for countries that seek to trade off a higher level of commitments in one sector against a lower one in another.

These deliberations have led to a reassessment of the benefits to be derived from a services agreement, both by those who were the main proponents and those who were initially unconvinced. As the ardor of the former tempered during the discussions, some of the later began to see material advantages. With mutual interests more apparent, there is now a large constituency in favor of an agreement, including most major traders among developing countries.

CONCLUSION

With complex issues to be resolved, it is not surprising that the systemic issues of how to improve the functioning of the multilateral trading system and how to strengthen the responsibilities of the GATT and its Secretariat have taken a back seat. Thus, the question of increasing the GATT's contribution to improved coherence in global policymaking, including strengthened cooperation with the IMF and the World Bank, has been left to some appropriate time down the road. Consideration of closer ties between the institutions also depends upon whether the GATT is to evolve toward a

World Trade Organization, which would bring all multilateral trade treaties under one roof.

Whatever form the GATT takes, a successful outcome of the Uruguay Round means increased responsibilities. This is so because the results need to be comprehensive if they are to set the trading environment—and hence help shape the external environment within which countries formulate their adjustment and growth objectives—for the next several decades. This has become increasingly clear with the difficulties negotiators have faced, including the possibility of losing the Round entirely. Thus, virtually for the first time, businessmen worldwide are making a concerted effort to voice their interest in not allowing the talks to be derailed.

Without a successful Uruguay Round, one of the main worries is that the trend toward bilateral and regional trading agreements is likely to accelerate and might do so in a way not supportive of the growth of global trade. Ideally, the formation of these pacts would work toward member countries' opening their markets globally as well, so that any trade diversion could generally be presumed to be offset by trade creation. It was on that basis, for example, that the Canada-United States Free-Trade Agreement was put forward. However, the belief that global trade creation may only be a major part of the dynamics of regional integration has given impetus to the expansion, if not formation, of these regional groupings (e.g., the recent spate of EC membership and association applications, the prospect of a European Economic Space, and the moves toward more free trade agreements in the Western Hemisphere). Moreover, if market access were reasonably assured on a regional basis only, production decisions within a country would be based on regional rather than on general market signals and could fall short of potential.

The recent resumption of the negotiations obviously constitutes a necessary, but not a sufficient, step toward success. It needs to be coupled with a genuine commitment to confronting and solving the underlying problems that have repeatedly stopped the Round. It would be ironic if the virtually worldwide trend toward allowing national economies to be guided by market signals were to be frustrated by an inability to allow these same signals to guide the complex workings of the multilateral trading system.

CHAPTER 7

The American Economy and
International Investment

This section is concerned with the political economy of international investment. Robert Kudrle, in "Foreign Direct Investment in the United States," reviews four recent books on the political economy of foreign direct investment. He notes that concern about excessive foreign investment in the United States focuses on four issues: national autonomy, political activity by foreign-owned firms, threats to national security, and the availability of foreign-supplied firms. Kudrle analyzes the effects of foreign direct investment in terms of production and competition, spillovers, taxation, income and factor shares, and the terms of trade.

The second article is by Phedon Nicolaides, who takes a liberal, neoclassical approach to international investment. Nicolaides argues that "foreign firms should not be prevented from entering a country's domestic market (i.e., the right of establishment) and once they are established in the domestic market they should not be subject to any special restrictions or requirements (i.e., national treatment)." He reviews the arguments concerning the effects of direct foreign investment on employment, trade, and technology transfer. He concludes that "the distinction between domestic and outside markets or national and foreign firms is hardly the basis for rational policies" in an increasingly integrated world economy.

25.   Foreign Direct Investment in the United States*

Robert T. Kudrle

SARA L. GORDON AND FRANCIS A. LEES. *Foreign Multinational Investment in the United States: Struggle for Industrial Supremacy.* New York: Quorum Books, 1986.

MARTIN TOLCHIN AND SUSAN TOLCHIN. *Buying into America: How Foreign Money Is Changing the Face of Our Nation.* New York: Times Books, 1988.

NORMAN J. GLICKMAN AND DOUGLAS P. WOODWARD. *The New Competitors: How Foreign Investors Are Changing the U.S. Economy.* New York: Basic Books, 1989.

EDWARD M. GRAHAM AND PAUL R. KRUGMAN. *Foreign Direct Investment in the United States.* Washington, D.C.: Institute for International Economics, 1989.

As recently as 1978, C. Fred Bergsten, Thomas Horst, and Theodore Moran were able to address the most urgent issues linking U.S. welfare and direct investment in a book called *American Multinationals and American Interests.*[1] A

decade later, the focus of policy attention had shifted almost completely. Scores of books and articles attempted to interpret the flow of incoming foreign direct investment (IFDI) that raised the 2.1 percent share of the U.S. nonfinancial corporate assets held by foreign-controlled enterprises to 10.6 percent over the period from 1977 to 1990.[2] Although the foreign role remains far lower in the United States than in virtually any other modern economy except Japan, it is growing rapidly. Moreover, when valued at estimated replacement cost or market value, IFDI by the end of 1988 was roughly half the value of U.S. direct investment abroad.[3] The United States now leads the world as both "source" and "host."

Increasing IFDI has generated alarm among opinion makers and the public. According to Massachusetts Institute of Technology economist Paul Krugman, "The political issue of the 1990s isn't going to be imports; it's going to be the

SOURCE: Reprinted from *International Organization,* vol. 45, no. 3, Summer 1991, pp. 397–424 by permission of the MIT Press, Cambridge, Massachusetts. Copyright © 1991 by the World Peace Foundation and the Massachusetts Institute of Technology.

* Research for this article was supported by the Center for Urban and Regional Affairs, University of Minnesota. I am grateful to Vijetha Dasappa, Robert Denemark, Earl Fry, Stephen Hoenack, Robert Hudec, Morris Kleiner, Stephen Krasner, Simon Reich, G. Edward Schuh, Susan Strange, and two referees for valuable comments on an earlier version of the article, which was originally prepared for delivery at the 31st Annual Convention of the International Studies Association, Washington, D.C., 13 April 1990.

[1] C. Fred Bergsten, Thomas Horst, and Theodore H. Moran, *American Multinationals and American Interests* (Washington, D.C.: Brookings Institution, 1978).

[2] In *Foreign Direct Investment,* pp. 10–16, Graham and Krugman present several alternative measures of the foreign role and explain their strengths and limitations.

[3] See Robert Eisner and Paul Pieper, "The World's Greatest Debtor Nation?" *North American Review of Economics and Finance* 1 (Spring 1990), pp. 9–32. Eisner and Pieper object strongly to the use of the term "debtor" to describe a negative net investment position overall. Only indirect (portfolio) investment involves debt. Moreover, published statistics that show the United States behind in direct investment mislead because they employ historical book values, and U.S. assets abroad are older than foreign holdings in the United States.

foreign invasion of the United States."[4]
A 1988 poll showed 78 percent public
support for limiting foreign investments
in business and real estate. Such stalwart
defenders of free enterprise as William
Safire and the late Malcolm Forbes have
suggested general controls, and Strom
Thurmond has sponsored them. With foreign investment, as with import penetration, some critics claim damage of the intrusion itself, while others allege lack of
U.S. access abroad.[5] Japanese investment
causes particular alarm, although it was
still less than 20 percent of total IFDI in
1989.

WHAT HAPPENED?

Direct investment essentially means the
multinational corporation,[6] and modern
theory assigns its spread to firm-specific
advantages that can be most profitably
employed by operation in more than one
country rather than by trading or licensing.[7] All of the books under review at

least implicitly agree that the share of
such advantages accruing to non-Ameri-
can firms has grown dramatically in recent years.

Firms go abroad almost entirely for one
or more of three reasons: to sell, to produce, or to learn. The first two involve
the efficient exploitation of the firm's assets, and the third is an attempt to gain
or augment them.[8] Over most of the postwar period, U.S. manufacturing and service firms invested overseas to market
and produce their wares where economically attractive or politically necessary.
As late as the 1970s, much foreign direct
investment coming to the United States
was at least partially motivated by the
desire to learn transferable production
and marketing lessons in the world's
most advanced market. The balance has
now shifted substantially. Thousands of

[4] Paul Krugman, quoted in "Foreign Firms
Build U.S. Factories, Vex American Rivals,"
Wall Street Journal, 24 July 1987, p. A6.

[5] A good account of current U.S. political
activity is Earl Fry's "Foreign Direct Investment in the United States: Public Policy Options," paper presented at the 31st Annual
Convention of the International Studies Association, Washington, D.C., 13 April 1990.

[6] Official data assign to foreigners any investment that is owned 10 percent or more by
a single foreign interest; this interest is typically a corporation. While the percentage
seems low, it is usually enough for control,
and the data apparently would change little
even if it were raised to 20 or 50 percent. See
Graham and Krugman's discussion in *Foreign
Direct Investment,* pp. 8–10.

[7] Hymer is credited with several of the original insights that were later refined and
expanded by Kindleberger and Caves. See
Stephen H. Hymer, "The International
Operations of National Firms: A Study of Direct Foreign Investment," Ph.D. diss., Massachusetts Institute of Technology, 1960 (published in 1976 by MIT Press, Cambridge,
Mass.); Charles P. Kindleberger, *American*

*Business Abroad: Six Lectures on Direct In-
vestment* (New Haven, Conn.: Yale University
Press, 1969); and Richard E. Caves, "International Corporations: The Industrial Economics
of Foreign Investment," *Economica* 38 (February 1971), pp. 1–27. Much of the foreign activity of U.S. firms since World War II can be
interpreted in terms of the diffusion of U.S.
innovations. See the following works by Raymond Vernon: "International Investment and
International Trade in the Product Cycle,"
Quarterly Journal of Economics 80 (May 1966),
pp. 190–207; and *Sovereignty at Bay: The Multinational Spread of U.S. Enterprises* (New
York: Basic Books, 1971). For a concise account of the growth of direct investment in the
context of international relations, see Robert
Gilpin, *The Political Economy of International
Relations* (Princeton, N.J.: Princeton University Press, 1987), chap. 6.

[8] A fourth motive, to escape or hide, also
generates some nominal multinationality. Foreign investment in so-called tax havens, such
as the Netherlands Antilles, developed almost
entirely because of the territory's legal and tax
structure and had little if anything to do with
the rest of its economy. In general, the strategy
pursued by a firm will obviously be partly
driven by the behavior of competitors and often by the pressures of source and host country
governments.

foreign firms in the United States exploit their preexisting advantages and adjust their production mix between source and host (or third) countries virtually as American firms have done for decades, while U.S. firms abroad are increasingly likely to learn valuable lessons beyond local tastes and customs. Deeper causes of the change include the slow U.S. productivity advance relative to foreign source countries and the concomitantly shifting relative shares of economic innovation. The rising ratio of IFDI to U.S. investment abroad can plausibly be interpreted as yet another manifestation of declining U.S. economy hegemony.

FOUR ACCOUNTS OF U.S. IFDI

In his recent review of the strategic trade literature, J. David Richardson notes that all contributors to the trade debate share one common policy criterion: "a high and rising standard of living."[9] A satisfactory evaluation of IFDI must necessarily rest on a broader base. Following a substantial literature, this review will consider the books' analyses of the autonomy and security as well as the prosperity implications of IFDI.[10]

IFDI plays an increasingly critical role in the integration of the world economy, a goal that the United States has championed with varying degrees of enthusiasm for nearly a half century. This essay will argue that most of the concerns raised about IFDI in the United States are either misdirected or exaggerated and that general apprehension may obscure the few areas in which policy attention could increase the already substantial U.S. net benefits. Moreover, adoption of the main policy initiatives advocated by all of the authors except Edward Graham and Paul Krugman would directly lower U.S. welfare and could seriously disrupt established and prospective international cooperation.

Each of the books presents a central dominant message that relates most closely to one of the three goals.

Foreign Multinational Investment in the United States

Sara Gordon and Francis Lees argue that the geopolitical role of the United States as a superpower demands a strong manufacturing base, some of which must remain independent of foreign ownership. Moreover, they attempt to develop spe-

---

[9] J. David Richardson, "The Political Economy of Strategic Trade Policy," *International Organization* 44 (Winter 1990), p. 112.

[10] The three goals are employed by Strange, Keohane and Nye, and Kudrle and Bobrow. See Susan Strange, "Transnational Relations," *International Affairs* 52 (July 1976), pp. 333–45; Robert O. Keohane and Joseph S. Nye, *Power and Interdependence: World Politics in Transition* (Boston: Little, Brown, 1977); and Robert T. Kudrle and Davis B. Bobrow, "U.S. Policy Toward Foreign Direct Investment," *World Politics* 34 (April 1982), pp. 353–79. A fourth goal, "national assertion," may also motivate behavior. See Keohane and Nye, *Power and Independence,* p. 45; the concept is further explored in Robert T. Kudrle and Stefanie A. Lenway, "Progress for the Rich: The Canada-U.S. Free Trade Agreement," in Emanuel Adler and Beverly Crawford, eds., *Progress in*

Post-War International Relations (New York: Columbia University Press, 1991), pp. 235–72. Following Johnson, some writers refer to autonomy and security as "noneconomic" goals because they do not involve privately consumable goods and services. See Harry G. Johnson, "The Efficiency and Welfare Implications of the Multinational Corporation," in Charles P. Kindleberger, ed., *The International Corporation: A Symposium* (Cambridge, Mass.: MIT Press, 1970), pp. 35–56. In fact, economists have long used national defense as an archetype of a collective good. See Francis M. Bator, "The Anatomy of Market Failure," *Quarterly Journal of Economics* 72 (August 1958), p. 370. Usage turns largely on the writer's relative emphasis on economics as the study of a particular set of human activities rather than as a methodology.

cific criteria by which IFDI can be evaluated. They try to compare foreign affiliates and domestic firms in several quantifiable dimensions to develop an overall index of "favorable contributions to the domestic economy." They also identify sectors of high-technology and military demand in which foreign ownership is deemed problematic.

Buying into America

Martin and Susan Tolchin, whose work is the only one to consider both direct and indirect (noncontrolling, portfolio) investment, appear most directly concerned with autonomy. They fear both the leverage that the holding of U.S. debt may give foreign governments and the influence that direct investors may already be exercising on the U.S. policy process. Their narrative often takes the form of dramatic and memorable vignettes. Sometimes this device works well, but frequently the reader is led to draw conclusions on the basis of inadequate information.[11]

The New Competitors

Norman Glickman and Douglas Woodward press for attention to a particular aspect of the prosperity criterion: high,

secure incomes for blue-collar workers and the economic stability of their communities. Their book focuses on the threats and promises that IFDI poses for this objective. Other considerations are touched upon, but this single yardstick dominates their evaluation of IFDI and of outgoing investment as well.[12] Virtually all of the authors' original research involves elaborate calculations of jobs "gained" and "lost" through employment shifts induced by foreign firms. The authors stress the similarity between U.S. firms and foreign firms and conclude that "the new competitors" are a symptom of U.S. economic decline rather than a cause.

Foreign Direct Investment in the United States

The previous three books share a common explicit assumption: when the restrictive conditions of perfect competition do not hold, no presumption about the benefit of IFDI should be made. Graham and Krugman start from a different position. They assume that "free market outcomes are innocent until proven guilty."[13] Graham and Krugman rest their presumption of gain on the role of direct investment as the handmaiden of trade and on the argument that (despite the implications of the other books) recent developments in trade theory do not overturn the case for openness from either a national or a cosmopolitan point of view.[14] They warn of the threat to prosperity from just those changes in policy,

---

[11] The Tolchins' account of Bridgestone's acquisition of failing Firestone facilities is compelling. But their interpretations are sometimes not only incomplete but also economically incoherent. They observe, for example, that the "slow pace of foreign reciprocity in encouraging U.S. outward investment further diminishes the hope of offsetting the current account deficit with more extensive overseas investments in foreign markets." They also offer the following argument: "Although it is not blamed as often as the budget deficit, the trade deficit—as excess of imports over exports—should also take some of the blame for contributing to America's new status as a debtor nation." Both quotes are from p. 181 of *Buying Into America.*

[12] Outgoing investment is discussed by Glickman and Woodward in chap. 6 of *The New Competitors.*
[13] Graham and Krugman, *Foreign Direct Investment,* p. 116.
[14] Comparative advantage retains central importance in modern trade theory albeit "complemented and to some extent supplemented" by newer approaches based on increasing returns. See Elhanan Helpman and

particularly the screening of IFDI, which are advocated in the other books. Overall, their brief yet comprehensive study builds on both careful analysis and previous scholarship in a way that puts it in a class by itself.

Some might question whether all four books are sufficiently scholarly to command consideration in these pages. Few would raise that issue about Graham and Krugman's work: serious scholars produced a concise yet comprehensive monograph with the imprimatur of a major research organization. Yet this book arguably rests on less original research than does that of Gordon and Lees or that of Glickman and Woodward. *Foreign Multinational Investment in the United States* is a pioneering, if ultimately unsatisfying, attempt by academic economists to evaluate IFDI from a comprehensive perspective, and *The New Competitors* is based on highly sophisticated research regarding employment issues. *Buying Into America* may appear most questionable, but the Tolchins brought to their task a formidable combination of academic and journalistic talent, producing a work praised by many influentials and selected as one of *Business Week*'s ten best books of 1988. If the impact on discussion by the attentive public is given any weight, the Tolchins are hard to exclude, despite their book's

general failure to analyze satisfactorily what it reports.

This essay will deal first with autonomy and security issues and next with prosperity issues, evaluating the analysis and prescription offered by the books on each subject. A final section will treat IFDI explicitly as an international relations problem.

AUTONOMY AND SECURITY

Autonomy issues provide much of the basis for global suspicion about IFDI—from the writings of the *dependentistas* to the protection of "cultural" industries from U.S. direct investment in the Canada-U.S. Free Trade Agreement. For the United States, however, autonomy concerns tend to be instrumental and focused on maintaining the will and the power to serve security, prosperity, or both.[15] Apprehension about security generates the deepest fears.

Paul Krugman, *Trade Policy and Market Structure* (Cambridge, Mass.: MIT Press, 1989), p. xi. Krugman is one of the major figures in the development of the modern theory upon which some writers have based new arguments for government intervention. Krugman, however, takes pains to distinguish theoretical possibilities from real situations and endorses an essentially free trade policy. See Paul Krugman, "Is Free Trade Passe?" *Journal of Economic Perspectives* 1 (Winter 1987), pp. 131–44. This scarcely settles the issue, of course. For a fair, complete, and recent account, see Richardson, "The Political Economy of Strategic Trade Policy."

[15] It might be useful to differentiate at least four types of challenge to autonomy from increasing international economic interdependence. First, economic interdependence diminishes the sense of being "master of one's own house" almost mechanically through the increasingly powerful web of market connections. The widely lamented inability of countries to pursue their own monetary policies is an example. When Glickman and Woodward observe that "direct investment has made nations more interdependent and allowed them less control of their own destinies" (*The New Competitors*, p. 276), they could just as well have been writing of trade or indirect investment. Such market linkages do not imply purposive foreign manipulation. Second, market penetration alone may alter tastes and values in ways that threaten national autonomy. Third, autonomy can be diminished by external manipulation of prices and quantities for specific foreign—usually state—purposes. Schacht's binding of several Balkan states to the Third Reich through trade leverage provides perhaps the most vivid historical example. And, fourth, autonomy can be lost from purposive foreign influence on culture or politics. IFDI contributes uniquely only to this fourth threat, although it can clearly magnify

General Concerns about Foreign Influence and Control

Disquiet about foreign influence pervades *Buying into America.* The Tolchins assert that "the ease with which foreigners purchase American newspapers is unique."[16] In so doing, they employ a rhetorical device with which the book abounds. Instead of arguing damage to the United States, they merely stress that many other nations do not follow U.S. practice, leaving the reader to conclude that foreigners are guarding their own well-being more successfully than Americans are. But the inference does not follow. Policy control over IFDI is propelled by the same political forces that generate import controls, and in neither case can we presume that protectionism increases national welfare. In fact, nowhere do the Tolchins argue that Rupert Murdoch and Robert Maxwell operate their publications in a way that consistently serves any foreign private or public power, nor do they suggest how this could be done.[17] Control in any sphere implies single-entity dominance or else collusion, and they find none. If a more subtle "orientation" bothers the Tolchins, they might consider the virtually global dominance of U.S. perspectives in news services and in popular entertainment.

The Tolchins are certainly right that the United States has consistently provided a regime of unsurpassed openness. Graham and Krugman explain that significant federal controls apply only to some activities subject to general regulation at the federal level (such as broadcasting and transportation); the states also impose some restrictions, mainly on the ownership of agricultural land.[18]

Some autonomy concerns stem not from present foreign ownership but from fears about future foreign control of the U.S. economy. Only Graham and Krugman address this issue. They assume that there is no reason to expect that the role of IFDI in the United States (expressed relative to the size of the U.S. economy) will in the near future exceed the share which accumulated in Europe over the postwar period and which has changed little over the last decade. They then forecast that when the share of foreign direct investment reaches a peak in the United States, the level will be lower than that presently observed in Europe, where a considerable amount of investment in the major European countries is intra-European and therefore considered "foreign" rather than domestic. In 1986, for example, foreigners controlled 7 percent of manufacturing employment in the United States, 13 percent in Germany, 14 percent in Britain, and 21 percent in France.[19]

---

the impact of the other three. The second and fourth categories may affect not only autonomy of action but also autonomy of thought by altering the perspective with which issues are viewed.

[16] Tolchin and Tolchin, *Buying Into America,* p. 24.

[17] Less than complete editorial independence by the Korean-owned *Washington Times,* cited by the Tolchins on p. 23 of *Buying Into America,* led to extremely damaging publicity.

[18] See Graham and Krugman, *Foreign Direct Investment,* pp. 95–107. For a more detailed account of U.S. controls, see Harvey Bale, Jr., "United States Policy Toward Inward Foreign Direct Investment," *Vanderbilt Journal of Transnational Law* 24 (Spring 1985), pp. 199–222.

[19] See Graham and Krugman, *Foreign Direct Investment,* pp. 24–26. When I undertook a static forecast based on only the time trend since 1978 as an independent variable, I found the current 11 percent foreign ownership of U.S. nonfinancial corporate assets climbing to over 20 percent by 2005. Such an extrapolation is useful mainly as the starting point for discussion, however. Data were taken from the Board of Governors, Federal Reserve System, *Balance Sheets for the U.S. Economy, 1945–89,* Washington, D.C., mimeograph, October 1990.

What should be made of the alarming scenario presented by the Tolchins that some shock could trigger a sudden conversion of foreign portfolio holdings—several times the size of the stock of IFDI—into controlling investment, causing foreign control to skyrocket? Glickman and Woodward deny the plausibility of such a development; they argue that anything shaking portfolio investors' confidence would cause capital flight and not conversion. More generally, most indirect investors do not regard direct investment as a close substitute.

While the future percentage of foreign ownership of U.S. industry is difficult to forecast and while some may be unpersuaded by Graham and Krugman's approach, none of the books makes a case for the critical importance of any particular aggregate or even sectorial threshold.

Data and Disclosure   General autonomy unease is heightened by fears about the inadequacy of data on foreign direct investment. The Tolchins attribute to unnamed "experts" the sensational and oft-repeated charge that "at least 50 percent of all foreign investment goes unreported."[20] Graham and Krugman's extensive evaluation of Department of Commerce data counters such claims; they argue persuasively that no substantial category of IFDI is significantly understated.

Buying Into America and *The New Competitors* argue strongly that more disclosure is needed about IFDI, but they differ in what that means. The Tolchins favor something like the approach of Representative John Bryant (a Texas Democrat), who proposed that foreign firms be required to disclose operating information even though the firms are not publicly traded in the United States.[21]

Glickman and Woodward remind the reader that the government information system for IFDI, in place since the mid-1970s, is based on the anonymity of individual firms, and they oppose the Bryant amendment, opting instead for a public reporting system of industry-level rather than firm-level data.[22]

Graham and Krugman argue that the government has virtually all of the data it needs, although more information, suitably aggregated to protect confidentiality, could be made available for research (see their Appendix A). Like Glickman and Woodward, they oppose the Bryant amendment, but they suggest that more than the principle of anonymity is involved: requiring public disclosure of operating information might discourage some foreign investors, partly because it would portend more restrictions in the future. The last argument is difficult to judge, but the circumstances in which disclosure alone would dampen foreign interest should be rare. As Graham and Krugman explain, all publicly traded firms in the United States must file 10K forms with the Securities and Exchange Commission, and these forms contain more detailed information than the Bryant amendment calls for.

The passage of the Bryant amendment seems largely a symbolic act without substantial impact. Discrimination against foreigners would result unless large, closely held U.S. firms were also required to make more public filings at the same time, and perhaps they should be.[23] More information might somewhat improve

---

[20] Tolchin and Tolchin, *Buying Into America,* p. 244.

[21] Ibid., p, 261.

[22] In *The New Competitors,* pp. 280–81, Glickman and Woodward complain about the inaccuracy of some of the data from the Bureau of Economic Analysis, but they give only one example of the kind of information they would like to be made public: the number of new jobs created by all foreign-owned firms by industry and state during a given year.

[23] In *Foreign Direct Investment,* pp. 113–15, Graham and Krugman suggest a possible in-

the bargaining prospects of organized labor with the affected firms,[24] but no private or public foreign threat would be uncovered.

Political Activity by Foreign-Owned Firms

The three most recent books all consider political activity connected with IFDI. But none draws a sharp distinction between levers of political influence which are available to foreigners in general and those which accrue to direct investors in particular. The Tolchins and Glickman and Woodward stress the influence of foreign-controlled political action committees (PACs) at the national level and the more varied influence of foreigners (depending partly on state law) in state and local politics.[25] Glickman and Woodward admit, however, that the PAC expenditures of most direct investors are quite modest.[26] Foreign and domestic firms alike use much more money to influence federal government decisions directly. For example, Glickman and Woodward discuss the lobbying of To-

shiba America's employees,[27] but this played only a minor part in the massive campaign to minimize penalties for insufficient monitoring of Soviet-bloc trade. Most important, the lobbying on Toshiba's behalf by affected U.S. firms stemmed from Toshiba's importance as a supplier; its direct investor role was relatively minor. This in no way denies that the case speaks volumes about economic interdependence and the permeability of federal decision-making structures.[28]

Despite widespread apprehension, relatively little has been suggested to curb the political activity of direct investors. The Tolchins clearly approve of Senator Lloyd Bentsen's efforts to disallow employee PACs of foreign-owned corporations on the grounds that foreigners should not participate in U.S. elections either "directly or through any other person."[29] Others have proposed that such

---

[27] Ibid.

[28] For an insightful account of the general problem, see Beverly Crawford, "Export Controls in an Interdependent World," Institute of International Studies, University of California, Berkeley, mimeograph, 1989. Even the Tolchins note that excessive political pressure can backfire (see Buying Into America, pp. 262–63). "Foreign influence" is viewed with alarm in every country; this point is developed in greater length in Robert T. Kudrle, "The Several Faces of the Multinational Corporation," in Ladd Hollist and F. Lamond Tullis, eds., An International Political Economy, vol. 1 of the International Political Economy Yearbook (Boulder, Colo.: Westview Press, 1983), pp. 175–97.

[29] See Tolchin and Tolchin, Buying Into America, p. 17. American employees of the firms (the only ones eligible to contribute) understandably regard such a restriction as an abridgment of their rights. And, as Glickman and Woodward note in The New Competitors, p. 273, the average PAC contribution of a foreign-owned firm in 1985-86 was only $796, which was less than the $1,000 ceiling on an individual contribution. The maximum PAC contribution per candidate was $25,000 per election.

ternational agreement on disclosure, which would probably be necessary to get complete parent firm information. Nonetheless, if the basic idea was accepted, nothing would inhibit unilateral U.S. action on both foreign subsidiaries and closely held domestic firms except a desire to trade U.S. reform for foreign concessions.

[24] Other things constant, a shift of foreign profits to domestic wages would raise national income.

[25] In Buying Into America, the Tolchins discuss at great length the successful campaign by foreign firms against various states' unitary tax laws, which effectively taxed firms for activity completely outside of the United States. The tale makes a poor example, however, because foreign (and domestic) multinationals' efforts were paralleled by strenuous executive attempts to control the practice in the name of federal supremacy in foreign affairs.

[26] Glickman and Woodward, The New Competitors, p. 272.

PACs be clearly labeled as "foreign."[30] The Tolchins also support the legislation that bans departing federal government officials from taking employment with foreign firms or governments for one year (legislation sponsored by Senator Strom Thurmond in 1988, subsequently vetoed by President Reagan, and finally passed).[31] Some have recommended broadening the categories of person who must register as agents of a foreign government and lengthening the banned employment period.

None of the books offers evidence of discernible influence by foreign-owned firms over public opinion or evidence of the effective use of the firms as a "fifth column" by foreign governments, despite the Tolchins' dated recounting of an apparent Soviet attempt to gain control of some banks in Silicon Valley.[32] Pat Choate has recently recorded the high volume of local charitable contributions by Japanese investors and the symbiotic relationship of investors and local politicians.[33] He fails to establish, however, that the political power against protectionism nurtured by the Japanese differs simply because the activity is foreign. Economic interdependence means that

many American jobs depend on undisrupted trade; the acceleration of interdependence by the very act of direct investment in the 1980s may have been the most effective Japanese political action of all.

Americans may resent the pursuit of profit by foreign firms, and the wisdom of minor policy emendations making political influence by foreigners marginally more expensive or less effective can be debated. But even the strongest proponents of such emendations cannot argue for a substantial result. The American system allows a strong voice by affected parties, especially powerful economic interests, even when they are foreign. Only a major departure in the nature of American government would alter that reality, and none of the books suggests fundamental change.

Specific Concerns about Defense Industries

The absence of well-developed argument and evidence on unique "influence" problems posed by IFDI in the United States may suggest the barrenness of the subject. Surprising, however, even an attempt to relate IFDI to defense-related industry performance can confront only a modest amount of systematic theory and observation.[34] A review of the literature suggests that four major considerations

---

[30] Tolchin and Tolchin, *Buying Into America*, pp. 18–19.

[31] Ibid., p. 258.

[32] Ibid., pp. 131–41.

[33] Choate's recent documentation of lavish expenditures by the Japanese for a variety of purposes comes much closer to making a general case for foreign influence than anything presented in the books under review. In addition to the PAC activities and federal lobbying on a massive scale, he records the considerable contributions from Japanese sources to sympathetic university voices and to other causes designed to gain a hearing for the Japanese position. But most of this activity aims at the trade relation, and its magnitude and effectiveness depend little on IFDI. See Pat Choate, *Agents of Influence: How Japan's Lobbyists in the United States Manipulate America's Political and Economic System* (New York: Knopf, 1990).

[34] Specific cases in which security threats were connected with IFDI tend to be few in number and sometimes admit to alternative interpretations. Hence, the postwar years offer at best only a few cautionary episodes, rather than a continuous record. Attempts to expand the number of observations require the examination of earlier periods in which technological conditions relevant to both security and business activity differed dramatically from those of the present. In *Foreign Direct Investment*, pp. 73–85, Graham and Krugman explore some material from earlier in the century in their security discussion, but they wisely refrain from drawing strong inferences from it.

may gauge the role of IFDI policy in defense sectors: the availability of the latest in defense-related technology; the physical availability of goods under adverse circumstances; the integrity of information and firm performance in national emergencies; and the costs and benefits of a more autarkic approach to the same industries.

High-Technology Assurance The books take a remarkable variety of positions on the implications of IFDI for national security. The authors of *The New Competitors* state simply that "there is no national security threat," since "foreigners have not taken over strategic industries and cannot do so under existing laws."[35] They point to the Exon-Florio amendment to the 1988 Trade Act, which allows the President to block foreign acquisitions with national security implications. In contrast, the Tolchins review the government's 1987 discouragement of Fujitsu's attempt to buy (already French-owned) Fairchild Instruments and warn of "the Pentagon's growing dependence on foreign suppliers."[36] Gordon and Lees also express skepticism about foreign takeovers on technology grounds.

Only Graham and Krugman discuss current U.S. security issues in light of a fundamental reality also recently stressed by Theodore Moran: foreigners now lead in six of twenty-two high-technology industries identified by the Pentagon, and a majority of those technologies play a key part in both civilian and defense production.[37] Their evaluation

also concurs with Moran's in warning of poor results likely from an attempt to duplicate the defense-related output of foreign-owned firms.[38] Both studies contend that access to technology and not ownership should principally concern U.S. policymakers. To ensure availability, Graham and Krugman argue that the United States could consider three options. It could make U.S. sales contingent upon licensing of the relevant technology to U.S. firms. It could require that the goods in question be manufactured in the United States. Upping the ante, it could mandate even more extensive U.S. activity. This might include not only U.S.-performed research and development (R&D) but also the widespread use of U.S. scientific and managerial personnel, so that the operation of the facilities would be minimally affected by any change in relations between the United States and the source country. U.S. choices would be guided by the degree of monopoly power of either foreign firms or source governments and by the potential consequences of the uses of that power.[39] The general approach implicitly assumes that the economic exploitation of new technologies requires access to the U.S. market. This will usually be the case.

Goods Availability Gordon and Lees' rhetorical question "How secure is the

---

[35] Glickman and Woodward, *The New Competitors,* p. 275.

[36] Tolchin and Tolchin, *Buying Into America,* p. 10.

[37] Theodore H. Moran, "The Globalization of America's Defense Industries: What Is the Threat? How Can It be Managed? Guidelines for a New Generation of Defense Industrial Strategists," Georgetown School of Foreign Service, Washington, D.C., mimeograph, 1989.

[38] See ibid., p. 39. Moran establishes the dangers of excessive determination to "go it alone" with a detailed history of the British "Nimrod" surveillance aircraft. The project continued for several years at high cost and marginal performance by contrast with available alternatives. Much of Moran's excellent study warns the U.S. military against "Nimrodization."

[39] The threat of using monopoly power can be real, as General DeGaulle found out when the United States prevented IBM and Control Data from cooperating in the French nuclear program. See Moran, "The Globalization of America's Defense Industries," p. 5.

supply of steel from South Korean facilities that are only hours away from Communist armored tank divisions?"[40] would have sounded alarmist even several years ago when their book was written, yet implicit in the question is the recognition that foreign sourcing has meaning logistically and not just jurisdictionally. Security-related performance requirements applicable to IFDI might in some cases have to include understandings about domestic production for reasons other than apprehension about the source country. In turn, appropriate analysis must employ information about the location and ownership of defense subcontractors, information that is presently inadequate.[41] But this concern applies equally to foreign-owned and U.S.-owned firms. Singling out foreign ownership as a problem related to "military surge demand," as Gordon and Lees do, seems to confuse trade protection and ownership policy.[42]

Integrity in Defense Information and Firm Performance   Only Graham and Krugman point out that foreign firms face far stiffer security rules than their purely domestic competitors face. Current ar-

rangements may leave the security risk greater with U.S.-owned firms; there has yet to be a "Walker case" involving a foreign-owned supplier.[43] Moreover, disloyal operation is an extremely remote possibility. It could exist only in limited form until the invocation of the Trading with the Enemy Act, after which the property would be taken over entirely by U.S. managers (and most managers in most subsidiaries are U.S. citizens anyway).

Independent Production   Should no activity remain exempt from foreign ownership on security grounds? Graham and Krugman deny expertise about "which specific activities, *if any,* the national interest requires be performed by domestically controlled firms."[44] They merely point out that "few Americans would feel comfortable" if a firm such as General Dynamics were owned abroad and that the President has had the power to block such an acquisition since the passage of the Exon-Florio amendment.[45] But is this enough? Could the United States be significantly advantaged by independent domestic development and the offer of sharing for political leverage? A complete discussion lies beyond this essay, but Moran argues that comprehensive independence would be dramatically expen-

[40] Gordon and Lees, *Foreign Multinational Investment,* p. 200.

[41] See Moran, "The Globalization of America's Defense Industries," p. 45; and Graham and Krugman, *Foreign Direct Investment,* p. 83.

[42] See Gordon and Lees, *Foreign Multinational Investment,* pp. 202–3 and 225. In eleven "military surge demand" sectors, Gordon and Lees suggest that foreign ownership should be subject to scrutiny, but they counsel only that "the relative merits" of domestic and foreign ownership should be considered. The reader is left hanging about how much "surge" might be needed and what criteria might be used to decide the degree (if any) of permitted foreign ownership. For a book that performs its policy analysis "not so much for domestic economic considerations but for strategic military reasons" (p. 198), this is a serious limitation.

[43] For details, see Graham and Krugman, *Foreign Direct Investment,* pp. 81–85.

[44] Ibid., p. 86; emphasis added. Although Graham and Krugman skillfully attack a range of proposals to increase control over IFDI, they seldom address relaxation of current restrictions.

[45] Before the passage of the Exon-Florio amendment, there was merely interdepartmental executive consultation by the Committee on Foreign Investment in the United States (CFIUS, established in 1975) concerning some acquisitions, although an executive expression of displeasure did prevent some takeovers. Legislation formally blocking a foreign acquisition would need to have been passed after the fact.

sive and would not ensure U.S. superiority anyway. The United States should instead maintain basic competence in all technologies but consider domestic duplication of foreign capacities only in the face of a monopoly so powerful that access to the U.S. market provides an insufficient lever to bring about cooperation. Moran sees the ultimate solution as international cooperation based on limiting extraterritorial claims by source governments and on nondiscrimination by nationality in the granting of R&D subsidies.[46]

In sum, the arguments made by Graham and Krugman against comprehensive independence in defense production seem far more persuasive in the 1990s than do the dimly adumbrated perils of foreign ownership alleged by the Tolchins and Gordon and Lees. The "autarkists" develop no persuasive scenarios, while the "assurists" present concrete policy alternatives for minimizing security dangers.

PROSPERITY

The last twenty years have seen vast development in both the theory of IFDI and the empirical studies of its impact on national economic welfare.[47]

Five Categories of Effect

For present purposes, five broad clusters of impact can capture most of what has been deemed important: effects related to products, production processes, and competition; positive or negative spillover effects; tax effects; effects on national income and factor earnings; and terms-of-trade effects. The books vary widely in the comprehensiveness of their economic discussion, but three conclude that federal screening can be justified partly on prosperity grounds.

Products, Production Processes, and Competition Foreign-owned firms offer new, better, or cheaper products that can be analyzed in the same partial equilibrium framework as domestic innovations or new imports.[48] When domestic production (as distinct from product availability) is considered, rent to domestic factors, including that from new exports, is added to the analysis.[49] Similarly, an increase in market power insufficiently compensated for by other positive considerations can lower welfare.

Only Graham and Krugman really stress the importance of the net contributions likely in these dimensions: innovations arrive more quickly and fully

---

[46] See Moran, "The Globalization of America's Defense Industries," pp. 44–46.

[47] This review concerns the impact of IFDI on a country that is highly developed economically. Evaluation for less developed countries can be vastly more complex. The classic statement on both political and economic issues remains Thomas J. Biersteker's *Distortion or Development: Contending Perspectives on the Multinational Corporation* (Cambridge, Mass.: MIT Press, 1978). Developments in economic theory and measurement through about 1980 are definitively examined by Richard E. Caves in *Multinational Enterprise and Economic Analysis* (Cambridge: Cambridge University Press, 1982).

[48] Partial equilibrium simply means that changes occur in one market and are confined there. The cost competitiveness of foreign products may result from partial importation, which in turn may be driven by comparative advantage or economies of scope and scale.

[49] The term "rent" is generally used in economics to refer to payments to a factor of production over and above those necessary to bring that factor to the economy or to a specific use. If, for example, a person who was willing to perform any forty-hour-a-week job for a minimum of $4 an hour is in fact employed at $5 an hour, that person earns $1 of rent per hour worked. Once an economic innovation has been made, *all* earnings that can be assigned to it are rent when no payment is necessary to sustain it.

through IFDI than through trade alone, and IFDI obviously plays a critical trade role in much of the increasingly important service sector. The arguments rest largely on deduction from general economic learning, however, rather than from the marshaling of specific evidence. The other authors may downplay or ignore these considerations because they are so obvious, but consequently the reader may give them too little weight.[50]

On the negative side, all four books sound warnings about monopoly, although none documents foreign achievement of significant U.S. market power through IFDI. The Tolchins think that Japanese investors in certain industries aim to crush domestic competitors.[51] Glickman and Woodward stress the quantitative insignificance of a concern

voiced by Gordon and Lees: the special role of government-owned or government-affiliated firms as "unfair" competitors.[52]

All except the Tolchins discuss competition policy explicitly. Graham and Krugman, who assign it a major role in maximizing the benefits of foreign investment,[53] criticize the laxity on mergers during the 1980s, a position anticipated in Glickman and Woodward's book.[54]

Those familiar with the substantial change in both academic thinking and judicial opinion on U.S. competition policy in recent years might wonder if recourse to antitrust resembles appealing to religion. Yet the moorings of policy follow-

[50] In *Foreign Multinational Investment,* Gordon and Lees suggest that expenditures on plant and equipment per employee can be used to compare the performance of foreign firms and domestic firms in the same industry. Although acquisition is the chief mode of entry for the overwhelming majority of new participants, most entrants intend to employ their specific assets to expand U.S. market share. It is hard to see why this expansion and the new plant and equipment expenditures that it implies necessarily yield superior social performance. Still more questionable is the relative profitability measure that Gordon and Lees also employ. Why should high profits be a sign of an unusually large social contribution? They could instead reflect monopoly power or rewards from gullible state and local officials. Another strong possibility is that foreigners are drawn to specific subsectors that are generally profitable to begin with.

[51] See Tolchin and Tolchin, *Buying Into America,* p. 9. On p. 21, the Tolchins repeat the complaint of a Tennessee politician that his state's top officials enticed Illinois-based Caterpillar's chief Japanese rival, Komatsu, to set up American manufacturing operations. On pp. 119–30, they also conclude that foreign banks have certain cost advantages over their U.S. competitors, but they do not explain why this leads to economic losses for the United States.

[52] In *The New Competitors,* p. 85, Glickman and Woodward point out that firms with government shareholders accounted for only 2.5 percent of total IFDI transactions between 1974 and 1981 and indicate that the percentage may be declining. They do acknowledge that state-related firms not only may enjoy subsidies but also may be particularly likely to be protected in their home markets.

[53] Graham and Krugman, *Foreign Direct Investment,* p. 121.

[54] In *The New Competitors,* pp. 294–95, Glickman and Woodward also urge a close look at such international joint ventures as the Fremont, Calif., project involving General Motors and Toyota. They repeat Reich and Mankin's question, "Would [the U.S. government] also have approved a GM-Ford deal?" but they make no attempt at an answer. See Robert B. Reich and Eric D. Mankin, "Joint Ventures with Japan Give Away Our Future," *Harvard Business Review* 64 (March-April 1986), pp. 78–86. In fact, the extremely different strengths of the participating firms in various strata of the "automobile market" provided grounds for government approval, as pointed out by Janusz Ordover and Carl Shapiro in "The General Motors-Toyota Joint Venture: An Economic Assessment," *Wayne Law Review,* vol. 31, 1985, pp. 1167–94. In *Foreign Direct Investment,* pp. 122–23, Graham and Krugman argue for especially stringent antitrust standards for both foreign and domestic defense suppliers.

ing the "antitrust revolution" of the 1970s—including a greater regard for market forces and a much more skeptical view of the singular importance of market concentration for policy—appear far sturdier than those they replaced. A high level of scholarly agreement now prevails about the important components of policy if not their relative weighing.[55] The possible importance of antitrust is suggested by Michael Porter's widely publicized recent study which concludes that the strength of domestic competition is the key to global marketing success.[56]

The behavior of Japanese firms in the United States relates both to competition policy and the terms of trade. Graham and Krugman warn that unless the import center of the products of Japanese firms begins to look more like that of U.S. firms in the same industries, "a 'Japan problem' could eventually arise in U.S. foreign direct investment policy."[57] In fact, the problem is broader, extending not just to imports but to sourcing from the Japanese-owned suppliers that have accompanied major manufacturers to the United States.

The traditional tale of market power by foreigners has imports displacing domestic products, after which import prices are raised above the levels prevailing before domestic competitors were "put out of business." Although that scenario typically lacks plausibility, a modern variant demands attention. Where economies of scale and of cumulative output are important, as in many high-technology industries, merely serving a large market over an extended period can yield increasing insulation from entry and large profits from prices that need not ever go up—because costs continue to fall. Initial foreign government subsidies or intrafirm cross-subsidization, perhaps based on discriminatory high prices in a protected foreign market, allow the "predators" to charge unbeatably low prices in the target market. Even if host rivals are not completely driven out of business, considerable profits could be transferred abroad at prices that could seem very reasonable.

"Industrial policy" aimed at identifying, fertilizing, and protecting certain U.S. industries might be infeasible, but preventing others from collusively stifling otherwise viable U.S. competitors and shifting profits abroad should stand as an important policy goal.[58]

Spillovers   Spillovers to the host country economy from increased management innovation, improved labor practices, and more R&D can magnify the gain from IFDI; a worsening in these areas can lower it. Attention must also be paid to the welfare-lowering possibility that IFDI will accelerate the diffusion of host country advantages to foreign competitors.

Positive spillovers (externalities) from

[55] Ease of entry and ease of exit join concentration as pivotal concerns. See the following contributions to a symposium in *The Journal of Economic Perspectives* 1 (Fall 1987), pp. 3–54: Steven C. Salop, "Symposium on Mergers and Antitrust"; Lawrence J. White, "Antitrust and Merger Policy: Review and Critique"; Franklin M. Fisher, "Horizontal Mergers: Triage and Treatment"; and Richard Schmalensee, "Horizontal Merger Policy: Problems and Changes."

[56] Michael E. Porter, *The Competitive Advantage of Nations* (New York: Free Press, 1990).

[57] Graham and Krugman, *Foreign Direct Investment,* p. 120; see also pp. 130–31.

[58] For a discussion of this issue in the context of the celebrated Matsushita case involving the decline of the U.S. television industry, see F. M. Scherer and David Ross, *Industrial Market Structure and Economic Performance,* 3d ed. (Boston: Houghton Mifflin, 1990), pp. 468–72. For an account that concludes that the Japanese action was definitely aimed at market power, see Kozo Yamamura and Jeanette VanDenBerg: "Japan's Rapid Growth on Trial: The Television Case," in K. Yamamura and G. Saxonhouse, eds., *Law and Trade Issues of the Japanese Economy* (Seattle: University of Washington Press, 1986), pp. 238–83.

IFDI are acknowledged in all of the works.[59] All recognize Japanese innovations in labor management relations and in labor training as unavoidable challenges that U.S. firms must meet to either maintain or gain the leading edge in many industries.[60] While Glickman and Woodward report evidence of low-skill U.S. activity in U.S.-Japanese joint ventures and of considerably less R&D spending per worker by foreign-owned firms in the United States than by their American competitors in several industries,[61] Graham and Krugman offer an analysis of manufacturing R&D that differs substantially. Looking at a broad range of industries, they find little difference in such spending between U.S.-owned firms and foreign-owned (or only Japanese-owned) firms in the United States, thus dispelling suspicion that foreign firms do their R&D at home. They also find little difference in value added or compensation per employee between these types of firm.[62]

All of the books except *Buying Into America* express skepticism about the frequent claim that IFDI through acquisition is transferring technology abroad to the detriment of the United States. But the claims are widespread and deserve comment. Why would the owners of a technology part with it for a price that somehow shortchanges the United States? Two possibilities stand out. If the technologies being profitably employed by the acquired firm were partly financed by U.S. taxpayers, untaxed rents are shifted to nonnationals.[63] One also hears claims that U.S. firms are too "impatient." In fact, there are international differences in the effective cost of capital to the firm, and these differences, which result partly from tax policies, may be driving the ownership of slow-payback technologies into Japanese hands.[64] Empirical work on these and related issues is overdue.[65]

The issue of "jobs," which Glickman and Woodward treat largely as a spillover, deserves special attention. It dominates their narrative and also heads every politician's list of concerns, but it makes a highly misleading yardstick for measuring the benefit of IFDI.

Economic progress involves the lessening of labor time to make a typical unit of output. Imagine the acquisition of a failing American firm by a foreign investor who prospers by selling the same quality and volume of product using labor much more efficiently, thus dramatically reducing employment. In most instances, the labor released will be hired again after a (usually short) period of unemployment. That rehired labor increases the output of the economy elsewhere, and the value of that increase may approximate the value of the firm's innovation. Most cases are much more complex, but the contribution of labor-saving innovation is fundamental. Unfortunately, the Glickman and Woodward

---

[59] Externalities are unmarketed costs and benefits to others from the action of an economic unit.

[60] Recent work by Reich favors foreign investment largely for this reason. See Robert Reich, "Who Is Us?" *Harvard Business Review* 66 (January-February 1990), pp. 53–64.

[61] Glickman and Woodward, *The New Competitors,* pp. 136–37.

[62] Graham and Krugman, *Foreign Direct Investment,* pp. 54–62.

[63] For a recent discussion of this and related issues, see Frank Press, "Scientific and Technological Relations Between the United States and Japan: Issues and Recommendations," paper prepared for the Commission on U.S.-Japan Relations for the Twenty-First Century, Washington, D.C., November 1990.

[64] See George N. Hatsopoulos, Paul R. Krugman, and Lawrence H. Summers, "U.S. Competitiveness: Beyond the Trade Deficit," *Science* 241 (July 1988), p. 307.

[65] See Press, "Scientific and Technological Relations Between the United States and Japan," p. 3.

approach, which dwells on immediate net employment changes from IFDI, leads the reader close to the opposite conclusion. And the approach is no more valid when all foreign firms are considered instead of a single investor.

Glickman and Woodward's major reservation about IFDI between 1982 and 1986 is that "foreigners contributed less than 1 percent of all U.S. job growth."[66] But even in the turbulent 1980s, reallocation of labor rather than permanent job loss was the issue. Despite the induced recession soon followed by the soaring dollar and the loss of international competitiveness, unemployment that stood at 9.6 percent in 1983 had dropped to 5.5 percent in 1988, reaching the lowest level in ten years.[67]

Glickman and Woodward fail to qualify the dominant criterion of immediate job impacts despite their frequently excellent discussion of other issues. In particular, they never face the latent contradiction between their concern with "competitiveness in manufacturing"[68] and their distaste for one of its most likely concomitants: temporary unemployment and the loss of rents embedded in the wages of many uncompetitive industries.[69]

Graham and Krugman's treatment of the employment issue will strike many readers as inadequate. How can Glickman and Woodward's principal preoccupation for over three hundred pages be dismissed in a few terse paragraphs with the conclusion that "the net impact of FDI on U.S. employment is approximately zero"?[70] Are all of those state ac-

---

[66] Glickman and Woodward, *The New Competitors*, p. 135.

[67] See ibid. Although Glickman and Woodward cite with disdain "Engine Charlie" Wilson's famous identification of the welfare of General Motors with that of the United States, they seem to equate national welfare with that of organized labor. For example, in their discussion of the impact of Japanese innovation on the automobile industry, they note without evaluation the traditional insistence of the United Automobile Workers on strict work rules as well as high wages. The Japanese are given considerable credit for innovation, but only when organized labor approved.

[68] Glickman and Woodward, *The New Competitors*, p. 162.

[69] See ibid., pp. 135–39, in which Glickman

and Woodward voice concern about pay levels and not just employment. U.S. income inequality increased substantially during the 1980s, partly as the result of a loss of rent that organized labor had been able to wrest directly from firm owners and indirectly from product purchasers in less competitive times and partly from a decline in the employment of unionized labor. The most careful recent research, however, assigns far more of the explanation to increased demand relative to supply of skilled workers. See Gary Burtless, ed., *A Future of Lousy Jobs?* (Washington, D.C.: Brookings Institution, 1990). An alternative explanation for the loss of high-paying jobs focuses not on rent but instead on unique environments in which labor can actually perform more work. Contributors to this "efficiency wage" literature offer a wide range of theoretical possibilities and empirical findings. See, for example, Erica L. Groshen, "Why Do Wages Vary Among Employers?" in Federal Reserve Bank of Cleveland, *Economic Review*, vol. 24, 1988, pp. 19–38; and Richard H. Thaler, "Interindustry Wage Differentials," *Journal of Economic Perspectives* 3 (Spring 1989), pp. 181–93. If the uniquely propitious environments could be identified, they might provide a basis for policy, but many economists believe that they are only mirages resulting from inappropriately controlled observation. See Jagdish Bhagwati, "U.S. Trade Policy Today," Columbia University, New York, mimeograph, 1989, pp. 24–27. In *Foreign Multinational Investment,* p. 4, Gordon and Lees claim that basic industries such as those producing steel and motor vehicles "provide an income for a large part of the population" and that without them there would be a "serious reduction in the standard of living." But they do not rest their case on literature of the kind just cited. They never explain how the decline of these specific industries affects general U.S. living standards.

[70] Glickman and Woodward, *The New Competitors*, p. 49.

tivities for international business development pursued in vain?

Graham and Krugman argue that the guardians of national macroeconomic stability will attempt to control overall demand at the "non-accelerating inflation rate of unemployment" (NAIRU), and because IFDI typically does not affect the NAIRU, it cannot affect employment. State and local officials may lure new business to combine with idle or underutilized resources, thus reducing unemployment by improving the match between labor supply and demand. But this enticement is unconnected with IFDI; any business will do.[71] Hence, the successful pursuit of these economic development policies, and not generally increased IFDI, modifies the NAIRU.

Tax Effects International convention gives the host country first crack at corporate taxation, and this alone provides a presumption of host gain from IFDI.[72] The welfare effects of taxes receive little attention in any of the books. The best-known effect, the gap between marginal social product and marginal foreign investor return caused by the corporate income tax, is neglected even in the Graham and Krugman study. The precise contribution would be difficult to isolate

for a period like the 1980s—a period dominated by large international capital flows, most of which were U.S. deficit demand driven—without an understanding both of the elasticities of supply and demand for capital among sectors and of the extent of "asset swapping."[73] Nonetheless, tax considerations add strongly to the presumption of U.S. gain from IFDI. As Richard Caves has memorably put it, "Beside the great issues of progress, sovereignty, and economic justice that swirl around [FDI], taxation sounds like a matter for petty minds that warm to accountancy. That instinct is squarely wrong, because it turns out that arrangements for taxing corporate net incomes constitute the dominant factor in the division of spoils between source and host countries."[74]

Gordon and Lees acknowledge the possible tax contribution of IFDI, but the discussion is marred by their apparent conclusion that foreign entry mainly displaces rather than adds to domestic activity. While this is generally true of employment effects, any increase in the size of the corporate capital stock made possible by IFDI generates additional tax revenues (above the costs of government services provided) that should be counted as national benefits.[75]

One possibly important point about taxation, raised but not carefully developed by Gordon and Lees, has recently created a furor in Washington: the point that profits can be transferred out of the

[71] While any new business (including start-up or "greenfield" IFDI) affects the result most directly, the same outcome can develop in many ways. For example, if plant and management are lured away from more normal areas in the domestic economy, the interaction of macropolicy and the workings of the labor market will restore employment there to the previous level.

[72] See G.D.A. MacDougall, "The Benefits and Costs of Private Investment from Abroad: A Theoretical Approach," *Economic Record* 36 (March 1960), pp. 13–35; and P. B. Musgrave, *Direct Investment Abroad and the Multinationals: Effects on the United States Economy* (Washington, D.C.: Government Printing Office, 1975).

[73] For example, if the dollar's fall in the late 1980s created increased demand for U.S. real assets based on money illusion, an exchange of financial for real assets between a foreigner and an American could take place with no tax impact whatsoever.

[74] Richard Caves, *Multinational Enterprise and Economic Analysis*, p. 226.

[75] In *Foreign Multinational Investment*, p. 221, Gordon and Lees' Table 7.9 combines tax shifts and tax increases to an unknown extent.

United States by the manipulation of intrafirm prices ("transfer pricing").[76] Insufficient monitoring of foreigners' tax liabilities reduces U.S. gains, and the Internal Revenue Service is tightening its surveillance.[77]

All of the books address one fiscal issue, and it provides a rare occasion of agreement; unfortunately, each offers poor counsel. They all contend that the tax concessions and subsidies offered by states and communities in competition with each other considerably lower the aggregate contribution of IFDI. Foreign firms typically first decide to locate in the United States and then determine where to operate, partly on the basis of local enticements. Glickman and Woodward propose that states improve their situation by insisting on specific elements of performance in return.[78] Graham and Krugman respond that not only might this action make state officials more willing to offer concessions but it would also undermine U.S. opposition to performance requirements in the General Agreement on Tariffs and Trade (GATT).[79] They advocate instead that state-level incentives simply be abolished, while Gordon and Lees propose that they be bargained away for foreign concessions. In fact, most states and localities are unlikely to relinquish voluntarily what they see as essential development tools, and the federal government will not interfere as long as incentives are nominally open to domestic and foreign firms alike (which is the invariable claim).[80]

Income and Factor Shares   With regard to economy-wide effects, a nonmarginal increment of capital should, ceteris paribus, both increase national income and change relative factor prices. According to most models, labor's wage should rise and the price of capital should fall. Perhaps understandably, none of the books deals with these impacts. Estimation would combine many of the same factors that bedevil an estimate of tax gains with further complications.[81]

Terms of Trade   Finally, effects on the ratio of export price to import price can be expected. These terms-of-trade effects are alluded to in all of the books, but only Graham and Krugman deal with the issue at all comprehensively. They report that the overall import content in manufacturing IFDI is about 2.5 times that for all of U.S. manufacturing and that Japan's ratio is more than 6 times the domestic U.S. ratio. They argue that some of the difference may come from misclassification and some from the phenomenon of essentially imported goods being partially fabricated in the United States. Import propensities may also be falling over time; many of the Japanese automobile manufacturers, for example, project

[76] In ibid., pp. 170–71, the authors claim, but do not demonstrate, that Japanese automobile sales in the United States in the mid-1980s were based on inappropriately high import prices.

[77] "Can Uncle Sam Mend This Hole in His Pocket?" *Business Week,* 10 September 1990, pp. 48–50.

[78] Glickman and Woodward, *The New Competitors,* pp. 246–51.

[79] Graham and Krugman, *Foreign Direct Investment,* p. 119.

[80] See Tolchin and Tolchin, *Buying Into America,* p. 21. In a recent discussion with Robert Hudec, he pointed out that federal action to block incentives for foreign firms alone could be justified as regulating foreign affairs, but such action would violate bilateral treaties ensuring national treatment.

[81] For an account that stresses such effects without attempting to estimate them, see John H. Makin, "The Effects of Japanese Investment in the United States," in Kozo Yamamura, ed., *Japanese Investment in the United States: Should We Be Concerned?* (Seattle: Society for Japanese Studies, 1989), pp. 41–62.

sharply increasing domestic content as they gain experience in the market.

Graham and Krugman estimate that the higher import propensity could, on extreme assumptions, cost the United States as much as 3 percent of the foreign purchasing power of the dollar. They might have explained more fully the tenuous basis on which this figure rests. It ignores that much of the current import content of U.S. production by Japanese-owned firms is replacing finished imports from Japan. Moreover, an analysis confined solely to the terms of trade must assume the availability of domestic substitutes that are equivalent in cost and quality. This begs a central question.

Export performance, too, must be considered against the baseline of no IFDI. In fact, all of the books at least implicitly acknowledge that improvements in product cost and quality spurred by foreign-owned firms may boost the sales of U.S. production in world markets, improving the U.S. terms of trade. Consider the potentially important exportation of U.S.-made "Japanese" cars to Europe.

Gordon and Lees, using trade data for a discussion of comparative import and export performance by foreign and domestic firms, stress the apparent balance-of-payments effects. This is an intuitive but seriously misleading approach. The trade propensities of various industries affect national welfare primarily by influencing the national terms of trade through the exchange rate. The balance of the current account reflects the mismatch between aggregate national expenditures and national production. Current account imbalances cannot be changed significantly by altering the export and import behavior of specific industries, a truth also ignored in most political speeches and much policy discussion.[82]

---

[82] One issue related to the U.S. current account imbalance is discussed in the three most

Screening and Performance Requirements

Only Graham and Krugman oppose the establishment of a government agency to screen IFDI. The Tolchins merely charge officials to discover "whether a specific investment poses a serious threat to U.S. interests,"[83] giving as examples hostile takeovers and threats to national security. No case is made for harm in either category.

Gordon and Lees also favor government screening, and they identify three parts of the economy in which there is a special need "to scrutinize foreign ownership carefully": four sectors in which the "performance" of foreign firms appears lower than that of domestic firms, eleven sectors that could be required for "military surge demand," and eight sectors of "high-tech" activity.[84] Unfortunately, their analyses of "performance" and "high-tech" issues make no persua-

---

recent books reviewed here. The Tolchins and Glickman and Woodward make much of the "debt-for-equity swap" at "fire sale" prices caused by the fall in the dollar's value after 1985. Glickman and Woodward also note and attribute to "observers" the view that "the Reagan legacy is 'America for Sale' at bargain basement prices." Graham and Krugman take sharp exception to that view. They use price and exchange rate comparisons to suggest that while U.S. assets may have been *overpriced* in the mid-1980s, there is little evidence that they have been underpriced since the dollar's fall. They concede that the surge of direct investment in the late 1980s could be linked to the level of the dollar, but only because of its previous overvaluation. They agree with Glickman and Woodward that exchange rate changes affect the timing of IFDI but have little effect otherwise. Compare Graham and Krugman, *Foreign Direct Investment*, pp. 35–37, with Glickman and Woodward, *The New Competitors*, p. 117.

[83] Tolchin and Tolchin, *Buying Into America*, p. 252.

[84] Gordon and Lees, *Foreign Multinational Investment*, p. 225.

sive case for government action, and they fail to establish either the volume of "surge capacity" needed or the criteria for foreign ownership.[85]

Glickman and Woodward propose a new screening agency colorfully dubbed MIRADOR (Multinational Review Agency and Department of Research). They argue that those involved in the interdepartmental executive consultations of the Committee on Foreign Investment in the United States (CFIUS) are bound to be overtaxed with the additional burden of overseeing the Exon-Florio amendment.[86] Hence, more coordinated research should be conducted by an agency that would also perform "economic impact analyses," publish detailed reports on "employment creation or destruction," and serve as a watchdog regarding the observance of labor laws and guidelines by foreign firms.[87]

MIRADOR would screen a limited number of large or militarily significant investments and give advice about denial to the President. *The New Competitors* makes no case whatever for reviewing defense-related investments, however, and offers employment as its only well-developed criterion for economic evaluation. Moreover, despite the authors' disclaimer that MIRADOR "should not be cast as a restrictive authority,"[88] Bergsten argued in 1974 that nothing could do more to politicize direct investment than attention focused on apparent employment effects.[89]

Graham and Krugman flatly oppose a new screening agency, preferring to rely on the CFIUS mechanism to enforce a very limited interpretation of the Exon-Florio amendment. Instead of blocking defense-related IFDI, they urge the imposition of domestic content and related requirements or compulsory licensing in narrowly defined circumstances.[90]

This reviewer concurs with Graham and Krugman here as well as on most other issues. No case has been made for the benefits of general screening, and more elaborate mechanisms offer increased scope for manipulation by special interests. Moreover, all of the proposed screening agencies would deal with individual firms in a situation of bilateral monopoly. Thus, if a firm were refused, it could come back with a more attractive proposal.[91] This could tend to generate de facto performance requirements, which the U.S. strenuously opposes in international forums.

Evaluation of the Prosperity Discussions

With regard to the prosperity discussions as a whole, all of the books except that of Graham and Krugman prove disappointing. Although Gordon and Lees claim na-

---

[85] The relations between the superpowers have changed dramatically since the book was written, but the same criticism could have been made in 1986.

[86] See footnote 45.

[87] See Glickman and Woodward, *The New Competitors,* pp. 294–302. The authors also favor an extension of plant closing notification to 120 days. This provision would apply both to foreign firms and domestic firms, however, and is logically unconnected with foreign economic policy as such, despite the 60-day provisions that were attached to the 1988 Trade Act.

[88] Ibid., p. 283.

[89] See C. Fred Bergsten, "Coming Investment Wars?" *Foreign Affairs* 53 (October 1974), pp. 135–51.

[90] In *Foreign Direct Investment,* pp. 121–25, Graham and Krugman decry the exclusion of foreign-owned firms from government-subsidized research consortia such as SEMATECH.

[91] U.S. practice would almost certainly make necessary a detailed and public account of the reasons for refusal. Even if reasons for rejection were not given, however, as during the era of the Canadian Foreign Investment Review Agency (1974-84), firms could make reasonable guesses on the basis of predecision discussions with officials and could then prepare and submit more attractive proposals.

tional defense as their central theme, their ambition to appraise IFDI in general yields evaluative criteria of mixed quality[92] and policy directions that seem both poorly motivated and vague. The Tolchins offer neither criteria for evaluating specific direct investments nor a summary judgment of overall economic effects. Their endorsement of screening apparently rests on a belief that someone can develop operational criteria for administrative discretion, but they provide none. While Glickman and Woodward acknowledge many considerations necessary for an overall economic evaluation of U.S. IFDI, their preoccupation with immediate employment effects makes MIRADOR a particularly alarming idea.

Graham and Krugman conclude that "the evidence does not shake the presumption that FDI in general makes a significant positive contribution to the U.S. economy."[93] Their treatment nominally

covers more economic bases than the other books, although much of the argument aims at what they regard as bogus attacks on IFDI, the beneficence of which is asserted far more than it is demonstrated. Their presentation will be most persuasive to readers already convinced by other literature about the importance of comparative advantage, scale and scope economies, increased competition, and the diffusion of labor skills, management techniques, and R&D results. Nonetheless, both the logic and evidence upon which many of their judgments rest are well developed elsewhere, and they can scarcely be expected to provide a complete guide to decades of learning.

Even Graham and Krugman fail to stress one significant trend: the nominal nationality of a firm is becoming an increasingly poor guide to its international employment distribution, trade behavior, ownership, and loyalty. A completely domestic firm may export less, import more, and have fewer domestic employees than a foreign-owned firm, which may also find an increasingly large part of its stock owned in the host country. Host government wishes may be resisted equally by both firms.[94]

IFDI AND INTERNATIONAL RELATIONS

The evaluation of policy initiatives so far has largely neglected America's international relations, but this downplays both

---

[92] Some of the measures used by Gordon and Lees in *Foreign Multinational Investment* could be important, but they offer no defense of their approach. A compensation per employee comparison, for example, could be used to counter the argument that foreign affiliates tend to preserve their heaviest human capital expenditures for "headquarters," although this interpretation is not offered.

[93] See Graham and Krugman, *Foreign Direct Investment,* p. 130. In his excellent comparative study of the automobile industry in four countries, Simon Reich argues that IFDI may "result in a reduction of domestic economic competitiveness." Those who claim that domestic firms offer superior economic performance must identify how much of this outcome rests on domestic ownership and how much on domestic production. Would a domestically owned firm engaging in substantial importation be preferred to a foreign-owned firm with greater domestic content? An understanding of the sources of superior performance takes on special urgency in automobile manufacturing and other industries in which multinational sourcing casts increasing doubt on the meaning of figures claiming to capture domestic unit output by country. More fundamentally, Reich's discussion does not really

deal with competitiveness as usually defined, since the quantitative role of overt protection and other forms of discrimination in preserving market share for domestic firms is not estimated. See Simon Reich, "Roads to Follow: Regulating Direct Foreign Investment," *International Organization* 43 (Autumn 1989), pp. 543–84.

[94] In "Who Is Us," Robert Reich provides a particularly persuasive statement of this view and also cites estimates that a quarter of U.S. pension funds will be invested in foreign-

the cause of much complaint and the perils of unilateral action.

Just as "reciprocity" became a battle cry for some U.S. trade policymakers during the 1980s,[95] it also emerged as a key issue in the foreign investment field. The Tolchins claim that "for foreign investment, the issues are clear, the inequities transparent, and the solutions obvious."[96] But the issues are far from clear. Two conflicting principles can be used to evaluate fairness for foreign investors: a country can grant foreigners only such access as is granted to its firms in the same industry abroad (reciprocity), or it

can treat foreign and domestic firms the same way in the same industry (national treatment). Graham and Krugman suggest U.S. territorial restrictions on bank operations by contrast with their projected absence in EC 1992 as an example where foreign insistence on reciprocity would have damaged the United States.[97] Furthermore, the United States has acknowledged that its partners may legitimately hold differing views about openness: the Canada-U.S. Free Trade Agreement permits certain asymmetrical ownership discrimination.[98]

Finally, although the Tolchins and Gordon and Lees claim that the United States is much less restrictive than other nations, the Organization for Economic Cooperation and Development (OECD) evidence cited by Graham and Krugman suggests otherwise. Despite some nominally greater oversight abroad, unprecedentedly little difference in practice now exists between the United States and its major industrial partners, with the possible exception of Japan (de facto, not de jure). They could also have noted that tensions between the principles of reciprocity and national treatment recede as the number of effectively restricted sectors diminishes because countries differ little in their treatment of national firms in most sectors. U.S. banking is important but not typical.[99]

---

owned companies within ten years. In *Foreign Direct Investment,* pp. 65–68, Graham and Krugman treat IFDI stockholders as completely foreign and thus miss the chance to stress the growing complexities of ownership. Although Simon Reich argues in "Roads to Follow," p. 581, that an autonomy threat is posed by IFDI because "foreign producers face a more realistic choice between exit or loyalty than do their domestic counterparts," exceptions are not hard to find in the United States. The American value added in the case of color televisions for sale in the United States is generally higher from foreign-owned than from U.S.-owned production. Reich's point may remain true for Japan, but one wonders how strongly national loyalties will persist in Europe after 1992. Moreover, as a general proposition, the argument implies that the domestic firms are not as "global" in Porter's sense as their foreign-owned competitors are. This raises some doubts about their economic performance prior to the testing of their loyalty. On firm typology, see Michael E. Porter, "Competition in Global Industries: A Conceptual Framework," in Michael E. Porter, ed., *Competition in Global Industries* (Boston: Harvard Business School Press, 1986), pp. 15–60.

[95] Various possible meanings of the term "reciprocity" are examined by Robert O. Keohane in "Reciprocity in International Relations," *International Organization* 40 (Winter 1986), pp. 1–27. For the term's use in international trade matters, see William R. Cline, *"Reciprocity": A New Approach to World Trade Policy?* (Washington, D.C.: Institute for International Economics, 1982).

[96] Tolchin and Tolchin, *Buying Into America,* p. 228.

[97] Graham and Krugman, *Foreign Direct Investment,* pp. 117–18.

[98] Kudrle and Lenway, "Progress for the Rich."

[99] In *Buying Into America,* the Tolchins note that Section 301 of the Trade Act of 1974 was expressly amended in 1984 to include action by the President to combat barriers to incoming investment. The same section in the 1988 legislation—"Super 301"—has concentrated world attention on unilateral U.S. measures. Japan continues to insist on reciprocity in the banking and financial industries (Office of the United States Trade Representative, *1989 National Trade Estimate Report on Foreign Trade Barriers,* Washington, D.C., mimeograph), and

The United States has taken the lead at the Uruguay Round in attempting to gain agreement on the treatment of IFDI and particularly the restriction of performance requirements; this adds a strike against the screening proposals made by all of the authors except Graham and Krugman.[100] Nonetheless, all of the authors except Glickman and Woodward explicitly consider international cooperation. Gordon and Lees endorse a "GATT for Investment" as a long-run goal,[101] but they adhere to "a weak version of industrial policy" based ultimately on U.S. defense needs.[102] Hence, they see realistic bilateral and multilateral cooperation as a kind of damage control device, as the United States joins other countries in the manipulation of trade and investment for national purposes. The Tolchins admonish U.S. policymakers to "work through the GATT as well as the OECD," but this

appears in the context of speculation about the use of unilateral investment restrictions to win foreign concessions on both investment reciprocity and trade issues.[103]

Graham and Krugman favor greater multilateral cooperation, but they hold little hope for a "GATT for Investment," in light of varied and stringent controls in many developing countries. Instead, they suggest an agreement among the "like-minded" OECD countries. The new experience of the United States as a substantial host country, Japan's declared openness,[104] common liberal policies promised as part of the EC 1992 Project, and the dispute settlement mechanism of the Canada-U.S. Free Trade Agreement create propitious conditions. They might also have cited increased commonality in competition policy.[105] Without it, the

---

the United States should certainly press for national treatment. Contrary to the tone of the accounts of the Tolchins and Gordon and Lees, however, one must search hard for other major targets for unilateral pressure within the developed countries. Gordon and Lees' *Foreign Multinational Investment* was prepared in the early to mid 1980s, however, when asymmetries such as that presented by the Canadian Foreign Investment Review Agency stood out more clearly. The efficacy of "Super 301" approaches to investment restrictions in non-OECD countries lies beyond the scope of this review.

[100] The U.S. position is well explained by Edward M. Graham and Paul R. Krugman in "Trade-Related Investment Measures," in Jeffrey Schott, ed., *Completing the Uruguay Round* (Washington, D.C.: Institute for International Economics, 1990), pp. 147–63.

[101] In *Foreign Multinational Investment*, Gordon and Lees cite the proposal made by Bergsten in his "Prepared Statement" for the U.S. Senate. See U.S. Congress, Senate Committee on Foreign Relations, *Hearings Before the Subcommittee on International Economic Policy*, 97th Congress, 1st sess., 1981, pp. 13–21.

[102] Gordon and Lees, *Foreign Multinational Investment*, p. 255.

[103] Tolchin and Tolchin, *Buying Into America*, p. 251.

[104] In addition to the difficulties of establishing distribution, foreign investors in Japan almost completely lack the entry mode generally favored elsewhere: acquisition. Japanese firms are not easy to buy, either by foreigners or other Japanese. On the evolution of Japanese policy, see Dennis J. Encarnation and Mark Mason, "Neither MITI nor America: The Political Economy of Capital Liberalization in Japan," *International Organization* 44 (Winter 1990), pp. 25–54.

[105] On the EC and the United States, see Douglas Rosenthal, "Competition Policy," in Gary C. Hufbauer, ed., *Europe 1992: An American Perspective* (Washington, D.C.: Brookings Institution, 1990), pp. 293–343. On North American similarities, see the following contributions to the "Symposium on North American Competition Policy," *Antitrust Law Journal*, vol. 57, 1988, pp. 397–445: Calvin S. Goldman, "Bilateral Aspects of Canadian Competition Policy"; Charles F. Rule, "Claims of Predation in a Competitive Marketplace: When Is an Antitrust Response Appropriate?"; and Joseph P. Griffin, "The Impact on Canada of the Extraterritorial Application of the U.S. Antitrust Laws." The considerably different Japanese case is discussed by Masu Uekusa in "Industrial Organization: The 1970s to the Present," in K. Yamamura and Y. Yusauba,

denial of entry through merger or acquisition by the host country on competition grounds could well generate conflict with the source.

A new agreement would aim to limit extraterritorial claims by source countries before conflicts erupt in the United States similar to those generated abroad over several decades by U.S. directives to its multinational corporations. Host countries would be encouraged to grant more clearly specified rights of establishment and national treatment while limiting the use of performance requirements and investment incentives.[106] Graham and Krugman eschew the development of elaborate GATT-like codes, however, favoring instead a short formal declaration of the rights and responsibilities of the principals, a regular forum for negotiation and consultation, and a compulsory dispute resolution mechanism similar to that established under the Canada-U.S. Free Trade Agreement.[107]

Graham and Krugman end their study somewhat surprisingly with a rousing call for international cooperation to avoid "investment wars," although their discussion has not anticipated any except possibly as the result of U.S. overreaction to the flood of IFDI or suspected Japanese perfidy. Nearly all of the book's logic and evidence suggest the desirability, but scarcely the urgency, of increasing the cooperation that is already reflected in a myriad of bilateral treaties.[108]

CONCLUSION: THE UNITED STATES AS AN ORDINARY HOST

The United States now lives with a sense of threat from IFDI similar to that first endured by most industrial countries decades ago. Although this foreign experience receives virtually no attention in the books reviewed, the lessons are generally reassuring and further affirm the basic position of Graham and Krugman.[109]

First, IFDI did not continue to grow in other major industrial countries but instead peaked at levels higher than many predict for the United States.

Second, virtually all studies of IFDI found positive effects on the host economies. Most important, the "entrenchment" of U.S. multinational corporations did not typically thwart subsequent advances by major domestic firms in the same industries.

Third, the practice of sealing off sectors against foreign penetration, often nominally on national security grounds, generally led to a high-cost duplication that was ultimately deemed unsatisfactory.

Fourth, the accumulated experience of various developed countries with sharply differing policies in earlier years led to an almost universal selection of unprecedented openness by the end of the 1980s. Perhaps most notably, the EC 1992 Project pronounces the final European verdict against most policies that distinguish investment solely on the basis of nationality of controlling ownership.

Finally, experience abroad suggests that the psychic bruises resulting from

---

eds., *The Domestic Transformation,* vol. 1 of *The Political Economy of Japan* (Stanford, Calif.: Stanford University Press, 1987), pp. 477–79.

[106] Performance requirements would be limited to industries with a direct national security connection. Most of these goals are familiar and echo previous suggestions; see, for example, Bergsten, "Prepared Statement."

[107] Graham and Krugman, *Foreign Direct Investment,* pp. 125–31.

[108] For a thorough discussion of these treaties, see Pamela B. Gann, "The U.S. Bilateral Investment Treaty Program," *Stanford Journal*

of International Law 21 (Fall 1985), pp. 373–459.

[109] Perhaps the best single source for country-specific studies is John H. Dunning, ed., *Multinational Enterprises, Economic Structure and International Competitiveness* (New York: Wiley, 1987).

being visibly outperformed by foreigners in one's own land need not be permanent. Indeed, they can serve to stimulate resurgence. This may stand as the most important lesson of all as the U.S. confronts *le défi japonais.*

Although each of the four books reviewed here sees the situation differently, all recognize the influx of foreign firms as a significant but still rather minor part of a much larger economic drama. In particular, all of the books agree that America's main economic problems are

still made in the U.S.A. However knavish the behavior of some of its international competitors, domestic problems such as the United States' unwillingness to pay for more current consumption with taxation, its low savings rate, and its inadequate system of training and education imply not just continued, but increasing, trouble in the years ahead. IFDI's various roles as messenger, menace, and savior should not distract Americans from larger, if more intractable, issues.

26. Investment Policies in an Integrated World Economy

Phedon Nicolaides

1. INTRODUCTION

Cross-border direct investment has been a major integrating force in the world economy during the last decade. Between 1983 and 1988 trade grew by 5 per cent while direct investment grew by 30 per cent in real terms (Julius and Thomsen, 1988; and Julius, 1990). In some years during the 1980s investment flows among OECD countries registered increases of more than 50 per cent in dollar terms (Akimune, 1991). As a result, it has been estimated that by 1989 the total stock of investment in the world had surpassed $1000 billion (JETRO, 1990). Almost 90 per cent of that investment was undertaken by just seven countries: the United States, Britain, Japan, Germany, the Netherlands, France and Canada.

Investment is also competing with trade as an issue of contention in public-policy discussions. While in the 1960s

and 1970s, it was developing countries that were concerned about foreign investment, during the last few years the stage of debate has moved to industrial countries. It is not hard to understand why investment has been receiving so much public attention. The United States, for example, has turned from a net exporter of capital to a net receiver of capital. Its ratio of inward to outward investment was 0.13 in 1961–70 while in 1981–88 it was 1.76. By contrast, in the same periods Japan's ratios were 0.43 and 0.03, respectively (Akimune, 1991). Indeed, Japan's outward investment has grown so rapidly and so spectacularly that in 1989 it became not only the world's largest creditor but also the largest direct investor in terms of annual flows.

The public's perception of the well-publicized investment cases, particularly in the United States, is that foreigners are gaining control of important national assets, while their economies, particularly that of Japan, are closed to third-country firms. This perceived conflict of interest

SOURCE: Reprinted with permission from *The World Economy,* vol. 14, no. 2, June 1991, pp. 121–137.

raises two questions. First, do host countries benefit from foreign investment? Second, should there be reciprocity requirements in investment?

In neoclassical trade theory, free trade maximises a small country's welfare and is the likely option for a group of large countries agreeing to refrain from predatory protectionism. Because of the complexity of determining optimum policies, strategic trade theory which has questioned the neoclassical assumptions has also leaned in favour of policy conservatism rather than activism (Baldwin, 1989).

My intention in this paper is to argue that similar answers can be given to the two questions above. An individual country most probably gains from inward investment. These gains may be increased by strategic policies that impose restrictions or other requirements on foreign firms. However, such gains are likely to be dissipated when other countries impose equivalent restrictions and when private firms take evasive action. The general policy prescription proposed in this paper is that foreign firms should not be prevented from entering a country's domestic market (i.e., the right of establishment) and once they are established in the domestic market they should not be subject to any special restrictions or requirements (i.e., national treatment).

Before arguing the case for a liberal policy on foreign investment, the following section sets the context for understanding investment decisions. It examines what motivates and what enables firms to invest in foreign markets and what these things imply for the nature of the markets in which multinational firms operate.

2. FOREIGN DIRECT INVESTMENT: THE NATURE OF THE MARKET

There are many different kinds of investment. The kind which is relevant for the purposes of this paper is investment which is undertaken by firms of one industrial country into the market of another industrial country. There are also many motives for this kind of investment. For example, it may be intended to replace exports (i.e., the product-cycle hypothesis) or to avoid trade barriers (i.e. the tariff-jumping hypothesis).[1] In general, however, investment among industrial countries serves to improve access to the markets of host countries or otherwise strengthen the market position of the firms that undertake it. Any assessment of how foreign firms should be treated must take into account this access-seeking objective and its consequences.

Investing in a foreign market is a risky activity. Local firms have the advantage of established relations with local customers, better knowledge of local consumer tastes and government policies and probably a more extensively developed network of local suppliers and distributors. Therefore, firms can invest abroad only when they own assets that give them a different kind of advantage and protect them from local competition until their knowledge of the local market improves. Usually such assets are intangible in nature (e.g., patents, proprietary production processes, management skills).

The possession of intangible assets both enables and further encourages investment because intangible assets can be moved to different locations so that production need not be tied to any particular country. Moreover, competition in the development of new assets (e.g., better information about local clients' needs) provides strong incentives to firms to design products that meet consumers' preferences and clients' needs more effec-

---

[1] For a recent review of the literature see Thomsen and Nicolaides (1991).

tively than those of their rivals. Tracking and responding to changing preferences and needs usually requires the establishment of some kind of permanent presence in major foreign markets.

The multinational company (MNC) exists precisely because it is not easy to trade intangible assets in open markets. It is difficult, for example, to write contracts for experience and newly-developed technology which is in the process of being adapted for commercial applications. The reasons that encourage corporate integration across national markets are similar to those that encourage vertical integration within national markets.[2] Some of these reasons are that production costs are reduced, information flows faster and the actions of individual units are more effectively coordinated.

Given that it is the possession of intangible assets that enables a firm to become multinational and that these assets are not readily available to all firms, it follows that MNCs operate in less than perfectly competitive markets. As is well known, in imperfectly competitive markets there is scope for governments to pursue a strategic trade policy in support of national firms.

Strategic trade policy has been examined in great detail by others (see the recent review by Lawrence and Schultze, 1990). By and large, their assessment is that in practice it would be exceedingly difficult to implement the theoretically-optimum policy that takes into account the true costs and benefits to the economy. Such costs and benefits are determined in part by the nature of the prevailing market imperfections, reactions of other firms, reactions of other governments and possible spill-overs into other industries. Strategic trade theory has not produced any general prescriptions for trade barriers or industrial subsidies.

Rather, each request for government intervention needs to be considered individually on its own merits.

Foreign direct investment weakens further the arguments for strategic trade policies. The reason is that investment blurs the distinction between foreign and national firms. Investment multiplies the links (both inward and outward leakages) between economies so that an assessment of true gains and losses from any particular policy becomes much more difficult. If trade policy becomes less effective in the presence of investment it may be thought that countries should instead pursue investment policies. The nature and effects of such policies are examined in later sections of this paper. Before turning to that issue Section 3 considers how foreign investment affects the economies of host countries.

3. EFFECTS OF FOREIGN DIRECT INVESTMENT

Investment influences the structure of the host economy. As a consequence, it affects, among other things, the host country's level of employment, the composition of factors of production (including technology and human capital), the nature of competition in domestic markets and the country's external balance of trade. Investment, of course, provides goods which could not otherwise be available to consumers through trade. Any assessment of foreign investment must compare this positive effect on the demand side with possibly negative effects on the supply side. This section focuses on the impact of investment on the supply side.

Public debate on the economic effects of foreign investment has focused almost exclusively on the level of employment and the balance of trade.[3] Yet, there is no

---

[2] See Kay (1991) for a review of the reasons for vertical integration.

[3] I do not examine here the debate on political or security repercussions of such things as

way of determining a priori the employment and trade effects of individual investment cases. This does not mean that
investment has no effect on them. It only
means that it is not generally predictable.

Nonetheless, a popular argument in favour of foreign direct investment is that
it generates jobs. A popular argument
against it is that it destroys jobs. Either
argument is wrong. In the short-term, the
overall level of employment depends on
macroeconomic conditions and policies.
In the long term, it depends on supply-
side conditions influencing labour mobility, retraining and so on.

It is true, of course, that investment affects employment in particular industries. In an economy which is close to full
employment and where there are no
firms competing with the foreign investor, investment will bid up wages and attract workers from within the industry
and from other industries. An increase in
real wages raises buying power and the
standard of living. In an economy which
suffers from unemployment and where
there are firms competing with the foreign investor, investment may create jobs
in one region but displace workers in rival firms in other regions. There is no
priori rule stipulating that the net effect
is either positive or negative.

The same can be said about the trade
effect of investment. Foreign firms and
governments claim that their investment
should be welcome because it helps to
reduce the host countries' bilateral deficits (e.g., US-Japan, EC-Japan). This is
bad economics answering bad economics. The correct answer, which for fear of
protectionist recriminations is not given,
is that bilateral deficits do not matter
while overall deficits reflect the gap in

domestic consumption and income, or
investment and savings.

There is another reason for not attach-
ing too much importance to the employment or trade effects of investment. Even
if the effects are negative, restrictions on
investment may exacerbate them and, in
any case, would not be the optimum policy for dealing with unemployment or
trade deficit problems. Consider what
would happen if restrictions were imposed on investment. If foreign firms
could replace their locally produced
goods with exports, local firms would experience a similar negative effect but the
local economy would be deprived from
any new job opportunities. The host
country's external balance could similarly worsen by a shift from investment
to exports, prompting the government to
impose restrictions on trade. But, trade
barriers are a third-best if not fourth-best
response to the problem of unemployment or external deficit. If protectionism
is a suboptimum policy-response to these
problems, there is even less justification
for resorting to investment restrictions for
the same purpose. What is ignored in
public policy discussions is that restrictions on investment for the purpose of
creating employment may also require restrictions on trade.

Of course, foreign firms may not be
able to substitute completely locally-pro-
duced goods with exports from their operations in other countries. But, the lower
the degree of substitution, the higher the
loss to the host country from forgone consumption of those goods.

Given the imperfections in the markets
in which multinational firms operate, the
interesting, and perhaps, crucial effects
of investment are those on the host country's resource endowment and market
structure. The question that really needs
to be asked is not whether foreign investment generates new jobs but whether it
differs from investment by domestic

---

foreign control of national assets. For a discussion of the relationship between economic
interests and security interests see Winters
(1990).

firms? Do foreign firms create low-quality employment? Do they drain the host countries' technological know-how? And, do they subvert competition?

Foreign companies, Japanese in particular, are often believed to establish low-skill, "screwdriver," operations whose aim is merely to assemble imported components within the host country's tariff wall. The finished products compete directly with those of local firms which may employ skilled workers and engineers. Even though investment does not have a systematic or identifiable effect on the overall level of employment it is still suspected of replacing engineering jobs with manual jobs.

As already explained, a firm which undertakes investment abroad needs to own unique intangible assets that enable it to survive competition in foreign markets. There are several reasons why investment entails a transfer of some of those assets from the home country to the host country. First, in many service sectors trade is either not technically feasible or cost-effective. Because the supply of these services requires close contact between their providers and consumers, foreign firms which want to supply non-tradeable services need to establish a permanent presence in local markets. They have to transfer their skills to local personnel. Apart from the national origin of the firm, investment in these services most probably has effects which are similar to those of corresponding investments undertaken by local firms. Most importantly, for many developing countries which lack human capital, investment in services is a major source of new human capital.

Transfer of skills, technology and other know-how also occurs in manufacturing investment. The magnitude and characteristics of this transfer vary from industry to industry and depend both on the nature of the market and the age of the investment. Complex or newly developed technology is more likely to be transferred within multinational firms than by other arrangements involving open market transactions. That is, complex technologies tend to spread geographically within MNCs without changing ownership. Mansfield and Romeo (1980) found that the technologies made available by US firms to their overseas affiliates were more modern than those sold or licensed to independent companies. Other studies have also found that intra-firm transfers involved more advanced technologies (Behrman and Wallender, 1976) and that new technologies were transferred more quickly to affiliates than to other firms (McFetridge, 1987). Therefore, the multinational firm is the major channel for the cross-border flow of new and advanced technologies.

This, of course, does not imply that every time a firm invests abroad it also transfers its latest technology. A firm, for example, many only intend to assemble components. Empirical studies on the conditions under which technology transfer takes place have indicated the existence of a correlation between transfers, the age of investment and host-country characteristics. Several studies have found that as subsidiaries become more familiar with their host economies they tend to receive more technology from their parent companies (Teece, 1976; Davidson, 1980; and Blomstrom and Zejan, 1981). More interestingly, there appears to be a positive relationship between the complexity of the transferred technology and the technological capability of the host country (Teece, 1976; and Kokko, 1990).

At first glance these findings may seem paradoxical. Why would MNCs be more inclined to send technology and other know-how to countries that are already technologically advanced? These results cease to be surprising when considering the MNCs survive global rivalry in imperfectly competitive markets by continually developing new assets. A country with a strong science/technology base is more likely to have innovative firms. A foreign investor would want to use that country's technology to compete more effectively. Moreover, it would need to use its own latest technology in competing. It would be able to do that because of the local availability of highly trained workers.

The fact that MNCs operate in imperfectly competitive markets and that investment is undertaken when market entry through trade is difficult, suggests an additional beneficial effect for host countries. Direct investment most probably intensifies competition, forcing local firms to become more efficient and innovative (Mansfield and Romeo, 1980). It can also drive them out of business, releasing their assets to more productive uses. In fact, a recent analysis of the impact of US investment in Europe concluded that the presence of American firms provided a stimulus to the revival of industries which had been more successful in the past (Cantwell, 1989). It is worth remembering that one of the main findings of the earlier studies on direct investment was that host countries experienced gains in productivity induced by the presence of foreign firms (Dunning, 1958).

It can be concluded, therefore, that in general, investment confers considerable benefits to host economies. It makes goods and services available at lower prices and/or larger amounts than were possible before the investment. It functions as a conduit for the flow of skills, information, technology and other know-how. It intensifies competition and accelerates the rate of innovation in local markets. Such benefits may not be present in *each* case of investment, but this does not constitute a *general* case against foreign investment.

4. POLICIES FOR MANAGING INVESTMENT?

For a large country free trade is preferable to no trade. A large country, however, also has incentives to influence trade to its advantage. Similarly, the existence of imperfections in the markets where investments take place may tempt governments to force foreign firms to transfer more of their technology and do more manufacturing of sophisticated products in their domestic markets. Any policy that seeks to influence foreign investment decisions by imposing restrictions or performance requirements on foreign firms must be able to make a distinction between national and foreign firms. Perhaps, this may be thought of as an obvious and trivial requirement. But, it is neither obvious nor trivial in a world in which MNC operations span many countries in many different forms.

There are statistical conventions on what constitutes foreign direct investment and how its national origin is to be determined. These conventions may or may not be economically meaningful. For example, an investment which is classified as Japanese may not be wholly financed by Japanese sources, nor need it involve transfers of only Japanese technology. Conversely, a firm which is classified as national may carry out a large proportion of its manufacturing operations in other countries. Therefore, in a world of multinational firms, origin need not coincide with the location which experiences the economic effects of the operations of a multinational firm. Moreover, the nationality of a firm need not coincide with the nationality of subsidiary firms in which it maintains share holdings.

These differences between the nationality of a firm and the location of its various operations reduce both the usefulness and effectiveness of policies that attempt to target foreign firms. For many purposes it would not be useful to target only foreign firms since in most OECD countries a sizeable proportion of national firms also have operations in third countries. For example, Julius (1990) has estimated that sales of foreign subsidiaries of US companies account for up to 20 per cent of US GNP.

Given that national firms have operations in other countries they would probably have to be targeted as well. If the objective of an investment policy is to bring about a particular economic effect in the host country there is no reason why it should focus exclusively on foreign firms. If, for example, a government perceives benefits in requiring foreign firms to manufacture locally at least 50 per cent of the products they sell in the domestic market, why should it not extend the same requirement to the products of national firms with overseas operations. It should be obvious that when pushed to their logical extreme these requirements are equivalent to policies favouring a move closer to autarky.

Even if it would be useful to target only foreign-owned firms it would still be hard to pursue a policy which could achieve its objectives effectively. The reason is that a foreign firm usually can choose from among several modes of investment. It can be the sole owner of a purpose-built factory, or it can establish a joint venture for the manufacturing of a new product, or it can have a local firm manufacture its products under its supervision, or it can manufacture under a local firm's brand name. The exact mode of investment will depend on the strategic objectives of the investor, the nature of its technology and the prevailing policies of the host-country government. Therefore, if policies change foreign firms would change their optimum mode of investment accordingly. Investments which are clearly identifiable as foreign may be-

come significantly less so after the implementation of restrictive policies on the activities of foreign firms.

An example of how interventionist policies blur the distinction between domestic and foreign products and firms is provided by some of the results of the EC's anti-dumping actions. Following a series of anti-dumping measures against their products in the 1980s, Japanese electronics manufacturers established both wholly-owned subsidiaries in Europe and joint ventures with the firms that lodged the dumping complaints. Such kind of investment may or may not have been a direct response to the anti-dumping measures. What is interesting is that firms like Olivetti, Philips, Siemens, Thompson and Groupe Bull have some of the products under their labels manufactured by Japanese firms. The question that EC trade authorities should ask is who gains from the restrictions on Japanese products and who gains from any subsidies to European firms?

5. LOCAL-CONTENT REQUIREMENTS AND TECHNOLOGY TRANSFER

A frequent restriction imposed on foreign firms concerns limits to the proportion of imported components they may use in products they manufacture in the host country's market. It should be noted that, with one exception, in the EC such restrictions affect only investments in depressed areas. Investments which qualify for subsidies under regional assistance programmes may be subject to various performance requirements (e.g., specified minimum duration of investment, employment targets, specified amount of extra-regional sales, etc). These performance requirements are not examined in this paper because they are not supposed to be administered in a discriminatory manner and also because there already exists a large literature on their impact on regional regeneration (see the literature cited in Bachtler, 1990). . . .

Local content regulations have a certain effect on investment. If it is assumed that in the absence of any restrictions, firms would choose the mode of investment that minimises their costs, a policy that forces them to change their preferred investment plans must also increase their costs. They will raise their local-content rate only if alternative ways of gaining access to a particular market are even costlier. In practice this means that exports are restricted by trade barriers. Therefore, a country which wants to raise the local-content of foreign manufacturing operations will also have to impose trade restrictions. As already mentioned above, a combination of investment and trade restrictions will bring that country closer to a state of autarky.

It may be thought that the cost of such restrictions is outweighed by the benefits of forcing foreign firms to transfer more of their technology. But, what is the evidence on the record of policies that attempt to force technology transfer? Most of the empirical analysis on the effects of investment policies has focused on the performance requirements administered by developing countries. This analysis has found little evidence that performance requirements have had any success in expediting the transfer of technology. In fact, these requirements appear to worsen distortions in host countries because they are as a rule accompanied by subsidies and other incentives which are intended to compensate MNCs for having to buy, for example, larger quantities of local materials (Greenaway, 1991). The few studies that have specifically carried out intercountry comparisons have found that technology transfers are inversely related to the level of distortions and costs imposed by host-country policies (Kokko, 1990; and McFetridge, 1987).

Most arguments in favour of some kind of performance requirements stress the importance of the positive externalities that are believed to be generated by the production of high-tech products and by R&D activities. Assume that such externalities do indeed create a virtuous cycle of new technologies, more competitive national firms and ultimately a higher level of prosperity. Are performance requirements the optimum policy for achieving that objective? There are several reasons why the answer is unlikely to be in the affirmative.

First, an optimum policy is the one which offsets directly the perceived market distortion and which has the least negative side-effects. If there are externalities in R&D, the efficient policy is to subsidise directly the local R&D operations of any firm irrespective of nationality.[4] Performance requirements which apply to foreign firms affect only part of the overall R&D activities within a country.

Second, MNCs respond positively to the technological capability of host countries. They voluntarily transfer more technology to the country whose technological capacity is perceived to be improving the competitiveness of their rivals. Hence, one way to encourage technology transfer is to support education and research in science and technology. Research and education are activities with pervasive positive externalities which should be attracting public support anyway.

Third, in a world of multinational firms the beneficial results of measures that target firms may appear in other countries (Blomstrom and Lipsey, 1989). Blomstrom (1990), for example, shows that Sweden has run for many years programs

---

[4] Even those who advocate trade management argue that the nationality of a firm should not be an issue of policy activism. See Tyson (1990).

assisting the R&D efforts of MNCs. In 1985 it had the highest level of R&D expenditure per unit of output among all the major industrial countries. Yet, Sweden's international competitiveness in high-tech products has actually declined over the past decade. Blomstrom's main explanation is that the firms that benefited from those support programs carried out the manufacturing of high-tech products in other countries.

It is still an open question whether the positive externalities of high-tech production emanate from the R&D stage or the manufacturing stage. The fact that such questions remain, implies that it cannot be simply asserted that either investment restrictions or subsidies will eventually boost the production and exports of high-tech products. Even if they do, they cannot be presumed to be the optimum policy for strengthening a country's technological capability.

6. RECIPROCITY INVESTMENT?

Some countries are more open to foreign investment than others. Yet, there is hardly a country which is completely free of statutory barriers to foreign ownership or involvement in certain industries. Even the United States which prides itself for its openness, severely restricts foreign investment in industries such as civil and maritime transportation, broadcasting and telecommunications (see Woolcock, 1991). Structural barriers are also pervasive in many countries. Feelings of unfairness are often aroused when domestic firms are taken over by foreign firms which are protected from takeovers.[5] For example, complex regulations protect Dutch and Swiss firms from hos-

tile takeovers. Cross-shareholdings by banks protect German and Japanese firms.

In practice, vulnerability to hostile takeovers is an issue only in two countries: Britain and the United States. Their problem is caused not so much by foreign predators but by the fact that their stock markets do not only provide capital but also discipline management. In those countries stock markets also function as markets for corporate control. But, the occurrence of hostile acquisitions is exaggerated. In 1987, for example, at the height of the merger wave in Britain less than five per cent of all mergers and takeovers were hostile. Takeovers by unwelcome foreign firms were even rarer.

Protection from takeovers does not necessarily confer an unfair advantage. Nicolaides and Thomsen (1991) explain why protection from takeovers has its hidden costs. Extensive involvement by banks in corporate affairs may afford firms the ability to take a long-term perspective on their investments but it also reduces their ability to react quickly to changing market conditions. More importantly, any firm has to pay the going market price for the firm it wants to acquire. If the firm which launches the takeover bid has some advantage that other firms do not have and, therefore, it is prepared to pay a price higher than that at which the market previously valued the target firm, the market will react accordingly and attach a monetary value to that advantage. In well-functioning, well-informed markets that advantage will tend to be dissipated. In the end the shareholders of the target firm will get a higher price than otherwise. Foreign bidding will raise the value of domestic firms and their sale will result in more wealth being transferred to the domestic economy.

However, the equilibrating function of the market does not make other countries more open to American or British investment. Hence, there may still be a role for

---

[5] Feelings of unfairness are also aroused when foreign companies are believed to benefit from access to cheap capital. The Appendix examines in more detail whether and how cheap capital confers a competitive advantage.

a reciprocity requirement in investment. The country which is prominent for its unusually low inward investment is Japan. The asymmetry between outward and inward investment in Japan is of the order of 33:1 (cumulative 1980-88). In comparison, the same ratio for Germany is 6:1, for France 1.5:1 and for Britain 2:1 (Julius, 1990). Yoshitomi (1991) explains this asymmetry as the result of the strong competitiveness of Japanese firms and the Japanese practice of building long-term relations between manufacturers and banks and between manufacturers and their suppliers and distributors (i.e., the "Keiretsu" system). Yoshitomi argues that the Japanese market is difficult to enter not because of discriminatory policies,[6] but because it is fiercely competitive and puts emphasis on high-quality products. He does not believe that the Keiretsu system discriminates against foreigners.

In a recent paper Dornbusch (1990) proposes that the United States retaliates against Japan unless the latter increases its imports by a specified amount. Dornbusch's rationale is that it is not statutory barriers that close Japan's market to foreign products but the invisible, structural, peculiarities such as the Keiretsu system. Unless Japanese firms are forced to buy foreign products they will never break out of their entrenched habits. Should a similar target be set for investment?

GATT has no rules on investment. The Uruguay Round negotiations on investment refer only to measures that have a trade effect. Although the OECD does have agreements which make recommendations about the treatment of foreign

investors, they are not agreements about liberalisation, nor are they backed up by GATT's elaborate dispute-settlement procedures. Hence, a country that wants to achieve liberalization in cross-border direct investment will have to act unilaterally. Apart from identifying and pressing for the removal of foreign discriminatory policies and statutory restrictions, it is difficult to see what else could be done that would bring benefits to the home country rather than its multinational firms.

The Japanese in particular would have no difficulty in establishing a few more joint ventures with foreign firms in Japan. They already have joint ventures and other cooperative agreements practically with all the American and European electronics, computer and automobile producers. Third-country firms may gain from new cooperative arrangements but it is far from clear how their home countries will benefit. This does not mean that home countries can never gain. The operations of Texas Instruments and ICI, for example, in Japan may provide the parent companies with revenue, technology and other information which are indispensable to the rest of their operations in other countries. As a result, their operations in the United States and Britain may prosper. But, are such benefits to the United States and Britain worth the costs of imposing restrictions on Japanese investment?

The answer cannot be an unqualified yes. The benefits from a pound's worth of investment in Japan will be spread to several countries (because TI and ICI are multinational). By contrast, the loss of a pound's worth of potential Japanese investment will be borne entirely either by the United States or Britain. Therefore, the validity of the argument for reciprocity very much depends on the existence of intangible benefits (e.g., access to technology) that can somehow succeed in generating more benefits in the longer

---

[6] Statutory barriers to foreign investment in Japan have largely been removed. Restrictions will remain in agriculture, mining, petroleum refining and leather processing. Special regulations affect entry into financial services and telecommunications.

term to the home countries than those that would be generated by Japanese investment of equivalent initial value. It is not impossible to think of a situation in which positive externalities from high-technology production spread more easily from the overseas operations of national firms than from the local operations of foreign firms. This implies, however, that reciprocity requirements would need to have specific technology-transfer objectives. As argued in previous sections, it is neither easy to target such externalities, nor to evaluate the cost and benefits of a policy that attempts to target them. Moreover, targeting externalities from high-technology production would entail a policy with considerable bureaucratic discretion.

The most powerful argument against reciprocity requirements, especially those with a high degree of decision-making discretion, is that they can easily be abused by other countries. There is no country which does not have a policy that some other country does not take offence to. The possibility that any one country becomes better off by the pursuit of reciprocity is much reduced when all major investing countries attempt to identify foreign policies that would justify their own restrictive measures.

7. CONCLUSION

I have argued in this paper that in general it cannot be presumed that foreign investment is detrimental to host countries and that discriminatory treatment of foreign firms is unwarranted and unlikely to be effective. This does not mean that the removal of foreign restrictions to investment should not be sought. But, this objective should not be confused with the pursuit of beggar-thy-neighbor policies under the pretext of correcting supposed market distortions.

There is another general conclusion that can be drawn from this paper. In-

vestment reduces the efficiency and desirability of trade policy that seeks to support particular firms or industries. As the distinction between national and foreign firms gets blurred, trade policy should instead be targeting the immobile factor of production. But, this raises the question: why should border measures be used to maintain employment or the quality of labour skills? In a world which is becoming increasingly integrated in many different ways, the distinction between domestic and outside markets or national and foreign firms is hardly the basis for rational policies.

REFERENCES

AKIMUNE, ?. (1991), "Japan's Direct Investment in the EC," in M. Yoshitomi. *Japanese Direct Investment in Europe.*

BACHTLER, J. (1990), "Grants for Inward Investors: Giving Away Money?" *National Westminster Bank Quarterly Review* (May).

BALDWIN, R. (1989). "The Political Economy of Trade Policy," *Journal of Economic Perspectives,* 3.

BEHRMAN, J. and H. WALLENDER (1976), *Transfer of Manufacturing Technology within Multinational Enterprises* (Cambridge, MA: Ballinger).

BLOMSTROM, M. (1990), "Host Country Benefits of Foreign Investment, mimeo, Stockholm School of Economics.

BLOMSTROM, M. and R. LIPSEY, (1989), "The Export Performance of US and Swedish Multinationals," *Review of Income and Wealth,* 35.

BLOMSTROM, M. and M. ZEJAN (1991), "Why Do Multinational Firms Seek Out Joint Venture?" *Journal of International Development,* 3.

CANTWELL, J. (1989), *Technological Innovation and Multinational Corporations* (Oxford: Basil Blackwell).

DAVIDSON, W. (1980), *Experience Effects in International Investment and Tech-*

nology Transfer (Ann Arbor, MI: University of Michigan Press).

DORNBUSCH, R. (1990), "Policy Options for Freer Trade: The Case for Bilateralism," in Lawrence and Schultze, An American Trade Strategy.

DUNNING, J. (1958), American Investment in British Manufacturing Industry (London: Allen & Unwin).

GREENAWAY, D. (1991), "Why Are We Negotiating on TRIMS?" in D. Greenaway et al. (eds.) Global Protectionism (London: Macmillan).

JETRO (1990), Current Situation of Business Operations of Japanese Manufacturing Enterprises in Europe (Tokyo: MITI).

JULIUS, D. (1990), Global Companies and Public Policy (London: Pinter for the Royal Institute of International Affairs).

JULIUS, D. and S. THOMSEN (1988), Foreign Direct Investment among the G-5, The Royal Institute of International Affairs.

KAY, J. (1991), "Managing Relations with Customers and Suppliers," Business Strategy Review, 2.

KOKKO, A. (1990), "Host Country Competition and Technology Transfer by US Multinationals," mimeo, Stockholm School of Economics.

LAWRENCE, R. and C. SCHULTZE, eds. (1990), An American Trade Strategy (Washington, DC: Brookings).

MANSFIELD, E. and A. ROMEO (1980), "Technology Transfer, Productivity and Economic Analysis," Quarterly Journal of Economics, 95.

MCFETRIDGE, D. (1987). "The Timing, Mode and Terms of Technology Transfer," in A. Safarian and G. BERTIN, eds., Multinationals, Governments, and International Technology Transfer (London: Croom Helm).

NICOLAIDES, P. and S. THOMSEN (1991), "The Impact of 1992 on Direct Investment in Europe," European Business Journal (forthcoming).

TEECE, D. (1976), The Multinational Corporation and the Resource Cost of International Technology Transfer (Cambridge, MA: Ballinger).

THOMSEN, S. and P. NICOLAIDES (1991), The Evolution of Japanese Direct Investment in Europe (Hemel Hempstead: Harvester Wheatsheaf).

TYSON, L.D. (1990), "Managed Trade," in Lawrence and Schultze, An American Trade Strategy.

WINTERS, L.A. (1990), "Digging for Victory: Agricultural Policy and National Security," The World Economy, 13, 170–190.

WOOLCOCK, S. (1991), "Trading Partners or Trading Blows," mimeo, The Royal Institute of International Affairs.

YOSHITOMI, M. (1991), Japanese Direct Investment in Europe (Aldershot: Avebury Press).

CHAPTER 8

The American Economy and International Debt

The articles in this section discuss the political economy of international debt. Esmail Hosseinzadeh, a member of the Union for Radical Political Economics, considers oil price rises, interest rate increases, the value of the dollar, the decline of commodity prices, and capital flight as causes of the debt crisis of less developed countries. He proposes partial debt write-off, compensation for lost export earnings, and capital repatriation as solutions to the debt problem.

The second article, "Developing Country Debt," was prepared by the U.S. Department of State. It argues that the global debt crisis is the result of several causes, including inappropriate domestic policies in debtor countries, excessively liberal lending policies by international banks, the 1979 oil price shock, increases in international interest rates, a decline in commodity prices, and the international recession. It also reviews the history of American proposals to deal with the issue.

27.   Global Debt: Causes and Cures

Esmail Hosseinzadeh

INTRODUCTION

Primitive accumulation of capital—whether capitalist or socialist—has appropriately been considered key to an industrialization "take-off." It played a cru-

SOURCE: Reprinted with permission of the Union for Radical Political Economics from *Review of Radical Political Economics,* vol. 20, nos. 2 and 3, Summer 1988, pp. 223–233. Copyright, Review of Radical Political Economics.

cial role in the early industrialization stages of Europe, especially of England; in the nineteenth century infra-structure building of the United States and Canada (largely funded by loans from Europe); in the primitive "socialist" accumulation in the Soviet Union; and in the reconstruction of Europe and Japan after World War II (WW II) through the Marshall Plan.

Viewed in this light, the tens of billions of petrodollars that were generated as a result of the oil price hikes of the 1970s constituted the potential for the largest primitive accumulation of capital to date which could be used for the industrialization of developing countries. Instead, the massive amounts of petrodollars (along with Eurodollars and the so-called "cheap money" of the early 1970s) found their way into the coffers of the big commercial banks and the pockets of the corrupt "leaders" of the borrowing countries, which triggered their external debt problem.

This study is an attempt to show the following.

(a) Contrary to popular perception, the oil price shocks of the 1970s did not cause the developing countries' external debt crisis, although they greatly accelerated that crisis. The major reason for the debt problem, in our opinion, was the shift away from official concessionary lending to private commercial bank lending.

(b) To the extent that petrodollars contributed to the debt crisis, the blame lies not with those dollars per se, but with the policy responses to them (i.e., policies of "recycling" and ways of using those dollars).

(c) Of the immense Third World debt, only a small fraction of the loans has actually been received by (and spent in) these countries. The major bulk of the debt has snowballed as a result of factors *exogenous* to their economies. Debtor nations are not responsible for this snowballed portion of the debt, and it therefore cannot be considered *"legitimate."*

ORIGINS OF THE WORLD DEBT CRISIS

Oil Price Shocks—Major Cause for the Debt Crisis?

The structure of the developing countries' external financial receipts in the post-war period has undergone considerable change. Whereas in the earlier part of this period the major bulk of those receipts consisted of official concessional finance, in the later part, especially after the late 1960s and early 1970s, commercial bank lending became the dominant source of those receipts. This gradual move away from concessional financing—consisting mainly of long-term, low-interest, project-related financing—to non-concessional, private bank lending is clearly reflected in Figure 27.1. It is obvious from this figure that while in the 1960-78 period the official development assistance (ODA) to developing countries decreased from 58 percent of their total external financial receipts to 30 percent private bank lending rose from about two percent to about 33 percent.

No doubt the oil price shocks of the 1970s accelerated this trend. But to view this contributory effect as the cause for skyrocketing of commercial bank lending, hence for the Third World debt problem, is challenging the reality of those developments. Evidence shows that the shift away from concessionary financing to private commercial lending—the major culprit in the debt crisis, in our opinion—took place prior to the oil shocks.

For example, Kristin Hallberg, using the official data of the Federal Reserve Board of Governors, shows that "real private bank lending grew 144 percent" between the years 1970-1973. Citing Charles Kindleberger's private correspondence (a renowned authority on international finance), she further shows that the expansion of commercial lending "coincided with the 'cheap money' push of 1971, when bankers looked to developing countries for riskier investments to maintain their income" (1986:9-10).

Several factors prompted the switch away from multilateral, official lending to commercial bank lending. Top among these factors was what might be called a weakening of Bretton Woods objectives. The essence of these objectives was to redress and expand the world capitalist

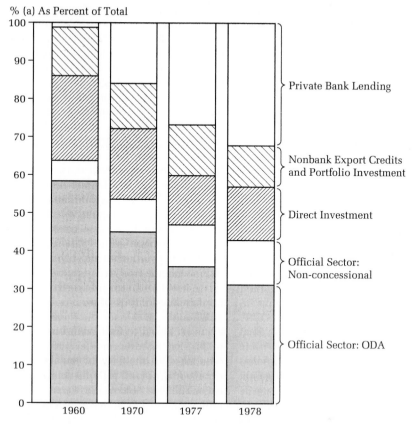

% (a) As Percent of Total

Figure 27.1
Long-Term Changes in the Structure of Developing Countries Total Net External Financial Receipts, 1960–78
SOURCE: OECD, Development Cooperation, 1979.

system which was badly shaken by the war and threatened by the spread of national liberation and other social movements in many parts of the world. To this end, the historic conference that convened in Bretton Woods, New Hampshire, in 1944, instituted the International Monetary Fund (IMF), the International Bank for Reconstruction and Development (World Bank), and a fixed exchange rate based on gold or the United States dollar. Although the original goal of establishing the IMF and the World Bank was to reconstruct the wartorn Europe and Japan, the United States

soon began to divert the resources of these institutions to the Third World.

To understand this interest of the United States in the Third World, we need to step back in time and put things into perspective. In the immediate aftermath of the war, the United States was not only challenging the expanding influence of the Soviet Union in the Third World, it was also trying to fend off or preempt independent national liberation and social movements in these countries, i.e., movements that had nothing or very little to do with the U.S.S.R. Furthermore, it was competing with its European allies over Third World markets and raw materials. Although these allies were weakened by the war and in need of the U.S. aid, they still controlled most of their colonial territories of the past and, in effect, kept U.S. capital out of those territories and markets.

Under these circumstances, where the Third World seemed at a cross-roads between capitalism and socialism (or something other than capitalism), the United States set out to block the latter road and coax, coerce, or force these countries to move along the former one. Thus its financial assistance to the Third World during this period was primarily based on geo-political and *long-term* economic considerations rather than short-term, cost-benefit calculations. And this is why most of the financial flows to these countries at that time were in the form of either outright aid or concessionary, development-related loans through multilateral institutions. The fate of Third World economies at this stage was too precarious to be entrusted with commercial banks.

By the late 1960s and early 1970s, this pattern of Third World financing changed as private banks began to lend to these countries on a commercial basis. A number of factors precipitated this switch: (a) the Cold war atmosphere and the fierce "East-West" rivalry in the Third World had subsided by this time, (b) most of the socio-political upheavals in ex-colonies and other less developed countries had also ebbed by the late 1960s, and (c) most of the developing countries had by now adopted a capitalist path of development. Whereas prior to this time private banks were reluctant to lend to developing countries because their economies were considered too volatile and their financial markets too unstructured, these banks now began to lend as most of these countries emerged as sovereign nations whose economies and financial markets appeared capable of absorbing substantial debt on a commercial basis. These favorable economic conditions for private bank lending were further reinforced by favorable political and legislative conditions as OECD countries (i.e., major industrialized capitalist countries) relaxed barriers that previously hampered commercial lending to developing countries: "Bank lending could [now] be expanded fairly rapidly, without the need to go through the legislative and budgetary processes of national governments" (Lomax 1986:8).

Commercial bank lending was further accelerated by a "natural" or "evolutionary" process of the accumulation of huge sums of finance capital in the coffers of Western big banks during the three decades of economic expansion and stability since WW II. This accumulation of bank capital was a culmination of several developments: the post-war expansionary cycle of the advanced capitalist economies; the Korean and Vietnam wars, which led to the flow of huge sums of dollars and/or Eurodollars into the hands of banks; the U.S. inflationary monetary policy that began under President Johnson, which led to the emergence of the so-called "cheap money" in the early 1970s; and, finally, the petrodollars of the 1970s. Part of the massive finance capital that resulted from these developments was bound to find its way to foreign lending, especially from the United States, where the Glass-Stegall Act prevented commercial banks from underwriting and selling corporate securities at home.

As these developments led to bank loan officers roaming the Third World pressing their wares, they also created favorable conditions and big appetites for borrowing in the non-oil developing countries. For the inflationary/expansionary cycle and the accompanied "cheap money" mentioned above, positively affected the economies of these countries. On the one hand, it raised both the amount and the price of their exports, on the other, it reduced the cost of borrowing, as it reduced the rate of interest.

This brief overview refutes the claim that the oil price shocks of the 1970s were the major cause for the global debt problem—although it does not deny their contributory or accelerating impact—since it shows that the expansion of bank lending as a result of those oil shocks took place within the general context of the expansion of bank lending.

POLICIES AND RESPONSIBILITIES OF THE OECD COUNTRIES AND THE LENDING INSTITUTIONS

Although the oil price shocks contained the immense potential for an international financial imbalance, and hence for the debt crisis, this crisis was not inevitable. The policy responses to the oil price hikes contributed more to the crisis than did the price hikes as such.

As far as the policies of the OECD countries are concerned, the flip-flop character of those policies was more responsible for the crisis than the policies themselves: policy responses of these countries to the first oil shock (1973-74) were diametrically opposed to their reactions to the second oil shock (1979-80).

The first major concern of these countries in the face of the 1973-74 oil shock was to maintain economic expansion "through joint expansionary policies which would maintain growth. . . . This argument reached its peak in the Bonn summit of July 1978 when the summit countries decided to adopt a locomotive theory of growth, with the major OECD countries agreeing to take action to help stimulate demand" (Lomax 1986:18). The second major concern was that the surplus resulting from the oil price hikes should be recycled toward the "deficit countries" so that their growth could also be maintained.

Unfortunately, these countries (in compliance with the wishes of the big private banks) also decided to expand the role of commercial banks in the projected recycling effort. As a supplementary step, they also decided to expand Eurocurrency markets, since Eurocurrency was the universal form of the surplus, and the surplus had therefore been converted into mainly Eurocurrency deposits.

To be sure, there was some opposition to the involvement of private banks on the grounds that these banks were not trustworthy in the matters of international trade and finance, and that therefore the recycling of the surplus ought to be accomplished through official, multilateral, concessionary financing. But the views that favored the involvement of commercial banks prevailed. These included the views of most OECD countries and the international organizations under their control, as expressed through the voices of their finance ministers or central bank officials. For example, the May 1974 issue of the *IMF Survey* stated:

Private markets have a basic role to play here, and it is to them that we must look for the main contribution in financing prospective balance of payment disequilibria. In the first instance, the Eurocurrency markets may be expected to be the main channel. These markets are well equipped to handle large volumes of funds, and they offer the flexibility and the anonymity that the lenders desire.

Denis Healey, the British Chancellor of the Exchequer, commended the role played by the commercial banks in recycling the surplus and strongly recommended the continuation of that role in his speech to the IMF in September 1977: "The commercial banking system has rightly played the main role in financing these deficits until now and has shown immense resourcefulness and flexibility in doing so."

Similar assessments and prescriptions were heard on the side of the United States. For example, William Miller, the United States Secretary of Treasury at the time, made the following recommendation in his speech at the 1979 IMF/IBRD annual meeting: "We all recognize that the private markets will . . . have to play by far the major role in channelling financing from surplus to deficit nations. Official institutions, including the IMF, play a vital role in this process, but it is essentially catalyctic in the nature."

Not surprisingly, the decision to expand the role of private banks and Eurocurrency markets led to an immediate and rapid expansion of both the share of commercial bank lending and of the Eurocurrency markets. Eurocurrency markets expanded in the 1973-82 period by almost six times, from $295 billion in 1973 to 1,689 in 1982 (Lomax, 1986:30, Table 2.8). And by 1984, "commercial banks' share of the total guaranteed medium- and long-term debt owed by non-oil developing countries to private creditors had risen to 86 percent" (Hallberg, 1986:12).

As a result of this easy monetary policy and vigorous expansion effort, the expansionary cycle that had started before the 1973-74 oil shock continued unhampered despite the recessionary or hindering effects exerted by the oil price shocks. The expansionary monetary policies (based on the locomotive theory) in the OECD countries, especially in the United States, positively affected the developing countries, even the non-oil ones. On the one hand, it kept the real interest rate very low, hence their borrowing cost very low, on the other, it raised their export earnings, both in terms of volume and prices. True, their debt was gradually building up, but there was no danger of a default as the steady growth in income, exports, and higher prices of primary goods during this period were reducing the external debt burden on these countries. Indeed, because

of low real interest rates and healthy export growth, their debt service ratio—the ratio of interest and amortization payments to export earnings—showed only moderate rises, from 16 percent in 1973 to 23 percent in 1980 (Lomax 1986:32, Table 2.11).

Thus, the 1973-79 period, the period between the two oil shocks, witnessed a healthy annual growth rate in the OECD countries, ranging on the average from 3.6 to 6.1 percent; in the non-oil developing countries, from 5 to 6.1 percent; and in international trade, an annual average growth of 5.5 percent (Ibid: 18, Table 2.5).

As noted earlier, the policy response of the OECD countries to the 1979-80 oil price hikes was diametrically opposed to their response in 1973-74. Instead of maintaining expansionary monetary policy in order to maintain the level of growth, of income and of world trade, these countries now resorted to tight monetary policy to control inflation. The pronounced expression of this new policy was Paul Volker's departure from the 1979 Belgrade IMF/IBRD conference before it was officially over in order to prepare the new monetary policy in October. The new policy created a ripple effect in the opposite direction of the previous period: interest rates shot up, growth slowed down and the recessionary cycle (of 1980-82) set in, and the export earnings of deficit countries began to drop.

The trade deficit of the developing countries was further aggravated by the shortening of the maturity period of their debt, on the one hand, and the protectionist policies of the OECD countries (prompted by high unemployment rates), on the other. There has been no alleviation of these factors that negatively affect Third World debt: the OECD countries' protectionist policies continue, the U.S. budget and trade deficits continue, and the demand for debtor nations' primary goods also continues to be very low.

The cumulative effect of these factors

was a jump in the debt service ratio of these countries from 20 percent in 1979 to 33 percent in 1982 (Ibid: 32, Table 2.11). The absolute amount of their foreign debt rose from $220 billion at the end of 1979 to 326 at the end of 1982 and 343 in 1983 (Ibid: 31, Table 2.10; Ibid: 52). Despite all the talk about solutions to the debt problem, this snowballing process of debt has continued unabated, and it now stands at about $1.2 trillion *(The New York Times,* 1 October 1988).

POLICIES AND RESPONSIBILITIES OF THE DEBTOR COUNTRIES

Only a small portion of the massive Third World debt has actually been received by (and spent in) these countries. The rest, the bigger portion, has accumulated due to factors exogenous to the economies of these countries. These factors included the rise in the international rate of interest, the rise in the U.S. budget deficit, hence in the value of the dollar, the decline in foreign demand for the debtors' primary goods, hence the fall in their prices, and, perhaps most importantly, the flight of huge sums of capital from these countries.

According to Peter Nunnenkamp's calculations, the combined effects of external factors on Third World debt in the 1974-81 period amounted to $570 billion, of which interest rate effects accounted for $133.49 billion, lost revenues due to depressed demand for their exports constituted $104.41 billion, and the terms of trade effect accounted for the remaining $297.45 billion—Nunnenkamp attributes about half of the terms of trade effect, i.e., half of the $297.45 billion, to the effects of oil price hikes (1986:59-67, Tables 22, 23, and 24).

A big chunk of the loan money was sent back out of the debtor countries to be deposited, invested, or used to acquire real estate abroad. According to an IMF estimate, some $200 billion may have

flown out of debtor countries by the end of 1985 (cited by Lochhead, 1987:13). *Time Magazine* estimated that the amount of capital that flew out of three Latin American countries between 1979 and 1984 was about $63 billion (28 billion from Mexico, 23 billion from Venezuela, and 12 billion from Argentina) (2 July 1984 [27]).

There is evidence of instances where the lending banks collaborated with corrupt officials of the debtor countries in the plunder of the loan money. The banks involved would lend money to these officials with one hand, and take it back with the other in the form of deposits that carried different titles and lower interest rates, making profits out of the differential interest rates (Schatan 1987:84-89).

But even excluding the part of the debt that is due to external factors, the remaining part, the part that was actually borrowed and somehow spent domestically, was quite substantial, amounting to tens of billions of dollars. What happened to it? How was it spent? What are its impacts on the economic development of these countries?

A major part of this money has been spent on consumption, often wasteful consumption of the military and luxury or unessential type, rather than investment and/or production. Borrowing from abroad is not good or bad per se; it all depends on how it is spent. If it is invested in projects that will yield a rate of return higher than the rate of interest paid for the borrowed capital, then borrowing can play the positive role of initial capital formation for productive investment, without the problem of repayment. This is a pivotal point in understanding the present crisis of the Third World: the borrowed funds were viewed not as capital to be invested productively, but as income to be used for consumption, or for financing the government's operating deficits. To the extent that some of these funds were formally invested in development projects, investment priorities and development policies were often perverse: building huge stadiums and sports complexes, buying synfuel plants to supply depressed oil markets, buying national airlines where citizens travel on the back of animals or ox-driven carts, and so on. Some of these pompous, grandiose, show-case projects—often undertaken in the name of building economic infrastructure, or as symbols of "national pride"—went as far as building whole new cities from scratch, such as Brasilia in Brazil and Abuja in Nigeria. "Nigeria is building itself a capital, Abuja, from scratch. The cost, by some estimates exceeds the nation's total sovereign debt of about $20 billion. Yet Nigeria has trouble making interest payments" (Lochhead, 1987:12).

A substantial amount of these countries' resources, borrowed or otherwise, is devoted to subsidizing "national" industries and enterprises, largely in the state sector but also occasionally in the private sector. While this policy is pursued in the name of promoting "national" industries, import-substitution, or economic self-reliance, in practice it falls short of achieving these objectives. Instead, by providing easy credit and windfall finances for inefficient and unprofitable enterprises, it aggravates the pattern of inefficiency and perpetuates the lack of competitiveness. It spoils the mismanaged "national" enterprises and their corrupt and inefficient managers by financial crutches. Import tariffs, credit control, exchange controls and similar restrictions are all part of this misguided (or, perhaps, hypocritic) nationalism.

Curtailment of foreign equity investment in a number of debtor countries—Mexico, Brazil, Nigeria, Ghana, and few others—and the turn to borrowing for financing investment projects has greatly contributed to both the external debt problem and the problem of inefficiency and slow growth. While this policy is celebrated as fighting imperialism and "dependency," it is in fact a policy of self-

defeat and self-delusion. For in the case of equity investment, investors provide not only funds, technology, and skills, they also take part of the risk of investment proportionate with their invested capital. Whereas in the case of investment through borrowing, the entire risk is shouldered by the borrower. True, foreign equity investment carries a foreign claim of ownership on part of the return to investment, but that is conditional on the success of investment (i.e., if there is a return over and above the cost of production). By contrast, debt carries no ownership claim, but the interest on the loan must be paid whether the investment is profitable or not.

LESSONS ON THE PAST, SOLUTIONS TO THE PRESENT, THOUGHTS FOR THE FUTURE

Solutions to the developing countries' debt problem range from that of James Baker's (previous U.S. Treasury Secretary) plan of eternal roll-over of the debt, on the Right, to that of Cheryl Payer's (the author of the *Debt Trap*) suggestion of total repudiation, on the far Left. We disagree with both these extremes. Instead, we believe that a just solution must take into account questions of *responsibility* for and *"legitimacy"* of the debt.

Our study showed that the developing countries' debt has been greatly inflated by exogenous factors like excessive interest rates, loss of export earnings, and capital flight. This inflated or snowballed part of the debt cannot be considered the responsibility of the debtor nations, and should therefore be repudiated as illegitimate. It is the responsibility and the business of the commercial banks and the corrupt "leaders" of the debtor nations—it is their baby, so to speak. Let them take care of it. Debtor nations should not pay for the sins of those who artificially inflated their debt. Nor should the taxpayers in the commercial banks' home countries pay for it. Thus, recent suggestions that imply transferring banks' debt risk to governments, and ultimately to tax payers, through tax incentives for discounted debt or government bond for debt-bond swaps, must be opposed.

Based on the notions of *responsibility* and *"legitimacy,"* deflation of the debt to its "legitimate" size can be accomplished through the following measures.

(a) Writing off of that part of the debt that can reasonably be attributed to excessive interest charges over and above the originally-agreed-upon fixed rate of six percent that prevailed before 1976. According to Schatan's calculations, an average differential rate of interest of four percent (ten minus six percent) resulted in $105-110 billion difference in Latin America's outstanding debt in the 1976-85 period (1987:109-110). If we extend his calculations to the present time, we will obviously come to a much higher figure.

(b) Compensating for the loss of debtor nations' export earnings as a result of the drop in the price of their raw materials, which has drastically turned the terms of trade in favor of industrialized countries. Schatan estimates that if "prices of raw materials had stayed at their 1980 level, export earnings would have been some $25-30 billion higher than they actually were; had this been the case, Latin America's borrowing needs would have declined by the same amount" (Ibid.).

(c) Repatriating all the capital that left since 1976. Again, according to Schatan's estimates, the flight of capital from Latin America in the 1976-85 period was in the range of $130-150 billion (Ibid.). Obviously, had this capital not flown out of the debtor nations, their need for borrowing would have been decreased accordingly. Since the capital to be repatriated will be spent/invested in domestic currency, the foreign currency thus recovered can be used for the repayment of the "legitimate" part of the debt.

Repayment of the rest of the debt (i.e., of the "legitimate" part of the debt) can be brought about by imposing a ceiling on the annual payments relative to the debtors' export earnings, e.g., 20 percent of their annual export earnings. Alternatively, it can be brought about through the measures delineated by Schatan: (i) transformation of the monetary value of the debt into its equivalent in raw materials and/or manufactured products—reasonable unit prices can be used for this purpose; (ii) a maximum yearly rate of interest of six percent, (iii) a 25-year period for repayment of the principal; (iv) stability of commodity unit prices throughout the whole repayment period (Ibid.).

Although the steps thus laid out will help reduce and eventually remove the developing countries' debt burden, they will not in and of themselves bring about a recovery of their depressed economies. Supplementary steps are needed to bring about such a recovery. This requires a futuristic vision and a globalist perspective of the international economy, a view that transcends the mercantalist type of economic nationalism, and appreciates the increasing integration and interdependence of the world economy. Based on such a view, we propose the following measures for the revival of the depressed developing economies.

(a) An International Marshall Plan-type Package of Development. Once the external debt is taken care of via the steps outlined above, the resources pulled together through this package will no longer have to go to the coffers of commercial banks, but to economic development via long-term, low-interest, project-related loans. Allocation and supervision of the funds thus created should be the responsibility of independent multilateral institutions. Needless to say countries like Japan and West Germany with trade surpluses can contribute more to this international pool of development funds. The considerable purchasing power thus to be created will not only have a take-off effect on the revival of the developing economies, it will also give a boost to international trade and the world economy as a whole, and will help reduce trade deficits of industrial countries like the United States. Such a "reflation" and revival of the world economy "is an easy thing to do," as Juliet Schor recently put it, "made difficult only by the opposition of wealth holders fearful of inflation, and companies wary of the effects of sustained growth on labor and other costs (1988:28).

(b) Changes in the Financing and Investment policies of the Developing Countries. As noted earlier, most of these countries have either banned foreign equity investment altogether, or have reduced it to a bare minimum. Instead, they have resorted to financing via borrowing. While this policy has been carried out under populistic posturings such as national independence, economic self-sufficiency, or curtailing the "exploitation of the periphery by the core," insidious motives can often be detected beneath such posturings: protection of the interests of the state bureaucracy and the class it represents, the so-called "national" bourgeoisie, from the more efficient foreign competitors. Motivations aside, this policy has been disastrous. It must therefore be changed, and a degree of foreign equity investment (in non-strategic industries) must be combined with investment via borrowing. Although this will give foreign investors a title of ownership of a part of the return to investment, they will in return share the risk of investment, bring funds, technology and know how. More importantly, it will force the inefficient domestic capitalists and public sector managers to be more competitive, and hence, more efficient.

(c) Exclusion of Commercial Banks. Just as in the United States the Glass-Steagall Act prevents commercial banks from getting involved in the manufacturing sector of the economy, so should a similar regulation prevent these banks from tampering with the developing

economies. It may be argued that it is economic suicide to shun the immense resources these banks possess. The answer to such an argument is simple: if the commercial banks want to help, they are welcome; let them join the international development pact suggested above and accept its rules and regulations. Or, alternatively, let them accept a ceiling on their interest charges established by the return to investments financed by their loans.

REFERENCES

CARDOSO, E. A. 1987. "Latin America's Debt: Which Way Now?" *Challenge* (May-June):11–17.

CAVANAGH, JOHN et al. 1986. *From Debt to Development: Alternatives to the International Debt Crisis.* Washington D.C.: Institute for Foreign Policy.

D'ARISTA, JANE. 1979. "Private Overseas Lending: Too Far, Too Fast?" in, *Debt and the Less Developed Countries.* Jonathan D. Anderson (ed.). Boulder, CO: Westview Press.

DORNBUSCH, RUDIGER. 1984. *External Debt, Budget Deficits and Disequilibrium Exchange Rates.* National Bureau of Economic Research Working paper No. 1336, (April). Cambridge: NBER.

HALLBERG, KRISTIN. 1986. "International Debt, 1985: Origins and Issues for Future," in *World Debt Crisis: International Lending on Trial.* M. P. Claudon. (ed.). pp. 3–42. Cambridge: Ballinger Publishing Co.

KHAN, MOHSIN S. AND MALCOLM KNIGHT. 1983. "Sources of Payment Problems in LDCs." *Finance and Development* (December):2–5.

LOCHHEAD, CAROLYN. 1987. "Western Money and Holes in the Third World's Pockets." Insight (31 August).

LOMAX, DAVID F. 1986. *The Developing Country Debt Crisis.* New York: St. Martin's Press.

NUNNENKAMP, PETER. 1986. *The Interna-*

tional Debt Crisis of the Third World. New York: St. Martin's Press.

SCHATAN, JACOBO. 1987. *World Debt: Who Is To Pay?* London and New Jersey: Zed Books.

SCHOR, JULIET. 1988. "The Great Trade Debate." *Zeta Magazine* (March):24–28.

TAYLOR, L. 1985. "The Theory and Practice of Developing Country Debt: An Informal Guide for the Perplexed." *Journal of Development Planning* 16:195–227.

UNITED NATIONS, UNCTC CURRENT STUDIES. 1986. *Foreign Direct Investment in Latin America: Recent Trends, Prospects, and Policy Issues.* New York.

28.   Developing Country Debt

U.S. Department of State

BACKGROUND

The ability of many developing countries to pay their foreign debt deteriorated in the 1980s. The United States and other creditors responded by developing a flexible, case-by-case approach. The United States has encouraged debtors to undertake economic reform and has persuaded banks, governments, and international financial institutions to support such efforts. In 1985, the United States introduced a debt strategy designed to improve and sustain growth in debtor countries (the Baker Plan). In March 1989, US Treasury Secretary Nicholas Brady outlined proposals for strengthening the strategy. In 1990, the United States complemented the Brady Plan with efforts to reduce official (government-to-government) debt and to encourage other creditor governments to do the same.

ORIGINS OF THE CRISIS

Several factors contributed to the debt crisis of the early 1980s. Inappropriate domestic policies in many debtor countries resulted in overvalued exchange rates, large budget deficits, heavy investment in inefficient public enterprises, and excessive restrictions on trade and investment. Many countries borrowed to promote consumption rather than build infrastructure or productive enterprises. Commercial banks often were lax in their oversight as they lent large amounts of "petrodollars."[1] External shocks such as the 1979 oil price jump, an increase in international interest rates, a drop in commodity prices, and recession in developed countries also hurt developing countries. Many borrowers relied on short-term, variable-rate loans that made them vulnerable to rising interest rates. (See Figure 28.1.)

BAKER PLAN

In 1982, the United States and other creditors developed packages to deal with the immediate cash-flow problems of major debtors arising from commercial debt. This approach succeeded in averting default by major debtor countries and in keeping the international financial system intact. By mid-1985, however, commercial lending to developing countries had declined sharply. Debtor govern-

SOURCE: U.S. Department of State Dispatch, July 29, 1991, pp. 556–557.

[1] Dollars earned from high price of oil.

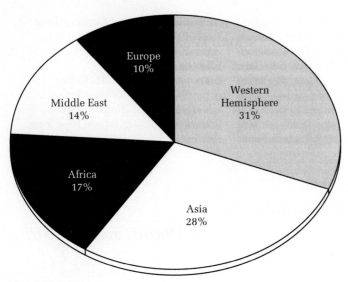

Figure 28.1
Developing Country Debt by Region, 1990
SOURCE: World Bank.

ments were concerned about poor economic growth.

In October 1985, the United States proposed the Program for Sustained Growth (Baker Plan), a broad, long-term strategy to restore creditworthiness of debtor countries by promoting sustainable economic growth. The program's main element, structural reform, was the pursuit of comprehensive economic policy changes leading to growth. A second element involved new commercial bank lending. The program also relied on new credits from international financial institutions that were linked more to economic reforms. These reforms permit market forces and private enterprises to play a larger role in the economy, encourage greater domestic savings and investment, reduce budget deficits, and liberalize trade and financial systems. The Baker Plan helped developing countries recognize that long-term growth requires a commitment to market-oriented policies.

Despite progress made under the Baker

Plan, low investment and capital flight continued, and commercial banks declined to provide new loans in a timely fashion. US banks reduced their developing country debt risk by adding to bank capital and selling or swapping some debt. An array of voluntary debt reduction mechanisms sprang up. Many debtor countries applied economic reforms inconsistently and failed to achieve adequate growth on a sustained, non-inflationary basis.

BRADY PLAN

In March 1989, Secretary Brady outlined a series of proposals to strengthen the US debt strategy. His proposals, while building on the Baker strategy, recognize the role of voluntary debt and debt service reduction as well as new commercial bank lending to provide financial support for economic reforms. The Brady approach also places more emphasis on new domestic and foreign investment and the repatriation of domestic capital.

Dramatic progress has been made under the Brady Plan. Seven countries (Chile, Costa Rica, Mexico, Morocco, Philippines, Uruguay, and Venezuela) have reached agreements that have debt-reduction options. Nigeria has a preliminary agreement, and bank negotiations are continuing with Argentina, Bolivia, Brazil, Ecuador, and Poland. Some countries, notably Mexico and Chile, are making progress toward attracting private foreign capital by their ability to regain access to international capital markets. The International Monetary Fund and the World Bank play a central role in this strategy by encouraging debtor policy reforms and catalyzing financial support.

Table 28.1   Developing Country Debt, 1990 ($ billion)

Brazil	115
Mexico	88
India	60
Argentina	60
Indonesia	53
Poland	42
Nigeria	35
Egypt	32
Philippines	29
Subtotal	514
Others	836
Total	1,350

Source: World Bank

OFFICIAL DEBT

The success of the enhanced debt strategy in gaining voluntary, market-based reduction of commercial debt has shifted some emphasis from commercial to official debt. Creditor governments have supported country reform efforts by rescheduling official bilateral debt, both interest and principal, through the Paris Club, an informal affiliation of creditor governments. In 1989, the United States announced a program to forgive up to $1 billion in economic assistance loans to Sub-Saharan African countries and other heavily indebted, low-income countries that are pursuing economic reform. The United States has forgiven more than $650 million owed by 15 African countries and is expected in 1991 to forgive $292 million owed by Bangladesh. The US Congress has provided authority for similar action on food assistance debt owed to the United States by relatively least developed countries. (See Table 28.1.)

In fall 1988, the Paris Club implemented the Toronto economic summit mandate to provide debt relief to Sub-Saharan African countries. The Toronto terms offer three options for providing

debt relief: debt reduction, extended maturities, or concessional interest rates. In 1990, these terms were extended to certain other poor countries on a case-by-case basis.

In response to a mandate agreed at the Houston economic summit in July 1990, the Paris Club devised more generous terms for lower middle-income countries—those severely indebted (i.e., debt more than 50% of GNP) but not poor enough to qualify for the Toronto terms. Congo, El Salvador, Honduras, Morocco, and Nigeria have received debt reschedulings on such terms, which extend the repayment period to 20 years with a 10-year grace period for official development assistance (ODA) and 15 years with an 8-year grace period for non-ODA loans.

In April 1991, the Paris Club agreed to a special rescheduling designed to reduce Poland's debt by 50% in the context of a multi-year economic restructuring agreement. The United States, citing the need to provide extraordinary assistance to Poland in its transition from a centrally planned to a free market economy, approved a 70% reduction. Creditor countries also have committed to a generous reduction of Egypt's official debt. The

United States forgave Egypt's military debt of $6.7 billion at the end of 1990.

ENTERPRISE FOR THE AMERICAS INITIATIVE

In June 1990, President Bush proposed the Enterprise for the Americas Initiative (EAI), an integrated program to increase free and fair trade, promote capital flows, ease debt burdens, and improve the environment. The EAI supports the process of democratic change and growing economic reform in the Western Hemisphere. To reinforce incentives for economic reform, the United States proposed to reduce existing non-military debts to the United States of Latin American and Caribbean countries that:

• Undertake macroeconomic and structural reforms;

• Liberalize their investment regimes; and

• Have negotiated agreements with commercial creditors (if commercial debt is a sufficiently large part of total external debt).

Interest payments on new, reduced development assistance and food aid debt would be made in local currency into an environmental fund in each country and used to support environmental projects identified by public/private local committees. A portion of non-concessional debt to the US Export-Import Bank and the Commodity Credit Corporation would be sold to facilitate investment and environmental or development projects.

CHAPTER 9

The Future of the World
Political Economy

The final section considers the future of the world political economy. Susan Strange, in "The Future of the American Empire," reviews three propositions in the literature on American hegemonic decline: (1) American power has declined, and will soon be matched or exceeded by the power of others; (2) great power decline is normal and explicable, especially given heavy military spending; and (3) declining hegemonic states create political instability and economic disorder in the international system. Strange rejects each of these propositions. She also calls for the creation of a symbiotic relationship between the United States and Japan.

Finally, Daniel Bell identifies four strong forces influencing the twenty-first century: the collapse of communism, the reunification of Europe, the end of "the American century," and the rise of the Pacific rim. He also analyzes world political and economic alignments according to four axes: East versus West, West versus West, North versus South, and East versus East. Further, he specifies two structural problems afflicting the world economy: high birth rates in the Third World and "the rising tension between the contrary pulls of the global economy and national policies."

29. The Future of the American Empire

Susan Strange

Make no mistake. Questions about American decline—true or untrue, avoidable or inevitable—which have been much in the public eye this last couple of years,

SOURCE: From *Journal of International Affairs,* vol. 42, no. 1, Fall 1988, pp. 1–17. Published by permission of the Journal of International Affairs and the Trustees of Columbia University in the City of New York.

are not just the subject of an academic debate, a kind of intellectual jousting match of absorbing interest to the protagonists but of only passing interest to the spectators. In my opinion, it is much more than that. This is one of the comparatively rare occasions on which the perceived outcome of an academic debate actually has some significance and impact outside the classroom and beyond the pages of professional journals. At the end of the day the apparent victor in the argument, and the broad conclusions that the spectators draw, will crucially affect decisions in the real world. It cannot help but affect the policy choices made in the future by people in business, banking and government, in the United States and in other countries around the world.

Personal, corporate and party policy-making decisions will vary according to the perceived outcome—whether the conviction becomes general that the United States is a superpower already in decline and destined to decline still further; or whether the view gains ground that the decline has been exaggerated and misunderstood and can be halted or reversed; or whether yet another interpretation takes hold, that there has not really been a decline at all, only a change in the basis of American power, as when a person shifts weight from one foot to another. Because perceptions of the debate will affect strategic choices by decision makers, and because those decisions will in turn affect the lives of ordinary people who have never even heard of any of the professors engaged in the debate, it seems to me a matter of such importance that it justifies return to a subject on which I have already written.[1]

At the time of writing, it looks as though the "school of decline"[2] as it has been called has thus far got the best of the intellectual joust. Although a few voices of dissent have been heard in America,

---

[1] Susan Strange, "The Persistent Myth of Lost Hegemony," *International Organization* 41, no. 4 (Autumn 1987): 551–573. Also see Susan Strange, "Still an Extraordinary Power: America's Role in a Global Monetary System," in Raymond E. Lombra and Willard E. Witte, eds., *Political Economy of International and Domestic Monetary Relations* (Ames, IA: Iowa State University Press, 1982), pp. 73–103.

[2] Peter Schmeisser, "Taking Stock: Is America in Decline?" *The New York Times Magazine* (17 April 1988): 24.

and though opinion outside the United States is still far from convinced that American power is declining, the challenges that have been made to the major propositions of this school have not registered much of a dent (see Figure 29.1). But the tournament is far from over and the verdict of the present and coming generations of students in the social sciences, and especially in international relations, has still to be given.

To that end, it may help first to disentangle the three major propositions of the school of decline. These are:

- American power, once predominant, is now less than it was, and, that it is (or soon will be) matched or exceeded by that of others.
- Such declines of great powers are normal and explicable and are to be anticipated, especially when such states are committed to heavy military spending.
- When such states do decline in power, one likely consequence is political instability and economic disorder in the international system.

Though distinctly separate, all three propositions are interrelated and thus often conflated in one argument. When that is done, the implications are strongly deterministic. For if indeed it is true that American power has declined, and if it is also true that such a decline is normal, even unavoidable, then the resulting disorder in the international system is also, in large degree preordained. This suggests that there is little that can be done about it. We have therefore to plan on uncertainty, anarchy, conflict and misrule and to behave accordingly. This is a counsel of despair not to be taken too lightly.

For readers to clarify their own thinking, therefore, the three propositions must first be considered separately, together with the refuting counter propositions, for it is not logically necessary to

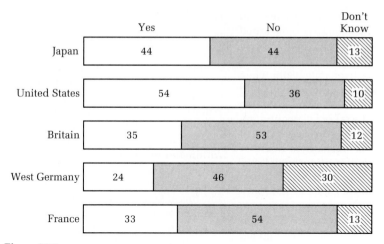

	Yes	No	Don't Know
Japan	44	44	13
United States	54	36	10
Britain	35	53	12
West Germany	24	46	30
France	33	54	13

Figure 29.1
Is U.S. Power Declining? (Public Opinion Poll)
SOURCE: *Daily Yomiuri,* 18 June 1987.

accept or reject all three. For example, the theme of Robert Keohane's *After Hegemony,*[3] and of much current literature by international economists, is that although American power has declined and although this has led to the erosion of international regimes, there is still a substitute for American hegemony to be found in international cooperation and the coordination of monetary and fiscal policies. Thus, accepting the first proposition does not necessarily mean accepting the third.

By laying out the main grounds on which I think each of the three propositions can be legitimately questioned, a different conclusion becomes possible. It is based on the analysis of structural power in international political economy which I have developed at greater length elsewhere.[4] It leads to the conclusion that although there are current weaknesses in

the American Empire, they are not irreparable and they are much less important than its continuing structural power. However, a necessary condition for the needed reforms is the development of a political will to change. And that will not come until it is more widely recognized that the school of decline has grossly overdone its Cassandra act.

To be fair, however, it has to be said that it is the simplifications and vulgarizations by the media and the politicians of what the gloomy academics have actually said that have been grossly overdone. Paul Kennedy, for example, in his epilogue quotes Bismarck to abjure determinism and to insist that the governments of states 'travelling on the stream of Time' may still 'steer with more or less experience.'[5] And although in public appearances he has sometimes weakened and pontificated confidently about international affairs, in his book he carefully plays the role of the nonpartisan histo-

[3] Robert O. Keohane, *After Hegemony: Co-operation and Discord in the World Political Economy* (Princeton, NJ: Princeton University Press, 1984).
[4] Susan Strange, *States and Markets* (New York: Basil Blackwell, 1988).

[5] Paul Kennedy, *The Rise and Fall of the Great Powers: Economic Change and Military Conflict from 1500 to 2000* (New York: Random House, 1987), p. 540.

rian, merely presenting his large body of data to the political scientists "concerned with the larger patterns of war and change in the international order" for them to analyze.[6] Time and again, when the reader looks more closely at the small print, there is found to be more common ground between the school of decline and its opponents (like myself) than would at first appear. For instance, I am in entire agreement with David Calleo that it is important for good European-American relations and for the security of the European frontier that the Europeans should assume greater responsibility for their own defense.[7] At the same time, I do not think this is made necessary by the declining ability of the United States to pay the costs, nor that it would necessarily result in such large savings on the U.S. defense budget. Rather, it is desirable because they can well afford it and because their present dependence on the Americans robs them of an independent voice on other matters of common concern.

Where I think we are all in agreement is on the critical nature of the present end-of-century decade. We share a common perception that mankind—and more particularly the governments it acknowledges as possessing the authority to make decisions—is standing at a fork in the road, at the end of a long stretch of comparative order and stability, and facing momentous choices in the way ahead. That is why there is shared concern to understand where we are now and how we got there and to seek in the lessons of history some guidance for future action. In the last resort, it may well be that this common concern is more significant than the differences of interpretation to which I now turn.

AMERICAN POWER

Paul Kennedy, in common with the rest of the decline school, starts from the age-old premise that "to be a great power demands a flourishing economic base."[8] Following Adam Smith the liberal, and Friedrich List the mercantilist, this is then interpreted to mean an economic base of manufacturing industry located within the territorial boundaries of the state. It is this interpretation of "a flourishing economic base" that is obsolete and therefore open to doubt. Smith and List are both long dead. More recent changes, noted by Peter Drucker,[9] among others, in the character of the world economy throw doubt on whether it is manufacturing that is now most important in developing the sinews of war; and, whether it is location within the boundaries of the territory that matters most.

My contention (which should surely be sustained by the champions of American service industries) is that it is the information-rich occupations, whether associated with manufacturing or not, that confer power, much more now than the physical capacity to roll goods off an assembly line. Secondly, I contend that the location of productive capacity is far less important than the location of the people who make the key decisions on what is to be produced, where and how, and who design, direct and manage to sell successfully on a world market. Is it more desirable that Americans should wear blue collars and mind the machines or that they should wear white collars and

---

[6] *Ibid.*, p. 536.
[7] David P. Calleo, *Beyond American Hegemony: The Future of the Western Alliance* (New York: Basic Books, 1987). See also David P. Calleo, *The Imperious Economy* (Cambridge, MA: Harvard University Press, 1982).

[8] Robert Gilpin, *The Political Economy of International Relations* (Princeton, NJ: Princeton University Press, 1987). See also Mancur Olson, *The Rise and Decline of Nations: Economic Growth, Stagflation, and Social Rigidities* (New Haven, CT: Yale University Press, 1982) and Robert O. Keohane, ed., *Neorealism and Its Critics* (New York: Columbia University Press, 1986).
[9] Peter F. Drucker, "The Changed World Economy," *Foreign Affairs* 64, no. 4 (Spring 1986): 768–791.

design, direct and finance the whole operation?

That is why all the figures so commonly trotted out about the U.S. share of world manufacturing capacity, or the declining U.S. share of world exports of manufactures are so misleading—*because they are territorially based.* Worse, they are irrelevant. What matters is the share of world output—of primary products, minerals and food and manufactured goods and services—that is under the direction of the executives of U.S. companies. That share can be U.S.-directed even if the enterprise directly responsible is only half owned by an American parent, and even, in some cases of technological dependence, where it is not owned at all but where the license to produce is granted or refused by people in the United States. The largest stock of foreign direct investments is still held by U.S. corporations—even though the figures are neither precise, complete nor comprehensive. The fact that the current outflow from Japan is greater than that from the United States merely means that the gap is narrowing. But the Japanese still have a long way to go to rival the extent of U.S. corporate operations in Europe, Latin America, Australasia, the Middle East and Africa, the assets of which are often valued at their historical prices not at their current values.

U.S.-controlled enterprise outside the territorial United States is still growing very fast in new fields of technology like software services, biotechnology, medical products, data retrieval, environmental management or new basic materials. IBM is still unrivaled in its field and has stayed so by strategic agility in overcoming its rivals and imitators. Genentech is still the world's biggest biotechnology corporation and Cray Research is the largest producer of supercomputers. What these leading American companies have in common is that more of their output is produced outside the territorial United States than is produced inside it.

For example, an estimate of middle-sized U.S. companies associated within the American Business Conference found that 80 percent of their revenues in 1986 came from production overseas, only 20 percent from exporting from the United States.[10] Two conclusions were drawn from their success. One was that Jean-Jacques Servan Schreiber had been quite wrong in seeing the "American Challenge" to the rest of the world as coming from the giant corporations like ITT or General Electric.[11] Today, the challenge is more likely to come from relatively new and smaller American enterprises. The other conclusion was that trade figures are not the best measure of competitiveness and that it would be better to judge by corporate world market shares.[12]

In these terms, Japanese companies just now beginning to shift production to America, Europe and mainland Asia are only following the American lead—and the trade figures so eagerly (and wrongly) watched for indications of competitiveness will soon begin to show it.

At this point some people will object that when production moves away from the territory of the United States, the authority of the U.S. government is diminished. At the same time, the same people sometimes complain against the "invasion" of the United States by Japanese companies, as if "selling off the farm" is diminishing the authority of the United States government. Clearly, both cannot be right. Rather, both perceptions seem to me to be wrong. What is happening is that the American Empire is spilling out beyond the frontier and that the very insubstantial nature of frontiers where pro-

[10] *Winning in the World Market* (Washington, DC: American Business Conference, 1987), p. 24.
[11] Jean-Jacques Servan Schreiber, *Le Defi Americain* (Paris: Denoel, 1967).
[12] "A Portrait of America's New Competitiveness," *The Economist* (4-10 June 1988): 57–58.

duction is concerned just shows the consolidation of an entirely new kind of nonterritorial empire.

It is that nonterritorial empire that is really the "flourishing economic base" of U.S. power, not the goods and services produced within the United States. One obvious indication of this fact is that foreign central banks last year spent roughly $140 billion supporting the exchange value of the dollar.[13] Another is that Japanese and other foreign investors financed the lion's share of the U.S. government's budget deficit by buying U.S. government securities and investing in the United States. An empire that can command such resources hardly seems to be losing power. The fact that the United States is still the largest and richest (and mostly open) market for goods and services under one political authority means that all successful foreign companies will want to produce and sell there and will deem it prudent also to produce there, not simply to avoid protectionist barriers but in order to be close to the customers. And the worldwide reach of U.S.-controlled enterprises also means that the capacity of the United States to exercise extraterritorial influence and authority is also greater than that of any other government. If only for security reasons, the ability of Washington to tell U.S. companies in Japan what to do or not to do is immeasurably greater than the ability of Tokyo to tell Japanese companies in the United States what to do.

This points to another major fallacy in the decline school's logic—its inattention to matters of security. The U.S. lead in the ability to make and deliver the means of nuclear destruction is the complement to its lead in influencing, through past investments overseas, the nature, modes and purposes of modern industrial production. Here, too, the gap may be narrowing as South Africa, Israel, India and others claim nuclear capability. Yet there is still no comparison between the military power of the United States to confer, deny or threaten the security of others with that of minor non-Communist states. That military power is now based far less on the capacity to manufacture nuclear weapons than on the capacity to recruit scientists, American or foreign, to keep ahead in design and invention, both offensive and defensive.

HISTORICAL PARALLELS

The decline school so far has succeeded in promoting the idea that history teaches that it is "normal" for great states and empires to decline, especially when they become militarily overextended;[14] or else when they become socially and politically sclerotic, risk-averse and resistant to change[15] or when they overindulge in foreign investment;[16] and for any or all of these reasons when they lose preeminence in agricultural and industrial production, or in trade and military capability.[17] In almost all this American literature on the rise and fall of empires, great attention and weight is characteristically (and for reasons of language and culture, perhaps understandably) given to the British experience. But the trouble with history, as the first great realist writer on international relations, E. H.

[13] Bank for International Settlements, *58th Annual Report* (Basle: Bank for International Settlements, 1988), pp. 187–189. See also news brief on Swiss National Bank President Pierre Languetin's statement, *Journal of Commerce* (22 February 1988): 7A.

[14] Kennedy, Calleo (1987).

[15] Olson (1982).

[16] Robert Gilpin, *U.S. Power and the Multinational Corporation* (New York: Basic Books, 1975) and Gilpin (1987).

[17] Immanuel Wallerstein, *The Modern World System* (New York: Academic Press, 1974) and Immanuel Wallerstein, *The Capitalist World Economy* (New York: Cambridge University Press, 1979).

Carr, rightly observed, is that it is necessarily selective—and that the historian selects facts as a fish shop selects fish, choosing some and discarding or overlooking others.[18] In this debate, the historical analogy between Britain and America is particularly weak; and the other examples selected for consideration show a strong tendency to concentrate on the empires whose decline after the peaking of their power was more or less steady and never reversed.

First, it is not too difficult to show that what Britain and America have had in common—such as a tendency to invest heavily overseas—is much less important than all the differences that mark their experience. Britain's economic decline, beginning around the 1880s, was the result of a neglect of the then advanced technologies—notably in chemicals and engineering. This neglect reflected the weakness and low status of manufacturing industry in British politics and society—a social disdain such as American industry has never had to contend with. Even more important was the effect of two long debilitating wars on the British economy, by comparison with which the American experience of Vietnam was a flea bite. It is arguable that the British economy, dependent as it was on financial power, would not have suffered so great a setback if the whole international financial system on which it lived and prospered had not been twice destroyed—first in the Great War and then in the Second World War. The interwar period was too short—and policies were also ill-chosen—to allow a reversal of this British decline.

Finally, there is the great difference between a small offshore island running a large territorial empire and a great continental power managing (or sometimes mismanaging) a large nonterritorial empire. The island state made the fatal mistake after the Second World War of relying on sheltered colonial and sterling area markets—with disastrous effects on the competitiveness of its export industries and even some of its old, established multinationals. The continental power's confidence in its ability to dominate an open world economy, plus the strong commitment to antitrust policies at home, has created no such weakening crutches for its major transnational corporations.

Secondly, any historical study of empires of the past fails to reveal any standard or uniform pattern of rise and fall. They are like trees. Some grow fast and fall suddenly without warning. Others grow slowly and decay very gradually, even making astonishing recoveries from shock or injury. One author, Michael Doyle, who has shared less in the media attention perhaps because his work lent itself less readily to deterministic interpretations, drew an important conclusion from an analytical survey of empires that included those of the ancient world as well as the later European ones. It is worth quoting:

> The historical alternatives had divided between persistence, which necessitated imperial development in both the metropole and the periphery, and decline and fall. Persistence in an extensive empire required that the metropole cross the Augustan threshold to imperial bureaucracy, and perhaps became in effect an equal political partner with the metropole.[19]

In plainer language, what I interpret this to mean is that the empires that lasted longest were those that managed to

---

[18] Edward Hallett Carr, *On History* (London: Macmillan, 1938).

[19] Michael Doyle, *Empires* (Ithaca, NY: Cornell University Press, 1986), p. 353.

build a political system suited to the administration of the empire out of one suited to managing the core. In addition, those empires that survived managed to blur the distinction between the ruling groups of the core and the participating allies and associates of the periphery. This is a notion closely related to Gramscian concepts of hegemony and explanations of the persistent strength of capitalist political economies.[20]

Michael Doyle's attention to the Roman Empire, which was much longer-lived than any of the nineteenth century European empires, is important for the debate. This is so partly because there have been so many conflicting interpretations of its decline, from Edward Gibbon and Thomas Macaulay to Joseph Schumpeter and Max Weber, and partly because most historians seem to agree that it passed through periods of regeneration and reform before it finally broke up in disorder. Michael Mann, for instance, recently identified one such period of reform and regeneration in the twenty years after the accession of Septimus Severus in AD 193:

> Severus began withdrawing crack legions from the frontiers to mobile reserve positions, replacing them at the frontier with a settler militia. This was a more defensive, less confident posture. It also cost more, and so he attempted financial reform, abolishing tax farming and the tax exemption of Rome and Italy.[21]

This comment by a sociologist is interesting because it focuses on two important elements of power in imperial states:

relations with key groups in the periphery, and the fiscal system by which unavoidable imperial expenditures are financed. When we consider the future of the American Empire, we find that these two issues are once again crucial to the outcome between Doyle's two alternatives—persistence or decline. Mann describes the Roman Empire as a "legionary empire," indicating that the role and character of the legions were important in explaining Roman power.

I would argue that America's "legions," in the integrated financial and production economy of today's world, are not military but economic. They are the corporate enterprises on which the military depends—as President Dwight Eisenhower foresaw in talking about the military-industrial complex. The American Empire in sociological terms therefore could be described as a "corporation empire" in which the culture and interests of the corporations are sustained by an imperial bureaucracy. But this bureaucracy, largely set up after the Second World War, was not simply a national American one based in Washington, D.C. A large and important part of it was and is multinational and works through the major international economic organizations such as the International Monetary Fund (IMF), the World Bank, the Organization for Economic Cooperation and Development (OECD) in Paris and the General Agreement on Tariffs and Trade (GATT) in Geneva.

The other feature of the Roman Empire that I believe is relevant to the current debate is that citizenship was not a matter of domicile, and that there were gradations of civil and political rights and responsibilities, ranging from slaves to senators, which did not depend on what we, today, understand by "nationality," indicated by possession or nonpossession of a passport. If we can once escape the corset-like intellectual constraints of the conventional study of international

[20] Robert W. Cox, *Production, Power and World Order* (New York: Columbia University Press, 1987).
[21] Michael Mann, *The Sources of Social Power, Volume One* (New York: Cambridge University Press, 1986).

relations and liberate our minds to ask new questions we begin to see new things about America's nonterritorial empire. Here, too, citizenship is becoming much more complex and graded than it used to be. The managers of U.S. corporations, in Brazil, for example, may hold Brazilian and not U.S. passports. But they are free to come and go with indefinite visas into the United States and they often exercise considerable delegated power in the running of U.S.-directed enterprises vital to the Brazilian economy. Participation in the cultural empire depends not on passports but on competence in the American language and in many cases participation in U.S.-based professional organizations—like the International Studies Association for example. Similarly, participation in America's financial empire depends on the possession and use of U.S. dollars and dollar-denominated assets and the ability to compete with U.S. banks and in U.S. financial markets.

Rather like a chrysalis in the metamorphosis from caterpillar to butterfly, the American Empire today combines features of a national-exclusive past with features of a transnational-extensive future. In military matters, it is still narrowly exclusive—though where advanced technology is concerned, even that is changing. Certainly, in financial and cultural matters, the distinction between first-class, passport-holding citizens and second-class, non-passport-holding participants is increasingly blurred. The peripheral allies have been unconsciously recruited into the American Empire.

This is why it is important for the current debate not to think that the mine of imperial histories has been finally and totally exhausted by Paul Kennedy, Mancur Olson and company. The variety of forms in which empires of the past have handled the personal identity question (citizenship), the territorial limit-of-authority question and the ideological con-

formity question calls for a lot more careful scholarly work. For instance, not so much has been done on the Austro-Hungarian empire of the nineteenth century, which lasted surprisingly long considering its backward economy. A comparison of the Napoleonic empire, which was militarily based and heavily hegemonic, with the Venetian empire so beloved of John Ruskin might be instructive. For while the one was ideological and comparatively short-lived, the Serenissima, being commercially based, was from the first strikingly nonideological and permissive in its dealings with Islamic infidels—and like the late Hapsburg empire surprisingly long-lived. One obvious feature of the American Empire, like that of Venice, has been that despite the political rhetoric on the subject of liberty, democracy and free trade, its governments have been remarkably unfussy on all three counts in their choice of allies and associates.

POWER AND SYSTEMIC DISORDER

The third proposition of the decline school has been the one under longest discussion among scholars in international relations. Over most of the past decade, the lead in these discussions has been taken by specialists in the study of international organizations (for example, Joseph Nye, Robert Keohane, John Ruggie and Ernst Haas). It seems to me that they share a wishful reluctance to admit that international organizations, when they are not simply adaptive mechanisms through which states respond to technical change, are either the strategic instruments of national policies and interests, or else merely symbolic gestures toward a desired but unattainable world government. This reluctance to admit the inherent limitations of international organizations leads them subconsciously to the conclusion that it must be hegemonic de-

cline that is the cause of economic instability and disorder and the coincident
erosion of earlier international regimes.

This is a proposition that does not
stand up well either to the record of recent international economic history or to
structural analysis of power in the international policy economy. I do not want
to repeat myself, but *Casino Capitalism*
was an attempt to show two things
(among others): there were more ways
than one of interpreting recent developments in the international monetary and
financial system; and, these developments of the last fifteen years or so could
be traced to a series of crucial (and mostly
permissive) decisions by governments.
Hence, the precarious and unstable state
of the global financial structure—which
has already been dramatically demonstrated once and probably will be so
again—was no fortuitous accident of fate
or history.[22]

Since that book was written, I find
confirmation that it was not a decline
of American power but rather a series of
American managerial decisions of dubious wisdom that accounts quite adequately for financial and monetary disorder, without any need to adduce the
decline of American hegemonic power.
Not only is this the theme of David Calleo's *The Imperious Economy*,[23] it is also
to be found buried in the text of Robert
Gilpin's chapters on international money
and finance:

> Beginning with the Vietnam war and
> continuing into the Reagan Adminis-
> tration, the United States had become
> more of a "predatory hegemon" to use
> John Conybeare's terms (1985), less
> willing to subordinate its own interests
> to those of its allies; instead it tended
> more and more to exploit its hege-

monic status for its own narrowly defined purposes.[24]

Gilpin repeats the point twenty pages
later, adding: "Most of the troubles of the
world economy in the 1980s have been
caused by this shift in American policy."[25]

It will not escape careful students of
this important text that Gilpin's historical
analysis, and the use of the word "mis-
management" with reference to American domestic and foreign financial policy, fundamentally contradicts his
concluding thesis that a stable and prosperous world economy in the future calls
for an American-Japanese condominium
because of lost American hegemony.[26]

Similarly, *States and Markets* extends
the definition of international political
economy beyond the conventional politics of international economic relations to
ask more basic who-gets-what questions.[27] In that volume I find that a structural analysis of the basic issues in any
political economy, when applied to the
world system, strongly suggests that on
balance American structural power may
actually have increased in recent decades. It has done so through four inter-
locking structures. These structures concern the power conferred by the ability to
offer, withhold or threaten security (the
security structure); the ability to offer,
withhold or demand credit (the financial
structure); the ability to determine the locus, mode and content of wealth-creating
activity (the production structure); and,
not least, the ability to influence ideas
and beliefs and therefore the kind of
knowledge socially prized and sought after, and to control (and, through language, to influence) access to and com-

---

[22] Susan Strange, *Casino Capitalism* (New
York: Basil Blackwell, 1986).
[23] Calleo (1982).

[24] Gilpin (1987), p. 345.
[25] *Ibid.,* p. 365.
[26] *Ibid.,* p. 339.
[27] Strange (1988).

munication of that knowledge (the knowledge structure).

Such a structural analysis suggests the existence under predominant American power and influence of an empire the likes of which the world has never seen before, a nonterritorial empire, whose only borders are the frontiers of the socialist great powers and their allies. It is not, in fact, such an eccentric idea. Two former U.S. secretaries of state recently wrote:

> Far into the future, the United States will have the world's largest and most innovative economy, and will remain a nuclear superpower, a cultural and intellectual leader, a model democracy and a society that provides exceptionally well for its citizens.[28]

WHAT, THEN, MUST BE DONE?

The power Henry Kissinger and Cyrus Vance describe is structural power. The objectives they advocate for the guidance of the next president lie not only in the field of foreign policy but in the political changes they judge necessary for the better management of the world economy and, consequently, for the creation of a more secure base for long-term U.S. national interests. Specifically, they mention a more efficient, trustful and well-defined relationship between the Congress and the White House, and a clearer definition, and limitation, of the role of the media in shaping U.S. policies at home and abroad. Such recommendations may suggest to the historian a transition to an Augustan system relying more on a career bureaucracy and less on the vagaries of party politics. The same point has been cogently made by Paul

Volcker, speaking as chairman of the National Commission on the Public Service.[29]

Curiously, perhaps, rather similar conclusions are to be found in the recent study by a Japanese journalist/scholar, Yoichi Funabashi, of international efforts at exchange rate management and policy coordination between the United States, Japan and the European Community (EC).[30] He suggests a greater and more responsible role in policy-making for the major committees in both houses of Congress—in other words, a more structured and formalized process of bipartisan decision making on crucial issues of trade and finance.

It seems that those individuals whose past professional experience in government or as informed observers best qualify them to judge do not share the enthusiasm for "international policy coordination" that has recently overwhelmed so many professional economists and some publicists. Summit meetings without long and careful preparation by officials, and Group of Seven market interventions without visible changes in economic management are not the answer. At this critical juncture in world affairs, the United States as hegemonic power has, as usual, to take the lead.

In the past two years or so, the Japanese have been conducting among themselves a lively and sometimes quite heated debate on their "identity," i.e., their role in the international political economy. According to Chalmers Johnson and others, despite some discussion of the possibilities of "Pax Nipponica" replacing Pax Americana (just as that in turn replaced Pax Britannica), such an outcome is not

[28] Henry Kissinger and Cyrus Vance, "Bipartisan Objectives for American Foreign Policy," *Foreign Affairs* 66, no. 5 (Summer 1988): 899–921.

[29] Paul Volcker, *Public Service: The Quiet Crisis* (Washington, DC: American Enterprise Institute, 1988).
[30] Yoichi Funabashi, *Managing the Dollar: From the Plaza to the Louvre* (Washington, DC: Institute for International Economics, 1988).

seen by most Japanese as lying within the realm of practical politics, if only because of the exclusivity of Japanese culture and the difficulties others have with the Japanese language.[31] Nor, because of the disordered and unstable state of world trade and finance, is muddling through on the basis of the status quo a very practical or desirable alternative.[32] A third option, "Pax Consortis" (the Japanese term for international policy coordination) has turned out to be more difficult to achieve than it sounds; "many meetings but little Pax," in Johnson's words.[33] Interest is, therefore, growing in the possibilities and nature of a joint U.S.-Japan hegemony. It does not mean splitting the world economy into three economic blocs, as in the 1930s. The economies of North America, Japan and Europe are far too closely intertwined with one another today to allow that. Nor, in the considered opinion of several influential elder statesmen in Japan, does it mean an equal balance of power between the United States and Japan. Naohiro Amaya, a former vice-minister at the Ministry of International Trade and Industry (MITI), for instance, calls it a "Pax Ameripponica," but adds that "if it were a company the United States would be president and Japan vice-president."[34] He does not think the opposite is possible.

What this implies, it seems to me, is that reforms should be set in motion that would create between the United States and Japan—now the world's major creditor and banker—the same sort of symbiotic relationship between senior and junior partner that the Americans developed with the British before, during and after the Second World War. Leadership—a term Charles Kindleberger, who started the whole hegemonic stability debate, has always used in preference to hegemony—rests with America.[35] But there has to be something more in it than there is now for Japan. And Americans have to make more strenuous efforts than they have made so far to tackle the dilemma of their two deficits—the budget deficit and the trade deficit. Unless they look as if they mean to do so, the sustaining flow of capital out of Japan into the United States is going to look precarious, inducing uncertainty and continuing volatility in exchange rates and interest rates. The markets will react accordingly. Consequently, not only must fat be cut out of the U.S. defense budget—at home as well as in Europe and the Middle East—something must also be done to encourage savings in place of the unremitting consumerism characteristic of the United States and some parts of its nonterritorial empire. Long-term assets underwritten in a basket of currencies and tax concessions for small savers are the sorts of policy instruments that need examination.

"New Deals" are needed internationally and not just nationally as in the 1930s. A New Deal with Japan would give better long-term assurance of financial support for the expenses of empire in return for more generous power sharing in organizations like the IMF, the World Bank, the OECD and the regional development banks in Asia and Latin America. A New Deal with Europe would exchange increased financial responsibility for the costs of NATO for "European-

---

[31] Chalmers Johnson, "The End of American Hegemony and the Future of Japanese-American Relations," unpublished manuscript (Cambridge, UK: 1988).

[32] Theodore Geiger, *The Future of the International System* (Boston, MA: Allen & Unwin, 1988).

[33] Chalmers Johnson (1988).

[34] Naohiro Amaya, "America in Decline?" *Look Japan* (May 1988): 6.

[35] See, for example, Charles P. Kindleberger, "Systems of International Economic Organization," in David P. Calleo, ed., *Money and the Coming World Order* (New York: New York University Press, 1977), pp. 15–39.

ization" (Calleo's term) of its command structure and some role, even if a minor consultative one, in arms control negotiations with the Soviet Union when they affect Europe. A New Deal for Latin America—in some ways the most solid part of the American empire—would take up the Japanese proposal, brushed too contemptuously aside at the Toronto summit, for a long-term solution of its chronic debt problems, in return perhaps for some commitments to liberalize trade and secure investments.[36]

[36] Since writing the above, I have found much concurrence of view in the Cuomo Commission's thoughtful report, *A New American Formula for a Strong Economy.* This stresses the interdependence of successful national economic regeneration with purposeful American policy initiatives on international trade and finance. See Cuomo Commission on Trade and Competitiveness, *The Cuomo Commission Report: A New American Formula for a Strong Economy* (New York: Touchstone/Simon & Schuster, 1988).

New Deals, however, do not drop like manna from heaven. They do not come about without political vision and inspiration, or without hard intellectual effort to find the sustaining optimal bargain. Optimal bargains are those that last because they go some way to satisfy the needs and aspirations of the governed as well as those of the governors. Only then can the power of those in charge of empires (as of states, local party machines or labor unions) be sustained over the long run. The next four years will show not only Americans but the rest of us who live and work in the American Empire whether the defeatist gloom of the school of decline can be dissipated. They will show whether the necessary vision can still be found in the White House for a series of global New Deals and whether the necessary intellectual effort to design and negotiate them will be generated not only in the bureaucracies, national and international, but in the universities and research institutes of all our countries.

30.   As We Go into the Nineties
Some Outlines of the Twenty-First Century

Daniel Bell

As we enter the 1990s, the outline of the twenty-first century, with respect to the configuration of issues and forces, already seems clear. We can identify four:

1. The collapse of communism
2. The reunification of Europe
3. The end of "The American Century"
4. The rise of the Pacific rim

SOURCE: Reprinted with permission from *Dissent,* Spring 1990, pp. 171–176.

Beyond these are other, more inchoate and indistinct forms, whose outlines are not as clear, though this does not mean they are of lesser importance. In some instances, as the twenty-first century unfolds, they may, indeed, prove to be the most disruptive. These issues are the following: the problems of poverty in the Third World (exempting East Asia now from that configuration), the fratricidal rivalries in the Middle East, and the rising ethnic and nationalist rivalries in many different parts of the world, as the older issues of class and imperialism recede.

How can we understand these new forces in some systematic way? Is there some framework that allows us to order them in some explanatory fashion? More than fifteen years ago, in seeking to provide a coherent picture of the world at that time, I set forth four "axes" along which the alignments might be understood. These were, schematically put:

1. *East vs. West.* This rivalry was principally between the United States and the Soviet Union and the forces grouped behind them in the NATO and Warsaw Pact alliances. The rivalries here were political and ideological, with the constant threat of military confrontation. This was the cold war.

2. *West vs. West.* This rivalry was principally between the United States on the one side and, on the other, Japan (putting her in this context within the West) and Germany. The rivalry here was economic.

3. *North vs. South.* Here were the OECD, or industrialized countries, versus the newly industrializing societies, the "Group of 77" within the United Nations, who were demanding a redistribution of world manufacturing capacity. The issues here were economic and ideological.

4. *East vs. East.* This rivalry was the Soviet Union against China, where the competitions were ideological and political with a thin threat of military conflict.

It was, and still is to some extent, a useful frame of reference.[1] The intention was to see which axis was salient, at what time. When this was first presented it was obvious that the East vs. West axis dominated all others. The West vs. West was only a dim cloud, and some writers

thought it improbable. North vs. South was very strident. And East vs. East was very strained.

Today it is likely that the cold war is finished. West vs. West, in particular the rivalry between Japan and the United States on economic issues, has become highly salient. But there is also now the rise of the various East Asian "tigers," such as Korea, Taiwan, and Thailand, to add to that competition. North vs. South at the moment is somewhat muted. And East vs. East is, for the while, quiet.

That analytical framework may still have some limited use. But there is now a new intellectual challenge to provide a different, coherent framework to encompass the new alignments as they are emerging. Whether this can be done remains to be seen. But before we can do so, there is much detailed analysis to explore.

EVENTS OF THE PAST DECADE

For almost fifty years after the Russian Revolution of October 1917, it seemed as if Marxism would sweep the world. Nothing so blazing as revolutionary Marxism had been seen, as some historians compared it, since the rise of Islam more than a millennium before. Here was a new faith system that had inspired working-class movements in Europe, sparked a revolution in China, become a model for intellectuals in Latin America and new elites in Africa, and so on. And now it has collapsed, in less than a decade, like a house of cards. It would take many volumes to analyze the reasons why. For the moment, let us deal with two related groups, one the Soviet Union, the other Eastern Europe.

There are, I would say, three factors, now conjoined, that account for the crisis in the Soviet Union:

1. *The failure of the economic model.* Soviet planning was rigid and inflexible and, beyond an initial start, it could not

---

[1] Much of this scheme was elaborated in my essay "The Future World Disorder" (1977), reprinted in my book *The Winding Passage* (Basic Books, 1980).

manage a large and complex economy. In an early essay Lenin said that planning was a simple affair. If there were 200 million Russians and each one needed two pairs of shoes, one produced 400 million pairs. There is, paradoxically enough, a *surplus* of shoes today in Soviet warehouses. But nobody wants them. They are too ungainly, shoddily constructed, and of poor quality. What the Soviet Union had, in the early five-year plans, was not "planning" but a *mobilized* economy based on *physical* targets. But there was no price mechanism to judge whether resources were being used efficiently. In fact, for dogmatic reasons, Soviet planners did not use the mechanism of interest rates (since interest was usury and exploitative) as a measure of the relative efficiency of capital. At the same time there were heavy subsidies on such items as bread and housing rents. But no one knew the true costs; more resources were devoted to bread, and because it was relatively cheap, the product was misused. Lacking a true cost and accounting system (and using a double-ruble system to divert resources for military use) Soviet planners had no measures of the deficits they were running and the inflation that was hidden. Today the economy is in shambles.

2. *The failure of ideology.* Ideologies are worldviews (weltanschaunungen) that mobilize their believers for a "cause" and provide a set of justifications on the basis of the "higher" goals. But the "revolutionary" goals of egalitarianism and of a classless society, and the ideas of socialized property, gave way, increasingly, to a "new class" of privileged, the *nomenklatura;* and the regime, particularly under Stalin, resorted to terror as a means of forcing compliance with its demands. The failure of ideology, when there are no other justifications, means a loss of legitimacy and the beliefs of the rulers and the ruled in their "right" to rule. For a period of time, the "patriotic war"

against Nazi Germany provided a social cement. But the resumptions of terror and privilege eroded those commitments.

3. *The crumbling of "empire."* What was little known is that the Soviet Union was the *only* nation that came out of World War II with extensive territorial gains, at a time when almost all the other imperial and colonial powers were surrendering their control over lands in Asia and Africa. Since 1940, starting with the Nazi-Soviet pact, the Soviet Union annexed Finnish Karelia, the Republics of Estonia, Latvia, and Lithuania, the Koenigsberg district of East Prussia, the eastern provinces of Poland, the sub-Carpathian district of Ruthenia from Czechoslovakia, Bukovina and Bessarabia from Romania, and the Sakhalin and Kurile islands from Japan.

In addition, badly drawn boundary lines within the older Soviet Union have left large pockets of ethnic rivalries, such as the Caucasus territory of Nagorno-Karabakh, which is heavily Armenian and Christian within the republic of Azerbaijan, which is Muslim. On the Black Sea, the small area of Abkazia wishes to secede from neighboring Georgia, while Georgia itself wants autonomy within the Soviet Union. And, more to the point, the most successful economic region of the Soviet Union, the Baltic republics of Estonia, Latvia, and Lithuania, are now demanding, if not freedom, then almost complete autonomy.

Almost twenty years ago, the Soviet dissident and writer Andrei Amalrik (who spent many years in the gulag and was killed tragically in an automobile accident) wrote a tract, *Will Russia Survive Until 1984?* It seemed odd and fanciful at the time. Now Russian politicians such as Boris Yeltsin (himself somewhat of an opportunist and demagogue) ask seriously whether the Soviet Union can last until 1994.

No one can provide an answer. It has

been the genius of Mikhail Gorbachev that he has recognized all the problems and sought to provide reforms through *perestroika*. He has, at the same time, recognized that the party cannot rule alone and has begun to create political structures with a degree of independent power. Even if Gorbachev succeeds, it is evident that the Soviet Union cannot remain an effective superpower and that the military and ideological threat it once posed, especially to Europe, has now largely receded. If he fails? There was once an old Soviet joke that said that when Stalin died he left two envelopes. One said, "In case of trouble, open this." Trouble arose and the envelope was opened. In it was a message that said, "Blame me." The other envelope said, "In the event of more trouble, open this." More trouble came and the second envelope was opened. It said, "Do as I did."

That is now impossible. Deng Xiaoping could still have the authority among the veterans of the Chinese revolution to give an order to shoot. Gorbachev cannot. His destruction of Stalin and the legitimacy of that "revolution" makes it impossible. Yet if Gorbachev fails, the greater likelihood is that of a right-wing, nationalist reaction, using the symbols of old Russia and seeking to mobilize the Soviet people on the basis of traditional symbols. But such a move would alienate the intelligentsia and the modernizing elements in the Soviet Union, and even if a right-wing force came into power, its economic base would still be weak.

About Eastern Europe: the news has been electrifying. Within a few months the communist regimes of Poland, Hungary, Bulgaria, East Germany, and Czechoslovakia have crumbled. The reasons are fairly clear. In almost no country had there been strong, indigenous communist forces. The regimes were *imposed* almost entirely from the outside and reinforced by Soviet troops. More than that, in the first decade after World War II, Stalin purged the leadership of most of the na-

tive Communist parties in a sweeping set of trials. In Czechoslovakia, there was the Slansky trial. In Hungary, the Rajk trial. In Bulgaria, the Petkov trial, and so on. In 1956, an independent Hungarian regime led by *communists,* such as the premier Imre Nagy, was suppressed by Soviet tanks, and Nagy was executed and buried in an unmarked grave until the poignant moment last summer when his remains were given a public, ceremonial funeral. In 1968, the Prague Spring, the effort of Alexander Dubcek to put forth the new idea of "socialism with a human face" was smashed by Soviet tanks.

Once *glasnost* and political reforms had begun in the Soviet Union, how could the older regimes hold out against change? They could not. In Hungary, the Communist party has dissolved itself, and only *5 percent* of its former members have joined a new Communist party. In Poland, the Communist party, though nominally guaranteed a majority of seats in the lower house, could not even gain enough votes to ratify that agreement, and a non-Communist is the prime minister of Poland, received with amiable greeting by Gorbachev himself.

From all that political rubble, one thing is clear. Whatever the formal adherence to the Warsaw Pact may mean, Eastern Europe is no longer a reliable force for the Soviet Union. Nor is East Germany. So far as Europe is concerned, the cold war is over and new configurations are about to begin.

WHAT OF THE FUTURE?

Let me turn, now, to the new configurations:

1. *The reunification of Europe.* The framework with which we have all been operating has been the idea of the European Economic Community, the twelve-nation "commonwealth" scheduled to come to fruition in 1992 and that, already, has taken distinct shape.

Now three new factors have to be taken

into account. One is the possible—and probable—reunification of the two Germanys into a single entity of eighty million persons, which will make it the most powerful economic unit of Europe. The second is the inclusion of Eastern Europe in a European trade bloc. And the third is the relation of the Soviet Union to Europe.

Historically, the Soviet Union has feared the emergence of a new, unified Germany. Historically, the two have been antagonists, even though a different set of dreamers, the German geopolitical strategists, such as Karl Haushofer, envisioned a new Eurasia, spanning the heartland of Europe and Asia and becoming the center of world power.

Although history has always been important in understanding the destinies of nations, it can also be misleading. England and France were enemies at the beginning of the nineteenth century and allies at the beginning of the twentieth. History has been important when *land* and *territory* were the goals of national states. Today these are less important than *technology.* The overriding need of the Soviet Union is for technology. And here, Germany, even a reunified Germany, becomes a useful partner. Already a deal had been struck ten years ago for a new pipeline that would bring natural gas from Siberia to Germany.

Until now, the Soviet Union has depended upon Czechoslovakia and East Germany for much of its manufactured products and for steel and machine tools. But both economies have become increasingly outmoded and incapable of supplying the Soviet Union with the new modern technology that it needs, particularly computer technology and telecommunications. West Germany becomes the "natural" source of this technology.

In effect, the logic of the economic interdependencies and needs, the huge timber, oil and gas, and mineral resources of the Soviet Union and the technology of Western Europe, dovetail into a pattern. Eastern Europe itself, if its industries are modernized, can provide the light industry (shoes and textiles) as well as the older manufactured products, including steel, as well as cheaper labor, for Western Europe.

These closer bonds would mean the destruction of the older NATO and Warsaw Pact configurations. England and France are bound to be wary of such moves—unless the security issue is completely resolved. Here the key is the Soviet Union. If Gorbachev takes convincing steps to reduce the Soviet military posture, then the economic logic can begin to operate. From his point of view, there is a contradictory problem. Reducing the military sector means freeing resources for the consumer sector. At the same time, the military has been an important power base for him—especially as the Communist party itself has become weakened. The military remains the major organized base of power within the Soviet Union. How Gorbachev manages these tasks will be decisive for his own retention of power, as well as for the necessary economic moves he has to make vis-à-vis Europe.

2. *The end of "The American Century."* The American Century was a phrase fashioned by Henry Luce—proprietor of *Time, Life* and *Fortune,* the most influential periodicals of their day—during World War II to herald a new and majestic role for the United States. Like all such ambitions, it had a mixture of idealism and economic self-interest. Luce, the son of Christian missionaries, whose early years had been spent in China, saw the American Century as fulfilling the Christian obligations of the United States to be "the good Samaritan," the helper of the poor and the needy. At its best, this was expressed politically by the Marshall Plan, which led to the economic reconstruction of Europe, and by substantial aid to Japan. As the cold war developed, the United States—which had begun to disarm after

World War II—became the military protector of both Europe and Japan against the Soviet Union. Its economic role became intertwined with its military role, creating what President Eisenhower called "the military-industrial complex." While military expenditure has never been the *necessary* basis for America's continuing economic growth, it has been an important one.

Four elements conjoin to reduce the centrality and power of the United States as the twenty-first century emerges: One is the reduction of the great power confrontations, and therefore the decisive political role of the United States as the "leader" of the world. Second is the rise of Japanese economic power, especially in the central high-technology sectors. Third are the low investment and productivity features of the American economy, which begin to sap its strength. And fourth comes the increasing difficulty of coping with domestic social problems such as crime and drugs, the aging infrastructures, and the declining quality of life in the central cities.

However, there has been a tendency, of late, to assume that the United States is almost "finished" as a major power. That would be misleading. The United States still maintains the general lead in technological *innovation*—if not always in development. (VCRs, facsimile, multivalve engines, and dozens of other products were created in the United States, though quickly developed elsewhere, as in Japan.) The United States maintains the foremost graduate education and scientific power of any country in the world. Japan, for example, has had strong universities but almost no graduate schools of any consequence. England and Europe, also with strong universities, do not have the scientific manpower and talent or the graduate schools of the United States. The United States remains the largest market for many export-led countries such as Korea to sell their products to. And in military and space technology, including aircraft, the United States maintains sizable leads.

The new free-trade pact with Canada and the growing integration of Mexican manufacture with U.S. industries provide a possible foundation for economic expansion. Nor should one ignore the political stability that provides a haven for jittery capital in other countries.

3. *The Pacific Rim.* What is evident here is the centrality of Japan as the major economic and financial power in the Pacific. And events in the last year have given Japan two "reprieves." One is the reduction of the Soviet military threat. In recent years, Japan has been under pressure from the United States to spend more on defense and military security. It has been yielding to that pressure. Now there is much less of that need. And the Soviet Union has even been making noises about returning some of the islands near Hokkaido to Japan, as a gesture of goodwill, and is seeking financial credits and technology from Japan. With the reduction of the Soviet threat, Japan is in a better position to resist American political and economic pressure on trade.

The second "reprieve" is China. The events in Tiananmen Square have, for the while, cut China off from the rest of the world. Historically, the United States, going back to the American Secretary of State John Hay, has always been *pro-China* in its policy. One of the "cards" open to the United States in recent years vis-à-vis Japan has been to develop political and economic relations with China. This was, particularly, the grand design of Henry Kissinger. And it would have led to a counterweight of U.S.-China relations to Japan and to the Soviet Union.

But as for Japan—and other East Asian countries—what is also evident is the recreation, with the cooperation of Australia and the Asian countries, of the old East Asia Co-Prosperity scheme. The industrialization of East Asia is proceeding rapidly, with Japan supplying most of the capital. A recent report of the Japan Center for Economic Research (October 1989) points out that in fiscal 1985 Japanese investments in manufacturing in Asian firms totaled $460 million. This increased 80 percent in the next year, and doubled the following one, and rose again by 40 percent in fiscal 1988. The total investments by electrical-machinery makers rose more than five times from 1985 to 1986 and have been increasing by 80 percent a year since then.

Given these emerging frameworks, what can one say, in summary, regarding the configuration of the twenty-first century as it is now appearing? I leave aside, as I said previously, the difficult questions of the increasing poverty and the widening gaps between the developed and the developing worlds, particularly in Africa. I leave aside the intractable passions of the Middle East. And there is the difficult question of the stability of the Soviet Union, given its economic and empire tensions.

North and South remain as an axis of division, which will likely become increasingly threatening after the first quarter of the twenty-first century. East vs. East is, for the while, in stasis, and much will depend upon the successors of Deng and even Gorbachev (who is likely to last, if he can surmount his difficulties, to the end of the century). And as for East vs. West, the United States and the Soviet Union may enter a period of détente.

The major new alignments that are coming into place are the regional blocs. These are economic-political units of a larger viability for nations to manage their problems of economic transition. A united Europe, a Continental North American economy, and a Japan-dominated Pacific region become the great land-mass units for economic, and even political, power. It would mean, if eco-

nomic logic also followed, the replacement of the dollar by a managed basket of the ECU (European currency unit), the dollar, and the yen as the mechanisms of exchange and trade balance.

One major caution: one cannot "predict" events and their outcomes, crucial as they may be; for example, the direction of China with the passing of Deng Xiaoping and his generation. One can only, as I have tried to do here, define "structural arrangements" to provide a grid for analysis.

If one looks ahead to the end of the century, there are two "structural" problems that loom quite large. One is demographic. In the United States, Western Europe, and Japan, we have aging populations. In most of the Third World countries—Algeria and Mexico are the prime examples—the youth cohort under seventeen years of age is between 40 to 50 percent of the population. Logically there are only three things one can do: take their people, buy their goods, or give them capital. All three pose difficulties that are not easy to resolve.

The second "structural" problem is the rising tension between the contrary pulls of the global economy and the national polities. Capital can flow easily; people cannot. No nation today controls its own currency and capital flows to take advantage of differential interest rates, cheaper labor, and better investment opportunities. But people, unless destitute or highly skilled, cannot move as readily; nor are many countries prepared to take them. More than that, as jobs slip away, the question before a regime is does it protect capital or people. In the United States we have seen this in the textile and automobile business and now in semiconductors. A large economy such as ours may be able to manage such transitions, but many cannot, and the fragmentation of many polities around the world because of economic difficulties, multiplied subsequently by ethnic clashes, increases the chances for what is called in the jargon of the Pentagon planner, "low-intensity conflicts."

These are the undertows and riptides in the world society. The interplay of demography, global economy, and national polity becomes the framework for trying to understand the problems of the twenty-first century.

Name Index

Subject Index

Agriculture, 9, 269, 276–87, 309–10
Aircraft, 169–70
Albania, 213
Algeria, 200, 385
American Telephone and Telegraph
  (ATT), 93
Argentina, 204, 225, 365
Asia Pacific Economic Cooperation
  (APEC), 215, 260–61
Association of Southeast Asian Na-
  tions (ASEAN), 215, 261
Australia, 261
Autarky, 241

Baker-Miyazawa Agreement, 181
Barter Trade, 261
Bolivia, 365
Brazil, 104, 204, 225, 238, 239, 267, 360
Bretton Woods Agreements, 1, 3, 5, 21,
  22, 47, 160, 181, 355
Bulgaria, 213, 230–38, 382
Burke-Hartke Bill, 271
Bush Administration, 57–58, 71–86,
  150, 208–26, 366

Canada, 98, 104, 255–58, 261
Capital accumulation, 8
Capitalism, 3
Cartels, 170–71
Carter Administration, 5, 208, 301
Central Intelligence Agency, 201, 211
Chile, 365
China, 4, 161, 192, 204, 258, 264–68,
  384
Common Agricultural Policy (CAP),
  278
Comparative advantage, 9
Conventional arms transfers, 223–34
Costa Rica, 365

Council for Mutual Economic Assis-
  tance (CMEA), 232, 235, 238
Countervailing duties, 241, 272
Czechoslovakia, 30, 213, 230–38, 382

Daimler-Benz, 178
Debt, Third World, 6, 214–16, 353–63,
  363–66
Defense spending, 50–70, 85
Deindustrialization, 152–54
Disproportionality, Law of, 7–8
Drugs, 218–19

East Asia, 192, 238–49, 258–61, 384–5
Eastern Europe, 230–38
Economic nationalism, xiv
Ecuador, 365
Energy, 211–12
Environment, 216–18, 234
Eurodollars, 5, 354
Europe, 13, 14–36, 174–82
European Economic Community
  (EEC), 6, 252–54, 286, 382
European Free Trade Association
  (EFTA), 252
European Monetary Union, 176, 180
Exchange rates, 159, 227–30
Export promotion, 189–90

Federal budget deficit, 71–86, 87–111,
  187–88
Federal insurance liabilities, 79–82
Federal Reserve, 107
Fiber optics, 167–68
Ford Administration, 105
Foreign direct investment, 159, 188–
  89, 213, 227–30, 316, 317–41,
  341–52
France, 4, 25, 29, 53, 59, 127, 178, 179